D1070948

150 YEARS OF

OPERA IN CHICAGO

WALKER BRANCH
THE CHICAGO PUBLIC LIBRARY
11071 SOUTH HOYNE AVENUE
CHICAGO ILLINOIS 60643

150 YEARS OF
OPERA

CHICAGO

ROBERT C. MARSH

Completed and Edited by NORMAN PELLEGRINI

NORTHERN

ILLINOIS

UNIVERSITY

PRESS

© 2006 by Northern Illinois University Press

Published by the Northern Illinois University Press,

DeKalb, Illinois 60115

Manufactured in the United States using acid-free paper

All Rights Reserved

Design by Julia Fauci

Complete permission credits are given on page 315

Library of Congress Cataloging-in-Publication Data

Marsh, Robert C. (Robert Charles)

150 years of opera in Chicago / Robert C. Marsh ; completed and

edited by Norman Pellegrini.

    p.   cm.

Includes bibliographical references (p.) and index.

ISBN-13: 978-0-87580-353-1 (clothbound : alk. paper)

ISBN-10: 0-87580-353-9 (clothbound : alk. paper)

1. Opera—Illinois—Chicago. I. Title: One hundred fifty years

of opera in Chicago. II. Pellegrini, Norman. III. Title.

ML1711.8.C5M37 2006

792.509773'11—dc22

2005036610

RO409528928

In memory of Alfred C. Stepan Jr., a noble friend of the arts

Contents

Preface

For many years, Robert C. Marsh wanted to write a book chronicling the presentation of opera in Chicago from its beginning to the present day, but it was only in the last ten years of his life that he was able to devote the time needed for concentrated research, reflection, and writing to accomplish the task. In the latter years of that effort he moved from Chicago to New Glarus, Wisconsin, and enlisted the help of a number of people, myself included, to track down missing facts and details he was unable to find without making even more of the trips back to Chicago than he did as he wrote specific chapters. He also asked me to read chapters as he completed them, openly asking for any comments or suggestions I might have.

When he died in 2002, his book was close to being finished, its fourteen chapters written but occasionally requiring some additional information, usually to complete chronologies or fill in details of a specific company or situation. I added text wherever I felt it was needed.

The largest amount of additions I have made is in Chapter 10, where specifics of performances over a number of seasons had to be noted. For those I was able to draw from reviews Dr. Marsh had written for the *Chicago Sun-Times,* so it is his voice that can be found in those evaluations. There was also a sizeable amount of detail needed to chronicle the most recent ten or so years of Chicago Opera Theater, and Carl Ratner, as he was writing his dissertation on that company, provided an exhaustive amount of articles and reviews concerning its history and fortunes.

It will be noted that footnotes to the text after Chapter 7 are sparse. Dr. Marsh was, by this time in the chronology, himself actively involved in Chi-

cago's musical life as music critic for the *Chicago Sun-Times.* Thus he drew from his own writings as well as personal contact with, and remembrances of, events of the years detailed in further chapters. In those chapters he does include—within the text—notations of specific references where applicable.

At Northern Illinois University Press, Mary Lincoln's interest in this book spurred the author to complete as much of it as he could, and her careful shepherding of it through the processes of publication has made its incarnation in its present form possible.

I am deeply indebted to Kaye Marsh, whose perseverance made it possible for me to obtain as much of the manuscript as Dr. Marsh had completed, and to Michael Hugos, whose computer wizardry allowed me to put the text in a form with which I could work. Ingrid Muller's careful reading of the finished writing and her suggestions in regard to it were invaluable. Robert Medina, of the Chicago Historical Society, was especially helpful in the acquisition of illustrations for use in this book, as were Robert Tuggle and John Pennino of the Metropolitan Opera Archives, and Susan Mathieson Mayer and Jeanne Fornari of Lyric Opera of Chicago. I wish to thank all of these people for their kindnesses as well as their assistance.

This book was a labor of love for Bob Marsh, as well as a demonstration of his devotion to Chicago and the best of what the city's artistic endeavors could and should accomplish. I am delighted to have been of assistance in helping bring his history, observations, and thoughts on opera in Chicago to a reading public.

—Norman Pellegrini

Author's Preface

My great-grandfather, the baron Heinrich von Marsch in his native Bavaria, could have heard the first operatic performance in Chicago. A "Forty Eighter," transformed into Henry Marsh—as a good revolutionary he believed European titles should be left in Europe—he arrived in Chicago, probably by water, in 1850, the year opera came to the city. He was thirty-nine, a man of culture and education (he was a musician and had attended Heidelberg), and would have seized the opportunity to hear opera in his new homeland. This is speculation, of course, based on nothing more concrete than family tradition, but he was a remarkable gentleman, and through my father's memories he is a presence in my life.

I have been attending operatic performances in Chicago and, in later years, other cities worldwide for more than sixty years. Thus nearly 40 percent of the time span encompassed in this history falls in the period of my own experience as an operagoer.

Those familiar with the meager literature on operatic production in Chicago will recall that one of the few good books is *Forty Years of Opera in Chicago* by Edward C. Moore, published in 1930. My title suggests that this book is intended, in part, to complete the story Moore began. Moore covers the four decades of opera in the Auditorium, 1889–1929, with particular emphasis on the resident companies that worked there from 1910 until the opening of the new Civic Opera House in 1929. Since he gives more than four hundred pages to what I must cover in a chapter, I cannot attempt to match the richness of detail he offers.

The present volume expands that time frame by 110 years. I move backward from Moore's beginning by 39 years and forward by 71. The 150th season since the first Chicago operatic performances (1999–2000) was also the 45th season of the Lyric Opera. From 1850 to 1910 Chicago was wholly dependent on touring opera companies. Resident companies rose and fell in the period 1910–1947. In 1954 the Lyric came and stayed. I appear to be the first his-torian of Chicago opera to include in detail the important contribution of touring opera companies in the present century.

Every Chicago opera historian is deeply in debt to a colleague of the past, George P. Upton, whose published memoirs and personal papers proved to be an invaluable guide to opera in the nineteenth century. In a way this history is seen through the eyes of three critics: Upton from 1850 to 1908; Moore from then to 1929; and the present author from 1939 onward. Upton and Moore both wrote for the *Chicago Tribune*. The *Chicago Sun-Times*, where I spent most of my professional life, was founded (as the *Chicago Sun*) in 1941. I joined its staff in 1956 and retired in 1991.

For many years the Lyric Opera had the remarkable policy of giving critics a pair of seats to every performance, which means that during the season I would be in the theater several nights a week, sometimes hearing an opera as many as five times. I do not believe that an opera production can be accurately evaluated on the basis of the first night alone. Indeed, I came to believe that the first night often was not as exciting as the dress rehearsal, although with rare exceptions I was banned from these events. Attending opera twenty-five or more times a season permitted me to write a final report that told not only how a production had appeared on opening night but how it had developed or declined during the course of its run. The practice of supplying press tickets for every night had to end as seasons grew longer.

The season of 1990 was the last I reviewed for the *Chicago Sun-Times*. The years 1991–99 are those in which I was a frequent visitor to the theater but lacked the close association previously possible. The chronicle of these later years thus has a somewhat different perspective.

As readers will discover, the reason the Auditorium was built as the chief cultural monument to the city's recovery from the great fire of 1871 is that there was already a firmly established operatic tradition that many felt must be preserved. Indeed, the Auditorium was not the city's first great opera house, but the second. Crosby's Opera House had preceded it and made a lasting impact. We cannot fully understand what happened after 1889 if we are unfamiliar with what happened before.

The argument for extending the history to the present is obvious. The Lyric Opera of Chicago is not only the most long-lived company in the history of the city but also the most important artistically and in its effect on the life of the community. For the first time, in the mature years of the Lyric, Chicago has become one of the great centers of opera production in the world. The importance of the company is not limited to its musical achievements. Examining the Lyric, we find an effective working solution to the problem of financing opera in the United States. By building a large, loyal, knowledgeable audience it has found the means to survive without significant government subsidy.

This history concentrates on operatic production by the major, professional companies that have had the maximum impact on the life of the community. It should be said that Chicago has always had a number of smaller opera groups, some ethnically oriented, some essentially opera workshops to give vocal students performance experience. The Chicago Opera Theater began in 1974 as an organization of this type but was transformed into an important professional production group. These smaller, marginally professional organizations are largely omitted for two reasons. The first—and the most practical—is that it is almost impossible to investigate their history. Few performances of this type were even mentioned in the press, and if these organizations had anything that might be called an archive, it never became part of a public collection.

Secondly, the social impact of these organizations is for the most part limited to the group directly involved. Measuring the importance of their performances on the community as a whole would be extremely difficult. There is one notable exception. The Lithuanian community has long supported an opera company that presents opera in Lithuanian. (Thanks to this group, in 1986 I heard my only staged performance of Rossini's *William Tell*. They also gave the only Chicago performances to date of Ponchielli's *I Lituani*—in 1981 and 1991.) By providing experienced singers for the chorus, that company contributed greatly to the young Lyric Theater.

Since this is primarily a history of fully staged opera,

only occasional reference is made to opera in concert form. A book must have a well-defined field, and for me real opera is opera in a theater or, possibly, opera in a well-made film or television program. But it should be noted that there has been a great deal of musically significant opera in concert form in Chicago, the principal producers being the Chicago Symphony Orchestra (both at Orchestra Hall and the Ravinia Festival) and the Grant Park Symphony concerts.

The problem of writing opera history is not finding detail but dealing with the masses of detail generated in a single season. What the historian must do is separate important events from commonplace happenings, significant lines of change from the routine of production. From the names of hundreds of now forgotten singers, the great voices must be recognized. Above all, the book must be readable—not a catalogue of old stage bills and reviews.

In part, this is a reference book. If, for instance, you want to discover what the public heard in the 1865–1866 season (a vintage year), you need only turn to Appendix B, which holds the "Annals of Opera in Chicago, 1850–2005." It is all there, and only the most important events need be recapitulated with appropriate commentary in the text.

I take the position that I need not duplicate here information that is easily found elsewhere. An overview of a season is not a series of reviews. Any reader wishing this much detail can find it in the newspapers issued a day or two after the first performance as listed in the "Annals." And the newspapers will frequently give fuller detail with respect to casts, conductors, directors, and designers and such.

The Mary Garden seasons were colorful, but they ended in January 1931. Is there anyone still living who remembers them? The question is their importance for the living, the lesson they may teach future opera producers in the city, as part of the larger question of the interaction of the opera producer and the public.

Work on this book began in 1983 with the hope that it would be completed in three years. I shall not enumerate the reasons why this did not take place, but they were good reasons, and in consequence the scope of the book now extends to a century and a half. It is open-ended. The significance of the new management of the Lyric Opera cannot be fairly judged at this time, but its announced plans and policies are discussed.

I am fundamentally prejudiced. A city with a successful opera company has a cultural resource that sets it distinctively apart from a city without opera, but the precise benefits that opera brings to the community are philosophical questions that should be examined with care. My consideration of these matters in the introduction is a sort of overture to the historical narrative that follows.

ACKNOWLEDGMENTS

A project of this magnitude, growing out of a lifetime of professional work, reflects the influence and assistance of many persons.

For my general understanding of opera I draw first on my experiences as a vocal student, learning how to sing and then realizing that my voice was not equal to sustaining an operatic career. To understand how a leading singer studies and creates a role, I owe much to Anna Moffo Sarnoff, Boris Christoff, and, most of all, to Tito Gobbi, who also showed me the responsibilities of the director. The friendship of Lesley Koenig gave further insight into the director's role.

For my understanding of the many facets of producing opera, I am in debt to four of the finest operatic conductors of the twentieth century: George Szell, Erich Leinsdorf, Sir Georg Solti, and James Levine. Their friendship was beyond price. I cannot begin to enumerate what they taught me.

In Chicago I had a long, thoroughly professional, courteous, and pleasant relationship with Ardis Krainik, and I have fond memories of candid, instructive conversations with Kurt Adler of San Francisco. Unfortunately, I found it difficult to talk with Carol Fox; with me she was never forthcoming.

In 1965 the Ford Foundation gave me a traveling fellowship that permitted me to study the new, smaller American opera companies and compare them with the older producers. This proved useful background for the preparation of this book.

For thirty-five years my primary professional responsibilities were as music critic of the *Chicago Sun-Times*. Anyone who has ever worked on a newspaper knows that success is always the result of collective effort. Without the skill and support of your colleagues you will never achieve anything approximating your objectives. Thus I could not possibly thank everyone who deserves my gratitude, but a few names are especially memorable.

Marshall Field IV, my publisher from 1956 to 1965, knew what I was trying to do and supported me fully. Throughout my years at the paper I was always work-ing for him, doing the job as he would have wanted it done. He believed there were people who might buy a newspaper because of a music critic, an idea that was rejected by editors and publishers who followed him. For roughly twenty-five years I worked in an environment that was indifferent, if not hostile, to the subjects I was writing about and the artistic objectives I held for the city. When for lack of space and support I could no longer maintain my professional standards, I took my leave.

Four editors, Milburn P. Akers, Quentin Gore, John (Dick) Trezevant, and Herman Kogan, were—in the 1950s and 1960s—a constant source of strength. The brief period after 1983 in the employ of Rupert Murdoch was the happiest in my later years with the paper. Murdoch, too, wanted the job done right and saw to it that I received the necessary means to succeed. Danny Newman, the press representative for the Lyric Opera of Chicago, was unfailingly the complete professional and loyal colleague.

Finally, outside the field of journalism, I must thank the medical staff of the University of Wisconsin Hospital, Madison, for diagnosis and treatment that made it possible to complete this book.

No project of this type can be attempted without subsidy to provide supplemental income during the months given to research and writing. It is extremely difficult for a person without a current academic appointment to secure research funds, especially for work in the humanities. Moreover, a history of Chicago opera is not seen in some quarters as a work of national significance. Newspapers, unfortunately, do not grant sabbatical leaves with even partial pay. I decided to fund the project with a number of smaller gifts from persons familiar with my work who saw the need for a book of this type. Eventually, the work was continued on my retirement income.

The project was established with a substantial contribution from the Stepan Chemical Company. Indeed, the support and friendship of the late Alfred C. Stepan Jr. was indispensable for the work to begin and a constant inducement to complete the book as he would have wished it. His daughter, Marilee Wehman, has been an invaluable sustaining force. Other important early gifts came from both Hope Abelson and her daughter Katherine, representing the Lester S. Abelson Foundation, and from the Anne P. Lederer Research Institute. The book was completed with major gifts from William B. Graham and Andrew Greeley.

Significant contributions came from Field Enterprises Charitable Corporation, Bell and Howell, the Crown and Pritzker Foundations, Louis Sudler, Boone Brackett, J. W. Van Gorkom, Sarah Zelzer, Sir Georg Solti, and James Levine. The United States Bankruptcy Court for the Western District of Wisconsin liberated me from debt, thus providing direct, practical support of a type I could not secure from the National Endowment for the Humanities.

I have received substantial assistance from the staff of the Newberry Library, Chicago, where I became a research associate in 1983, and from Philip Gossett and the staff of the Regenstein Library of the University of Chicago, the librarians of the Chicago Historical Society, Brenda Nelson-Strauss of the Chicago Symphony Orchestra Archives, the Wisconsin Historical Society, the Mills Music Library of the University of Wisconsin, Madison, and the music department of the Cambridge University Library. During the final period of work, when illness limited my mobility, I received significant assistance in research from Virginia Davis and Wynne Delacoma of the *Chicago Sun-Times* and from Andrew Karzas. Dr. Carolyn Guzski, a colleague in operatic history, generously shared the results of some of her research.

Finally, Norman Pellegrini, who after Marshall Field IV best understood my objectives as a critic, undertook the responsibility of answering some important questions in Chicago libraries and reading the entire text with a critical eye. During the months in which I was unable to travel to Chicago, his assistance was indispensable, as was his agreement to complete this book if I was unable to do so.

—Robert C. Marsh
New Glarus, Wisconsin, 2001

150 YEARS OF

OPERA IN CHICAGO

Introduction

In Berlin you can, in a matter of moments, walk from the Staatsoper on *Unter den Linden,* dedicated in 1743 as Frederick the Great's temple to the muses, to St. Hedwig's Cathedral, consecrated in 1773 to the glory of God. We find similar juxtapositions in many other European cities. For the eighteenth-century mind it was perfectly logical that the two buildings should stand together, one a monument to humanistic culture, the other a glorification of the transcendent and divine. Both were architectural symbols of a system of values.

Neither could plausibly be called a place of entertainment. For entertainment one went to a less demanding setting. To understand fully what was transpiring, both the opera and the cathedral required one to become fully involved in the events one witnessed. Passive pleasure seeking would go unsatisfied.

Opera is theater in its highest form, with the union of words and music, music and drama, serving to lift the events on the stage to the greatest significance and intensity. The intention of a great operatic performance is that we look two ways, outwardly to the stage and inwardly to our own most private thoughts and feelings. Ideally, we go to the opera house to discover ourselves. Every opera that has demonstrated the power to survive, to communicate forcefully with persons of many social and cultural origins in different periods of history, does so because there is a common humanity we all share that this work of art touches, illuminates, and enhances as the events on stage take place.

The greatest art has the capacity of being understood on several levels. There is the simple, straightforward experience of some artifact, perhaps a picture, a work of music, or spoken words, and on that level there may be comprehension and gratification. But with repeated experience, closer scrutiny, longer association, it may well be understood that the first impressions, although valid, were superficial, that there are other, more fundamental and universal things here, and we grow in our intellect and humanity as we learn to discover them. Thus a late Rembrandt self-portrait, first seen as a fine representation of an older man, becomes a universal image of humankind surveying life and the world with the understanding that years of sorrow, joy, and growing wisdom may bring. It is the face of one who knows the human condition and has come to terms with its demands. It is the artist as the image of the humanist ideal.

Great art has the capacity to produce a transcendent experience. It has spiritual force. The impact is no less than the moment for a devout believer when the priest at mass administers communion. The opera house, thus, itself exists on several levels, and on the highest it is a sacred place where, as Aristotle said of the theater he knew, through a catharsis of pity and fear we see ourselves in a blinding light of truth and insight.

Americans today are living in a society oriented toward entertainment that demands nothing except a mindless, socially conditioned response. One hears the laugh track in the sitcom and responds. One can be completely passive, avoiding any interaction with the entertainer, and simple pleasure seeking will be gratified. There is no stimulus to growth or introspection, and still less are you invited to extend the content of the entertainment to a perspective on the world and the human condition. One laughs or smiles, and the entertainer's objective has been achieved. There is minimal brain activity.

It would be unrealistic to think that through the centuries opera audiences have not contained their share of persons who came only to be entertained, who were unwilling or unable to understand the meaning of a great performance on its highest level. It probably would be equally unrealistic to fail to see that a person may start going to the opera for one reason and, as experience of the operatic theater grows, continue for reasons different from those that prompted the initial visit. An opera house is a constant invitation to personal growth and discovery. Moreover, the range and depth of the operatic repertory today intensifies these results. There is no question that in the past many went to the opera to be diverted by the acrobatics of celebrated "singing machines," and there is no question that such performances could be impressive for all their lack of profundity. But the experienced operagoer was unlikely to be confused about the fact that opera exists on several levels. There was *La sonnambula,* but before that there was *Don Giovanni.*

Neither can there be any question that for many years, especially in the United States, the artistic purpose of the opera house often seemed subordinated to a social function: providing the rich with a showcase for their wealth. What this history reveals is that the rich, however wealthy they might be, cannot by themselves sustain a major opera company. The value of its work must penetrate deeply into the community, for both filled boxes and a packed gallery are essential for a firm base of operations.

Opera makes demands. In the past it has made some unreasonable ones, primarily that operagoers (unless they are familiar with the work) prepare for the performance in a manner that is not required by any other visit to the theater. In the final years of the twentieth century, with the general use of supertitles in American theaters, the language barrier has been eliminated. What is happening on the stage is at last verbally intelligible. The jokes are funny; the anguish is real. Supertitles over the stage or—even better—titles at seat level (as they are in the Metropolitan Opera House) permit the listener to enjoy the union of language and music the composer imagined and still be fully involved in the action.

The newly rich operagoer of the past, who neither understood nor enjoyed the music, who could not comprehend the action, but who went to the theater to flaunt possessions, is practically gone. Whether you enjoy the opera or not is a personal decision, but in most American theaters there is no excuse for not understanding the words. In Chicago the introduction of supertitles in the mid-1980s might be said to be a decisive element in creating completely sold-out seasons.

Nineteenth-century America was initially concerned with conquering a continent, bringing commerce (if not civilization) to the vast spaces between the two oceans. As the century ended, the cry arose that the nation was absorbed in materialism. What Helen L. Horowitz calls "the single minded absorption of business men in their private affairs,"[1] undermined religion, values, and, indeed, encouraged social and political corruption. The countermeasure was to direct wealth to philanthropic ends: universities, libraries, art museums, and symphony orchestras. The true leaders, the civic elite, were told they were obliged to provide the essentials for a cultural and intellectual life, and tax laws were written that rewarded them for philanthropic works.

In the 1890s, opera, both grand and light varieties, was widely regarded as commercial entertainment. It appealed to the lower instincts and supported materialism. Thus at the turn of the century opera thrived in three large cities, New York, Chicago, and San Francisco, where there were enough people of great wealth so this showcase was desired and could be financed. The great growth of serious music in the early part of the twentieth century primarily involved the symphony orchestra. The symphony was regarded as spiritually uplifting. Opera did not fully gain this prestige until after World War II. Time cleansed it of its bonds to the base and material, and small opera companies began to function all over the map. By the end of the century one finds American opera producers offering seasons with larger repertories than ever before. The symphony orchestra established the concept that serious music must be subsidized, and the newly founded opera companies now drew on philanthropic resources previously reserved for "spiritually pure" enterprises.

With this growth comes the appreciation that a city with an opera company has a civic resource that deserves the widest appreciation and support. The opera company must have an appropriate theater in which to work, an orchestra (in smaller cities now often drawn from the ranks of the local symphonic ensemble) that can play demanding music well, and support groups—chorus, supernumeraries, scenery shops, stage crews—that can work on a secure professional level. Most of all, it must have a management that can use these resources effectively and a budget that permits it to engage high-quality singers, rehearse them adequately, and offer strong, unified productions.

Opera was well established as a part of European life long before it was first heard on the North American continent, but Americans have a gift of importing things and quickly absorbing them into the national life. (Young persons are horrified to learn that in my youth pizza was unknown. Now many think it was invented [if not perfected] in Chicago rather than Naples.) It is difficult to say when opera became a part of the American theater rather than an imported delicacy, but the construction of the Metropolitan Opera House in 1883 is probably as good a date as any. The assimilation of opera into the national life was strengthened by the composition of American operas. That process began with *Leonora* by William Henry Fry in 1845, beginning a long succession of works, until today there is a small but solid body of high-quality operatic scores by American composers.

There are few experiences in life than can rival the inner exaltation that comes in the climactic moments of a superlative operatic performance, when the force of the drama rises through the evening in a long ascending arc that seems to lift one upward, ever upward, until the action is resolved. In the final moments of *Die Meistersinger,* for example, we witness the triumph of the good, the beautiful, and the true and seem to feel a transcendent cosmic pulse that assures us that God is with us and all is well. Shakespeare in his greatest moments cannot surpass this. For a start, he lacks a chorus and orchestra.

Opera is a product of Western civilization, but it belongs to all humanity. It is interesting to see, for example, how it is finding a place in Japanese life. For me it is the universal human dramatic form. Its audience is growing, its importance is becoming more widely understood, its necessity is widely recognized. The operas I know best, many of them operas I have known and studied for more than sixty years, are an essential part of me; I cannot imagine life without them. On the secular level (the cathedral is still needed), I have found opera to be the fundamental key to the enrichment of life. And I am one of millions.

1

The Roots of a Tradition

1850–1864

Sometime during the final week of July 1850, a ship from Milwaukee brought to Chicago exotic creatures it had not known before: opera singers. The place would never be the same again.

Chicago, ironically known as the "Gem of the Prairie," was born to be an opera town. An intense zest for life, frequently seasoned by greed and lust, drove the young city, and this was the very stuff of which opera was made. But even in 1850 those passions could be dressed in an elegant façade as one went, with friends and family, to the theater.

The first professional operatic performance was heard in Rice's Chicago Theater at 8:00 p.m. on Monday, July 29, 1850. The work was Vincenzo Bellini's *La sonnambula (The Sleepwalker),* composed in 1831 and enormously popular. It gave a prima donna the opportunity to display her flamboyant vocal skills and, moreover, it had a happy ending.

The performing group, a hardy quartet of three singers and (one assumes) a pianist, were billed as the Manvers, or the Manvers-Brienti, Italian Opera Company, although one comes to suspect that the closest it had ever been to Italy was London's Soho Square. Eliza Brienti was the soprano. The tenor, Charles Manvers, had been to the United States a decade before as part of a group of British singers who appeared in eastern cities. The bass is identified variously as Guibel, Giubeti, and Guibelei. Most likely Guibel was the real name. The fourth member, a gentleman named Lippert, was the accompanist or, when an orchestra was available, the conductor. A Chicago singer, Miss Mathews, was cast in a supporting part, and members of the chorus played the briefer roles. It would appear that the performance was bilingual, with the principal singers presenting the Italian text and the others singing in English.

Linguistic mixtures of this type were commonplace in the mid–nineteenth century.

The reason Milwaukee did not hear a *complete* opera before Chicago was that although it had a chorus and a string quartet, it lacked an orchestra. The visitors, apparently engaged by a local impresario, were heard in concert, singing excerpts from *La sonnambula* as well as Bellini's *Norma* and Donizetti's *The Daughter of the Regiment (La Fille du régiment).* Reviews suggest that some of this repertory was sung in English. At least three such programs were given with success in a week starting in mid-July, after which the troupe boarded ship and sailed some eighty miles to Chicago, where greater triumphs beckoned. Travel by water was by far the fastest and most comfortable way to make the journey. The roads, when they deserved that description, were unpaved. The only railroad ran westward to Galena. (Milwaukee finally heard an opera, Lortzing's *Zar und Zimmermann,* in 1853.)

La sonnambula proved to be the first opera performed in what was to become another of the nation's most important opera towns, San Francisco. It was heard, in January 1851, from the Pellegrini troupe, a hardy collection of European singers and instrumentalists, who had come by ship to claim their share of the golden bounty. Scenery was improvised and, again, there was a locally recruited chorus. But costumes and music were on hand and, most important, so was an audience.

The *Chicago Journal* welcomed the Manvers-Brienti company with the report, "This troupe have won golden opinions from the public and press." The "rare skill" of the singers was attested in their reviews. "We bespeak for them a multitudinous welcome." Performances were scheduled for July 29, 30, and 31, 1850.

A fully-staged opera for Chicago required some preparation. Presumably the troupe brought its music, which was given to the musicians who normally played for the theater, and a chorus had been hastily recruited. The scenery must have been provided by the theater owner, John B. Rice, who apparently was able to deal with the striking visual effect of the final scene, when the sleepwalking heroine safely passes over a fragile bridge crossing the mill wheel.

Chicago's first important music critic, George P. Upton of the *Tribune*, was an undergraduate at Brown University in 1850 but later investigated this landmark event carefully. He reports in his memoirs that the artists had arrived "some days previously," which suggests that care had been taken to rehearse the local talent.

It was an elegant opening night. Upton tells us: "The theater was crowded. The ladies were out in full force, dressed in the prevailing circumference of style at that time, and those belonging to the swell set were distinguished by their lorgnettes. Most of the gentlemen were dressed in faultless evening suits, for the swallow-tail was an everyday coat in those days."[1]

To preserve the proper moral tone (specifically to prevent solicitation for prostitution) no woman was admitted without a male companion. Rice ran a high quality operation. Prostitution was commonplace, the practical consequence of a population of thirty thousand with three thousand more men than women. But there was to be no whoring in John Rice's theater.

What sort of theater was this? Externally it was a two-story wooden building, eighty feet long and forty feet wide, that might have served any number of less glamorous functions than housing opera. It stood in the center of the city on the south side of Randolph Street, midway between Clark and Dearborn. The site is now a monument to municipal government.

Chicago's *first* theater was a makeshift affair, a performance space created by remodeling part of the Sauganash Hotel. It opened in 1837. It met the need for entertainment but attracted "a very rough element of the population."[2] Drunks in the audience were commonplace, fights were not infrequent, and prostitutes were readily available. It was precisely what you might expect in a place of amusement in a male-dominated frontier town. There were few sidewalks, and the streets were unpaved. The river was an open sewer flowing into the lake, which served as the water supply. Every Summer brought cholera. Archi-

THEATRE.

N. B CLARKE................STAGE MANAGER.

Engagement of the Opera Troupe.
MISS ELIZA BRIENTI,
MR. MANVERS,
MR GUIBELI.

On MONDAY Evening, July 29, will be acted
I A SOMNAMBULA.

Count Rodolpho,	Mr. Guibeli.
Elvino,	Mr. Manvers.
Amina,	Miss Eliza Brienti.

Concludes with a
Pas De Deux,   Mr. & Mrs. Gilbert.

Admission to Boxes, 50 cents—Pit 25   Doors open at 7½; Curtain rises at 8 o'clock.

Advertisement for the first performance of opera in Chicago, 1850

tecturally the young city was undistinguished. It was the boom town atmosphere that attracted young men from the eastern states. If you could stand the smell and the lack of amenities, it offered the clever businessman limitless opportunities.

Such genteel citizenry as there was rejoiced when John Rice gave it a chance to enjoy cultivated amusements. He was born in Maryland in 1809. His family were farmers, but he yearned for a more exciting life and at twenty ran away to Philadelphia, where he became an actor. In 1837 he married Ann Warren, the daughter of an established theatrical family, but this failed to advance his career as a performer. Apparently deciding he was better at running theaters than performing in them, he turned to management. Before coming to Chicago he had a theater in Albany, New York, and may also have run a theater in Buffalo. A chain of theaters was forming in the western states, and performers of some reputation from the east might make the circuit, or part of it, appearing with the local company. Albany and Buffalo were the eastern links, and there were theaters of importance in Detroit and Cleveland. St. Louis, Natchez, and New Orleans, easily reached by Mississippi riverboats, completed the series.

Rice felt that with a population of thirty thousand Chicago belonged in this chain despite travel being more difficult. There was a public ready for refined entertainment, and a producer that met its standards would be a success. He engaged an alderman named

The first Rice's Theatre

John B. Rice

Updyke, who was a builder as well as a politician, to design and construct his theater, and the work began in early May 1847, with the opening the following month, on June 28. It was called variously the Chicago Theater or the New Theater, but there was no old theater. Rice had built the first building in the city intended specifically for theatrical presentations. There could not have been earlier operatic performances because there was no suitable place to house them.

The theater was on the second floor. Presumably the space at street level was used for commercial purposes. The *Chicago Journal*, which got an advance look on June 26, hailed "the internal arrangements" as "admirable." The design was described as following the "plan of the coliseum," which suggests a horseshoe-shaped hall. There was a pit for a small orchestra. "A full view of the stage can be obtained from every part of the house. . . . The boxes are elegantly furnished and fitted with carpets and settees, rather resembling a boudoir or a private sitting room in a gentleman's house." The final judgement was that the building was "tasteful and commodious," a "striking exponent of Western industry and enterprise." It probably had about 350 seats, divided between the circle of boxes, where a seat cost fifty cents, and the main floor, where seats were half that price. An upper tier of seats—probably quite small—was designated for "colored persons" and also cost twenty-five cents. It is odd that a northern city in which only 1% of the population was of African American descent would feel the need for segregated seating, but Rice apparently found it desirable.

Theatrical managers could enter polite society, but actors could not. Buskers and mountebank thespians, who earned from $10 to $15 a week, were welcome on the stage but not in the drawing room. The core of the repertory in Rice's theater from its opening weeks was Shakespeare, but it was supplemented with plays of the most ephemeral nature, the nineteenth-century version of the sitcom. The billing changed frequently.

The first opera performance in the city on July 29, 1850, was an instant success, the universal topic of conversation in the upper strata of society. The *Journal* of July 30 rhapsodized about the "excellent house" and "music of the highest order executed with exquisite grace." Brienti's face was "so eloquent in her favor to begin with, and her voice, now soft as a vesper sigh, now loud and shrill as a clarion" charmed the listener. The male voices were found to be of "admirable power and tone," but it is clear that, for this anonymous critic, the prima donna ruled the stage.

In the spirit of flamboyant nineteenth-century criticism, the review concluded that the cast "could make harmony and melody that Apollo would not hesitate to accompany on his ocean-tuned harp." The true quality of the performance must remain forever a matter of conjecture, but it is really unimportant. So far as the Chicago public and press were concerned, it was a tremendous success. Opera had come to the city in a way that ensured it would return.

The following evening the work was to be heard again, and the house was full. All went well until the opening moments of the second act, when cries of "Fire!" were heard from the street. Kelly's Stable on Dearborn Street was in flames, and the blaze soon spread to the theater. The fatal combination of horses, hay, lanterns, and wooden buildings set Chicago burning many times before the monumental conflagration of 1871 that leveled practically everything. This blaze of 1850 destroyed twenty buildings in the heart of the city.

Rice came to center stage, assured his audience they had ample time to leave the theater, and, indeed, evacuated the hall without incident. One piece of lore

about the event tells of an Englishman who had fortified himself for the evening with a dinner sparkling with wine. As the flames spread, he sat alone in the front row, shouting "Bravo!" for the verisimilitude of the presentation. Assured it was reality, not stagecraft, he took his leave, jubilant and unsinged.

The company had in haste removed all it could from the building: scenery, props, costumes, and possibly music. Even so, much was lost. The theater was a ruin in half an hour (a scene "eloquent of destruction and alarm," as the *Journal* described it), and Rice was left to contemplate that he had $1,000 insurance coverage on a $7,000 investment. But Rice was so esteemed in the community that on August 3, 1850, a benefit concert was given at City Hall or at the City Saloon (depending on the source consulted—the latter is more probable). It yielded $60, the box office receipts of an average night. The opera singers participated, along with local musicians.[3]

Who made up the audience that welcomed opera so warmly? In 1850 nearly half the population of Chicago had been born in America. The rest were recent European immigrants. The largest ethnic group was Germans—"Forty-Eighters," as they were called—building new lives after the unsuccessful revolution in their homeland. They mixed with the older German settlers, some of whom had American roots that went as far back as the eighteenth century. Twenty percent of the population (40% of the new arrivals) was Irish.

There was a distinct difference between the two groups of immigrants. The Irish were primarily tenant farmers who had been unable to sustain themselves in their homeland. The Germans cut across social divisions from the titled to the peasant, spurred on by their political beliefs. Arriving in Boston or New York, you crossed New York State to Buffalo, where a lake steamer would take you to Detroit. From there a Michigan Central Railway train carried you to New Buffalo on the eastern shore of Lake Michigan, where a second ship made the short journey to Chicago.

Apart from recognizing its significance for Chicago, one is tempted to try to reconstruct the tour of this allegedly Italian company. I suspect the group came from England, and its members may all have been of English birth. Brienti is, indeed, an Italian name, but Eliza is solidly British, as are the other names. I suggest they came through Buffalo and Detroit, where they may have offered concerts, and from Detroit proceeded to Milwaukee. What happened to them after the Chicago disaster? They may well have lost the necessities of producing opera, but they were probably able to continue concertizing. One historian says, "They gave a few performances in nearby towns to recoup their losses and quietly evaporated from the scene."[4]

They probably continued to St. Louis (an easy journey) and from there by steamboat to New Orleans, where they could be assured of a welcome. From a port of this importance, a return to England would present no difficulties. This is, of course, outside the story of Chicago opera, but the tour of this company was probably a significant early event in the history of opera in the United States, and it deserves recognition.

Operatic singing might have returned to Chicago later in 1850 when Jenny Lind, a genuinely international operatic celebrity, made a much acclaimed American tour under the management of the greatest champion of exotics, P. T. Barnum. He offered her expenses and $1,000 a performance, an extraordinary fee in those days, but, as it proved, one she had no difficulty earning. She was thirty years old and had been an opera star of the first magnitude for nine years. She came to the United States after a series of triumphs in London. Despite her skills on the stage, opera had lost its attraction for her, and she wished to become a concert artist. Unfortunately, her concert career never surpassed her operatic successes.

Before 1847, when a concert was to be presented in the city, one of the larger saloons was taken over for the evening. But Jenny Lind, a woman of exemplary moral fiber, could not sing in a saloon. Apart from the fact that it could not possibly—even at the outrageous price of $2 a ticket—bring in enough money to pay her fee, it would have been a demeaning experience. Lind, whose much heralded moral qualities were exemplified by her philanthropy, in 1850 gave $1,000 to a Swedish church, St. Anagarius, under construction in Chicago. But to the dismay of the city fathers, she did not choose to sing there. Chicago had a burned-out theater, but St. Louis had a hall, and St. Louis got her. On her second tour, in the latter half of 1851, she was scheduled to come to Chicago, but later decided not to travel west of Cincinnati, which could be reached in a comfortable Ohio River steamboat.

Jenny Lind was remarkable among nineteenth-century opera singers in that she had two names. Most of her colleagues, unless they came from a family such as the Patti clan that produced more than one artist of stature, apparently preferred to be known by their last names only. In some cases the professional name was a disguise. For one thing, it offered protection against the prejudice some felt was directed at American singers. But genuine Italians, for a variety of reasons—privacy, image, prestige—used only their family name. The practice continues today in casual conversation, but everyone knows that Callas was Maria and Sutherland is Joan. A century before, these intimate details might not have been familiar to the public at large, and the opera historian may find them difficult to learn.

Lind arrived in the United States in September 1850 and on the eleventh sang to an audience of seven thousand at Castle Garden in New York City. Late in November she began a journey that extended to Havana on the South and St. Louis on the west. Freshman Upton of Brown University in Providence, Rhode Island, heard her and was infected, along with thousands of others in this country and in Europe, with "Jenny Lind Fever." It was one of the things that prompted him to give his life to music.

Lind's programs set a pattern later adopted by Caruso. She did not appear alone. There was a baritone and an instrumentalist to fill out the evening. She never appeared in opera in the United States and limited her programs to two arias at the most. Her popularity was based on what were called "folksongs," although many were the work of song composers. She gave her public eloquent realizations of music that was easily accepted and enjoyed, such as "Home Sweet Home," "The Last Rose of Summer," and the like. Barnum was not out to raise the cultural level of the nation but to make money, and music with the lowest common denominator of middle-class comprehension best served this purpose.

For the greatest part of the nineteenth century, the prima donna was supreme. She drew huge audiences and obtained fees that, in terms of purchasing power, far exceed anything earned today in an age in which managers and tax collectors take their share of every dollar. Adelina Patti in her prime demanded $5,000 a performance, preferably in gold Swiss francs and paid in advance.

The first tenor to compete successfully with celebrated sopranos was Italo Campanini, who in 1882 negotiated a fee of $1,000 a performance, the highest price ever paid for a tenor in the United States at that time. The next tenor to receive that kind of money was probably Jean de Reszke, who made his American

Italo Campanini

debut in Chicago in an 1891 production of *Lohengrin*. Succeeded early in the new century by Enrico Caruso, he opened the way for today's era of the tenor. Now it is three tenors, not three sopranos, who fill baseball parks for their televised concerts.

Midway into the nineteenth century, the rivalry between Chicago and St. Louis had become intense. St. Louis proclaimed itself the "Gateway to the West" and had, indeed, profited mightily from its location at the meeting of two great river highways, the Mississippi and the Missouri. In the first half of the century water provided the easiest means of travel. But the wide Missouri was not of much use if you wished to go to California, and with the completion of the transcontinental railroad in 1869, Chicago, the great meeting point of the eastern and western railways, began an explosive growth that permitted the rapid reconstruction of the city after its destruction in 1871.

In 1850 the great cultural bastion of the nation was New York City. At first a reflection of British culture, it had ballad opera in the eighteenth century as part of a lively theatrical tradition based on works that are almost wholly forgotten. Italian opera, as exemplified by Rossini's *The Barber of Seville (Il barbiere di Siviglia)*, arrived in 1825. The first opera house in the mid-continent had opened in New Orleans in 1796. It was essentially a French theater. New Orleans had a secure operatic tradition through the nineteenth century.

Chicago, it must be remembered, was a rough frontier town for the first third of the nineteenth century. Virtually the entire population had been wiped out in 1812 by Indians in the employ of the British, and recovery was slow. Upton puts it well: "When it is remembered that Italian opera was inaugurated by the Garcia troupe in New York as early as 1825, and New Orleans had regular seasons even before that time, it may seem odd that opera was a long time in reaching Chicago; but in 1825 there were more Indians than white men here, and when New Orleans was enjoying its regular seasons of opera there were hardly a half-dozen whites outside the walls of Fort Dearborn."[5]

Indians and a military garrison did not make up a promising operatic public. What made opera possible was the arrival of a level of stability that produced a class of educated, prosperous citizenry that sought the kind of emotional and intellectual stimulation opera could bring. Rice cleared the site of his ruined theater and began rebuilding. The new structure was to be brick rather than wood, and it was a hundred feet in length, considerably larger than its predecessor. It cost $11,000. There were fourteen hundred seats, three tiers of boxes, and a saloon. By this time gas lighting had come to Chicago's main streets and the buildings beside them. The construction took somewhat longer than planned, and the opening did not take place until early February 1851.

If Chicago missed Lind, it was among the first American cities to discover Adelina Patti, the *prima donna assoluta* of the century. Patti was born in Madrid in 1843 to a Sicilian father and a Roman mother and, as an infant, was brought to New York. Upton writes, "There was not an impulse, an influence, or a purpose in her early life that was not musical." Her entire family was involved with opera. Her mother was a prima donna, with *Norma* considered her finest role. All the women sang. Adelina's two older sisters, Amalia and Carlotta, both appeared professionally. The child Adelina began public appearances at seven.

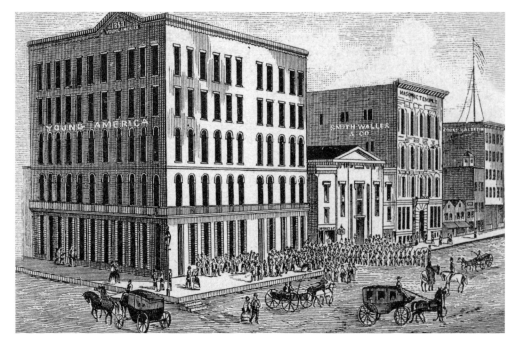

The Young America Hotel and the second Rice's Theatre

Tremont House

The Tremont House at Lake and Dearborn, a hotel that took pride in its Italian marble, responded to the burning of Rice's theater by remodeling its ballroom as Tremont Hall, a room for music as well as dancing. The ten-year-old Patti made her formal debut there in 1853, although she had sung previously in a program in the dining room of the hotel. Upton recalled "a somewhat delicate, pale-faced, dark-browed child" who sang "bravura arias with the utmost ease and facility." Thirty-six years later she was to dedicate the Auditorium, the great theater that symbolized Chicago's cultural rebirth after the fire. Her truly final American tour, the last of many farewells, was in 1906.

It was in October 1853 that Chicago heard what I suspect was an opera company with a number of authentically Italian-born singers. The population of the fast-growing city had by then risen to 60,650. Rice, undaunted by his previous operatic venture, welcomed to his new theater a group that called itself the Artists Association. Presumably it came from New York, making use of the rail link that in 1852 joined the tracks of the Illinois Central Railway with those of the Michigan Central near the state line. The Michigan Central had been extended to Toledo, and in 1853 it joined the railroad from Cleveland to the east. The Illinois Central proceeded into the city on pilings at the lakeshore, to reach a terminus at the river at what is now lower Wacker Drive.

There were four leading singers: a prima donna, Signora Rosa De Vries; a tenor, Signor Pozzolini; a baritone, Signor Taffanelli, and a bass, Signor Colletti. Maria Callas's pointed query many years later "Who needs mezzos?" was here answered graphically by the absence of a second lady among the featured artists. The company was advertised in a spare-no-superlatives style as forty singers and instrumentalists "under the magic direction of the most distinguished master and composer of European fame, Sig. Luigi Arditi." Arditi (1822–1903) made his career conducting opera in northern Europe rather than in Italian theaters and is now remembered as the composer of one work that has endured, the song "Il bacio" ("The Kiss"). This youthful debut was the first of many visits to Chicago, his finest hours being the Mapleson seasons some thirty years in the future.

It was commonplace in the nineteenth century that singers could not read music. Arditi was respected for teaching his singers their parts. Theodore Thomas recalls, "I can remember singers of great renown who did not know the name of a note."[6]

Thomas remembers that "Arditi, a small, nervous, energetic man, was in touch with his orchestra." In the performance you realized that "he knew his music, and one could instantly perceive that he had pounded it over many times with his singers . . . until they knew their parts well enough to go into an orchestral rehearsal." One hazard of this system is that singers might have memory lapses and skip a page or more of their part, requiring the conductor and orchestra to catch up with them.

The repertory consisted of three works: *Lucia di Lammermoor, La sonnambula,* and *Norma,* with each opera originally scheduled to be heard once. Apparently, public demand for tickets produced some repeat performances, but not enough to balance the books. Rossini's *Stabat Mater* closed the season on a note of piety, albeit one expressed in thoroughly operatic terms. The casting procedure was apparently that which was characteristic of smaller European companies of the day, in which the first soprano took the lead opposite the first tenor, and so on through the available talent until the roster was complete.

Rice's new theater had to be paid for. Prices had now risen to $2 for the boxes and dress circle, down to fifty cents for an unreserved place in the gallery. For Rice the engagement was a total failure. His budget estimates were faulty, and he could not take in enough at the box office to cover his costs. An extra performance of *Norma* was added in the hope that it would produce enough money to let the singers return to New York. Rice recouped his losses by booking an animal act featuring monkeys and dogs, an entertainment that earned him $1,000 in a week's run. Even so, he considered this an undignified way to make money and announced he would never again offer attractions of this type.

Opera in Chicago in the nineteenth century was show business. No one thought it required subsidy. But it did require singers. Chicago was an importer of opera and was to remain so until 1910. Opera could be presented when there were companies on the road that felt the inclination to travel west. In 1858, when the city had grown to ninety-three thousand, Rice left the theater for the larger and more dramatic world of politics. He was elected mayor of Chicago (1865–1869) and then sent to Congress. (He died, an honored citizen, in 1874.) His place as an impresario was taken by J. H. McVicker, who had been part of the chorus for the original *La sonnambula* performance in 1850. In 1857 the first McVicker's Theatre

James H. McVicker

The first McVicker's Theatre

had been built in a no-expense-spared manner on Madison Street, west of State Street. McVicker brought a troupe up the river, the New Orleans English Opera Company.

The meaning of the name is not self-evident. An English opera company did not necessarily come from England. This one certainly did not, nor was it committed to the works of Anglo-Irish composers. Rather, it sang operas (many of them Italian scores) in the English language. Today standards of musical purity demand that in this country an opera be given in either the original language or in English translation, but this practice dates only from the middle of the twentieth century. Prior to that you produced an opera in whatever language was most convenient. *Faust* was sung frequently in Italian, for example, and Mary Garden, the grand lady of Chicago's first resident opera company, sang both *Tosca* and *Salome* in French. No American opera company could deal with an opera in a Slavic language.

The common practice in Europe was to sing the operas of a nation's composers in the original language and translate works by composers of other countries. Thus, in German theaters, everything was sung in German. Mozart's *Don Giovanni,* for example,

became *Don Juan.* But there was no American operatic repertory. Translating everything suggested that operas in English would be accessible to the audience, a hope that was rarely realized. Moreover, the use of an English text more or less eliminated singers whose native language was not English.

Prices were going up. McVicker's theater, which held two thousand persons, had cost $85,000. Boxes were now $5, although seventy-five cents would buy a good seat. Racial segregation remained. There were two galleries, each offering twenty-five-cent seats, and blacks were required to sit in the upper one. The African American population of the city had substantially increased, and since many were slaves seeking refuge from southern masters, no exact count was possible.

The distinctive things about this engagement are the extent of the repertory—nine operas were heard, eight of them new to the city—and the unusual feature that the company had no tenor. Miss Georgia Hodson sang the male leads opposite Miss Rosalie Durand, with the two ladies exemplifying vocal stamina by appearing nightly. The company had three conductors, one of them twenty-three-year-old Theodore Thomas, who would return under happier circumstances for nearly fifty years.

The engagement began on September 27, 1858, with *La sonnambula,* which was beginning to look like Chicago's opera (although it was quickly to be eclipsed). Donizetti's *The Daughter of the Regiment (La Fille du régiment)* followed on the twenty-eighth, and Auber's *The Crown Diamonds (Les Diamants de la couronne)* was heard on the twenty-ninth. Rossini's *The Barber of Seville* was offered September 30. The first of two performances of *The Bohemian Girl* (by Michael William Balfe, 1808–1870) opened October 1, and October 2 brought more Auber, *Fra Diavolo.* The company then took Sunday off. It returned on October 4 with what I surmise was Rossini's *Cinderella (La Cenerentola),* proceeded with Weber's *Der Freischütz* on the sixth and seventh,[7] and *Il trovatore* on the eighth. A repeat of *The Bohemian Girl* on the ninth concluded the run.

Anyone who has written music criticism in the latter part of the twentieth century has heard agonized complaints from artists about the severity of the attacks to which they are subjected in the press. But contemporary music criticism is mild compared to what the nineteenth-century critic might write when his indignation was aroused. It would appear that, apart from giving the city an opportunity to hear (after a fashion) some important music for the first time, these performances were really bad. The critic of the *Journal* reached a particularly high peak of eloquence in his treatment of *Il trovatore,* the first Verdi to be heard in Chicago. The opera, he found, "was shrieked, screamed, groaned and killed. The whole performance was below mediocrity. The properties were miserable, the action tame, the music inharmonious, false, and discordant. *Il trovatore* is far beyond the capabilities of the troupe, and we trust they will not again allow the charge of murder to rest upon them." It should be noted that the critic evidently was familiar with the score. Nineteenth-century critics may have had more venomous pens than their twentieth-century successors, but in many cases they were better educated musically.

Things were to improve quickly. Four months later in the same theater "the fashion and chivalry of the city," as Upton described them, were to encounter authentic grand opera in an Italian season that proved so successful that Chicago now appeared to the eastern managers as a profitable place to visit. In a quarter of a century the transition from an Indian trading town to a place making some claim to culture and social refinement had been achieved.

Contributing to the change was that it had become reasonably easy and comfortable to travel from Chicago to New York. There were now two rail lines. On Christmas Day 1858 the Pittsburgh and Fort Wayne Railway began service between its station at Canal and Madison Streets and eastern cities. These rails were still new in February 1859 when Maurice Strakosch (1825–1887) arrived as conductor and director of a touring company. Strakosch was a graduate of the Vienna Conservatory and had come to New York in 1848 as a teacher and pianist but was destined to be transformed into an impresario. His younger brother, Max, was also a pianist and would become an important opera producer in New York. Maurice was the brother-in-law of Adelina Patti, married to her oldest sister, the soprano Amalia. Beginning with these 1859 performances Amalia became a stalwart of Chicago opera, a gracious and attractive woman, who possessed a beautiful voice and was completely reliable as a performer.

Maurice Strakosch   Max Strakosch

In addition to his talented wife, Strakosch introduced Chicago to some important Italian singers. Teresa Parodi had been brought to New York from London by the impresario Max Maretzek as a rival for Jenny Lind. She was a robust Italian woman, tall and dignified. Pasquale Brignoli, who was making his Chicago debut, was a dominant Italian tenor in New York and points west for many years. Chicago came to adore him for the elegance and beauty of his voice. Nicolo and Ettore Barili, Junca, and the senior Amodio were also heard. Significantly, there were a number of Americans: Cora Wilhorst, Henry Squires,

Marietta Piccolomini and Pasquale Brignoli

and, most important, Pauline Colson, a "pretty and vivacious" young woman, as Upton saw her, who delighted her audiences.

In short, Strakosch came to Chicago with artists of genuine stature, beginning a tradition that made it possible for Chicago to hear sooner or later nearly all of the best that New York had to offer. I surmise that Strakosch imported at least the principal players, if not all of the orchestra required, since Chicago might not have had musicians who could quickly master difficult and unfamiliar music and perform it on the level he expected.

The engagement, which ran from late February to mid-March 1859, consisted almost entirely of new repertory: the first performance of a Mozart opera, *Don Giovanni*, and major Verdi operas: *Ernani, Rigoletto, La traviata*, and, finally in an adequate presentation, *Il trovatore*. Donizetti was represented by three new works: *Lucrezia Borgia, La favorita (La favorite)*, and *Poliuto*, as well as *Lucia di Lammermoor*. Bellini's *I puritani* had its first local production, and *Maritana*, by William Vincent Wallace (1812–1865), which was a popular score in the English repertory, may also have been heard.[8] From the standpoint of the audience, the most important new work was the opera that was to drive *La sonnambula* from the hearts of the Chicago public, *Martha*, by far the most popular opera composed by Friedrich von Flotow (1812–1883).

Reminiscing, Upton writes, "When Colson sang *The Last Rose of Summer* and kissed her rose directly at the people, they simply went frantic and kept her singing it until she was nearly exhausted, not to mention Brignoli's patience."[9] *Martha* had a strange history. An operatic treatment of a ballet-pantomime, it was first presented in Vienna in November 1847 as *Martha oder Der Markt zu Richmond*. It is one of the most translated operas in history and, in consequence, an opera that—except in German-speaking countries—is almost never heard with its original text.

Its first London production (1849) was in German, but in 1858 it was heard in both Italian and English. In New York it was heard in English in 1852, in German in 1855, and in Italian in 1859. In the United States it was generally done in English unless it featured a major Italian artist, such as Caruso, in which case it was sung in that language. The Chicago première seems to have been basically an English version, although Brignoli apparently chose to sing his arias in his own language.

Brignoli, who played the role of Lionel on these evenings, gives us a key to operatic staging in a period when most people went to the theater primarily to hear voices. "To hear him sing *M'apparì* and *Il mio tesoro*," Upton recalls, "or the music of Manrico or Edgardo, was to listen to vocalization of absolute beauty, to an exposition of bel canto of the Italian romantic school as perfect for a tenor as Adelina Patti's for a soprano." But he was awkward, "an indifferent actor," always nervous and, in love scenes, "would implore [the soprano] not to touch him." A modern director would find him impossible, however beautiful the singing.

The opera subscriber of today hears a group of operas over a period of several months. In the nineteenth century it was a different story. A company would come to the city and, if you wished to hear all the new or important repertory, you might be in the theater four or five nights a week for two weeks or more. Since every night the theater was dark was a night that lost money, it was an endurance contest for singers, orchestra musicians, and critics, and Upton's records suggest that, hardy soul that he was, even he occasionally felt unequal to attending everything.

Binge operagoing was inevitable if the impresario put his profits ahead of graceful living. Consider this 1859 season at McVicker's. It probably was felt desirable to begin with music Chicago had encountered before, Donizetti's *Lucia di Lammermoor*, heard six years earlier. It opened the engagement February 21 and returned three days later. The first of the new Donizetti works was staged February 22, with Parodi as Lucrezia Borgia opposite Madame Strakosch and Junca. Brignoli was the tenor.

The following evening brought the Verdi team: Colson as Violetta, Brignoli as Alfredo, and Amodio as the elder Germont in *La traviata*. The work was only six years old. When it was first heard in New York in 1856, clergymen condemned its theme and promised it would have an adverse effect on public morals. No opera, not even *Salome* in 1910, seems to have altered Chicago's morals in the slightest, and *La traviata* was welcomed as the masterwork it is.

There was a new Bellini score on February 25, *I puritani,* with Cora Wilhorst opposite Brignoli and Amodio. Brignoli insisted he never sang high C in order to spare his voice, but apparently he thought nothing of appearing five nights in a row. The matinée on February 26 brought a second Donizetti score, *Poliuto,* with Parodi and Brignoli proving their endurance. Henry Squires, an American tenor, was the Duke in *Rigoletto,* with Nicolo in the title role and Wilhorst returning as Gilda. On Sunday, February 27, one gathers, all rested, even Strakosch, who appears to have been conducting everything.

Monday, February 28, brought *Il trovatore* as it should be—with a tenor. Brignoli presumably sang the part of Manrico as written (no high Cs), Parodi was Leonora, and Amodio, Di Luna. The work was repeated twice, March 4 and 7. As we shall see, *Il trovatore* quickly became the most popular serious large-scale opera in the local repertory.

Following it, on March 1, was the magnificent piece of froth that was to delight the public for decades: *Martha,* with Colson, Madame Strakosch, Brignoli, Junca, and Nicolo. It was repeated two nights later. After the luxury of a night off, Parodi returned on March 2 to sing *Norma* with Madame Strakosch, Brignoli, and Junca. And Brignoli was back the next day, with Colson, in *La sonnambula.* This was a Saturday, and if *Maritana* was heard from this company, it would have to have been a matinée (the record is unclear). Again there was a day of rest.

March 8 introduced the last of the Donizetti works new to the city, *La favorita,* with Parodi and Brignoli paired. They were back the next night in *Ernani.* The following two nights belonged to Mozart's *Don Giovanni,* with Barili in the title role, Parodi as Donna Anna, Madame Strakosch as Donna Elvira, Colson as Zerlina, and Brignoli as Ottavio—one of his finest roles. Junca played Leporello, Nicolo the Commendatore. The season closed March 11 with a series of operatic excerpts sung as a benefit for Strakosch.

Looking back from 1908, Upton delights in the innocent enthusiasm of the public over its "first season of real opera." Remember, he urges us, "they lived in the days of operatic Arcadia, where melody was born and where the art of bel canto still lives. . . . The orange had not been squeezed. Full dress was not imperative. Seats were not five dollars each. Opera was something new and fresh. . . . They had not heard of music dramas, motifs, the dramatic recitative opera, or music of the future."[10]

George P. Upton

What sort of opera was this? It was not at all like that of the late twentieth century. When one goes to the opera today, even in a smaller city, one expects to see a performance that has been produced rather than assembled. It is supposed to be an artistic, dramatic, and musical unity, the realization of ideas from a conductor, stage director, scenic designer, costume designer, lighting specialist, and other skilled personnel. In Madison, Wisconsin, the level of expectation exceeds that of New York audiences a century ago.

It must be remembered that before the mid–twentieth century performances rarely had that character. Opera was mostly about singing. One could assume that anything offered by a touring company had been sung previously on the road after one or more performances in New York. But usually a touring company did not bring scenery. A theater then was supposed to have stock scenery, a set of painted canvas drops covering basic situations such as the interior and exterior of a castle, a fashionable drawing room, a church, a city square, and so on. It also had swords, costumes, furniture, and other stage properties.

Leading singers had their own costumes for their roles. The first great American prima donna, Clara Louise Kellogg, whom we shall meet presently, spent a fortune on hers (she aspired to be the best-dressed woman in the theater), but her satins might not go with the character she was portraying. Such stage direction as there was came from the conductor. Most familiar operas had evolved a standard presentation, so a newcomer from another continent could walk onstage, size things up, and take an appropriate place with a dramatic gesture.

Although Theodore Thomas and European guests held the idea that the orchestral music should be played as effectively as possible, with the accuracy, refinement, and nuance associated with a symphony orchestra, most of the time audiences probably heard a hastily prepared ensemble furiously sight-reading under a conductor whose primary job was to accompany the money makers, the singing machines on stage.

Of course there were exceptions, but most of them were found in Europe. Wagner was a demanding conductor of great skill, and so, one gathers, was Verdi. As the century ended, Nikisch in Budapest, Mahler in Vienna, and Toscanini at La Scala and later at the Met revolutionized standards. But the first fifty years of opera in Chicago and operatic performances since the mid–twentieth century are very different in character.

There were three more opportunities to hear opera in 1859. The Cooper English Opera Troupe arrived April 11 to play in North's Amphitheater on Monroe Street, "a huge barn-like structure," as Upton saw it, unsuited to high-quality opera. It offered repertory the city already knew well and had heard in better performances. The new music was an oratorio, Haydn's *The Creation (Die Schöpfung),* and a concert of operatic excerpts included the first opportunity to hear a substantial part of Donizetti's *L'elisir d'amore.*[11] Silence fell until early December, when the city's first opera war broke out. There were two rival companies in the city. The Escott and Miranda English Opera Group returned Lucy Escott, Brookhouse Bowler, and

Kate Duckworth of the Cooper troupe and brought Miranda ("a very popular tenor," according to Upton) to McVicker's. The Italian company had Parodi and a strong tenor, Sbriglia, but it was generally not a terribly exciting group of singers. It booked the Metropolitan Concert Hall on the northwest corner of LaSalle and Randolph Streets. The dedicated operagoer was zigzagging between the two theaters until December 16. The Italians had to work on a small, concert-type stage, and "it required considerable skill and ingenuity to secure operatic illusions." Eventually the war "ended in the rout of the Italians, who were very poorly managed."[12]

On opening night, December 5, your choice was between *The Bohemian Girl* from the English troupe or *Il trovatore* from the Italians. If this does not seem to be any choice at all, recall that in the mid–nineteenth century *The Bohemian Girl* was regarded as an important work. "I dreamt I dwelt in marble halls" and "Then you'll remember me" were music to rival Martha's "The Last Rose of Summer" in popular favor. By 1910, when resident opera came to Chicago, it had vanished from the repertory. Balfe was no rival for Puccini.

The Italians continued with *Ernani,* and the English replied with *Maritana.* On December 7 the English countered with their *Il trovatore,* and the Italians staged *Norma.* And so it went. Three performances of an 1810 opera by John Davy (1763–1824), *Rob Roy MacGregor,* an English work that has achieved ultimate obscurity, followed. The Italians gave *Poliuto* December 10 and retired from the field. The English remained to present *Guy Mannering,* an 1816 work mainly, but not completely, by Sir Henry Bishop (1786–1855) and then invaded Italian repertory with Bellini and Donizetti.

In 1860 Chicago stood astride rail lines from east to west, and local merchants now sneered at St. Louis as "a fur trade town." Traveling salesmen, soon to become a part of American folklore, sallied forth to sell anything and everything Chicago merchants might supply. April saw the venerable Sauganash Tavern on the West Side at Lake Street and Market Street (now Wacker Drive) torn down, and in its place rose the Wigwam of the Republican Party. There, a month later, "Honest Abe, the Rail Splitter" was nominated to run for president of the United States.

After Lincoln's election there was little interest in opera as the nation tensely awaited the resolution of the differences between the North and the South.

Colson appeared briefly in Donizetti's *Don Pasquale.* In April 1861 a small troupe with Brignoli and other established people was heard in repertory that could be produced with minimal forces and piano accompaniment. Upton called the performances "excellent but unremunerative."

When on April 15 Lincoln called for seventy-five thousand volunteers to serve three months, it was clear that the nation had more important business before it than opera. The sword had been drawn for bitter conflict. Upton became a war corespondent (ideal training for someone planning to write music criticism in Chicago).

Between April 1861 and June 1863, when the New York impresario Jacob Grau lit up McVicker's for three weeks, Chicago counted opera among the wartime casualties. In the 1860s Jacob Grau's name on a stage bill had the same authority as that of Sol Hurok a century later. When a manager as important as Grau had come to realize there was money to be made in Chicago, the prestige of the city was established.

Upton says of Grau, "He made many artistic pretensions; indeed, from the fervor with which he did so, one might infer that he was sacrificing himself on the altar of art for the sake of the people, and that he was spending his money without a pang in order that the public should have Italian opera as the composer desired." Upton concluded this was a fraud. "His methods indicated a very commercial soul. . . . When business was good, he never appeared in newspaper offices but sent his nephew (Maurice Grau, who was to become a more important impresario than his uncle); but when business was bad, he was a frequent visitor, and long and piteous were his tales of woe, and most sorrowful were his complaints of the ingratitude of the public after all he had done for it. Then dark hints would follow that it might be his last season, for he was convinced that Chicago did not appreciate his efforts." In the long run, as Upton saw it, he "brought many fine artists to Chicago and produced opera in a good style."[13]

In June 1863 the important new work was Rossini's *Moses in Egypt* (*Mosè in Egitto*), a major representation of an aspect of the composer virtually unknown to American audiences today. Halévy's *La Juive* was also introduced. The city had its first encounter with Meyerbeer, represented by *Dinorah* and *Robert le diable.* The Verdi works included *I vespri siciliani* and *Un ballo in maschera,* both new. *Don Giovanni* was sung twice, the only repetition in the run.

The indefatigable Brignoli was the leading tenor, Vera Lorini (born Virginia Whiting) the soprano, and Amodio and Susini the baritone and bass, respectively. An Irish tenor, McAffery, Italianized himself as Macafferi. The schedule was hectic—a typical opera binge. Grau believed in keeping his singers, and his public, busy. Opening night was Monday, June 15, with *Lucrezia Borgia,* followed by five different operas in five nights and a Sunday of silence. The new week began with *I puritani* and was as crowded as its predecessor, but the sabbath was honored. *Don Giovanni* was heard Wednesday, June 24, and the following Tuesday. *Un ballo in maschera* opened the final week. *Moses in Egypt* was sung at midweek, and the series closed July 4 with *Robert le diable.*

The city had been opera-starved, and thus, despite the length of the run, tickets sold well. The casts had the stamina to deal with the schedule. It was typical of the times: the nineteenth-century opera singer was made of strong stuff. Since Grau made money, he was back at McVicker's on February 1, 1864, for nine performances in ten days. Lorini again was the principal soprano, Morensi (Kate Duckworth, transformed) the contralto, Tamaro the leading tenor, Morelli (who sang Don Giovanni) the baritone, and Hartmann the bass. The repertory was familiar. *Il trovatore* was heard twice. The run began with Donizetti and Bellini, followed by *Martha, Un ballo in maschera,* and *Don Giovanni.*

Things went so well that Grau was back in May for twelve performances in thirteen days. The singers were essentially the same as those he had brought earlier, but this time the repertory included three works new to the city, the most important of them Gounod's *Faust,* which in 1883 was to open the Metropolitan Opera House in New York. For a large segment of the public it came to represent the summation of romantic opera. We must remember that in the mid–nineteenth century few singers of other than French birth sang opera in that language. *Faust* for many years was an Italian opera. The same applied to Meyerbeer, represented this time by *Robert le diable,* which opened the second series on May 9 with Steffani in the title role. The *Faust* offered Tamaro as the aged protagonist, Morelli as Mephistopheles, and Lorini as Marguerite. On May 16 practically the entire resources of the troupe were expended on Meyerbeer's *Les Huguenots,* which was being heard in the city for the first time. The run continued with *Don Giovanni,* again with Morelli, and closed with Auber's *La Muette de Portici* under the title of the first English performance, *Masaniello.* This was another successful engagement. Grau was pleased. You could make money producing opera in Chicago.

There was a brief summer season in July 1865 from the Philips Opera Company, consisting of two comic operas, *The Barber of Seville* and *Don Pasquale.* Brignoli, always ready to take to the road, was the tenor in largely Italian casts. In the grand tenor manner, Brignoli made a great deal of money, spent it, and died broke. Upton met him for the last time in 1884. Patti was to sing that night, but Brignoli could not afford a ticket and would not ask for a pass. "I sang with Adelina when she made her debut [1859]," he recalled. "Tonight she must transpose her part. Old Brignoli can sing his where it is written. Adelina gets $5,000 a night; old Brignoli gets fifty cents." He died in New York a few weeks later. The age of the tenor was yet to come.[14]

A new period in the history of Chicago opera begins with the opening of Crosby's Opera House on April 20, 1865. The war had ended, and the arts were ready to flourish again.

Surveying the more than thirty scores heard in Chicago during the first fourteen years of operatic production, one must first observe that the musical diet was remarkably well balanced. Four different musical traditions were represented, and none dominated. The division between German, French, Italian, and English/Irish composers was nearly equal.

Secondly, the high quality of the music heard was impressive. Nearly half the works remain in the repertory of American opera houses, and others are scores that turn up with reasonable frequency in Europe; the third that is produced no longer is generally the weakest material. Here the blow falls heaviest on the English/Irish composers, all of whom are gone. The primary casualties from the Continent are Meyerbeer, who has been unfashionable for nearly a century, and the French light-opera composer Auber.

One of the staples of the nineteenth-century repertory in the United States and in England was the (facetiously named) "English *Ring*": *The Bohemian Girl, Maritana,* and *The Lily of Killarney.* The first two works were introduced to Chicago in 1858 and 1859, respectively; the third arrived in 1868. None appears to have been able to compete with *Martha.*

Chicago preferred Italian opera, and it preferred new opera, as represented by Verdi, to the older bel canto tradition. *Il trovatore,* Verdi in his purest form, was the most popular work in the repertory. Five other Verdi works were known, but the full range of his work was not discovered until the twentieth century.

Surveying the scene, we conclude that the consistent Chicago operagoer in 1864 knew the work of the major Italian composers of the older school. Bellini, Donizetti, and Rossini had all been adequately represented. Indeed, this hypothetical Chicagoan knew the serious Rossini of *Moses in Egypt,* an aspect of the composer denied the majority of later listeners, and there was familiarity with Mozart's *Don Giovanni.* New music outside of Italy was represented by *Faust,* the most incorrigibly popular opera of the nineteenth century. The distinctive German operatic tradition was represented by its first great success, *Der Freischütz.*

The gaps are obvious, the greatest of them Wagner (who was to appear in 1865). But it was a solid foundation on which to build, and its strength would soon be proved.

2

The Crosby Years

1865–1871

In 1865, Chicago, with a population of about 250,000, had an opera house nearly as large as La Scala, Milan. This was partly American bravura, but it also reflected the fact that midway in the nineteenth century opera in America was commercial theater. It was supposed to be produced at a profit, even if this was often more a hope than a reality. In any case, the more seats you had to sell, the more income the box office could yield.

The person responsible for this new citadel of the muse signed himself U. H. Crosby, and he was one of a number of shrewd Yankees (the greatest was Marshall Field of Pittsfield, Massachusetts) who saw Chicago as a glorious place to make money.[1] Born in 1831, Uranus Crosby left his home on Cape Cod and came to Chicago in 1850. His cousin Albert, two years his senior, had arrived in 1848 and prospered selling tea and liquor. By 1850 Albert had the largest distillery in the western United States, at Chicago Avenue and Larrabee Street. He was a businessman. Uranus was strongly committed to the arts. He had missed the initial performance of *La sonnambula,* but he was present for later operatic seasons. He soon felt the obligation to establish opera in the city on a proper scale. Less interested in money than in elevating the cultural level of the community, he nonetheless realized money was essential for the realization of his goals and went to work with his cousin. Together they made a fortune as distillers and importers of alcoholic beverages. Their chief product was probably corn whiskey, the staple libation of the frontier.

In May 1860, sensing the inevitability of war, they were delighted to learn from a drunken politician that hostilities would bring a tax on liquor. They surmised that the tax would be applied as the spirits came out of the still, before they had suffered an

evaporation loss in the warehouse. The cousins had their warehouses full before the first shot was fired. Since they had a superior product, aged longer than their competitors' wares, they could demand a premium price. And because the monies rivals had to turn over to the tax collector were considerably higher than what the Crosbys paid, the Crosby pockets were enriched all the more. From this golden hoard, Chicago opera flowered as it never had before.

A symbol of the nation's triumphant rebirth following the Civil War, the new opera house was directly across the adjacent block from Rice's theater of 1847, standing midway on the north side of Washington Street east of Dearborn. The frontage of the building was 140 feet, and it was 190 feet in depth. A second building, 90 feet wide, on State Street housed commercial rentals and, on the fourth floor, Beethoven Hall, a concert room with one thousand seats. It opened seven months after the large theater, in November 1865.

The architect for both projects, William W. Boyington (1818–1898) was responsible for a number of important buildings of the day, among them the first University of Chicago. His lasting monument is the waterworks and water tower, which survived the fire and stand today at the intersection of Chicago and Michigan Avenues. The opera house was one of his biggest projects and presented problems he had not had to face before. Uranus took him to Italy, where the San Carlo Opera House in Naples and the Teatro Regio in Parma provided examples of how such a building should be designed and decorated.

The façade, which Upton characterizes as "the French style, common in public edifices at the time,"[2] offered space for stores at the street level. The commercial spaces (each 30 feet wide and 190 feet deep)

Uranus H. Crosby

Albert Crosby

Crosby's Opera House at its opening, 1865

Crosby's Opera House auditorium

flanked both sides of the entrance to what Crosby called the "temple of art" and were occupied by three music merchants: the Kimball piano company, the Root and Cady music store, and Julius Bauer & Co. The fourth held Kinsley's restaurant, an establishment reflecting Crosby's belief that his patrons would like to dine elegantly a mere step or two away from the theater. Kinsley's became a shrine for those devoted to oysters and ice cream.

The main entrance was crowned with statues representing painting, sculpture, music, and commerce, dedicating the building to a synthesis of business and the arts. The façade was made of Athens marble. Fragments of it, hauled away after the fire, may be found in lakefront landfill on the south side of the city. The hidden sidewalls were presumably brick. One went through the main entrance and up a flight of stairs to the auditorium, which was shielded from street noise by buildings of equal height on both sides and by studios for music teachers at the front of the building on the second and third floors, a feature suggested by the architecture of Italian opera houses.

In 1867 the twenty-six-year-old Florenz Ziegfeld, father of the future Broadway producer and one of the city's most popular music teachers, moved his Academy of Music to these opera house spaces. After the fire, in a new home, he founded Chicago Musical College, now part of Roosevelt University. The fourth floor and a shallow attic behind a mansard roof contained an art gallery and ten studios for artists. At the time of the fire Crosby had an apartment in this part of the opera house. Rental of the commercial and studio spaces was reported to be worth $30,000 a year.

Arriving at the head of the stairs, operagoers passed a ticket taker. They then entered the grand foyer, its walls covered with light blue damask and adorned with mirrors and ornamentation. Statues by Leonard Volk symbolizing music and drama framed the three large double doors into the auditorium. The main floor of the theater was divided into three sections: orchestra, parquet, and dress circle. There were six proscenium boxes, an innovation for the city. Fifty more, furnished and decorated to meet the most exacting taste of the day, were placed in the front of the balcony circle. The family circle lay behind. For the opening performances Crosby reserved a large number of these seats for "respectable colored persons," who were charged seventy-five cents admission but given a ticket for a lower price if it was beyond their means.[3] There was a total of three thousand seats.

The proscenium contained a fresco, a copy of Guido Reni's *Aurora,* and was flanked by other frescoes representing Comedy and Tragedy. Portraits of twelve eminent composers were set in sunken panels in the domed ceiling, completing the decoration of the house. Illumination was by gas, but the lighting was indirect, which heightened the splendid effect. This, many insisted, was the most beautiful room in the city.

Looking back from 1908, when the Auditorium was considered close to obsolete, Upton recalled Crosby's theater as "rich and artistic . . . a model of comfort, convenience, and safety. It was a combined opera house, art gallery, and home of arts and crafts on which money had been expended lavishly [$700,000] and of which Chicago was very proud. It was just such a structure as Chicago needs today."[4] Upton admired the Auditorium when it was new, but apparently felt in time, as others did, that its splendid

acoustics did not compensate for a lack of intimacy.

Crosby's Opera House was a classic, compact, horseshoe-shaped hall, and, as with most theaters of this type, the acoustics were considered excellent. Lighting and the facilities for operatic production were of the most modern design. Built-in treadmills and overhead tracks made the movement of scenery fast and easy. No New York theater had as many gaslights—the number ran into the hundreds—with reflectors that permitted a wide range of new effects. There was an automatic system to spray water on the stage in case of fire, and fire exits were provided to State Street and the roofs of adjacent buildings. A steam-powered ventilating system energetically exchanged the hot air of the auditorium with cool, fresh air from outside. And the artists rejoiced at the size and appointments of the dressing rooms, some of which even contained a small piano.

The dedication of the hall, scheduled for April 17, 1865, was intended by Crosby to be one of the great events of the year. He had engaged the Italian opera company of the New York Academy of Music, which was on tour under the management of Jacob Grau. Grau was "deeply impressed with the importance of the occasion"[5] and scheduled the longest opera season in the history of the city—forty-two performances in seven weeks. Subscriptions were sold until April 13, after which the public could buy tickets for individual performances. Like some Lyric Opera seasons to come many years later, nearly every seat was sold before opening night. The company arrived by rail from Cincinnati on April 10, and preparations for the opening began at full speed. Ladies had been told not to wear hoop skirts, and gentlemen were informed they must wear full dress, announcements that caused some consternation among those who did not already possess appropriate garments.

These matters were quickly overshadowed on the morning of April 15 when the city learned of the assassination of President Lincoln. The opening must be postponed, and April 20 was set as the new date. Pouring rain did not prevent this from being "one of the most brilliant audiences ever assembled in Chicago."[6] Everybody who professed to be anybody in the city was there: George Pullman, the railroad tycoon; Marshall Field, the merchant prince; Joseph Medill, publisher of the *Tribune;* the hotelier Potter Palmer; and theater owners Rice and McVicker. They were all on the list. The critic Upton had been seated in the midst of these eminences, a gesture that would never be repeated in a later day. Moved by the splendor of the theater, the audience called for Crosby to speak. He complied and then gave the stage to George C. Bates, a golden-tongued member of the bar, who produced a roll of paper and read an "Inauguration Ode" by W. H. C. Hosmer, to the growing distress of his listeners.

Finally there was *Il trovatore*. Carl Bergmann conducted a cast with Carlotta Carozzi-Zucchi the soprano, Morensi the contralto, Bernardo Massimiliani the tenor, and Fernando Bellini the baritone. Their names evoke little magic today, but they were celebrated, highly paid artists, hailed by Upton as "a superb troupe." Grau supplied the sets and costumes (although in those days they might be used for more than one opera). The principal artists usually wore their own costumes, which may or may not have been suitable dress for the characters they were playing. Apparently it was felt that Chicago could not supply a pit band equal to performing this music, so Grau brought his own orchestra, probably about forty players. There was no stage director. The idea of a production designed as a unity and directed in a style consistent with that design did not exist. Opera was still about singing, and the staging was of secondary importance.

Upton complained that *Il trovatore* was now familiar to the point of being hackneyed (it was to be the second most frequently heard opera in the century) but that the performance was superb. It was not inappropriate that the engagement should feature two American singers. One of them, Morensi, as noted earlier, was born Kate Duckworth but apparently felt that pretending to be European would enhance her career. The second night brought *Lucia di Lammermoor* and, more important, the Chicago operatic debut of a woman who wanted to be known as an American prima donna, Clara Louise Kellogg, then twenty-two years old. Kellogg, born in South Carolina, made her debut in New York in 1861 and in 1863 sang Marguerite in the first New York performance of *Faust*—a role she was to repeat throughout her career. (*Faust* was the work most frequently produced in Chicago in the nineteenth century.) In 1867 she was engaged by Colonel James Henry Mapleson (of whom we shall hear more later) to make her London debut in *Faust* and triumphantly established that America could produce singers of the first rank. In addition to having a lovely, well-trained voice, she advanced an idea that she shared with a number of other American singers: that the success of her performance depended not only on the quality of her singing but on the dramatic force with which she defined and projected a character as well. This produced a sharp contrast with Italian artists, who were primarily concerned with vocal display.

Clara Louise Kellogg

On April 27, six days after her Chicago debut, Kellogg proved to be a truly virginal Marguerite when *Faust* entered the season's repertory. (In her memoirs she observes that she did not feel either Marguerite or Lucia was particularly bright.) Morensi was Siebel, Guglielmo Lotti played the title role, and Bellini (a fine singing actor) gave Mephistopheles a swagger and sophistication the city had not seen in the character before. Here, and in other evenings of the series, the audience felt it was encountering a familiar opera in a performance so superior to those it had known in the past that its conception of the work must be revised.

Kellogg was the most conspicuous soprano of the series, rivaled only by Carlotta Carozzi-Zucchi, who sang the heavy Italian roles. Moreover, Kellogg showed her skills in both bel canto and more recent repertory. She sang in *I puritani,* but she was also Gilda in *Rigoletto.* She did not reject lighter, popular scores like *Martha, The Daughter of the Regiment,* and *Fra Diavolo* and proved a delightful Zerlina in *Don Giovanni.* One yearns for a worm hole in time that might permit a contemporary listener to discover exactly what these performances were like. It is instructive that even in the opening weeks of an inaugural season such as this, where curiosity alone might be expected to sell tickets, only one of twenty-one operas (Donizetti's *Linda di Chamounix*—another Kellogg vehicle) was new to the city, so it was felt desirable for the bill to change every night. *Fra Diavolo* and *Martha,* the two certain successes, were given five and four performances, respectively. *Il trovatore,* then the most popular of the serious works, got two evening stagings and a matinée. *Don Sebastiano* (another Donizetti opera), *Norma,* and *Faust* were heard three times. *Linda di Chamounix,* the new work, was scheduled for three performances, but the first one had to be replaced by a last-minute switch to *Lucia di Lammermoor* because the tenor could not reach the city in time. Like most impresarios, Grau was cautious. He liked to stick with what had sold well in the past.

Grau also was attracted by the opportunity to create a new effect. In *Un ballo in maschera,* on May 5, rather than engaging supernumeraries to fill the stage in the final scene, he invited the fashionable audience in the boxes and the seats nearest the stage to join the small group of maskers he had placed on the stage so that they could be an active part of the gala event at which the Count (sung by the tenor Francesco Mazzoleni, who was making his Chicago debut) would meet his death. It was, Grau felt, "the event of the season," although on other nights he spared little to produce vivid, large-scale theatrical effects.

The run progressed from April to June with a militantly Italian repertory. Its forty-two performances were nearly four times the number of the opening series of Chicago's Lyric Theater eighty-nine years later. The only French operas were *Faust* and *Fra Diavolo,* both sung in Italian. The only Austro-German composers were Mozart *(Don Giovanni)* and Flotow *(Martha),* both also sung in Italian. The great rivalry was between the new—Verdi, with ten performances—and the old—Donizetti, with twelve performances, Bellini with five. Donizetti was, briefly, the most popu-

lar composer. By the close of the century his reputation was to rest almost entirely on *Lucia di Lammermoor.*

Several of the operas had important choral music, and Grau imported his usual motley crew from New York. "No manager," Upton later observed, "ever brought together a more venerable aggregation of signoras and signors than he. . . . Some required only a steady supply of pasta to keep them contented" but "others were a mob of chronic fault-finders, ready to rise in revolt on the slightest pretext, and most ready to rise just before the curtain rose." Grau's solution— offered, one trusts, facetiously—was that "the only way to be sure of a performance was to kill one of them whenever two or three were seen with their heads together, otherwise you would have to pay them whatever they demanded or kill yourself."[7]

After the inaugural performances Grau departed briefly for Cincinnati. But there was money to be made in Chicago, and a second, short series from June 5 to 20 completed the dedication of the house. These performances included the second new work of the series, *La forza del destino,* which was billed as the American première of a new Verdi score. *Forza* had been composed for St. Petersburg and was first sung there in December 1862. Rome heard it the following year, and Vienna heard it a few days before Chicago, but it was on the stage at Crosby's before it was presented in London, Paris, or, for that matter, Milan. Grau's claim of a première appears to have been exaggerated. He had offered the work in New York the preceding February. Otherwise the repertory was picked up from the previous weeks, and, for all the fanfare about new works, the score most frequently performed—five times—was the lasting favorite, *Fra Diavolo* (which died, with the Ravinia Opera, in 1931).

On June 12 Generals Ulysses S. Grant and William Tecumseh Sherman were honored with a performance of *The Daughter of the Regiment.* Upton, who was present, observes that "neither of the war heroes seemed to be very deeply engrossed with the doings of the vivandiere and her companions until the 'Rataplan' was sung. . . . I do not think either of them cared greatly for music."[8]

Crosby then had to face the reality that he knew how to sell whiskey but that producing opera was a different matter entirely. Grau made money; Crosby didn't. Even with sold-out houses, he was the last to be paid—if he was paid at all. Income from performances had proved inadequate to cover the expenses of maintaining the theater. Opera required one to think of patronage rather than profits—patronage on a greater scale than he could supply.

Remarkable as it was, the opening of Crosby's Opera House was not the beginning of opera in 1865. Those performances, presented by Leonard Grover, had begun at McVicker's on January 2 of that year when the German population was rewarded by the visit of what Upton called "the first German thoroughly equipped opera troupe" to the city. In a German company, German singers sang their native language, even in the popular Italian operas. The artists, recruited from a number of German theaters, were good and much easier to deal with—and pay—than Italians. Grover provided Chicago's first encounter with an opera by Richard Wagner. The work, heard on January 13, was *Tannhäuser,* with an undersized orchestra and a heavily cut performance of the Dresden version of 1845 rather than the more recent 1861 Paris text. Grover could not supply a ballet. This was the year when Europeans could hear *Tristan und Isolde,* and the arrival of Wagner's music in Chicago was overdue. But although Wagner's name was seen on the dome at Crosby's Opera House, Grau apparently would not tour with an orchestra large enough to play a Wagnerian score and feared that he would not find extra musicians of adequate quality in Chicago.

This was a long season, nearly three weeks, with a repertory of fifteen scores for a total of twenty performances. Familiar works were *Faust, The Barber of Seville,* and *Don Giovanni.* New works in the January series were Boïeldieu's *La Dame blanche* and Meyerbeer's *Les Huguenots,* both sung in German. Original German works in the repertory were *Fidelio, The Magic Flute (Die Zauberflöte),* and Flotow's *Stradella,* which was unable to challenge the popularity of *Martha,* also heard, apparently for the first time, in the original language.

After the festive opening, Crosby's theater offered no more opera until September, but the season 1865/66 became a sustained opera binge, a test of how much music of this type the audience could support. The autumn began with the arrival of Campbell's and Castle's English Opera Troupe at the Academy of Music. They offered Balfe and Wallace for four weeks. On October 12 they gave a performance of *Maritana* at Crosby's theater before an audience of less than fifty persons, but they tried again with *The Bohemian Girl* and enjoyed somewhat greater success. The Rosa Cook English Company then briefly passed through town, followed by the Smith and Zuporis English Opera Troupe for a week's performances that contrasted *Faust* with the same Balfe and Wallace staples just heard from Campbell and Castle. Upton was unimpressed by these shows.

Apparently feeling that he had a public in the Midwest which would buy anything, Grau was back in November for Crosby's second season with what Upton describes as "a heterogeneous collection of mediocrities gathered from everywhere, including No Man's Land."[9] There were a few singers of consequence in the group, the chief of them Lucy Simons, who made her debut in *L'elisir d'amore* on the twenty-first to provide one of the few bright moments of the run. This was the first complete performance of the work in Chicago, but the *Tribune* review was skeptical about the score's prospects for survival. (Lyric Opera of Chicago was still doing it in 2000.) *L'elisir, La traviata,* and Gounod's *Sapho* were the only operas not included in Grau's offerings of earlier months.

When Grover's Grand German Opera Company returned for two weeks in December, it came to Crosby's with different singers but much the same repertory as during its visit in January. Eleven works were heard for a total of thirteen performances. The orchestra and chorus were poor and the casts were of uneven quality, but as the series progressed, quality improved. Crosby wanted a performance of *Tannhäuser,* but poor advance ticket sales caused Grover to cancel it. The single Wagner performance of *Tannhäuser* in Crosby's theater did not come until 1871.

If one should ask dedicated operagoers of the 1990s what they considered the greatest year for opera in Chicago, they might think of one of the Lyric's best seasons or the legendary days of Mary Garden, but I am inclined to argue for 1865. Here was a city of 250,000 with an extraordinary new opera house—a theater that might have been in use a century later had it survived—that in the space of a single year heard thirty-seven different operas with a total of approximately one hundred performances. The Lyric in its forty-fifth season offered eighty-five performances, but in a metropolitan area of 8.5 million persons. And it produced not forty, but eight, operas.

In 1865, about 300,000 opera tickets were printed for a population of 250,000 persons. The public was offered more tickets than would have been required to send every adult man or woman in the city to the opera once and still leave space for tourists. Clearly, the opera audience was a much smaller group of dedicated individuals who attended several performances in the course of the year. A few (other than music critics) might actually have heard all the thirty-seven works that were presented.

The most frequently sung opera in 1865 was *Faust,* with eleven performances from various sources. Assuming all tickets were sold, that gave Chicago an active opera audience of 33,000, 13% of the population. In its forty-fifth season the Lyric gave a popular opera twelve times to an audience of 42,000. But with the Lyric no work received less than nine performances.

Who made up the audience of 1865? My suggestion is that many were foreign-born, with the Germans—the Forty-Eighters—a significant part of the total. Consider the case of my great-grandfather, who was born in 1811 and would have been fifty-four years old, in the prime of his life, when Crosby's Opera House opened. For all I know, he might have been in that opening night audience. I also suspect that a significant portion of this German group consisted of German Jews. The Jewish population was well assimilated into German life, and the assumption that a German immigrant was a Christian is unjustified. This was Chicago's greatest operatic audience. In the 1860s it was in midlife, in the 1870s it was aging, and by the 1890s it was largely gone. It was not replaced for nearly a century, and as it disappeared the demand for opera declined sharply.

Many of the Europeans thought of opera as a cultural resource funded by the state. For my great-grandfather in his youth, the Bavarian treasury met the bills. The American idea of opera as business for profit was alien. With the 1865 season opera in Chicago reached a saturation point. The commercial importance of opera was diminishing because of oversupply, and the market regulated itself with a decrease in the number of performances offered in later years. So we witness a vicious cycle in which, if the opera producer offers performances of the quality needed to attract the finest audience, he loses money. If he resorts to entertainment that offers the promise of balancing the books, he may be accused of abandoning the cause of musical art.

Today opera in Chicago must compete with other forms of serious music and a wealth of commercial mass entertainment and professional sports that did not exist in 1865. One can ask, theoretically, how many of these operagoers would have appeared at the box office had they been offered television, films, or football. (In the 1860s there were occasional recitals and symphony concerts, and the theater of the spo-

ken word was more important then than now.) If the Lyric were to offer enough performances of an opera to reach 13% of the present population, it would have to stage the work 265 times during the season. This, of course, is absurd. No opera company in the world offers a single score in anything approaching this number of performances in one year. In 1865 opera had achieved the level of social penetration associated today with a highly successful musical show such as *The Phantom of the Opera,* which can offer as many as seven performances a week. In that case an expensive production is mounted, but if the show plays long enough, it amortizes the investment and becomes profitable. The flood of opera in 1865—and the red ink that flowed many nights—led to a bleak winter of 1865/66.

Crosby's Yankee ingenuity and Midwestern taste clashed when he realized that the opera house was not going to be the moneymaker he had anticipated. In the postwar era costs had increased and profits had shrunk—or disappeared. "He had spent money extravagantly," Upton observes, and, "knowing little about the details of the operatic business, he was at the mercy of managers," who "had been slowly but surely dragging him to the verge of bankruptcy. . . . He was generous to a fault, and undoubtedly his generosity had been abused more than once . . . since the brilliant inauguration night."[10]

But there was more to it than the high cost of presenting opera. Uranus had long cut a figure as the wealthy bachelor. He had been living in the most expensive hotel suite in the city, belonged to all the best clubs, and spent $15,000 a year for the upkeep of his personal stable of horses. As 1865 came to an end, Crosby's financial situation was so grim that he authorized the liquidation of his real estate holdings, securities, and personal property to pay his debts.

Grau was back in January with five performances of Meyerbeer's *L'Africana (L'Africaine).* Upton recalled that "the performance was mediocre, but being a novelty, it drew crowds." The observation is significant. The audience of 1866 did not reject new works. On the contrary, perhaps growing tired of the bombardment of *Faust* and *Il trovatore,* it was especially open to something new.

In an effort to make money with popular entertainment, the opera house was filled on April 17 for "a great Ethiopian extravaganza"—Skiff and Gaylord's minstrel show. Crosby was unhappy. He had not built his theater for performances of this type. In May

Ghioni and Susini offered what Upton calls "a scratch company" (today it would be "pickup" company) for a short run, with Max Strakosch as the director. All the repertory was familiar except for what Upton found "a delightful little opera," *Crispino e la comare* by Luigi Ricci (1805–1859) and his brother, Federico Ricci (1809–1877). There were three performances, and the local audience was receptive, but it proved to be only a passing fancy.

Ghioni and Susini, again with Max Strakosch in charge, returned to light up Crosby's on Christmas Eve 1866 with a season that was to run through January 11 of the new year. Crosby may have been aware of the shortcomings of the troupe but engaged it because it was the only one on the road. *Il trovatore* was heard on opening night, followed by *Crispino e la comare,* *L'Africana* (three times), *La favorita* on New Year's Eve, and *Norma* on January 1. *Fra Diavolo* followed on the second (with a repeat), then a procession of familiar scores. Some excellent singers were in the casts, but apparently the series was hastily thrown together to get as many operas as possible before the public.

It is mistaken to assume that what was offered was always what was most desired, especially in a season that lost money. Impresarios, like many managers today, tended to follow the public rather than lead it, and their choices of what would sell were often based on nothing more than anxiety and guesswork.

If the lessons of the following decade are valid, what Chicago may have been most curious about in the late 1860s was Wagner, but his works were expensive to produce, hence risky—something to be avoided, if possible. But if you avoid what you can sell and produce what you cannot sell, your losses may be even greater. In 1865 there were five Wagner operas the city might have heard, but one had to wait until 1896 before all of them had been staged in Chicago. By that time Wagner's *Ring* cycle, first heard in Bayreuth in 1876, had had its local première.

It became clear that the only way the opera house was to make money was to have it managed by a professional, and in 1866 C. D. Hess, who considered it the best theater west of his base in New York, accepted a five-year lease on the house with the assumption that he would keep it functioning. When touring opera was available it would be heard. The rest of the time he would select the most promising attractions on the road.

Crosby's problem was how to recoup his investment in the theater. The gimmick, as a later genera-

tion would call it, was the formation of the Opera House Art Association. For $5 you could purchase an engraving or a lithographed copy of a painting and also received a lottery ticket that might bring you the opera house as a prize. Lotteries were popular, and in this one the curse of gambling was overcome. The ticket was a reward for spending $5 for enriching your home with a fine work of art. The art may have cost Crosby twenty-five cents, but—due to the popularity of the scheme—a copy of Huntington's *Mercy's Dream* became the showpiece of many a prairie parlor.

With nicely calculated ambiguity, Crosby never said precisely what the winner was to get. Most ticket holders thought they had an opportunity to own the building, but it is clear that Crosby never intended to part with the four walls and income from the commercial spaces. If you read the fine print, the prize was the portion of the structure occupied by the theater, a far less desirable reward. Some important (and some worthless) works of art housed in the building were also to go to the winners. More than three hundred prizes would be awarded.

If the lottery was conceived from the beginning as a swindle, it must be said that Crosby carried it off with real finesse. "In the spring of 1865," the prospectus—probably written by himself—tells us, "Crosby completed his opera house at a cost of $600,000." Due to great expenses over his original budget "and other unforeseen costs which it is unnecessary to state, he became financially embarrassed and only succeeded in his purpose of giving to Chicago this noble work of art at the sacrifice of his fortune."[11] The *Tribune* bewailed that the "sublime conception" of the opera house should end in "the disastrous failure of its proprietor."

The Opera House Art Association was to remedy this injustice. There were 210,000 tickets available (considerably better odds than the present Illinois State Lottery offers), of which Crosby retained the 25,000 that remained unsold—roughly one chance in eight of winning. The public fancy was attracted by the idea and sales were good, but not good enough to permit a drawing in October 1866, when the lottery was originally to be held. It was rescheduled for January 21, 1867, shortly after Ghioni and Susini had ended their run. Some players gathered together in pools, many of them with raffish names like "Bloody Tub" and "Kiss Me Quick," trusting that if they had enough tickets, they were sure to win something.

When the day arrived, the city was packed with

ticket holders gazing at the glittering reward they felt they would soon grasp. The drawing took place on the opera house stage. One spinning circular drum contained all the ticket numbers, another contained the numbers of the prizes. Numbers from the larger drum would be drawn until the smaller one was empty.

Crosby was lucky. He won a fine bust of Lincoln and two of the best paintings in the collection. Others were pleased to carry away a genre painting typical of the period, such as *A Scene in the Tyrol* or *The Sultan's Daughter*. With the 113th spin of the drums the opera house came up as the prize. The winner was not in the hall. Indeed, he was never seen by the press or the public. Identified as Abraham Hagerman Lee of Prairie du Rocher (a village south of St. Louis in the backlands of remote Randolph County), he later announced in a letter to a St. Louis newspaper that he was surprised by his success but really had no use for an opera house. Lee was no simple farmer. In the Civil War he had been a colonel in an Illinois regiment. His wife, who may have been the one who bought the ticket, was French.

To avoid "unpleasant notoriety," as he told the *Chicago Republican* after the event, he came to the city and sold Crosby the ticket for $200,000. He then vanished. To skeptics, he was a phantom: he never existed, and most certainly the $200,000 was never paid; the lottery had been a confidence game of monumental proportions. The figures are impressive. Crosby's theater had cost $700,000, about $600,000 to build and roughly $100,000 to furnish, but lottery tickets worth at least $900,000 had been sold. The cost of running the lottery was perhaps $10,000.

The $200,000 payment to Lee was, in fact, genuine. In 1867 Lee built a mansion near Prairie du Rocher, which survived until 1970. But neither Lee nor his wife lived to enjoy it long, for both were gone in 1869, when Lee's business partner acquired the property. His family lived there until 1935.

Through the lottery the public had paid back Crosby all his costs in constructing his temple to the glorious union of the arts and commerce and left him in possession of the building. He was saved for the moment, but public opinion was against him, and the wisest move appeared to be to sell the opera house. Albert Crosby cared very little for the arts, but he was a successful and respected Chicago businessman with a brewery, a distillery, and substantial real estate holdings. Ownership of the property would enhance his prestige. In 1867 he bought the opera house from his cousin for an undisclosed sum. Uranus retained his apartment, but Albert was now in charge.[12]

The lottery over, public imagination was again attracted by opera. In the spring of 1867 Strakosch returned with what was now called the Grand Italian Opera Company. Chicago was offered five operas in six days, all familiar items. *Il trovatore,* with Euphrosyne Parepa-Rosa and the veteran Brignoli, once more opened the series, followed by *Norma, The Barber of Seville* (which was heard twice), *Don Giovanni,* and *Don Pasquale.* Parepa (her hyphenated named followed her marriage to Carl Rosa) was a soprano of monumental build and serene temperament, blessed with a pure, lyric soprano, which had been carefully trained in all the vocal styles of the day. She spoke five languages and happily toured wherever her music might be desired. Much of her work was in recital rooms, but her contribution to opera in England was probably the most important of the day.

It was Strakosch again for a brief autumn season, this time with a group called the La Grange and Brignoli Grand Italian Opera Company. There were twelve performances, opening October 28 (with *Il trovatore,* of course) and offering what appears to be the last mighty array of bel canto scores. There were performances of *Norma, I puritani, Lucrezia Borgia,* and *Lucia di Lammermoor. Ernani* was heard alongside the two Dons, Pasquale and Giovanni, *The Barber of Seville,* and *Martha. Il trovatore, The Barber of Seville,* and *Don Pasquale* were heard twice.

There was no opera during the holiday season 1867/68, but February brought a company formed by Grover and Max Maretzek. The run opened with *Ernani,* but the big event was the second night, when Minnie Hauk made her debut in *Crispino e la comare.* The previous season she had made her New York debut at the age of fifteen, and in 1869 she was to be a sensation in Paris. Mapleson engaged her for London, and the career of the second internationally acclaimed American soprano was well launched. In Chicago in 1867 she was back the next evening as Gounod's Juliet, one of her great roles, and she was heard later in the week in *Fra Diavolo* and *Faust.* The indispensable *Il trovatore* and *Lucrezia Borgia* completed the offerings.

In March 1868 the Richings Grand English Opera Company took over the house for two weeks with lighter repertory. Everything was sung in English, and although the offerings included *Faust,* the emphasis was on lighter opera: *Martha, The Bohemian Girl,* and

Minnie Hauk

work in the repertory, Meyerbeer's *The Star of the North (L'Étoile du nord)* was heard on October 16. Things less likely to be encountered in a later day were the same composer's *Robert le diable* and Verdi's *I vespri siciliani.*

One notes with mixed emotions that the financially most successful production in the history of the opera house was *Humpty Dumpty,* a successful New York "burlesque pantomime," which Hess booked in 1868 to keep the theater lit. It played to standing-room-only crowds for three weeks and returned, with similar success, the following year. Albert was delighted to see the money pouring in.

The dust from these performances had hardly settled when the Richings Grand English Opera Company rolled back into town with much the same repertory it had offered in March. *Crispino e la comare* was heard uncut and in English, and then it vanished from the stage until 1884. The interesting new work announced, Lortzing's *Zar und Zimmermann,* may have been canceled. There was some serious fare, *Norma, La traviata,* and *Il trovatore,* but it was outweighed by *Martha* and a full "English *Ring*": *The Bohemian Girl, Maritana,* and *The Lily of Killarney.*

Emphasis on lighter fare continued in the new year when in January 1869 Sallie Holman's Opera Bouffe Company passed though the city with performances of *Martha, The Crown Diamonds,* and *La Grande Duchesse de Gérolstein.* March brought the Susan Galton English Comic Opera Company with French light opera in English. Among the works was an item by Offenbach rarely heard, *Robinson Crusoé.* (How many singers did it require?) The performances were mediocre, the audiences indifferent. April was given to Jacob Grau's Grand French Opera Bouffe Company, which offered six works, concentrating on Offenbach. Upton found the shows filled with filth and foolery. Albert Crosby was delighted by the box office success of the run and the fact that this was the kind of opera he could enjoy. And that's all there was until July, when Brignoli came back for two performances, in *The Barber of Seville* and *Lucia di Lammermoor.* Upton found the troupe incompetent and the performances disasters, "an unmitigated fiasco from beginning to end and an imposition on the public."

Echoes of the past were evoked when on October 8, 1869, Jenny Lind, now forty-nine and apparently vocally past her prime, finally appeared in Chicago, not in recital, but in an Irish play, in which she sang several songs. Those who were eager for more serious

such. Upton found a new score, *The Doctor of Alcantara,* by Julius Eichberg (1824–1893), "a pretty little opera." April brought the Grand Parisian Opera and Ballet Company from New Orleans with three works by Offenbach: *La Grande Duchesse de Gérolstein, La belle Hélène,* and *Orphée aux enfers (Orpheus in the Underworld).* In May Brignoli was back for a single performance of *Don Pasquale.* September brought a two-night stand from Bateman's French Opera Bouffe Company with *La belle Hélène* and *La Grande Duchesse de Gérolstein.* But it was not all *divertissements.* In 1868 the theater housed the Republican National Convention that nominated Ulysses S. Grant of Galena, Illinois, to be president of the United States.

The combination of Max Maretzek's German and Italian troupes opened for business with the predictable *Il trovatore* and the equally predictable Brignoli on September 28, 1868. The rest of the singers are of no particular interest today. The single new things might have been gratified in October that the principal billing of the autumn was the Parepa-Rosa Grand English Opera Company, which brought its own twenty-nine-piece orchestra. Carl Rosa and his wife, the soprano Euphrosyne Parepa-Rosa, were the directors of the company. The run opened with *Maritana* on a list dominated by *The Bohemian Girl, Martha,* and other crowd pleasers. But there was also the first local performance of *The Marriage of Figaro (Le nozze di Figaro)* (which demonstrated the capability of the company), and, of course, there was *Il trovatore.*

The fundamental differences between Uranus and Albert surfaced in November when Lydia Thompson and her British Blondes burlesque played the opera house. As Upton puts it, the theater now offered "a curious medley of entertainments," including animal acts and Swiss bell ringers. Theodore Thomas and his orchestra were in town, but they had been exiled to Farwell Hall. McVicker's was offering Joseph Jefferson in *Rip Van Winkle.* You could even hear George Armstrong Custer lecture on how to conquer the West (his fateful meeting with Crazy Horse at Little Big Horn was eight years in the future). Albert Crosby saw the building as more than an opera house. It was the largest and finest theater in the city, and for a shrewd Yankee businessman the important thing was not prestige rentals; Albert gladly settled for those that promised to keep it rented—a job Hess did well. If there was to be a profit, band concerts and promenade concerts were scheduled, and the hall was used for charity balls.

From the standpoint of the moralists, Lydia Thompson and her blondes defined the low point of 1869. This, it must be noted, was a different sort of burlesque than what the brothers Minsky purveyed on State Street in the next century. The ladies of 1869 wore tights and, by our standards, were plump demoiselles with piano legs. In the 1860s sexy meant healthy, and healthy meant fat. The fashion models of today would have been regarded as prime candidates for tuberculosis. The striptease belonged in the distant future. Even so, the defenders of virtue flamed with indignation, but business was so good that the troupe returned in 1870. As the *Chicago Times* saw it, the opera house had become "a den of prostitution and lust that defies public decency in this city." Some sixty years later when, a few blocks to the south at the Star and Garter, Margie Hart, the greatest of the strippers, was offering *divertissements* of a much different type, the moralists had accepted the inevitable.

The caution at Crosby's was shared at McVicker's, which early in 1870 offered a short, unexciting season of familiar works. The Parepa-Rosa troupe returned briefly in April 1870 with essentially the same repertory as during its previous visits, except for the first Chicago performance of Weber's *Oberon,* which proved a great success despite the small orchestra. And they were back again in autumn, with *Les Huguenots* on the now familiar list. This time the troupe did not bring an orchestra but, to save money, assembled a group of Chicago musicians, many of them students, which proved totally inadequate to the demands of the repertory. Albert Crosby was not going to be fleeced by New York opera managers, and apparently the English troupes were the only groups whose fees were low enough that he could pay them and make money. Their principal singers, most of them forgotten names today, cost far less than comparable Italians. But if things got too bad, people refused to come to the theater. Albert considered the possibility of remodeling the building and turning the theater into office space, but he was persuaded to keep trying to make the opera house profitable. One notes, however, that when the theater was in ashes, he showed no interest in rebuilding.

It is possible that Italian opera was not making money in the manner impresarios expected because everyone was offering the public a tight little repertory of what was regarded as certain box office successes, ignoring that a larger and more sophisticated audience might become tired of them or, at least, unwilling to hear them more than once a year. Chicago went from the autumn of 1868 to the winter of 1871 on a lean operatic diet, dominated by Offenbach and English opera. The primary reason, apparently, was the fear of losing money. Offenbach was cheap, easy to produce, and would sell.

In February 1871 Max Maretzek brought the New German Combination Troupe to the theater, opened with *Don Giovanni,* and proceeded through a repertory that contained some lighter works *(Martha, La Dame blanche)* but also dealt with much weightier things. For a start, on February 17 he finally staged *Tannhäuser,* the only Wagner performance in the history of the theater. It was played by an orchestra of twenty-five pieces Maretzek had brought from New York, and obviously there was slight suggestion of the texture of Wagner's orchestration. The casts—experienced artists—were satisfactory. There was less familiar music: *La Juive* and Nicolai's *The Merry Wives of*

Windsor. The staples included *Fidelio, Il trovatore, Faust, Les Huguenots,* and the first Chicago performance of Rossini's *William Tell (Guillaume Tell),* which, unfortunately, was introduced to the city in the bad Italian text rather than the original French, although it is possible that it was sung in German.

Max Maretzek

In the final opera season under Crosby management, the Grand English Opera Combination Troupe offered a mixed grill of eleven operas, some serious (the second and last Chicago performance of *Oberon*), some less so. *Les Huguenots, Der Freischütz, Il trovatore, The Marriage of Figaro,* and *Fidelio* complete the serious works. *The Bohemian Girl, Martha, Maritana,* and *Fra Diavolo* are the lighter scores, except for a mysterious item that was the last opera heard in the theater, George Frederick Bristow's *Rip Van Winkle.* A well-known figure in the musical life of New York, Bristow (1825–1898) cultivated American subjects but wrote music dominated by European influences.

Ignoring its aberrations, one may plausibly argue

that Crosby's Opera House was, to use a phrase fashionable a century later, the first American cultural center. It was to be a home for serious music, opera, and concerts, and in its brief life it served that purpose well. In 1870, when Theodore Thomas brought a sixty-piece orchestra of high quality to the hall, it proved to be as fine a home for symphonic music as it was for opera.

The first Chicago Philharmonic Society was formed in 1850, drawing on the resident musicians who had made the presentation of *La sonnambula* possible, but its performing ensemble was a chamber orchestra. True symphonic music came to Chicago in 1853 when a touring orchestra of Forty-Eighters (the Germania Society) played Beethoven's Symphony No. 2 as the principal work on their program. Further efforts to establish a local orchestra followed, but Chicago lacked musicians of the quality necessary for a first-class symphonic organization.

Theodore Thomas first visited Chicago in 1854, but his influence really began in November 1869 when he brought his Central Park Garden Orchestra from New York—"forty pieces, perfectly trained" as Upton describes them—which quickly dominated symphonic music in the city. The reincarnation of the local Philharmonic Society current at the time gave up and canceled the balance of its season. Thomas began the association with the city that was to lead to his founding of the Chicago Symphony Orchestra in 1891. Crosby's was the key to this Chicago connection.

No one could suspect that Bristow's *Rip Van Winkle* would be the last opera heard in the theater, but Crosby's, which most assuredly began with a bang on April 20, 1865, ended with a comparative whimper on March 25, 1871. The house was closed for the summer for renovation and redecoration. It was to become "something rich and strange," at the cost of $80,000 for new seats, carpets, and elaborate refurbishing. The season was to begin October 9 with the first concert by Thomas and his New York orchestra, and on the eighth they were on a train headed for Chicago.

Upton recalls the autumn as "hot and sere, and furious burning winds passed across the prairie. Week after week passed without rain. . . . The whole city experienced a feeling of depression and a presentiment of something terrible to happen."[13] It was, indeed, a tinder box awaiting a spark, a city—in many cases hastily built of wood—courting disaster. Back from his vacation and ready for the autumn rounds of music,

Upton was invited to a ceremony at 7:30 p.m. when the opera house was to be ceremonially lighted again.

Things did not go as planned.

"I was there at the appointed time," he recalls in his memoirs, "in company with others who were enthusiastic in their appreciation of the brilliant transformation which had been effected, and over the seemingly brilliant prospects of the season 1871/ 72."[14] Hardly had the ceremony ended than the participants must have become aware that a windblown wall of flame was advancing resolutely eastward from the west side of the city, much of which had already been devastated.

I have a fantasy about Upton's response to this. I speculate that he hurried to the *Tribune* office, which was only a step or two away from McVicker's Theater, salvaged his day books, walked up State Street, and watched the opera house go. The manuscript books he rescued, which contained his personal record of music in the city, became one of the primary sources for this history.[15] In my fantasy Upton moved toward the lake and headed north toward Fullerton Avenue (the city limit at that time) to find a congenial taproom not yet aflame where he might shed a tear and drink a ceremonial libation to the world he had lost. In the days after the fire, he reported, "many . . . musicians fled from the city, for they felt that music would be the last of the phoenix brood to rise from the ashes."

"Three or four hours" after the ceremonial reopening Upton saw the opera house in flames. The fire, he suggested, was like Sherman's definition of war—hell. "The beautiful structure seemed to melt away. I saw it a little distance off, when it first burst out into flame. It did not seem to catch fire at any particular point. It was as if a huge wave of fire swept over and devoured it. . . . Gone with all its memories and association with nights of pleasure!"[16]

On their arrival the next morning, Theodore Thomas and his orchestra found their train stopped at 22nd Street. There was no place for them to go, no hall in which they might play, no public to attend. Thomas led a retreat to Joliet, where he and his musicians stayed until their St. Louis engagement began. For Thomas the loss of income from the Chicago concerts was a devastating blow, but he and his group were back the next year and many years thereafter.

For some, Crosby's Opera House was like Wagner's Flying Dutchman, always sailing under a curse. Nothing ever went as planned, from the tragedy that delayed the original opening to the final ironic scenes of renewal instantly followed by destruction. For Upton it was, and remained in memory, a treasure. "Even conceding the superior adaptation of the present Auditorium to the production of opera," Upton wrote later, "it is doubtful if Chicago will ever have a more comfortable, convenient, and enjoyable audience-room or one with more perfect acoustics than Crosby's."[17] Those who knew it insisted for many years that it was one of the great theaters of the world and perhaps the most important loss to the city the fire produced. And it was the respect for a great hall these memories sustained that led, in large part, to the construction of the Auditorium in 1889. Unfortunately, it came too late for the audience that had supported Crosby's theater to derive much benefit from its existence.

A city with less inner energy than Chicago might have been destroyed. But Chicago was hard to kill. It had survived other fires, it would survive this one. Scarcely had the ashes cooled than rebuilding began. Opera was heard again in 1872. And eighteen years after the great blaze, when the Auditorium opened its doors, Chicago again could claim what was briefly the most modern opera house in the world.

It should be noted that Crosby's Opera House made only a slight contribution to the growth of the contemporary repertory. Of the sixty-six operas heard in the theater, only twenty-five are likely to be encountered today, and nearly all of these are works that had been performed in Chicago before Crosby opened his doors. In the absence of subsidy or patronage, the management had been forced to put emphasis on things that looked like they might attract the widest possible audience and make money. The untried and expensive, symbolized by the works of Wagner, could not be attempted.

Crosby appears to have done little to advance the cause of American opera, though at least the beginnings of an American corpus had been written. William Henry Fry (1813–1864), for instance, had composed five operas, any of which could have been given in Chicago, but none was.

3

A Tradition Rebuilt

1872–1889

Upton's dire prediction that after the fire musicians would leave Chicago proved partially correct. Some left for good, some departed only to return when things improved, and some, like Upton himself, unwilling to accept defeat, stayed. There was a concert, a makeshift affair in a makeshift hall, as early as December 14, 1871. Chicago, including the local arts community, was hard to kill.

Rebuilding began as soon as the ashes cooled. In 1872 Chicagoans saw the construction of some two hundred churches. The largest number of new religious buildings was Roman Catholic, evidence of the strength of the Irish, immigrants from southern Germany, and the French and Italian populations. There were four synagogues. About fifty schools, public and private, of various academic levels were constructed. (The most important university in the region, Northwestern University, founded in 1851, was in Evanston and thus unaffected by the fire.) Nine theaters were built, several of which were called opera houses, although few proved to be of any importance in that role. Perhaps half the group was marginally suited for the presentation of opera. And, to show where the interest of the community really went, more than fourteen hundred new saloons opened for business. Since Edwards's city directory was a respectable publication, the number of bordellos rebuilt or reestablished is not printed, but we many assume that the shrines to Venus returned as quickly as those to Bacchus. Culture was important, but so was vice. The crucial thing was that they could live together.

Chicago had been prospering as a center for transportation and commerce. Here the rails to the Pacific, completed in 1869, and the rails to the Atlantic met. First things came first. The prosperity of the nation demanded that the city be quickly restored. Writing for *Harper's Magazine*, Upton felt that music was now regarded as recreation, something one could put aside while facing the work of rebuilding. "There was neither time nor opportunity for musical culture," he reports. There were probably more high-quality operatic performances in the seasons 1865–1867 than in the seven years from 1872 to the arrival of the Mapleson Company in 1879.

More than a dozen theaters had been destroyed in the fire, but for opera the loss of Crosby's and McVicker's was by far the most important. Uranus Crosby apparently felt the party was over. He had money in bank accounts and the shirt on his back, but everything else lay in ruins. He bought a railroad ticket and after twenty-one years in Chicago, at forty, returned to Massachusetts where, as Upton put it, "he ended his days." He had nothing further to do with opera but pursued various business ventures at home and in New York City. When he died in 1903, he was honored in Chicago as one of the city fathers. If, because of the lottery, he was a crook, he was one of the most successful in the history of a city where devious behavior had also become a fine art.

Albert Crosby stayed in Chicago, collected what insurance he could, and rejoiced that although his opera house and distillery were gone, he had the only working brewery in town—at 23rd Street, safely south of the fire. He had managed to save some paintings from the opera house, and his greatest regret was that the public had never seen the house in its refurbished form. He pursued his business interests, punctuated by long periods of travel, until 1887, when he returned to Massachusetts, leaving a number of large debts behind. In 1895 his creditors found him, and he declared himself bankrupt. Freed of debt, he survived until 1906.

C. D. Hess was wiped out by the fire. The physical assets required for his autumn opera season, as well as his personal belongings, were in a warehouse on the north branch of the river. Music, costumes, scenery—all uninsured—went up in flames. But he remained an opera producer and was back in Chicago in 1879.

For seventeen years Chicago had no place for opera comparable to what it had lost. Several theaters, none of them completely adequate in that role, competed for rental by touring opera troupes. Some, like Meyer's Opera House on Monroe Street between State and Dearborn, or the North Side Opera House at Clark and Kinzie (both opened in 1873), never presented a serious operatic performance.

The first opera after the fire was in the Globe Theater (1,890 seats) at 56 South Dearborn, the first appropriate hall to be opened after the blaze. The original Globe was located on Desplaines Street. The fire created an opportunity to move to a more central location. The Grand German Opera Company arrived there on February 12, 1872, for an announced two-week run that began with *Il trovatore*. The event marked the debut of Theodor Wachtel, notable for the magnitude of his voice and the fervor of his passions, as Manrico. Presumably, he sang the role in German. The theater was nondescript, and the orchestra and chorus were a scratch group of local talent. *Les Huguenots* and *Martha* were announced for February 16 and 17, respectively, but Wachtel had overtaxed his vocal chords. The balance of the season was canceled, and the Globe was never used for grand opera again.

The Academy of Music at 81 South Halsted Street, an extreme example of the horseshoe-shaped hall, had been ready for business in January 1872, but since the public thought of it as a theater on the west side, it was quickly eclipsed by new houses in the central area. Nonetheless, a French opera company that arrived there in April with five works by Offenbach appears to have had reasonable success. And that was the 1871/72 opera season.

The years between the fire and the opening of the Auditorium have been regarded by some historians as a gray page in the artistic life of Chicago, but they contain some things of considerable musical interest, especially after New York's opera war, the rivalry between the Metropolitan Opera House and the Mapleson troupes, was played out partially in Chicago. The primary problem was not the lack of a public. Many of the people who had supported opera at Crosby's Opera House were still in Chicago, still eager to hear music. This was an operatic public in which perhaps half the members were European-born. It remained predominantly German in ancestry. One of the foremost elements in the support of opera in the city was the Forty-Eighters. Those who had survived the Civil War were, as noted earlier, in vigorous middle age in the 1860s, getting older in the 1870s, and starting to disappear from the scene in the 1880s.

The Auditorium, although a great monument to the city's rebirth, actually did not introduce a renewal of interest in opera but a decline. The great new theater came too late to benefit those who might have appreciated it the most. The Auditorium was really built not for them but for their children, and that generation, it quickly proved, was not as deeply involved with opera as its parents had been. Opera for the Forty-Eighters was popular entertainment. It reached out to the general public and attracted enough listeners so that despite difficulties it survived without subsidy. Lighter works—Offenbach and his French colleagues, and the works of Gilbert and Sullivan—soon proved formidable rivals for public attention.

Increasingly, grand opera was considered elitist. In the 1870s we see widespread interest in works that entertained while making no pretense to be art and that could be staged effectively with singers of less than operatic stature. The operatic repertory failed to grow as it had in the past. After the opening of the Auditorium, grand opera became more and more the distinctive entertainment of the rich. An opera house was the ideal place for the display of wealth. You did not want it to be especially innovative. The very rich liked the idea of learning a few dozen works in adolescence and surviving through life on this musical education. The middle class welcomed new music. But a shrinking middle-class audience meant a shrinking demand for tickets.

A new McVicker's (1,990 seats) opened in 1872 on Madison Street between Dearborn and State with a brief appearance of what seems to have been a scratch company from out of town, the Maretzek Italian Opera Company. It had a small orchestra supplemented by two pianos and began its run on October 11, with Jessica M. Haskell as Leonora in *Il trovatore* and Harry Gates as Manrico. *I puritani* was also produced. The series was decidedly a mixed bag.

There was another *Il trovatore* on January 9 from one English Grand Opera Company that sailed into Chicago (and the Academy of Music) with this and

The second McVicker's Theatre

Text view of the second McVicker's Theatre auditorium

the usual collection of *Martha*s, *Maritana*s, and their kin. Upton notes in his daybook that the season was a failure—very poor houses. The lack of celebrated singers may have been a reason. There followed a short French opera series at Aiken's Theater on West Washington Street.

Finally McVicker's came up with a Grand Italian Opera Company capable of presenting nine works in twelve days. *La favorita,* on February 3, marked the debut of Pauline Lucca, a remarkably appealing Viennese artist who combined splendid musicianship with a lovely voice and exceptional skills as an actress. She appeared again a week later in a new score, which was to remain popular for eighty years, Thomas's *Mignon.* Clara Louise Kellogg starred as Philine, with Lucca in the title role, one of her great successes. In the manner of the day, it was sung not in French but in Italian. The two ladies appeared (as Donna Anna and Zerlina) in *Don Giovanni* on February 7. A week later they were paired (as Cherubino and Susanna) in *The Marriage of Figaro* against an all-Italian cast.

Mignon, the new score, drew an audience of forty-one hundred (one must wonder where McVicker put them all). The next night *Il trovatore* (again with Kellogg) drew a small house and left a meager $741 at the box office. But lest one hastily conclude that the old standbys were not able to sell, *Fra Diavolo* on the twelfth pulled four thousand listeners. This was not the record for the run; fifty-six hundred heard *Faust* on February 5. For many, real opera was still preferable to French farce or English comic opera fare.

The problem, at least in part, was money. In November 1873 Max Maretzek refused to bring his opera company to Chicago, insisting that he could not make money if the most expensive ticket had to remain $4. In 1873 good box office receipts for a week were $20,000, and on that base one could pay a star of Kellogg's magnitude as much as $1,500 a performance. This was more than Mary Garden commanded in 1910. Indeed, $1,500 was a good fee at the Metropolitan midway into the next century. Nineteenth-century impresarios would say that one of the problems of today's opera producers is that the houses are too small. A capacity of six thousand (some of it, presumably, standing room) for a popular opera like *Lucia di Lammermoor* was highly desirable.

A short run of the Oakes Burlergo Opera Company in May 1873 returned Lucca in the role in which she had the greatest success in February, Marguerite in *Faust.* She and Kellogg repeated their earlier successes in *Mignon* and *Don Giovanni,* and Lucca added *The Daughter of the Regiment* to her local repertory. Upton reported that the series was very successful, and the impresarios presented Lucca with a diamond cross, a gesture that probably was not appreciated by Kellogg, with whom she was said to have had difficulties.

Strakosch rose to the challenge of making money in Chicago and brought his company to McVicker's in December. Kellogg appeared in practically everything, but Lucca was nowhere in sight. *Martha, Faust, Lucia di Lammermoor, The Bohemian Girl, The Marriage of Figaro,* and *Il trovatore* were Kellogg's vehicles. *Rigoletto, Fra Diavolo,* and *Maritana* had to struggle along without her. The soprano in those works was Jenny Van Zandt, an American, presumably the older sister of Marie Van Zandt, who made her Chicago debut in 1891. Strakosch's optimism was justified. He made money.

The most determined, and possibly most optimistic, theater owner was Richard M. Hooley, an unconquerable Irishman who in 1870 bought a theater at 119 North Clark Street. Built in 1860 as a concert hall (it was home to the Chicago Philharmonic Society), it was renamed Hooley's Opera House. Unfortunately, it

The second Hooley's Theatre

Richard M. Hooley

The Grand Opera House, 1880

never housed an opera before it vanished in flames.

Undaunted, Hooley rebuilt. The new Hooley's (1,184 seats, facing Randolph Street between Clark and LaSalle) opened in 1872. It was roundly condemned by out-of-town managers—the pit was too small, the wings too shallow, the fly loft too low. For a number of years it lost important bookings to McVicker's. Since opera producers were not coming to him, Hooley decided to show off his house by producing his own opera, a single performance of *Il trovatore* on December 21, 1873. It had no immediate effect, but, starting in 1884, Hooley's was the choice of the New York impresarios visiting the city from the Metropolitan Opera House, and thus, in terms of the number and importance of the performances, this theater may be regarded as the city's principal opera house in the five years before the opening of the Auditorium in 1889. Programs from the Met season of 1888/89 name it the Chicago Opera House—not Hooley's Theater.

In 1891, realizing that opera had moved out for good, Hooley's was refurbished as a playhouse and reopened as Power's Theater. It continued to be lit regularly for another thirty-one years. In 1924 it was torn down to create a new site for the Sherman Hotel, which, some sixty years later, was razed to house the present State of Illinois Building.

The site at 119 North Clark (which Hooley had vacated) was rebuilt after the fire as Tom Foley's Billiard Hall, and in 1874 it was further remodeled as the Coliseum Beer Garden. But showbiz was to conquer. In 1878 it was again rebuilt as Hamlin's Theater, and in 1880 it was renamed the Grand Opera House. It had seventeen hundred seats and was the most long-lasting of the opera houses of the 1870s—the only one known to the author. A substantial amount of touring opera was heard here. Early in the new century the theater was acquired by George M. Cohan as a Chicago base for his shows and became Cohan's Opera House. Under that name, in 1916, it housed the Diaghilev Ballet Russe during its first American tour. Cohan sold the theater in 1927, and it reverted to the name Grand Opera House, which it retained, except for a short period as a movie house (the RKO Grand) in the 1940s. In its last years it housed several successful plays. Along with the Erlanger—an excellent legitimate theater next door—it was demolished in 1958 to clear the site now occupied by the Daley Center.

But McVicker's was the destination of the Grand Italian Opera Company that arrived on January 12, 1874. It brought the first Chicago performance of *Aida* on January 16 with Italo Campanini, who was to become the highest-priced tenor of the day, as Radames. The size of his vanity was rivaled only by the size of his voice, and he would willingly sacrifice beauty of tone for volume. He excelled in *Carmen* and was one of the few Italians to sing the title role in *Lohengrin.* Annie Louise Cary, one of the most respected American singers before the public, was cast as Amneris, and the celebrated European diva Christine Nilsson, who was to open the Met as Marguerite in *Faust* in 1883, sang that role for Chicago the following night. She

was also heard in what some considered her greatest role, Valentine in *Les Huguenots.* The run contained the fashionable novelty *Mignon* but was dominated by staples such as *Don Giovanni, La traviata,* and *Lucia di Lammermoor.* When Chicago got opera, it got much the same opera as New York. Nilsson's fame became so great that eventually she demanded, and got, the same $5,000 fee Adelina Patti received.

Some independent producer, who admired Auber's *Masaniello,* gave it a run of six performances at McVicker's from March 30 to April 4. Upton apparently considered these events beneath his notice.

The 1874/75 season brought a series of operas by the English Grand Opera Company to McVicker's in October. Kellogg, converted to the cause of opera in English, had formed her own company in 1873 and brought it to Chicago in October of the following year. She was conspicuous in now familiar roles as Susanna in *The Marriage of Figaro* and Zerlina in *Don Giovanni,* and she was heard in *Lucia di Lammermoor, Martha, Faust, Fra Diavolo,* and *Mignon,* which was sung for the first time in English. She continued to alternate with Van Zandt. Other American singers associated with the troupe were Joseph Maas and William Castle.

McVicker's was lit by Strakosch in January with casts that surrounded Cary with Europeans. January 18, 1875, brought the Chicago debut of Marie Heilbronn in *La traviata.* She returned later in *Faust, Mignon,* and as Susanna in *The Marriage of Figaro.* Belgian by birth, the New Grove Dictionary of Opera observes, "she was immensely gifted and very attractive in appearance, but her private life intruded upon her career." She died at the age of thirty-five. Two years before her death she sang the première performance of Massenet's *Manon* in Paris.

Strakosch's box office receipts reflect an audience that is eager to support new operas but has grown tired of the staples. Thus, Heilbronn notwithstanding, his opening-night *La traviata* drew only $566.00, *Faust,* two nights later, fetched a mere $596.00, and *Ernani,* two nights after that, brought in only $576.00 at the box office. *Aida,* still new to Chicago, drew $763.00; *The Barber of Seville,* old stuff, produced a mere $496.00. The only familiar scores to rival the new music were *La sonnambula,* which had not been heard in five years, with $1,787.00, and *Lucia di Lammermoor,* with $1,341.00. Compare that with $3,347.00 for the return of *Lohengrin* and $1,730.00 for *Mignon.* The first performance of *Ruy Blas* by Filippo Marchetti (1831–1902) apparently created little excitement, bringing only $337.50 in ticket sales on January 30—the end and the absolute fiscal low point of the series.

Possibly frightened by Strakosch's tales of financial difficulties, little opera toured in Chicago in 1875/76. The season was dominated by the English. Kellogg's company arrived at Hooley's Theater on January 3 with Kellogg in *The Bohemian Girl.* She was back two nights later in *Mignon,* and two nights after that in *Fra Diavolo.* January 10 brought her in a new role, Edith in Balfe's *The Talisman* (an opera you are quite unlikely ever to hear). Starting January 12, at two-night intervals, she appeared in *Lucia di Lammermoor, Martha,* and, on January 17 in Benedict's *The Lily of Killarney.* Two nights after that she was again Figaro's Susanna. Between these appearances the menu offered standard English opera fare, with George Conly joining the casts and Van Zandt, Castle, and Maas featured again. Viennese light opera was briefly represented when *The Rose of Tyrol* had a short run in March. Many listeners probably felt they were on short rations.

Strakosch had another try at McVicker's in the autumn of 1876. It was a short, cautious visit, from October 30 to November 10, and the most interesting thing was the first Chicago performance of Rossini's *Semiramide* on November 6, with Palmieri in the title role. The *Barber*'s sad fate in 1875 did not prevent its return along with *Martha,* and even *The Bohemian Girl.* There were also the—one senses, mandatory—*Il trovatore, Faust,* and *Lucia di Lammermoor.* And, as if that did not satisfy the presumed insatiable demand for the familiar, Strakosch (allied with the ever optimistic Hess) was back in December with a short series of opera in English, notable for the first Chicago performance of *Carmen.* The Richings Bernard Opera Company brought a longer English series to Haverly's Theater on April 30 with *Maritana,* followed by *The Bohemian Girl, Martha,* and *Fra Diavolo.* As a concession to other tastes, *The Marriage of Figaro* closed the run on May 5. *Martha* and *The Bohemian Girl* fluttered by in April.

The first really good period for opera came in 1877/78. The Pappenheim-Adams German troupe arrived at Hooley's with serious fare. Pappenheim was the soprano, Adams the tenor. *Lohengrin, Fidelio, Les Huguenots,* and *Faust* were heard, together with the first Chicago performance of *The Flying Dutchman.* Hardly had the run begun when the Susani-Kellogg Company took over with opera in English at McVicker's with its production of *The Flying Dutchman* on November 29, offering Kellogg as Senta. Meyerbeer's *The Star of the North* (also with Kellogg) was an additional novelty. Otherwise the repertory was predictable.

In a spring Italian season at Hooley's in 1877 Strakosch courted popular taste with Kellogg in *The Bohemian Girl* (the one English score in the repertory), but otherwise dealt with such eminently marketable items as Kellogg in *Il trovatore,* as Aida, and in *Mignon* and *Don Giovanni.* And a passing moment of summer opera brought Brignoli in *Don Pasquale,* introducing opera to Haverly's Theater at 104 West Monroe.

The autumn of 1878 brought a good Italian series at McVicker's. The principal event was *Carmen* (in Italian, of course), with Kellogg in the title role. Pay her and she would sing anything short of Isolde. Cary was the mezzo-soprano. The rest of the series, with Kellogg bountifully on view, was well-established scores.

The decisive event of the decade took place in January 1879 when Colonel James Mapleson arrived with the Italian Troupe from Her Majesty's Theater in London. Mapleson offered a direct link to opera not only in New York but in Europe as well. This was exactly what the city needed for operatic performances on the highest artistic level.

New York produced opera; Chicago consumed it. The older and larger city had the resources, financial and artistic, to sustain a major company. After 1868 it was clear that Chicago had the wealth and the public to support only short seasons, the kind of opera that ideally was provided by a large company on the road. Chicago had become, for all practical purposes, a second home for the major New York producers. From 1879 to 1886 Mapleson was the most important figure in Chicago opera. After he retired, companies from the Metropolitan Opera House dominated the scene for twenty-four years.

New York had nearly a quarter-century head start on Chicago as an opera town. While opera was struggling to establish itself in Chicago, New York enjoyed opera in one theater or another the year round. The first successful opera house in New York opened in 1847. On January 6, 1851, it housed the première of an opera written in the United States, *Giovanna Prima di Napoli,* by Adelina Patti's brother-in-law, Maurice Strakosch. If he expected her to lead it to fame, he was mistaken. She never sang a note of it.

This was not the first American opera to be produced; *Leonora* by William Henry Fry had that distinction. The work was his second opera. His first, *Aurelia,* never was performed, but *Leonora*—written in collaboration with his librettist brother, Joseph—was produced in Philadelphia on June 4, 1845. (His last opera, *Notre Dame of Paris,* was also given in Philadelphia, in 1864—shortly before he died of tuberculosis—and was conducted by no less a musician than Theodore Thomas. There were five Fry operas in all, but heavily influenced as they were by the Italian bel canto tradition, they were considered dated. Was there no such thing as an American musical idiom? Its discovery would take a long time.)

In 1854, New Yorkers hailed the new Academy of Music on Irving Place at 14th Street, which they proudly claimed to be the largest opera house in the world. It had forty-five hundred seats—twice the number of that of most large European theaters—and featured what a later day would call continental seating on the main floor: there were no aisles; one entered a row of seats from the side.

The Academy was to be used for a variety of musical events and was similar in many ways to the Academy of Music in Philadelphia, which opened in 1857. Long respected as a concert room (the home of the Philadelphia Orchestra), the Philadelphia hall was felt by some to be the finest opera house in the United States, and until the start of the twenty-first century it served the community in both roles.

Mapleson (1830–1901), the most colorful figure in the rather brightly hued group of nineteenth-century opera producers, leased the New York Academy in 1878 for five years (rent was $175 a night when the house was lit) and began to offer opera with the gifts of a great showman. He had become manager of Her Majesty's Theater in London in 1862, and it remained his base, with interruptions, until 1889. But he had additional worlds to conquer. By 1879 he was the dominant operatic producer in the English-speaking world, presenting seasons in both London and New York and reaching out to promising locations in the United States. Eventually he toured westward as far as San Francisco.

Born in London, he entered the Royal Academy of Music at fourteen to study violin. Some two years later he was working in the pit of Her Majesty's Theater. Balfe, the composer of *The Bohemian Girl,* was the conductor. "It had already occurred to me to quit the comparative obscurity of the orchestra for a bril-

Colonel James H. Mapleson

liant position on the stage; and this idea was encouraged by Balfe, who during the intervals of operatic business, gave me singing lessons." A tenor, he found himself a job in 1848 in a company presenting concerts in the British provinces. After playing Salisbury, the singers retired to nearby Stonehenge, where "among the Druidical remains" the prima donna Henriette Sontag sang *Casta Diva.*

To finance further vocal studies, he became a critic for a paper called the *Atlas.* These earnings in hand, he went to Italy, where he made his debut. As Enrico Mariani, he sang Manrico in *Il trovatore* in Verona. After returning to England in 1854 he suffered vocal problems, submitted to surgery, and "found myself deprived alike of tonsils, uvula, and voice." In 1856, at the age of twenty-six, he transformed himself into a manager.

His visit to America in 1879 was less a tour than an invasion. The company—"some 140 persons"—sailed from Queenstown on the last day of August with Minnie Hauk, Alwina Valleria (an American soprano Mapleson had championed), and the Hungarian soprano Etelka Gerster on board. There was also the most celebrated Italian tenor, Italo Campanini, and Giuseppe Del Puente, one of the leading Italian bass-baritones, as well as an Irish bass, A. J. Foli, and Arditi, the conductor.

Gerster achieved fame almost overnight after her debut in 1876 but destroyed her voice in less than ten years in an unsuccessful effort to surpass Patti. She

Architectural drawing of Haverly's Theatre

opened the Chicago season in *Carmen* with Campanini as Don José and Del Puente as Escamillo. When Chicago first heard her, she was in her prime, and although lacking as an actress she made Bizet's gypsy a striking character. Hauk had been heard in Chicago before. She now returned in triumph. On January 15 she sang Cherubino in *The Marriage of Figaro* (Mapleson's wife, Marie-Hippolyte Rôze, was Susanna, and the two ladies did not get along) and returned on January 21 as Marguerite in *Faust*. She closed the run on January 25 as Violetta in *La traviata*. Most members of the troupe were Italian singers better known in Europe than the United States, and although they appear to have been artists of high quality, they are largely forgotten.

Mapleson also brought what he called "a magnificent chorus of some 60 select voices, together with the whole of the corps de ballet and a principal dancer." The American musicians' union prohibited him from importing a London orchestra, but Mapleson soon learned that American players were to be preferred in any case. Embarkation was complicated by the fact that "some of the Italian choristers had been assured by Irish humorists that the streets of New York were infested by crocodiles and wild Indians; and these they were most unwilling to encounter."

Chicago received Mapleson rapturously. It is unlikely that any New York impresarios had visited the city with forces this large or of such high quality. Ballet had been conspicuously lacking. Mapleson recalled, "During all this visit to Chicago there was one unbroken line of intending buyers waiting to secure tickets at the box office." He recalled providing wood fires to keep them warm in the evening that frequently consumed as much as $20 worth of wood a day, a large amount of fuel in 1879.

The company, first known as the Italian Troupe from Her Majesty's Theater, was later billed as Her Majesty's Opera Company, which suggested a closer bond to the crown than really existed. Mapleson's military commission came from the queen; it represented not the regular army but the London militia, a volunteer organization. His relationship to the organization was probably more social than military. He was one of those in charge of the officers' mess, a duty he appears to have discharged with enthusiasm.

Of the Chicago theaters, Mapleson selected Haverly's. Originally named the Adelphi Theater, it burned and was reopened a year later. In 1878 J. H. Haverly purchased and renamed the property and op-

Pictorial diagram of the auditorium of Haverly's Theatre

erated it until 1882, when it yielded to new construction, a theater on Monroe Street west of Dearborn named the Columbia, which then became Mapleson's choice. The Columbia burned down in 1900.

The Haverly (about 2,400 seats) was not constructed to hold the capacity audiences Mapleson attracted. At a performance of *I puritani* in the second week of the run, he reported, "the house was so crowded that the outer walls began to crack, and, in the managerial room where I was working, I could put my hand through one of the corners where the two walls met." The Chicago building code of the day obviously left some things to be desired. "I communicated with Carter Harrison, who was then Mayor. He at once proceeded to the theater, and, without creating any alarm, and under the pretext that the house was too full, caused upwards of a thousand people to leave the building. So pleased were they with the performance that they all refused to have their money returned."

Mapleson delighted that he had had "one of the most successful Chicago seasons on record." Battling gout, he sent the troupe off to St. Louis with his son Henry in charge. Even by contemporary standards,

Mapleson's first American season was a formidable undertaking: 164 operatic performances and 47 concerts (with an additional 135 operatic performances and 48 concerts in England). He visited Boston, Chicago, St. Louis, Cincinnati, Baltimore, and Washington, D.C., in addition to giving two long series of performances in New York. In Chicago there were 14 performances from a repertory of 11 operas. On the basis of this success Mapleson returned to become an annual visitor, and with him the artistic standards of Chicago opera and New York opera became indistinguishable.

Upton describes Mapleson as "a typical Englishman, tall, broad-shouldered, well made, rosy faced," with military whiskers and manner. "He was very pompous and haughty. . . . As he stood before me for the first time in my little office he seemed to fill it. He laid his card upon my desk and as I read the name with its prefix and suffixes I felt I was in the atmosphere of royalty. He was quite gracious on this occasion" [presumably 1879], "as he wished favors."

In the classic manner of music producers, Mapleson's relations to the press were thoroughly opportunistic. "The Colonel had three forms of address,"

Upton recalls. "If he were seeking favors, it was 'My dear fellow,' with a conventional smile; if he were on good terms with you and the occasion was social, it was 'My boy,' with measured dignity; if he were not on good terms, it was 'Sir' very haughtily."

Upton encountered both extremes early in the 1879 series. Soon after the initial meeting, displeased with a review, "he stalked into my room and threw his card upon my desk with the words, 'Take my card to the editor-in-chief, sir.' The worm, thus addressed, turned and said, 'Take it yourself, sir.'" Upton was not to be intimidated. The *Tribune* knew that if a critic was to function well, he must be protected from persons advancing their personal interests. It would have been desirable that editors of a later day always remembered this.

A second British contribution to the city was the arrival in January 1879 of a touring company with Gilbert and Sullivan's *H.M.S. Pinafore.* The public loved it. "Pinafore Fever," as it came to be called, was an intense, but ultimately harmless, affliction on a national scale. The January run was followed by two amateur productions in February, after which a professional troupe arrived from New York in May for more hearings. It had to compete with three amateur stagings and a fourth version with a cast of children. In July it was sung in a German translation. There were three more productions before the year's end. When the touring D'Oyly Carte company appeared in 1880 with additional Gilbert and Sullivan repertory, the popularity of *Pinafore* began to decline, especially when stronger works like *The Mikado* and *Patience* became well known. But *Pinafore* was revived from time to time.

Karl Strakosch, nephew of Maurice and Max Strakosch, followed in his uncles' footsteps as an entrepreneur. His visit to McVicker's in March was an occasion to say farewell to Kellogg, whose voice (at thirty-seven) was now past its prime. She appeared in *Les Huguenots* on opening night, March 17, was back two nights later in *Mignon,* and returned as Carmen on March 22. Carmen was not one of her good roles; she was much too ladylike to play Bizet's gypsy convincingly. The previous evening, at a farewell gala, she sang Elsa in the first act of *Lohengrin.* Although light opera came to Hooley's in April, Kellogg really closed the season. Her operatic career had lasted only sixteen years, but it established without question the right of American singers to hold center stage in their own country. She sang a few concerts, and in 1887—at the

age of forty-five and in the unlikely locale of Elkhart, Indiana—married Karl Strakosch and retired for good. It was a happy marriage, which lasted fifty years.

Strakosch was back at McVicker's in October 1879 with a short Italian season, offering now familiar fare and largely forgotten artists. Emma Abbott, born in Illinois, brought her company for a brief series in December. The way was clear for Mapleson to return in January and sweep everything before him. And that is just what he did.

We must accept Mapleson as a lover of fine voices, especially those best served by Italian opera. In terms of repertory he was rarely an innovator. Opening night on January 12, 1880, brought *Martha* with Campanini and Cary, surrounded by leading singers from Mapleson's London troupe, few of whom retain any reputation today. Campanini and Del Puente are the voices best remembered from *La sonnambula,* staged the following night. They turn up regularly through the run, with Del Puente memorable as Mephistopheles in *Faust* on the seventeenth. He sang opposite Brignoli in *Lucia di Lammermoor* on January 19.

Brignoli was back for some of his final appearances in the city in September when Emma Abbott returned, bringing her company to the Grand Opera House and opening with herself in *The Bohemian Girl.* Brignoli was in that cast, presumably singing a role in English, but returned in his true metier the next night as Manrico in *Il trovatore.* As a proof of stamina, he sang Edgardo in *Lucia di Lammermoor* the following evening. That may have been too much for him, since he did not appear in the rest of the run.

Campanini, Gerster, and Cary were the most celebrated artists in the third Mapleson season, which opened at Haverly's Theater on January 31, 1881. *Aida* served as a monumental inaugural evening, and on February 3 Mapleson, for once, introduced an important new opera to the city, Boito's *Mefistofele.* Both Campanini and Cary were in the cast. The title role went to Novara, whose fame has passed. February 9 may have been a particularly fine night with Del Puente as Don Giovanni and Cary as Zerlina. The next night Campanini sang Lohengrin (in Italian, I assume) with Gerster as Elsa.

The remarkable event in the run of the Beauplan Opera Company, which arrived at McVicker's on March 21, was that French operas were sung in that language. The run began with *Les Huguenots* and continued with *La Juive, Faust, Carmen,* and the original (and finer) text of *William Tell.* Italian repertory was apparently also sung in French, thus we have *Le Trouvère* rather than *Il trovatore.*

There was no more opera until January 1882, when Mapleson was back for two weeks with the same mixture as before. Then there was an operatic drought of a year until January 1883, when Mapleson returned for a week. The series is notable primarily for the Chicago debut of one of the great American sopranos, Lillian Nordica, in *Faust,* an opera for which she proved to have a special affinity. November brought the Boston Ideal Opera Company with a repertory of four works, one of them *Mefistofele.*

In 1883, when Chicago was best known for railroads and meat packing, each of the world's great cities had its special claim to distinction in the arts. London was the citadel of theater, Paris the stronghold of the visual arts, and St. Petersburg the bastion of ballet. Vienna remained, as it had been for more than a century, the primary font of instrumental music. Milan, in a divided Italy, could not set world standards in opera; that distinction belonged to New York.

The problem in New York was that the opera had become the prime showcase for wealth, and the preferred setting for that display of affluence was a box. The Astor Place house had not had many boxes, hence its replacement by the Academy of Music. (Cynics observed that the majority of box holders never heard the first act of any work. After a long and gracious dinner, they breezed in at the first intermission.) The wealthy wanted a theater that, in its decor and amenities, rivaled the new Opéra opened in Paris in 1875. They were in an admirable position to get what they wanted, and they called it the Metropolitan Opera House. It was basically a real estate venture, capitalized by the sale of seventy boxes at $15,000 each. The box owners were not to become music producers. The house would be made available to an impresario, who would present a season. The Metropolitan Opera Company of today dates from a reorganization in 1908.

Mapleson viewed the construction uptown with scorn. As the new theater opened, on October 22, 1883, he countered Gounod's *Faust* with a still popular old opera, Bellini's *La sonnambula.* "My audience is the Faubourg St. Germaine [*sic*] of the town," he announced. "My rival, I understand, is supported by a number of rich persons who want some new ways of spending money." The success of the opening performance did not surprise or impress him. It had "a fine cast, and perfectly trained, since all these artists had played under my direction and did not require a rehearsal."

Mapleson's weakest point was his dedication to Italian opera, a repertory based on the star system and the fading idea that one went to the theater not so much to hear an opera as to hear a celebrated voice. Adelina Patti was his greatest asset. No singer of this century could rival her fame—or her fees. Part of the Patti legend is that she never attended rehearsals, a stipulation that would make an operatic career impossible today. Her maid attended and told Patti where she was supposed to stand in important scenes. It should also be noted that her fame rested on the beauty of her voice. She had a trim figure and expressive eyes, but a long nose and pointed chin dominated her face. Singers who followed her to fame early in the new century—artists such as Lina Cavalieri—combined a beautiful voice with an equally striking appearance.

Adelina Patti

Mapleson first met Patti, accompanied by her brother-in-law and manager—perhaps (some suggested) her lover, possibly her Svengali—Maurice Strakosch, in 1861. He had been a pupil of Giuditta Pasta, hailed as the greatest of all Italian prima donnas, and had taught Patti Pasta's ornamentations and cadenzas. We must remember that the nineteenth-century prima donna was expected to excel in florid singing, trills, and fireworks, and Patti preferred operas in which singing of that type was expected. Later in her career she tried *Carmen* with disastrous results, but, surprisingly, she won success as Aida.

"The little lady from America arrived," Mapleson recalls, "and sent me up her card." She insisted that, if given an opportunity to sing, "she felt sure she would draw money." Mapleson requested an audition and was given a rendition of "Home Sweet Home." "I saw," he writes, "that I had secured a diamond of the first water." But before he could find a theater and a group of singers to make up an Italian company, Patti had run out of money and signed with a rival management. The following year, down to the last two pounds in his pocket, Mapleson secured a lease on Her Majesty's Theater, the finest in London, and on this basis assembled a notable company of singers and flourished.

For Mapleson—and Mapleson alone—the *prima donna assoluta* Patti would occasionally sing without advance payment of her fee. Sooner or later she was always paid, but Mapleson's skill in dodging creditors possibly was exceeded only by Richard Wagner's. Patti's monetary demands were possible because of her unsurpassed drawing power at the box office. If she demanded $5,000, she produced $10,000 in ticket sales, usually enough to cover the remaining costs and leave a margin of profit. But in 1883, with the battle with the new Metropolitan Opera House fully engaged, she declined to offer Mapleson credit.

La traviata was to be heard on the second night of a Boston engagement. "That afternoon about two o'clock, Patti's agent called upon me," Mapleson recalls, "to receive the $5,000 for her services that evening. I was at low water just then, and inquiring at the booking-office found I was $1,000 short. All I could offer was the trifle of $4,000 as a payment on account."

The sum was refused, and Mapleson was told his contract with Patti was canceled. Two hours later the manager was back. "Madame Patti," he reported, "does not wish to break her engagement with you, as

she certainly would have done with anyone else under the circumstances. Give me the $4,000 and she will make every preparation for going on the stage. She empowers me to tell you that she will be at the theater in good time for the beginning of the opera and that she will be ready, dressed in the costume of Violetta with the exception only of shoes. You can let her have the balance when the doors open and the money comes in. Direct she receives it she will put her shoes on and at the proper moment make her appearance on stage."

When the manager reappeared, Mapleson had $800 to give him. "I handed it to my benevolent friend," he wrote, "and begged him to carry it without delay to the obliging prima donna, who, having received $4,800, might, I thought, be induced to complete her toilette pending the arrival of the $200 balance."

Patti put on one shoe. "Send her the $200, and she will put on the other," Mapleson was told. Moments later the box office yielded the $200, the other shoe was put on, and, "her face radiant with benign smiles," Patti went onstage to join the cast of the opera—which had already begun. She sang brilliantly. All was saved. Rudolf Bing, one suspects, would have strangled her. Mapleson, apparently, did not really mind all this. "Patti," he wrote, "is beyond all doubt the most successful singer who ever lived." Her fees bought her a castle in Wales, and her fame kept her before the public in annual farewell tours long after she had retired from opera. Her actual farewell was in the Royal Albert Hall, London, in 1914. She was seventy-one, and her voice still filled the house.

Often in the 1883 season, after paying her and the other cast members, Mapleson had less than $25 for himself. But in New York in those days $25 paid for a decent hotel room and a good meal. He was a true English sportsman. It was the thrill of the great game that excited him, not the profits. And Patti, despite her collection methods, was a loyal lady. She did not sing at the Metropolitan until 1892—twelve performances in a single season, a small fraction of what she had done for Mapleson. She then concentrated on concerts, which she found considerably more profitable than opera.

If Patti made money for Mapleson, she also represented some 45% of his costs. She brought in the dollars, but then she took them back. He hung on for three more years, spending more and more time on the road. But as the sheriffs, lawyers, and bill collectors descended on him, he fled the country, defeated, in 1886 with the cry, "I cannot fight Wall Street." The Academy of Music ceased to be of importance as an opera house after Mapleson's departure, but it could be used for other purposes; it survived until 1929.

Chicago could do nothing but profit from the opera war. Both Mapleson and his rivals needed to tour, and Chicago welcomed them. The first impresario at the Met in 1883/84 was Henry Eugene Abbey, whose experience was in the theater of the spoken, rather than the sung, word. As he saw it, the economics were simple. An opera was prepared for New York and given there as many times as it might be expected to fill the house. Without further preparation it could then be taken on the road to gross further box office income. In that initial season at the Met, *Faust* was sung sixteen times: ten in the Metropolitan Opera House and six times elsewhere (twice in Chicago).

Early in 1884 both Mapeleson's troupe and Abbey's company from the Met found themselves not only in the same city, Chicago, but in the same hotel. Circumstances decreed they could not be at the same theater. Abbey was at Hooley's, Mapleson at the Columbia, and this time Mapleson had Patti. Presenting her in Chicago guaranteed that he would lose money because the Columbia had more than a thousand seats less than the Academy of Music and the box office income would be proportionately lower. But Mapleson was probably willing to take the financial loss to triumph artistically, and triumph he did. Upton felt some of the Met productions had sunk into butchery and called Abbey's run the worst-managed opera season Chicago ever had.

There were good reasons. Abbey did not bring productions from New York; he insisted they would not fit the Chicago stage. So, in contrast to the fresh decor Mapleson provided, Abbey's audiences saw shabby old scenery they might have viewed in various circumstances many times before. The level of musical preparation went from the best to the worst. *Faust* with Christine Nilsson was excellent—and why not, it had opened the Met in October. *Lucia di Lammermoor* on the second night marked the Chicago debut of Marcella Sembrich, who was not to tour with the company again until 1898. She was also heard in *The Barber of Seville, La traviata,* and *Martha.* The following evening *Lohengrin* (in Italian) was so bad that Nilsson was laughing, and the tenor, Campanini, walked off the stage, refusing to sing the final scene against the vile sounds emerging from the orchestra

and chorus. (The *Met Annals* says, "The final scene was omitted because Campanini fell ill.") But in *Don Giovanni* on January 24 of that year Abbey introduced Amelia Materna, one of the great Wagner singers of the day, one of the few who had studied with the composer. The range and power of her voice were extraordinary.

In terms of the future, the most important event of the series may have been the Chicago debut on February 8 of the twenty-three-year-old conductor Cleofonte Campanini, the younger (by fifteen years) brother of the tenor, who was to become one of the central figures in the early years of resident Chicago opera.

Mapleson, with record advance sales, arrived on January 28 with Patti. On opening night she sang the Ricci brothers' *Crispino e la comare,* which had been briefly popular some twenty years before, then continued with powerful scores: *Lucia di Lammermoor, La traviata, Rigoletto,* and, inevitably, a rival *Faust* to set Abbey reeling. Unfortunately, Patti's success also set his other leading soprano, Gerster, in flames. Patti could not sing every night. Mapleson had to have a second soprano of first rank. Gerster was persuaded to honor her contract for Chicago and even appeared with Patti in *Les Huguenots* on January 20. Upton was impressed with Mapleson's casts but felt there was room for improvement in his productions. "It is about time that an earnest protest be entered against the policy of using great names as a cover for shabbily mounted and carelessly produced worn-out operas." But *Faust* remained the most frequently produced work in the Chicago repertory, and in the next century it was still going strong. The grim truth is that operas get worn out for critics before producing that effect on the public at large because the critics, for obvious reasons, hear them every time they are produced.

Abbey's losses for the first Met season were $600,000, a monumental sum for 1884. Was the new house to stay dark for its second year? The conductor Leopold Damrosch went to the box holders, pointing out that the high cost of Italian opera was due to the fees of the artists. His proposal was that he engage a company from German theaters, where singers were paid an annual salary rather than per performance and had free time. He would conduct everything, and, following German practice, everything would be sung in that language. With a $4 top price—20% less than Abbey demanded—a season of fifty-seven performances would end up in the black. Nearly half the performances were Wagner, and the New York public greeted them with an enthusiasm that guaranteed success. Unfortunately, Damrosch's plans imposed physical demands he could not meet. He conducted fifty-two performances without a break and on January 9 (after *Lohengrin*) collapsed with pneumonia. He died on February 15.

His twenty-three-year-old son Walter took his place and began a notable career. As a child in the 1930s I recall Dr. Damrosch, then in his seventies, presiding over an orchestra on the NBC music appreciation broadcasts. Preparing his listeners for a Wagner excerpt, he would hold forth in a robust German accent on "gods and goddezzes." When Walter Damrosch came to Chicago in March 1885, he offered a more cosmopolitan repertory, including Rossini's *William Tell*, Auber's *La Muette de Portici*, and Boïeldieu's *La Dame blanche*—all in German.

Mapleson's finest hours in Chicago were probably a two-week opera festival in 1885 in which Patti was to be heard in several of her finest roles. The performances were to take place in the Interstate Industrial and Exposition Building, a large and imposing structure possibly inspired by London's Crystal Palace (but with less glass), built in 1872 as a temporary structure in Grant Park on Michigan Avenue at the foot of Adams Street. William W. Boyington, who had designed Crosby's opera house, was the architect. It opened in 1873 to house an exposition honoring "the material and cultural progress of Chicago and of the Northwest." There were three imposing entrances with a dome over each doorway and long, arched halls, which were used to present everything from prize pigs to the wonders of art. It became such a useful facility that its temporary status was forgotten. Its dedication to culture was not.

The Interstate Industrial and Exposition Building

In 1877 Theodore Thomas created a beer garden at one end of the building for his summer concerts. The combination of the atmosphere and the music was all a heavily German community might desire. "Chicago," he later commented, "is the only city on the continent, next to New York, where there is sufficient musical culture to enable me to give a series of fifty successive concerts." With these programs he established the foundation for the Chicago Symphony. The hall welcomed more than instrumental music. In 1881 it was home to a successful German *Sängerfest*. Thomas used this as an inspiration for two May Festivals, in 1882 and 1884, which were very well received. Although Mapleson made a career of bringing European talent to the United States, he regretted that he never was able to take Thomas and his orchestra to Europe, so superior were they to any ensemble that might be heard in London.

These rentals gave the hall a renewed lease on life, made all the stronger in 1884 when the building housed both the Republican and Democratic political conventions. It was finally torn down in 1892 to create a site for the Art Institute of Chicago.

Mapleson arrived in the dead of winter in 1885 to mark out personally the dimensions for the opera house to be constructed for him within the building (where Thomas's beer garden had once flourished). Dankmar Adler and Louis H. Sullivan, who on the basis of this success were later to build the Auditorium, were the architects. At a banquet in his honor at the Calumet Club, where he was hailed as the emperor of opera, he announced that his greatest success would be achieved in Chicago the following spring.

Enthusiasm for the project was so great that a real opera house was built within the Exposition Building, a lavish gesture for a festival that was to last only two weeks. When Mapleson visited it, he was "astounded at its surpassing grandeur." The proscenium was sixty feet high with an opening of seventy feet. The stage apron was twenty feet deep, and the orchestra pit held 155 musicians. There were six thousand seats with two tiers of proscenium boxes, two balconies, and fifty feet of depth for standing room. It was needed. Audiences were as large as twelve thousand people. More than $50,000 were taken on the first day tickets went on sale.

On April 14 and again a week later Mapleson presented *Aida* on a scale that possibly never has been surpassed in the city. Patti, of course, sang the title role, with Nicolini as Radames. The Triumphal Scene called for 500 supernumeraries as captured Ethiopians, a military band, a supplemental chorus of 350, and 600 state militia as the Egyptian army. As the press saw it, "The promises made by the Festival Association have been fulfilled to the letter." A few nights later Patti was equally triumphant in *Faust*. Inaugurating what was to be a grand tradition, this was billed as "her farewell visit to America." Four years later, for (one presumes) her usual fee, she was opening the Auditorium.

Patti alternated with an American soprano, Emma Nevada, who was making her Chicago debut. Her repertory included *La sonnambula, Lucia di Lammermoor,* and *Rigoletto.* Characteristically, the company was largely European. In the course of the festival, 190,000 persons attended an opera. Later opera producers might look back wistfully at that number. At the close of the series Mapleson was called to the stage by the mayor, Carter H. Harrison, and given "the freedom of the city." One of the strangest mistakes in Upton's account is his statement that Mapleson died six years later, that is, in 1891. In fact, he lived another decade. The correct date of his death is 1901.

Mapleson, on his departure, expressed his hope to return year after year to this city "whose history has been the wonder of the world" to "some vast opera hall" where thousands could hear this music in an appropriate setting. His declining finances made this impossible, although he did produce further opera in England. The key figures in the local power structure heard or read the call for a new opera house, and for Ferdinand W. Peck it had special significance. In 1885 he had advocated the construction in Chicago of a great hall that would belong to all the people and provide a home for noble events, including grand opera. Mapleson's festival in the Exposition Building had been an experiment to see if audiences existed for performances of this type. The answer appeared to be positive and unequivocal. Adler and Peck went to work, and in 1889 the Auditorium was a reality.

The final Mapleson season, in February 1886, offered Patti and familiar repertory but is notable for one of the great onstage confrontations between a prima donna and a megalomanic tenor. The lady was the formidable Minnie Hauk, and her antagonist an Italian gentleman, Luigi Ravelli. Their confrontation was in the third act of *Carmen* (which, of course, was being sung in Italian). Ravelli's old trick was to interpolate a high note that invariably dazzled the public, and Hauk's reply, less to preserve the integrity of the score than to avoid being eclipsed, was to seize him in a tight embrace and squelch the interpolation for lack of air. Ravelli screamed for her to let go and tried to push her into the orchestra pit. The audience loved it.

Mapleson had to tighten security for two repeat performances, during which the two singers kept a safe distance from one another. Hauk, fearing the use of a real knife in the final scene, revised the action so she was stabbed offstage. In his memoirs Mapleson asked, rhetorically, "What could the public think of an opera company in which the tenor was always threatening to murder the prima donna, while the prima donna's husband found himself forced to take up a position at one of the wings bearing a revolver with which he proposed to shoot the tenor the moment he showed the slightest intention of approach-

ing the personage for whom he is supposed to entertain an ungovernable passion?"

In 1886 the Met toured under Hermann Grau (the uncle of Maurice) and came to Chicago in March with Wagner's *Rienzi* and Karl Goldmark's *Die Königin von Saba,* both new, and neither likely to establish a place in the repertory. The rest was standard fare.

With Mapleson out of the way, Theodore Thomas was persuaded to take charge of a newly formed American Opera Company which would tour and would give opera in English. Ballets were also to be offered.

"I believed in the idea," he wrote later, "and I knew it would also give my orchestra a permanent engagement, and relieve me from the responsibility of paying salaries. My hopes, however, were soon doomed to disappointment, for it soon became evi-

Theodore Thomas

dent that there were peculiarities of management which neither art nor business could long endure." What a wonderful phrase! The fact that Thomas had no business interests in the company did not protect him, after its demise, from several years of "lawsuits brought against me by its victims."

Thomas brought the company to Chicago in May 1886 with a short but cosmopolitan repertory that included Gluck's *Orfeo ed Euridice* (presumably in the French version), Delibes's *Lakmé,* and two Wagner operas, *Lohengrin* and *The Flying Dutchman.* The same repertory returned during a second visit in December, as well as *Aida, Les Huguenots, Faust,* and *The Merry Wives of Windsor.* Rubinstein's *Nero,* which the company did produce, was not staged until the New York run of 1887.

Walter Damrosch was invited to assemble a company and come to the city but could not engage the singers he needed. Instead, Chicago heard *The Mikado.* Then darkness fell. There was no grand opera worthy of the name in 1887/88.

As if to reward the public for its patience, April 1889 brought a return of the Met, where Wagner now reigned supreme. "There is no hope," wrote the critic Henry Theophilus Finck, "for the Italianissimi who sign for their macaronic arias and the Ernani and Gazza Ladra soup." Educated at Harvard, Finck had been to Bayreuth for the première of the *Ring* in 1876 and ruled the music desk of the *New York Post* for forty years.

Operas of the *Ring* cycle had entered the Met repertory as early as 1885, but in 1889 the company staged the entire cycle and, in a triumphant gesture, brought it to Chicago. It could not, however, bring the Met scenery. None of the stages to be visited could hold it. Simple touring sets had to be built. Edmund C. Stanton now ran the company, and its two greatest assets were the conductor, Anton Seidl, a member of the inner Wagner circle, and Lilli Lehmann, perhaps the greatest dramatic soprano of the day. Seidl felt Wagner could replace Italian repertory only if, at least at the beginning, the works were of comparable length, so he made cuts—some of them falsely attributed at a later date to Artur Bodansky, the Met's great Wagnerian of the early twentieth century. The Met did not present an uncut *Ring* until the 1898/99 season.

Stanton did not want to bring the *Ring* to Chicago during Holy Week, so he booked the troupe into Milwaukee, which heard the cycle April 16–20. There was

Lilli Lehmann as Brünnhilde in *Die Walküre*

no performance on the nineteenth, Easter Sunday, which was felt to be an inappropriate occasion for *Götterdämmerung.* When the company got to Chicago on April 22, it presented four operas in four nights, since Lehmann, unlike most sopranos, could easily sing the three Brünnhilde roles in a row. She had been a Rheinmaiden in the original 1876 production of the cycle at Bayreuth. In the winter of 1889 she married Paul Kalisch, both the Siegmund and the Siegfried of the cycle, and billed herself as Lehmann-Kalisch. Much of the rapid acceptance of the Wagner operas can be attributed to her. The power and beauty of her voice, shaped by a remarkable technique, was irresistible for many. Emil Fischer was the Wotan and the *Götterdämmerung* Hagen of the cycle, Felice Kaschowska was Sieglinde, and Max Alvary sang Loge.

Any listener who felt unequal to four nights of the *Ring* in a row could attend repeat performances of *Siegfried* and *Götterdämmerung* at the close of the run, after *Tannhäuser, Die Meistersinger,* and Beethoven's *Fidelio* had been heard. *Lohengrin* completed the repertory.

In the 1980s one might find Chicago newspaper executives who thought a music critic's job was to attend a performance and write three pages of snappy prose informing the reader whether he had liked it or not. It was all completely subjective and supposed to be entertaining. In the nineteenth century it was a different matter. The instructive thing about the press response to the 1889 *Ring* is that the major critics were musically well qualified. They knew the works. If they had not heard them at Bayreuth, they had heard them in New York, and they at least had the piano scores, since they were aware of the cuts. Indeed, following the first performance of *Das Rheingold* in Munich in 1869, there had been considerable interest in the cycle in the Chicago German community, and there was sympathy for Wagner's hope to build a festival theater in which to present it. Patrick Carnegy states that one such proposal came from Chicago,

presumably around 1870.[1] Since Wagner was not a linguist, any offer from outside a German-speaking country would not be considered seriously. Both Chicago and London were declined, and the plans for the Bayreuth theater were begun in 1871.

Das Rheingold runs only two-and-a-half hours, so with a curtain time of 7:45 there was no need to trim it. But with performances of the other operas scheduled to end at 11:00, a large amount of music was cut out of the second act of *Die Walküre; Siegfried* lacked both the bear in act 1 and Erda in act 3 (although Erda was heard in New York); and in *Götterdämmerung* there were no Norns, no debate between Brünnhilde and Waltraute, and no exchanges between Hagen and Alberich. On the other hand, Brünnhilde had a real horse.

This was a mutilated *Ring,* but under Seidl what was heard was impressive. The richness of the orchestration was reduced, since the pit held only sixty musicians.

The Met proved it could do things Mapleson would never attempt, but it did not make money. The company lost $2,500 on the engagement. Still, this was an improvement on Milwaukee, where, possibly because of the devout, the red-ink figure had been $4,000. Artistically, it was an impressive way to close the seventeen seasons between the fire and the opening of the Auditorium. The city was about to learn what it meant to have a real opera house again.

4

The Met West

1884–1910

The 1960s will be remembered as the decade of cultural centers, the most important of which remains Lincoln Center in New York City, which opened in 1962. But if we consider this concept in its broadest aspect, one of the first true cultural centers in the United States was the Auditorium in Chicago. It was built on a lavish scale with the expectation that it would house a resident opera company and symphony orchestra, neither of which existed at the time. Moreover, it was to be a symbol of rebirth that, in eighteen years, the city that had been ashes and ruin in 1871 was now a center of wealth and power with few peers in the United States. It was, and remains, a monumental building, a symbol, an affirmation that Chicago was dedicated to higher things than just commerce.

The Auditorium was the work of what today would be regarded as young men. Dankmar Adler, who has been hailed as an acoustical genius, was forty-two, and Ferdinand Peck was his contemporary. Louis Sullivan was in his thirties. Assistant to both architects was an apprentice in his teens—Frank Lloyd Wright. It was Wright who later hailed the building as "the greatest room for opera and music in the world—bar none." (With one qualification: an acoustical reflector onstage is essential for concerts and recitals. Many would still insist he was correct.)

The Auditorium was built on a beach. Today construction would begin by sinking caissons into bedrock, but in the 1880s this was impossible. Instead, after a hole of suitable dimensions was dug into the sandy soil, a huge raft of heavy timbers was constructed with the idea that if the weight of the building was evenly distributed, it would simply float on the soft substructure. This worthy goal was not achieved because of a later decision to build a tower

to hold the tanks for the hydraulically propelled elevators. The raft tipped slightly, and the floors and staircases of the theater have never been dead level.

The Auditorium was built primarily as an opera house. As Theodore Thomas later was to complain, it did not contain the offstage spaces required by a symphony orchestra. The design of the stage reflected current practices in operatic production, where scenery was painted on canvas sheets that, propelled by the muscles of stagehands, flew up and down from a stage loft. Three-dimensional scenery pieces were small. The width of the stage opening could be adjusted by panels in the fire curtain, but there were no wings of any real depth. When you walked offstage, you soon encountered a wall. For these reasons the hall was considered out of date as early as 1908.

The great innovative feature of the building was that it was the first large theater in the world to use electric lighting. Those who saw it after its restoration asked why all those bare light bulbs were so proudly displayed, but in 1889 you did not conceal a light bulb. First, because of their carbon filaments (the bulbs for the restored theater had to be especially made) the light was a soft yellow color, and secondly because they were the newest thing, something to exhibit with pride.

Essentially this was a solid masonry building with steel employed to arch wide spaces and keep the number of supporting pillars in the theater to a minimum. Acoustically it was truly a wonder. A singer—or speaker—at the front of the stage could be heard with perfect clarity and all desired force in the last row of the upper gallery. There was a huge main floor, an abundance of boxes, and a large balcony. At the top there were two galleries, the uppermost suspended in part from the ceiling. I have always suspected it was

The Auditorium Theatre and Hotel Building

Inside the Auditorium Theatre

added to the original design to provide segregated seating for blacks. If so, they could take satisfaction in the fact that the sight lines were excellent and the sound was marvelous—equal to many a more expensive seat. I used to love to sit there.

With both galleries in use the hall seated more than four thousand, but curved panels could be lowered to cut the galleries off, and with this modification about one thousand seats were lost. Apparently after 1910 the galleries were normally closed; the Chicago audience did not require the full capacity of the house. From the standpoint of the music producers, it was, unlike the makeshift theaters in use since 1872, a real opera house. The stage could hold any production in use at the Metropolitan, the orchestra pit easily contained a full Wagner ensemble, and, best of all, it was a place where you could make money. Sell four thousand seats on an appropriate scale and the most expensive production still could yield a profit.

Local tradition was that opera houses were dedicated by oratory, and so it went on December 9, 1889. Ferdinand W. Peck, who was the first to advocate the project, was graciously permitted by the politicians to say a few words. In 1886 Peck had founded the Chicago Auditorium Association, with the city's greatest merchant prince, Marshall Field I, its chairman. Construction was made possible by the sale of $2 million in stock and $900,000 in bonds.

Peck, following the example of Crosby's Opera House and the Metropolitan Opera House in New York, insisted that the theater be combined with commercial spaces, in this case a hotel. The theater was encircled and soundproofed by rooms facing the street. Unfortunately, the hotel was never the success it was hoped to be. Rivals a few steps away offered a larger number of private baths and other amenities.

Sullivan's decorations are one of the great beauties of the building, and the public rooms of the hotel were notable for their elegance. Wright, visiting Roosevelt University in the 1940s, surveyed the former hotel dining room (now a library) and glared at the columns encased in navy gray paint. "Under that muck," he declared, "is solid Honduras mahogany."

The fact that politicians (not always the liveliest act in town) dominated the opening proceedings may account for the modest ticket prices—$3 top. Mayor DeWitt C. Cregier was a principal speaker, followed by the president of the United States, Benjamin Harrison, and Governor Joseph W. Fifer of Illinois. Harrison hoped the theater might call "people away from cares of business to those enjoyments and entertainments which develop the soul of men and inspire those whose lives are heavy with toil; and in this magnificent and inspired presence, lift them for a time out of dull things and into those higher things where man should live." It was rhetoric typical of the time.

What music do you offer an audience of civic leaders, politicians, and solid citizens? "Home Sweet Home," of course, and to sing it you engage the most celebrated operatic artist of the age, Adelina Patti. This was her first stop on a tour undertaken by Henry E. Abbey, who first brought the Met to Chicago in 1884. Patti really wanted to do this tour, which was to take her to San Francisco and Mexico, and as a magnificent gesture she reduced her fee to $3,500 a performance and a percentage of the house. It exceeded $5,000. At these bargain rates, she still went home with $160,000 from the tour.

Her appearance was prefaced by choral numbers and a dedicatory ode. "Home Sweet Home" might express sentiments shared by all, but Patti was Patti, and she could not quit the stage without demonstrating the things she could do vocally that few dared to rival. So there was a staple of her concert programs, "Swiss Echo Song," by one Karl Anton Florian Eckert. It had a simple line of melody on which all manner of ornamentation and trills might be imposed, and, hearing them flawlessly executed by Patti, you knew with whom you were dealing.

Here, for the first time in this history, we encounter a theater that still stands. Abandoned as Chicago's principal opera house in 1929, the Auditorium survived by booking shows that required a large hall, the last of them—just before the nation entered World War II—a festival of comic excesses called *Hellzapoppin*. In the war years the hall was taken over as a recreational center for servicemen (part of it used as a bowling alley), and then was abandoned as a ruin. At war's end the hotel spaces became Roosevelt University, and some insisted that the building be remodeled and the theater be turned into classrooms and a parking garage. Many who realized that the theater, although obsolete as an opera house, was a civic asset not to be lost, joined Mrs. John V. Spachner, who in seventeen years raised $2.25 million and saw the house reopened by the New York City Ballet on October 31, 1967. Harry Weese was the architect in charge of the restoration, which became a continuing process.

On December 10, 1889, when opera was first heard, all this lay far in the future. The hall belonged to Abbey and his associate, Maurice Grau. (Both were impresarios associated with the Metropolitan Opera House, and Quaintance Eaton, in *Opera Caravan,* her history of Met touring, regards these first performances as a Met tour, although it is not so treated in the company's official annals.)

In 1889/90 the official impresario of the Met remained Edmund C. Stanton, who brought his company to the Auditorium for eighteen performances in April 1890. Patti is not listed in the 1889/90 Met roster. From 1884 to 1891 all operas at the Met were sung in German, and although one can imagine Patti as the forest bird in *Siegfried,* German operas (and German texts) were not her choice of repertory. She made her official Met debut in April 1892 as Rosina in *The Barber of Seville.* Her career there was very short. She could make far more money concertizing. Her annual farewell tour was an impressive money-maker from 1895 to 1906.

Abbey had three big stars. In addition to Patti there was Lillian Nordica and the supertenor Francesco Tamagno, Verdi's original Otello, who made his American debut in that role on January 2, 1890. (Some references wrongly consider his debut to be his first appearance at the Met in 1891.) In a run that lasted until early January, the first operatic performance in the new theater was Gounod's *Romeo and Juliet,* with Patti and Luigi Ravelli as the lovers. Patti returned to sing *Lucia di Lammermoor, Semiramide, Martha, La traviata, La sonnambula,* and *The Barber of Seville.* Tamagno sang in *Otello, Il trovatore,* and *William Tell.* Abbey's production of *Otello* preceded its first production by the Met, which also took place in the Auditorium. Nordica's greatest success was *Aida.* There were twenty-two performances in all, heard by an audience of more than a hundred thousand persons. Some $233,000 came in at the box office. Chicago was opera-dazzled.

Abbey pushed his luck by concluding his tour with a return to Chicago for six performances in March. Patti added *Linda di Chamounix* to her local repertory and repeated *Lakmé* and *Semiramide. L'Africana (L'Africaine)* with Tamagno was new, and he sang *Otello* twice. But this time there were empty seats.

When Stanton appeared for three weeks, with Damrosch conducting, nearly everything in the repertory changed dramatically. Like Abbey, he offered *William Tell.* Italian repertory was otherwise represented by *Un ballo in maschera,* and *Norma* and *La Juive* were heard—all of them in German. There were five operas by Wagner, Mozart's *Don Giovanni*—in the German text commonly called *Don Juan*—Beethoven's *Fidelio,* and two less familiar works, Peter Cornelius's *Der Barbier von Baghdad* and Karl Goldmark's *Die Königin von Saba.* Lilli Lehmann's Elisabeth in *Tannhäuser* was the vocal performance most likely to be remembered. For the German population, which had weathered a four-month inundation of Italian and French music, it was a blessed change of style. Every one of the fourteen operas had been heard in New York. Packing them into a train for performances in Chicago was good business.

In the 1890s New York could not support long seasons. In 1890/91, as Stanton bowed out in his sixth year, the Met offered seventy-nine performances from a repertory of seventeen works, an average of somewhat less than five performances of each score. The company did not tour. Chicago, after the grandiose offerings in the Auditorium the previous season, had a total of only ten operatic performances worth noting. In the spring of 1891 there was a week of Wagner from a scratch company, and apparently it was successful, since it was repeated in autumn.

Not surprisingly, the first music producer to provide the Auditorium with a permanent tenant was Theodore Thomas. He owed this to Charles Norman Fay, a utilities magnate, who in 1877 on his first visit to the city was attracted to one of Thomas's Summer Garden Concerts in the Exposition Building and, as he later wrote, "for the first time I heard a great orchestra." By autumn, Fay was a resident of Chicago and a regular figure at Thomas's concerts. In 1881 the two men became friends.

In New York, during a lunch at Delmonico's restaurant in 1889, Thomas appeared depressed. The failure of the American Opera Company had wiped out his savings and caused him to lose his orchestra. He could no longer engage his musicians by the year but had to hire a scratch orchestra. Thomas's projects were never to be confused with not-for-profit organizations. He kept his orchestra intact by playing a series of New York concerts and going on the road. To avoid financial losses he was, he complained, condemned to tour constantly, winter and summer, year after year, and at fifty-three the strain had become too great.

Fay was curious. Major Henry Lee Higginson had founded the Boston Symphony in 1881 on the model of orchestras he had heard in Europe. Although the New York Philharmonic (founded in 1842) was older than the Boston orchestra, it played considerably fewer concerts and was not permanent, in the sense that the musicians had to have other work in order to survive. Was there no one in New York to play a role similar to Higginson's in Boston? "No," Thomas replied. New York philanthropy ran to other lines, and in music, if it went anywhere, it went to opera. Fay put the crucial question. Would Thomas come to Chicago if it gave him a permanent orchestra? Back came the much quoted reply: "I would go to Hell if they gave me a permanent orchestra." Thus the Chicago Symphony was conceived over coffee and—probably—cigars.

As Thomas was to write later in his memoirs, establishing a permanent orchestra of high quality in Chicago was no simple task. About ninety musicians were required. (Thomas, one must remember, was a champion of Richard Strauss.) Although there were capable professional musicians in Chicago—most of them string players—there were not enough to meet his needs. Where would he find a contrabassoon except in New York? Eventually he negotiated a deal with the Chicago musicians' union for an orchestra of eighty-six members, with twenty-four from Chicago. The initial response was that this new ensemble, initially called the Chicago Orchestra, was inferior to the Theodore Thomas Orchestras of the past, but by the close of the first season the old level of performance was in place.

Thomas set two conditions for Fay. He should have absolute control and could make his programs without any consideration of possible ticket sales. Secondly, since touring any distance with an orchestra of this size would produce traveling costs in excess of any likely profits, few journeys would be much farther than Milwaukee.

The orchestra was to be engaged for twenty-eight weeks and play a regular series of twenty Friday afternoons and twenty Saturday nights. In addition, the orchestra was to play popular concerts and join the Apollo Club in choral music. There were to be no entangling alliances with piano manufacturers, and a guarantee fund of $50,000 was to be available for the first three seasons. On this basis the Orchestral Association was established in 1890, with Marshall Field the first of those to guarantee $1,000 a year for the support of the ensemble.

Thomas still had reservations. "The conditions at that time were very unfavorable to success," he wrote in his memoirs. The city had 2 million inhabitants, but most of them were poorly paid, manual laborers.

"The cultivated class," he wrote, "is comparatively small," a view that others might hold into the new century. For the first season a box holding five persons cost $500 for the twenty concerts. Subscriptions were $30, $20, and $10, but since the hall was so large, it never sold out; those wishing single tickets could always gain admission. This is why, when Orchestra Hall was planned in 1903, it was originally made too small, and a gallery as steep as some upper reaches of the Jungfrau was hastily incorporated into the design to provide a more reasonable number of seats.

The deficit for the first season was $53,600, an ominous portent for Thomas, who had hoped the concerts might be self-sustaining in time. Debating the matter with his guarantors, Thomas challenged them. Did they want programs comparable to those played by the Boston Symphony? Civic pride, if not musical culture, required them to say yes. Then Thomas pointed out that several of his programs of the first season had not contained a symphony, that the surest way to sell tickets was to engage a celebrated soloist, and, if money was to be the issue, that soloists and popular concerts were the way to draw a larger public. To the enduring credit of his backers, they insisted that he stick to his standards, and they would pay the bills. For the second season the loss was down to slightly over $51,000, for the third it was $49,000. In anticipation of a fourth season, a fund for the orchestra was established with the expectation that an annual subsidy would be essential. "Never," Thomas wrote, "was I ever asked by our directors to lower [the orchestra's] artistic standards in order to gain the patronage of the multitude."

Experience proved that the Auditorium was designed primarily for the presentation of opera. Some visiting companies used Thomas's orchestra, which provided the musicians with welcome additional work. The best client for these services proved to be the Metropolitan, which quickly realized that it could save money by using an orchestra based in Chicago rather than importing and housing its New York musicians. Of necessity, the Chicago Orchestra concerts were fitted in around other bookings. The building lacked a space for a music library, instrument storage, and an area in which the players could change into concert dress and get warmed up for the performance. What it needed most of all was something unknown in the period, an acoustical reflector to keep the music of the orchestra from being diffused backstage and to project it into the hall. Thomas concluded

Jean de Reszke as Romeo in *Romeo and Juliet*

Édouard de Reszke as Mephistopheles in *Faust*

that the Chicago Orchestra needed a home of its own, and the project to build Orchestra Hall was begun. It was dedicated in December 1904.

The story of Chicago opera from 1890 to 1910 can be quickly summarized. The Auditorium became mostly the western base of companies from the Metropolitan Opera, which visited the city nineteen times in this period. It was artistically and economically sensible to tour with already prepared and performed productions.

But the companies from the Met did not, by any means, have a monopoly on the resources of the house. The Grand French Opera of New Orleans came up the river twice (in 1899 and 1900) for a stay in Chicago, and the Boston Opera was a visitor in 1910. There were further visitations from New York when an impresario hired a group of singers and decided to try the road.

In 1891/92 leadership at the Met passed to a trio of impresarios, the redoubtable Abbey, Maurice Grau, and John B. Schoffel. They obviously felt the potential of Chicago had been seriously underrated and began in November with a five-week season in the Auditorium prior to opening in New York in mid-December. Their great strength was the brothers de Reszke, Jean (perhaps the greatest tenor of the nineteenth century) and his brother Édouard, a bass. Both made their American debut in *Lohengrin*, opening the Chicago season on November 9, 1891, with Theodore Thomas's orchestra in the pit. Jean, naturally, sang the title role; Édouard was the King. Emma Eames, who was also making her American debut after great success in Europe, was Elsa. The same trio was heard in *Romeo and Juliet* on November 16 and in *Faust* on November 26. The de Reszkes returned in *Les Huguenots*. Chicago heard the first Met performance of *Otello* with Jean. Apparently unsure if this new work was to be a success, this was an out-of-town tryout with stock scenery. The work was repeated in New York on January 11. Now confident it would remain in the repertory, the Met built a production that appeared in the 1894/95 season with Tamagno in the title role in New York and Chicago. As the Chicago run continued, Édouard was Plunkett in *Martha* and Leporello in *Don Giovanni*. The Chicago Orchestra traveled with the Met to Louisville for three performances.

Other repertory, cast with capable, if largely forgotten, singers, included Gluck's *Orfeo ed Euridice,* Meyerbeer's *Dinorah,* Bellini's *Norma,* and Thomas's *Mignon.* The ticking bomb was the first Chicago performance of a *verismo* opera, Pietro Mascagni's *Cavalleria rusticana* on December 4, 1891, with Eames as Santuzza. It was an exciting view of a new day to come. On December 9 a gala of operatic excerpts was given to mark the first anniversary of the opening of the theater. After a series like this, one could claim that Chicago was being given opera of the same quality that one might expect in New York or in leading European theaters. Was it prepared to support it?

Abbey and his colleagues had to wait until 1893/94 to find out. In August 1892 fire destroyed much of the interior of the Metropolitan Opera House, and the season was canceled while the building was restored. In Chicago, 1893 was the year of the World's Columbian Exposition, which had no place for opera. Abbey, Schoffel, and Grau brought a "grand historical spectacle" called *America.* It had allegorical ballets depicting events in history and a grand panorama of the arts, of science, and of invention, from Franklin's lightning rod to Edison's phonograph. Opening in March, it had played one hundred performances by mid-July.

The Abbey group was back in March 1894 for twenty-seven performances, with the Chicago Orchestra transferred once more to the Auditorium pit. Again the series opened with the brothers de Reszke, but Abbey also had Nellie Melba, Nordica, and two Emmas, Eames and Calvé (as Carmen, her great role). Calvé was the first to sing *Carmen* in French in Chicago; until then it had been heard in Italian. Indeed, considering the company as a whole, Chicago had not heard such a concentration of vocal talent in a number of years. Fifty years later Chicago opera might have one or two major artists in leading roles, but it could not fill out a cast with experienced artists in a manner comparable to the Met of the 1890s. Opening night was virtually the same as the opening of the New York season, *Faust* with both the de

Reszkes and Eames. *The Marriage of Figaro* brought Eames and Édouard de Reszke as the Countess and Count. Jean de Reszke headed the cast of *L'Africana* and *Lohengrin,* with Eames as Elsa. Melba sang in *Lucia di Lammermoor* and *Romeo and Juliet* and played Gilda in *Rigoletto.* Calvé was Mignon and sang Santuzza in *Cavalleria rusticana.* Nordica sang *Aida* and joined the de Reszkes in *Les Huguenots.*

The public support was generous, and the three impresarios were back with another long season (twenty-two performances) in 1895. Since the Chicago Orchestra was on tour, the Met brought its New York musicians. The novelty was a new opera by Verdi, *Falstaff,* with Victor Maurel making his Chicago debut in the title role and with Eames as Alice. Maurel was also heard as Don Giovanni, and Eames was Desdemona to Tamagno's Otello. This time Nordica joined the de Reszke brothers in *Les Huguenots.* Much of the repertory and casting was the same as during the previous season. The Met performances were followed by a week of Wagner from Walter Damrosch, who, I surmise, made use of Thomas's orchestra. Things must have gone well, because he was back in November for two weeks with what I call a "short" *Ring* cycle, one without *Das Rheingold.*

The Abbey company may have feared that the demand for opera in Chicago had largely been met for that season, since, when they returned in March 1896, it was for just two weeks, and only one Wagner opera was given. Again the Chicago Orchestra was touring, and the Met ensemble was heard. Opening night was *Faust* with the de Reszkes; Melba was Marguerite. The three were later heard in *Les Huguenots.* De Reszke and Nordica proved a sensation in *Tristan und Isolde,* and Calvé once more sang Carmen and Santuzza. Maurel and Melba were heard as Rigoletto and his daughter. The most talked-about incident of the run took place on March 20 when *Romeo and Juliet* was interrupted by what the Met annals call "a deranged man," who managed to get on the stage and threaten the principals, Jean de Reszke and Melba. He was taken away by the police.

Abbey died on October 17, 1896.

In February 1897 the Grand Italian Opera Company returned for four weeks and twenty-five performances. Again they had Calvé as Carmen, Jean de Reszke in *Les Huguenots* and *Tristan und Isolde,* and Pol Plançon as Mephistopheles in both *Faust* and *Mefistofele.* Both brothers de Reszke appeared in

Lohengrin and *Siegfried*. The novelty was the first Chicago performance of Massenet's *Le Cid,* with both de Reszkes and Plançon. With casts like that you would expect the house to be packed, but business must have been bad, since Chicago did not hear another Met season of that length until Giulio Gatti-Casazza (usually referred to as just Gatti) brought the company in the spring of 1910. This time the Chicago Orchestra not only played for the performances in the Auditorium but went on the road for five performances in St. Louis, two in Louisville, and eight in Cincinnati.

Giulio Gatti-Casazza

There was no Met season in either New York or Chicago in 1897/98. Opera in Chicago during that season consisted of nine performances in March of conventional repertory from Damrosch and Ellis. In 1889/90 Grau became the sole manager at the Metropolitan. He held on until 1902/03, cashed in his chips, and retired to Europe, by the standards of the day a wealthy man. He was succeeded by Heinrich

Conried (1903–1908). The company was then reorganized into its present form, and Gatti began his twenty-seven years as general manager. He was on salary. The profits now went to the company.

Damrosch and Ellis arrived in Chicago in March 1898 with Melba in *La traviata, The Barber of Seville,* and *Faust*. Johanna Gadski, who had made her American debut with Damrosch in 1895, was heard in *Tannhäuser, Die Walküre* (opposite the Brünnhilde of Nordica), *Siegfried, Lohengrin,* and *Die Meistersinger*. Later that year Melba was to begin seventeen seasons as a leading soprano at the Metropolitan. *Les Huguenots* offered Melba, Nordica, and Giuseppe Campanari at the head of its cast.

Grau tried three weeks (twenty performances) in Chicago, opening in November 1898, and this time the Chicago Orchestra was back in the pit. His opening night, November 7, provided the American debut of Ernestine Schumann-Heink as Ortrud in *Lohengrin* and as both Fricka and Waltraute in *Die Walküre*. Marcella Sembrich, returning for the first time since 1884, sang in *The Barber of Seville, La traviata,* and *Lucia di Lammermoor*. Nordica was heard as Aida and Brünnhilde. The roster of male singers included the debut of Herman Devries, who was to end his days as a Chicago music critic. Chicago first heard him on November 8 as Capulet in *Romeo and Juliet*.

The Charles A. Ellis Opera Company arrived from New York in February 1899 with a new opera by a new composer—*La bohème* by Giacomo Puccini. Moreover, Nellie Melba (one of the early champions of the role) was Mimì opposite a tenor named Pandolfini, whose fame has passed. It was a vision of the future. For an audience of that day, Puccini was a radically modern composer, who flouted traditional rules of harmony and composition. Melba also appeared in *Faust* and *Romeo and Juliet*. She was to sing Micaëla in *Carmen,* but laryngitis took her from the cast. Gadski took her place and appeared in other operas: *Tannhäuser, Lohengrin,* and *Siegfried*—which might be expected—but also *Cavalleria rusticana*—which might not. It was an exceptional range of roles. *Cavalleria*—affectionately known as "Cav"—was combined with *Pagliacci* in what came to be a classic double bill. In the late nineteenth century it was not unusual for productions of *Siegfried* to stand alone. Later it was rarely heard, except as part of a *Ring* cycle.

The Grand French Opera of New Orleans appeared in March with Gounod's *La Reine de Saba,* Donizetti's *La favorite* (in its original French text—the preferred, but rarely heard, version of the opera most often given in Italian as *La favorita*), and Verdi's *Le Trouvère (Il trovatore)*. The singers were good, but the most celebrated French singers were working for the Met.

Apparently, as Grau saw it, 1898 was enough of a success to justify an engagement of three weeks, beginning in November 1899. This time there were twenty-two performances. Again the Chicago Orchestra was in service, and this time it began with the Met on tour, giving a performance in Indianapolis, three performances in Louisville, and four in Cincinnati. On November 24 some of the Chicago musicians reinforced the Bach Orchestra (a chamber ensemble) in Milwaukee for a performance of *The Barber of Seville* while the main force played *Die Walküre* in the Auditorium. The relationship with the Met may have ended because the Chicago musicians often taught in the afternoon and were accustomed to 10:00 a.m. rehearsals. The singers did not want to rehearse before noon.

Casting was strong. Calvé was Carmen and Marguerite in *Faust*. Sembrich was Susanna in *The Marriage of Figaro* and Zerlina in *Don Giovanni;* Antonio Scotti made his debut as Don Giovanni. Nordica was Venus in *Tannhäuser* and Leonora in *Il trovatore*. Schumann-Heink repeated her dual roles in *Die Walküre,* and Eames was Elsa in *Lohengrin*. Jean de Reszke was conspicuously absent. Apparently Grau lost money this time, something he hated to do (he was producing opera in order to *make* money), and his final three visits to Chicago lasted only about two weeks each. Grau had no real competition when it came to artistic quality, but he was not the only impresario bringing opera to the city. The Castle Square Opera Company, which Upton considered beneath his interest, appeared regularly at the Studebaker from 1899 to 1903. (I omit it from the annals.) Its heavy crowd pleasers were works such as *The Sultan of Sulu* and *The Black Hussar,* but it cautiously ventured into deeper water, offering *The Bohemian Girl, Martha,* and *Aida* in 1899, *Lucia di Lammermoor* and *Faust* in 1900, and *La traviata* and *Carmen* in 1902. This repertory returned in its later seasons, but *Tristan und Isolde,* which it attempted in 1900, was abandoned—probably for excellent reasons—after a single season.

There is a myth that the 1890s and the years before World War I represent a golden age of opera: incredible voices singing to a large and thoroughly appreciative audience, and that, compared to this, we are living in a lesser era. It simply is not true.

One cannot question that some remarkable voices could be heard at this time, but listeners of today might complain that many of these artists made no pretext of acting or joining their colleagues to create dramatic situations onstage.

In the season 1899/1900 the Met functioned from November through April, but the company was kept together by touring. The first performances were in Los Angeles, and there were three weeks in San Francisco. The trip home involved stops in Denver, Colorado; Lincoln, Nebraska; Kansas City, Missouri; and Minneapolis, Minnesota. Opening night in New York was December 18. There were nineteen performances in Philadelphia, spaced through the season, and the final tour, beginning April 1, took the company to Boston, Pittsburgh, and Cincinnati before it arrived in Chicago.

How much opera was given in New York? Eighty performances. In 1999/2000 the Met stayed at home and gave three times as many performances in its Lincoln Center house. This reflected impressive growth in the size of the audience, but the character of the audience had changed as well. This was an educated, well-dressed audience of some affluence, but it came to the opera to attend a performance, not put on a performance of its own advertising its wealth.

The New Orleans company was back in March 1900 with two novelties by Louis-Étienne-Ernest Reyer, *Salammbô* and *Sigurd,* in what proved to be their only Chicago performances. *William Tell* was sung in its original French text. *Cavalleria rusticana* was on a double bill with Massenet's *La Navarraise,* and Massenet's *Manon* was heard for the first time. Otherwise, the repertory largely duplicated the performances of the previous year. The public enjoyed a change from German and Italian fare.

Grau returned in April 1901 with the first local staging of *Tosca*, which had had its United States première at the Met on February 4. Scotti was Scarpia, and one may assume it was an intensely dramatic performance, with Milka Ternina and Giuseppe Cremonini as Tosca and Cavaradossi. *Don Giovanni* was heard, again with Scotti in the title role, Édouard de Reszke as Leporello, and Nordica as Donna Anna—a noteworthy cast. Jean de Reszke was back opening night to sing *Faust* with his brother and Melba. This was the Chicago debut of Louise Homer (as Siebel), who was to be one of the Met's most important artists for nineteen years. The de Reszke tenor was heard again in *Les Huguenots* and in *Lohengrin,* with Schumann-Heink as Ortrud, Nordica as Elsa, and Damrosch conducting. Melba sang *Lucia di Lammermoor*. It was a short season, but with a generous display of talent.

December 1902 provided a wild interlude. Mascagni had been persuaded to assemble an Italian troupe and tour the United States with his incorrigibly popular *Cavalleria rusticana* on a program including excerpts from his perennially unsuccessful *Iris.* It was not a happy tour—its practical consequences were that Mascagni achieved the distinction of being the only composer of great reputation to be arrested in Chicago. After the performance the company came to him, begging to be permitted to return home, and in a grandiose gesture he paid them off and put them on a train for New York, where a ship bound for Italy presumably could be found. The backer of the tour promptly charged the composer with embezzling funds (the proceeds of recent appearances) for this purpose and denying the backer the income from engagements that now must be canceled. A friendly judge produced a settlement, and Mascagni declared that nothing could persuade him to return to the United States. He was, however, happy to go on receiving dollar royalties for the performances of his works.

To make his stay in March 1902 as attractive as possible, Grau offered a *Ring* cycle, the first in thirteen years, and this time with the regular Met scenery and a full Wagner orchestra in the pit, Damrosch conducting. Schumann-Heink played the Rheinmaiden Flosshilde, Erda, and Waltraute. Édouard de Reszke was Hagen in *Götterdämmerung.* On tour, the Norns Scene and the Hagen-Alberich Scene continued to be cut, presumably to keep the work within a more normal time frame. Elsewhere in the schedule was *Aida* with Eames and Homer, *Cavalleria rusticana* with Calvé as Santuzza (she also sang Carmen), and some attractive Mozart: *The Marriage of Figaro,* with Eames and Sembrich, and *The Magic Flute,* with Sembrich as the Queen of the Night, Eames as Pamina, and Homer as the Second Lady. Sembrich was cast in *Manru,* an ill-fated opera by Ignace Jan Paderewski that died after five performances.

Grau returned for the last time in April 1903 and offered a nicely balanced series of fifteen operas, among them a short *Ring,* with Nordica as Brünnhilde, Schumann-Heink as Fricka, Waltraute, and Flosshilde, Alois Burgstaller as both Siegmund and Siegfried, and Anton Van Rooy as Wotan. Alfred Hertz conducted. Schumann-Heink was Brangäne to Nordica's Isolde, and Magdalene to Gadski's Eva in *Die Meistersinger.* There was a *Magic Flute* with the same cast as that of the previous year. Sembrich sang *The Daughter of the Regiment.*

Grau's successor, Conried, offered his first (and longest) Chicago season beginning in March 1904 with *Die Walküre,* conducted by a Bayreuth stalwart,

Felix Mottl. He dominated the engagement, again offering the city a short *Ring* cycle and two Mozart operas, *The Magic Flute* (with Plançon as Sarastro and Sembrich again the Queen of the Night) and *The Marriage of Figaro,* with Gadski as the Countess and Sembrich as Susanna. Sembrich would later return in *L'elisir d'amore* and *The Barber of Seville.* There was more Wagner, *Lohengrin* (with Gadski as Elsa) and *Tannhäuser,* conducted by Alfred Hertz. Enrico Caruso, who had made his debut with the company in November, sang *Tosca* in Philadelphia but declined traveling as far west as Chicago. Eames, Journet, and Scotti made a memorable trio in *Faust,* and once more there was Calvé in *Carmen* and *Cavalleria rusticana.* Apparently Conried regretted the decision to stay this long and never returned for more than one week during the remainder of his tenure at the Met. Gatti was more optimistic. His first Chicago season in April 1909 lasted two weeks.

The San Carlo Opera Company appeared for the first time in February 1907 with what was to be its predictable fare, Italian opera from capable, but less expensive, Italian singers. *Les Huguenots* was the only work of other than Italian origin.

One cannot fault Conried for denying Chicago the best the Met had to offer, and if business was bad—as presumably it was—his decision to reduce the length of his Chicago stays was justified. The seasons 1904–1908 were some of the shortest of the century, but they contained great moments, none more exciting than opening night, March 20, 1905, when Caruso made his Chicago debut with Sembrich in *Lucia di Lammermoor.* Caruso was back two nights later in *Pagliacci,* with Scotti as Tonio. March 24 brought *La Gioconda* with two formidable ladies, Nordica and Homer. Caruso was to sing in twenty-three operatic performances in Chicago, twenty-one with the Metropolitan from 1905 to 1910 and two appearances with the resident company in 1911.

When Caruso was onstage, Italian opera dominated, but the eight performances of the run were balanced toward German repertory. There were two performances of *Parsifal* with Nordica as Kundry and one of *Die Meistersinger,* and even *Die Fledermaus* was heard, with Sembrich as Rosalinde. Eames sang *Tosca,* which proved just as sensational as it had at its première.

There were three more Caruso performances in 1906: *Faust,* with Eames and Plançon; *Carmen,* with Fremstad and Journet; and *Martha* (in Italian), with Sembrich and Homer. Arturo Vigna conducted all of these early appearances. Homer sang Ortrud in *Lohengrin.*

Caruso opened the 1907 series with *L'Africana* and went on to sing Rodolfo in *La bohème* and play Radames to Homer's Aida. To close the nine-performance series he was back in *Pagliacci*. Between those first two performances Conried introduced his most potent soprano star, Geraldine Farrar, first as Madama Butterfly and then as Elisabeth in *Tannhäuser*. Carl Burrian and Johanna Gadski sang *Tristan und Isolde*, with Schumann-Heink as Brangäne.

There were only eight nights of opera in Conried's final season, 1908, but, again, he planned to fill the theater by offering his biggest stars. Opening night was *La bohème* with Farrar, followed by *Il trovatore* with Caruso and Eames. Caruso was back in *Pagliacci* and in *Iris* (an opera he liked, even if the public did not). Farrar reappeared in *Faust* and *Mignon*. Wagner was represented by *Die Walküre* and Gustav Mahler's production of *Tristan und Isolde*. Mahler consented to conduct the work in Philadelphia, but a journey to Chicago was beyond him. Alfred Hertz took his place. Mahler never appeared in Chicago.

Writing in 1908, Upton regrets that "opera seasons during the last eight years have not only been less frequent, but they have steadily diminished in length."[1] By his count, in the nineteen years since the Auditorium was dedicated, the average number of operatic performances a year had been fifteen. This was a far cry from 1865.

My explanation is that early in the twentieth century opera had ceased to be mass entertainment. The great audience of the mid–nineteenth century was gone. Since the French Revolution the primary support of live theater had been the middle class, but throughout the 1890s the middle class listeners turned to things they found amusing but less demanding than opera. The younger audiences of the day enjoyed music theater that was unabashedly entertaining: Gilbert and Sullivan, French light opera, and what today we would classify as Broadway shows. If they went to the opera, they might buy a ticket for the Castle Square Opera Company, which, despite the fact that Upton did not take it seriously, settled into the Studebaker Theater with a vast repertory of works on different artistic levels. Everything was in English, and business was good from 1899 to 1908.

Opera became the theater of the affluent. Chicago went the way New York had gone decades before. The people who provided the company with its primary financial support went to the Auditorium to present an image of conspicuous consumption, enthroned in a box for all to admire or envy, and listened to music they probably felt was too good for the masses. Of course, opera was not totally abandoned by the bourgeoisie; it could not survive a season without their ticket purchases. But they paid their money, took their seats, and stayed in the background. The impressive thing is that they heard a great deal of important music.

When Gatti decided to leave La Scala and go to the Met, he knew the man he needed to succeed, and he got him. One of the great events in the history of the company was the debut of Arturo Toscanini in a new production of *Aida* on November 16, 1908, which opened the season in the New York house with Caruso as Radames. Toscanini had conducted Caruso's La Scala debut in 1900, and they were a powerful combination. Scotti was Amonasro, Emmy Destinn sang Aida, and Homer was Amneris. Unfortunately, Caruso was not part of the Met tour this season.

Toscanini made his Chicago debut on April 12, 1909, with *Aida*. Destinn sang the title role, with Homer as Amneris. Three nights later he conducted *Madama Butterfly* with Geraldine Farrar (who was to become his lover for seven years). On December 10, 1908, Toscanini directed *Götterdämmerung* at the Met, with Erik Schmedes as Siegfried, Olive Fremstadt as Brünnhilde, and Homer as Flosshilde. All of the four operas of the *Ring* cycle were heard that season (though not in sequence), with Hertz conducting in New York. (Toscanini never conducted a full *Ring*; *Das Rheingold* was not in his repertory.) Apparently it was felt that this *Götterdämmerung* could be cut. The maestro was told he could have either Norns or Waltraute and, under protest, chose the Norns Scene. When the opera was repeated in Philadelphia on March 25, 1909, with Hertz, it was the other way around. When Toscanini conducted it in Chicago the following April 24, with Gadski as Brünnhilde and Georg Anthes as Siegfried, the Norns were again on view.

Elsewhere in the run were *Die Walküre* (with Gadski and Homer), *Tannhäuser, Tristan und Isolde* (with Gadski), and *Parsifal* (with Fremstad) from Hertz, who also directed *The Marriage of Figaro,* with Scotti as the Count, Johanna Gadski as the Countess, and Marcella Sembrich as Susanna. The novelty from Hertz's baton was Smetana's *The Bartered Bride,* sung in German. *Faust* represented the French repertory, and Italian operas included *Falstaff, Il trovatore, La bohème* (with Farrar), and *Pagliacci*. The casts were essentially the same as those offered in New York.

On December 9, 1909, the Chicago Grand Opera Company was organized, with fifty business leaders contributing $5,000 each to a guaranty fund. Harold F. McCormick, the head of the International Harvester Company, chaired the organization, which announced that its first season would be presented in the Auditorium in the autumn of 1910.

In January 1910 Chicago was visited by the newly formed Boston Opera Company. This was a noble endeavor to establish a resident company in another city where opera had usually come from the Met on tour. Its brief history seemed to prove that, at least early in the century, Boston was not an opera town. It could support a few performances as well as a lot of theater from out of town, but in the long run it was happy to give the responsibilities of production to other cities. Its musical glory was its symphony orchestra, which for many years had been unsurpassed in the nation.

To house the new company, an opera house was built—"the first Unitarian opera house," as some called it—a well-proportioned redbrick building with decorative accents in white. It opened on November 8, 1909, and lasted nearly fifty years. The Boston Opera vanished into bankruptcy early in 1915. The Met was back in April 1916, delighted with the new Boston theater, and returned two years later. Other touring companies would include Boston bookings, but the principal source of opera in Boston from 1918 to 1929 was Chicago. Chicago companies visited the city for ten seasons and a total of 143 performances, the largest number in any city visited except New York (216) and Philadelphia (189). Apparently Chicago continued to tour to Boston after the move to the Civic Opera House. So if the Auditorium was the "Met West," the Boston house became the "Auditorium East." Under the management of the Shuberts, the theater hung on into the 1950s, when, rumored to be structurally unsafe, it was torn down in 1958.

For its two weeks in Chicago, the Bostonians chose French and Italian repertory, with the exception of a performance of *Lohengrin.* Opening night featured *Aida,* but the growing popularity of Puccini was demonstrated by the presence of both *La bohème* and *Madama Butterfly,* each given two performances. The *verismo* revolution was further demonstrated by a production of *Pagliacci.* As a gesture to the tour, *Les Huguenots,* which had not been included in the Boston season, was added. The singers apparently were all capable people whose names mean little to audiences of today. Boston was to have its share of stars: the conductor Felix Weingartner, Luisa Tetrazzini, Leo Slezak, Nordica, Melba, Caruso. Even Mary Garden appeared there. But they were never part of a second Chicago tour.

Faced with increased competition, in the 1909/10 season the Met increased its forces to include a double orchestra, offered performances in two New York theaters, and toured on the most lavish scale, including eighteen performances in Paris. When Gatti brought the Met to Chicago for a nearly month-long visit in April 1910, agreements had been made that meant the New York company would never return to the Auditorium and, as it turned out, would not be heard in the city for thirty-three years. He offered twenty-five operas, including such unfamiliar fare as *Germania,* by Alberto Franchetti (1860–1942), and *Il maestro di cappella,* by Johann Florian Deller (1729–1773). This time there were several repeat performances—two *Butterfly*s with Farrar, for example.

Caruso sang nine times. He began by repeating his performance of the opening night of the Met season (November 15, 1909), singing *La Gioconda* with Destinn and Homer on April 4, 1910, with Toscanini conducting. Two nights later Caruso returned in the first of two performances of *La bohème.* Three days later he was back to sing a matinée of *Germania.* On April 13 he joined Toscanini in *Aida* (Destinn sang the title role). He appeared twice in what many considered his primary role, Canio in *Pagliacci.* Unfortunately, Chicago never heard Caruso with the Tonio of Antonio Scotti. On April 20 Caruso was heard in *Faust;* his Marguerite was Alma Gluck.

One can feel at times that theaters still ring with the echoes of past performances, and part of the magic of the Auditorium—magic that inspired its restoration after World War II—was that in the right frame of mind one could almost hear Toscanini and Caruso in *Aida.* The only other place in America where that magic also remains is the Academy of Music in Philadelphia.

Toscanini conducted *Otello* with Slezak in the title role, Alda as Desdemona, and Scotti as Iago. Slezak was Radames in Toscanini's first *Aida* on April 8, and *Madama Butterfly,* on April 11, paired Toscanini with Farrar in the title role. *Die Meistersinger,* on the eighteenth, featured Slezak as Walther to Gadski's Eva. Hertz conducted *Lohengrin* (with Fremstad), *Tannhäuser* (with Fremstad as Venus and Destinn as Elisabeth), *Die Walküre,* and *Parsifal* (with Fremstad as Kundry). And there was standard fare with less than superstar castings. It remained a spectacular demonstration of the potential of the Met company, a challenge to the new Chicago troupe to present something comparable. The days of the "Met West" had ended. There were thirty-three performances, a number the Lyric Opera of Chicago did not reach until its tenth season in 1963.

In the 150 years examined in this book, opera began as mass entertainment and then became the showcase for wealth and social status. In the final third of the twentieth century it became what it ought to be, a distinctive art form for those who can understand and enjoy a union of music and theater on the highest level.

In the sixty years, 1850–1910, in which Chicago looked to New York as its principal source of operatic music, audiences were offered somewhat more than a hundred works. The distinction between grand opera and light opera, which existed well into the twentieth century but was now starting to disappear, makes precise classification difficult. Tossing everything into a general category such as music theater creates even more perplexing problems. *Die Meistersinger* and *The Bohemian Girl* have very different artistic objectives that are pursued by very different artistic means. When was *The Bohemian Girl* last staged by a major opera company? The Met, one notes, has never staged it at all. It has not been heard in Chicago since 1925. And does either work belong in the same category as *La Périchole,* which, at least in the past century, was considered entertaining but not serious? This has not affected its durability. For five seasons the Met had delightful success with *La Périchole. Naughty Marietta* (1910) was enormously popular music theater and survived to become a successful sound film, but its composer, Victor Herbert, never would have imagined it in an opera house.

Nineteenth-century operagoers undoubtedly attended both serious and light opera, although it is impossible to estimate the degree to which the two audiences overlapped. In the 1880s thousands flocked to Gilbert and Sullivan who would never be caught attending Benedict's *The Lily of Kilarney,* let alone Wagner's *Lohengrin.*

Of the operas in the 1850–1910 repertory, roughly a third may be regarded as dead. No living listener is likely to have heard them onstage, and, more to the point, no living opera producer is likely to show any interest in presenting them. Some fifty-five works were produced in only one or two seasons, and most of these are forgotten. But there are exceptions. Although Verdi's *La forza del destino* was staged only once, this did not prevent its eventual assimilation into the repertory, and although Rossini's *Moses in Egypt* had only a single staging, it does not diminish its importance.

On the other hand, there are more than forty operas from this period that any major opera company might produce next season without anyone regarding the matter as unusual in any way. These are operas that—when the right artists are available or when some producer or conductor takes interest—are revived. Thomas's *Mignon,* Verdi's *I vespri siciliani,* and Halévy's *La Juive* are cases in point.

Then there are scores that achieved almost instant popularity and remain firmly placed in the present-day repertory. *Il trovatore* and *Faust* were produced in some forty seasons. *Don Giovanni* was part of twenty-two seasons, *Aida* (a late arrival, in 1871) in twenty, as was *Lohengrin. La traviata* was heard in eighteen seasons. Even so, one must be impressed by the small size of the repertory. Verdi, for example, is represented primarily by seven works. One obvious consideration is that expanding the repertory costs money. Productions must be built. Singers must be coached in new roles (remember that few of them could read music). Orchestras must be prepared. This was commercial theater; expenses such as these reduced profits.

It is significant that, in general, Gresham's law does not apply to opera: strong scores displace weaker works. The first performance of *La bohème* was the death knell of *The Bohemian Girl.* Works once popular like *Martha* were swept off the stage by the new Italian scores, the growing significance of Wagner, and, in time, Richard Strauss. In the 1860s the opera most listeners wanted to hear was *Il trovatore.* In the middle of the twentieth century, nothing surpassed *Tristan und Isolde* for audience appeal. Both, undeniably, are great works, but they reflect very different approaches to music and theater.

In the half century 1950–2000 more than twice as many works were heard than in the years 1850–1910. Since the number of performances did not increase proportionally—there were some forty-five operatic performances in 1965 as opposed to more than seventy the century before—the number of stagings of even the most popular works declined. And it was no longer *Faust* that kept impresarios in business, it was *Madama Butterfly.*

As we turn to the work of the resident Chicago opera companies in the years 1910–2000, we will note, especially after 1950, the regular assimilation of new works into the repertory. Opera in the year 2000 is in a healthy state. There is life after Richard Strauss. Any review of recent seasons in American opera houses will establish that point very well.

5

A New Tradition

1910–1929

For sixty years Chicago heard opera by importing performances—most of them from New York. In 1910 it finally had what it had long desired, resident opera. San Francisco, another of America's most important centers of opera, had to wait until 1923 for similar autonomy.

The process began in 1909—with the importation, in large part, of a New York company. Karleton Hackett, the music critic of the *Chicago Evening Post,* began a series of articles insisting that the years of dependency on New York should end. If Chicago could produce a symphony orchestra that rivaled any other ensemble of this type in the nation, it could produce opera of comparable stature. This was optimistic indeed. Opera production is far more complex and sophisticated than presenting symphonic music. Music critics do not progress very far in ventures of this type unless they have their publishers behind them, and Hackett was firmly supported by his employer, John C. Shaffer, who began talks to implement the project.[1]

New York was in the midst of an opera war. Oscar Hammerstein had made a fortune manufacturing cigars, but his real interest was the theater. In 1889 he built the Harlem Opera House on 125th Street between Seventh and Eighth Avenues, and this led to further such projects in 1890, 1892, and 1895. His passion was producing opera. In March 1890 he presented a week of opera in the Harlem theater featuring Lilli Lehmann of the Metropolitan, and the success of the venture prompted a short season of opera in English the following October. It was a box office failure. He decided to move downtown and built his first Manhattan Opera House on a 34th Street site, later to become Macy's department store. When he began presenting opera there in January 1893, he had no competition; the Met was rebuilding after a cata-

strophic fire the previous August. But Hammerstein cut an announced eleven-week season short after two weeks of mediocre productions. It was not just a matter of producing opera. It was producing opera on a level the New York public would support.

That enterprise had to wait until 1906. The Metropolitan Opera House stood between 39th and 40th Streets facing Broadway, bounded on the west by Seventh Avenue. Five blocks away the second Manhattan Opera House was built facing 34th Street, between Eighth and Ninth Avenues. And there, in February 1906, Hammerstein presented his first real season. His intent was perfectly clear. Successful opera made money. As he saw it, the Met under Heinrich Conried was in a state of stagnation, emphasizing singers rather than new and adventurous repertory and minimizing risks (just as the Lyric Opera of Chicago was to do later in the century by offering the public fewer performances than the city was prepared to support). If Hammerstein could present livelier fare, he could put the Met out of business. Encouraged by his initial successes, he invaded the Met's principal touring market by building an opera house, the Academy of Music, in Philadelphia in 1908.

There is a myth that Hammerstein's New York company toured to Chicago, but John F. Cone establishes that Pittsburgh and Cincinnati were the western limits of these excursions on the road.[2] Delighted with the first season of his Philadelphia venture, Hammerstein visited Chicago. In the autumn of 1909 he was conferring with Chicago's John C. Shaffer. As he saw it, Chicago, too, would get a modern opera house (he considered the Auditorium outdated), and he would bring a notable company to fill it. But Chicago must raise $500,000. Shaffer agreed, provided that Chicago be represented by three persons on a seven-member board of directors. Hammerstein would have none of it. He ran a one-man show; there were no directors in New York or Philadelphia to tell him what to do. Hammerstein, on his own, looked for possible sites for a Chicago theater, or pretended to, but nothing came of his investigations. Hammerstein's son Arthur later said that the Chicago inquiries were intended to produce an intervention from the Metropolitan, to force it to overextend itself. Presumably as a political gesture, Hammerstein even paid $5,000 for a sixty-day option on a possible theater site. The Met did not take the bait, and, as it soon turned out, it was Hammerstein who was overextended.

Shaffer turned to the president of the Metropolitan, Otto Kahn, who agreed to duplicate Hammerstein's offer and accepted the principle that leading Chicagoans who were supporting the company should have a voice in its affairs. On the basis of the negotiations with Kahn it was announced on November 4, 1909, that the Chicago company had been formed on a financial basis of $5,000 subscriptions from forty-nine prominent citizens. This fund of $245,000 was matched by $235,000 from a group of wealthy New Yorkers, and the new company was capitalized. Shaffer was to work with Andreas Dippel, who had long served the Met as a competent tenor who could sing almost all the standard roles on short notice. He was now managing director of the Met but would come to Chicago, a brilliant strategic move that ended the internal battles between Dippel and the artistic chief of the company, Giulio Gatti-Casazza. This placed in the Chicago management a person who would protect the Met's interests.

Kahn, impressed by the size and acoustics of the Auditorium, decided a new opera house was unnecessary, that a little remodeling could produce any necessary changes. With Kahn's assistance, the Chicago Grand Opera Company bought out the balance of the lease on the theater, held by the Klaw and Erlanger syndicate. The remodeling took place, and a twenty-week season, secured by some $500,000 in cash reserves, was planned for 1910.

After formal incorporation on December 9, 1909, officers were elected. Harold F. McCormick of International Harvester became president; Charles G. Dawes, vice-president and treasurer; Charles L. Hutchinson and Philip M. Lydig, secretaries; Clarence H. Mackay, chairman of the board; and John C. Shaffer, vice-chairman. Three of the seven men, Kahn, Lydig, and Mackay were New Yorkers. Inconspicuous, but involved in the new company, was Samuel Insull. The most powerful force behind the scenes was McCormick's wife, John D. Rockefeller's daughter Edith. Her great personal wealth, dedication to opera, and her unquestioned position as the head of local society gave her every opportunity to get things done as she wished.

The 1909/10 season marked the close of the New York opera war. Like Mapleson twenty-five years earlier, Hammerstein had to accept that he could not fight Wall Street. His second Philadelphia season had lost $100,000, and he was prepared to sell his theater there to the Metropolitan, which was interested in something more modern than the venerable

Edith Rockefeller McCormick

Academy of Music. The Met's countermove was that it wanted more than the Philadelphia theater, it wanted to buy out Hammerstein and remove him from opera production in New York for ten years. If the Met felt he would not live that long, the conjecture was correct: he died in 1919.

Hammerstein was not going to surrender in person. Arthur became his legally empowered alter ego. In April 1910 Hammerstein senior sailed for Europe. He was going to Egypt, he told the press. He had learned there was a two-headed singer there, both a soprano and a contralto, so he could get two voices for one fee. It was a brave piece of gallows humor. Hardly had the elder Hammerstein arrived in Europe than his son sold the company, the theater, the production rights, and the productions to the Met for $1.2 million, which, it is now generally felt, came from Kahn.

The Hammerstein family again became important in New York musical theater when—quite a few years later—Arthur's nephew, Oscar Hammerstein II, emerged as the lyricist for a long series of notable Broadway shows. The Manhattan Opera House was eventually remodeled as Manhattan Center and functions today as (among other things) a ballroom and one of the city's principal recording studios.

Under the agreement the Met received the music, scenery, properties, and rights (if protected by copyright) to the forty operas Hammerstein had staged. Many were works well established in the Met repertory; some were things the Met had no interest in staging. *Elektra,* in 1910, was the last important première in the Hammerstein house. The Met, which had had an unfortunate experience producing *Salome,* apparently regarded it as another nasty modern opera by that man Strauss. It did not present *Elektra* until 1932.

It is impossible to document the disposition of these things in detail today, but the assumption must be that the largest part of the material remains of the Manhattan Opera Company came to Chicago. One need only see that the Chicago Grand Opera Company began its first season less than eight months after the demise of the Hammerstein company and that eighteen of the twenty-one operas presented had been in the Hammerstein repertory. For all practical purposes, twenty-one productions could not possibly have been designed, built, and painted in that time, but three (*Madama Butterfly, La fanciulla del West,* and *Un ballo in maschera*) could have been managed. In the early Lyric years people traditionally spoke of "the old Chicago Opera scenery," but, more accurately, they should have said "the old Manhattan Opera scenery." Hammerstein's legacy to the Chicago opera public, unintended as it may have been, was a significant contribution to opera well beyond the middle of the century. The striking décor for *Don Giovanni* that framed the Lyric Opera's "calling card" performance in 1954 had first been seen on 34th Street in New York on December 12, 1906.

The first resident companies felt obliged to produce a lot of repertory because the audience was small and to keep it coming back they had to constantly offer something new. At the end of the century the audience was large enough so that the repertory could shrink from twenty-one to eight productions, each of which had a run long enough to amortize a large part of the production costs. What Chicago had was essentially an Italian opera company with capable Italian singers (and quite a few of other ancestry) who are all but forgotten. In the first season fourteen of the twenty-one works were sung in Italian; the remainder were in French. This established a pattern that continued, with some variation, through the Auditorium seasons. Over the years the number of German operas ranged from none to nine, with an average of three. There was a certain amount of opera in English.

Massenet's *Thaïs* was new to the city, was instantly popular, and received the largest number of performances—six. Another new work, Puccini's *La fanciulla del West,* was given five performances, as were *Aida* and *Pagliacci.* Gustave Charpentier's *Louise,* Debussy's *Pelléas et Mélisande,* and *Tosca* were considered worthy of four hearings (they were vehicles for Mary Garden), but nearly everything else vanished after two or three stagings. Four operas were prepared and sung only once. This is just about the best possible way to lose money with an opera company.

The first performance of opera in Chicago from a resident company was heard on November 3, 1910. There was no oratory comparable to earlier events of this type, but Dippel said a few words at the close. The opera was *Aida,* with Amadeo Bassi as Radames, Jeanne Korolewicz in the title role, Eleanor de Cisneros as Amneris, and Mario Sammarco as Amonasro. Dippel had begun his Chicago career by engaging Hammerstein's principal conductor, Cleofonte Campanini (a sometime colleague of Toscanini at La Scala) as general music director of the new company, and he was in charge opening night. He was a violinist, and it was his custom to conduct from a first-violin part, because, one surmises, it was a cue sheet that involved far less page turning.

The cast names mean little today, but the Chicago Grand Opera Company had produced a civic event of the first magnitude. "Chicago took its opera and took it hard," Edward C. Moore reports. "The newspapers fairly turned over their whole editions to the opening."[3] The idea of anything comparable happening fifty years later, when newspapers were dedicated to commercial mass entertainment, is inconceivable. The performance was hailed as a triumphant success. Then came Mary Garden in *Pelléas et Mélisande* and what Moore called "a new page in operatic history."

The new prima donna was challenged a few days later by a triumphant tenor in the first of two performances of *La bohème:* John McCormack sang the role of Rodolfo. An apocryphal story has McCormack urging his leading lady in the final act, "For God's sake, die. I need a drink." Later in the month he was singing the Duke in *Rigoletto* for three performances, a revelation for those who thought of him primarily in terms of his recordings of Irish songs. He had sung one season for Hammerstein and, after his Chicago debut, appeared briefly at the Met, but he did not wish to compete with high-powered Italians like Caruso.

There were other notable voices. Melba sang Mimì later in the season, but with another tenor, and she was also heard in *La traviata*. Gadski was cast as Aida, and a single performance of *Les Huguenots* brought her back in one of her celebrated roles, Valentine. The Met was represented by two of its brightest luminaries, Geraldine Farrar and Antonio Scotti in *Tosca* and *Madama Butterfly*.

The great event of the season, management hoped, would be the local première of the new Puccini opera *La fanciulla del West*. It had been offered to Garden, who viewed it suspiciously and turned it down. Carolina White sang the title role as convincingly as the libretto would allow. Puccini loved exotic locales, which was fine except when his work was performed in that place. He did not guess that parts of *Madama Butterfly* were obscene to the Japanese, and neither did he suspect that Americans, who felt they knew all about the Wild West, would find the Italian version unconvincing and occasionally funny. The final performance was sparked when a cast change put Caruso, who two nights earlier had sung *Pagliacci,* in the role of Dick Johnson. Unfortunately, on the way back to New York he caught a cold, which put him out of action for several weeks. The Met management insisted that henceforth he give his American services exclusively to them.

White earned $350.00 a performance, and her services to the company brought her $8,437.00 for the season, a generous income for 1910. Garden cost $1,400.00 a performance (a lot less than Patti, but still a lot of money), and after forty-seven performances (including the tour) she returned to Paris with $65,800.00. Paris paid her more but did not give her as many performances. The deficit was twice the guarantee fund: $101,038.54. Singers cost $165,214.29 for the season (39% of the total went to Garden). Garden cost nearly twice as much as the entire orchestra, which received $32,122.87, and the musical staff (including Campanini) added $24,918.63 to the expenses. Management salaries added up to $15,173.73. Interestingly enough, $15,280.00 was paid in royalties on music protected by copyright. Puccini was a rich man, and even Strauss's *Salome* earned money for its composer.

With Hammerstein out of the picture in Philadelphia, in 1910 one saw a Chicago-Philadelphia Opera Company, which meant that on January 19 it went on tour. There were fifty-five performances in Philadelphia, only eleven less than in Chicago in a series that went on until early April. New York heard eleven performances, Baltimore was offered ten. During the Chicago season the company visited Milwaukee and St. Louis. Chicago had become a major source of opera for five other cities, and the company spent more time on the road than it did at home. This is in sharp contrast to the Lyric Opera, which, for all practical purposes, has never toured at all. Some will insist that it is one of the reasons the Lyric is still around.

In Chicago's popular culture the years 1910–1929, when resident opera flourished in the Auditorium, are the Mary Garden seasons, so it is appropriate to begin with her and her career in the city. But, as further examination will quickly reveal, there was much more to Chicago opera in those years than the Garden performances, and one might argue that other singers, such as Rosa Raisa and Amelita Galli-Curci, made a more forceful and lasting contribution to Chicago opera. Fyodor Chaliapin was the highest paid artist of these years, earning more than twice Garden's fee. Still, for many, from her debut at the Auditorium (which she came to love) on November 5, 1910, until her final Chicago appearance in the new Civic Opera House (which she thoroughly disliked) on January 24, 1931, Garden personified opera for the people most responsible for bringing it to the city. It was a romance of some twenty years, probably unparalleled elsewhere, between an audience and an artist. For her public, opera existed to provide opportunities for "our Mary" to practice her art, which went far beyond singing to the limits of mass hypnosis. Witnessing her create a character and develop a role, it was felt by many, was the most intense and gratifying experience the musical theater could bring. Repertory was selected to provide her with vehicles for her magic.

She was a master of surprise, self-promotion, and publicity to the degree that she made Maria Callas, who was not without talent in these fields, look like an apprentice. Musically she could do as she pleased. If she wanted to sing *Tosca* in French, switching to Italian for "Visi d'arte" (it really sounds better in that language), of course she could. Why not? And if everyone else was singing Italian and the exchanges with Scarpia sounded funny, who cared?

In the great tradition of passionate romances, Garden's love of Chicago was not on the level of its love for her. Of course it provided secure annual engagements and a lot of money (what singer could resist that?), but her great love always was Paris, where her career began and her art was first given full recognition. Home was an apartment at 148, avenue Malakoff. She could not forget New York, where Hammerstein had made her a star, and which hailed her when she came on tour with the Chicago company, or Boston, where she was given unqualified acclaim, and where she sang her final performance with her Chicago colleagues. She never sang at the Met, possibly, as she claimed, because "they never asked me." "They never needed me" might be the better answer. They had Farrar.

Mary Garden was born in Aberdeen, Scotland, in 1874 and died not too far from her birthplace in 1967. She always retained in her speech the distinctive sound of her native place. In her later years she suffered from senile dementia, and her autobiography is filled with imaginary things, such as a Paris performance of *Manon Lescaut* with Caruso (the opera was not in her repertory).[4] She was one of the greatest singing actresses ever to face an audience, but the actress was more important than the singer. Physically she was slight, perhaps five feet four inches in height, but she used her body so skillfully that she easily

dominated the stage. She was not a beauty, but she knew how to make one think she was. The voice could range from mediocre to brilliant in the space of a single performance. When she taught, she taught acting, not vocal, technique. Her phonograph records, as a group, are disappointing.

Mary's father brought the family to the United States in 1880. She lived briefly in Brooklyn, in Chicopee, Massachusetts, and, after a brief return to Scotland, in Hyde Park (then a southern extension of Chicago), where as a teenager she sang the leading woman's role in *Trial by Jury*. Vocal studies followed, with Mary's success so evident that she secured a wealthy patron. In 1897, with her patron's support, she sailed for France. Henceforth Paris was to be the center of her musical life.

A close friendship with the American soprano Sibyl Sanderson, who lived in France, proved invaluable. She was engaged by the Opéra Comique and selected as a cover singer (understudy) for Marthe Rioton in the new opera *Louise,* which was in rehearsal. Midway in the performance of April 10, 1900, Rioton had to withdraw because of a cold. Garden took her place and created a sensation with her singing of "Depuis le jour." A career had been launched.

The Mary Garden who came to Chicago ten years later was an established performer with twenty-two roles in her repertory. As she saw it, her career was still based in France, although she had been one of the major assets of Hammerstein's company. Her one engagement in London was a disaster. She was known by reputation but had no career in central Europe and never sang in Italy. It is unlikely that she expected the reception Chicago would give her or that the bond would last so long. Even so, through her Chicago years she spent the greater part of her time in Europe and alternated her operatic roles with recitals, which, in time, have become overshadowed by her stage performances.

In her career, Mary Garden sang 1,187 operatic performances from a repertory of thirty-five works. Nearly a third are by Massenet, a composer with a gift for writing a Garden vehicle. Fifteen of the thirty-five are operas you might hear today. Thirteen were (at least from her viewpoint) failures, operas that lasted for six performances or less. Five of these catastrophes took place in Chicago. The worst disasters, *La Marseillaise,* by Lucien Lambert (1858–1945), and *Princess Osra*, by Herbert Bunning (1863–1937) (both two performances), took place in Paris and London, respectively.

Two of the failures in the group, Massenet's *Don Quichotte* and Thomas's *Hamlet* have survived; they just weren't Garden things. That category can be illustrated by *Aphrodite,* composed by Camille Erlanger (1863–1919), which she sang sixty-three times, but only once in Chicago. Opinion was that you saw a lot of flesh but heard little music of interest.

Thirty-five percent of her appearances was in three now well established operas that entered her repertory long before her Chicago debut: Charpentier's *Louise* (175 performances), Massenet's *Thaïs* (144 performances), and Debussy's *Pelléas et Mélisande* (106 performances). If you add Massenet's *Manon* (72 performances), Bizet's *Carmen* (69 performances), and Massenet's *Le Jongleur de Notre-Dame* (67), you have the first six items in her repertory in terms of frequency of presentation. Together they make up more than half of her operatic engagements.

Despite her problems with it in the United States, she sang *Salome* sixty-one times. The Strauss score was her only German opera. She used a French version the composer had prepared for her. He had hoped she might be interested in the role of Octavian in *Der Rosenkavalier,* but he was wrong. A French *Rosenkavalier* was out of the question, and Garden in a German role of this length was unthinkable. Mozart did not exist for her (one must wonder what she might have achieved with Zerlina and Cherubino), but she gave twenty-two performances to a second-rate American opera, *Natoma,* by Victor Herbert (1859–1924). She sang one Verdi opera, *La traviata,* and one Puccini, *Tosca*—both in French. Italo Montemezzi's *L'amore dei tre re* became a staple, and her only Italian role. Ironically, she had to sing only two acts. In the third she is onstage, but playing a corpse; not the typical Garden performance.

She arrived for her first Chicago season on, one assumes, a French ship. Fellow passengers were the tenor McCormack and one of the Met's prize conductors, Gustav Mahler. It is difficult to imagine what, if they met, they might have said to one another. From her suite in the Blackstone Hotel, a short step from the theater (she found the Auditorium Hotel uncomfortable), she was teasing the press with talk of an imminent marriage, which never took place.

The *Chicago Daily News* said of her debut that she dominated the house "with power more effective than merely vocal pyrotechnics could have attained. Her conquest was complete and the great audience gave her all the honor that many recalls could compel." Since the opera was *Pelléas et Mélisande,* opportunities for vocal pyrotechnics were few. Her impact came from the manner in which she created and projected a role. It was also due to the fact that—wherever else corners might be cut—Garden operas were always carefully prepared. But although Mélisande proved to be one of her greatest roles (she sang it in the opera's world première at the Opéra Comique in Paris in 1902), it consistently drew the poorest box office of all the basic Garden repertory.

Nothing in the season created a commotion—or drew more interest—than her scheduled appearance as Salome on November 25. Strauss based his opera on a play Oscar Wilde had written in French. From our present perspective, this is typical degenerate art of the Mauve Decade, and Strauss, who had had bad luck with his two earlier operatic libretti, saw it as an eminently stageworthy piece and draped it in appropriately sensuous and uninhibited music.

The Metropolitan had staged the opera in January 1907, with Olive Fremstad in the title role and a member of the ballet performing the "Dance of the Seven Veils." Ever meticulous, Fremstad decided that to play the final scene correctly she had to know how much a human head weighed, and she went to the city morgue to find out. The answer was twelve pounds. If Fremstad was ready for *Salome,* the Met audience was not. After an enormous hue and cry it was withdrawn after the initial performance.

Hammerstein gleefully announced it for January 28, 1909, with Garden singing and dancing. Cleofonte Campanini conducted, and the orchestra was enlarged to 117 musicians. Garden's performance, hailed by one critic as "a conception of incarnate beastiality," dazzled the public, which included a number of the Met's principal supporters. The house was sold out for ten New York performances that season and three in Philadelphia. No widespread moral decline was observed as an aftermath. The work returned four times in the 1909/10 season, which also contained the successful American première of *Elektra,* sung, for some reason, in French by Mariette Mazarin ("Agamemnon! Père!"). Even in the French version, Garden would never consider singing such an unglamorous heroine.

In Chicago, main-floor tickets were hiked to $7—because of the "Dance of the Seven Veils," wits insisted. Conservative critics were appalled. Upton, in his classic tome on the standard operas, found *Salome* "repulsive and unclean." Strauss had indulged in "a riotous squandering of genius in orchestration and constructive musicianship upon dramatic rottenness." The vocal writing displeased Upton, who felt the singers had no opportunities, while the orchestra "bears the heat and burden of this orgy of strange technique and complex cacophony."[5] This was nothing like Verdi, and, sadly, it was time for Upton to retire.

Garden insisted her performance was artistic, not voluptuous, that the "Dance of the Seven Veils" "was not a hoochi-koochi dance at all." This had no effect on Arthur Farwell, the head of the Law and Order League, who was offered a free ticket but declined. "I am a normal man," he insisted, "but I would not trust myself to see a performance of *Salome*."

Garden's rejoinder was, "Anyone whose morals could have been corrupted by seeing *Salome* must already have degenerated."

Chicago's chief of police found the performance disgusting but not immoral. "There is no music to it," he concluded. Considering that this was, after all, an opera, it is strange that almost no one seemed interested in the music. It was Garden's physical appearance, her gestures and body language, that fascinated the public. A second performance was packed, but, to end the outcry, a third was canceled. One more full house, this time in Milwaukee, viewed the work without incident. "It wasn't risqué at all," the *Morning Telegraph* reported.

Garden, at least, had a severed head to which she might sing. When Sir Thomas Beecham offered the first London performance of the work the following month, censors demanded the silver platter be empty. Garden felt that with her "immoral shows" there was no place for her in London opera. Hammerstein commented ironically, "I don't know what could be done to 'tone down' *Salome*, especially the head scene, unless maybe they'd give the head a shave and a haircut." It should be noted in passing that not far from the Auditorium, in the Levee, Chicago had long had the most celebrated red-light district north of New Orleans. An annual directory of the establishments and women was published. Targeting the hypocrisy of her reception, Garden, in a moment of pique, said she would not sing in Chicago again: it accepted vice on the grand scale but was too unsophisticated for Strauss's opera.

The opera remained a staple of her repertory, although Garden did not sing it in Chicago again for eleven years. In September 1911 she sang *Salome* at the Paris Opéra five times, wearing a costume considerably more revealing than the one she had worn in America. It explained her love for the city and, one may assume, its love for her.

Over the years Chicago was gradually introduced to the Garden repertory. It is instructive to note that she appeared far less frequently than her reputation might suggest. Nearly everything she did in 1910 was a local première. In addition to the Debussy and Strauss scores she also introduced the city to *Louise* (perhaps her greatest role) and *Thaïs*. The Garden performances of *Louise* were uncut; after her departure, revivals omitted two scenes. Accurate control of lighting cues was almost impossible in the Auditorium, and the errors in the initial *Thaïs* were ludicrous, but Garden's portrayal of the courtesan, which produced steadily shrinking costumes, became one of the great box office attractions of Chicago opera.

"The women of America made my career," she announced in 1949. "They took their husbands to see my *Thaïs* or my *Salome*, when men wanted to go to the movies. But when they saw Thaïs was nearly nude, they took the opera glasses away from the ladies and kept them all evening. The men learned that opera could be made interesting."[6]

She was studying German, she told the press, and hoped to have both Elsa and Isolde in her repertory. (Neither ever happened, of course.) Meanwhile, to offer one familiar thing, she sang Marguerite in *Faust*, a role that did not reveal her at her best, vocally or dramatically. But she succeeded against real competition. Farrar was with the company, singing *Tosca* and *Madama Butterfly*.

It is instructive to compare the 1910/11 offerings of the Chicago Grand Opera Company with those of the Metropolitan that season. Chicago had 21 productions in a season that ran from November to its departure for Philadelphia in mid-January. The Met had 30 productions in a season that ran from mid-November to the end of April. Chicago gave 64 performances in addition to 8 concerts and 2 nights of ballet. The Met gave 185 opera performances and several concerts and dance events. Four of the operas in the Met repertory were new. The remaining 26 were scores the orchestra had played before and, presumably, could play again with minimal rehearsal.

As late as the close of the twentieth century many European cities had one orchestra that was based in the opera house but played a certain number of symphony concerts. Until late in the century this was the practice in San Francisco, where the opera and the symphony shared the same hall and the symphony season began when the opera season ended. The Vienna Philharmonic is drawn from the orchestra of the Staatsoper. London and Berlin were examples of cities that maintained separate orchestras for operatic and symphonic music, and Chicago adopted this practice from the start. The Chicago Symphony Orchestra had musicians who had worked for operatic touring companies that did not bring an orchestra, but an opera orchestra had to be created. This was possible because tours usually gave the musicians about six months of work. In 1910 the Chicago Symphony was housed in Orchestra Hall, often performing the same night as an operatic performance. Under Frederick Stock it had played Salome's dance in two seasons. No one at the opera had seen the music to *Salome* before, and it was a demanding score. Indeed, the newly recruited opera orchestra had to start out with seven different works in as many days, operas as demanding as *Pelléas et Mélisande* and *Louise*—a situation in which a high level of performance would be impossible under the union rehearsal rules of a later day. But there must have been many hours of rehearsal.

When the Met prepared a popular opera, it was assumed the work would run a while and recoup production costs. Chicago could do so only to a more limited extent. It gave five performances of *Aida,* and there was a sixth in New York. Between New York and tour dates, the Met presented that work eleven times. Four of the operas in the Chicago repertory were prepared and sung only once in the city. The Met would not present a work it felt could not support a repeat. For the Met this was a profitable season; it made about $100,000. Chicago lost money both at home and on the road. As the first season ended, prophetic souls might say that you cannot sustain an opera company with an audience of wealthy people who are infatuated with a single operatic personality. The swells and Mary Garden were not enough. What was needed was a true ensemble and an audience more deeply rooted in the community.

The 1911/12 season opened with a dismal staging of *Samson and Delilah,* and the arrival of Garden as Carmen was welcome. The following night, even she was eclipsed by the local debut of Campanini's sister-in-law Luisa Tetrazzini in *Lucia di Lammermoor.* Tetrazzini remained in the city only two weeks but sang five operas (the others were *La traviata, The Barber of Seville, Rigoletto,* and *Lakmé*), creating a sensation that echoed through the autumn. Unfortunately,

she did not get along with her brother-in-law, and she appeared with the company in only two seasons.

Maggie Teyte was as petite as Tetrazzini was monumental, but the voice was full and strong. She excelled as Cherubino in *The Marriage of Figaro* and Antonia in *The Tales of Hoffmann,* and she was one of the few good things in *Quo Vadis?,* an opera by Jean Nouguès (1875–1932). It was a Roman spectacle filled, Moore says, with "greatly noisy and unimportant music."[7] It lasted one season. Massenet's *Cendrillon* (the Cinderella story) had Garden as the Prince and Teyte as the heroine. The opera was heard only two seasons, but the Prince's ballroom eventually provided a new set for the first act of *La traviata.*

Early in 1911 Garden went on a concert tour that extended as far west as Denver, traveling in a private railway car with her own entourage. Her Carmen produced speculation whether it was accident or design that in the final moments of the opera her skirt should start to part company with her, revealing a lot of leg. This was an area in which she could easily outshine Farrar, whose legs were best concealed.

Massenet's *Cendrillon* and *Le Jongleur de Notre-Dame* (both casting Garden in male roles) were new French scores. *Jongleur* had originally been written for a tenor, but Garden persuaded the composer to let her do it, an assignment that, presumably, required her to learn juggling. Finally she turned to an American opera, Victor Herbert's *Natoma,* which she championed resolutely and sustained with the sheer force of her presence. Everyone, starting with Campanini, was ready to hail a compelling American opera, and since it has long been assumed that successful composers of popular music should also be the source of the serious American works, who was better qualified than Herbert? Over the years the score was heard thirty times, but it had a weak libretto and was eventually dropped from the repertory. It was never produced at the Met, although one is compelled to note that even weaker operas have graced that stage. Garden's pay was raised to $1,600 a performance, and her efforts in Chicago brought her $80,000. Apparently she was worth it. The loss for the season was slightly under $6,000.

In contrast to the Herbert opera there was the American première of Ermanno Wolf-Ferrari's (1876–1948) *The Jewels of the Madonna (I gioielli della Madonna),* a large serving of lasagna, which was to be a local favorite well into the 1920s. Wolf-Ferrari's *The Secret of Suzanne,* which was to prove enormously popular later at Ravinia, was a happy little frolic. (The secret was that the lady smoked, and the Anti-Cigarette League was aghast.)

On a more serious level, the company produced its first Wagner, *Die Walküre*. Schumann-Heink (Fricka) is the only name in the cast likely to be recognized today. She returned as Ortrud later in the season when *Lohengrin* entered the repertory. Campanini demonstrated that he could conduct Wagner in the closing week of the season when *Tristan und Isolde* was heard with Fremstad as the Irish Princess.

Although the *Titanic* disaster was on their minds, the singers who came from Europe in 1912 all arrived safely. The impressive debut of the third season was a baritone, Titta Ruffo, who revised everyone's idea about *Rigoletto* and proved that the role of Tonio in *Pagliacci* could carry as much weight as the celebrated tenor lead. Ruffo also was heard in the title role of *Hamlet*. His merits were not unrewarded. He earned $2,000 a performance, considerably more than Garden. Teyte was a fragile Mimì in *La bohème* and returned (without Garden) in *Cendrillon*. She won respect for her performance in English in *The Cricket on the Hearth*, an attractive little score by Karl Goldmark (1830–1915), which died with one performance. Schumann-Heink was Nordica's Brangäne in *Tristan und Isolde* and returned in *Die Walküre*. As the mother of several children, she may have found her greatest delight in playing the witch in a New Year's production of *Hansel and Gretel*. Tetrazzini repeated *Lucia di Lammermoor* and *The Barber of Seville*. Garden was in Chicago less than a month (although she earned $67,200 for the season), and her repertory was familiar, with one exception. Early in 1913 she sang *Tosca* for the first time in Chicago, wearing a red wig, a green dress, and a blue scarf. Striking, if not outrageous, costumes were her specialty. She was determined to catch the eye of the audience.

The company had insisted it was paying too much in royalties. As a result there had been no Puccini in 1911/12, but agreements were reached and his music was back. Moreover, the city heard for the first time the opera that had established the composer's career, *Manon Lescaut*. White sang the title role. Campanini wanted to expand the repertory backward as well as forward and in January gave a concert version of one of the earliest operas, Monteverdi's *Orfeo*. It was beautifully achieved, but the public was indifferent. The company closed the season with its longest tour, playing New York and the West Coast, and actually made $68,000 doing so.

Garden as Tosca opened the 1913 season, with Vanni-Marcoux as Scarpia. Two nights later they were back in *Don Quichotte*, a work well suited to both of them, but it did not prove a great audience success. Other new Garden scores were *Manon* and *Monna Vanna*. *Monna Vanna*, composed by Henri Février (1875–1957), is not much of an opera (it is about a medieval siege of Pisa by the Florentines and, like *Pelléas et Mélisande,* is based on a play by Maeterlinck). Garden was able to make it a success. Poor Carolina White insisted she was overworked and underpaid, but she never came close to catching up. In 1913/14, when her salary finally was raised to $600 a performance, Garden was still $1,000 ahead of her. Eventually White abandoned the Chicago company for vaudeville.

The most impressive debut of the 1913/14 series was the youthful Rosa Raisa as Aida. Campanini was impressed but also somewhat concerned about the sheer volume of her voice. Could it be blended in ensembles? (In later seasons she was known facetiously as "Raisa de roofa.") She returned as Mimì in *La bohème*, a role few would associate with her. But this was not the only surprise of the season. Teyte was heard as Madama Butterfly and Humperdinck's Hansel. Schumann-Heink sang one of her rare Italian roles, Azucena in *Il trovatore*. Ruffo was miscast as Don Giovannini and proved that opposite Garden in *Thaïs* he did not appear at his best. The critic Eric DeLamarter, who in 1918 was to become associate conductor of the Chicago Symphony, wrote, "It [Ruffo's performance] is carefully guarded from anything approaching dramatic action." Two performances were enough. Ruffo was happier playing Rossini's Figaro and Franchetti's Cristoforo Colombo with Raisa.

A legacy of the English opera companies of the past century was a vocal minority that demanded opera in English. Campanini responded with a Saturday night series that not only was in English but at half the regular prices. Moore comments ruefully that instead of "the educational stimulus and rapt enthusiasm" the advocates of opera in English predicted, "the series was greeted with calm demeanor and lack of interest."[8] Still, the Chicago season apparently did well—the deficit was roughly $8,000—but it ended with a western tour that was a financial disaster, $150,000 worth of red ink from an operation that was supposed to break even if not make money.

The 1912/13 season was the end of a chapter. Dippel left the company in April 1913; he could not get

Ernestine Schumann-Heink on a Chicago sidewalk, 1914

cided that the prudent thing for the opera company was to declare bankruptcy, skip a season, and return reorganized. This meant the new Chicago Opera Association would start off free of debt. The financial problems were largely due to singers' contracts that had to be renegotiated or paid. Under the contracts in question Garden was to earn $80,000 a year, but Tetrazzini, at $2,000 a performance, was more highly paid. Schumann-Heink, McCormack, and the tenor Lucien Muratore (whom Garden considered "a horrible man") were paid $1,200. Fremstad and Gadski were in the $1,000 range. Poor Maggie Teyte got only $400. Campanini received $30,000 a season; Dippel had made only $22,500. The largest single debt was to Harold McCormick—$260,000 advanced against the costs of the season. Presumably he gladly wrote it off.

In the absence of a 1914/15 season from a resident company, Milton and Sargent Alborn brought their troupe from the Century Theater, New York, to play a six-week season of French and Italian operatic staples from November 23 to January 2. (The eight-week season originally announced appears to have been shortened because ticket sales did not reach the expected level.) Apparently all performances were in English, and once more the opera-in-English advocates proved they were better at arguing their cause than buying tickets. Although it is impossible to give detailed data on casting, English-speaking artists from the Metropolitan (some of them known from Ravinia) were given prominent roles. It is probable that the unemployed Chicago opera orchestra was used. The source of the sets is a mystery. It is noteworthy that Chicago was not totally without opera in 1914/15, but artistically the series appears to have been unimportant. One should also note that a popular opera like *Madama Butterfly* was given a run, in this case six performances. Apparently this was more than the public would support, at least without Farrar.

The Chicago Opera Association (as it was named now) opened its first season in November 1915. It had a $110,000 guarantee fund and the backing of the city's leading citizens. Farrar was the glamorous figure of the autumn, singing Tosca, Carmen, Madama Butterfly, and Marguerite in *Faust*. In late December she joined McCormack in *La bohème*. He reappeared in mid-January as Don Ottavio in *Don Giovanni,* one of his finest roles. Garden, who was vigorously supporting the French war effort, did not appear. Two of her specialties, *Louise* and *Monna*

along with Campanini any more than he could with Gatti-Casazza. Dippel favored German music over Italian repertory; Campanini felt differently. But there was more than this: a decisive break with New York. Otto Kahn remained on the board, but henceforth this was to be a Chicago company with Harold McCormick the principal backer. Nominally Harold was in charge, but it was generally felt that in this case opera was a collaboration of husband and wife, and much of the money that flowed to the company through Harold's hands actually originated in Edith's fortune. The opera company was to become their personal enterprise, and, as long as they could afford it, it prospered. They bought out the New York stockholders. Their man, Campanini, was given charge of the entire operation, including business matters, which really were not his strong point.

When Garden sailed for Europe in May on the *Kaiser Wilhelm II,* Caruso, Scotti, Farrar, and her lover, Toscanini, were fellow passengers. War in Europe was imminent. The Germans on the ship were likely to become enemies soon, but one could trust German ships not to hit icebergs. McCormick de-

Vanna were heard, but no other artist could erase the memory of what she had done with them. Melba returned as one of her favorite heroines, Mimì. Conchita Supervia, a jewel of a Spanish mezzo-soprano, made her debut in Massenet's *Werther* and later returned as, in Moore's words, "a nice girlish little Carmen" and a remarkable Mignon in the Ambroise Thomas opera. Muratore was apparently one reason for the ill-conceived American première of Saint-Saëns's *Déjanire*. It lasted two performances. It should be noted by operagoers of the twenty-first century that in 1915 theaters did not announce the entire season in advance, which made it difficult to secure subscriptions to other than boxes. If an opera did not sell, it was pulled from the repertory and something more promising was put in its place.

The United States was not at war, but there was growing hostility toward things German, which McCormick chose to ignore. As the third opera of the season he staged *Tristan und Isolde,* with Francis Maclennan (an American tenor) and Olive Fremstad in the title roles and Egon Pollak conducting. Fremstad had left the Metropolitan in 1914. Gatti-Casazza was disturbed by "the limitations of her repertoire" in a period in which the demand for German opera was likely to vanish. In late November Pollak conducted *Das Rheingold,* the opening of the first *Ring* cycle from a Chicago company. Moreover, McCormick insisted the Wagner scores be uncut, a problem for members of the audience who were not accustomed to Wagnerian time spans. Schumann-Heink was Erda. *Die Walküre, Siegfried,* and *Götterdämmerung* followed in early December, the latter bringing Fremstad as Brünnhilde and Schumann-Heink as both the First Norn and Waltraute. But the debut of Florence Easton as Brünnhilde in *Siegfried* had a powerful impact. Unfortunately for Chicago, she soon joined the Metropolitan Opera, where she sang until 1936. None of the names of the other singers would mean much by the end of the century, but the performances were well received. They were not repeated. It was unnecessary; McCormick had seen them.

Wagner's great patron, King Ludwig, had operas performed for him alone, although one suspects some of those performances were really dress rehearsals. He had the Bavarian state treasury behind him, but, even so, he eventually encountered difficulties. Even with a seemingly inexhaustible well of McCormick money to draw on, producing the *Ring* for one performance of the cycle was economic madness.

This did not stop McCormick from doing the cycle again the following year. (Again it was uncut, and again each opera was heard once.) *Parsifal,* the final Wagner of the season, brought Fremstad as Kundry and received a second performance. None of these operas were in the Hammerstein repertory, which means a production had to be designed and built, a substantial addition to the cost of the season.

Although Campanini was always eager to go to New York, no tour was planned for 1916. When the opera vacated the hall, it was taken over by the Diaghilev Ballet on its first American tour (financed by Otto Kahn), which introduced Chicago to Stravinsky's masterpieces *The Firebird* and *Petrouchka.*

Poster for the 1915 Chicago Opera Association *Ring* cycle

The opening night of 1916 brought Raisa as Aida, one of her memorable roles. Two nights later she was back as Maddalena in *Andrea Chénier,* and in later weeks she returned in *Cavalleria rusticana* and, surprisingly, as Alice Ford in *Falstaff.* She found herself trapped into doing Riccardo Zandonai's *Francesca da Rimini,* an opera with the unusual combination of a potentially strong libretto (the story comes from Dante, after all) and a weak score. Worst of all, a battle scene was required, and it proved a disaster. As Moore recalls, "When a couple of arrows wafted themselves up to the blue sky, stuck there, and remained sticking until the end of the act, and when a few large catapult balls sailed over the wall and down on the struggling throng, hitting chorus men on the head and bouncing gently to the stage without apparent damage to anybody or anything, the audience shouted with glee. . . . Two more performances were given to see if the audiences would keep on laughing. They did."[9]

Farrar returned in 1916 as Carmen and in a new vehicle, Engelbert Humperdinck's *Königskinder,* which the audience loved. Her repertory also included *Madama Butterfly, La bohème,* and *Tannhäuser,* the one Wagner score for which the company had inherited Hammerstein sets. Garden, who expressed nothing but contempt for German submarines, was back in December 1916 to sing *Carmen, Thaïs, Le Jongleur de Notre-Dame,* and *Louise* and to introduce a work by Massenet, *Grisélidis. Parsifal* returned, again with Fremstad as Kundry. This time the *Ring* became a series of Sunday matinées, and attendance was poor. Most things German had become unpopular.

Both Campanini and Gatti-Casazza wished to advance the cause of American opera, and one must commend them for their efforts as well as share their disappointment over their lack of success. A second work by Victor Herbert was staged, *Madeleine,* "a pretty but unimportant piece," according to Moore. Another première scheduled for the season was *Venise,* an opera by Raoul Gunsbourg (1859–1955), but the work was lost with the destruction of the ship bringing the score to the city. Moore remarks, ironically, "in view of the same composer's *Le Vieil Aigle,* as done later, there began to be opinions that something might be said in favor of war."[10]

The most celebrated soprano of the autumn was Amelita Galli-Curci, who made her extraordinary debut on December 1, 1916, in *La traviata* and again won tremendous success two weeks later in *Romeo and Juliet,* with Muratore. January brought her in *The*

Geraldine Farrar rehearsing in the Auditorium with a flock of geese for a 1916 performance of Humperdinck's *Königskinder*

Barber of Seville and *Lucia di Lammermoor.* The sheer beauty of her voice was enough to drive audiences into a frenzy of admiration, but she was also a fine musician with a splendid stage presence, and this made her a real match for the glamour girls.

Harold McCormick was troubled by criticism that the opera was more about social display than music. He sent a note to each box subscriber, saying: "It has been suggested that evening dress not be worn this season of opera performances, and thus lend respect to the artistic features and dispense with the emblem of the social feature heretofore enjoyed."[11] His anxieties were appropriate. Early in the 1917/18 season, presumably as a social protest, Galli-Curci's first appearance in *Dinorah* (a work she had not sung previously in Chicago) was interrupted by the malfunction of a pipe bomb that had been placed under the last row of seats on the center aisle. A fireman grabbed the bomb and rushed it to a gutter outside, where it sputtered into silence. Campanini, at the first sign of danger, plunged the orchestra into "The Star-Spangled Banner." The audience rose, sang, and remained calm. It was soon reassured the danger had passed. The bomber was eventually found and jailed.

Although the nation was at war—and thus there was no German opera—the 1917/18 season was as ample as those of peacetime and continued from November 13 to January 19. It got off to a strong start.

Mascagni's *Isabeau* with Raisa was a retelling of the Lady Godiva story, but those eager to see a quantity of bare flesh were disappointed, although there was enough interest to sustain the work for four performances. It was followed by *Lucia di Lammermoor,* with Galli-Curci. Raisa then returned in *Aida,* and Melba was heard in *Faust.* Galli-Curci was then heard again in *Dinorah.* Melba's contribution to the season also included *La bohème,* and Raisa appeared in *Les Huguenots* and *The Jewels of the Madonna.* Galli-Curci sang *Lakmé, The Barber of Seville,* and *La bohème.* Georges Baklanoff's first appearance as Scarpia in *Tosca* redefined the role for Chicago audiences.

Again there was an American opera, *Azora, Daughter of Montezuma,* by Henry Hadley (1871–1937). It had an American cast and a production to rival *Aida.* What made Campanini's efforts to promote American opera even more commendable was that the Chicago audience, possibly put off by the libretto, offered little support. The house was "filled with paper"—the show business euphemism for free seats. For the second performance the main floor held subscribers and five persons who had bought tickets. Even so, the work was taken to New York on tour and was received with some interest.

Two Garden specialties were heard in December without Garden. Geneviève Vix sang *Le Jongleur de Notre-Dame* and *Louise.* Moreover, she had the courage to repeat the Massenet score in January after Garden had rejoined the company. When Garden passed through town briefly early in 1918, it was for only five performances, all of them familiar repertory.

The war was over (but there was still no German opera) when the 1918/19 season began on November 18. Raisa and Galli-Curci dominated the early part of the season. The important debut, it later became clear, was that of the conductor Giorgio Polacco, who presided over opening night and was to have a long and influential career in Chicago opera. He launched the season with Galli-Curci in *La traviata.* She never strayed from earlier successes: *Lucia di Lammermoor, The Barber of Seville,* and *La bohème,* the latter with John McCormack. Raisa was hardly more adventurous. She concentrated on *Il trovatore, Aida, Tosca,* and *Cavalleria rusticana.* Garden was back in January 1919 with two works by Février: *Monna Vanna,* followed in mid-month by the world première of *Gismonda,* based on a play of Sardou. A production had been built, and the première was done in style, but the opera only lasted for two Chicago performances.

Massenet's *Cléopâtre* had received its American première in Chicago early in 1916 but was not a success. Garden picked it up in January 1919 and eventually was to sing it eighteen times, seven of them in Chicago. The opera has long disappeared from the international repertory. The season ended with another opera that was destined to have a short life, *Le Chemineau,* a work by the French composer Xavier Leroux (1863–1919). Despite obvious merits and a core of vocal admirers, it remained poor box office downtown but gained a following at Ravinia.

Harold McCormick wrote his friend Charles Dawes, "The season has been a great success in every way except financially." He hoped to reduce the annual loss from $70,000 to $25,000.[12] In 1919 subscriptions to boxes dropped to 65 from 160. "When the boxes are empty it evidences unconsciously that it is not fashionable to attend the opera," he complained. The company met the problem by making the seats available to members of the army and navy.

On May 11, 1919, after an absence of eight years, Caruso returned to Chicago to sing in Medinah Temple. His fee for these events was $7,000, $4,500 more than he asked for an operatic appearance in New York. But the concert could be put in the largest hall available, which gave the impresario a chance to make money. The evening opened with a violinist, Francis Xavier Cugat (who was to go on to other things), playing the sort of bijou piece one heard on the parlor phonograph. He was followed by a soprano, often Nina Morgana, who sang an aria with a small orchestra. Finally Caruso appeared with an aria. This sequence was repeated three times. For Chicago Caruso sang "Celeste Aida," "O soave fanciulla," and "Vesti la giubba"—staples of his recorded repertory—and, with piano accompaniment, a group of songs.

Harold and Edith McCormick, realizing that the opera had to have working funds, offered interest-free advances against the earnings of the season, and as these earnings became more precarious the size of the advances grew. We have the figures for four years: 1916, $60,000; 1917, $250,000; 1918, $317,600; 1919, $426,000.[13]

Opening night in 1919 brought Raisa in a new work, *La Nave.* Italo Montemezzi, who wrote it, had had one success in the international repertory and came to conduct the première, hoping for another. It received a lavish production, another case of pouring a large sum (in this case, $60,000) into a work destined for a short stage life—two performances.

Tito Schipa at a Chicago railroad station, with unidentified animals on his shoulder

Left to right—Alessandro Dolci, Rosa Raisa, Giacomo Rimini, and Italo Montemezzi rehearsing with Montemezzi for a 1919 performance of his opera *La Nave*

Edward C. Moore *(left)* playing cards with a group of opera singers

Cleofonte Campanini

The work was defeated by a bad libretto. Later in the season Raisa was to sing *Tosca* and *Un ballo in maschera,* but she was less visible this autumn than in the recent past.

Galli-Curci did not appear until December, but she brought new repertory, *La sonnambula,* which the city had not heard in forty-five years, and *Don Pasquale.* There were familiar things as well: *La traviata, Lucia di Lammermoor,* and *The Barber of Seville.*

The return of Titta Ruffo in *Pagliacci,* combined with the debut of Tito Schipa in *Tosca,* challenged the prima donnas with two exceptional male voices. Schipa was also cast in *La sonnambula* and *Manon.* Garden offered a review of her staples and in January 1920 added as new music the Montemezzi opera with real lasting power, *L'amore dei tre re,* in the first of her thirty-four performances of the work. The intensity she brought to the character was remarkable even for her.

The conductor Gino Marinuzzi arrived in Chicago from the winter season in South America determined to introduce Puccini's newest creation, *Il trittico.* It had its Chicago première on December 6, 1919, with Raisa doing her best to sustain *Suor Angelica,* an opera that, Puccini notwithstanding, was not to be heard again for seventy-eight years. Raisa was rewarded with an opportunity to sing *Norma,* an opera that had been out of the repertory for more than a quarter century, which suited her unique talents.

The brief stage life of Reginald De Koven's *Rip Van Winkle* brought renewed conflict over opera in English. As Moore recalls, "The most ingenious argument discovered was to the effect that (1) no Americans knew how to sing their own language; (2) even if they did, American audiences had debased their ears so long listening to tunes in an unknown tongue that they did not know how to recognize their own language when they heard it."[14] As Moore saw it, the singers were overcome by De Koven's heavy orchestration.

A significant development, supported by Campanini, was the cultivation of ballet for its own sake. Serge Oukrainsky and Andreas Pavley, alumni of the St. Petersburg company, were resident in Chicago and went to a local composer, Felix Borowski (1872–1956) for a score. The work was *Boudoir,* and it was well received. Even more noteworthy is the production in the opera season of the ballet *The Birthday of the Infanta,* based on a play by Oscar Wilde, with a score by one of the most important Chicago composers, John Alden Carpenter (1876–1951). Ruth Page danced the title role, her first great success, beginning a long and important career of bringing dance to the city.

Garden was the conspicuous legacy from the Hammerstein company, but in retrospect it appears that a far more significant acquisition was Campanini. Garden came and went. Campanini stayed through the season, building an orchestra, defining standards, and revealing a broad musical vision combined with a faultless sense of style. Seasoned in his youth in Italian theaters, he was perfectly at home in French, Italian, and German repertory. He had two advantages over the other great maestro from Parma, Toscanini. Campanini had a more cosmopolitan outlook, and although his spoken English was flawed, apparently he had an excellent bilingual secretary, since his English correspondence is excellent. He was not a visitor. He made himself part of American musical life.

Garden praised him. "Nobody could touch Campanini," she said. "Nobody in the world. He was the most consummate artist in every way, not only as a conductor. He had faultless taste in choosing operas and filling the roles with people who were absolutely right for them."

His devotion to Verdi was demonstrated in 1913, the centennial of the composer's birth, when Campanini returned to the composer's birthplace to underwrite a Verdi cycle. Impressed by this gesture, Edith Rockefeller McCormick joined with him in sponsoring a new opera by an Italian composer. When it became clear in the 1919/20 season that Campanini was seriously ill, he received the best medical treatment Chicago could offer, with Harold McCormick paying the bills. It was to no avail. He died on December 19, 1919. His funeral took place in Holy Name Cathedral, and a memorial service was held in the theater the day before as a civic tribute.

His death was a decisive turning point in the history of the company, which was now left without an artistic head, and created a situation that produced political intrigue. Another conductor, Gino Marinuzzi (1882–1945), became artistic director but lasted only a year. Dealing with singers became an impossible burden to him. For opening night 1920 Marinuzzi scheduled the first of three performances of his own opera, *Jacquerie,* on which he had lavished a $50,000 production. Yvonne Gall and Edward Johnson, major talents, played the leads. It was an expensive show of vanity, which the McCormicks were apparently prepared to underwrite.

Garden made her first appearance in Camille Erlanger's *Aphrodite,* a work she had first sung with the company in New York the preceding February. One nearly transparent costume was felt by some to be the most interesting thing in the show. Four performances of established Garden items completed her contribution to the season.

Raisa was expanding her repertory. She sang Elsa in English in *Lohengrin* and Desdemona in *Otello* in addition to the expected *Aida, Cavalleria rusticana,* and *Il trovatore.* Galli-Curci broke no new ground. Charles Marshall's debut in the title role of *Otello,* with Ruffo as Iago, was possibly the greatest sensation of the autumn. Ruffo joined Raisa in *Andrea Chénier* and was heard as Rigoletto, but his appearance in Leoncavallo's last opera, *Edipo re,* demonstrated the sad truth that the composer, eighteen years removed from *Pagliacci,* was written out.

Johnson sang *Pagliacci,* and a recording suggests he could rival any celebrated Italian in that work. He showed his range as an artist when he took on another major role (never heard in Chicago) as Walther in *Die Meistersinger.* His most important Chicago affiliation proved to be the Ravinia Opera. Schipa went his way through *La traviata, Lucia di Lammermoor, The Barber of Seville, Lakmé,* and *Mignon.* There were two performances of a heavily cut *Die Walküre.* The season ended with the most expensive transcontinental tour ever undertaken by an American company. It presented the new management with a substantial debt.

Chicago heard Caruso for the last time, again in Medinah Temple, on October 3, 1920, his last month of concentrated work. He sang with the Met five times in November and seven times in December; *La Juive* on December 24 was the last performance of his life. For the Chicago date, "Cielo e mar" and "O paradiso" were possible substitutions for works heard the previous year. Apparently Caruso kept his choices open to the last moment. Again there were songs. Toscanini, who was touring America with the La Scala orchestra, heard the December 24 New York performance and immediately knew something was gravely wrong with the tenor, but Caruso, in the grip of the thoracic infection that was to kill him, concealed the gravity of his situation from the casual listener. Surely few in Chicago that October sensed they were attending his farewell.

The management issue was resolved on January 14, 1921, by naming Mary Garden director (she preferred "directa") of the Chicago Opera Association, inheriting a $300,000 deficit. She would now be paid an estimated $2,500 a night for her performances but

would not receive a salary for her administrative work. One of her objectives, she stated, was to prevent the company from being completely dominated by Italian singers and Italian opera.

Mary Garden and Harold R. McCormick, 1921

Her most serious failing as a manager proved to be her inability to judge how much talent she needed to produce a season. She hired many more singers than the schedule required, from thirty-seven in 1920/21 to fifty-four the following season. Someone would be brought from Europe for one performance. One mezzo-soprano was paid for eight performances but actually sang only two. Gadski arrived and never got to sing. She was offered the promised fees to cancel her contract but chose to sue the company for a half million dollars, claiming her reputation had been damaged. Methodical planning was not Garden's forte.

But Garden was still in good form as a singer. Her repertory for 1921/22 again consisted of things she had offered previously, and on December 28, 1921, she sang *Salome* once more. Again there was an outcry over its obscenity. It vanished from the repertory until 1934.

This was the year of Prokofiev's *The Love for Three Oranges.* The work had been commissioned before Garden took over the company. Cyrus and Harold McCormick were interested in recent Russian music, although it turned out their taste ran more to Glière

1921-22
Grand Opera Season

MARY GARDEN, General Director

WORLD'S PREMIERE—SPECIAL PERFORMANCE
FRIDAY EVENING, DECEMBER 30, AT 8.

The Love for Three Oranges

A Fantastic Opera in Four Acts and Ten Scenes,
with a Prologue.
Words and Music by Serge Prokofieff, after the Fairy Tale
by Carlo Cozzi.

The King of Trifle, king of an imaginary kingdom..Edouard Cotreuil
The Prince, his son.................................Jose Mojica
The Princess Clarice, niece of the King.............Irene Pavloska
Leandre, Prime Minister............................William Beck
Trouffaldino ....Octave Dua
Pantalon ....Desire Defrere
The Magician Tchelio...............................Hector Dufranne
Fata Morgana, a witch..............................Nina Koshetz (debut)
The Devil Farfarello...............................James Wolf
Smeraldine...Jeanne Schneider
The Creonte ....Constantin Nicolay
The Master of Ceremonies...........................Lodovico Oliviero
Linetta   {   { Frances Paperte
Violetta   { the Princesses...... { Philine Falco
Nicoletta   {   { Jeanne Dusseau
The Herald ....Jerome Uhl
Ridicules, Comiques, Lyriques, Tragiques, Empty Heads, Devils.
Incidental Dances by Corps de Ballet.
Orchestra Under the Direction of the Composer, Serge Prokofieff.
Mise-en-Scene Established and Staged by Jacques Coini.
Scenery, costumes and properties especially designed and executed
for this production by Boris Anisfeld.

Mason & Hamlin Piano Used Exclusively.
In the interest of the art, encores are not permitted.

above—Set for act 2, scene 2, of *The Love for Three Oranges*, 1921

left—Program listing for the world première of *The Love for Three Oranges*

Salome, 1921: Mary Garden as Salome; Hector Dufranne as Jochanaan; *far left*, Jose Mojica as Narraboth

than Prokofiev. Cyrus McCormick arranged for the visa necessary for Prokofiev to visit the United States in 1918, and three years later, on December 30, 1921, Chicago had the world première of the Prokofiev opera that came (the composer conducting) with performances in French. Fourteen days earlier Prokofiev had been the soloist in Orchestra Hall for the world première of his Piano Concerto No. 3, performed with Frederick Stock and the Chicago Symphony Orchestra. Prokofiev was given the full treatment for his opera. Garden spent $100,000 for the production and spared nothing on the staging, which was elaborate and visually striking.

The work was too much for her and, it seems, the Chicago public, which had been flooded with neoromantic music at the expense of other contemporary styles. Moore found *Love* "an opera ahead of its time."[15] Prokofiev, who apparently knew little English, complained in French that Garden "turned out to be a director who liked to make generous gestures but was chiefly concerned with her own roles and was never available when wanted."[16] His relationship with the company left him with $1,000 and an aching head, he later remarked. After a New York performance Garden was told the scenery was falling apart, and she ordered it destroyed on the grounds that no one would want to see this opera again. Actually the work was produced with success in Germany (in German) in 1925 and went on to recognition in the Soviet Union. Chicago audiences of the mid-century found it quite attractive.

Chicago welcomed its first radio station in 1921, KYW, a Westinghouse subsidiary, and the inaugural broadcast from the Auditorium on November 11 offered Garden singing an aria, presumably "Un bel dì" from *Madama Butterfly.* Why she would select an excerpt from an opera not in her repertory (and in Italian at that) is somewhat mysterious, but the station management may have insisted on something well known, and thanks to the parlor phonograph "Un bel dì" met that requirement. She may have had her revenge by singing it in French.

The 1921/22 series began with Giorgio Polacco, who was destined to become Campanini's successor as principal conductor, directing *Samson and Delilah.* The following night Raisa sang *Tosca,* and Polacco then returned with a memorable debut, his wife, Edith Mason, as Butterfly. She would be back in *Romeo and Juliet.* Garden did not appear until the fourth night, when she sang *Monna Vanna.* Raisa of-

fered a surprise in January when she sang in *La fanciulla del West,* and though perhaps few thought of her as Elisabeth in *Tannhäuser,* she sang the role with great success. Her other repertory consisted of things by now familiar. The same could be said of Galli-Curci, who reappeared in January after triumphantly opening the Met season with Beniamino Gigli. Schipa was regularly on view, and in expected roles.

Harold McCormick had predicted that 1921 would be his last season. Moore says of Garden's year, "If this was the most exciting season of the Chicago opera, it was also the most expensive."[17] McCormick was true to his word. Before he made his exit, he paid the final bills (they came to $1 million) and presented the company with another $1 million in scenery, props, and music he had acquired as principal stockholder.

He was fatally attracted to Ganna Walska, who had approached him in New York in the autumn of 1919, seeking an engagement with the Chicago company. Quite rightly, he referred the matter to Campanini. A soprano of questionable musical achievement, whose proven skill was the ability to collect and shed wealthy husbands, she soon had McCormick in her spell, and he went seeking a divorce. As proof of his love, Dedmon reports, "he sent to her chateau near Versailles one of every kind of machine International Harvester produced."[18] Secretly she had probably always wanted a combine, but McCormick was not ready for marriage. At fifty-one he felt the need for physical rejuvenation and midway into 1922 underwent a secret operation to restore his gonads. According to Dedmon, society wits parodied Longfellow:

> Under the spreading chestnut tree,
> The village smithy stands.
> The smith a gloomy man is he;
> McCormick has his glands.

Thus fortified, he married Walska, who, in her autobiography, reports that she found him to be a hypochondriac. Only active sex could convince him of his health. His new wife was so concerned "with the richness of the soul" that his wish "to seek further for a gross and limited pleasure" was unacceptable to her. Surprisingly enough the marriage lasted until 1931, and McCormick, sadder, poorer, but not necessarily wiser, searched for new interests, film actresses for a start.

Edith came to an equally bad end, trusting her fortune to a slick-talking real estate promoter. Her brother came to her rescue and moved her to the Drake Hotel, where she got by as best she could on $1,000 a day. She died in 1932. Both McCormicks were better off, and probably happier, when they were producing opera.

It would be a mistake to think that all the remarkable operatic performances of the 1920s came from the resident companies. Sol Hurok, Mapleson's logical successor, destined to be the greatest impresario of the new century, was permitting his enthusiasm to run riot. His successes with Anna Pavlova and Isadora Duncan do not belong to this history, but his devotion to the Russian basso Fyodor Chaliapin permitted American audiences to become fully aware of the stature of this remarkable artist.

Fyodor Chaliapin, with Sol Hurok

"In the spring of 1922," Hurok recalls in his memoirs, "I walked about in a roseate haze. Chaliapin had come and gone, leaving me breathless and somewhat in the red."[19] Pavlova's success had balanced his books, and with this false sense of security he was ready for what he called "bankruptcy à la russe." He heard of an entire Russian opera company, ninety-three artists stranded in Tokyo by the revolution, that had painfully made its way to California. Abandoning the slightest semblance of prudence, he signed them up. When Chaliapin returned in 1923, Hurok could offer something Moscow could not duplicate because, as he said, "Moscow did not have Chaliapin and I did." The great man would be surrounded by a company of his own countrymen and -women, offering *Boris Godunov* in its original language, something no other American opera producer could duplicate.

Hurok met the company in Chicago, was "appalled at the shabby sets and costumes," but put on a series of performances and "cheerfully advanced the Russians the money to live on during the summer." The 1922 performances were in March while the Chicago company was on the road. The repertory included a staple or two, *Carmen* (presumably in Russian, an unusual experience) with Ina Bourskaya, for example, but concentrated on Russian fare: *Boris Godunov* (without Chaliapin this first time), Tchaikovsky's *The Queen of Spades (Pique Dame)* and *Eugene Onegin* (both new to the city), and heady stuff like Rimsky-Korsakov's *Sniegurochka (The Snow Maiden)*, Dargomïzhsky's *Rusalka,* and Nápravník's *Dubrovsky.*

In May 1922 Edward Ziegler of the Metropolitan reported to his boss, Gatti-Casazza, a discussion he had had with Garden in New York. She had wanted to see if Chicago could borrow the Met production of Umberto Giordano's *Madame Sans-Gêne,* which that company had produced (for Farrar) in four seasons, starting in 1915. The sets no longer existed, and the project was dropped. One may speculate whether Garden saw the work as something for herself. (Ravinia staged it in 1926.)[20]

When the Chicago company returned from its tour on April 23, 1922, Garden had stepped down as directa. The company faced reorganization and a new name. With the departure of McCormick, in the 1922/23 season Samuel Insull became president of the Chicago Civic Opera. Publicly he was not critical of Garden's work, but the new company was soon to prove to be his and his alone. Like Garden, he felt the opera audience should be found in the telephone book, not the social register.

Samuel Insull

Insull came to Chicago in 1892 to head the Edison Company and quickly became one of the most influential men in the business community. Born in London, he had developed his love for opera, skrimping to buy the cheapest seats at Covent Garden. If opera was for the swells (as Upton had put it), Insull would never have been able to attend. Such an attitude, he felt, did not serve the best interests of either opera or the community. For all his wealth and power, Insull respected the middle and working classes and defended their right to be part of the cultural life of the city. Edward Moore comments, "Mr. Insull was always of the firm opinion that opera, its enjoyments and advantages, should by no means be confined to one particular class or a group of classes. He greatly preferred to think of its effect on the community as a whole, realizing the while that in order to have a general effect, it must be given a general patronage."[21] He believed that a firm audience base running through all levels of society must be built. This is still true.

Insull began attending opera soon after his arrival in Chicago, and with the establishment of a resident company he became a guarantor. He had little respect for Gold Coast society but treated it with civility. Like Edith McCormick, he never touched alcohol, and there was little room in his life for fancy parties.

As time passed, he became increasingly important in the operations of the opera company and in 1922

was the natural choice to assume the presidency. When he took over, he could rightly claim that a city of 2 million depended on his companies for electricity, gas, and transportation, both within the city and by way of electric interurban railways. One of his first moves was to increase the number of guarantors to three thousand by reducing the sum to be pledged.

Insull was actively in charge of things with a committee of experts from the staff to review all decisions. The five most highly paid artists, Garden, Galli-Curci, Raisa, Baklanoff, and Schipa were to receive their usual fees, but some of the others had been dismissed, and the rest had accepted a 50% pay cut.[22]

Insull realized that the Auditorium was a liability. The hotel, with few private baths (like Garden, visiting artists preferred to stay down the street at the Blackstone) was in difficulty. If the building went bankrupt, the assets of the opera company in the theater probably would be seized.

If Insull did not see opera as a showcase for the wealthy, neither did he view it as a mad enterprise that inevitably lost huge sums of money. True, it required subsidy, but it could be run in a businesslike manner, and losses could be held to a minimum. This required expanding the audience and keeping the seats full, the keys to the success of the Lyric Opera later in the century. Eventually his grand design was to be fully revealed in his plans for a new opera house.

The reorganized Chicago Civic Opera Company began on November 13, 1922, with as impressive a sequence of major singers as the city had heard in some time, and kept it up until January 20. Opening night offered Raisa in *Aida,* followed by Garden as Carmen and Mason in *La bohème.* Mason was back in the exotic item of the season, Rimsky-Korsakov's *The Snow Maiden,* in English. The Hurok performances had, of course, been in Russian, and now the lack of a language barrier apparently greatly increased the appeal of the work. Garden was back with *L'amore dei tre re,* and Raisa again sang Wolf-Ferrari's *The Jewels of the Madonna.* Wagner was represented by *Parsifal,* conducted by Ettore Panizza, who had just joined the company. It did not sell and was withdrawn after two Chicago performances, but it resurfaced on tour. *Die Walküre* in December met a similar fate. Finally there was *Tosca* with Raisa. The month advanced with Raisa in *Il trovatore,* Mason in *Madama Butterfly,* and then Raisa in *La fanciulla del West* and Mason in *Rigoletto.* Raisa was to return later in the series in *La forza del destino* and *La Juive,* which had not been heard in more than twenty years.

There were three major debuts, starting with Claudia Muzio, who sang *Aida, Il trovatore,* and *Pagliacci* (all with ferocious success) within one week. Louise Homer, long a stalwart of the Met, made a powerful impression as Azucana in *Il trovatore.* The third debut was Chaliapin in *Mefistofele.* He sang the opening scene with the lower half of his body invisible in black tights and the top glowing with luminous paint. Nothing in the season surpassed that—not that the ladies weren't trying. Galli-Curci offered seven of her finest roles, and Garden could be seen twice as Tosca. Schipa remained the dominant tenor.

The most far-reaching innovation of the season was the effort to broadcast opera. Here the Chicago company was well ahead of the Metropolitan, which did not broadcast a performance until 1931. The Met, however, is still broadcasting, and, although Chicago opera broadcasts continued well into the decade on the new NBC network, Chicago opera was off the air for many years. Inevitably the question was raised, if they can get the music for free, will they stop buying tickets? The answer, of course, is that there is much more to opera than the music: Garden on the air and Garden onstage were very different things.

Hurok's 1922/23 tour began in Boston in the autumn, and losses ran from $3,000 to $5,000 a week. When the troupe reached Chicago, it took over the Auditorium for a month, beginning in mid-February. Hurok advertised "Russian opera at popular prices—the most tuneful opera in existence with all-star casts." The theater had no bar, so intermission imbibers had to make their way to the Congress Hotel though a passageway under the street called Peacock Alley. Nightly Hurok attended his show, and, nightly, across the street, he staged a party where the press and cronies "came and ate and drank with me and shared my happiness." Chaliapin, who made $3,500 (a good middle-class annual income) for each performance and sang as often as three times a week, was "among his own people, who treated him like a god," and he was completely happy. But all was not well, Hurok adds. "For four delirious weeks I walked on air while my pockets were quietly emptying to the tune of $60,000."

Something had to be offered that might fill the four-thousand-seat house when Chaliapin was not singing Boris, and it proved to be a piece of froth, Valentinov's *A Night of Love,* which Hurok's advertising proclaimed had "taken Chicago by storm" and, at

least, gave him something to sell. The operetta had nothing except the title in common with the later film starring Grace Moore. When the Russians departed, it vanished as well—forever.

The 1923 Hurok repertory combined staples such as *Carmen* and *La Juive* with Dargomïzhsky's *Rusalka* and genuine novelties such as Rimsky-Korsakov's *Christmas Eve* and *The Tsar's Bride* and Tchaikovsky's *Mazeppa.*

Chicago had not been able to present *Boris Godunov* in 1922/23 because it lacked a production, so that honor had gone to Hurok. By November 1923 the work was ready, and Chaliapin was on hand to sing it, but while the Hurok production had been in Russian, this one was in Italian except for the part of Chaliapin, who, of course, sang the Russian text. He repeated his success in *Mefistofele* and returned in January in one of his favorite roles, Basilio in *The Barber of Seville.* In the *Tribune,* Moore announced that "as a specimen of makeup it beat everything in a dozen years. . . . The mere sight of him was worth a trip to the theater."

Louise Homer, who had retired from the Metropolitan in 1918 after twenty years as a leading singer, decided to return to opera and began the first of several notable seasons in Chicago. She first won success in *Samson and Delilah* and reappeared as Amneris in *Aida.* Mason joined Chaliapin in *Mefistofele* and was also heard in *Manon* and *The Snow Maiden.* Raisa offered new fare in *L'Africana,* the opera by Giacomo Meyerbeer (1791–1864), then returned to staples. As it proved, this was Galli-Curci's last season (she got into a nasty fight about her future repertory), but there was a lot of her: *Lakmé, Dinorah, La traviata, Lucia di Lammermoor,* and *The Barber of Seville.* (She sang at the Met until 1930.)

Muzio offered a substantial repertory: *Monna Vanna, La forza del destino, Mefistofele, La traviata,* and *Aida.* Garden did not reappear until the end of the year, when she returned with three of her established works. An important debut was that of Claire Dux, but she was thrust into a poorly prepared staging of *Königskinder* on Christmas Day and thus robbed of the success she deserved. Two weeks later *Pagliacci* brought her deserved recognition.

In a way, the oddest events of the autumn were two performances of *Siegfried* under the Chicago Symphony's conductor, Frederick Stock. Stock delighted in tampering with other men's music, and he decided the opera was much too long. The high point of the work was the Siegfried-Brünnhilde duet at the close, and the audience must wait far too long to get there.

Stock trimmed about a hour from the score (first to go, one speculates, were Alberich and Erda), but it was not a box office success and soon left the repertory.

Insull's efforts to produce opera in a businesslike manner were achieving results. In terms of dollars, 74% of the maximum box office income was realized (an increase of more than $150,000 over the previous year) with attendance at 84% of capacity despite the number of performances having increased from seventy-two to ninety-one. The deficit was $325,000, and the guarantors covered it. People were buying tickets.

The people who had made 1923/24 a success predictably returned the following autumn. Raisa had opening night with *La Gioconda*. She was back as Aida, sang Elisabeth in *Tannhäuser,* and repeated *La Juive, Otello, Cavalleria rusticana,* and *The Jewels of the Madonna.* Muzio was heard as Tosca and Aida and joined Chaliapin in *Mefistofele.* Mason again sang *Madama Butterfly.* As an innovative turn, she used her own daughter as the child Trouble. Homer appeared in an ill-considered revival of Meyerbeer's *Le Prophète* and repeated Delilah. Garden revived *Werther* but otherwise offered familiar staples, including *Pelléas et Mélisande.*

There were new faces. Elvira de Hidalgo, now remembered as the teacher of Maria Callas but then a major star in her prime, sang her most popular role, Rosina in *The Barber of Seville.* In 1925 she would repeat the role at Ravinia. Gladys Swarthout, destined to be a film star and one of the major singers of the next two decades, sang a collection of roles: Lola in *Cavalleria rusticana,* Musetta in *La bohème,* Feodor in *Boris Godunov,* and Stephano in *Romeo and Juliet.* She went to Ravinia in 1927. Henry Weber, who was to be an important part of Chicago music for some twenty-five years, made his conducting debut in *Tannhäuser.*

Chaliapin returned as Boris and sang both devils, Gounod's Mephistopheles and Boito's Mefistofele, but unfortunate disagreements with the company caused him to take his leave for good, although at $3,500 a performance he was the highest paid artist in the company. He could match that elsewhere.

As the series closed, Insull reported with regret that the deficit was $75,000 higher than the previous year, although attendance continued to increase. Moreover, the new company was requiring far less subsidy than its predecessor. Touring had been made profitable. The company demanded $15,000 a performance, and a local committee guaranteed the fee, so an annual tour budget that now came to nearly $1 million was covered. The Chicago

opera, like the Metropolitan, was functioning as a national company, but Chicago went to many smaller cities that the Met never played.

Being businesslike meant, in part, controlling costs, and Insull decided the company needed a warehouse for its existing productions and workshops for the creation of new ones. It would own its own space for necessary functions that had previously required rented housing. A half-million-dollar bond issue paid for the work, then began to generate significant savings, and the warehouse, at Dearborn and 26th Streets, still serves the Lyric. In 1978, when the Lyric was in precarious financial straits, a mortgage on the warehouse helped keep the company functioning.

In retrospect, the 1925/26 series must be called the season of *Der Rosenkavalier.* Strauss finally came into his own in Chicago as the composer of an enjoyable and only slightly scandalous work. It was hardly new. Europe first heard it in 1911, and it quickly was produced at the leading theaters. It reached the Metropolitan in December 1913, with Alfred Hertz conducting and a production designed in Vienna.

Conductor Giorgio Polacco and his wife, soprano Edith Mason, in Chicago, 1922

Perhaps the most remarkable thing about the Chicago production is that it had a real stage director, Charles Moor, who was imported from Scotland to do the job. A *Rosenkavalier* in which the singers improvised their stage business would be an impossible mess, although the Chicago companies had offered any number of messes of that type, not only because normally they had no one permanently on the staff who was primarily responsible for staging, but also because operas were put together in such haste that a real director would have no time in which to do his job. Moreover, the greatest stars, such as Garden and Chaliapin, had absolutely no need for such services, and many in the audience were apparently content with singers who stood still and followed the conductor.

Polacco conducted with a strong cast: Raisa as the Marschallin, Mason as Sophie, Olga Forrai as Octavian, and Alexander Kipnis as Ochs. Moor's efforts were so successful that he became a permanent part of the company. Raisa reappeared four nights later in her more traditional repertory, *Un ballo in maschera,* with *Aida, Falstaff,* and *Il trovatore* following, but she broke with convention to sing *Madama Butterfly,* a score that many felt belonged to Mason but that Raisa projected forcefully.

Manon Lescaut was a Puccini opera oddly neglected in Chicago, but it had its second staging, with Muzio as the ill-fated beauty. Later Muzio performances were in *Il trovatore* and *Andrea Chénier.* Mason sang in *Rigoletto, Martha,* and *Faust.* Homer repeated her success as Delilah.

In January 1925 Garden sang *Salome* in Seattle. The police, eager to defend public morals, reported that "the show was better than the movies" with "a nifty dance."[23] Garden must have felt vindicated.

In December 1925 she offered Chicago new repertory, an opera whose libretto was based on Tolstoy's novel *Resurrection,* with music by Franco Alfano (1875–1954). *Risurrezione* won one of the greatest successes of recent years with an undistinguished score. It was an opera Garden was to sing fifty-four times in the closing phase of her career. *Werther, Carmen, Louise,* and *Pelléas et Mélisande* completed her contribution.

This was the year of *Namiko-San,* an opera so obscure it is not to be found in Loewenberg's *Annals of Opera,* in which more than half the titles are of works you are certain you will never see or hear. The composer of *Namiko-San* was Aldo Franchetti, the nephew of Alberto (1860–1942), the better-known composer of that name, two of whose works had been heard in

Chicago. The libretto (in English) is taken from a Japanese play, *The Daimyo.* The soprano was a Japanese lady, Tamaki Miura, who wanted something in her repertory besides *Madama Butterfly.* The problem was the ending. The soprano's head is severed by a samurai so adept at decapitation that it remains in place, at least until she has completed a climactic high note, and then drops and rolls across the stage.

Any experienced music critic can think of several ladies he would like to see cast in that role, but Miura, who wanted to sing more than the première performance, insisted that the libretto be changed. Her wish was granted. She and the work survived three performances by the Chicago company, and the following year she took it on a national tour. Another interesting aspect of the opera was that its composer became a naturalized American citizen just a few days before the première, a feat accomplished through frantic machinations behind the scene so that the work could be billed as an American opera!

In November 1925 Louis Eckstein, the chief executive of the Ravinia Company, wrote to Edward Ziegler, the assistant general manager of the Metropolitan: "There is so much in the papers these days about the Chicago Opera that I can only send you a clipping here and there which may be of interest. Confidentially, there is great dissatisfaction, much criticism on the part of the public and many empty seats." Eckstein doubted if the city could support a twelve-week winter season. Moreover, he complained, "much butting in by women affiliated with the management, and much internal strife and jealousies are adding to the chaos."[24]

Moore noted, "In Chicago it is by no means uncommon to present thirty-five different operas in a period of ten or twelve weeks. In Europe they would not give that many in forty weeks."[25] But in Europe there was an audience, and a much larger percentage of the population attended opera, which is why it so commonly received government subsidy on some level. In the final decades of the nineteenth century we see the rise of commercial mass entertainment, which was to rival opera for the public's attention, and by the close of the twentieth century it would foster the charge that operatic and symphonic music were for an unimportant elitist minority. Moore tells of a prominent Chicago bootlegger who was gunned down by the competition (a not uncommon event in Chicago during the 1920s) and was found to have four opera tickets in his pocket. Criminals with class might be considered a distinctive product of the Chicago cultural environment.[26]

Insull ended the season with the announcement that a new guaranty fund of $500,000 a year must be in place by 1927. (He got $520,000—the support was there.) Costs were increasing. A new union contract had given the members of the orchestra a minimum of $119 a week (which came to $1,428 a player), roughly $120,000 a season for the ensemble. Reasonably confident that the company was economically secure, on December 9, 1925, Insull addressed the Association of Commerce with the plea that opera in Chicago required a new theater, "a home for grand opera of such monumental character that it would be a credit to this great city of which we are so proud." In fact, architects were already at work on the preliminary design; Insull was not the kind of man to leave his dreams unfulfilled. Less than four years later, on November 4, 1929, the new house opened.

The 1926/27 series began with another star parade. It opened with Muzio in *Aida,* went on to Raisa in *The Jewels of the Madonna,* then to Mason in *La bohème.* The following night *Risurrezione* provided Garden with her first appearance, after which she sang three of her staples and introduced *Judith,* one of the four operas composed by Arthur Honegger (1892–1955). Many found the music far too modern, but Garden was able to make the work convincing. Raisa had a busy year, singing *La Juive, Cavalleria rusticana, Un ballo in maschera,* Donna Anna in *Don Giovanni*—a role few would associate with her—and making a second appearance in *Der Rosenkavalier.* Muzio returned in *Il trovatore.* Mason sang predictable things, *Madama Butterfly* and *Faust. Boris Godunov* remained a popular opera, and it was back, but in Italian, with Vanni-Marcoux in the title role. There was another brave try at American opera, *A Witch of Salem,* by Charles Wakefield Cadman (1881–1946). The audience found it unattractively grim.

In the light of the Eckstein letter it is instructive to read *Opera Topics,* the company's promotional newspaper, for the 1926 holiday period. "Happily," it reports, "the season has progressed since [the opening week] with a calm perfection marvelous indeed. . . . Rich and entrancing has been the feast of beauty spread before us." The company was trying to build a subscription audience apart from the box holders, but with modest results. If it was felt that self-serving prose of this type would do the job, it was mistaken.

A critic of the later decades of the century might envy the space given his colleagues of the 1920s, but

Claudia Muzio in Chicago, sewing, 1927

some chose to fill it with rhetorical fluff—writing more descriptive than evaluative. Moore at the *Tribune* is the voice most appealing to readers of a later day. Reading his colleagues, one is made aware of the revolutionary effect of Virgil Thomson on American music criticism.

It is instructive to compare the Chicago company and the Metropolitan at this point in history. The Met was essentially an Italian company, run by Giulio Gatti-Casazza for nearly twenty years. Gatti certainly had learned some English in that period, but he kept it to himself. All negotiations had to be in French or Italian. But if, officially, he did not know English, it was a matter of public knowledge that he knew how to make money. The Met ended the 1926/27 season with a record profit of $141,000. Why, one may ask, is this sort of thing no longer possible? The answer is stagehands, musicians, chorus, and ballet, groups that traditionally received meager pay then and, through unionization, greatly increased their income, with a proportional increase in production costs.

Hurok decided the United States was not ready for Russian opera, but a simple matter like bankruptcy did not stop him from going on the road again with Chaliapin in 1926. The great basso wanted to tour with Rossini's *The Barber of Seville*. Asked why he would choose as a vehicle an opera in which he played Don Basilio, a supporting role with only one aria, he thundered, "Do you buy artists by the yard?" A company was engaged with Elvira de Hidalgo as Rosina, George Dubrovsky as Figaro, and "a Lithuanian tenor named Bobrovich" as Almaviva. Chicago had heard both Chaliapin and Hidalgo in these roles, but that did not deter Hurok's plans.

Chaliapin in a smaller role was not good box office, or, perhaps, as Hurok speculated, "America was not ready for Italian opera either." Chaliapin caught cold, returned to New York "for four or five weeks" to nurse himself, "and the company and orchestra sat in St. Louis drawing salary and not playing." It was the ultimate manager's nightmare, a $120,000 disaster. Unable to pay his rent when he returned to New York, Hurok spent a few nights sleeping in Central Park, a fate Mapleson had avoided.

In January 1927 Insull told the guarantors of the company that the new theater was to be on the river between Madison and Washington Streets, facing what was then Market Street, the city's principal area for wholesale produce merchants. (Wacker Drive was still in the future.) A hundred years earlier this had been a swampy place much favored for hunting game birds. Later in that century the north end of the site had held the city's first hotel, which gave way to the Wigwam (in which—as noted earlier—Abraham Lincoln was nominated for the presidency). While waiting at Washington and Wacker for a bus to take them to the subway, today's operagoers can recall that Lincoln was nominated right across the street.

November 3, 1927, presented a dilemma for both the audience and, especially, music critics, since Muzio in *La traviata* at the Auditorium was in direct competition with the Boston Symphony Orchestra and the first Chicago appearance of Serge Koussevitzky at Orchestra Hall. The next evening brought Henry Weber in charge of *Tannhäuser*, an opera Chicago audiences continued to view coolly. One reason, I suspect, is that the original, rather than the Paris, version was used. *The Snow Maiden* had been transformed from a French opera to an English one and assigned to Weber, with Mason starring. Her other castings for the season were in *Madama Butter-*

fly, Faust, Martha (with Schipa, who had made the work something of a specialty), and as Alice Ford in *Falstaff. A Witch of Salem,* introduced the previous season, was back for a second try at success. The public still found its gloomy subject unappealing. Raisa was again in the *Falstaff* cast and predictably returned in *Aida, La Gioconda, The Jewels of the Madonna,* and, for New Year's Eve, *Die Fledermaus,* in English, with a stellar group of singers. It proved a welcome diversion. Muzio was heard as Aida, Tosca, and Leonora in *Il trovatore,* but achieved her greatest effects in a work staged for her, where the beauty of her voice was combined with yards of pale blue chiffon. The opera was *Loreley,* by Alfredo Catalani (1854–1893).

Garden had sung "The Star-Spangled Banner" at a Paris reception for the hero of the day, Charles Lindbergh, but only after carefully checking the words. For 1927/28 she offered familiar things and an opulent production of Massenet's *Sapho.* That opera had been considered somewhat scandalous when it was first heard in 1897, but thirty years had passed, and these were the supposedly Roaring Twenties. Moore said that "the music promptly began to contest the place of *Monna Vanna* in the list of unimportant operatic scores. Dramatically most of its value had died out years before."[27] But this was a Garden vehicle; it was supposed to succeed. The public heard it three times.

As the 1928/29 season opened, the new opera house was under construction. "The old guard was out in force," Karleton Hackett reported, "and waxed sentimental, as is the habit of old-timers, over the glories of the past: Calvé, Nordica, Melba, the de Reszkes and Caruso." *Carmen* brought Maria Olszewska as a controversial heroine. She was far more successful as Ortrud in *Lohengrin.* Her Elsa was Marion Claire, who had made her debut three days earlier in *La bohème.* Claire's marriage to Weber in January 1929 was the great backstage romance of the company. The admiration of Robert R. McCormick, the publisher of the *Chicago Tribune,* kept her and her spouse on the radio in a weekly show, the *Chicago Theater of the Air,* until the 1940s. Generally the format was an operetta trimmed to fit into fifty minutes, with an intermission talk in which McCormick proclaimed his distinctive, very conservative views on the state of the world. In the 1940s Claire was far better suited to *The Student Prince* than *Lohengrin.*

An important debut was that of Eva Turner, who sang *Aida* the first week and returned in *Un ballo in maschera* and as Sieglinde in *Die Walküre.* Polacco conducted the performance, which had Alexander Kipnis as Wotan and Frida Leider, one of the great German dramatic sopranos, making her debut as Brünnhilde. She returned as the Marschallin in *Der Rosenkavalier* with Kipnis as Ochs and Mason as Sophie. Olszewska was Octavian, one of her important non-Wagnerian roles, as was Donna Anna in *Don Giovanni*, which Polacco conducted. Mason was also cast in *Romeo and Juliet, Faust, La bohème,* and as Zerlina in *Don Giovanni.* Raisa achieved enormous success in two performances of *Norma.*

Sapho returned as Garden said farewell to the Auditorium with established repertory. Honegger's *Judith* was revived without creating much enthusiasm. Insull wished the Auditorium torn down—it was potential competition for the new theater. That was one of the few things he failed to get. He felt that the last performance in the theater should be the same as the first, *Romeo and Juliet.* This time it was Mason rather than Patti as the tragic heroine. The Auditorium lowered the curtain on January 26, 1929. Moore recaptures the moment: "Miss Mason and Mr. Hackett sang their loveliest, and in one of the entr'actes Mr. Polacco signaled the orchestra, which played *Home Sweet Home* and *Auld Lang Syne,* the nearest thing to the recall of Patti. The house rose to its feet, and some of the spectators, including Miss Garden, sang as many words as they could remember."[28]

The theater had been Chicago's opera house for nearly forty years. After more than a century it still serves the cultural life of the city. Insull's Civic Opera House was seventy-one years old when the twenty-first century began, and it may well be in service on its centennial. The first Metropolitan Opera House in New York was torn down in its eighty-third year.

Hurok began to recoup his fortunes in New York with a series of Sunday afternoon performances of opera in concert form. Dazzled that he was actually making money again, he heard the Lorelei songs of another stranded opera company, German this time, and in the 1928/29 season the German Grand Opera Company went on the road, 150 strong, to ten cities, with the *Ring.*[29] Gadski was the principal soprano. Sonia Sharnova, who was to become a staple of Chicago opera and, in later years, a leading vocal teacher, was the principal contralto, and Karl Jorn was the leading tenor. Ernest Knoch and Walter Rabi were the conductors. The company arrived at the Auditorium in February 1929. Press and public were enthusiastic, and admirers of the Auditorium rejoiced that its days as an opera house had not ended. But it would never hear another season like the ones of the past.

6

The Ravinia Opera

1912–1931

After twenty seasons of successful production, the Ravinia Opera gave its final performance just as it was achieving recognition as the nearest American counterpart to the great music festivals of Europe. In 1931 it was easy to dismiss it as another victim of the Great Depression, and, after 1936, when Ravinia was reborn as a successful summer festival of symphonic music, it was natural to delegate the opera seasons to a musty past. But the perspective that the passage of time provides reveals that these impressions were misleading. The demise of the Ravinia Opera was due to more than a depressed economy, and its influence on opera in Chicago, and on opera in the United States, was greater and more lasting than might first appear.

Summer music festivals are now a staple part of musical life in the United States, but there never have been many summer opera festivals. Ravinia was the first of the type. The Lyric Opera of Chicago might not have prospered in its early years without the pioneering at Ravinia. It is time that these matters be reexamined and reappraised.

What was opera doing at Ravinia in the first place? What chain of events put a successful company twenty-five miles from the established locale of Chicago operatic performances?

It all began with a railroad. The invention of the electrical trolley car, and the subsequent development of the electrically powered railway coach, produced at the turn of the century a brief but significant period in which, in the absence of highways, many major cities and larger towns were linked by electric interurban railways. Chicago became a hub for travel of this type, with lines extending to three points of the compass. (Operations to the east were partly obstructed by Lake Michigan.) The northern line, which had its terminus in Milwaukee, Wiscon-

sin, was primarily responsible for the Ravinia Opera.

One way to increase business for an interurban railroad was to build attractive places along the right-of-way for people to visit. Ravinia Park was intended as a center for well-mannered amusement. The area took its name from the numerous ravines into which small watercourses descended from bluffs to flow into Lake Michigan. A plot of thirty-six acres, the park was bisected diagonally by the A. C. Frost Company's Chicago and Milwaukee Electric Railway. Originally the western part of the site was left to trees. The park buildings were in the eastern triangle, and the electric train, which here ran parallel to the Chicago and Northwestern steam railway, took you directly to the entrance.

Construction began in 1903. When the park opened in 1904, it offered as its primary attractions a large carousel, a baseball diamond with a spacious grandstand, a fountain illuminated by electric lights, a theater of one thousand seats with a pipe organ, and a noble structure called the Casino (which, however, was dedicated to food, drink, and dancing rather than gambling). Promotional literature was rhapsodic: "Equipped with every facility for attracting people of taste and refinement, Ravinia Park and its theater are located in Highland Park, Illinois, on the Chicago and Milwaukee Electric Railway." The business of transporting visitors from the city was shared by the two railroads and was assured by the fact that in 1904 there was not a mile of paved country road in the United States. Suburban visitors might arrive at the park by car on village streets, but compared to the train, a drive to or from the city would have been slow and vexatious.

The initial hope that the park might be operated year round quickly vanished. Its appeal as a summer attraction was enhanced in 1905 by the construction

The entrance gate to the Ravinia Festival during its years as an opera producer

of an outdoor music pavilion with a concave acousti-cal reflector. The theater was intended for the spoken word but was troubled by the same problems that fol-lowed its reopening in mid-century. It could be oppres-sively hot in the summer months. Withdrawn from service in 1915, it became a warehouse for opera scenery. For its return to use in 1957 it was extensively refurbished and later was air-conditioned to function as a recital hall. It is the only structure of the original park to survive. Visitors to Ravinia today find them-selves in a setting dominated by recent landscaping and construction. Nothing evokes the opera nights.

Promoted as "Chicago's Summer Capital" and "a place of entertainment for people of culture and re-finement," experience quickly proved that the public responded to Ravinia most enthusiastically when it offered serious music. Walter Damrosch brought the New York Symphony there in 1905 and returned for five years. A typical program of 1906 opened with Beethoven's *Egmont* Overture and proceeded to the Symphony No. 41 *(Jupiter)* of Mozart. Concerts during

the later opera seasons were on a less demanding level. Ravinia also welcomed the orchestras of Chicago and Minneapolis, as well as lesser ensembles. The concert pavilion became the center of activity. But popular as they were, the concerts were not able to make the enterprise profitable. Faced with this and other ventures that had failed to generate the ex-pected earnings, the A. C. Frost Company went into receivership and began to sell its assets.

In 1911, fearing redevelopment along lines they considered undesirable (with a rail-side park at nearby Fort Sheridan a horrible example), a group of local resi-dents formed the Ravinia Company and bought the land for $105,000, with half the funds obtained from the sale of stock and the balance a mortgage loan. Louis Eckstein was elected president. The following year a group of socially prominent women formed the Ravinia Club to keep "Ravinia Park up to its old ideals." Mrs. Harold McCormick was the honorary president, and Mrs. Frank McMullin, the wife of the founder of the Ravinia Company, the active chief executive.

The first significant decision of the new administration was to remodel the music facility, converting the old band shell from a quarter sphere to a proscenium stage and placing 1,420 seats under a roof—a theater without walls. Peter J. Weber was the architect. The result was a charming place, built of heavy brown timbers and illuminated by Japanese lanterns. After a fire in 1949 in which it was completely destroyed, Ravinia veterans would refer to it nostalgically as the Old Pavilion.

There was no amplification of the sounds from the stage; suitable electronic equipment came into existence only with the development of sound motion pictures late in the 1920s. But when the air was still and was laden with an optimum amount of humidity, the music might carry some distance on its innate acoustical energy. There were listeners on the lawn, as there are today, and apparently they heard enough to make the journey worthwhile.

At the opening of the century, opera still could be promoted effectively as popular entertainment. In mid-June 1911 a group calling itself the Aborn Grand Opera Company was presenting Puccini's *La bohème* at McVicker's Theater in the Chicago Loop for a two-week run (six nights a week, matinées Wednesdays and Saturdays) of the type one would expect from a musical show. In July, Ponchielli's *La Gioconda* could be heard at the White City amusement park on the south side. The new and larger Ravinia stage offered the possibility of presenting scenes from operas, and the management felt it might profit by adding several such programs to the 1911 schedule. Typical of the times, the singers were in costume, but scenery and props—if any—were minimal. You went to the opera to hear singing, and the physical production could be simple, even primitive. The Chicago Concert Orchestra, a group that, I suspect, was recruited largely from the ranks of the Theodore Thomas Orchestra (as the Chicago Symphony was then known), was heard, with Chevalier N. B. Emanuel conducting. The company consisted of a half dozen singers established in the Chicago area: Lois Ewell, Vera Allen, Barbara Wolf, David Duggan, William Beard, and Carver Williams. There was a chorus of thirty voices. Admission to the park was twenty-five cents, and reserved seats, scaled from twenty-five to seventy-five cents, were offered.

Frederick Stock and the Theodore Thomas Orchestra opened the series. The opera programs began the week of July 16 with three performances of the third act of *Aida*, three performances of the third act of

Faust, and a night offering the prelude and Bridal Chamber Scene from *Lohengrin*. Later weeks added excerpts from such repertory staples as *Martha, Carmen, Faust, Thaïs*, and *The Tales of Hoffmann*. Ravinia tradition (and the available records) tell us the first complete opera performances were in 1912, which means the 1911 version of *Pagliacci* was limited to the first act, a practice Ravinia was to follow until 1915.

The change that transformed Ravinia from a concert series to an opera festival took place in 1912. On August 21 a Ravinia audience heard a performance of Mascagni's *Cavalleria rusticana*. A single act dedicated to adultery and revenge, set in rural Sicily, it had received twenty-one productions in Chicago since it was first heard in 1892. If the intention was to test Ravinia as a site for fully staged opera, this was a work that was certain to draw well at the box office. It was a success, and it began a series of performances not surpassed in survival power until 1975.

Opera was not by any means the only attraction of the summer. Ravinia showed silent motion pictures, among them Sarah Bernhardt in *Camille*. The season had begun with concerts and dance. Emil Oberhoffer directed the Minneapolis Symphony with dance interludes by Lydia Lopokova, who was billed as a member of the Imperial Russian Ballet, although she was to become far better known as a celebrated dancer of the Diaghilev Ballets Russes. From there she acquired a different type of celebrity as the wife of John Maynard Keynes. The Chicago orchestra under Frederick Stock took the Pavilion stage on July 14, playing afternoon and evening programs daily. The following week Lopokova returned to dance, with Stock conducting. If this failed to appeal to you, theaters in the Loop were offering *Uncle Tom's Cabin* and a new Viennese operetta, *The Merry Widow Re-Married*. Those who wanted more action might attend the combined Buffalo Bill and Pawnee Bill Wild West Shows.

In 1912 one could take a Chicago and Northwestern train from the Loop at 7:30 in the evening and arrive promptly for a performance at 8:15, in about a third of the time that might be necessary to make the journey by road. Even today a driver would be fortunate to arrive that quickly. The steam train back to the city left the park at 10:40. General admission had now risen to 35 cents.

Culture Ravinia-style blossomed the week of July 28 with the opening of a five-week season of what was called grand opera. There was a regular change of repertory for a total of thirty-five performances. Thirteen different operas were presented, but only *Caval-leria rusticana* escaped major cuts, although some of its choral pages may have been trimmed. This was the age of the spring-driven phonograph, which chopped operas into four-minute segments suitable for one side of a 78 rpm shellac disc. Ravinia liked the idea of tabloid opera, paring favorite works to their essentials. Thus *Madama Butterfly* was reduced to its first act, *Faust* shrunk to act 3 (traditionally known at Ravinia as the Garden Scene), and *Tosca* was compressed into act 2. There is every indication that most of these programs were essentially the same as the summer before, but now there were costumes, props, and a minimal amount of scenery. Wagner excerpts were heard in the symphony concerts. The response was strong and positive. This was the kind of music the Ravinia public most wanted to hear.

Ravinia had a resident company. Gustav Hinrichs was the conductor, with a handful of singers who did everything in the manner of a small European provincial theater. The festival management concluded the season with the assertion in the final program book that "nowhere in the United States has such a varied and comprehensive program of high grade summer music been given. . . . The impressive array of offerings has met with splendid response," and, despite some cool weather, the park "has had the most prosperous season of its career." At first this may seem to be extravagant self-praise, but, if you survey the American musical scene in 1912, you realize that Ravinia could rightly claim that there was little to rival it either in this country or, for that matter, in Europe.

In retrospect it is astonishing that Ravinia became the home of a successful opera festival, because as an opera house the Old Pavilion left much to be desired. Never designed with opera in mind, it had an inadequate pit and neither a fly loft nor wings. The stage was shallow, and scenery consisted of painted canvas

The stage of the original Ravinia Pavilion

flats. An occasional prop and some scenery (largely furniture, I surmise) could be borrowed from the company downtown. Since the Auditorium and, after 1929, the new Civic Opera House used painted canvas drops that "flew" (a type of scenery totally unsuited to the Ravina stage), Ravinia had to provide its own sets. Only the simplest lighting effects were possible. Today, with a strong trend toward minimalism in operatic design, the old Ravinia stage might be regarded as an interesting challenge, but in the first decades of the century, when quantities of realistic scenery were the usual expectation, it could not compete with the downtown companies in terms of decor. At Ravinia the primary emphases were on the natural beauty of the park and outstanding singing. The 1912 company was about twice the size of the previous year: two sopranos, two mezzos, three tenors, two baritones, and a bass. Lois Ewell of the 1911 series returned. A newcomer, Louis Kreidler, was just about to make his New York debut at the Metropolitan, where he sang twenty-seven performances in two seasons. Frances Ingram was to sing at the Met from 1919 to 1921. The other singers, one assumes, were from the greater Chicago area. It is difficult to estimate the quality of these Ravinia performances, since the Chicago newspapers regarded them as suburban events. René Devries of the *Evening American* surfaced in a music magazine to observe that "Miss Abercrombie was not very successful" as Butterfly, but if he was comparing her to Geraldine Farrar, who virtually owned the role at the Met, this was only to be expected.

By and large the Ravinia formula worked. We must take the viewpoint of 1912 to appreciate that it offered an attractive blend of well-established staples from the previous century (to name only *Faust, Aida, Martha, Thaïs,* and *Lohengrin*) with new music—verismo opera—represented by *Cavalleria rusticana, Pagliacci, La bohème,* and *Madama Butterfly.* Mascagni and Puccini were strong, innovative forces, sweeping many an established older work away with their musical and dramatic force.

While companies downtown plunged into bankruptcy, the Ravinia Opera offered longer and more elaborate seasons. Its survival from 1912 to 1931 can be attributed to three things. Until its final crisis, it had secure financial backing and good artistic leadership. It had a loyal audience. Most of all, it had charm. The ambience of the place is suggested, but not duplicated, by performances today. It was something totally different from any conventional opera

house. Claudia Cassidy, whose career as a Chicago music critic extended from the 1920s to 1990, wrote retrospectively in 1985, "Ravinia Opera in its bosky intimacy . . . was the real thing in high style with a special flair for the intimate, the instinctively elegant, and, on certain nights, the indelibly combustible. The special luxury was the rapport."[1] Otto H. Kahn, one of the great patrons of opera in the early decades of the century, observed that if Ravinia were plucked up from where it is and set down somewhere in Central Europe, people would make pilgrimages from all over the civilized world to visit it.[2]

The park was the ideal place to experience the magic of a perfect summer night. In Europe the principal summer festivals are dedicated to high art, *Kultur.* Here the evocative power of the music was immediately intensified by a setting that radiated the spirit of romance. It was a place to be in love, or to fall in love, or to remember when you last fell in love, or

Louis Eckstein

hope to fall in love again. This could be recalled in the early years of the present Ravinia Festival, founded to provide the Chicago Symphony with a summer home. When I first encountered the Old Pavilion in 1938, three years after Eckstein's death and two years after the beginning of the symphonic festival, it was unchanged except that the blue velvet curtains were gone and the stage now held a concert set. The old ambience was intact. The gateways still read Ravinia Opera.

The central figure in the new organization was Louis Eckstein, a Chicago businessman with a home nearby. Eckstein told his friends he had once been a musician, although his fortune was based on a number of ventures, primarily publishing and real estate. Within a short time, Ravinia became his other self. A strongly inner-directed person, he preferred to run his own opera company with the help of a few congenial friends, and the repertory that evolved probably represents his personal preferences. The strengths and weaknesses of the festival both go back to the fact that essentially it was a one-man show. A place on the board of the floundering Chicago Grand Opera Company downtown is unlikely to have been attractive to him. Cassidy quotes him as saying, "Some men have a yacht. I have Ravinia."[3] At Ravinia, Cassidy recalls, he played the *grand seigneur,* "welcoming us all as he stood beside the bed of Rosy Morn' petunias (in front of the Old Pavilion)—dark jacket, white trousers, straw boater, gold headed cane."[4]

And Ravinia had railroads, although the original bond between the park and electric trains was the stronger tie to success. Even the improved highways of the 1920s would not have invited, or permitted, a great influx of Chicago patrons in automobiles, and Northwestern Station was on the far west side of the Loop, beyond the walking distance of many operagoers. The electric train was close at hand. In 1916, renamed the Chicago, North Shore, and Milwaukee Railroad, the electric line became part of the utilities empire of Samuel Insull. One of his first moves to develop its potential was to acquire the right to use the tracks of the Chicago elevated railway, and in 1919 there was a North Shore Line station by the elevated structure on Adams Street at Wabash Avenue in the Chicago Loop. You could board the train as far south as 63rd Street. Listeners from the south side of the city could easily reach Ravinia, while the northern extension of the line invited participation from those living as far away as Milwaukee.

Sir Thomas Beecham said of Ravinia in a later day that "it was the only railway station with a resident orchestra." There was, for many years, an abundance of trains, and they made noise. More important, they ruled the schedule. During the years of the opera festival, although the program might be filled with advertisements for automobiles, the electric train remained supreme. The North Shore Line special back to Chicago could not leave much later than 11:00 p.m., so the opera had to be over by then. This meant cuts, sometimes ingenious snippets here and there, but often massive deletions such as the second act of *Lohengrin.* Purists today would be up in arms, but in the middle of the century, even at the Metropolitan Opera in New York (where train schedules had no influence on artistic policy) large cuts were accepted.

A siding at the park held a special North Shore Line train for those returning to the city and intermediate points. Orchestra members who hastened to change their clothes and grab their instruments might jump on board in the final moments before it began a quick, clean, inexpensive run to the city. So it remained through the Ravinia Opera seasons and the early decades of the later symphonic festival. Service to the park ended in 1955, and the railway ended all operations in 1963. With the completion of expressways to the city in 1961, Ravinia belonged primarily to those with automobiles, although Metra trains on the old Chicago and Northwestern tracks still stop at the park in the summer months.

From 1913 onward, Ravinia may be regarded as an evolving opera festival, moreover, a festival of a distinctively American type. European summer music is heard in a theater under conditions very similar to the winter season. At Wagner's shrine in Bayreuth, Germany, you wear formal dress and assume a manner appropriate to a confrontation with serious art. Outdoor summer music is an American innovation, based on the expectation of an essentially friendly climate and the belief that the special qualities of a summer night should be exploited and—if possible—enhanced. You may dress casually in the park. You are there to enjoy yourself.

In 1913 Ravinia described its offerings as grand opera and concerts. The Chicago Symphony Orchestra was engaged for the summer (although it is doubtful that the full winter personnel was present), with Attilio Parelli in charge. Ruth St. Denis offered *Dances of the East,* and intermissions were timed so that one could view a film in the theater. A typical work was

Parelli's own opus, *A Lovers' Quarrel,* which was not merely in one act but probably could be played in less than an hour. It shared the bill with the St. Denis dance program and short selections of light concert fare such as the *Poet and Peasant* overture. Right up to the final concert program on August 23, 1931, Ravinia orchestra programs largely avoided longer works, especially the symphonies and concertos familiar from the winter symphony programs. They offered instead the kind of bland musical diet the Boston Pops orchestra performed before Arthur Fiedler became its conductor in 1930. Stock sometimes rebelled—for example, on July 7, 1915, he played the Beethoven *Pastoral* Symphony in its entirety, but such departures were rare. When the orchestra began its Ravinia concerts in June 1936 with a Beethoven symphony and music by Debussy and Stravinsky, it was offering a completely new level of programming.

When a longer opera was offered, it still had to be short enough to fit the limited time. In 1913 *Cavalleria rusticana* apparently was once more sung uncut, and Parelli's score was given in its entirety. Leoncavallo's *Pagliacci* was again represented by the first act alone, although the program book thoughtfully gives a synopsis of the missing second act. *Madama Butterfly* became, for the first and last time, a serial, with three performances of act 1 and three later nights given to acts 2 and 3. Two scenes were all you heard of *Lucia* or *Thaïs.* Flotow's *Martha* was reduced to the third act. The Prison and *Miserere* Scenes gave the listener all he was to hear of Verdi's *Il trovatore.* Once more the Garden Scene exemplified *Faust,* and the Nile Scene became the essence of *Aida. Lohengrin* now included music from the second act, and *La bohème, The Tales of Hoffmann,* and *Rigoletto* were given in dramatically abridged form. A Ravinia idiosyncrasy was that "Hoffmann" was always spelled in English with one *n.* Big cuts at Ravinia can often be detected from the program books; small cuts are impossible to establish. Some of the music used at Ravinia probably came from the library of the opera company downtown. There is no way, when examining the orchestral parts, to determine cuts made by Ravinia and those made by other productions. Whatever orchestral material Ravinia might have owned apparently was destroyed, along with most of the records of the festival, in 1957.

It would be impossible under the union rules of today to offer a schedule of the type Ravinia demanded. In 1913 there were afternoon concert programs with changing repertory every day. Thursday had a children's concert, a Ravinia tradition that continued to the end. There were also seven evening performances, usually combining an operatic excerpt with more concert music. There may have been some rotation of musicians, but the orchestra never had a day off, working probably for less than $100 a week. Somewhere along the way there had to be a few rehearsals. In 1914 Monday concerts occasionally yielded to rehearsal time, and in 1915 they were gone. In 1916 Monday became a concert night rather than an opera evening, a tradition that continued with occasional variation until 1927. Tuesday afternoon concerts ended in 1915; the Wednesday events were last heard in 1916. In 1917 Thursday remained a children's matinée, and Friday afternoon became student artists' day. Afternoon concerts on Saturdays and Sundays remained until 1924; Sunday concerts survived to the end. Stock played his Saturday night popular concerts in Orchestra Hall without rehearsal into the 1940s, and I suspect Ravinia musicians always did a lot of sight reading. They might respond that it was better than six shows a day in a motion picture theater or, worse, a vaudeville or burlesque house.

The singers and the solo dancer appeared almost nightly. In 1913 all the singers were new except Kreidler, who sang the prologue and Silvio in *Pagliacci.* Florence Mulford, Phil Fein, and William Schuster all shared Kreidler's ties to the Metropolitan Opera. Eckstein's casting was still making use of American voices and Midwestern talent, but he was also beginning to see the Met as a reservoir of artists, many of whom welcomed summer engagements. The cultivation of this opportunity produced, in time, a fairly stable Ravinia company. In the end some of the most celebrated artists of the Metropolitan Opera saw Ravinia as a summer home.

Typical of these was Louis D'Angelo, who was to sing at Ravinia up to the final performances. He joined the company in 1914. Three years later he began a long affiliation with the Met. Kreidler and Schuster remained as other representatives of the New York house. Eckstein continued his search for the right sopranos. Of the new women in 1914, the soprano Beatrice La Palme survived, to reappear in 1915. Cordelia Latham was the chosen mezzo. All the tenors of 1914 failed to return, but Kreidler and Schuster were back. The summer of 1914 introduced *Carmen* to the Ravinia repertory in a production that showed neither the beginning nor the ending of the work—it offered just the two middle acts. Eventually, in 1916, act 4 was added, but right up to the last performance in August 1931 Ravinia's *Carmen* lacked the first act. The reason is easy enough to explain: Ravinia could not muster the choral forces and supernumeraries the work required. But think of it musically: sixteen productions in which neither the "Habanera" nor "Seguidilla" was sung!

A complete listing of the works, performance dates, and cast lists for the full span of Ravinia opera performances from 1912 to 1931 has been published in my *Annals of the Ravinia Opera* within four issues of *Opera Quarterly* 13, no. 3, through 14, no. 2 (1997–98). In those pages I demand that a listed Ravinia opera performance offer at least 40% of the score.

The repertory for 1915 was notable for the demise of tabloid opera. Of seventeen works produced, sixteen make the 40% level (or better). The one exception, Wolf-Ferrari's *The Jewels of the Madonna,* was represented by act 2, the only music from this score ever sung at Ravinia. It retained this truncated form through its final performances in 1929. Basically the 1915 works are repetitions of music established and accepted in previous seasons. The most interesting exception is that the 1915 repertory contains Balfe's *The Bohemian Girl,* one of the incorrigibly popular nineteenth-century operas that had fallen before new verismo works. It received three performances and three more in 1916, then was heard no more in Highland Park. The ears that once were delighted by "I dreamt I dwelt in marble halls" now rejoiced to "Un bel dì." A grand moment in opera that Ravinia had felt unequal to staging was the *Aida* Triumphal Scene. Two brave efforts centering on the ballet were made in July 1915, but apparently they were considered unsuccessful.

The distinctive thing about 1916 was that Ravinia was now functioning more or less like a traditional opera company. Six works were heard in their entirety, and twelve were given on the 40% level or above. The only fragment was the one that was to last, act 2 of *The Jewels of the Madonna.*

Ravinia now had a conductor of real stature, Richard Hageman, who directed opera at the Metropolitan in seasons from 1908 to 1937. Nine of the productions went to him. He also was affiliated with Chicago Musical College as a professor of voice. His career ended in Hollywood, where he composed film music. Two tenors, Orville Harrold and Morgan Kingston, came from the Met, as did the baritones D'Angelo and Millo Picco and the basses Schuster and Henri Scott.

At the end of its first five years Ravinia had largely defined its repertory, and the works that delighted its early audiences returned summer after summer to the end. The pattern was dominated by the most popular operas of the previous century. Verdi, for example, was known for *Aida, Rigoletto, La traviata* and *Il trovatore.* His predecessors Donizetti and Rossini were each represented by one opera, *Lucia di Lammermoor* and *The Barber of Seville,* respectively. German opera comprised Wagner's *Lohengrin* and two works sung in Italian, Wolf-Ferrari's *The Secret of Suzanne* and Flotow's *Martha.* There were five French operas: Gounod's *Faust,* Bizet's *Carmen,* Offenbach's *The Tales of Hoffmann,* and Massenet's *Manon* and *Thaïs.* And then there was the new music, verismo works by Leoncavallo, Mascagni, and Puccini.

In 1917 Hageman was joined by Gennaro Papi, who had made his debut at the Met in 1915 and was to conduct there regularly until 1941. He remained with the Ravinia Opera until the final curtain, and his ability to produce dramatic, musically exciting performances under summer working conditions was a central element in the success of the company. This time there was no big turnover in the artist listings. Thirteen of the twenty-one singers had appeared the previous summer. Significantly, Eckstein was now getting the kind of sopranos he needed for maximum effect. Edith Mason, who was to be a major attraction at the Met from 1915 to 1936, opened the summer season as Nedda in *Pagliacci,* with Kingston as Canio, Picco as Tonio, and D'Angelo as Silvio. Later she was to be heard in *Faust* (with Harrold), *Carmen* (with Marguerite Bariza in the title role and Kingston as Don José), *Madama Butterfly* (with Giordano), and *La bohème* (with Kingston). Florence Macbeth, one of the prizes of the Chicago opera downtown, was heard as Lucia, with Harrold. Marie Rappold, a Met stalwart since 1905, was Leonora in *Il trovatore,* with Kingston. Roughly half the company was now imported from New York. Two French operas—both nineteenth-century staples—were added to the repertory: Thomas's *Mignon* and another Gounod, *Romeo and Juliet*—both with Macbeth.

In an inspired move, Eckstein brought Claudia Muzio to Ravinia for the summer of 1918, immediately following her Met debut. She got the opening night, *Aida* (with Kingston), and largely dominated the summer with later appearances in *Il trovatore, Pagliacci, Tosca, Faust, Cavalleria rusticana, Manon, La bohème, L'amore dei tre re, Madama Butterfly,* and even *The Secret of Suzanne.* Harrold was her tenor in the Gounod and Massenet works; otherwise she was paired with Kingston through the summer. Mason was back briefly for two performances in late August. There was no war of the prima donnas. Whatever restrictions World War I possibly imposed at Ravinia had vanished by the summer of 1919. Prohibition might have come early to Ravinia. Beer advertisements disappeared from the program in 1916, replaced by the images of two gentlemen clinking glasses of a "wholesome, refreshing, thirst quenching, non-alcoholic" libation called Pablo. "You can't tell the difference" (a thoroughly questionable claim) heads the page. Other pages in later summers hail Buck, "the nippy, foamy-flavor rich cereal beverage" that was unlikely to put Al Capone's illegal Cicero brewery out of business.

The most conspicuous thing about the 1919 artists roster is that it was not only headed by one of the monumental stars of the Metropolitan, Antonio Scotti, but practically the entire company was made up of singers who were working, or were to work, in the Broadway house. Of twenty-one artists, only three never sang in the New York theater. Eckstein had a finely crafted mixture of established people and new voices. In addition to stars such as Scotti, Florence Easton, and Léon Rothier, there was, for example, Philine Falco, who was to make her Met debut in 1927 after distinguished summers at Ravinia.

L'Oracolo had been written by Franco Leoni (1864–1949) for Scotti; he sang the première at the Covent Garden Opera, London, in 1905, then starred in the New York première at the Metropolitan in 1915. Scotti sang it at the Met for thirty-five years, and the work was his through to the final performance in 1933, which came to Ravinia as a production of the Scotti Opera Company, with a Metropolitan cast of Easton, Ingram, Harrold, Rothier, D'Angelo, and Derman. Following Met practice, it was billed with *Pagliacci* for its three performances; the final one brought Scotti as Tonio. Many felt that Scotti's greatest role was Scarpia, and it is ironic that in a summer with three performances of *Tosca* he never appeared in that opera at Ravinia.

In 1921 Mario Chamlee and Charles Hackett, leading tenors of the Metropolitan, began their long association with Ravinia, and Margery Maxwell joined the sopranos. Claire Dux and Queena Mario came in 1922, along with Giuseppe Danise and Vincente Ballester. Tito Schipa, since 1919 one of the great stars of Chicago opera, made his Ravinia debut in 1923, along with another stalwart from the Auditorium, Désiré Defrère. Armand Tokatyan, Giacomo Lauri-Volpi, Elisabeth Rethberg, and Ina Bourskaya, some of the brightest stars of the Met stage, added Ravinia to their triumphs. More Met celebrities followed in 1924: Lucrezia Bori, Giovanni Martinelli, and Mario

Basiola. Rosa Raisa, a prize of the Loop company, was at Ravinia in 1925, as was Elvira de Hidalgo. Fausto Cleva was the chorus master. Ruth Page, who was later to perform the same services for the Lyric, took over the Ravinia ballet in 1926, and Edward Johnson joined the roster of tenors. The young Gladys Swarthout came to Ravinia in 1927. In 1928 Yvonne Gall joined the company, and Defrère became stage director for the season. This group of artists carried Ravinia through its final season. There was talent in abundance, and it was the kind that does not come cheap. Moore remarked, "Mr. Eckstein makes a practice of engaging the most famous artists in the most lavish manner."[5] Ticket prices were now up to $3.50 for a reserved seat.

In its first five years Ravinia presented music from twenty-one operas, and all but two of these scores were represented in more than one year. Eleven more works were added in the next five summers, and ten more followed in the years 1921–26. At the end, after twenty seasons, Ravinia had offered fifty-four operas in whole or part, and only eight of these had received a single production. The Ravinia repertory was remarkably stable. Some 40% of the works produced were heard in half the Ravinia seasons or more. A core of eighteen operas, a third of the repertory, was heard in at least 70% of the seasons. Seven operas, *Aida, Cavalleria rusticana, Faust, Il trovatore, La bohème, Madama Butterfly,* and *Martha,* appeared in some form every summer.

It is fair to assume that Eckstein was self-indulgent and mixed a sense of box office values with his personal taste. The glaring omission in the Ravinia repertory is German opera. Wagner and Strauss demanded larger orchestras than Ravinia normally employed, but why no Mozart when he was being represented regularly by the companies downtown? I assume the simplest answer is that Eckstein didn't like Mozart. And, in a similar vein, apparently he didn't like Verdi's *Falstaff.* But why, with Martinelli in his company, he never offered Verdi's *Otello* is incomprehensible.

His innovations are interesting. Some reflect the fashions of the companies downtown, but some show real imagination in seeing possibilities for Ravinia. Henri Rabaud's *Mârouf,* for example, a failure at the Metropolitan, was a success in Ravinia's more intimate setting. Deems Taylor's *Peter Ibbetson* sold out its six performances.

Although the Depression undoubtedly played a part in the demise of the Ravinia Opera, it is questionable whether it was the primary factor. In retrospect, the

Ravinia Opera seems to have failed for essentially the same reason as its predecessors downtown, the Chicago Grand Opera Company of 1910–1913 and the Chicago Opera Association of 1915–1921. The Chicago Civic Opera was founded in 1922 and, like Ravinia, became a casualty in 1931. In all four cases, maintaining the company required a higher level of subsidy than the community could provide, and that high subsidy level arose from the disparity between production costs and box office income. The festival was devoured by a dragon of backstage expenses.

By comparison, the Metropolitan Opera today, in a seven-month season, offers some two dozen operas. The most adventuresome, such as Glass's *The Voyage* and Weill's *Mahagonny,* nonetheless will be heard at least five times. The most popular, such as *La bohème,* can have as many as sixteen performances. This gives a rough average of nine performances for each score, thirty-six thousand seats sold, generating enough box office revenue to balance the books on a practical level of subsidy. Ravinia in its final summer presented thirty-five works, an outrageous amount of repertory. Twenty percent of these scores were prepared for a single performance, a certain way to generate a large deficit. Of the thirty-five productions in the 1931 season, only ten were offered three or more times. By any Harvard Business School standard, this was bad management. The problem arose from the compulsion to keep the house filled and the belief that this demanded frequent changes of repertory. Eckstein, like most of the Chicago opera managers of his day, apparently was terrified that he was going to run out of audience and was convinced that the loss produced by high production costs was not as serious as income lost from unsold tickets. This is a telling fallacy. A loss is a loss, and the wise manager chooses the smallest loss he must sustain. In 1931 the deficit was some $280,000. About $85,000 came from Eckstein's friends, but he paid the rest and—I am sure, reluctantly—turned off the lights. He could have increased his available subsidy by opening up the organization and recruiting guarantors, or he could have enlarged his public. But he took neither of those routes.

How well did Eckstein know his audience? He felt he was dealing with a core group of six or seven thousand dedicated patrons, and he had to keep them coming back. What he had done, in fact, was make the affluent, well-educated suburban public aware that opera was theater in its most exciting form. These people did not demand an annual repetition of all their favorite scores, and they were open to new things, as the success of *Peter Ibbetson* indicates. One of Eckstein's weaknesses was his low-key advertising policy. In its early years Ravinia received minimal attention in the Chicago press. Downtown music critics rarely reviewed the performances. When the celebrated singers arrived in the 1920s, the critics arrived with them. But to the end, Eckstein made poor use of the opportunities provided by the media.

In 1930 Moore said, "[Ravinia] has the potent achievement of fine art; it has the informal, comfortable atmosphere of a country club; it competes with no other operatic institution on earth."[6] As Moore wrote this, Ravinia was beginning to draw a considerable number of visitors from other cities. Unfortunately, in another year it was to vanish.

A suburban dweller of 1920, looking downtown, saw opera dominated by the social-register set—old money, first families. The board was headed by a McCormick flanked by a Dawes and a Field. Going to the opera was a ceremony. You dressed up, took your place in your box, and you were seen. Ravinia's ambience was very different and far more inviting. I can document this from my own family. My mother and her sister, neither of whom would have dreamed of setting foot in Harold McCormick's theater, began their operagoing at Ravinia, enjoyed it, and became potential public for future producers who offered opera in a congenial setting.

The middle class has been the primary support of the live performing arts since the late eighteenth century. The aristocracy might occupy the boxes, but it was the middle class that filled the house and made the enterprise economically feasible. When the Lyric Opera of Chicago began in 1954, eight years after the demise of the last resident Chicago opera company, it was locked in the same pattern that brought disaster to all its predecessors. In 1955 *Madama Butterfly* with Maria Callas could not be counted on to sell more than 10,500 tickets, filling the house three times. The ratio of production costs to ticket sales still pointed to long-term bankruptcy. The solution was to enlarge the potential audience, to sell, not ten thousand, but forty thousand tickets. The new market was the suburban public, the audience Eckstein to a very large degree created and diligently cultivated for twenty summers. He was a visionary, a pioneer, and, in some ways, rather like a prospector who finds the gold mine but is unable to tap its fullest resources. Ravinia failed, but it pointed the way to success.

7

A New Theater

1929–1947

Ironically, Chicago built two opera houses just as international practices in staging called for a new type of design. The Auditorium had a deep stage but practically no offstage areas to the right and left of the proscenium. It was intended primarily for scenery that disappeared into a stage loft when no longer required. But the opening of the new century brought the introduction of solid scenery pieces that had to be moved offstage and stored. The nostalgia-minded insisted the Auditorium was one of the city's great buildings (it still is today) and therefore remained a perfectly appropriate home for a Chicago opera company. Indeed, when restored to use in 1967, there were those who felt that it should again house opera in the city. The proposal was completely unrealistic.

The Auditorium might have remained in use for more than forty years had Chicago opera been in the hands of someone other than Samuel Insull. The new Civic Opera House was his distinctive creation. Originally, the new theater was to have more seats than the Auditorium but fewer boxes, an unpopular change. Insull liked the idea of combining the theater with commercial spaces, but he wanted business rentals rather than stores. The theater was to be part of a huge office building costing some $20 million. The new opera house was not to face the fruit and vegetable market there at the time, but a European-type plaza. "It cannot be purely monumental," Insull insisted. "It must be commercial, not only self-supporting, but profitable." Insull sold $10 million worth of stock in the project and borrowed the rest of his budget from the Metropolitan Life Insurance Company, confident that rents from the office space would pay the mortgage and subsidize the opera company.

Such plans were possible because the location, between the west side of the El Loop and the river, was filled with nondescript buildings; a site would not be expensive. Market Street real estate, by downtown standards, was cheap, and the area was crying for renewal, which the opera house would initiate. Although the new theater was on the direct route suburban commuters followed between the LaSalle Street financial district and the Chicago and North Western railway station, audiences in the early seasons complained that the new opera house was far removed from the civilization of the eastern side of the Loop. One of the first steps to improve things was the construction of Wacker Drive after the market had been moved westward. But the plaza never materialized. For many years the opera house faced storage tracks of the elevated railway and the home of Hearst's local newspaper empire. Both have vanished.

The Civic Opera House proved to be a glorious expression of the Chicago of its day. The building, with its tower, rose to forty-two stories. Moore saw this as "an enormous civic poem," but its financial difficulties in the Depression years left the noble vision of business supporting opera unfulfilled.

If you like art of the 1920s, as those of us born in that decade often do, the building would never fail to impress. If you didn't—and there have always been opinions of this type—it was gaudy and pretentious. Seen from the west, the building had the appearance of a huge chair, which some called Insull's Throne. Inside it was a gilded marble palace with a grand foyer encircled by a balcony at the level of the box seats, the two floors united by grand staircases worthy of any major European theater. Unlike many European houses, inside the theater one was not especially conscious of the boxes, and there were twenty-one fewer of them than at the Auditorium. Moreover, they were located under the balcony and provided

The Civic Opera House, photographed from the rear, showing "Insull's Throne"

limited opportunities for display, an agonizing discovery for former dwellers of the Golden Horseshoe. There were 112 fewer seats than at the Auditorium, and, of the 3,472 seats in place in 1929, 48% were on the main floor. (Only 27% of the Auditorium's seating was similarly located.)

A second theater, the Civic, on the Washington Street end of the building, seated 878, a size that later in the century proved to be too small for most commercial musical or theatrical events. As the century ended it was absorbed into the larger theater to provide additional rehearsal and backstage space.

There was an orchestra pit that could hold 120 musicians—large enough to accommodate Wagner and Strauss orchestras—and, as circumstances required, it moved up and down. The stage machinery, state of the art for its day, was still functioning after a fashion in the Lyric years. Since the scenery of the older Chicago companies was still to be used, the new house had one of the highest stage lofts in the world (140 feet), and drops for an entire season could be hung and lowered as required. Ample space was provided for costumes, wigs, and props to be stored and, when necessary, manufactured. A large rehearsal room duplicated the stage. The Auditorium was lacking nearly all of these amenities, although by 1880s standards its stage machinery was impressive. The magician Harry Houdini, who frequently rented the place, liked to disappear into the stage on one side of the proscenium and pop up through a trap door on the other.

"If," Moore recalls, "during the first few years of the Chicago Opera there was ever a time when a change of lighting was made on its proper cue, neither memory nor record records the fact. It was nearly a perfect score of errors."[1] In the Civic Opera House the prompter and the lighting technician sat side-by-side in a booth at the stage apron, and a highly sophisticated lighting system could be controlled instantaneously from a switchboard.

The stage, 120 feet wide at the proscenium, had generous storage areas on both sides and, except on rare occasions when a set of great depth was used, the rear. There were 75 feet from the steel curtain to the rear wall. Solid scenery pieces, provided they were not too large, could be rolled away and kept for their next use. But here the hall quickly fell behind the times, for it became the tendency to use scenery pieces of increasingly larger size. By the final decades of the twentieth century many productions could not be borrowed from other companies because there was no doorway large

enough to get them into the theater. And once inside, they took up space that might be required for other works in the current repertory. Eventually the problem was solved by creating a new doorway and moving the backstage wall to Washington Street.

The traditional shape of a European opera house was a horseshoe, a large main floor rising from the orchestra pit to the rear entrances and encircling boxes or, on the upper levels, shallow balconies. At the very top a deeper balcony might extend to the rear. Theaters of this type might be found all over the continent, usually with a seating capacity of about two thousand. They were considered acoustically satisfactory, and voices of less than monumental strength could be heard effectively.

The most important theater of this type in the United States, although it was larger than most of its European counterparts, was the original (1883) Metropolitan Opera House in New York. In Chicago, most theaters built between the 1860s and the close of the 1880s were basically of this design, Crosby's Opera House being the most successful.

The two opera houses standing in Chicago today, the Auditorium (1889) and the Civic Opera House (1929), are fundamentally rectangular rather than horseshoe-shaped. Their architectural lineage goes back to the original Gewandhaus in Leipzig, which was built for symphonic rather than operatic music. The two surviving rectangular concert halls deeply influenced by their acoustical principles are the Vienna Musikvereinssaal and Symphony Hall in Boston, Massachusetts. The Vienna hall is often praised as the finest in the world.

Symphony Hall is the masterpiece of the first great American acoustician, Walter C. Sabine, of Harvard, who felt the curved walls of the horseshoe-shaped theater provided undesirable reflections and concentrations of sound while failing to reflect sound from the stage and orchestra pit to the seats in the rear of the theater. The Auditorium had a horseshoe of boxes set within the rectangle, and this tended to mask the basic shape of the structure. The Civic Opera House has always looked unequivocally rectangular and long. On the main floor it is, I am confident, the longest opera house in the world. However, the rectangle tapers toward the stage, and a deep proscenium provides architectural enhancement of sound from the stage and the pit.

The architects of the new opera house recognized the fact that, although the Auditorium was dated in many ways, it remained a superlative acoustical environment for opera. Experience proved that for recitals and orchestra concerts the stage loft had to be blocked by an appropriate acoustical reflector on stage. Thus modified, it became one of the few halls that functioned effectively for both opera and symphonic music. Opera houses must not have so much reverberation that the words sung cannot be heard clearly, while symphonic music is best when hall resonance prolongs tones by two seconds or more.

The objective was to build a new hall with essentially the same acoustical properties of the old. Paul E. Sabine, following a family tradition of acoustical research, was engaged as a consultant. For the architects—Graham, Anderson, Probst and White—the ceiling of the Auditorium, which rose in stepped, shallow arches from 45 feet at the proscenium to 65 feet at the rear of the hall, served to eliminate echoes and standing waves; it also served as a huge sound reflector with some surfaces projecting direct sound to the balcony and gallery seats and others providing diffused sound to the theater as a whole. Although the ceiling of the new opera house was flat rather than curved, a similar stepped pattern from the proscenium to the rear was adopted, and the side walls were divided into equal bays.

Basic Sabine principles demanded that the side walls be broken surfaces. Sound coming to them would be reflected or absorbed, but it would follow a different path from that of its origination. A combination of decorated surfaces and draperies achieved this result, an important consideration, since boxes and balconies were set quite far to the rear of the hall. It was felt that, as in the Auditorium, the quality of the sound in the upper parts of the hall was more than satisfactory. If there was an acoustical problem anywhere, it was on the main floor under the boxes, where the side walls reflected less sound than had been calculated.

When put into service, the Civic Opera House proved to be a splendid hall, but it was significantly different from the Auditorium. The latter remained a warm, resonant concert room, while the new theater was dry, with about 1.4 seconds reverberation time as Sabine measured it on completion. Most troublesome for singers was that the rear wall was so distant that nothing ever came back to the stage. It was like singing out-of-doors. Experience with the hall made it possible to learn how much voice was required for a desired effect, but newcomers had a tendency to sing louder than necessary.

November 4, 1929. The Civic Opera House opens with a production of *Aida*, starring Rosa Raisa *(far left)*. This same set was used when Zinka Milanov sang the role here thirteen years later.

The Auditorium, for all its glories, was a dark hall. The Civic Opera House was bright and new and filled with light, a dazzling transition into a new day. No one expected it to be in use for more than a century, although with recent remodeling there is now every likelihood that it will. In 1929 the year 2000 seemed very far away.

Insull, aware of the orations that had opened Crosby's Opera House and the Auditorium, forbade any speeches on opening night. The audience, which had paid $6 for a seat in the front of the main floor and $5 for a place at the rear (1870s prices), produced $16,500 at the box office. No one could recall a more glittering throng: men in formal dress surrounded by women adorned with the finest jewels and most fashionable gowns affluence could provide. No one would have guessed that less than a week before, the stock market had plunged into the depths.

This audience was clearly more curious about the theater than the music it was to hear, although the performance, *Aida,* with Rosa Raisa in the title role, Charles Marshall as Radames, Cyrena Van Gordon as Amneris, and Cesare Formichi as Amonasro, promised to be a festive event. Giorgio Polacco conducted.

Insull stated his principles in the program book. "Merely to build a beautiful house and give it the best equipment possible was not the fundamental idea of this undertaking. That idea was, and still is, to give opera an abiding place in Chicago, and, through the Chicago Music Foundation . . . make Chicago a music center worthy of its place in the world's affairs." The opera house had been given to the foundation as a gift, and income from the building was to liquidate debts and underwrite operatic production. This grand design lasted nearly twenty years, but Insull did not live to see its demise; his utilities empire collapsed in 1932. As he left the scene, a friend, thinking of the opera house, assured him, "You've built a monument that they can't tear down."

This is not the place to discuss or judge Insull's business principles or practices (no court found him guilty of wrongdoing), but one cannot question his love of opera and his vision and skill as a builder. He spent his final years in Europe. Nine years after the opening of the opera house, in July 1938, he died at seventy-nine of a heart attack in a Paris subway train. He was nicely dressed and, according to the police report, had eight cents in his pocket. Ironically, for many years there was no likeness of him in the theater. Eventually justice was done, and a portrait emerged from obscurity to be hung on the box floor.

Looking back through the history of the twentieth century, it is difficult to imagine a worse year to inaugurate a new operatic venture than 1929. The Roaring Twenties had ended with the crash of the stock market, and the nation plunged into a three-year ride into the depths. The Great Depression was to last a decade. Hardly had recovery started than war flamed up in Asia and then in Europe. Those of us who lived through these days, clinging tenaciously to cultural values, needed more than ever the nourishment of great art.

The victim of difficult times, the first fifteen seasons in the new Civic Opera House were the least distinguished in the history of Chicago opera and therefore need not be treated in great detail. Twice there was no season from a local company. An occasional bright hour was produced by exceptional singing, but from 1933 to 1946 resident Chicago opera on many nights swung from mediocrity to disaster. It was the longest, bleakest period in the cultural history of the city, a wasteland produced by the interaction of multiple causes. There was the brutal economic reality of the Depression, with banks failing, households pauperized, and a legion of unemployed that came to include many respectable middle-class families. After 1939 war prevented the international exchange of singers, and the artists who came to the United States as a result of the rise of fascism invariably gravitated to New York.

The Chicago Symphony, although imperiled once or twice, survived because its matinées were an established institution to serenade the wives and daughters of the hog butchers and steel makers. Sustained by a board that was really a gentlemen's club of the first families, the trustees kept costs to a minimum (the orchestra rarely traveled farther than Milwaukee) and generally could raise any necessary funds from within their own circle. The conductor, the beloved Dr. Frederick Stock, had no aspirations to either the salary or the fame of such eastern rivals as Toscanini and Stokowski. His death in 1942 introduced the greatest period of artistic crisis in the history of the orchestra. Distinguished European conductors were in the United States and available, but in the eyes of the symphony trustees nearly all of them were Jewish and hence socially unacceptable in a Midwestern setting where antisemitism was deeply ingrained in the upper levels of society.

Opera rested on a far more perilous foundation. The audience was small, and the affluent patrons who supported the early Chicago companies had largely vanished from the scene. Moreover, its great star attraction was leaving. Mary Garden made her exit at the close of the 1930/31 series. When it was announced in February 1932 that there would be no Chicago opera season the following autumn, she declared that Insull had killed opera in Chicago. Newly allied with Arthur Judson and Columbia Concerts, she was gone and, more to the point, so was the Garden fan club. There was no generation of young socialites eager to take their place. Harold Mc-Cormick was no longer prepared to write big checks. Insull's empire collapsed a few weeks after the demise of his opera company.

For those accustomed to Lyric Opera financial statements—even those of the early years—Chicago opera in the late 1930s and 1940s was operating on shoestring budgets and failing for sums that in a later day would hardly have paid Carol Fox's expense account. Attendance was low. Money was tight. Quality was a luxury one could rarely afford. On this basis it was difficult to sustain an audience (let alone build one), and the astonishing thing is that opera survived as long as it did. As it is, the Chicago company was reorganized three times.

The Chicago Civic Opera Company lasted ten years, the most long-lived of the resident opera producers in the period 1910–1946. It bridged the move from the Auditorium to the Civic Opera House and bequeathed to its successors scenery, furniture, props, wigs, and costumes that made the Lyric Theater possible in 1954. The three companies that succeeded it in the years 1933–1946 were all artistic and economic failures. The key to the situation can be seen in table 1.

What is immediately clear is that after 1932 the length of the opera seasons was dramatically curtailed and the public was offered, at the most, about half the number of performances staged in earlier years. The 1944 season was a quarter of the length of that of 1930, but the number of works produced did not decline proportionately. There were thirty operas presented in 1930, fifteen in 1945. Most of them were heard twice. Two were given three stagings, and two more were sung only once. The ratio of production costs to box office income, even if the production was haphazard, was a sure formula for financial ruin. The cost of preparing operas became ridiculously out of proportion to their possible box office earnings. In short, the companies required a higher level of subsidy than the community was able (or willing) to supply.

TABLE 1—NUMBER OF PRODUCTIONS AND PERFORMANCES BY CHICAGO OPERA COMPANIES, BY SEASON

Company	Season	Productions	Performances
Chicago Civic Opera	1929/30	32	81
	1930/31	33	90
	1931/32	27	83
	1932/33	0	0
Chicago Grand Opera	1933/34	18	26
	1934/35	21	43
Chicago City Opera	1935	20	29
	1936	28	36
	1937	33	46
	1938	30	46
	1939	27	44
Chicago Opera	1940	23	37
	1941	19	25
	1942	18	27
	1943	0	0
	1944	12	23
	1945	15	30
	1946	15	30

Mary Garden did not like the new Civic Opera House. According to her autobiography, "When I looked into that long black hole I said, 'Oh no!' It was no real opera house at all, more like a convention hall. We had absolutely no communication with the public." Other singers would deny that. Garden's dislike of Insull did not improve matters.

She sang in the Civic Opera House for two seasons but brought nothing new to her first appearances in the new house. Her repertory was all staples: *L'amore dei tre re, Louise, Le Jongleur de Notre-Dame, Thaïs,* and *Pelléas et Mélisande.*

The 1929 season had, of course, been planned before the crash and thus, except for the new house, greatly resembled those that had immediately preceded it. *Aida* had been a splendid beginning. Mascagni's *Iris* proved a worthy vehicle for Edith Mason, but it remained an opera more admired by singers than the public, which vastly preferred to hear Claudia Muzio in *La traviata*. Muzio was back in *Il trovatore;* Raisa sang *Norma* and *Tosca*. Frida Leider was heard as Isolde, with Alexander Kipnis as King Marke and Theodore Stranck, whose local career proved short, as Tristan. Leider, Maria Olszewska, Mason, and Kipnis were the principals in *Der Rosenkavalier,* and Leider was Brünnhilde in *Die Walküre.*

Impressive as the opening of the Civic Opera House had been, there still was opera in the Auditorium in the 1929/30 season. The response of 1929 ensured that in February 1930 Hurok's German Grand Opera Company was back with the *Ring, The Flying Dutchman, Tristan und Isolde,* and—for contrast—Mozart's *Don Giovanni,* sung in German as *Don Juan.* Johanna Gadski, Sonia Sharnova, and Carl Jorn returned. Gotthold Ditten was the principal baritone, and Carl Braun the principal bass. Hans Blechschmidt was the first conductor.

If Sol Hurok's memoirs are to be trusted, he had an artist hastily recruited in Chicago to sing Mime in *Das Rheingold* but had lost the only singer who knew the role in *Siegfried.* The first act of that opera, therefore, had to be cut. The conductors Blechschmidt and Ernest Mehlich refused to have anything to do with the project. The third conductor, Ernest Knoch, agreed to produce a two-act version, and Milwaukee heard the opera in this form. "Nobody stoned us," Hurok recalls,[2] and the effect of the Siegfried-Brünnhilde duet, with Johannes Sembach and Gadski in fine voice, saved the evening. But apparently Hurok knew better than to try this in Chicago. Alexander Larsen is given as the Mime in the Chicago program. How much of the role he actually sang is a matter of conjecture. Since, as Hurok observes, "no performance of Wagner is ever given as he wrote it—except possibly in Bayreuth,"[3] one may surmise that the practice of trimming the scores, still common in this period, was followed. Jorn and Juliette Lippe were Tristan and Isolde, with Sharnova and Richard Gross as Brangäne and Kurwenal, respectively. Manuel Salzonger was the Dutchman, with Margaret Bäumer as Senta. Franz Egenieff was Don Juan.

The 1930/31 and 1931/32 Chicago series seemed to have been planned in defiance of the Depression and, as a result, produced two of the largest deficits in the history of local operatic production. Part of the problem was greatly reduced box office income. The company was at the mercy of single-ticket buyers, some of whom were indifferent to the offerings, and

some of whom were newly poor. You did not buy opera tickets with money needed for groceries.

The 1930/31 season opened with a new work destined to last only three performances, *Lorenzaccio,* by Ernest Moret (d. 1949) and went on to much more important matters when Lotte Lehmann made her Chicago debut as Sieglinde in *Die Walküre,* with Leider as Brünnhilde and Paul Althouse as Siegmund. Lehmann was later heard as Elisabeth in *Tannhäuser* and Eva in *Die Meistersinger.* Leider appeared in *Der Rosenkavalier* and *Don Giovanni.* An American singer, John Charles Thomas, created a sensation when he made his local operatic debut singing Tonio in *Pagliacci* and joined Raisa in *Un ballo in maschera.* Muzio appeared in *La forza del destino, Il trovatore, Otello, Aida, L'amore dei tre re,* and *Cavalleria rusticana.* The novelty of the series was *The Bartered Bride,* sung, one assumes, in German.

You would expect a musical bounty of these proportions to succeed, but, although a good seat cost about $4, the deficit exceeded $1 million. Part of that was a lavish production built at the cost of $42,000 for *Camille,* by Hamilton Forrest (1901–1963), a Chicago composer. The public wanted to be impressed by the music, not the scenery, and the work vanished after four performances. It was Garden's final Chicago disaster. In contrast, Massenet's *La Navarraise,* the last opera she was to introduce to Chicago, became a local favorite and was heard regularly long after her departure.

During the 1930/31 season, in addition to the new works, Garden again sang in Alfano's *Risurezzione* and Debussy's *Pelléas et Mélisande.* She made her final Chicago appearance on January 24, 1931, in *Le Jongleur de Notre-Dame,* but her real farewell was on February 6, when she sang *Camille* with the touring company in Boston. Again it was a disaster; she should have made her exit from the American scene in one of her great roles. Twenty years of affiliation notwithstanding, not a single official of the Chicago company was present to say goodbye.

Garden was fifty-seven when she said farewell to Chicago, but she continued to sing opera in France until her formal retirement (after a Paris performance of *Risurezzione*) in May 1934. She filled her time with a variety of engagements, among them a much acclaimed Debussy program with Serge Koussevitzky and the Boston Symphony in December 1931, vaudeville on the Loew circuit in 1933, and master classes at Chicago Musical College in 1935. Until 1937 she was engaged to find vocal talent for Hollywood.

By then she had moved to the Left Bank. Her new Parisian apartment at 44, rue de Bac was her home until 1940, when, perhaps fearing the fall of France, she fled to Scotland, which became her base for the rest of her life. In 1946, during a period in the United States, she was hired to teach French to a young singer named Beverly Sills. In her later years she became a pathetic figure, trading on her reputation but unable to show a new public how that reputation had been made. Little of her wealth remained at her death.

Hurok's third German season, 1930/31, took him to the new Civic Opera House under the management of one of the legendary Chicago impresarios, Bertha Ott. Gadski still was the major star, surrounded by talent (some of it American) from leading German theaters. "With its second American tour, last season, the German Grand Opera Company established a secure and unchallenged reputation as one of the foremost organizations ever presented in this country," the advertisements modestly proclaimed. Although the press had been good and the public response enthusiastic, Hurok was cautious this time. There was *Die Walküre,* but no *Ring* cycle. *The Flying Dutchman* and *Tristan und Isolde* were repeated from the previous year, and d'Albert's *Tiefland* was the novelty.

Hurok felt genuine gratitude to Gadski. "Despite her heroic voice, she was not heroic in stature. Offstage she was an old fashioned German hausfrau. . . . She was a fine Wagnerian artist who was equally at home in French and Italian opera. . . . Her death in an automobile accident . . . was a painful shock to me."[4]

Summing up, he concludes, "I felt we had conquered the United States for German opera that winter. We had done a good job, my bank balance was as robust as it had ever been, and for the second time in my life I knew when to stop."[5] Hurok had learned that dance could draw as well as opera at the box office and was much cheaper to produce. His last great operatic venture was his alliance with the Metropolitan Opera National Company in 1965.

In contrast to the troubled Chicago company, in 1930/31 the financially secure Metropolitan produced some 225 operatic performances, in addition to a number of concerts, from a repertory of forty-five works— ten more works than Chicago, but 135 more performances. This way one could avoid big financial losses.

Plans for 1931/32 were aimed at increasing ticket sales by offering a somewhat lighter and more entertaining season. Tickets now ran from $1 to $6. In 1931 $6 bought a week's groceries. Polacco bowed out

as artistic director to be replaced by Herbert Witherspoon, best known in the city as the president of Chicago Musical College. He believed in quality, at least in terms of vocal talent. The season opened on November 2 with Muzio in *Tosca.* She would return in *Aida, La traviata, La bohème,* and *Cavalleria rusticana.* Jan Kiepura, a great favorite in the large Polish community, was in evidence in *Rigoletto* and *La bohème. Tristan und Isolde* combined Leider, Althouse, and Kipnis, who could also be heard in *The Magic Flute, Parsifal, Die Meistersinger,* and *Lohengrin* (the latter two with Lehmann). Raisa was back in *La Juive* and *Cavalleria rusticana.* There was room in the repertory for unusual works, Leoni's *L'Oracolo* and *Mona Lisa,* by Max von Schillings (1868–1933), which was new to the city. Both were well received, but it did not make much difference.

As the final performance arrived on January 29, the message of doom was clear. With another deficit of more than $1 million, a guaranty fund of at least $500,000 a season was needed, and it could not be raised. After ten years, what had looked like the most secure resident opera-producing organization had gone broke. The new Civic Opera House went dark. Opera in 1932/33 consisted of a performance of *Aida* in Soldier Field, a 102,000-seat stadium. The best shows in town were two political conventions from which the incumbent president, Herbert Hoover, and a challenger, Franklin D. Roosevelt, emerged to face the public.

Opera, it was theorized, had only superficially penetrated American life: it was basically a European art form, separated from American audiences first by barriers of language and second by the representation of societies very different from our own. Films—and they were now beginning to speak—permitted instant cultural identification. Actually, with the Western world in an economic slump, opera's need for subsidy was creating problems even in Europe.

Chicago was not giving up. In 1933 the Chicago Grand Opera Company, which, as it turned out, was to last only two years, was incorporated, and a five-week season announced. The city would hear considerably less opera than it had been offered in the recent past, but it was hoped there was an audience of sufficient size to keep the house reasonably full. Gennaro Papi was the chief conductor; Paul Longone, an experienced operatic administrator, was the general manager.

The 1933 season led off with a debut and strong Puccini: Maria Jeritza in *Tosca,* a role she all but owned at the Metropolitan, and Elisabeth Rethberg making her downtown debut as Butterfly. Raisa sang the first Chicago performance of *Turandot,* a role she had played in the world première of the work at La Scala (Toscanini conducting) in 1926. Raisa was also much in evidence with *Tosca, Aida, La Gioconda,* and her well-established *Cavalleria rusticana* on view. Mason sang two Puccini heroines, Mimì and Butterfly, Harriet in *Martha,* and Marguerite in *Faust.* Maria Jeritza appeared in *Lohengrin.* The novelty this time was Rimsky-Korsakov's *Le Coq d'or,* presumably sung in French. Tickets were cheap; for the first time in decades you could hear an opera for the price of a movie. Main-floor seats went for $3. But the budget was one-fourth of those of previous seasons. For 1934 main-floor tickets went up to $4, but these were still the prices of the previous century.

Jeritza was the real show the following year. This time *Turandot* was hers for opening night. She went on to *Tosca, Lohengrin,* and another heroic effort to present *Salome.* Jeritza's version of the heroine was someone who went headfirst into Jochanaan's prison to relish the sight of his decapitation. Rough stuff. Giovanni Martinelli sang *Il trovatore, Aida, Pagliacci,* and *La forza del destino.* Mason triumphed in *La traviata* and reappeared as Butterfly. Lehmann and Paul Althouse appeared in *Tannhäuser.* There were two notable debuts, Lauritz Melchior as Tristan and Ezio Pinza as both Don Giovanni and Gounod's Mephistopheles. The *Tristan* production was conducted by a dedicated Wagnerian who, nonetheless, had little experience in the opera house: Frederick Stock of the Chicago Symphony. Between Stock and Melchior (who probably never learned all the music), the third act was very likely reduced to about forty-five minutes.

Money problems led to the end of the company, but this time the supporters of opera rallied, and a new organization, the Chicago City Opera Company,

The Civic Opera House auditorium, named The Ardis Krainik Theatre in 1996

was formed in time to offer a 1935 season. The critic Karleton Hackett was named president, but illness claimed him after a single year. The new company sought continuity with the previous resident producers of opera and listed Harold F. McCormick and Samuel Insull as former presidents. Jason F. Whitney headed the City Opera Company with Robert Hall McCormick as vice-president. The directors were a diversified group, containing a successful merchant, Nathan Goldblatt; a celebrated pianist and teacher, Rudolph Ganz; and a man of many skills who was in time to lead the Chicago Symphony trustees, Louis C. Sudler. To make the performances more accessible to a large public, the most expensive ticket again was only $3, still a significant sum when a comfortable middle-class income was $3,000 a year. But cutting box office income meant cutting production costs, and, as it turned out, the operas were hastily thrown together on minimum budgets. Chicago expected something better.

Papi was now sharing conducting with the Americans Henry Weber and Leo Kopp. Saving money on conductors' fees was, it was felt, a good way to economize, and both these men—who had first appeared in 1934—were considered acceptable. Neither of them had anything approaching Papi's experience, and their ascendancy in following seasons was to cripple the company with a lack of strong leadership in the pit. But Papi was still conducting in 1935 when Boito's *Mefistofele* was heard with Pinza in the title role. And Pinza was back as Don Giovanni. Familiar castings returned: Mason in *Martha;* Raisa in *Turandot, Aida,* and *Cavalleria rusticana;* Lehmann in *Lohengrin* and *Der Rosenkavalier.* The greatest disaster of a generally disastrous season was *Gale (The Haunting),* by Edith Leginska (1886–1920), a British-born, socially prominent local musician. John Charles Thomas never bothered to learn his role thoroughly, and the single performance, which was heavily subsidized by her friends—with the composer conducting—was at best a reading rehearsal. The greatest impact of the season came at the end: two performances of a new opera by Respighi, *La fiamma,* with Raisa in top form.

Early in 1936 Chicago saw its first production of Gershwin's *Porgy and Bess.* The Theatre Guild had presented the world première performances in New York and Boston the previous fall, and they sent a touring company to the Erlanger Theater in Chicago for two-and-a-half weeks. Original cast members appeared: Todd Duncan was Porgy, and Anne Brown was Bess;

John W. Bubbles was Sportin' Life, and Warren Coleman sang Crown. Alexander Smallens, who conducted the première performances, led the Chicago engagement.

The 1936 Chicago City Opera Company season provided a slight recovery from the previous year but still pointed the way to financial disaster. There were twenty-eight productions, and seventeen of them were heard only once. Apparently it was felt there was enough of an operatic audience in the city to sustain three nights of *La bohème* and *Mignon* and two stagings of *Martha, La Juive, Die Walküre,* and *Louise.*

What is interesting is that newer repertory was felt to be more attractive than staples. Thus there is only one *Faust* and just one *Madama Butterfly,* but there are two performances each of the following: *Jack and the Beanstalk,* in the world première of this Louis Gruenberg (1884–1964) opera; *La fiamma;* and *The Bartered Bride.* Nine houses sold out. One of them was a repeat of *La bohème,* in which Galli-Curci returned to opera (sans rehearsal) after six years of vocal difficulties (which were not over). She decided her operatic career was finished.

Martinelli, who was about to add *Otello* to his Met repertory, sang the work with Tibbett and Mason. Mason again was a lovely Violetta in *La traviata* and Margherita to Pinza's Mefistofele. Those must have been notable evenings. Raisa returned in *La fiamma,* but her singing was not up to her earlier seasons. Pinza and Helen Jepson were cast in *Faust,* and Jepson returned in *Martha* and *Louise. Tannhäuser,* with Marjorie Lawrence and Althouse, at least had some good singing, as did a hastily assembled *Die Walküre,* with Melchior and with Marjorie Lawrence as Brünnhilde. Melchior returned to sing *Lohengrin* with Rethberg, who joined Martinelli in *Aida.* If you traveled to New York, you heard them in something approximating a real production. Chicago could not afford a luxury of this type. And in New York you heard Wagner from a Mahler disciple, Artur Bodanzky, not Henry Weber.

Still, by 1937 the effort to make the opera attractive to a larger audience was showing success, and audiences combined Upton's "swells" with solidly middle-class citizenry. *Aida* was a conventional but exciting opening night with Martinelli and Rethberg, and Martinelli returned in the second production as Saint-Saëns's Samson and in the third as Manrico in *Il trovatore.* There were four important debuts. Kirsten Flagstad joined Melchior in *Tristan und Isolde,* bringing the city one of the Met's all-time star combinations. Being stuck with Weber in the pit may have kindled her enthusiasm for Edwin McArthur. (She was to return to America as Isolde in this theater a decade later with Artur Rodzinski and the Chicago Symphony.) Melchior and Flagstad were heard later in *Tannhäuser.* Helen Traubel, who would succeed Flagstad at the Met during the war, was introduced in Walter Damrosch's *The Man without a Country.* She returned with Melchior as Sieglinde in *Die Walküre,* with Flagstad singing Brünnhilde. Grace Moore chose *Manon* and *La bohème* to introduce herself to Chicago opera. Lawrence Tibbett joined Mason and Martinelli in *Otello.* In February Jussi Bjoerling had made his Vienna debut in *La bohème* with Jarmila Novotná; in Chicago his Mimì was Marion Claire. He also sang the Duke in *Rigoletto,* with Tibbett in the title role.

Between this season and 1958, Bjoerling was to give thirty-five operatic performances in Chicago and appear regularly as a recitalist. He was back in 1938, 1940, and 1941 in those two roles. During the war his activities were largely concentrated in Scandinavia, although, politically naïve, he sang once in Germany and would have appeared again at the Vienna Opera if he had been permitted to sing Italian roles in Italian. (During the war the policy there was that everything was to be in German.)

What was wrong with this season was that it was not a Chicago opera company at work as much as a series of shows imported from the Met, with well-prepared Met principals working with Chicago scenery, a third-rate Chicago orchestra, and frequently an inadequate conductor. The sensational event in 1938 was the long overdue Chicago debut of Beniamino Gigli, who returned to the United States after an absence of six years. He sang *Martha,* a relatively easy opera, with Jepson. Four weeks later he was back in a more demanding role, *Andrea Chénier,* with Rose Bampton, who was also making her debut. Gigli's Met career ended with performances in 1938/39. He could go on singing Neapolitan songs into old age, and though his 1938 Chicago appearance was a great success, the glory days of his career were past.

Jepson, Tibbett, and Martinelli opened the season in *Otello,* followed by Martinelli in *Aida.* Eva Turner joined him in the second and third performances and sang Turandot, one of her great roles. Flagstad appeared in *Tristan und Isolde,* this time with Paul Althouse, Weber again conducting, but in *Lohengrin* she had her favorite American conductor, Edwin Mc-

Arthur. With her backing, he was to appear at the Met six times in the next three years. Pinza was Gounod's Devil; Tibbett was Rigoletto. Ticket prices were up, with $4.40 now the top of the scale.

As war drew near in 1939, the artistic director Paul Longone died in France. The season was complete on paper, and Weber became music director, a job he was to hold for two years. He conducted the opening night, *Boris Godunov* (in Italian, naturally) with Pinza. Grace Moore sang the last performances of *Louise* the city was to hear in the century. Gladys Swarthout, who had made a strong impression at Ravinia, was back for her first downtown season, offering a lady-like Carmen, with Kiepura as Don José. She was more effective in *Mignon* with Pinza and Tito Schipa. Flagstad had McArthur conducting for her *Tannhäuser* and *Die Walküre.* He was also in charge on November 24 when Martinelli sang his only German role, his one and only Tristan to Flagstad's Isolde. It was well received, but for reasons not entirely clear, he did not add it to his Met repertory. In a way this is sad because he may have known all of the third act.

Audiences had been elegant but less than capacity. No real effort had been made to reach out to younger people, and it is not surprising that they found other forms of music more interesting. Continuing financial problems called for yet another reorganization. The 1940s opened with the arrival of the Chicago Opera Company, the last of the ill-fated troupes to make the Civic Opera House their home. Weber promised a new level of production values, opera as the city had known it twenty years before. At season's end he decided this was an unrealistic goal and resigned.

Long before its opening night the company engaged Giovanni Cardelli to prepare a report on the artistic and managerial procedures of Chicago opera producers. It was a private document, intended to circulate among the directors of the company. Cardelli apparently was part of the local musical scene and was familiar with operations at La Scala, Milan.[6] Some of his omissions are, in the light of present practices, startling. He sees no need for subscriptions and does not feel the management of the company requires the services of a full-time fund-raiser. These two items alone could be enough to explain why resident Chicago opera, plagued by the Depression and then war, disappeared in 1946. Cardelli's view of the repertory is essentially Italian, and his wish that some operas be cut and librettos revised would now go contrary to contemporary thought. Far more significant is that virtually none of his recommendations seem to have been put into effect.

"Opera in Chicago," he stated, "is, beyond all possible question, the worst to be found in any major opera house." He said that the previous Chicago opera companies were directing their productions to far too small an audience and that the audience was not responding because the productions were "given with consistent and total disregard for ensemble and other fundamentally consistent parts, other than two or three top ranking stars with whom it might be possible to add lustre to a cast." "The real, fundamental reason" for limited public support was "that the quality of the performances, the choice of operas, the casting and the presentation do not justify the public's attendance."

He found the new theater, although not the equal of the most modern ones in Europe, adequate, "but an intelligent realization of the limitations of [the technical facilities] is indispensable to the solution of the problem of taking full advantage of them." Unfortunately, "one of the company's major problems is that production is entirely in the hands of non-specialists, even though opera is one of the most highly specialized undertakings known to man. . . . Through an inadmissibly stupid error in design . . . it is not possible to store two complete shows in the theater at one time." That meant backstage costs for truck crews and stagehands would always be high.

"The wardrobe department is one of the theater's chief glories: yet it is not always fully exploited, due to the absence of a single person familiar with historical accuracy [in costume]. Swords nearly always are from a different period than the costumes with which they appear." One strange problem was a panoramic painting of the crucifixion that hung at the rear of the stage behind the cyclorama and interfered with it. It was eventually removed and found a permanent home in Forest Lawn Cemetery in California.

La Scala, he observed, offered ten to fourteen operas in a season of fifty-four performances with an orchestra, chorus, and staff "infinitely better trained" than their Chicago counterparts. And, "the present chorus is so bad from every conceivable point of view, that it need not even be considered in any project for the future of opera in Chicago."

By presenting six performances in a week, Chicago, he said, "is in the position of feeding the public more than it can possibly digest." San Francisco, in contrast, gave only four performances a week. The star system, he found, encouraged large fees that created the need to change casts and to replace expensive singers with less costly artists for repeat performances. That made the repeats difficult to sell. He argued that the first performances could have used at least twice as many rehearsals as they were being given; repeats (despite cast changes) usually were not rehearsed at all.

"The pressing danger is two-fold," he writes. "First that the existing system degenerates to a point where nothing less than a total rebirth will suffice, and secondly that the public should become so exasperated and discouraged by an apparently endless repetition of the same inexcusable blunders, that it will no longer believe in the actual reform when and if it does make its belated appearance."

The reforms never took place. Nothing less than collapse, years of silence, and rebirth in the form of the Lyric was sufficient to bring about a change.

For a start toward excellence, the 1940 series had major conductors, starting with two giants making their local operatic debuts. (Both directed the Chicago Symphony at Ravinia and were later to become music directors in Orchestra Hall.) Artur Rodzinski led *Salome* with Rose Pauly, a last-minute replacement for an ailing Marjorie Lawrence. Lawrence did sing Carmen—an unexpected role she did well—and Brünnhilde in *Die Walküre,* where, if she was given the chance, she rode a horse in the second act. Her athletic skills made it all the more tragic when she was stricken with polio in 1945. Fritz Reiner led more Strauss in *Der Rosenkavalier,* with the local debut of Risë Stevens, an irresistible Octavian. Pinza sang Don Giovanni with another new conductor, Paul Breisach, who was about to go to the Met.

Again *Aida* provided an opening night, this time with the debut of Zinka Milanov in the title role, opposite Martinelli and Thomas. A Flagstad-Melchior-McArthur *Tristan* followed. *La traviata* paired Jepson with fellow Americans: the tenor James Melton, who was popular with the public (a regular American boy, he had a museum of old cars), and Thomas as his father. Maurice Abravanel was another fresh face as the conductor. Rose Bampton and Martinelli carried *Il trovatore,* and Jepson, Abravanel, and another American tenor, Richard Crooks, appeared in *Manon.* Both tenors were new to Chicago. *Pagliacci* was strengthened with Martinelli as Canio and Jepson as Nedda, but Thomas was ill-cast as Tonio and even more seriously out of his depth as Scarpia in *Tosca,* opposite

Kiepura's unlikely Cavaradossi. Grace Moore was heard as Manon, one of her established Met roles, and, for her first time, as Flora in Montemezzi's *L'amore dei tre re*. The composer conducted and zealously coached her for the part. Bjoerling appeared briefly as the Duke in *Rigoletto*. He was back, in recital but not opera, in February 1941, his last Chicago appearance until after the war. He rejoined the Met late in 1945.

Giovanni Martinelli taking over the artistic directorship of the Chicago Opera Company from Fortune Gallo, 1940

Two months before the opening, Martinelli was named artistic director of the company, but it appears to have been largely a ceremonial appointment. The man who was really running things was Fortune Gallo, whose budget-produced San Carlo Opera operated in the nineteenth-century tradition and actually made money. But that was achieved by cutting corners in a manner many found inappropriate for a company charging high ticket prices.

Before the 1941 season ended on December 13, the nation was at war. It was a short series, drawing heavily on things heard in the recent past. There was a fresh note on opening night, *Un ballo in maschera* with Martinelli, Thomas, and Rethberg. Lily Pons made her debut with her current Met vehicle, Donizetti's *The Daughter of the Regiment*. Four days before Pearl Harbor Licia Albanese sang Butterfly with a real Yankee *vagabondo*, Melton, as her Pinkerton. The

opera was to drop out of the repertory for four years; America had worse things in store for Nagasaki. But then came Swarthout as Carmen, Pinza as Mephistopheles, Martinelli and Tibbett in *Otello*, Martinelli in *Pagliacci* and *Aida*, Moore in *Tosca*, and Melchior in *Lohengrin* with a seasoned Met conductor, Emil Cooper. Ticket sales were good.

In 1942 *Lakmé* was scheduled to open the season, with Lily Pons in the title role. She became ill a few days before opening night, so Martinelli called on his colleague and great friend Zinka Milanov, who agreed to hurry into town to sing the title role in the substituted *Aida*, doing so without rehearsal. The remaining cast held the same principals scheduled to do the Delibes opera: Martinelli sang Radames; Tibbett was Amonasro; Anna Kaskas was Amneris; and Alexander Kipnis sang Ramfis. Martinelli was on hand for *Otello* and *Pagliacci*. An attractive *La traviata* offered Jarmila Novotná, with Melton and Tibbett. Melton was also heard in *Lucia di Lammermoor* and one of his specialties, *Martha*. Richard Crooks sang Faust opposite Albanese. Kiepura delighted the Polish community in *Halka*, an opera by their countryman Stanislaw Moniuszko (1819–1872). Notable vocal debuts were Dorothy Kirsten as Micaëla in *Carmen* and Jennie Tourel as Mignon. Fausto Cleva, who eventually was to run the company, made his downtown conducting debut. He presided over Moore's appearances in *La bohème* and in *Tosca* with Martinelli.

Producer-entrepreneur Cheryl Crawford dispatched a touring company of *Porgy and Bess*, which landed in Chicago at the Studebaker Theatre in November 1942 and stayed until the middle of January 1943. Etta Moten was Bess this time, and Avon Long, who was to become the Sportin' Life of choice in productions for years to come, made his first Chicago appearance in that role. Todd Duncan (Porgy), Warren Coleman (Crown), and the conductor Alexander Smallens were back. The *Tribune* found the production an improvement over the original one seen in 1936.

Few opportunities existed in opera for American black singers in the 1940s, and in response the National Negro Opera Company came into existence. It visited Chicago in 1942 with *Aida* and in 1943 with *La traviata*, but it could not meet the standards of the established professional companies.

Early in 1943 the Met returned in force for the first time in thirty-three years, and later in the year it was announced that the next opera season would come from them. That story is told in the next chapter.

What proved to be the final three seasons of the Chicago company began in October 1944. Fausto Cleva was now the artistic director. The series celebrated an opera star who was also a movie star. Gladys Swarthout, who sang Carmen on opening night, had enjoyed a reasonable success in pictures, but nothing to compare with Jeanette MacDonald, who appeared at the matinée of November 4 as Gounod's Juliet and was back on November 15 as the composer's Marguerite. The voice was lovely, well produced, and surprised the doubters by being more than ample to fill the house. Cleva and Pinza contributed to the success of the *Faust* in which Raoul Jobin sang the title role.

Martial Singher was Pelléas, Tibbett was Golaud, and Bidú Sayâo was Mélisande when the Debussy opera was revived after fourteen seasons. Eugene Goossens, a major conducting talent, was in charge. Sayâo joined Cleva for a striking *La traviata.* Kirsten Thorborg made her debut as Fricka in *Die Walküre,* which featured Traubel as Brünnhilde and introduced Astrid Varnay as Sieglinde. Flagstad was now isolated in Europe, but even without her support McArthur was still invited to conduct. Thorborg sang Azucena to Milanov's Leonora in *Il trovatore.* Another significant debut was Leonard Warren as Rigoletto.

Zinka Milanov in her dressing room, about to carve a slice of pineapple, before performing in the Chicago Opera production of *Tosca,* November 13, 1945

Sayâo's success in 1944 gave her opening night in 1945, the title role in *Manon.* Martinelli and Swarthout, who had sung in *Carmen* together in 1944, returned to do it again. Martial Singher and Thorborg returned in *Parsifal.* (Wagner was not banned in the postwar season.) George Szell was to have conducted but walked out, skeptical about the quality of the Chicago orchestra. Fritz Stiedry stepped in and made a strong impression with his local debut. Bruno Walter was invited to conduct *La forza del destino.* He then returned to lead a Met cast (Pinza, Brownlee, and Novotná) in *The Marriage of Figaro. Pelléas et Mélisande,* which had proved to survive without Garden, was back with the 1944 cast and conductor. Milanov returned, this time as Tosca.

One might have hoped that after the war the 1946 season would open the way to happier days. Cleva had been a strong force as artistic director. A board headed by John D. Allen and Abner J. Stilwell contained important names. The season was short, but Cleva had worked diligently to raise standards and, with Europe once more accessible, introduce new artists: Italo Tajo, Ferruccio Tagliavini, and Janine Micheau. The postwar opening night—*Aida,* naturally—had a celebratory quality. Milanov sang the title role and Tajo was an impressive high priest. *La bohème* with Kirsten followed.

There was an important conducting debut, that of Erich Leinsdorf. In later years he recalled one of the most unusual experiences of his career. It was in Gruenberg's *The Emperor Jones,* a spectacular vehicle for Tibbett, on the third night of the season. "In some scenes he was the only one on stage. The day of the dress rehearsal he was drunk in his hotel room, so in these places the curtain would rise, the lights would go up, and no one would appear. The orchestra went right on playing. The music was new to them, and I enjoyed the extra rehearsal. In due course the lights faded and the curtain came down. I must add that for the performance Tibbett appeared in fine form and delivered a powerful characterization."

Leinsdorf was back the next afternoon to lead Traubel and Set Svanholm in a *Tristan* with, miraculously, a complete third act. Two weeks later he conducted *Carmen* for Swarthout, whose repertory for the season also included Mignon. Tagliavini made his debut when *Madama Butterfly* returned to the repertory, with Kirsten in the title role.

Bjoerling appeared after six years, again as the Duke in *Rigoletto.* His conductor on October 5 was Nicola Rescigno (of whom we shall hear much more later). Warren sang the title role. Two nights later Bjoerling again appeared with Rescigno, this time in *La bohème.* Rescigno directed the repeat and also presided over the performance of *Lucia di Lammermoor* that introduced Patrice Munsel and Richard Tucker to Chicago audiences. Micheau, Tibbett, and Armand Tokatyan appeared in *La traviata.*

These were things worthy of support, but the support was not there. The deficit came to about $150,000 (more than $1 million at the end of the century if one adjusts for inflation). Private philanthropy and the still largely untouched world of business support could not produce the funds, and resident Chicago opera abruptly ceased. The General Finance Corporation, which had acquired the Civic Opera building on most favorable terms, came forward in 1948 and paid off the creditors, a splendid gesture.

8

New York Takes Over

1943–1954

Writing for the *Musical Courier* after the 1942 season, a senior Chicago critic, René Devries, conscious that the Ravinia Opera had become in its later years a summer job for artists from the Metropolitan, observed that the downtown company had gone much the same way. Its artistic director, Giovanni Martinelli, was one of the Met's biggest stars, and its performances often duplicated offerings of the current Met season with the same key castings. "We sometimes feel a nostalgia," he confesses, "for the long era when Chicago boasted a company of its own, when singers were honored to call themselves members of the Chicago opera."

In 1942 the most important part of the artists roster—some 40%—came from the Met: eight sopranos, two mezzos, five tenors, six baritones and basses, and one conductor. These singers had leading roles. Comprimario parts were often given to artists of the San Carlo Opera Company.

Chicago still had some room for individuality. The 1942 series offered one performance of *Halka* with Jan Kiepura, honoring the city's large Polish community. But the seventeen other operas in the repertory were all staples of the Met, and a dozen of them could be heard that season in the New York house. New York also heard works by Wagner and Strauss that apparently were considered too expensive for the Chicago company to produce.

Devries's dismay rose to greater heights when he learned in September that in the 1943 season Chicago would present no opera at all. The problem was not money or attendance. The deficit for 1942 had been low, $25,000 (petty cash in later years), but this was the year in which Insull's grand scheme to sustain an opera company with the earnings of an office building came to an end. Old debts were liqui-

dated by the sale of the Civic Opera House to the General Finance Corporation. By the time the lawyers and accountants were through, the people needed for an opera company had vanished. Fortune Gallo, the general director in 1942, went back on the road with his San Carlo troupe.

Anticipating this situation, the Met came to Chicago in March and April 1943, visiting the Civic Opera House for the first time with fourteen performances from a repertory of thirteen operas. General Manager Edward Johnson was prepared to offer the city the best he had to give—the best in the world in those grim days. The first performance was *The Marriage of Figaro,* with Bruno Walter conducting and Herbert Graf directing. Chicago had not heard opera from a conductor of Walter's international reputation for many years. Ezio Pinza sang the title role with Bidú Sayâo as his bride, Jarmila Novotná was Cherubino, and John Brownlee and Eleanor Steber played the Count and Countess. The author is not reading old program books but recalling music he heard, music that has lived in his memory for more than fifty years and contained performances that have never been surpassed. Chicago had not encountered casting of this strength for twenty years.

Devries may have been unhappy over the demise of the Chicago Opera Company, but a Philadelphia critic, Max de Schauensee, saw it differently. The Met's general manager, Johnson, he said, "realizes that Chicago is one of the cities of the United States that cannot and will not do without grand opera. What is more, without plenty of it."

Walter, Pinza, Brownlee, and Novotná returned in *The Magic Flute,* which, in those days, was heard in an acceptable English translation. Charles Kullman sang Tamino. Walter's gift for Italian opera was heard in *La forza del destino,* which offered Lawrence Tibbett's impassioned portrayal of Don Carlo. Sir Thomas Beecham presided over *Carmen,* with two French singers, Lily Djanel and Raoul Jobin, in the leading roles. *Tannhäuser* was conducted by George Szell, with Lauritz Melchior and Helen Traubel, who returned, with Erich Leinsdorf conducting, in *Tristan und Isolde.*

La traviata was heard twice—with two casts. Helen Jepson and Licia Albanese were the Violettas, with Charles Kullman and Tibbett in the second cast. Zinka Milanov and Giovanni Martinelli were heard in *Il trovatore.* Bruna Castagna sang Amneris in *Aida. The Barber of Seville* was offered with an all-star cast: Nino Martini as Almaviva, Sayâo as Rosina, Brownlee as Figaro, and even Pinza as Don Basilio. No Chicago company could cast a singer of that reputation in a supporting role. Four nights later Pinza was back as Don Giovanni. There was even a *Boris Godunov,* conducted by Szell, with Alexander Kipnis. It was a dazzling series. The character and quality of opera in Chicago had improved spectacularly.

When the Met was formally invited to replace the resident company during the 1943/44 Chicago season, it leaped at the opportunity. An audience was there. So was a large and modern theater, a facility far superior to many it visited on the road. The Met was not adverse to closing a season with its books in the black. As recently as 1939/40 it had made a profit of $171,000.

As the Met saw it, supplying opera to Chicago was economically sound. The cost of shipping scenery and costumes was far less than that of preparing a production. This time it had the formal sponsorship of the Chicago Opera Company. Even so, it was not a good year for touring. The nation was at war. Travel, especially on the scale demanded by an opera company, was difficult. But Johnson felt he had a commitment to return to Cleveland, where audience loyalty could not be doubted, and if he was going to be that far from New York, he would do two weeks in Chicago, stopping for a week in Cleveland, then offering a single performance in Rochester on the way home.

The argument was simple: Why not go back to the way things were in the nineteenth century? Why should Chicago throw together makeshift productions and import Met stars to sell tickets when, for less money, the whole show, well prepared and performed several times previously, could be brought from New York?

And so an opera war began, and one might say that it did not end until 1962. A reorganized Chicago

Opera Company was back in 1944 with Fausto Cleva—an established conductor at the Met—as its general artistic director. He remained so for three years until the demise of the company after its 1946 series. His first season was heralded by a campaign to sell certificates, ten in a $10 book, which could be used to buy tickets thirty days before the box office opened to the general public.

Fausto Cleva

The Met, in the midst of what many see as one of its golden decades, was formidable competition. In April 1944 it opened its Chicago season with *Tristan und Isolde,* with Melchior and Marjorie Lawrence, Beecham conducting. It offered *Parsifal,* an opera the city had not heard in thirteen years, with Melchior as Parsifal and Kipnis as Gurnemanz. There was *Tannhäuser* with Lawrence as Venus, Rose Bampton as Elisabeth, and Melchior in the title role. Walter again conducted *The Magic Flute.*

The repertory was diversified, with a good mix of strong and popular French and Italian works (*The Tales of Hoffmann,* with Beecham, Patrice Munsel,

Djanel, and Steber, and *Tosca* with Grace Moore). Beecham conducted *Mignon,* with Jennie Tourel in the title role and Patrice Munsel as Philine. Both were making Chicago debuts in this series. Albanese, Kullman, Brownlee, and Pinza were the principals in *La bohème.* Walter conducted *Un ballo in maschera* with Jan Peerce, Leonard Warren, Kirsten Thorborg, and Milanov. It would be many years before Chicago heard a comparable cast again.

In July 1943, what was billed as the Gallo and Zelzer Opera Company had presented both *Aida* and *Carmen* (one performance each) in Soldier Field, a 102,000-seat stadium. Presumably emboldened by the success of that venture, on three consecutive days in June 1944, the San Carlo Opera Company brought *Aida, La traviata,* and *Il trovatore* to the same place, again with one performance of each opera.

In December of that year Cheryl Crawford brought back her *Porgy and Bess* production to Chicago, this time for a week's stay at the Civic Opera House. Though Todd Duncan was back in the cast as Porgy, and Etta Moten, Avon Long, Warren Coleman, and Alexander Smallens were back with their contributions, the production had lost its magic.

For 1945 the Met's Chicago season was less than a week, but there were *La bohème* with Albanese and Peerce, *Norma* with Milanov, Pinza as Don Giovanni, and *Die Meistersinger* with Steber, Thorborg, and Kullman. A week in 1946 began with a coal strike that produced dim-out regulations nationally. The proximity of the river became a blessing. The freighter *Mainsheet Eye* was chartered and tied up behind the opera house. Its two generators fed five hundred watts into the Met's touring switchboards, and although *Tannnhäuser* was not as brightly lit as one might desire, it could be performed. Fritz Busch made his Chicago debut as the conductor. Walter conducted *The Magic Flute,* with Pinza as Sarastro, and repeated his *Un ballo in maschera* of 1944. Melchior and Astrid Varnay were the Siegmund and Sieglinde in *Die Walküre;* Traubel sang Brünnhilde. The weekend—and the end of the strike—brought *Der Rosenkavalier,* conducted by Szell, with Irene Jessner as the Marschallin, Risë Stevens as Octavian, and Steber as Sophie. Emanuel List was Ochs. It was a performance I shall remember to the end of my days. A Chicago company could never have duplicated it. With the Met you had a season, short though it was, that held the local company to a standard it could not meet.

The Chicago Opera Company lowered the curtain for the last time in November 1946, and the city once more belonged to New York impresarios.

A group called the United States Opera Company, headed by Ottavio Scotto, announced its plans to offer "opera in the great tradition," opening a five-week season on January 6, 1947. Ruth Page was to be the ballet mistress and Danny Newman the press representative. (Both were to make careers at the Lyric.) Most of the fifteen singers were Europeans, some of them (Anni and Hilde Konetzni, Max Lorenz, and Nicola Rossi-Lemeni, for example) celebrated artists. *Turandot* was to be given with a Greek-American soprano unknown in the United States. Her name was Maria Calas (later she added a second *l*).

Money problems caused one delay after another, and Scotto, a respectable professional in opera production, was fearful because his primary support came from a New York lawyer, Edgar Richard Bagarozy, who apparently suffered grave reverses on the stock market and was headed for bankruptcy. Union problems erupted, and the company went broke. Stranded far from home, the singers were desperate, and Claudia Cassidy suggested they offer a concert, with the proceeds going to their assistance. Newman went to work selling tickets and, without advertising, realized about half the possible dollar income from the house. The event took place on the Civic Opera stage on February 5, 1947, with piano accompaniment. Callas, who had remained in New York, did not appear, but even so, the city had rarely seen such a parade of talent in concert. A profit of $4,300 gave each of the singers enough money to return to Europe. Most of them never came to the United States again. Bagarozy was to reappear in 1954, with disastrous results the following year.

A new group, called Opera Theater, offered a short season in April 1947, notable for the first American performance of Benjamin Britten's *The Rape of Lucretia* (which it presented again the following year in a three-production season). In June 1947 the impresario Harry Zelzer, as manager of the group, wired Igor Stravinsky (through his publisher) about projected stagings of *Mavra, L'Histoire du soldat,* and *Pulcinella* in October. Stravinsky indicated his availability to conduct and asked for details of the productions. Apparently they could not be worked out to the satisfaction of all parties. It was a lost opportunity of some significance.[1]

Artur Rodzinski, the music director of the Chicago Symphony Orchestra for the 1947/48 season, had, in his decade directing the Cleveland Orchestra, combined operatic performances with symphonic programs. His Orchestra Hall schedule included in concert form the long overdue, first Chicago performance of *Elektra*. The opening scene was cut, but Gertrude Lawrence (recovering from polio and singing from a wheelchair) was triumphant. (Chicago did not see *Elektra* on the stage until 1975.) In November 1947 Rodzinski offered a fully staged performance of *Tristan und Isolde* in the Civic Opera House with Flagstad and Svanholm as the principals, with the Chicago Symphony in the pit. Its official goal, which apparently was not achieved, was to earn funds for the orchestra's pension fund. But it made a more important point: that with forces of the stature of the Symphony and Rodzinski as a leader, Chicago could rival the Met in the most demanding repertory. This hope of Rodzinski's became one of the justifications for his dismissal early in 1948. The orchestral trustees announced that they had no wish to become involved in establishing an opera company. With Rodzinski's departure the fondest hopes for Chicago opera collapsed. The city was back to the situation that had prevailed until 1910.

In April 1947 the Met had offered *The Marriage of Figaro,* with Busch conducting and Pinza again in the title role; *Boris Godunov,* this time with Pinza; and a nice mixture of popular Italian and French scores, among them *Madama Butterfly* with Dorothy Kirsten and Kullman, *La bohème* with Peerce and Sayâo, and *Faust* with Kirsten. And then, having won the field, it abandoned it for two years. The company wished to expand its touring to the Far West, and Chicago was bypassed in favor of visits to Dallas, Denver, and Los Angeles, all of them regarded as potentially profitable markets.

The trustees of Insull's Chicago Music Foundation and a group of civic leaders functioning as the Committee for Opera in Chicago addressed the situation by inviting the New York City Opera Company to present a season at the Civic Opera House in 1948. It arrived on the scene when Chicago needed it the most. In 1943 delinquent taxes gave the city of New York possession of Mecca Temple on West 55th Street, a fanciful structure constructed by the Shriners. The city's dynamic mayor, Fiorello H. LaGuardia, came from a musical family (his father had played accompaniments for Patti). He was easily persuaded to put the nearly twenty-seven hundred seats to use in the cause of the serious arts.

In March of that year the New York City Center of Music and Drama was incorporated, a private non-profit organization. Originally intended to function as a presenting, rather than a producing, organization, its directors soon realized that to meet the objective of offering high-quality events at prices the general public could easily afford, it had to prepare its own shows. An opera company thus became an integral part of the design for the Center, which after 1948 was also to house George Balanchine's New York City Ballet.

The troupe, first known as the City Center Opera Company, gave its first performance on February 21, 1944. László Halász, a Hungarian with a razor tongue and the tact of a crocodile, was initially the director and principal conductor. A champion of opera in English, he wanted to offer fresh, lively productions that would appeal to listeners who might easily be put off by the usual operatic conventions. He created a tradition of innovation that remains with the company.

During a span of nearly three weeks, opening with Brenda Lewis in *Salome* on December 1, 1948, Chicago was offered fifteen operas in a well-balanced repertory from Mozart to Menotti. It is frequently suggested that, from 1946 to the appearance of the Lyric Theater eight years later, Chicago was without opera. But, although it was without a resident company, there was a reasonable amount of opera to be heard. Anyone who—like the author—was living in the city at that time will affirm that.

The City Opera was never a company for swells and made no effort to compete with the Met for expensive European talent. Basically it was an ensemble composed primarily of American singers. The City Opera was the first major company in New York to provide opportunities to African American singers. In 1946, nine years before the Metropolitan engaged Marian Anderson, Camilla Williams became the City Opera's first Butterfly. She sang the role twice in Chicago. Later in the series she returned in *Aida*. A double bill of Menotti's *Amelia Goes to the Ball* and *The Old Maid and the Thief* revealed a dedication to American opera. *Amelia,* on December 4, 1948, marked the local debut of Julius Rudel, whose Chicago career was to continue to the end of the century.

The City Opera felt no obligation to produce established box office successes. Thus, with Jean Paul Morel conducting, it offered *Pelléas et Mélisande,* with Maggie Teyte. A few nights later there was Tchaikovsky, *Eugene Onegin.* One can surmise neither of those two sold out, laying the foundation for Danny

Newman's scorn for fickle single-ticket buyers versus subscription purchasers. James Pease sang the title role in an admirable, fast-paced production of *Don Giovanni* that made use of an ingenious unit set. Joseph Rosenstock, another stalwart of the company, was in charge of *The Marriage of Figaro,* in which Pease again had the title role. It had a strong cast, with Walter Cassel and Frances Yeend as the Count and Countess, Virgina MacWatters as Susanna, and Frances Bible as Cherubino.

It was a good season, welcome for its variety and quality. Many felt that if New York could bring to Chicago opera on this level, maintaining a resident company was unjustified. Moreover, it was opera without subscription and with reasonably priced tickets, directed, as in New York, to a middle-class audience. If wealthy suburbanites wanted to attend, they were welcome, but the success of the venture did not depend on their patronage. It was appropriate that Insull's foundation should sponsor this season. This was opera in the spirit Insull respected.

In 1949/50 Chicago had two opera seasons, a long one from the New York City Opera in the autumn and a short one from the Met in May. Rosenstock opened the City Opera series on November 23 with *Der Rosenkavalier.* Maria Reining sang the Marschallin, with Bible as Octavian, Haskins as Sophie, and Lorenzo Alvary as Ochs. Reining returned in more Strauss, *Ariadne auf Naxos,* with MacWatters as Zerbinetta and Rudolph Petrak as Bacchus. The New York company did much to establish this opera as a repertory work in the United States. The big surprise was Prokofiev's *The Love for Three Oranges* in its first American production since its world première Chicago performances in 1921. It had been heard in Europe. Ahead of its time in 1921, in 1949 it was strongly cast, and it was a success. Again there was a Menotti evening, *The Old Maid and the Thief,* combined, this time, with *The Medium.* Popular works heard in 1948 completed the repertory.

The Met opened its final Johnson season here with Ljuba Welitsch and Bjoerling in *Tosca* (Bjoerling returned to sing the Duke in *Rigoletto*), followed by Stevens in *Carmen* and Albanese and Giuseppe di Stefano in *La traviata.* (Those who think di Stefano made his Chicago debut with the Lyric in 1954 are mistaken.) There was *Die Meistersinger,* conducted by Reiner, with an excellent cast headed by Set Svanholm and Astrid Varnay. The two visitations from New York added up to twenty-seven performances from a repertory of seventeen operas, considerably more than the Lyric produced in its first seasons.

In 1950/51 Chicago again had two opera seasons. The autumn belonged to the New York City Opera, which arrived in November and stayed two weeks. Harry Zelzer was identified as the Chicago manager, and Danny Newman as the publicity director. *The Love for Three Oranges* had been such a success that it opened the season on November 15. *Turandot,* which had not been heard in the city for a dozen years, was the novelty of the series, which otherwise consisted largely of works familiar from previous series.

This was Rudolf Bing's first season as general manager of the Metropolitan, and tour policies changed. Bing wanted to make money, which meant playing in venues like the Cleveland Public Auditorium, huge places quite unsuited to opera but with lots of seats to sell. The Met was in Chicago for three days in May and did not return for three years. It offered two performances of *Die Fledermaus* (the first in the city since 1927), as well as *La traviata* and *La bohème,* the latter with Victoria de Los Angeles in what appears to have been her first and last Chicago opera performance.

The City Opera was back for a little over two weeks in November 1951, opening with *Manon,* conducted by Morel. *The Love for Three Oranges* returned, as did the usual favorites. Rosenstock directed *The Marriage of Figaro,* with Pease in the title role. For the 1952 series City Opera introduced two artists later associated with the Lyric, the conductor Tullio Serafin, who led performances of *Tosca, Aida,* and *Faust,* and the bass Nicola Rossi-Lemeni, who was making his debut and was billed as a guest from La Scala, as Mephistopheles. Rosenstock conducted Bartók's *Duke Bluebeard's Castle* (in English), with Pease and Ann Ayars. The Bartók opera was almost unknown in the United States, and to offer this work was a brave gesture indeed. *The Love for Three Oranges* was back for the fourth time. Menotti's *Amahl and the Night Visitors* was performed on a double bill with the Bartók. The young Thomas Schippers conducted the Menotti, and later in the run he returned to conduct Menotti's *The Consul,* a powerful work new to the city. The remaining repertory was familiar, but the company wanted to see whether a popular opera could support a short run, and thus *Carmen* was heard three times.

In June 1952 a production of *Porgy and Bess* came to the Civic Opera House for a little over three weeks. In a book of memoirs he has written, Danny Newman tells the full (highly interesting) story of the production's arrival in Chicago, and how the appearance assured its subsequent international tour and triumps. Here we will mention only a few details, including the fact that it introduced two extraordinary young talents to Chicago: Leontyne Price as Bess, and William Warfield as Porgy. Cab Calloway was Sportin' Life, John McCurry was Crown, and Alexander Smallens conducted. (The production returned in 1954).

What proved to be the last New York City Opera season in seven years opened on November 18, 1953, with Rossini's *La Cenerentola* in its first Chicago performance in ninety-five years. Bible sang the title role. This time there was no reference to the Committee for Opera in Chicago; this was a collaboration between Rosenstock, who was now the general director of the company, and the impresario Zelzer.

One of the great historic moments of Chicago opera took place on November 19, 1953, when the tenor David Poleri, one of the company regulars, who had been having differences with Rosenstock, walked off the stage in the final scene of *Carmen*, leaving the lady to kill herself. He was not fired on the spot and even returned to sing *La bohème* with Schippers on November 25, but his reputation suffered badly.

Rigoletto, on November 28, provided a Chicago debut for Norman Treigle. He was to become one of the great artists of the New York company. *Hansel and*

Harry Zelzer

Gretel, a specialty of the old Chicago opera, had not been heard for thirteen years when it returned with Schippers conducting. And there was a *Madama Butterfly* with a Japanese soprano, Michiko Sunahara, in the title role and another Japanese singer, Kazuko Matsuchi, as Suzuki. *Die Fledermaus* was an excursion into lighter fare. The season lasted about a week and a half, and that was the last opera the city heard until the Lyric Theater presented its "calling card" the following February.

In May 1954 the Met rolled into town, booked as a Zelzer attraction, performing in the Civic Opera House. Danny Newman had joined the Lyric, and Harry Zelzer was denouncing him for supporting the new company that threatened to rob the Zelzer organization of the monopoly on opera in the city. But it was inevitable that the Zelzer monopoly should end. He lacked the financial resources to offer an extended opera season of the type the city needed. Six shows were about his limit, and, as the series demonstrated, he was afraid to offer anything but the most familiar repertory. To make a profit, he had to sell out. He bet on tenors: Richard Tucker in *Faust* and *La bohème,* Jan Peerce in *Lucia di Lammermoor* and *La traviata.*

Looking at the half dozen operas he presented in May 1955, you had to ask, "Who could possibly lose money with Stevens and Tucker in *Carmen?*" Tucker also carried the show in *Andrea Chénier,* and there was a *Manon*—small departures from the most familiar repertory. Peerce and Dorothy Kirsten were heard in *La traviata;* Peerce and Albanese carried *La bohème.*

There were five operas in May 1956. Of the greatest interest were *Die Meistersinger,* conducted by Rudolf Kempe, and a *Boris Godunov* with Cesare Siepi, conducted by Dimitri Mitropoulos. Milanov sang *Aida,* and Stevens and Tucker sang *Carmen.* Steber and Roberta Peters brightened *Die Fledermaus.*

The novelty of the 1957 series was *La Périchole* with Munsel, in a new production by Cyril Ritchard, led by Morel. Stevens and Mitropoulos joined forces for a sizzling *Carmen;* George London was Escamillo. The other four shows were also repertory staples, but at least Renata Tebaldi was seen in a new production of *La traviata,* the best of the Italian offerings. Zinka Milanov in *Il trovatore,* Licia Albanese in *Madama Butterfly,* and a routine *La bohème* completed the group.

Because he could sell it as a benefit, Zelzer got brave in 1958 and opened with *Eugene Onegin.* Mitropoulos conducted, and George London was masterful as the Byronic hero. A fairly uneven realization—despite heroic efforts in the pit by Max Rudolf—of *Der Rosenkavalier* followed. *Samson and Delilah* was unconvincing, but Roberta Peters brightened *The Barber of Seville*. Nicolai Gedda, making his local operatic debut, was notable in *Faust,* with Morel conducting. The discovery was *Madama Butterfly* staged by a Japanese director, Yoshio Aoyama, who spoke no English but insisted that things be done in the Japanese manner. For example, Butterfly tied her ankles together before slitting her throat so she would not fall in an undignified manner. (Contrary to common belief, Japanese women do not commit hara-kiri.) When he returned to direct the work for the Met National Company, dissatisfied with the way the Japanese costumes looked, Aoyama demanded Japanese underwear as well as outer garments. Antonietta Stella and Carlo Bergonzi, still completely Italian in spirit, were the principals. Mitropoulos again conducted.

That was the last time the Met played the Civic Opera House. In 1960 Bing announced that the company had "dropped Chicago from its present touring plans." The Civic Opera House was too small, he said. The Met was accustomed to touring to cities that did not have resident opera companies but rather local Met fund-raising organizations. Sponsorship by an independent impresario such as Zelzer was unusual, and he had to be permitted to show a modest profit. This meant that the Met lost money. So for two seasons Chicago looked for opera to its new resident company, and the Lyric, delighted not to have out-of-town competition, grew.

The New York City Opera returned for three dates in March 1960, celebrating the Ford Foundation's American opera project, with sponsorship from the Ford Foundation, the Lyric, and a local foundation. Carlisle Floyd's *Susannah* was heard for the first time, as was Douglas Moore's *The Ballad of Baby Doe,* and Kurt Weill's *Street Scene* was introduced to the city. The role of Baby Doe became the Chicago operatic debut of Beverly Sills. The series, so very different from what anyone else was bringing to Chicago, drew many curious and, eventually, gratified listeners. Attendance was 88% of capacity, proving once more that there are those who want only standard fare and there are those who would welcome something else. Here the public was ahead of the majority of the critics, who gave the impression they would settle for nothing less than masterpieces.

Weill, of course, was the most experienced composer of the group, and *Street Scene* was carried by a strong libretto (a play by Elmer Rice) rather than the score. *Susannah,* with Phyllis Curtin in the title role, Richard Cassilly as her brother, and Norman Treigle as the lusty evangelist Olin Blitch, showed a lasting value later demonstrated in time.

The Met had promised that it would seriously consider returning to Chicago if a "suitable hall" was available. The arrival on the scene of the new, large Arie Crown Theater at McCormick Place lured the company back in May 1961. But construction of the Arie Crown ran behind schedule, and the plaster in the theater was still wet on opening night.

It was never entirely certain just what the Arie Crown Theater had been designed to house, but apparently it was events in which the actors all were wired with microphones. It certainly wasn't an opera house. The four performances began with a routine *Aida.* A revival of *Martha,* dampened by the cancellation of Victoria de Los Angeles, was lost in the vast spaces. But a *Turandot* with Birgit Nilsson and Franco Corelli (who could take on the Grand Canyon if necessary) was exciting. Kurt Adler replaced Leopold Stokowski as conductor. Anna Moffo, who made her American debut with the Lyric, returned triumphantly as a major star of the Met in the opera with which she was most closely associated, *La traviata,* with Peerce. Adler again conducted.

If the acoustical problems went unsolved, the money issues apparently were under control, since Bing agreed to return in May 1962. This time he offered four Italian staples: a routine *Madama Butterfly;* Moffo in one of her major roles, *Lucia di Lammermoor;* Leontyne Price as Tosca; and Bergonzi in *La forza del destino.* With artists of this stature there was some fine singing, but as a whole the performances were disappointing. The public that bought tickets in 1961 didn't know anything about the hall. This time they knew it was dreadful, and many stayed away.

The Met packed up its scenery and, seventy-eight years after its first Chicago performance, vanished down the tracks, never to return. In all, the company had offered some 470 performances (some of them concerts) to Chicago audiences. The Lyric Opera of Chicago reached that number in its fifteenth season, 1969. Finding a comparably precise date for the Ravinia Opera is complicated because many works were cut, but the 470 figure can be said to have been reached in twelve seasons, by the summer of 1923. Few operagoers today, if asked which Chicago area company was the first to produce more opera than the

Metropolitan, would name Ravinia. In fact, few opera-goers today are aware that a Ravinia Opera ever existed.

Again, for two seasons, the Lyric was without competition. Then in 1964 Zelzer brought back the New York City Opera for twelve performances at McCormick Place. The run began on November 29 with *Die Fledermaus* and *The Merry Widow* back to back, matinée and evening, and because of illness in the cast Sills sang the lead in both performances. John Reardon, an excellent singing actor, was her Danilo. Both works were repeated.

The run continued a month later, on December 26, with Sills in *La traviata.* Another last-minute cast change introduced a young Chicago area singer, Sherrill Milnes, as the elder Germont. He returned as Valentin in *Faust.* Another new artist, Tatiana Troyanos, was Siebel. George Shirley, a notable young African American tenor, sang the Duke in *Rigoletto,* and Martina Arroyo, a great African American soprano, was heard as Butterfly. Treigle, one of the most remarkable members of the company, played four very different roles: Mephistopheles, Escamillo, Sparafucile, and Mozart's Figaro. Also in the *Carmen* cast were Beverly Wolff and another tenor who was to go on to other worthy things, Richard Cassilly.

And that was the last bid of a New York company to gain a Chicago foothold. Later in the decade Chicago was to become a stop on three cross-country tours. The short-lived Met National Company made springtime visits to the city briefly in 1966 and 1967 with reasonable success, and the American National Opera Company lit the Civic Opera House for three performances in the autumn of 1967, when the Lyric had been closed down by labor problems. Under Sarah Caldwell's direction it offered the first Chicago performance of Alban Berg's *Lulu* and ingenious stagings of *Tosca* (using photographs of the actual places in Rome) and *Falstaff.* The ill-fated Marie Collier (at the age of forty-four she plunged to her death from the fourth-floor window of a London hotel) sang Puccini's heroine. Peter Glossop sang the title role in the first performance of *Falstaff,* but the second went to a wide-ranging musician, who, among other things, had once been a Chicago music critic—Andrew Foldi.

Other companies would appear briefly in years to come, but for more than thirty years Chicago opera was to be Lyric Opera, and it is the history of that company we must now pursue.

9

The Lyric Theater
1954–1955

What set Chicago apart from New York in the mid-1950s is that enterprising individuals could accomplish remarkable things without going to the great power brokers of the local establishment. If your ideas were exciting and your initial efforts showed promise, enough of the public would be interested that support could be rallied.

The Lyric Theater was founded by as unlikely a triumvirate as one might imagine: an ambitious but unproven conductor eager to advance his career, a young Irishman with a questionable sense of the value of money, and a failed vocal student who was determined to make her way, somehow, in the world of opera. But they were in Chicago, a place where determined people can make their presence known. The founders of the Lyric, Nicola Rescigno, Lawrence Kelly, and Carol Fox, were able to put on a show, win over the public, and establish a company.

The senior member of the group was Rescigno. He was born in 1916 and was a professional who had conducted in Chicago with the San Carlo Opera Company and in the final seasons of the Chicago Opera Company. Giorgio Polacco had recognized his talent and assisted him in starting a career. Having an opera company of his own in a big American city in the manner of his former boss, Fausto Cleva, was the kind of chance he may have been searching for. Kelly and Fox can best be described as ambitious amateurs.

Kelly, one gathers, was delighted with the possibility of putting on shows, engaging important singers, and realizing his ideas on the stage. Fox was not looking for a place where she might sing. Apparently she had given up those ambitions sometime earlier. But if she was not to win recognition for her voice, she would win respect for her power—and how she used

it. Rescigno wanted to be the grand maestro, Kelly the great producer, and Fox the tsarina.

Both Kelly and Fox came from families with sufficient wealth to be regarded as society in the broader sense. Fox's father manufactured office furniture; his business ended when the site of his factory disappeared under the Kennedy Expressway. Kelly was in insurance and real estate. They knew important people, but society editors would not regard them as good copy.

Born in 1926, Fox received her formal education at the Latin School, a private establishment offering the first twelve grades to the youth of the so-called Gold Coast. Soon after graduation in 1941, rather than going to college, she went to Europe for vocal study. America's involvement in the war brought her home, and she continued her studies in New York. In 1942 she may have had a modest debut in Chicago society, but none of her classmates who were asked about it recalled the event or, for that matter, had strong memories of Carol. Giovanni Martinelli was her mentor in New York, and he lived to see her triumph at the Lyric, where Fox put him on a largely symbolic advisory board. Fox was coached also by Rescigno, and she turned to him when she learned of efforts in Chicago to reestablish resident opera. Together they scouted possible sources of support and, in the course of this, met Kelly, who soon became a close ally.

Kelly, born in 1928 to a real-estate developer and a mother devoted to opera, was the fifth son in a big Irish family. Business took them to Florida, where Kelly studied piano and performed briefly in public. Artur Schnabel gave him a few lessons and became his cultural hero. But Kelly did not see himself as a professional pianist, and his interests shifted from the keyboard to opera. At fourteen he was back in

Left to right—Nicola Rescigno, Carol Fox, and Lawrence Kelly, at the time they created Lyric Theater, 1954

Chicago, where he attended Loyola University and Chicago Musical College. He considered becoming a lawyer, until his father's death in 1950 put him in charge of the family business.

For three years the trio dreamed and talked and planned, with the hope of returning resident opera to Chicago. A landmark meeting took place in box 8 of the Metropolitan Opera House on February 22, 1952. The opera was *The Marriage of Figaro*, conducted by Fritz Reiner, with Cesare Siepi, Nadine Connor, Victoria de los Angeles, John Brownlee, and Mildred Miller. Probably aglow, they retired to the Waldorf-Astoria Hotel, talked all night, and went forth now dedicated to a mission. Their next step was the incorporation of the Lyric so that it could raise funds. In 1953 Rescigno left the board of directors, dissatisfied with the company's plans. In the end it became clear that there was no alternative to actually producing an opera and showing the public what you could do. When it was decided to offer a "calling card" performance in 1954, Rescigno was invited to direct it.

Kemper Insurance, the owner of the Civic Opera House since 1948, was supportive. Resident opera in

the theater would lower taxes. But uncertain whether these people had the money to pay the rent, only one date was released to them, Friday, February 5, 1954. The spell of Mozart still ruled and the opera was to be *Don Giovanni*, a work notoriously difficult to cast. When the announced performance sold out, a second date on Sunday, February 7, was quickly offered. The old decor in the Chicago opera warehouse was good, as were the costumes.

The Chicago Symphony was playing Thursday night and Friday afternoon under Bruno Walter, which means the musicians had been working at their best. The first Lyric orchestra was made up of nearly all Symphony people, but it never happened again. Reiner, at the time music director of the Chicago Symphony, would not tolerate sharing his musicians with an opera company, and they were banned from accepting further engagements of this type. Stage direction went to the man who had staged the last work of a resident opera producer in that theater (the Rodzinski-conducted *Tristan und Isolde* of 1947), William Wymetal.

In the initial program book Fox is named as president of the Lyric Theater and Kelly as secretary-treasurer. Some eighty persons are listed as members of the Lyric Guild. There are three guarantors and nine sustaining members, as well as lists of patrons, subscribers, and members.

Rescigno, who was given no title, did the casting. He knew that the key to success was experienced singers who could do good work with limited preparation. Nicola Rossi-Lemeni's Don Giovanni was a dramatic, larger-than-life sex symbol. His Leporello, John Brownlee, had been the Don in the Glynde-

boune recording that taught this opera to a generation. The three ladies, Eleanor Steber (Anna), Irene Jordan (Elvira), and Bidú Sayâo (Zerlina; in her last appearance ever in a staged opera) each projected a strongly drawn character, and the other men, Léopold Simoneau (Ottavio) and Lorenzo Alvary (Masetto), matched them all the way. The production was based on the premise that true professionals, given the basic requirements of a successful performance, won't let you down. An honored guest was Rosa

Eleanor Steber, as Donna Anna, greeting well-wishers backstage following Lyric Theater's calling-card performance of *Don Giovanni*

Raisa, who starred in the production of *Aida* that opened the Civic Opera House in 1929.

The two performances lost $924—"a mere nothing," Kelly told the press. (With some additional contributions the figure dropped to $286.) The Lyric Theater had offered its calling card, and the public had accepted it enthusiastically. The press was consistently good; "a big, bold, joyous performance," said the *Chicago Tribune*'s Claudia Cassidy, whose civic booster spirit went into high gear. No one in town wanted resident opera back more than she did, and if this was a possible source, it could claim her strongest support.

Riding the crest of the wave, Lyric brought Danny Newman on board. Not only had he been the press agent in the last year (1946) of the most recent attempt to form a local company (the Chicago Opera Company), but he had a wealth of publicity and personal representation experience in matters of presentation and audience development on many performance fronts behind him already. He was invaluable in helping Lyric lay a firm groundwork for cognizance and support of the new endeavor. His wisdom and initiatives were to be vital keys in Lyric's survival and growth into the twenty-first century.

Shortly after the calling card performance Fox was off to Europe to engage artists for a season in the fall. She was blessed with a historic situation that was not to last. First, this was what Italians now regard as a golden age of singing. Second, the Italian opera season did not begin until December. November was a month in which singers, many of whom had spent at least part of the summer in Argentina, caught a brief glimpse of their Italian homes. But there are few artists who will not sacrifice such reunions for an appropriate fee.

Fox came home with contracts for the services of, among others, Rosanna Carteri, Giulietta Simionato, Giuseppe di Stefano, Tito Gobbi, Gian Giacomo Guelfi, Nicola Rossi-Lemeni, and—the real treasure—Maria Callas. As one critic observed, it looked more like La Scala than an American company. The most significant contribution of the Metropolitan was Steber.

Why, when she was getting offers from all over, would Callas decide to come to a new American company? The answer is simplicity itself: money. In 1954 the unwritten rule in American opera was that no one was to pay more than the Met's official top fee of $1,000 a night. In fact, the official top fee was a fraud perpetrated for negotiation purposes. For example, in 1956 the Met was paying Jussi Bjoerling $1,500 a performance, but a side agreement with management called for an additional stipend of $500 for an unusually demanding role. Callas's husband and manager, Giovanni Battista Meneghini, had demanded $12,000 for six performances, plus travel expenses. Fox countered with $10,500 ($1,750 per performance), and he agreed. Most of these artists from Italy were new to the American stage but not to American listeners. They had figured prominently in the proliferation of complete operatic recordings following the introduction of the long-playing record, and they were preceded by a reputation based on recordings. The prospect of hearing Callas live, unedited, and in her American debut, stirred the blood.

Lunching one day in the Biffi Scala in Milan, Callas was approached by a friend who had just returned from America and reported the intense anticipation of her debut. "I hope I don't disappoint them," she said.

She didn't.

The secret of the Lyric Theater seasons was the same as the secret of the calling card performances: offer the public an evening vocally so powerful that shortcomings in other areas will be overlooked. Fox bargained that Callas would put the new Chicago company on the international musical map, and she was right. The Callas presence was worth every cent it cost.

The three-week initial season of Lyric Theater opened on November 1, 1954, with Bellini's *Norma*. Callas sang the title role with Simionato as Adalgisa, Mirto Picchi as Pollione, and Rossi-Lemeni as Oroveso. Callas had recorded the work in April and May of that year, and Dario Soria, who headed the Angel Records publicity team, was deeply involved in promoting this Lyric production. Cassidy, whose criticism in the *Chicago Tribune* frequently was a florid description of what she had heard, wrote, "She sang the *Casta Diva* in a kind of mystic dream, like a goddess of the moon briefly descended." In the *Chicago Sun-Times*, Felix Borowski went beyond Callas to view the production as a whole and announced that "the city has raised an operatic voice which deserves to be heard around the world." Since Borowski had been present from the beginning of resident opera in Chicago, these were words to be respected.

James Hinton Jr. wrote in the magazine *High Fidelity* in terms that meant something to a musician. As Hinton heard it, "From the purely vocal standpoint her Norma . . . was much as it sounds on records, which is to say, flawed. . . . There is the same veiled, bottled up feel to some tones, and some

Nicola Rossi-Lemeni and Maria Callas in *Norma,* the opening production of Lyric Theater's first season, November 1, 1954

unsteadiness to others. The real point is that these blemishes seemed extremely unimportant in the total theatrical context, for she is a person of such authority all ordinary scales of value are useless as measures of her achievement."

It must be added that this was one notable achievement in a group of notable achievements. For example, Hinton writes: "Simionato's Adalgisa was, in its way, as impressive as Callas's Norma."

For those who think of Callas in terms of her fiery exit in 1955, it is appropriate to recall that from the moment of her arrival in Chicago she was totally involved in the works she was to perform, a fully cooperative team player fully committed to whatever was necessary to achieve success—even if it meant singing "Casta Diva" nine times in rehearsal. Offstage, Callas did nothing more effective to win the affection of the public than to be seen frequently with her father, George, still a strikingly handsome man and a reminder that she was American-born. Since Meneghini knew no English, his social contacts were limited.

So here was a fabulous operatic event, and how many people were to hear it? The Lyric Theater in this respect was no different from the other Chicago companies that walked the narrow path to financial ruin between 1910 and 1946. Chicago once more had an opera company, but it lacked an appropriate operatic audience. *Norma* was repeated on November 5, 1954. It was safe to estimate that seven thousand people might want to hear it. To hope for anything beyond that was risky.

In the Civic Opera House the opening night of *Norma* brought a group of eminent singers of the past to the theater: Edith Mason, Eva Turner, Rosa Raisa, and Giovanni Martinelli. Polacco came to hear his protégé. It is said that—unnoticed in the crowd—Mary Garden was present. She had spent most of 1954 in the United States, and if she was there, no one from the Lyric knew it. She slipped through the city a silent ghost of vanished seasons. Earlier in the year she had gone to the abandoned Auditorium and stood silently on the stage. She was eighty years old. Nearly all her great audience was dead, and she, gaunt and simply dressed, would hardly be recognized as her former self. After the performance of *Norma*, Michael Turnbull reports, Garden turned to the accompanist, Bill Browning, and said of Callas, "Listen carefully, son. There's not been anything like this since I was up there. . . . She is a great actress, she is a great singer, but she acts on impulse. That's very dangerous."

Her comment is illuminating. Callas acted with her voice. In her recordings, although the visual dimension of the performance is lacking, the union of the words and the musical line conveys the intensity of her performance. This is not the case in most of the Garden recordings. The impact of Garden's great performances was in the visual dimension—apparently every gesture was carefully planned. The voice alone cannot evoke what we know from those who were present, that those were performances of the highest dramatic impact.

Callas and Meneghini checked into a housekeeping apartment at the Ambassador West, and when not at the theater she attended to marketing and cooking like a good Italian wife. Life offstage became more involved on November 4, when an attorney filed a $300,000 suit on behalf of Edward Richard Bagarozy, who, with his wife, had in 1946 offered Callas vocal coaching and legal advice in New York. The following year, before returning to Europe, she had signed a management agreement with him.

She was to appear in court on November 8. Instead, she denied that the Bagarozys had done anything to advance her career, and on November 8 she turned up not in court but on stage with Léopold Simoneau and Tito Gobbi in *La traviata*. Singing carried the show, but it was obvious in an opera with many comprimario roles that the Lyric lacked experienced people for these assignments. Again there was one more performance, on November 12. Hinton did not feel the role suited her. "Belief in the idea of Miss Callas lying poor and neglected in a furnished room is too much to ask of any audience."

Callas's greatest success of the autumn, in part because it brought forth her finest singing, was *Lucia di Lammermoor*. For Hinton, "the tone was almost always free and clean, and the brooding, tragic side of the character, so seldom more than hinted at by most Lucias, was completely projected."

"No previous interpreter of Donizetti's score imbued the Mad Scene with so much heart-gripping poignance," Borowski wrote in the *Sun-Times*. The second performance, on November 17, closed with a seventeen-minute ovation and twenty-two curtain calls. Callas said, "I have been touched by God's finger."

There were five other productions that autumn. On November 3 Tito Gobbi made his Lyric debut, appearing in *The Barber of Seville*. The role was a specialty. It had served for his American debut in San Francisco in 1948, and he had even made a film of the opera. Simionato was a lively Rosina, and Léopold Simoneau played the Count.

Twenty-five years later, in reviewing the Lyric's silver anniversary, Claudia Cassidy would refer to Tito Gobbi as "practically the Lyric's godfather." It was an apt description. From his first appearance at the Lyric until his death thirty years later, beyond his many appearances onstage (and his later activities as a stage director), he was an adviser, entrepreneur, friend, and confidant to the company, a vital force both behind the scenes and publicly in the Lyric's artistic growth and its imprimatur as a major opera company.

Part of Chicago operatic myth is that in 1954 the city heard *Tosca* with the Callas-di Stefano-Gobbi cast of the incomparable 1953 recording. It did hear a *Tosca* with di Stefano and Gobbi, but the title role was sung by Eleanor Steber. Without Callas it was still a powerful performance.

Rosanna Carteri was the striking Mimì of *La bohème*. Simionato returned in a *Carmen* far more Italian than French. It had a mixed reception.

The surprising element in the 1954 repertory is an American opera, *The Taming of the Shrew*, by Vittorio Giannini (1903–1966), in its first full-scale staging. Fox, it can be assumed, had been unaware of the existence of the score, and its presence is probably due to Rescigno. With its all-American cast, headed by Thomas Stewart, it was a welcome contrast, a delight for the adventurous element of the public, and a clue to what the Lyric Theater might have produced in later autumns.

There were, of course, no sets in the old Chicago opera warehouse for *The Taming of the Shrew*. Gerald Ritholz scrounged around for likely-looking stuff and staged the opera out of things originally intended for *Mignon, Il trovatore, Romeo and Juliet,* and a few other works, including *Boris Godunov.*

William Wymetal directed everything. Rescigno conducted six of the eight scores. *Carmen* and *La bohème* went to Jonel Perlea, a seasoned maestro. In terms of the long-term achievement of the company, nothing more important happened in 1954 than the arrival of Michael Lepore as chorus master. Later he was to produce marvels season after season.

The balance sheet was frightening. There were sixteen shows, and attendance was 84%, with *Taming of the Shrew* most responsible for unsold tickets. (Without it, the figure would have been 90%.) Expenses were $224,294 for producing the season, and $287,676 for other operating costs. Income was $216,438 from

ticket sales, $57,240 from contributions and other sources. This left a red figure of about $239,000. Balancing the books required 47% subsidy, a figure in the fatal range that had destroyed seven previous opera companies in the Chicago area. But it could be raised. Lyric guilds now had some 650 members, and the city was excited to the degree necessary for fund-raising to succeed. As Hinton put it, "a real old fashioned grand opera season was what Chicago needed."

Callas returned to La Scala, which paid homage to her in January 1955 by spending $140,000 (the largest sum ever at that time for a new production) to revive Spontini's *La Vestale,* a bel canto score from 1807 that had little to recommend it except the opportunities it provided for the singer of the leading role. Opening night the house went wild, as only an Italian audience can, and Callas lifted it to greater heights at the close of act 2 by collecting carnations that had been flung on the stage and presenting them to Toscanini, who was seated in a stage box. The Old Man, who used to insist that flowers were for race horses and corpses, was sufficiently impressed to respond graciously.

A more ambitious Lyric season was planned for 1955. The number of productions increased to twelve (two of them triple bills) in five weeks, the number of performances to twenty-five. Callas opened on October 31 once more with Bellini, this time in *I puritani,* in a production borrowed from Palermo. The work had been popular in the nineteenth century but had not been heard in Chicago since a Mapleson production in 1886. Callas had recorded the work in 1953, and di Stefano and Rossi-Lemeni of that cast were with her. Making his Chicago debut was the comprimario tenor Mariano Caruso, who was to become a Lyric institution. *I puritani* provides opportunities for spectacular singing, and in a Callas-crazy city it was a success. Critic Roger Dettmer of the *American* threw objectivity to the winds and wrote, "I am a slave in her spell."

For her next assignment, on November 5, Callas sang major Verdi, *Il trovatore,* with Jussi Bjoerling making his Lyric debut as Manrico and with a great Italian mezzo-soprano, Ebe Stignani, as Azucena. William Wildermann, who was to sing bass roles with the company for many years, also made his first appearance. Every element was present for a memorable evening. This was the only occasion when Bjoerling and Callas appeared together. On the afternoon of November 8, before the second performance, Callas signed a contract with the Metropolitan Opera that she would open its next season, on October 29, 1956. And she did, for an undisclosed, but assuredly generous, fee.

Then came *Madama Butterfly*. Callas had recorded the work at La Scala (with Herbert von Karajan) that August. Her Chicago performances were the only times she sang it on the stage. To believe Irving Sablosky in the *Chicago Daily News,* she was "a fully trained member of the Kabuki Theater." This success probably should be attributed in part to the director, Hitzi Koyke. Here di Stefano was her Pinkerton, Robert Weede her Sharpless. The powerful realization of the tragic Japanese heroine, vocally explicit in the recording, was now fully revealed, and the enthusiasm of the audience was boundless.

Opening night was November 11, with a repeat scheduled for November 14. But the response was such that Kelly and Fox went to Callas and begged her to do it a third time. In 1955 the Chicago operatic public had grown to the degree that you could actually hope to draw 10,500 persons to hear Callas in *Madama Butterfly*. There was no danger of an empty house. When the box office opened, the line stretched to the corner, then around the corner, and back to the bridge at the rear of the theater.

With the final curtain, another drama began. The Bagarozy lawsuit remained on the books. Meneghini refused to consider a settlement. Federal process servers had been haunting Callas since she arrived in the city. To secure her contract, the Lyric had agreed to protect her from Bagarozy, but it could not hold due legal procedure at bay indefinitely. From the cloud of charges and countercharges one may surmise that a deal was made. After the last performance the papers might be served, and after her final bow, Callas found a U.S. Marshal in her dressing room.

"I will not be sued!" she is reported to have said. "I have the voice of an angel! No man can sue me." The civil rights of angels have never been precisely defined in Chicago. The papers were thrust at her, and, as the marshal turned to leave, photographers—conveniently present?—captured her blazing with rage. When she had dressed, Kelly and Meneghini slipped her out of the theater by a side door and proceeded to the apartment of Kelly's brother, where they spent the night spewing venom in all directions. At sunrise they gathered their possessions, drove to the airport, and took the first plane out—it went to Montreal—that offered a connection to Milan.

Kelly was convinced that Fox had admitted the process servers to the theater to destroy his friendship

Maria Callas shouting at a process server who had just delivered his subpoena, immediately after her last performance of *Madama Butterfly* (and her last appearance at Lyric Theater), November 17, 1955

with Callas, and Callas readily accepted that Fox was the betrayer. (I wonder whether Fox might have been tempted to offer a reprisal for Callas's abandoning Chicago for New York.) Process servers or no process servers, she was not going to return in 1956, but Fox probably felt she still needed her to keep the young company afloat.

When passions cooled, Meneghini had to face the truth that, if his wife was to have an American career, this lawsuit must be resolved. His stubbornness made the issue more costly and stressful than necessary. Rossi-Lemeni, caught in similar circumstances, made a deal for $4,000. The Callas suit was settled out of court for an undisclosed sum in November 1957.

On October 29, 1956, Callas made her New York debut at the Metropolitan Opera in *Norma*. "No fee," she remarked, "is high enough for singing that role." Some of the local press, oblivious to the world west of the Hudson, tried to claim it was her American debut. In fact, Callas sang at the Met in three seasons,

1956/57, 1957/58, and 1964/65, offering four roles: Lucia, Norma, Tosca, and Violetta in *La traviata,* for a total of twenty-one performances. In Chicago she sang six roles for a total of twenty-five performances.

In the end Callas deserted Fox, but not Chicago. She returned to the Civic Opera House in January 1957 for her first American concert, six arias (Bellini to Verdi) in a benefit performance for the Alliance Française. She demanded and got the Chicago Symphony to accompany her. Fausto Cleva conducted. She played the role of the prima donna magnificently, her throat encased in diamonds, wearing a white ermine coat as foil for dramatic gestures. When not needed, she draped the garment over the rail of Cleva's podium.

Tullio Serafin at a rehearsal in Chicago, 1955

All was forgiven. Chicago was no longer "a city of Zulus" but a place to which she was delighted to return. "I love Chicago. How can you hate an entire city for what a few people [presumably the Lyric management and the federal government] have done?"

When she returned for a second such appearance in 1958, Norman Ross, one of her closest friends in her Lyric years, hosted a champagne supper, possibly with the hope that she could be persuaded to return to sing opera. The society columnist Cholly Dearborn observed, "Tonight's gathering possesses all the potentialities of a Lucrezia Borgia poison ring party."

In November there actually was an effort to begin talks. Fox, who had just given birth to her daughter Victoria, offered to go to any of the cities where Callas was scheduled to sing, suggesting as possible repertory *Anna Bolena, Thaïs, Macbeth,* and *Il Turco in Italia.* Time passed with no response.

Callas, it must be understood, was always entirely involved with herself and her work. The important men in her life, Meneghini and later Aristotle Onassis, provided her with an opportunity to be totally self-centered. Apart from her musical training, she had very little education. Her methods were intuitive rather than intellectual or analytic. Wally Toscanini, the daughter of the Maestro and one of the great figures in Milan society, did much to launch the Callas career but found her a banal woman who had never escaped a middle-class upbringing. When her singing career ended, Callas had no larger interests to which she might turn. "I don't understand," Wally Toscanini said, "how an artist of such sensitivity and talent onstage could be so devoid of personality in real life. She was a very dull woman."

Chicago had to wait nearly twenty years for a third concert. After 1958 Callas was never again heard in the city during her vocal prime.

Remarkable as Callas's contributions to the 1955 season were, she was not the only star of first magnitude. At La Scala her greatest rival was Renata Tebaldi. Callas suggested that she be invited to Chicago, but although the two ladies had to share the same dressing room, their paths never crossed directly. Hard on the opening night of *I puritani* followed *Aida* with Tebaldi, Gobbi, and a tenor no one in Chicago ever heard again, Doro Antonioli as Radames. Callas appeared at the *Aida* performance, a vision of high fashion, and it is said that in the Nile Scene, as Tebaldi prepared to launch her high C, Callas dropped a diamond bracelet and drew attention to her box as she

was searching for it with a flashlight. Since the boxes are set fairly far back in the Chicago opera house, many were oblivious of the event.

So long a season required two conductors, and Fox may well have gone to Callas for advice. In any case, the Lyric hired the man who had presided over Callas's Italian debut in August 1947 at the Verona Arena, the now seventy-six-year-old Tullio Serafin, one of the truly grand maestri of Italian opera.

The Callas *Trovatore* was followed on November 7 by a Tebaldi *La bohème,* with di Stefano, Gobbi, and Rossi-Lemeni. Again Serafin conducted. In turn, the Callas *Butterfly* was succeeded on November 12 by a *Rigoletto* with Bjoerling, Gobbi, and an American soprano, Teresa Stich-Randall, as Gilda. In the cast, as Giovanna, was a typist from the Lyric office, Ardis Krainik. Rescigno conducted. Serafin returned to conduct *Faust,* with Bjoerling, Rossi-Lemeni, and the Marguerite of Rosanna Carteri.

The two triple bills of singing and dance appear to have been Rescigno's project. He conducted both of them. Vocally most memorable in the first bill was Puccini's *Il tabarro* with the debut of Carlo Bergonzi; Gobbi sang the sinister bargeman. The work was a clear success, but this did not prevent it from remaining unheard for another forty-one years. In Monteverdi's masque *Il ballo delle ingrate* and her dance version of *The Merry Widow,* Ruth Page, who had presided over dance at the Ravinia Opera, affirmed her new role with the Lyric.

The second bill featured a bloody *Cavalleria rusticana,* with di Stefano and Bergonzi alternating as Turiddu to Ebe Stignani's Santuzza. Fresher fare was *Lord Byron's Love Letter,* a one-act opera by Raffaello de Banfield (b. 1922) from a Tennessee Williams play, with Astrid Varnay. Page's ballet of *Il trovatore* completed the evening.

For the final week the Lyric turned to its basic product, Italian opera, with three scores. Donizetti's *L'elisir d'amore* offered Léopold Simoneau and Carteri with Serafin, who returned to direct Bergonzi, Robert Weede, and Dorothy Kirsten in *L'amore dei tre re.* The season closed with Bjoerling in one of his finest roles, Riccardo in *Un ballo in maschera,* with Gobbi and the debut of Anita Cerquetti as Amelia. Rescigno conducted.

The company was doing good work, but it was losing a lot of money. Operating expenses were up, amounting to $619,906, and an increase in income to $415,518 again left more than $200,000 worth of red ink. The Lyric paid creditors with money it had deducted for income tax, which meant that eventually the biggest debt was owed to the Internal Revenue Service, which promptly froze Fox's and Kelly's bank accounts. By 1957 the money was raised and books balanced, but it was grim for a time. What saved the situation was that having seen resident opera once more—and on a level far above that of the companies of the 1940s—the city was not prepared to give it up.

In the end, the Lyric Theater was destroyed not by debt but by an internal power struggle that revealed the fundamental instability of the governing troika. In mid-January 1956 the Lyric board authorized that three-year contracts be issued to Rescigno (who had been restored to the board of directors), Fox, and Kelly. In 1954 and 1955 Rescigno had been compensated for his services as a conductor, and after March 1955 Fox and Kelly had been paid $150 weekly as compensation and for expenses. Under the proposed contracts Fox and Kelly were to receive $10,000 annually, and Rescigno was to be paid $7,500 plus conducting fees. Rescigno was to submit a draft of a contract that would serve as a basis for the other two members. He did so on February 12.

Rescigno's draft contained language that one might expect to define the job of the artistic director of an opera company. He had the right to approve or disapprove the choice of repertory, artists, and other matters central to the production of the 1956 season and the two following seasons. Fox called it a veto clause. Rescigno replied that, if he was the artistic director of the company, he was responsible for what it produced; he was the one to approve artistic decisions.

The truth of the matter is that, from the start, titles at the Lyric were decorations rather than definitions. Fox saw herself as the founder of the Lyric, and as the general manager she was the chief executive of both the business and the artistic side of the company; Rescigno was an employee. Bruno Bartoletti, who later held the title for many years, was never an artistic director of the Lyric in the sense that James Levine is the artistic director of the Metropolitan Opera. Fox, when piqued, might refer to Bartoletti as "the flute player" and Ardis Krainik as "the secretary"—after years of distinguished service. Part of the problem may have been Kelly's sexual orientation. In the beginning, there is reason to think that Fox would have welcomed a closer involvement with him. When this proved impossible, she married a physician, C. Larkin Flanagan.

When on February 17 Kelly—as treasurer of the Lyric board—refused to sign salary checks until the contract issue was resolved, Fox ordered the locks on the company office and the combination of the company safe to be changed. Kelly was denied access to the company books, and he and Rescigno were not to receive mail sent to them at the company office.

On February 22 Fox summoned the board of directors to authorize her to sign checks on all the company bank accounts. The authority was denied because the board was deadlocked. Fox had invited Claudia Cassidy and her associate Seymour Raven to the meeting, and it is reported that Cassidy challenged Rescigno, saying she would "run him out of town" if he did not sign a contract waiving the right of approval over Lyric productions. In short, he was to hold the title of artistic director, but the actual power of the office would belong to Fox. Of course, Cassidy had no business being at that meeting, and the rest of the Chicago press had not been aware of these conflicts.

But the Lyric crisis exploded in the press, with Cassidy the outspoken advocate of Fox's cause. Fox came forward with a public statement that can be seen as a small masterpiece of hypocrisy: "I regret all this more than I can say. Mr. Kelly, Mr. Rescigno and I have worked successfully in the past on the basis of agreement, respect and trust. What destroyed this happy arrangement I do not know." The Lyric, she said, would give Rescigno all he requested—except veto power.

Cassidy and the *Tribune* came out vigorously for Fox. Roger Dettmer and the *American* became advocates of Kelly and Rescigno. The *Sun-Times* and *Daily News* remained neutral, which, as later events proved, Fox viewed as a hostile position. For Borowski, critic for the *Sun-Times,* "the squabble over who will bring opera to Chicago in 1956" had become "as murky as the second act of *Rigoletto*."

On March 8 Kelly issued a statement indicating a deadlock resulting from a stacked and stalemated board had existed since February 22. As he saw it, two members, who were Fox appointees, should resign so that the remaining board members could proceed to the presentation of a 1956 season. He wrote, "While Miss Fox has done an excellent public relations job until recently for Lyric Theater, her current actions make it clear that she seeks complete authority which would prevent our performing as we have hitherto-fore. We feel strongly, because of experiences over the past three years, that Miss Fox is not equipped to take control from the people who have performed these duties satisfactorily without her interference."

Fox then proceeded to engage artists for the autumn of 1956 as an officer of the Lyric, but in case the Lyric came to an end, on March 8 a new entity, the Opera Theater Association, was incorporated, functioning out of Lyric's offices. Pro-Fox members of the board wished to initiate an orderly transfer of assets (including artists' contracts) from the Lyric to the Opera Theater Association.

In April the Opera Theater Association sued the Lyric Theater, requesting that its assets be turned over to the new corporation. Kelly, through his attorneys, said the purpose of the suit was to destroy the Lyric and "enhance the ambitions and aspiration of Carol Fox to be known and publicized as the sole 'creatrix' and sole 'founder' of the Lyric."

On May 2, Judge John J. Lupe of the Superior Court, on the basis of $15,000 in payments, dismissed the suit of three creditors seeking receivership of the company. He then dismissed Kelly's suit. Fox said that the board might be reunited if Kelly and Rescigno "would be satisfied with contracts without those unbearable clauses."

Cassidy, in her history of the first twenty-five Lyric seasons, sings a similar tune. "It was sad to lose the brilliant imagination of Larry Kelly and the flowering of Nicola Rescigno's lyric talent." But she dismisses the battle for control with the statement that "temperamental differences blew up a storm."

For Kelly and Rescigno, the wisest course was to acknowledge Fox's victory and leave Chicago. In 1957 they founded the Dallas Civic Opera, with Kelly as general manager and Rescigno as artistic director. Their trump card was Callas, who sang for them three seasons. Dallas proved that Kelly was wonderful at production and hopeless at staying on budgets, but Texas loved his work, and the bills were paid. He died young, in 1974, of cancer. Rescigno, who had never realized the promise of his youth, reappeared to conduct Donizetti's *La favorita* in 1974 and the overture to *Don Giovanni* at the Lyric's twenty-fifth anniversary gala in 1979 (which was disappointing).

10

The Fox Years

1956–1981

With Lawrence Kelly and Nicola Rescigno out of the picture and with Carol Fox in full charge, with her board behind her, the Lyric Theater became the Lyric Opera of Chicago. The company was organized along traditional lines. Leonard Spacek was the president, and there were sixteen directors. Fox, as the general manager, was an employee of the board, although she rarely conveyed that impression. In her view, the board worked for her.

In retrospect, the most remarkable thing about that first year of the "new" organization was that it happened at all. In March the company seemed to be in ruins, yet at 8:00 p.m. on October 10, 1956, there was an opening night, and thereafter for five weeks there was a season. And it was a season with an ample measure of remarkable things. Much of it would be eclipsed by the Lyric's achievements in later years, but for the Chicagoans who bought tickets that year, it was filled with discovery. There were eleven operas and, reviving a tradition from the past, a gala concert on November 10.

Fox had hired some remarkable talent. In addition to major singers who had appeared with the Lyric before, there were Birgit Nilsson, Inge Borkh, Mario Del Monaco, Richard Tucker, Ludwig Suthaus, and Paul Schöffler. Danny Newman reported that Tito Gobbi had now acquired a special role with the company. Dedicated to Fox, Gobbi kept close watch on the European operatic scene and recommended promising individuals for Lyric engagements.

The list of artists from Chicago includes Ardis Krainik among the mezzo-sopranos and Billy Mason among the tenors. Little did either suspect that their Lyric careers would culminate in rather different jobs. And the young Bruno Bartoletti, making his Ameri-can debut, could hardly have guessed that he would be conducting at the Lyric into the next century.

Important as these people were, the new name that was to mean the most in terms of the immediate artistic growth of the company was Georg Solti. He was forty-four, the head of a major European theater in Frankfurt, supremely talented, ambitious, enterprising, and dedicated to quality. He was not unknown to the Chicago audience, having made his debut in 1954 in concerts with the Chicago Symphony at the Ravinia Festival.

The foundation on which every operatic performance rests is the orchestra. For two seasons the Lyric had made do with a group of local professionals, but no one had had the time to shape them into a real ensemble. Solti, a master orchestra builder, conducted nine of the twenty-five performances of the autumn. In this and the season to follow it was he who created the Lyric Opera orchestra as a major asset of the company. Asked for the key to his success, he replied, "Patience. Lots of patience." The musicians were not bad, but they were inexperienced. They did not know the repertory and might be unfamiliar with the style. Solti's success is documented in a recording for British Decca based on the gala.

Opening night brought out one of the finest productions in the old Chicago Opera warehouse, the 1910 sets for *La fanciulla del West,* a production so fine that the Met borrowed it in 1961. Dimitri Mitropoulos, one of the Met stalwarts, was in the pit for his only Lyric engagement, conducting music he never played in the New York house. Because he excelled in Mahler and Schoenberg one might fear that he would be uninvolved in Puccini. Not so. In this, the composer's "American" opera, the richness of color and harmony was fully developed.

Eleanor Steber, one of the great Minnies, was the girl, and Mario Del Monaco cut the right figure as her bandit lover. Gobbi, who might profitably have studied a few John Wayne movies, was the pursuing sheriff and romantic rival, Jack Rance. The image of Steber riding onstage in the final act with a pistol in each hand proved unforgettable. Lyric revived this work in 1978 and 1990 but never did it greater justice. Aldo Mirabella Vassallo directed *Fanciulla* and five other productions; the rest went to William Wymetal.

Steber, Del Monaco, and Gobbi were back on October 16, 1956, in *Andrea Chénier*. This was familiar Italian fare, right out of the warehouse, as was *Il trovatore* on October 23 with Herva Nelli as Leonora, Jussi Bjoerling as Manrico, and Ettore Bastianini as Di Luna. Bartoletti appeared in the pit for the first time, probably recommended by Gobbi, who had heard him conduct Rossini's *Moses in Egypt* in Lisbon and been impressed. Bartoletti conducted four productions that season.

His debut was overshadowed by that of Solti on October 17 in *Salome*, the first German opera to be produced by the Lyric. A scandal in 1910, when this decor was used for Mary Garden, *Salome* in 1956 became a study in obsessive passion. Inge Borkh had the voice and the body essential for the role, and she was ably matched with Ramón Vinay as Herod and Alexander Welitsch as Jochanaan. But what put it all together and carried it to its tragic crest was the Solti baton. Many, leaving the theater, asked themselves, "Is that the orchestra we heard last season?"

It was a one-two punch. Solti was back on October 20 with the Lyric's first Wagner, *Die Walküre*. There was a good, old production in the warehouse to frame a spectacular new voice on the stage: Birgit Nilsson, not yet an international superstar, but already a superb artist. She was Brünnhilde to Paul Schöffler's Wotan, and the first act brought Ludwig Suthaus and Borkh as Siegmund and Sieglinde. Ardis Krainik is immortalized in the photograph showing her in Valkyrie dress as Rossweisse. Solti's power and sweep as a Wagner conductor was shortly to be documented in his recording of the *Ring* operas, but to encounter him live in a theater was an extraordinary experience.

It was felt that the production of *La traviata* in the warehouse was too old to be used again, so Fox went to Palermo for scenery. Steber sang Violetta, with Léopold Simoneau and Bastianini singing the younger and older Germonts. Caring for the dying Violetta in the final act was Krainik, transformed from Rossweisse to Annina.

Solti went from Strauss to Wagner to Mozart, and on October 29 led the Lyric's second *Don Giovanni*. Eleanor Steber, Nicola Rossi-Lemeni, and Simoneau of the 1954 cast returned. The rest were not quite up to the previous standard, but Solti made it all work.

From then on the season was dominated by Renata Tebaldi. Today she is regarded as a legendary figure, and, undoubtedly, there have been few more beautiful voices. But while Callas was an actress with an incredible sense of stagecraft, Tebaldi could take direction only up to a point; what dazzled her audiences was what she could do with her voice.

On October 30 she sang *Tosca* opposite Bjoerling and Gobbi—a great night. (Billy Mason had sung the shepherd in 1954, and this production marked his second Lyric season in that role.) Tebaldi closed the season with *La bohème*, again with Bjoerling. It was ravishing to the ear. Her finest performance was in *La forza del destino*, with Solti proving he was one of the most powerful and idiomatic Verdi conductors of the day. Tebaldi was surrounded with her peers: Giulietta Simionato, Bastianini, and Nicola Rossi-Lemeni.

Then Richard Tucker made his Lyric debut. Since Fox (as a matter of policy) would not engage American singers if she could cast an Italian in the role, Tucker's presence was a cause for special rejoicing. (Over the years Italy, in response, gave Fox a medal and an unprecedented $20,000 grant for her advocacy of Italian opera.) Harry Zelzer, as part of his vendetta against the company, used his influence with the Hurok management to prevent Hurok artists from singing with the Lyric. As a result, Tucker's brother-in-law Jan Peerce never appeared in a Lyric production. Gobbi got a second chance to sing Seville's barber opposite Simionato and Simoneau, a show more or less picked up from the previous season.

By June the Lyric had realized 80% of the previous year's sale of subscription seats, and here the guiding hand of Danny Newman was already paying rich dividends. He was a master of promotion, and he had ties—nationally as well as locally—to all kinds of institutions and individuals who could enhance the visibility and imprimatur of the company.

Newman's basic tenets were promotion and, especially, audience subscription, dating from when he was fourteen and selling his first subscriptions door-to-door for a civic theater group called the Mummers of Chicago. The experience convinced him that growth and longevity in any performing company hinged on the institution's ability to sign up an audience for the full season of its offerings, thereby ensuring sold seats for whatever the company would present. In the case of the Lyric it led, through consistency and fine-tuning, to seasons virtually sold out before the curtain went up on opening night. (And it should be noted that Newman's book, *Subscribe Now! Building Arts Audiences through Dynamic Subscription Promotion,* to this day never out of print since its first edition in 1977, has become a "bible" for thousands of arts organizations that have both survived and thrived because of Newman's ideas and personal efforts.)

The Lyric Opera of Chicago offered three series in 1957, and the company was doing the best box office business to date. As it turned out, 93% of the seats were sold for thirteen productions—a new record—and three of them were heard three times. Solti was to conduct three operas; Serafin was back to do four. Gianandrea Gavazzeni made his debut and led two works; Bartoletti prepared three. Aldo Mirabella Vassallo was the stage director for eight Italian operas. Solti had Hans Hartleb for *The Marriage of Figaro* and *Don Carlo,* his two greatest successes. Vladimir Rosing, who had been Sir Thomas Beecham's stage director at Covent Garden, did three works.

Musically the season had a strong opening, *Otello* with Del Monaco as the Moor, Gobbi's unsurpassed characterization of Iago, and Tebaldi as a lovely Desdemona. The conductor Tullio Serafin concentrated on his singers, and they gave the audience something to cheer. The old production was still attractive.

The great American debut of the autumn, providing the moment most likely to be remembered, came on October 16 in *La bohème.* Anna Moffo, twenty-five, radiantly beautiful and exquisitely poignant as Puccini's tragic heroine, was vocally and dramatically dazzling. Even a stand-up-and-sing character like Bjoerling became so involved with the music and the drama that he was weeping real tears as the final curtain fell. Gianandrea Gavazzeni conducted. Moffo was back as Philine in a revival of Thomas's *Mignon* with Simionato in the title role. Tebaldi and Bjoerling were the principals in a routine *Manon Lescaut.* The classic double bill of *Cavalleria rusticana* and *Pagliacci* apparently gave the audience all it expected. Simionato was Santuzza. In the Leoncavallo one was more impressed by the complex character Gobbi made of Tonio than Del Monaco's somewhat wooden Canio. But then came *Andrea Chénier* in a battered old production led by Gavazzeni that nonetheless gave Del Monaco, Tebaldi, and Gobbi a frame for a unified, dramatically

Danny Newman

intense performance. After that season Del Monaco shifted his American career to the Metropolitan.

Encountering Eileen Farrell and Tucker in *La Gioconda,* one heard two singers mightily acclaimed in New York who, indeed, sang beautifully but had little concept of how to turn this involved plot into a drama. Maria Tallchief appeared in the *Dance of the Hours.* As a concession to Tebaldi—who saw the piece as a vehicle for herself—Fox staged Cilea's *Adriana Lecouvreur,* improvising a production out of the warehouse. Giuseppe di Stefano, Gobbi, and Simionato were assets and joined Serafin in expending great talent on somewhat trivial material. Di Stefano was put to better use in *Lucia di Lammermoor* with Moffo, who was poignant in the title role, but neither could make up for indifferent staging.

The only Austro-German opera of the season was Mozart's *The Marriage of Figaro,* with Solti, Walter Berry in the title role, Moffo a beguiling Susannah, Steber as the Countess, Simionato as Cherubino, and Gobbi as the Count. For its full potential and unified style, more rehearsal was in order. Really solid Italian opera came in Solti's version of *Un ballo in maschera,* with Bjoerling and Anita Cerquetti, a singer whose career was all too short (1949–61). Solti then turned to the greatest success of the season, *Don Carlo,* in the first new production offered by the Lyric. Cerquetti, Bjoerling, and Gobbi were a grand trio of principals, joined by Boris Christoff in his debut with the company. His masterful realization of Philip II promised marvels to come.

Backstage at *Don Carlo*, 1957; *left to right,* Boris Christoff and Jussi Bjoerling

Looking backward at the season, Cassidy was unhappy. There were some fine things, she wrote on December 1, but also there was "a growing uneasiness as evidence piled up that the Lyric has ceased to develop and has begun to decline. . . . the Lyric has increasingly begun to produce the kind of opera it was organized to protest," the indifferently staged productions of the 1940s.

Now, after opening seasons filled with promise, she writes, "the Lyric management blew sky high. . . . I never quite understood it and always regretted it." This was Cassidy avoiding responsibility for consequences of one of her political moves. The problem was quite apparent: Fox did not have the full qualifications to run an opera company. "What she needs," Cassidy writes, "is a musical director or artistic director of the highest quality. The way things are now, each visiting conductor and stage director seems to take full charge. If they are first rank, we are in luck. Otherwise we revert to provincialism. The Lyric, like the Chicago Symphony, does not exist to follow public taste but to lead and develop it."

What Cassidy failed to say was that Fox had such a person on her payroll—Georg Solti. But the Cassidy-Solti dynamic had become troublesome. Cassidy praised Solti's first year at the Lyric (and claimed she was the one who had suggested Carol Fox invite him to the Lyric in the first place), but as Solti's second Lyric season progressed, Cassidy turned against him.

The most prevalent explanation centers around an incident that occurred when Solti conducted *The Marriage of Figaro* and played the recitatives from the podium. Either because the lights at the podium were not practical for him to see the score, or as a point of vanity (Cassidy took the latter explanation), a light shone down from above the conductor and made him more visible than he might otherwise have been. Cassidy felt this was gauche, and she was critical of him on that occasion and for the remaining operas he conducted that season.

On the one hand, Solti—like George Szell before him—supposedly said he did not take Cassidy's judgments seriously. On the other hand, he knew how powerful Cassidy was and how influential her opinions were to Carol Fox. Roger Dettmer, then the critic of the *American,* said later that Solti said he would be crazy to come back and "let her kill me more" and even rejected not only an invitation from Fox to return to the Lyric, but any further invitations for Chicago engagements (including one to become the Chicago Symphony's music director when Fritz Reiner retired, then died, in 1963) until Cassidy had left the *Tribune.* In 1969, when he took the Symphony position, Solti did say, "Cassidy was out to get me. She kept me from going to the Chicago Symphony when Reiner retired. But this time [1957] she did me a great favor. If I had remained as chief conductor of the Lyric, I never would have been offered the Chicago Symphony Orchestra again."

Another view of the situation reports that Cassidy influenced Fox to keep Solti from further Lyric dates and that Cassidy lobbied for Artur Rodzinski (whom she had championed, but who had been dismissed from the Chicago Symphony in 1948 after only one season as its music director) to become Lyric's music director. In any event, Rodzinski did conduct at the Lyric in 1958. The drawback was that, at sixty-six, he was a dying man.

In June of 1958 the *Lyric Opera News* announced that "General Manager Carol Fox has named Pino Donati as her musical assistant." He was present in Chicago, preparing the fall season. It was a brilliant,

Machiavellian move on Fox's part. Before coming to Chicago, Donati had been a seasoned Italian operatic impresario, who could be expected to know all the things, theoretical and practical, needed to run a company effectively. Fox was protected. Donati had directed a major Italian opera house (the Teatro Comunale in Bologna) and had been general manager of the summer opera festival in his native city of Verona. Well educated at the Milan conservatory, he was the composer of two operas and had written music criticism for Italian periodicals. Throughout his Chicago years (he died in 1975) Donati professed to know no English, hence the press was told he could not be interviewed. And since the press was never allowed to see him in action, it was always conjectural what he did. Obviously he did a lot. He dealt with stage crews, orchestra members, and the backstage musical staff—through interpreters. Invariably cordial and polite, he conveyed the impression that in the Italian repertory he could put any standard work before the public with a practiced hand.

The 1958 season opened on October 10 with Gobbi as Verdi's Falstaff. Moffo was Nanetta, and the merry wives were a wonderful trio: Tebaldi, Simionato, and Annamaria Canali. Serafin, in what proved to be his last season, conducted. He had grown extremely frail and had to be assisted into the orchestra pit and to the chair from which he conducted, but once the stick was in his hand he was transformed. The performance was broadcast on WBBM AM/FM, restoring Chicago opera to the air after decades of silence. Rudolph Ganz, the elder statesman of Chicago music, provided commentaries.

Eyebrows lifted when it was announced that the Russian conductor Kiril Kondrashin, who had shared Van Cliburn's Moscow triumphs, was to direct *Madama Butterfly*. He faced Italian veterans Tebaldi, Canali, and Di Stefano, and he proved in the first rehearsal that he knew the work down to the last hemidemisemiquaver. Traditional liberties ended. They sang what Puccini had written. It was completely fresh and miraculous. Di Stefano, ever the tenor opportunist, maneuvered Tebaldi in the final duet of act 1 so her concluding high note went to the back of the stage and his went straight out to the audience. (If he had done that to Callas he probably would not have lived to sing act 3.)

This was Tebaldi's only Chicago opera for 1958. Bing liked to claim that the Lyric was too dependent on talent from the Met (it wasn't), when, in fact, he

Left to right—Bruno Bartoletti, Carol Fox, and Pino Donati, 1963

was busy stealing established artists from the Lyric. Tebaldi went to him first in 1955; in 1959 she had no time for Lyric engagements. Fox promised her *Fedora* (which Bing would never have revived) and got her back in 1960. But the day of those informal negotiations was ending. Bing had the financial resources to make long-term commitments, and Tebaldi responded. Fox had limited financial reserves and often had to make a casting on the basis of whoever was available at the last minute. And the European calendar was changing. Opera seasons were opening earlier, and if singers were in Chicago, they were unavailable for rehearsals at home.

Nilsson was back in *Turandot,* with Serafin conducting, and a handsome production from San Franciso in which Di Stefano was Calaf and Moffo a poignant Liù. Vladimir Rosing handled the stage like a master. Every act blazed with color, every act had movement and thrust apart from the music, and the drama built resolutely to the final climax.

The Lyric went from its best to its worst two nights later with a well-cast *Il trovatore,* entrusted to Rodzinski's assistant Lee Schaenen, late conductor of the New York City Opera. He had such stalwarts as Bjoerling, Bastianini, and Simionato, and he displayed them in a context of capricious tempos and an insecure ensemble. For contrast Chicago had Serafin

above—Falstaff, 1958; *left to right*—Renata Tebaldi, Tito Gobbi, Annamaria Canali, and Giulietta Simionato

left—Birgit Nilsson in costume as Turandot backstage at the Metropolitan Opera, with Rosa Raisa. Both ladies sang Turandot several times in Chicago, Raisa's 1934 performance introducing the work to the city, Nilsson's 1958 appearance marking Lyric Opera of Chicago's first production of the opera.

again with a double bill of *Pagliacci* and *Gianni Schicchi*. It was really Gobbi's night. His sinister Tonio dominated the Leoncavallo (despite Di Stefano's histrionics), and then the comic Gobbi revealed himself in Puccini's comedy of cross and double-cross. Moffo was Lauretta, the character with the aria everyone knows.

November 1 brought the first of three performances of *Tristan und Isolde* from Rodzinski. For those who heard the previous one in 1947 with the Chicago Symphony, there were obvious shortcomings. The important thing was that they didn't care. The musicians in the pit were giving them everything they had, and, after two seasons with Solti, that was a great deal.

Before arriving in Chicago, Rodzinski had said to me, "You know, in 1957 they invite me to do something Italian, and I said anybody can do that. Give me a real assignment. So they came back with *Tristan*. And I asked, 'Can the orchestra play it?' 'Yes,' they told me, 'the orchestra is in great shape.' So we will see." Rodzinski's heart was growing weaker by the day. When he sailed from Italy, he stood at the rail and told his son Richard that he would never return. In rehearsal he adopted a familiar technique, learned in his Philadelphia years from Stokowski. An associate, Schaenen, conducted the preliminary sessions, and Rodzinski sat in the front row, the score in his lap, supervising. He elected to make the cuts Toscanini had made at the Metropolitan, which lessened the burden somewhat.

The cast was as fine as one might put together in a period in which there was no outstanding Tristan tenor before the public. Karl Liebl sang the role and sang it effectively, holding his own with Nilsson, who was to become the greatest Isolde of her generation. Grace Hoffman was Brangäne, Walter Cassel sang Kurwenal, and William Wildermann was King Marke (whose censure was substantially trimmed). As in 1947, Wymetal directed, with the same old Chicago opera decor.

There were high-quality professionals on the stage, and Rodzinski flooded the audience with music that swept everything before it. The singers opened their mouths and hearts and gave Wagner's great song of love and death their full commitment. At various times critics have announced that the Lyric had come of age, but nothing was more exciting than this quantum leap into a new dimension of opera. We knew now that Lyric was not just a skillful Italian company. If it put forth its best effort, it could do anything.

Hardly had the applause faded than Rodzinski was filled with anxiety. He had done it once, but could he do it again a week later? The second performance was not as good as he wished, although few in the audience would complain. He went to Fox, begging for a short orchestral rehearsal before the final performance on November 10. All the time she had to give him was an hour that afternoon. And, as he described it that evening, "For that hour I give them hell."

The third *Tristan* was surely as fine as the first, perhaps finer, but at the ultimate cost. In his dressing room afterward Rodzinski was gray and limp with fatigue. In his eyes you read the satisfaction of achievement. He had given everything to this music. Isolde's *Liebestod* had been *his* immolation scene. He remained in Chicago a few days, then fled to a Boston hospital, where he died seventeen days after his final performance.

Rodzinski had been scheduled to lead *Boris Godunov* with Christoff, set to open on November 17. When it was obvious that the conductor could not prepare the score, Georges Sebastian took over, saved the day, and offered a strong performance, in which Christoff excelled. The old Chicago production, with the Kremlin onstage for the Coronation Scene, was still beautiful. By the time of the last performance Rodzinski was dead.

Serafin and Steber were strong elements in *La traviata,* and Gobbi and Simionato offered an acceptable *Barber of Seville,* despite Schaenen's conducting. Sebastian presided over *Rigoletto* with Bjoerling, Gobbi, and Moffo heading a strong cast. He was back, as were Bjoerling, Gobbi, Simionato, and Leonie Rysanek, for the final production of the season, *Aida.* Both were Italian staples, but the *Rigoletto* was a success, and the *Aida* little more than routine.

In 1959 Fox lured Margherita Wallmann, one of Vienna's most respected directors, to Chicago with the expectation that she would be staging *Der Rosenkavalier.* Instead, she found herself in charge of a new production of *Carmen,* designed by Piero Zuffi. A Viennese colleague, also making his debut and thoroughly in command, was the conductor Lovro von Matačić, who was to become a major asset to the company. Jean Madeira was the gypsy firebrand, with Di Stefano as Don José. The French baritone Ernest Blanc sang Escamillo, but both the musical and dramatic dimensions of the role gave him difficulties.

The production of Verdi's *Simon Boccanegra,* which Chicago was hearing for the first time, came from the

Lyric Opera's 1959 *Così fan tutte* cast with Carol Fox. Standing, *left to right:* Fernando Corena, Leopold Simoneau, Carol Fox, conductor Lovro von Matačić, Elisabeth Schwarzkopf; seated: Walter Berry, Sylvia Stahlman, Christa Ludwig

Rome Opera and proved that when the Lyric went shopping internationally for sets, it could find attractive productions. Strongly cast, the opera proved a remarkably effective vehicle for Gobbi as the doge and Margherita Roberti and Tucker as the lovers. This was impassioned grand opera. *La Cenerentola,* basically an ensemble piece, was dominated by a coloratura-mezzo, Anna Maria Rota. In looks and style it was pleasantly old-fashioned. The public viewed it with polite indifference. *Turandot* returned with Nilsson and Di Stefano, Gavazzeni conducting, but it was no match for their performances under Serafin the previous year.

Von Matačić had two other assignments, Janáček's *Jenůfa,* with Gre Brouwenstijn, and *The Flying Dutchman,* with Nilsson as Senta. Rome was responsible for the sleazy *Dutchman* decor, and poor judgment brought the otherwise weak cast, but von Matačić and Nilsson gave their best, and the chorus was excellent. There was no *Dutchman* production in the Lyric warehouse, and here (and in *La Cenerentola*) Fox decided to borrow rather than build. *Jenůfa* was a more substantial success, a forceful presentation of a major twentieth-century work. The production and director came from Covent Garden, as did key members of the altogether excellent cast. But it was von Matačić and an orchestra playing as it had for Rodzinski a year before that made this an evening filled with opportunities for discovery, which, history demonstrated, were insufficiently appreciated. There was no more Janáček for twenty-seven years, although the box office disaster of the series was not this work but the Rossini.

After the first performance of *Un ballo in maschera* in the Bostonian version, I congratulated Nilsson (who had sung Amelia with Di Stefano). "I love these Italian roles," she said. "They are so light and easy on the voice." One can wonder how many Italian sopranos would regard Amelia that way, but then, they never sing Brünnhilde. Gobbi was in his element as Renato; Bartoletti conducted. Alas, after her Met debut and the corresponding increase in her fees, few could afford to hire Nilsson for the Italian operas she sang so well.

The discovery of the season was a Mozart opera Chicago had never heard before, *Così fan tutte,* in a production with sets from San Francisco but practically everything else from Vienna. Josef Krips and von Matačić shared the conducting assignment. The three ladies were Elisabeth Schwarzkopf, Christa Ludwig, and Sylvia Stahlman (a major American talent), and the gentlemen were Léopold Simoneau, Walter Berry, and Fernando Corena. Adolf Rott directed. It was pure gold. One might ask, If the Lyric can function on this level, why settle for anything less?

Unfortunately one had to settle for considerably less before the season was over. *La Gioconda* provided another chance to hear Farrell as the lady with the mysterious smile, and though she sounded beautiful, she was wooden opposite Tucker, whose acting skills were hardly superior to hers. *Thaïs,* revived in an ancient production, was nearly a total disaster despite the presence of Leontyne Price onstage and a fine conductor, Georges Prêtre, in the pit. The Massenet magic of days past never reappeared. Price, singing the role for the first time, was miscast.

That season, Ardis Krainik played three brief roles. It was her farewell as a singer with the company, but already she had become an important figure behind the scenes. She was, in effect, Fox's (largely unsung) assistant, and that was an assignment that covered a great deal of territory. As Danny Newman described it years later, Fox put Krainik "into half a dozen different positions but Ardis never gave up what she did before, she just added on. She 'married' Lyric Opera and served it wholly. She did everything possible for its benefit and learned everything one could learn about producing opera. One could see, even in the earliest days with Lyric Opera, that she was an extraordinary person."

In terms of box office dollars, 1959 attendance was down a little over 6 percent from 1958, and the average of twenty-seven performances was some 84% of capacity. Fox announced this had been a season "for

the critics"—meaning the press had demanded of her that she take these losses. I replied (*Chicago Sun-Times,* December 6, 1959), "A season of opera is not produced for the critics. There are only four of them. They have no choice about attending. And anyway, they get in free. An able management produces opera for the public, but in such a way that the critics will applaud the way in which it is done." Moreover, a season for the critics suggests that some effort was made to get the critics to suggest what they would like to have done. Nothing remotely like this took place.

I wrote further, "The departures that characterize this season 'for the critics' were the disappearance from the Lyric roster of the majority of its established stars and the substitution of a repertory largely made up of less familiar scores. My idea of a season 'for the critics' would involve the Lyric producing from its own resources operas distinctively imaginative and enterprising either as repertory or stagecraft, such as Wieland Wagner's Hamburg version of *Carmen* with Kirsten Meyer making the title character a long-legged floozy like the Dietrich of *The Blue Angel.* The Lyric, unfortunately, came up with nothing even approximating this."

Lyric's *Carmen* was conservative and traditional. *Jenůfa* was imported from Rafael Kubelik's revival of the work at Covent Garden. And *Così fan tutte* came from Vienna.

In March 1960 Lyric Opera of Chicago brought the New York City Opera to the Civic Opera House for a three-night run of Chicago premières of important American works. Phyllis Curtin took the title role, and Norman Treigle was Olin Blitch, in Carlisle Floyd's *Susannah;* Beverly Sills was Baby Doe, Walter Cassel was Horace Tabor, and Frances Bible was Augusta in Douglas Moore's *The Ballad of Baby Doe;* and Weill's *Street Scene* was headlined by Elisabeth Carron as Anna Maurrant, Frank Porretta as Sam Kaplan, and Joy Clements as Rose Maurrant. Julius Rudel conducted the first and third operas; Emerson Buckley led the second one.

Announcing the 1960 season, Lyric Opera anticipated the largest number of subscribers in its history, the secret being the most conservative repertory offered by any major American company. Tickets for seven nights of opera could be obtained for as little as $17.50, and time payments were offered. Ten works were in the repertory, and subscriptions ran through the season on Monday, Wednesday, and Friday. The Saturday performances were reserved for single-ticket buyers. Every cast contained at least two or three major stars. Top price for the main floor was $9.00, and the house was scaled to $2.50 in the upper balcony. A college teacher earning $5,000.00 a year could afford a $6.00 balcony seat. Mail orders moved most of the non-subscription seats before the box office opened in October.

A powerful cast brought artistic glory to *Don Carlo* on opening night in 1960. This was the product of interaction between the conductor, Antonino Votto, who was making his Lyric debut, the director, Christopher West, and such forceful musical and stage presences as Richard Tucker in the title role, Tito Gobbi as Rodrigo, and Boris Christoff as King Philip. Margherita Roberti, whose Lyric career was all too short, was poignant as Elisabetta, and Giulietta Simionato, who had gone to the Met the previous year, returned in triumph as Eboli. Roberti also sang two of the season's stagings of *Aida*.

Leontyne Price really showed her stature when she sang the title role in *Aida*. Carlo Bergonzi was Radames, Simionato was Amneris, and Antonino Votto conducted. The scope and spirit of the work were well realized. Price was to return in November for an effective *Madama Butterfly*.

Eberhard Wächter created a vivid impression as the Count when he made his debut in *The Marriage of Figaro* with Berry, Ludwig, Rita Streich, and Schwarzkopf, with Josef Krips conducting. This was Lyric proving it could offer Sacher torte as well as cannoli. Renata Scotto made her American debut in *La bohème* with Tucker and sang Micaëla to Jean Madeira's Carmen, with Di Stefano and Robert Merrill. Von Matačić offered vigorous support. His great night proved to be *Die Walküre* with Hans Hotter, Jon Vickers, Nilsson, and Ludwig offering outstanding performances. Vickers and Gre Brouwenstijn lifted the first act to romantic heights, the Wotan-Fricka debate was not a bore, and the third act gained in power as it progressed. The Valkyries were not always equal to the demands of their music, and von Matačić conducted a finer performance than his orchestra was able to play.

Gobbi's malevolent Scarpia returned with Tebaldi and Di Stefano in what, apart from Gobbi, was a rather routine traversal of *Tosca*. The gentlemen then joined her in *Fedora*, which she had demanded as a reward for her return. A play by Sardou, intended for Sarah Bernhardt, it was fine for Tebaldi's voice but very slight in its demand for characteriza-

tion. In the climactic moment when Di Stefano (who was singing at his best) was telling her why her fiancé was murdered, she was rearranging her costume. She was not the most dramatically involved of singers. Gobbi made a memorable appearance on a bicycle. Fox knew better than to build a production. The sets, improvised by Gerald Ritholz, included the Garter Inn from *Falstaff*. Despite the presence of Tebaldi, Tucker, and Gobbi, *Simon Boccanegra* lacked the dramatic intensity of the previous year. One way Fox saved some money was that she gave a large number of secondary roles to Americans rather than importing singers from Italy to perform this music. The advantage of the Italians was that they were experienced artists, who had sung these roles many times. The young Americans often required more rehearsal and direction than they received.

For the publicists, the great event of 1961 was opening night, when Joan Sutherland made her debut as Lucia di Lammermoor with Tucker. There were lots of high notes, but the opera was dramatically unconvincing. Vickers was the strongest element in a fairly routine *Andrea Chénier*. Real excitement came in the third production, *Mefistofele,* which Boris Christoff restored to the repertory after an absence of twenty-five years. Bergonzi was Faust, Ilva Ligabue, Marguerite, and Ludwig was Helen of Troy. Votto conducted this opera and the two previous ones. For many the work was a discovery. A second discovery followed. Christoff, Bergonzi, Ludwig, and Farrell were the principals in *La forza del destino*. It was a powerful evening despite Farrell's limitations as an actress.

Mozart and Beethoven took over, with Peter Maag in charge. *Così fan tutte* again glowed with Schwarzkopf, Ludwig, Stahlman, Simoneau, and Berry, a marvel of a cast. *Don Giovanni* combined Wächter's swashbuckling seducer with Teresa Stich-Randall as Donna Anna, Irmgard Seefried as Zerlina, and the bounteous presence of Schwarzkopf and Lisa Della Casa alternating as Donna Elvira. Simoneau and Berry completed the principals. For *Fidelio* the powerful combination was Nilsson and Vickers, with Seefried, Berry, and Hotter.

One of the delights of these seasons was Christoff's appearance in supporting roles. Like Chaliapin, he liked to play Basilio in *The Barber of Seville*. It was a cast offering arrivals and departures: Sesto Bruscantini making his American debut as Figaro, Simionato singing her last role with the Lyric as Rosina.

Leontyne Price as Madama Butterfly, 1960, with Mildred Miller (left) as Suzuki

Jon Vickers as Florestan in *Fidelio*, 1961

Renata Tebaldi and Tito Gobbi in *Tosca*, 1960

Then came *The Harvest,* part of a Ford Foundation project to commission American operas and support their first production. Asked to pick an American composer, Fox was at a loss. Donati might have heard of George Gershwin, but he was unavailable. They turned to the composer of the one full-length American opera the Lyric had staged, Vittorio Giannini. There was nothing especially American about his libretto, a rather ordinary tragedy of rural lust, and the score, with some intense lyric moments, could have been written by an Italian living in Italy. The composer conducted a good cast, with the young Marilyn Horne in the leading role and Geraint Evans making his debut in a part rather different from those he played in later years.

Cassidy called the work a disaster, but it was a craftsmanlike score of a type many more celebrated composers had written, and it was no more successful than the American scores Campanini had sponsored more than forty years earlier. The economic failure of the work made the strongest impression on the company. Two performances would have been adequate, but there were four, with an abundance of empty seats. The Ford Foundation achieved the exact opposite of its worthy objective, and the cause of American opera was set back many years. When the cause was revived, the Chicago Opera Theater would be responsible.

Christoff had long wished to do *Prince Igor,* and as he departed in 1961 he was told the work was scheduled for the following autumn. He asked who would sing the title role. "Why, you will," he was told. He explained that Igor is a baritone role and said he would sing both Galitsky and Konchak. Fox and Donati, for whom Russian opera (*Boris Godunov* excepted) was an unknown land, hastily engaged a fine Russian-American singer, Igor Gorin. Oscar Danon conducted an able cast, and Rosing directed. The real challenge of the score was one of the longest and best-known ballet scenes in opera, the Polovtsian Dances. Ruth Page and her troupe rose to the occasion by importing a newly arrived Russian dancer who already was famous for his recent defection from Soviet Russia, Rudolf Nureyev, who easily dominated the stage. Still, the great image of the production, possibly the great image of his Lyric career, was Christoff as Konchak, with a real falcon perched on his wrist.

Christoff was back in the next opera, singing Colline in *La bohème*. "I like the role," he told me. "I understand Colline." Tucker was Rodolfo. *Tosca* brought Gobbi as Régine Crespin's nemesis. *L'elisir*

d'amore benefited from the presence of Alfredo Kraus. But these three shows, all conducted by Carlo Felice Cillario, revealed a disturbing tendency in the Lyric: the depth of casting was not as consistently great as in the past. One heard Italians of lesser reputation and, one assumes, lower fees.

Mozart was still first class. *The Marriage of Figaro* cast Gobbi as the Count, Lisa Della Casa as his Countess, Rita Streich as Susanna to Renato Capecchi's Figaro, and Teresa Berganza as a delectable Cherubino. Peter Maag, currently the Lyric's Mozart man, was in charge of what proved to be an elegant evening. *Samson and Delilah* had been planned for Simionato and Vickers. Both canceled, and Chicago got Rita Gorr and Hans Kart. They were acceptable— Gorr far more than that—and conductor Pierre Dervaux provided strong leadership. He remained for the final two productions, *Rigoletto,* with Tucker heading a not very exciting cast, and *Orfeo ed Euridice* in the Paris version, with Gabriel Bacquier and two glorious ladies, Della Casa and Streich.

In retrospect, the level of vocal talent available to the Lyric in its first ten seasons is astonishing, and it becomes apparent that the continued success of the company—despite the occasional hastily assembled production—came from the quality of the singing it could offer on its best nights. For Italians, these were years of true gold at La Scala, and prior to the Milan season many of the finest artists were in Chicago, demolishing large steaks at the Italian Village restaurant (a sort of unofficial club), where they often preferred American beef to their native cuisine.

As to the ladies, Callas has been discussed, but Renata Tebaldi sang in six seasons of the first decade and played a dozen roles. Chicago heard the cream of her repertory. Giulietta Simionato, probably the greatest Italian mezzo of the day, sang in six seasons and thirteen roles. Among the tenors, Giuseppe Di Stefano appeared in six seasons and a dozen roles. Carlo Bergonzi sang seven roles in three seasons. The celebrated tenor roster was not dominated by Italians. Jussi Bjoerling was with the company four seasons, from 1955 until 1958. He sang only eleven operas in the final two decades of his career, and Chicago heard him in nine of them, including the last he ever learned—Don Carlo. Richard Tucker, America's pride, was heard in seven seasons and eight roles. Jon Vickers, the greatest Canadian singer of his generation, made his debut in 1960 and was heard on an almost annual basis for the rest of his career.

Boris Christoff, truly the principal bass, appeared in seven seasons between 1957 and 1963, singing ten roles. But among the men there was no one to rival Tito Gobbi, who appeared in nine of the first ten seasons, playing nineteen roles. Christoff never sang at the Metropolitan. He would not join a production that was running but insisted on taking part in the rehearsals, and Rudolf Bing would not agree to this. Gobbi appeared in the New York house in twelve seasons but sang only four roles. Both of these remarkable artists (they were brothers-in-law, married to the daughters of a distinguished music critic) belonged distinctively to Chicago.

The Lyric was good at getting people at reasonable prices before they made a Met debut and their fees doubled. Birgit Nilsson came to the Lyric in 1956 and sang six roles in five seasons. Anna Moffo made her American debut with the Lyric in 1957 and was back two more times for a total of nine roles. And Leontyne Price, whom the Lyric first heard in 1959, sang four roles before departing after 1960. Elisabeth Schwarzkopf did not go to the Met until 1964, but she sang with the Lyric in 1959, 1960, and 1961 in a total of three roles, two of them things New York never heard from her. She would have returned in 1962 if the Lyric had given her *Der Rosenkavalier,* but Fox felt the company was unequal to the task. Bing was prepared to stage *Rosenkavalier,* and Schwarzkopf sang it for him.

In those early years artists did not need to be engaged long in advance, and the Lyric planned on a fairly casual season-to-season basis, announcing its autumn repertory early in the year. Bartoletti recalls Fox asking Tebaldi early in 1960 what she would like to sing next year. "Oh, Carol," was the reply. "Why don't we do *Fedora?*" (It had not been heard in Chicago for thirty years.) A production was ready for two performances in late November.

By the spring of 1962, the Billy Mason who had sung the offstage shepherd boy in *Tosca* in Lyric's earliest seasons had become Bill Mason (William, of course, but virtually everyone calls him Bill), a young man in his early twenties, who contacted Ardis Krainik to see if there was any work for him at the Lyric Opera. She suggested he come back in October, and when he did, he was named the assistant to Pino Donati, the man he was to refer to later as his mentor and second father. Mason spoke some opera-libretto Italian but crash-coursed his way (mainly through on-the-job training) into speaking the language fluently in a company in which it was almost a first language. Quickly he became immersed in all elements of opera production. Donati's heart attack in 1969 brought Mason deep into matters of rehearsal scheduling, and he took that task over completely when Donati died in 1975. Mason remained at the Lyric until 1978 (with a few gaps), holding various positions through the years, among them assistant stage manager, assistant director, stage manager, and production stage manager, dealing with both the administrative and physical elements of getting productions onstage.

The Lyric Opera of Chicago ended its first decade in 1963. Bartoletti conducted a Verdi score beloved in Italy and virtually unknown in the United States, *Nabucco.* The Met had produced it once (three years earlier), and the Lyric borrowed its decor. Gobbi and Christoff headed the cast. A two-performance wonder, Danica Mastilovic, sang Abigaille. Chicago opera was on the air again; *Nabucco* was broadcast.

In addition to *Nabucco* Fox offered Christoff roles in *Fidelio* and *The Barber of Seville.* "Is that all you have for me?" he asked. The reply was yes. On his arrival he found *Faust* in the repertory, with another Bulgarian bass, Nicolai Ghiaurov, usurping one of the great Christoff roles, Mephistopheles. Christoff was furious. For him, Ghiaurov was always "that Communist." He refused to go and hear him sing but would ask colleagues, "Is that Communist really any good?" Eventually there was a painful scene in public, all the more difficult because his brother-in-law Gobbi defended Fox, and later they came to blows (but over a family, not an artistic, matter). Christoff departed, never to return, but his European career continued to flourish. For many in the Lyric audience it was an irreparable loss. Ghiaurov notwithstanding, the *Faust* actually was not very good. The production, an import, was unattractive, and the performances were routine. Ghiaurov had things to learn. Guy Chauvet sang the title role with Andréa Guiot as Marguerite. Pierre Dervaux conducted.

Vickers and Crespin were the principals in *Fidelio.* The other German score of the season was *Tannhäuser,* with the "Black Venus" seen at Bayreuth, Grace Bumbry, Crespin as Elisabeth, and Dimiter Uzunov in the title role. Vickers and Gobbi were the driving forces in *Otello,* with Sena Jurinac in her Lyric debut a lovely Desdemona. Vickers and Tucker alternated in *Un ballo in maschera,* with Crespin and Bumbry. Two Italian standbys brought Alfredo Kraus and Teresa Berganza in *The Barber of Seville* and Kraus and Fernando Corena in *Don Pasquale.*

In an interview in 1963 with Peter Jacobi, Fox was asked why the Lyric did not have a full-time artistic or music director. Actually it did—Donati—but after the conflict with Rescigno Fox was unwilling to offer anyone else the title in case they might take it seriously. "Why?" she replied. "Rudolf Bing doesn't have one. I've spent twenty years studying music. Am I not capable of artistic direction?" A newcomer from out of town might destroy the company. "We must keep in mind what the public will accept, and I think that those of us who have been connected with Lyric are more capable of doing that than a newcomer not familiar with Chicago taste."[1]

But Fox did, at the end of the 1963 season, ask Bartoletti to become the company's artistic director. Bartoletti told her he could never do that because it would be a slight to Donati. The compromise was that Donati and Bartoletti were named artistic *co*-rectors, and that situation prevailed until Donati's death, at which time Bartoletti became the sole artistic director, holding the post for quite a few years to come.

Régine Crespin and Richard Tucker in *Un ballo in maschera*, 1963

The Chicago repertory was nearly 70% Italian, as opposed to 52% at the Metropolitan and 49% in San Francisco. At the New York City Opera Italian works made up less than a quarter of the productions. Fox's reply was that Italian singers were generally more available and standard Italian works were certain to produce the 90% attendance the company felt was essential. German opera required different singers, different conductors, and two German works a season were apparently all the box office could maintain. Producing twentieth-century opera was risky. New productions must be borrowed or built, longer rehearsals would be necessary, and the public reaction might be difficult to predict. What succeeded in San Francisco might fail in Chicago. One got the impression that in the last analysis, money questions dominated most issues. "Opera costs money. Our problems are financial." And a board of businessmen wanted to sustain conservative policies.

Five of the nine operas of Lyric's 1964 repertory were Italian. The season opener, *Il trovatore,* proved that even an all-star cast can yield a lukewarm performance. Only Grace Bumbry's Azucena stood out for vocal and dramatic force, while Ilva Ligabue, Franco Corelli, and Mario Zanasi offered passable, but not particularly interesting, performances.

Donizetti's *La favorita* was presented in a full-scale production of the Paris version of 1840, ballet included. Fiorenza Cossotto made her American debut as Leonora, and by the fourth act she sang freely with a warmth and color well suited to the role. Alfredo Kraus made the best of the generally unrewarding role of Ferdinand, but better stage direction could have helped Ivo Vinco's and Sesto Bruscantini's otherwise solid vocal performances achieve better dramatic results. The ballet offered some excellent dancing by Kenneth Johnson and Patricia Klekovic.

Grace Bumbry and Franco Corelli were back as Carmen and Don José, and while Bumbry was the best reason for seeing the production, Corelli was giving direct, intense singing and acting in the confrontation scenes of the second and fourth acts.

In its eleventh season, this was the third time the Lyric offered Verdi's *Don Carlo,* as usual in Italian and without the Fontainebleau Scene. Tucker, Gobbi, Leyla Gencer, and Ghiaurov gave their all in a grand-manner production that profited from Bruno Bartoletti's strong conducting.

The year 1964 marked the centennial of the birth of Richard Strauss, and the Lyric presented *Ariadne auf*

Reri Grist as Zerbinetta and Irmgard Seefried as the Composer in Lyric Opera's first *Ariadne auf Naxos,* 1964

Naxos. It was only the second time it had offered the composer's music. The conductor Eugen Jochum, in his Lyric debut, shaped an idiomatic and beautiful performance. The principal ladies were outstanding: Régine Crespin grew ever more impressive through the evening as the Prima Donna/Ariadne; Reri Grist was a marvel vocally and dramatically as Zerbinetta; and Irmgard Seefried shone as the Composer. The seasoned veterans Erich Kunz, Gerhard Unger, and Morley Meredith kept the comedy spinning, and Jean Cox (as Bacchus) and Crespin gave the opera a radiant finale.

Renata Tebaldi returned after three seasons, in *La bohème.* Her voice was not as fresh as it had been in earlier years, but this time she gave Chicagoans a more involved, concentrated, and consistent Mimì than they had seen from her before. Renato Cioni, Sesto Bruscantini, and Luisa De Sett headed the lively group of bohemian companions, and Pierre Dervaux conducted with a good sense of Puccini's idiom.

The Lyric returned with its calling-card opera, *Don Giovanni,* and the production could be taken as proof that, on a good night, the company could command a style and a standard that spoke resoundingly for its years of growth. The sets of Franco Zeffirelli, on loan from Dallas, were evocative, as were the good looks and uncommonly high level of acting found in the principals. Nicolai Ghiaurov made us believe he could be the most celebrated Don Giovanni since Pinza, Erich Kunz was—as ever—the perfect Leporello, and Josef Krips had the orchestra playing with a high polish and crisp Mozartian style. Teresa Stich-Randall (Donna Anna), Phyllis Curtin (Donna Elvira), and Nicoletta Panni (Zerlina) contributed well-defined characters and lively singing, and Theodor Uppman gave Masetto some welcome dignity rather than the usual portrayal of him as a yokel.

La Cenerentola was considerably better than at Lyric's first try five years earlier. Teresa Berganza was the centerpiece of an excellent cast, spinning Rossini's

Geraint Evans as Wozzeck, 1965

vocal filigree to perfection and reveling in the wise, feline character of the heroine. Renzo Casselato was ideal as her clever prince, and Sesto Bruscantini, Giorgio Tadeo, and Renato Cesari responded to Riccardo Moresco's direction, avoiding slapstick and farce. Carlo Felice Cillario's conducting was another plus.

Crespin, Tucker, and Gobbi were back for *Tosca,* and they were well matched vocally and dramatically, each bringing out the best in the others. The Lyric ended its season with empty ticket racks and with a public solidly behind it.

In 1965 the Lyric Opera took a major step, which opened new horizons for the company and its audience. The Chicago public had the impression that Bruno Bartoletti's interests lay solely in Donizetti, Verdi, and Puccini, but the management of the Lyric knew otherwise. Bartoletti was passionately interested in twentieth-century opera and had been pressing for its inclusion in the Lyric repertory from his earliest days of influence with the company. Bartoletti was certain that Carol Fox realized Lyric's future had to include a broadening of the repertoire, but he felt also that she did not know what directions to take. He insisted that for both the growth of the company and for what he called "the *cultural* people of the city"—the audience beyond those seeking only the standard repertoire—the Lyric must do operas such as Alban Berg's *Wozzeck,* and when he became artistic codirector with Pino Donati in 1963, that was an opera he proposed. Fox was skeptical, Donati even more so, but Bartoletti prevailed and *Wozzeck* was given as the seventh of Lyric's 1965 offerings. The production—at Bartoletti's further insistence—was the same one for which he had conducted in Florence two years earlier, designed by Luciano Damiani and staged by Virginio Puecher (a student of the brilliant Giorgio Strehler).

If Donati was wary, he realized nonetheless the importance of what was for the Lyric at that time an extraordinary amount of rehearsal time. It all paid off. This was a true fusion of stage and pit. The opera was given in English, with Geraint Evans affirming every dramatic and vocal truth of the score, abetted by a like-minded cast and orchestra.

Wozzeck was presented in three acts, and after each of the first two Fox told Bartoletti, "It's a disaster. Many people are leaving the theatre because they detest it." It was only when Bartoletti asked the orchestra to stand before the beginning of the last act that Fox, and even Bartoletti himself, realized the impact the performance was making. Bartoletti said later in an interview, "It was the longest applause in the history of our theatre." When the opera ended, the audience stayed, stood, and cheered. Not only had Bartoletti made his point that the Lyric should present twentieth-century opera; he demonstrated another major belief of his, that effective staging was vital to the full realization of opera's musical-dramatic mission.

Lyric offered another novelty that season, a double bill of Ravel's *L'Heure espagnole* (in its first Chicago performance since 1928) and Carl Orff's *Carmina Burana* (in its only Chicago-staged version of the work to date). Direction and staging played an important part in the success of both productions, and, in the Orff, Michael Lepore's chorus and Ruth Page's choreography and dancers demonstrated they were among Lyric's greatest resources. Teresa Berganza and Alfredo Kraus were a complete delight in the Ravel, and Jean Fournet's authoritative conducting of both works contributed to an exciting evening of music and dance.

The season had begun with Lyric's second staging of Boito's *Mefistofele*. This time the title role went to Nicolai Ghiaurov, who was the strongest figure onstage. Alfredo Kraus and Renata Tebaldi, as Faust and Margherita, were effective without creating any particular sense of poignancy. Elena Suliotis made her American debut as Elena, and her richly colored voice became more impressive the longer she sang. Nino Sanzogno, in his Lyric debut, conducted with the sure hand of a seasoned maestro.

Three Verdi operas were given. *Simon Boccanegra* was splendidly effective as both music and drama. Tito Gobbi's singing and stage direction were major forces in the success of the production, and Ilva Ligabue, Renato Cioni, and conductor Bartoletti were all at their best. Raphäel Arié's debut performance as Fiesco brought beauty of voice and nobility of character to the role. *Aida* was better heard than seen, with staging that piled cliché on cliché, so much so that the Triumphal Scene drew laughter from the audience. Leontyne Price, singing with less richness and depth of tonal color than she had shown previously in the title role, acted with new, fussy and meaningless gestures that robbed her performance of the basic simplicity and force seen in her 1960 characterization. Fiorenza Cossotto and Ettore Bastianini were the vocal standouts, while Giorgio Casellato, in his American debut as Radames, exhibited a sizeable voice, but he needed better musical and stage direction. The season closer was *Rigoletto*, which rarely rose to a level better than routine. Alfredo Kraus sang especially well as the Duke, but Cornell MacNeil seemed to tire as the opera progressed, and Renata Scotto tended to be a bit shrill, erratic in pitch, and unsympathetic as Gilda.

There were two Puccini operas that season. Mirella Freni made her (previously postponed) debut in *La bohème,* exhibiting everything necessary to make the role of Mimì her own, but receiving scant support from her colleagues. Franco Corelli's robust tenor and heroic stances were wrong for the part of Rodolfo, and the three other bohemians appeared to be underplaying their roles on the assumption that Corelli would dominate the stage. Neither the conducting nor the staging rose above routine. Renata Scotto was considerably more successful in *Madama Butterfly* than she was that same season in *Rigoletto*. Her characterization was complete and her voice was pure and clear in all registers, at its best in high pianissimos. Renato Cioni's Pinkerton was well sung but stiffly acted. Sesto Bruscantini as Sharpless and Nedda Casei as Suzuki headed a strong supporting cast.

Another French opera given in 1965 was *Samson and Delilah*. Jon Vickers sang with powerful radiance and played Samson with great dignity. Grace Bumbry's Delilah conveyed the twists and turns of the character with a voice that changed with graded perfection to suit each mood. Jean Fournet conducted.

The 1966 season of the Lyric Opera of Chicago began with a powerful, if maddeningly truncated, staging of *Boris Godunov*, here an abridged version of the Rimsky-Korsakov edition. Bruno Bartoletti proved (as Toscanini had done years earlier) that an Italian conductor could give a warm, impassioned, idiomatic reading of this very Russian opera. Nicolai Ghiaurov's enormous, superbly produced voice was used with taste, but his characterization lacked the full haunted, demoniac quality the role asks for. William Wildermann returned to the Lyric after an absence of several years, providing a splendid Pimen. Carlo Cossutta was Grigory, and Ruza Pospinov made an admirable Lyric debut as Marina. The true protagonist of the drama for many is the people, and Michael Lepore's chorus portrayed them well. Nicola Benois's beautiful sets suggested the color and majesty of old Russia.

The biggest news of the season was the company's presentation of extraordinary operas from the seventeenth and twentieth centuries, both of them in their Chicago premières. In its only staging of Monteverdi's *L'incoronazione di Poppea* to date the Lyric achieved an unfolding sequence of sight, sound, and motion that seemed about perfect, but the audience was not pre-pared to follow or understand the work; they were fa-miliar with Verdi and Puccini, but not prepared for sev-enteenth-century Italian opera, in which the emphasis is not on action but on the development of the vocal line. (This was long before supertitles, and the Lyric did not offer a libretto of the opera.) Evelyn Lear made an impressive Lyric debut in the title role and was beauti-fully supported by another American, Sylvia Stahlman, as well as by strong performances from Teresa Berganza, André Montal, Lothar Ostenburg, William Wildermann, Oralia Dominguez, and Margaret Rog-gero. Bruno Bartoletti's conducting deserved laurels, as did the decor and overall production.

Until this season the only Prokofiev opera Chicago had seen was the one that had received its world pre-mière in the city, *The Love for Three Oranges*. Perhaps because of the success of *Wozzeck* a year earlier, Bruno Bartoletti convinced Carol Fox that a contemporary work even less familiar to the American audience than the Berg masterpiece was, nonetheless, worth produc-ing. And so Chicago saw its first production (again the only one to date) of Prokofiev's *Angel of Fire*. Felicia Weathers's vocal characterization of the heroine, Re-nata, made a deep impression, as did Virginio Puecher's staging of the Luciano Damiani production imported from Rome. The Lyric applied its best efforts to a score that needed, and got, a strong representation.

Strong female leads and idiomatic conducting from Nino Sanzogno gave an otherwise prosaic *La Gioconda* some needed lift. Elena Suliotis was the Gioconda, Fiorenza Cossotto proved herself the finest Italian dra-matic mezzo-soprano of the day as Laura, and Elena Zilio, in her American debut, did her best to create more than the cardboard character so often found in La Cieca. Renato Cioni as Enzo was excellent when he embraced the role's bel canto aspects, but often he pushed his voice into hardness. Gian Giacomo Guelfi's Barnaba and Ivo Vinco's Alvise were conventional vil-lains, and the *Dance of the Hours* was uninspired.

Two Verdi operas were given. Jon Vickers was to have sung all four performances of *Otello* but was re-placed by the British tenor Charles Craig for some of them (including opening night) due to Vickers's in-disposition. Craig was a dramatic tenor with a fresh, strong voice and the skill to bring the role to life. Raina Kabaivanska was Desdemona, and Tito Gobbi was both the stage director for the production and its Iago. He was in fine voice, and he offered a deeply etched characterization. His staging was particularly effective in the opera's final scene.

Though *La traviata* grew progressively better as it went along, overall the production tended to be dull. Margherita Rinaldi in the title role exhibited a voice of generous size and dulcet tone, but there seemed to be greater dramatic potential than was realized here. Alfredo Kraus and Sesto Bruscantini sang well, but their characterizations left one wanting deeper in-volvement. Mario Rossi, making his American con-ducting debut, elicited a high degree of playing from the Lyric orchestra.

Eugen Jochum returned to the Lyric to conduct the company's first offering ever of Mozart's *The Magic Flute,* and he gave the opera a sensitive, relaxed read-ing. Erich Kunz as Papageno dominated the scene every time he was onstage, sparking a production that otherwise lacked the polish and class to present this opera at its best. Claire Watson and Ernst Haefliger as Pamina and Tamino, respectively, sang well but of-fered fairly placid characterizations. Mady Mesplé, the Queen of the Night, and Karl Ridderbusch, Sarastro, did not cope fully with the demands of the music.

Bizet's *The Pearl Fishers* was given four perform-ances. Christiane Eda-Pierre's Lyric debut as Lêila re-vealed a voice of beauty and a charming stage pres-ence, while Alfredo Kraus and Sesto Bruscantini, as the two men who love her, sang well but otherwise offered little to bolster the basically slight plot. Jean Fournet conducted.

Lyric once more presented an evening of ballet and opera. Alfredo Casella's *La Giara* was the curtain raiser, with somewhat predictable Ruth Page choreography but excellent performances by Erik Bruhn and Patricia Klekovic. Mascagni's *Cavalleria rusticana* was the evening's opera, dominated by Grace Bumbry's sympa-thetic, if insufficiently intense, Santuzza. Gianfranco Cecchele was Turiddu, and Gian Giacomo Guelfi sang Alfio; both were convincing if somewhat unsubtle. Nino Sanzogno conducted both productions.

Italy suffered devastating floods midway into the Lyric season, and on November 21, 1966, virtually all the artists in residence at the Lyric at the time—including the company's chorus and ballet corps—donated their services for a benefit concert for the survivors, presented to an audience that filled the Civic Opera House. The program was given in three parts, containing excerpts from operas currently be-ing presented onstage, art songs from the recital repertoire, and operatic music heard in other seasons. Approximately $50,000 was raised for the cause.

When the curtain went down on Lyric's last perform-ance in 1966, no one on either side of the footlights had even the vaguest inkling that it would be almost two years before the Lyric would again produce an opera.

In 1967 there was a direct confrontation over whether expansion of the Lyric season was to be determined by management or by the company's orchestra and its union. Spurred by the efforts of the Metropolitan Opera orchestra for year-round employment, the Lyric musicians felt their season should double in length. Negotiations began in December 1966 with an initial union demand for a twenty-week season, salary increases, reduced hours, and other expensive gains. The Lyric responded that it was prepared to give the orchestra what it felt it could afford but it could not commit itself contractually to pay money in excess of what it could raise. Although it had been making regular progress in operating income, the Lyric had yet to meet a budget of the size it would take to meet such demands.

The Lyric's stated estimate at the time that a twenty-week season would play to only 57% of capacity had to be viewed with skepticism, as the company in its advertising referred to the many thousands of nonsubscribers who were unable to get tickets to the operas they wished to hear. A conservative policy of calculated underproduction was being protected. Faced with what they said was a choice between producing more opera than the public might support and creating a shortage of tickets, the specter of unsold tickets weighed the decision in favor of underproduction. Lyric's attitude was that when it was felt that a sufficient number of frustrated ticket buyers were waiting to get in, additional performances would be given.

It was a time when symphony and opera orchestra musicians across the country were making inroads in correcting what had for many years been unfair working conditions, too little compensation, and management dominance. The Chicago union leadership decided it was time to stand its ground and thus was astonished (as was the Lyric audience) when the 1967 opera season was canceled on March 2—the deadline for the Lyric to disengage itself from commitments for artists, scenery, costumes, and other matters. Talks continued with the hope of negotiating a contract for 1968, but it was only when Chicago's mayor, Richard J. Daley, finally stepped into the discussions that the orchestra musicians abandoned their militant stance and agreed to a contract for that year that added five more performances. In the meantime, public loyalty to the company, coupled with disapproval of the union's tactics, produced some $325,000 in contributions to keep the Lyric afloat during the dark year.

Administrative costs were only $307,784 that year, leaving a surplus—the company's first—of some $15,000. When performances resumed in the autumn of 1968, most of the artists originally scheduled for the previous year were engaged for the roles they were to have sung in 1967.

On October 31, 1967, the Auditorium, after more than two decades of absence from the life of the city, was reopened, triumphantly restored to its prewar state. It was almost the eightieth anniversary of the start of its construction. The proposal was made that the Lyric move its operations to the old house. It is notable that the opening-night performance was neither concert nor opera, but George Balanchine's *A Midsummer Night's Dream,* danced by the New York City Ballet. As a home for ballet, the historic theater was unsurpassed.

Chicago always has had its share of people with misguided nostalgia for old halls. The inescapable fact was that the Auditorium was unsuited to presenting opera with twentieth-century stagecraft, and it was abandoned in 1929 for excellent reasons that still held. The restored hall—with an appropriate acoustical reflector—was an excellent venue for concerts and recitals. It even held some touring opera troupes. But its principal attraction, as time proved, was to provide a home for long runs of large-scale musical shows like *The Phantom of the Opera.* Here its ample seating, excellent sightlines, and still marvelous acoustics were as impressive as ever.

The Lyric reopened its doors to the public on September 27, 1968, with a production of *Salome* achieved with a degree of visual impact and stagecraft characteristic of Lyric's best hours of previous years. There were a number of new players in the orchestra, and Bruno Bartoletti's conducting demonstrated both his firm, powerful grasp of the score and his gifts as an orchestra builder—a talent long considered one of his prime contributions to the company over his many years of association with it. The realistic, explicit staging yielded great visual and dramatic impact, and Felicia Weathers looked and sang the title role to great effect. Hans Hopf and Astrid Varnay were ideal as Herod and Herodias, and Gerd Nienstedt had the vocal authority the role of the prophet John the Baptist required.

The number of productions was now down to eight per season (a practice that continued through 1974), but none of them had less than five performances, and some had six.

A Stravinsky double bill reaffirmed Lyric'c commitment to twentieth-century opera. The staging of *Oedipus*

Rex may have contained more action than Stravinsky intended, but its basic, sculptural effect was striking. Mirto Picchi as Oedipus and Donald Gramm as the Messenger offered ample illustration of how purely vocal characterization can define and develop a dramatic situation. Lyric's production of *Le rossignol* was half transformed into a ballet that subordinated music to spectacle. Three of the principal singers—Christiane Eda-Pierre (the Nightingale), Ottavio Garaventa (the Fisherman), and Oralia Dominguez (Death)—were banished to the pit and replaced on stage by dancers, whose actions often distracted from the vocal line. Sets, costumes, and visual effects were impressive in themselves, but the vocal dramatics of Stravinsky's score were slighted.

The remaining six operas were Italian, the most effective of them Verdi's *Falstaff*. Tito Gobbi's staging was stylistically consistent from beginning to end. His performance in the title role showed a voice youthful enough to soar when it needed to, and when at the end of a phrase it might run a bit dry, he was canny enough to make that add to his characterization. Norman Mittelmann's beautifully controlled singing as Ford was one of the great joys of the production. Raina Kabaivanska and Stefania Malagù were the merry wives, with Lydia Marimpietri and Ottavio Garaventa as the young lovers Nanetta and Fenton, contributing lovely singing and distinct charm.

The season's other Verdi was *Un ballo in maschera,* back for the fifth time in fourteen seasons, this time in an uneven production. Act 2 was a near disaster; there were long intermissions, and only in the final act was the direction strong enough to create an effective stage picture. Renato Cioni as Riccardo produced a larger, but less refined, tone than in earlier Lyric appearances, and he was willing to sacrifice bel canto to characterization when he portrayed the dying man. Peter Glossop was an especially effective Renato, with Sylvia Stahlmann's Oscar vocally and dramatically sparkling. Luisa Maragliano's appearance as Amelia showed a large voice with some lovely sounds, but her acting was rudimentary.

Fiorenza Cossotto as Adalgisa dominated Lyric's production of Bellini's *Norma,* her incandescent vocal quality putting even her well-above-average colleagues in the shade. Elena Suliotis as Norma appeared to pace her performance to conserve her voice for the last act; rarely did she sing with the freedom and warmth of expression that Cossotto summoned. Gianfranco Cecchele's opening scene as Pollione was

his best, his voice large and commanding, and Ivo Vinco's two scenes as Oroveso (with chorus) were well sung. The stage direction was conventional, but Nino Sanzogno had the orchestra playing accompaniments of refinement and clarity.

Lyric's 1968 production of Donizetti's *Don Pasquale* was a distinct improvement over the company's 1963 presentation of the opera. Alfredo Kraus was again Ernesto, but this time there was a beauty and focus of tone in his voice not heard in the role five years earlier. Geraint Evans was Don Pasquale, and that excellent singing actor made the most of his characterization. Reri Grist sang well as Norina, but the stage direction in the final act made her appear viperish and cruel. Sesto Bruscantini's adroit portrait of Dr. Malatesta was a highlight, and Bruno Bartoletti set a brisk pace, making his orchestra play with a lightness and brightness that made the most of Donizetti's rhythms and tunes.

There were two Puccini operas. *Tosca* was the third production of the season; the sets—on loan from Rome—were said to be an exact copy of those in the 1900 première of the opera. Unfortunately, the staging seemed a throwback to that earlier time: singers faced the audience while addressing people behind them, and lavish freedom for traditional gestures and grimaces was in evidence. Antonietta Stella made her Lyric debut as Tosca, playing it with insight, passion, and a voice of silken luster. Her Cavaradossi was Renato Cioni, who had grown impressively as an artist since he was first heard several seasons earlier. Gian Giacomo Guelfi had the unwelcome assignment of succeeding Tito Gobbi as Scarpia, a role that had been Gobbi's alone since the first Lyric production of *Tosca* in 1954. But Guelfi was strong enough to make the central conflicts of the action stand out boldly. Bruno Bartoletti set hard-driving tempos—in contrast to his far broader realizations later, especially in the 1990s.

Renata Tebaldi was scheduled to star in *Manon Lescaut.* By most accounts, she was in excellent voice at the dress rehearsal, but by the time she taxied to her hotel from the theater that night she was feeling the first signs of a flu attack that was in full bloom by the next morning. Lyric postponed the opening for a week, and at noon on the day of the first performance it looked as though she could appear. Later in the day, though, she felt she lacked the necessary strength, and, as it turned out, Tebaldi sang in none of the five performances the Lyric presented. Luisa Maragliano, who had sung in *Un ballo in maschera* earlier in the season, was her replacement, and her performance here was in every way an improvement over her Amelia. The Lyric debut of a young man named Plácido Domingo in the role of Des Grieux demonstrated what was already known elsewhere, that he was one of the best young tenors of the day, with the voice, stature, and dramatic savvy to be a major star. Carlo Badioli's Geronte was an artfully played old rogue, presented with skillful vocal projection if rarely with singing, a model representation of the qualities of a fine character actor.

The 1969 Lyric season was typical of the period. It went from admirable to awful, presenting the public with the dilemma that the company must be supported (otherwise you lose the good things it brings) and the question of whether it couldn't sustain a more consistent artistic standard. Attendance was the highest of any Lyric season, 95.4%, and twenty-five of the forty-one performances were sold out. Fox could not complain of a lack of public support. One million dollars came in from subscribers, with an additional $345,000 from the box office, but Fox obviously felt she must economize on certain of her productions.

Bartoletti dominated the opening weeks. He once more showed a remarkable flair for Russian opera with the first Chicago performances of *Khovanshchina,* a colorful, panoramic work left unfinished at Mussorgsky's death and made viable by Rimsky-Korsakov. Ghiaurov sang the principal role, Prince Ivan Khovansky, with the American debuts of Lubomir Bodurov as Galitsin and Boris Shtokolov as Dositheus. Ruza Pospinov-Baldani took the role of Marfa. Staging came from Nicola Benois. Ruth Page choreographed some fine dancing, and Michael Lepore's chorus, singing in Russian, exceeded all expectations.

Black sopranos dominated the next two works: Grace Bumbry as Verdi's Lady Macbeth and Felicia Weathers as Butterfly. The latter was an acceptable but unadventurous recycling of the Puccini drama. *Macbeth* was major Verdi, new to the city. Bartoletti was determined to reveal its strengths, and a strong cast projected the drama with due force.

A major acquisition from Europe, Anja Silja, was Senta to Thomas Stewart's Dutchman in *The Flying Dutchman,* with Christoph von Dohnányi (who was to become her husband) conducting. Musically it was splendid, but this was a modern, school-of-Wieland-Wagner production, asking more of the technical resources of the old Chicago house than could always be supplied.

The Lyric's ability to stage standard Italian repertory was upheld in *The Barber of Seville,* with Marilyn Horne as Rosina, Geraint Evans as Bartolo, and Sesto Bruscantini as Figaro. Peter Hall supplied the sets, and Gobbi's direction kept the action brisk while avoiding slapstick excesses. *Cavalleria rusticana* paired Fiorenza Cossotto with Franco Tagliavini to good effect.

Mid-season brought two failures. *I puritani* had some good singing from Alfredo Kraus and Margherita Roberti, but the production was a dreary old wreck, and the characterizations a reminder of operatic acting of an earlier day. Gobbi long entertained the fantasy that Don Giovanni was one of his finest roles, but the sure grasp of character, so conspicuous in his Scarpia, was missing here. He was permitted to sing, as well as direct, the opera, with Ferdinand Leitner conducting, Peter Hall sets and costumes, and a strong cast including Judith Raskin (who died in 1984 at the early age of fifty-six) as Zerlina, Ilva Ligabue as Donna Elvira, and Claire Watson as Donna Anna. Evans understood the character of Leporello. The bottom dropped out with a ballet, *El amor brujo,* of which the less said the better.

Despite the overall Italianate bent of the Lyric repertoire over the years (and the continuous characterization of the company by many as "La Scala West") Carol Fox always claimed that her favorite opera was *Der Rosenkavalier.* In 1970—and for the second straight year that the Lyric had offered a Richard Strauss opera as a season opener—she gave Chicago its first *Rosenkavalier* in a dozen years. Lyric staging, which had been improving with every new season, here found a new level of excellence with sets by Günther Schneider-Siemssen, costumes from the Cologne Opera, and Hans Neugebauer's superb handling of the stage action. With a strong cast, and with conductor Christoph von Dohnányi's tastefully expert pacing and understanding of the opera, the work was beautifully presented. Christa Ludwig was the Marschallin as Strauss described her, a woman in her early thirties, vibrant, sexy, attractive, yet wise to the world. Yvonne Minton and Patricia Brooks as Octavian and Sophie were totally convincing both vocally and dramatically, and, as Baron Ochs, Walter Berry mercifully presented the character not as a dirty old man but as a country beau: rural nobility in pursuit of fun and games—and a wealthy wife. One of the reasons the Lyric had waited so long to stage *Der Rosenkavalier* was that the opera's orchestral demands are so daunting, and in this first attempt at the task the Lyric orchestra could not always meet the music on the level it requires.

Birgit Nilsson returned to Lyric as Puccini's Turandot after nine years of absence from opera in Chicago. One marveled once more at the overwhelming strength and beauty of her voice as well as her commanding presence as the Chinese princess. Felicia Weathers's Liù was a sensitively drawn character, and Franco Tagliavini's Calaf was passionate and well acted, but neither was heard at their vocal best. Highly stylized choreographic details were often dramatically ludicrous, and the staging was slick and professional, but calculated.

A number of cuts in the score and a lack of character in the voice of Cristina Deutekom in the title role led to an overall disappointing *Lucia di Lammermoor*. But Richard Tucker's Edgardo was a standout, the celebrated ping in his voice never more in evidence than here.

Montserrat Caballé and Nicolai Gedda made their Lyric debuts as the lovers in *La traviata*, and it was a happy meeting. Both voices soared, Caballé's musicality proving to be especially gorgeous. Pier Luigi Pizzi's opulent new production beautifully evoked the demimonde of 1850 Paris as well as a fresh, but not overbearing, realism in the opera's second-act country setting.

Bruno Bartoletti's commitment to music of the twentieth century was witnessed at its best when the Lyric offered the American stage première of Britten's *Billy Budd* in its 1961 revised version. Theodor Uppman, who had created the title role ten years earlier in London, was close to perfection, and Geraint Evans's Claggart was outstanding. Richard Lewis sang well but acted less freely as Captain Vere. Much of the scene painting of *Billy Budd* is to be heard in the orchestra and chorus, and Bartoletti and his forces projected it with sustained intensity.

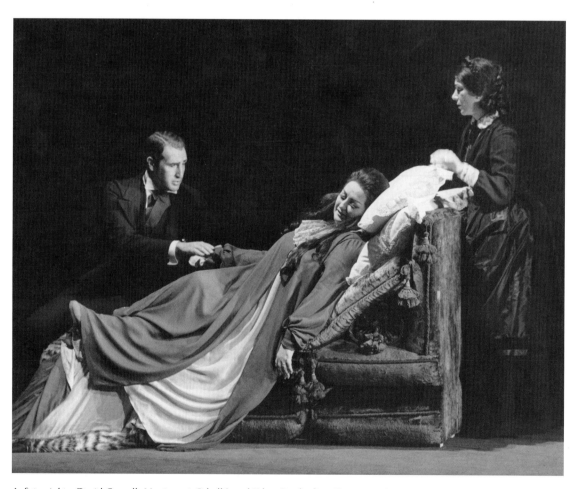

Left to right—David Cornell, Montserrat Caballé, and Edna Garabedian-George, in *La traviata*, 1970

Left to right—Joan Sutherland and Marilyn Horne in *Semiramide,* 1971

Musically, *L'Italiana in Algeri* is Rossini at his happiest, and Lyric's production of it—here in its Chicago première—was a delight in every way, with Marilyn Horne at her best in a role that could have been written for her extraordinary bel canto gifts. She was supported to the fullest by vocal and comedic contributions from Giuseppe Taddei, Lydia Marimpietri, Ottavio Garaventa, and Domenico Trimarchi, as well as stylistic and theatrical excellence from the conductor, Argeo Quadri.

The season's second Puccini score was *Madama Butterfly* in the same staging seen in 1969. The performance was more routine than involving. Edy Amadeo replaced the scheduled Felicia Weathers in the title role (illness was the cited reason), and she and Franco Tagliavini as Pinkerton gave performances notable for neither great achievement nor great failings. Domenico Trimarchi as Sharpless was the best of the principals, and Florindo Andreolli, a valued stalwart at the Lyric in character tenor roles for many years, here as Goro seemed able to steal any scene he wanted to claim.

The last offering of the season brought a double bill of one-act operas, both of them dating from 1918.

Bartók's *Bluebeard's Castle* and Puccini's *Gianni Schicchi* abound in robust melodic writing that soars to full-bodied climactic passages in which the orchestra is blended masterfully with the vocal line, and the Lyric put them in the hands of experienced people with good track records for the musical and dramatic course of each. Virgino Puecher designed and directed a powerful production of the Bartók, which was sung in English. David Ward as Bluebeard and Janis Martin as his overly inquisitive wife, Judith, projected the words with great clarity and with masterful musical force in their interpretations. Tito Gobbi directed and starred in the Puccini, a performance filled with the spontaneous laughter generated by a really funny show. Ottavio Garavento and Lydia Marimpietri as the young lovers sang agreeably, but a strong singing actor in the role of Schicchi can dominate the action, and Gobbi did just that. Bartoletti conducted both scores with a great feel for the character and flow of each.

Highlights of the 1971 Lyric Opera season were new (and beautiful) productions of two of the most popular operas in the Italian repertory, the first

Curtain call for Lyric's 1971 *Don Carlo; left to right:* Sherrill Milnes, Fiorenza Cossotto (partially hidden), Carlo Cossutta, Pilar Lorengar, and Nicolai Ghiaurov

performances in Chicago in seventy-eight years of a late Rossini score, and the launching of a *Ring* cycle.

Maria Callas had made forays into revitalizing interest in bel canto repertoire, and Joan Sutherland and her husband, the conductor Richard Bonynge, and Marilyn Horne continued to make strides in convincing the late-twentieth-century operagoing public how beautiful and powerful music from this period could be. The latter three brought Rossini's *Semiramide* to open Lyric's 1971 season and gave the city a revival that had audiences cheering. Overcoming a convoluted, silly plot, the commitment and virtuosity of the Sutherland-Horne-Bonynge combination gave dignity and moment to what otherwise could seem clumsy and pretentious. Opening night was broadcast live, locally, by WFMT, "Chicago's Fine Arts Station," and in the then current sonic rage, quadrophonic (and stereo) sound. It was WFMT's first airing

of a Lyric Opera production and the start of a fruitful collaboration between the opera company and the station, which continues to this day.

New productions of Verdi's *Rigoletto* and Puccini's *Tosca* came next. Pier Luigi Pizzi designed them, the *Rigoletto* nobly reflecting the time, mood, and prophecy of the opera, the *Tosca* at once traditional but highly imaginative and well suited to the needs of a good director. Piero Cappuccilli's full-bodied, theatrically moving rendering of Rigoletto's "Cortigiani, vil razza dannata" was the vocal highlight of that production, with Gail Robinson's Gilda and Alfredo Kraus's Duke tasteful if not particularly exciting. Tito Gobbi directed *Tosca* and sang its Scarpia (effectively, as always), with Carlo Bergonzi strongly conveying the drama of the role of Cavaradossi through his voice—here at its prime—and the natural dignity he always displayed in his characterizations. Janis Martin was Tosca, singing well but lacking the Italianate power Gobbi and Bergonzi brought to their roles.

Alfredo Kraus returned for Lyric's first production of Massenet's *Werther* and gave one of the best-sung and most strongly acted performances of his Chicago career to date. Tatiana Troyanos, an attractive young woman with a dark, pleasing voice, was Charlotte, but her characterization was too cool to accept her as the object of a grand passion. Jean Fournet, Lyric's sure hand for French repertory, conducted a well-paced performance.

Verdi's *Don Carlo* returned (with the all too usual cuts), bringing with it the Lyric debuts of Pilar Lorengar as Elisabetta and Sherrill Milnes as Rodrigo. Lorengar was perhaps the loveliest and most sympathetic figure the Lyric ever had in that role, but she had sung more brilliantly in previous appearances elsewhere. Milnes was young, American, and good, but he seemed to have a lot to learn about his role at that stage in his career. It was Fiorenza Cossotto as Eboli who seized vocal honors, while Hans Sotin offered some fine singing as the Grand Inquisitor. Nicolai Ghiaurov was not in his best voice this time as King Philip. Lotfi Mansouri's staging offered one novel, if curious, twist. Instead of Carlo's being wafted away by the ghost of Charles V at the end of the opera, here he was surrendered to the Inquisition.

It was especially noteworthy that Chicago heard two different productions of *Das Rheingold* (of all Wagner operas!) in the same year. Sir Georg Solti gave a concert performance of it with the Chicago Symphony in April 1971, and Lyric staged its first production of the work in November of that year. That marked the beginning of a complete Wagner *Ring* cycle from the Lyric, with one opera given each season. The musical dimension of *Das Rheingold* here yielded the most powerful and rewarding aspect of the production. Ferdinand Leitner's conducting was the greatest success of the evening, with his orchestra playing better than at any time previously in the season. Sets were by Ekkehard Grübler, with direction by Hans-Peter Lehmann. The staging followed neither the romantic/literal nineteenth-century tradition nor the postwar Bayreuth symbolic/austere approach, but rather was reminiscent of the 1930s. Costumes might be characterized as Wagner kitsch, and there was a general lack of a consistent interpretive outlook transformed into a style. If the cast could not quite match that of Solti's recorded *Ring* cycle, there was Gustav Neidlinger's remarkable Alberich, Grace Hoffman's regal Fricka, Hans Sotin's impressive Fafner, and Jeannine Altmeyer's effective Freia.

From the first notes of the overture to Rossini's *The Barber of Seville*, conductor Bruno Bartoletti made it clear that he was ready to give the audience a musical account of the score with elegance and style. But from the beginning of the action onstage, director Tito Gobbi made it clear that he was going to present a version in which musical values were sacrificed to keeping the stage bouncing and the audience laughing. Few of the cast could deliver a singing performance of prime quality, and few of them had a natural flair for comedy. Hermann Prey, so effective as Mozart's Figaro, sang well but here was lacking the light touch for this kind of Italian comedy, while Marilyn Horne (whose previous Rossini performances in Chicago were so effective) offered an over-the-top interpretive outlook. Of the principals, only Ottavio Garaventa's Almaviva was a reasonably well sung and well-defined character.

The combination of Wieland Wagner set designs, Hans-Peter Lehmann stage direction, Christoph von Dohnányi conducting, and Anja Silja vocal dramatics yielded all the elements of a powerful evening of opera when the Lyric presented Richard Strauss's *Salome* as its final production of the season. On balance, it was the finest of the three presentations of the work in Lyric's history so far. Silja looked wonderful, sounded great, and dazzled in her every motion onstage. Gerd Nienstedt gave a bold portrait of Jochanaan, and Ragnar Ulfung and Sona Cervena made impressive Lyric debuts as Herod and his quarrelsome wife.

On opening night of Lyric's 1972 season, Carol Fox, apparently caught up in the festive air of the occasion, made announcements about the 1973 repertory (most notably that it would contain Britten's *Peter Grimes*) and of Lyric's considering a spring opera season in the Civic Theater (the small theater alongside the Civic Opera House). Moreover, she expressed the expectation of Lyric's commissioning an opera for the nation's bicentennial in 1976.

The opera onstage that September evening was a Verdi rarity, and one of its cast was making an important American debut. *I due Foscari* received its Chicago première, with the twenty-six-year-old Katia Ricciarelli its soprano star. The opera itself is almost totally static, and the evening certainly belonged to the singers onstage that night. The thrills of the evening came in moments such as Ricciarelli's first scene when she sang in the grand soprano manner with the promise of a great career ahead. To match her, there was Franco Tagliavini doing the exciting things an Italian tenor is supposed to do (and with three major opportunities to bring down the house).

Birgit Nilsson as Brünnhilde in *Die Walküre,* 1972

Rounding out the principals, Piero Cappuccilli sang with nobility and beauty. Once more, WFMT broadcast opening night to the Chicago area.

The second installment of Lyric's one-opera-per-year *Ring* cycle, Wagner's *Die Walküre,* brought important additions to the previous season's *Das Rheingold,* including Birgit Nilsson's Brünnhilde, Hermin Esser's Siegmund, and Janis Martin's Sieglinde. Overall, though, Lyric's 1960 staging of the opera was more successful, with a stronger group of artists (Nilsson excepted) and a better production. It was presented in the Neo-Wieland-Wagner style, but not done with flair or distinction.

What in 1970 was in every way a highly successful new production of *La traviata* was revived in 1972 as a slapdash copy of its former self. A very ordinary group

of singers gave stereotyped operatic acting at its most conventional, with routine conducting and playing. Celestina Casapietra was Violetta, Franco Bordoni the elder Germont. Three different Alfredos appeared in the six evening performances: Giorgio Merighi sang on opening night; Franco Tagliavini (an improvement) sang the next three; and Wieslaw Ochman appeared in the final two. Maurizio Arena conducted.

This season James C. Hemphill, a longtime supporter of the Lyric Opera, gave the company a beautiful new production of *La bohème* with sets by Pier Luigi Pizzi—so beautiful and effective that it is still being used whenever the Lyric revives the opera. On this occasion, Bruno Bartoletti's conducting and Giorgio De Lullo's stage direction kept the music and dramatic action smooth and convincing throughout, and Gil Wechler's lighting effects were entirely natural, never intrusive. Marina Krilovici was a young, attractive Mimì, displaying an exciting and powerful voice coupled with fine acting ability. Giorgio Merighi sang and acted with greater distinction than he had in *La traviata,* and Elena Zilio's Musetta and Julian Patrick's Marcello were further assets.

For its third Italian opera in a row, the Lyric presented another new production (again from James C. Hemphill, here in collaboration with Lee A. Freeman). Verdi's *Un ballo in maschera* had complex but effective sets by Robert Darling and stage direction by Tito Gobbi. This time we saw seventeenth-century Boston onstage (Indians and all) rather than eighteenth-century Stockholm. The level of singing was exceptional, with Martina Arroyo making her Lyric debut as Amelia, Franco Tagliavini singing the role of Riccardo, and Sherrill Milnes portraying Renato. Christoph von Dohnányi paced the work well, and the orchestra responded with strong, bright playing.

Dohnányi returned to lead a well-focused, idiomatic performance of Mozart's *Così fan tutte* in a Jean-Pierre Ponnelle production, its sets evocative of Watteau and Gainsborough, providing an ideal frame for the action. The cast was marvelous, everyone looking right, singing right, and acting right, radiating the proper spirit of the work. Ryland Davies and Tom Krause were the young men, Margaret Price and Anne Howells the sisters, and Geraint Evans and Urszula Koszut the plotters.

Two twentieth-century masterpieces closed the season. Debussy's *Pelléas et Mélisande* had not been seen in Chicago in twenty years, and if, on this occasion, the opening night audience at first had trouble settling into the atmosphere of this haunting work, the magic soon began to work. The union of Desmond Heeley's remarkable setting, Paul-Emile Deiber's direction, and Jean Fournet's conducting truly fired the imagination. Jeanette Pilou was more sensual and womanly than most Mélisandes, and Richard Stilwell was more openly in love with her as Pelléas, but both of them sang well. Raphäel Arié's Arkel was an especially beautifully drawn character.

The 1965 production of Berg's *Wozzeck* returned, once more sung in English, again with Bruno Bartoletti conducting, Virginio Puecher directing, and Geraint Evans in the title role. The performances verified the continuing artistic growth of the Lyric and its orchestra. Evans's portrayal was again profoundly moving, and this time his Marie was Anja Silja, who was vocally and dramatically outstanding. Frank Little portrayed the Drum Major, and among these three principals the balance of power between the characters was more fully drawn than in the earlier production. This time there were five performances of the opera as opposed to only three in 1965.

Despite general audience and critical approval of the Lyric Opera of Chicago and its product, as well as growing subscriptions numbers, the company's financial condition was not as closely watched by Carol Fox as it should have been. Administrative costs of all kinds behind the scenes continued to grow at a worrisome pace in relation to the company's various sources of income, but Fox seemed oblivious to that. In an interview with Speight Jenkins (himself destined to become an opera manager) titled "Carol & Co." (in *Opera News,* November 1972), Fox said, "We're after a total artistic package. Our original goal was to put on opera at the highest and best level we knew. Now the idea is the same but our scope is different. In the beginning we had little money and we spent it on artists. Only recently have we expanded into better rehearsed productions, therefore better conductors, more rehearsal time, therefore better directors, and a better overall visual appeal." But the situation was considerably more complicated than that, as time proved.

Like Carol Fox, Alan Stone was a singer, but unlike Fox he had had a real, if modest, professional career. He wanted to produce opera, and in January 1973 had a try with a group called Pilot Knob Opera Company, whose offerings ranged from dreadful to mediocre. Significantly, Pilot Knob offered not standard fare but Nicolai's *The Merry Wives of Windsor.*

The Lyric Opera opened its 1973 season with Donizetti's *Maria Stuarda,* an opera never given before in Chicago. A reigning soprano of the day in Donizetti, Bellini, and early Verdi was its star: Montserrat Caballé sang the title role, and it was the last time she appeared with the company. Viorica Cortez made her Lyric debut as Elisabetta (Queen Elizabeth I of England). As historical drama, *Maria Stuarda* leaves much to be desired, but it *is* a "singer's opera." On opening night the singing was inconsistent, with Caballé starting superbly but weakening as the opera progressed, and Cortez beginning tight-voiced but becoming considerably more attractive in quality and consistency of sound as the opera progressed. Franco Tagliavini sang the role of Leicester, and that extraordinarily versatile artist, Donald Gramm, as Talbot brought a character boldly drawn and well sung. Bruno Bartoletti conducted his judiciously edited version of the score.

A major step up in Lyric Opera broadcasting began this season as WFMT started presenting live local broadcasts of the opening nights of all eight productions, continuing at this point to offer them in four-channel (and stereo) sound.

The Lyric gave its first staging of Massenet's *Manon,* doing so in a handsome new production (yet another one given to the company by the generous James C. Hemphill) designed by Jacques Dupont. The score is almost always cut for today's audiences, but the Lyric said their *Manon* was "not as badly cut as most." Teresa Zylis-Gara's French was not as idiomatic as it should have been, but she put the dramatic meaning of a phrase across with the consistency of a real artist and sang Manon's music with taste, style, and a bright, attractive sound. Alfredo Kraus's Des Grieux was a worthy foil to his highly successful Werther of two years earlier, and Jean Fournet's conducting was wholly commendable. Two Americans almost stole the show. The voices of Julian Patrick, who sang Lescaut, and Donald Gramm as Count Des Grieux rang through the house with impressive force and dramatic power, and both played their (sharply contrasting) roles with the assurance that comes from knowing both the character and the music thoroughly.

This season's *Tosca* had Teresa Kubiak bringing out the emotional complexity of the title character and offering some lovely singing in the bargain. Tito Gobbi gave his usual, powerful Scarpia characterization, but the Cavaradossi of Franco Tagliavini seemed somewhat superficial and lacking in involvement.

Left to right—Elena Zilio, Julian Patrick, Ileana Cotrubas, and Luciano Pavarotti, in *La bohème*, 1973

Two more first stagings for the Lyric followed. As its fourth opera of the season, another Donizetti score was given, this time *The Daughter of the Regiment,* sung in the original French. Joan Sutherland, Alfredo Kraus, and Spiro Malas had sung their roles frequently enough with each other that there was a sense of happy togetherness throughout, with Sutherland more relaxed and effective onstage than one remembered her from previous appearances. Regina Resnik as the Marquise de Berkenfeld knew how to capture and hold your eye even when the stage was full of people and a celebrated tenor or soprano was pouring out a high note only a few feet away. It is sad that another great mezzo-soprano and actress, Jennie Tourel (who died just a month after her last performance in this production), made her only Lyric appearance ever in the one-line character of the Duchess of Crakenthorp.

To continue the *Ring* cycle begun two years earlier, Wagner's *Siegfried* had its first performances on the Lyric stage. Though the Lehmann-Grübler production

team did its best work so far in the series, there were still far too many directing and visual mishaps to give the production very high marks. Jean Cox played the title role well but could not match the great Siegfrieds of the past, and much the same could be said of Theo Adam's Wanderer and Gerhard Unger's Mime. There were, however, two outstanding talents on view at their best: the conductor Ferdinand Leitner, who kept the musical standards of the performance at an artistic level needed to sustain Wagner's ideas, and the soprano Birgit Nilsson, whose stunningly sung Brünnhilde sent shivers running up and down the spine.

Bizet's *Carmen* was given a production marred by careless direction, hit-and-miss conducting, and a situation in which none of the major singers was at his or her best.

Lyric's *Der Rosenkavalier* returned, this time with two Marschallins, who had significant differences between them. Christa Ludwig sang the first and fourth performances, Helga Dernesch the other four. Ludwig, basically a mezzo-soprano, touched everything with the skill of a great artist and made her character a sexy lady, thus creating a strong triangle in the Marschallin-Octavian-Sophie relationship. Dernesch, a tall and handsome woman, who looked regal and sang with great strength and splendor, was nonetheless a more maternal Marschallin and did not convey the full nuances of the Hofmannsthal libretto. Judith Blegen was the ideal Sophie, clearly having her character's mind and music all figured out to the last flick of an eyebrow. Opening night found the Octavian of Charlotte Berthold a smaller-voiced, less complete and convincing character than those of the other female principals, with Hans Sotin's Baron Ochs lacking insight and simplifying the character to a degree that touched too little on the more complex person Strauss and his librettist envisioned. Ferdinand Leitner conducted, eliminating some cuts and slowing tempos down from what Christoph von Dohnányi had chosen in 1970. The second performance ran some fifteen minutes shorter than the first, and it had a more relaxed atmosphere overall, with Berthold considerably more forceful and Sotin lighter and funnier than before.

On paper (and in retrospect) this year's final Lyric offering, *La bohème,* should have marked two stunning debuts: Ileana Cotrubas in her first appearance in America; Luciano Pavarotti in his first Lyric production. She brought genuine pathos and some lovely singing to the role of Mimì, while Pavarotti sounded constricted in the first act, belting out high notes without regard for their proper musical value. Their singing of the duet in act 3 was an improvement over what had gone before, and the Death Scene brought its familiar emotional tug. (Both artists were to go on to greater Lyric triumphs in years to come.) At the dress rehearsal of act 2, as they watched Luciano Pavarotti continually eating roast chicken (provided for realism) at the table in the Café Momus Scene, Carol Fox and Ardis Krainik became so hungry they sent assistants out during the performance to bring lunch in for them as soon as the act would end. (When it was over, Pavarotti brought the remaining chicken to his dressing room, finishing it before act 3.)

In 1974 the Lyric launched its professional artist development program for young singers aiming for an operatic career. Called the Lyric Opera Center for American Artists (LOCAA), it holds annual auditions (which have grown to attract as many as five hundred aspirants as the program has developed over the years) leading to the selection of a dozen hopefuls for a twelve-month residency, renewable at Lyric's discretion for a maximum of two more years. The participants are immersed in all aspects of singing, acting, movement, language, master classes, and so forth with coaching from Lyric's own personnel as well as from visiting artists of each Lyric mainstage season. The students work on and understudy roles presented in the Lyric season as well sing minor parts in some of those productions. There were those who called the program an inexpensive way for Lyric to get comprimario talent for its mainstage presentations. Even if there is some truth in the charge, it must be said that a number of the LOCAA alumni have gone on to bigger things.

In April 1974 Alan Stone, who had learned from missteps with the offerings of his Pilot Knob company the previous year, was back on the operatic scene, this time in the five-hundred-seat auditorium of Jones Commercial High School (which remained his company's mainstage location through 1976) with a workshop group he called Chicago Opera Studio and a production of *Così fan tutte* that had excellent young singers and genuine charm. Six performances cost $8,000 to produce.

None of the three previous Lyric stagings of Verdi's *Simon Boccanegra* produced anything comparable in effect to the one with which the company opened its 1974 season. It is a difficult opera to stage, but here it built resolutely from start to finish, with dramatic symmetry and logic that made it as psychologically and dramatically convincing as this opera is ever likely to be. The combination of Pizzi sets, De Lullo direction, and Bartoletti conducting delighted the eye, mind, and ear. The orchestra pit at the Civic Opera House had been expanded, placing the musicians in a more favorable acoustic setting and permitting the sound to blend and grow with resonance before being dispersed into the house. The orchestra never sounded better. Verdi calls for big voices in this opera, and the Lyric provided them in Martina Arroyo's radiant Amelia, Carlo Cossutta's heroic Adorno, Piero Cappuccilli's deeply felt Boccanegra, and Ruggero Raimondi's incisive Fiesco. David Clatworthy proved exactly the sort of singing actor to give the brief but pivotal role of Paolo its full significance.

Nearly thirty years after its London première, Benjamin Britten's *Peter Grimes* received its first Lyric production, a staging that is still spoken of today as one of Lyric's finest hours. Jon Vickers's Grimes cried out to the heart of the listener, and his powerful voice and personality rang through the house. Geraint Evans sang the role of Captain Balstrode and, with Ande Anderson, directed the production in an excellent realization of the opera in its larger outlines as well as its wealth of small details. The primary conflict in the opera is between Grimes and the townspeople, and Michael Lepore's choristers provided a consistently remarkable job of singing and moving about the stage, simultaneously defining characters; it was as if everyone were playing a role. Their onstage and offstage cries of "Peter Grimes!" in the final act were hair-raising. Teresa Kubiak was Ellen Orford, singing with convincing musicianship and sense of drama. Further, the vocal and dramatic quality of all the lesser roles, sung by performers including Morley Meredith (Swallow), Donna Petersen (Mrs. Sedley), Lili Chookasian (Auntie), and Patricia Guthrie and Helen-Kay Eberley (the two "nieces"), was consistently high.

The *Peter Grimes* production was a gift to the Lyric and the San Francisco Opera jointly from the Gramma Fisher Foundation of Marshalltown, Iowa, an institution that, over the years, has made an enormous impact on American opera through its gifts of productions, each one designated to be shared by a number of companies rather than being granted to a single organization.

Two contrasting Donizetti operas appeared on the Lyric stage this season. *La favorita* is a grand, tragic opera with an absurd plot but a lot of opportunity for vocal display (90% music; 10% theater); *Don Pasquale* is a grand, comic opera filled with echoes of Rossini. Nicola Rescigno, one of the founders of the Lyric and its principal conductor in 1954 and 1955, was back for the first time in nineteen years, leading a performance of *La favorita* that was well-paced and building to the big, dramatic moments Donizetti calls for. His Leonora, Fiorenza Cossotto, proved once more that she was one of the finest mezzo-sopranos of the age, though her acting was wooden (as was that of her husband, Ivo Vinco, in the role of Baldassare). Piero Cappuccilli, confronted with the fairly static role of King Alfonso XI, exhibited the stage sense to bring his character to life, and Elena Zilio as Inez had the stage to herself for a pleasant scene midway in the first act. The ballet company created for the Lyric by Ruth Page, which had served the company so well in its early years, had been disbanded earlier in an economy wave, but a new group, headed by Maria Tallchief, appeared in this opera. It had talented and well-trained dancers, but clearly they had things to learn.

Alfredo Kraus was the tenor in both Donizetti operas, exhibiting little dramatic flair in *La favorita* but being a more convincing character in *Don Pasquale*. He sang well in each of the two operas. In fact, everyone in *Don Pasquale* was in excellent vocal form, making one feel it would be unlikely to hear a performance of the opera better sung throughout. In his American debut, Wladimiro Ganzarolli mercifully brought dignity and charm to the title character, who in so many productions is made a grotesque buffoon. Other principals were Ileana Cotrubas and Vincenzo Sardinero, and Ezio Frigerio designed an ingenious set within a set (another James C. Hemphill gift to the Lyric) in which a platform stage placed in an Italian palace seemed to be offering a performance for royalty.

Verdi's *Falstaff* returned, with Geraint Evans this time, in a performance in which one found the fat knight too old and fragile, too deep in his cups, for his lecherous designs on the wives of Windsor to be convincing. Ilva Ligabue (Alice), Thomas Stewart (Ford), Lili Chookasian (Dame Quickly), and Luigi Alva (Fenton) offered the kind of consistently rewarding singing that sustained the evening, but Peter Maag's conducting provided unsure orchestral support. A substantial upgrading of lighting equipment in the Civic Opera House had been made over the months preceding this Lyric season, and here Gil Wechsler's use of it (he was the one who pressed for and supervised the improvements) made the charming Franco Zeffirelli settings even more effective than they had appeared before.

Riccardo Chailly made his American opera debut conducting a performance of *Madama Butterfly* that hardly heralded the more impressive things he was to do later. His Butterfly, Marina Krilovici, a handsome woman who looked the part, did not sing it well, and Giorgio Merighi gave a weak, unconvincing portrayal of Pinkerton. Even Yoshio Aoyama's staging did not come up to the level it had achieved in the past.

An opera not seen in Chicago in forty-five years was revived for one of its reigning stars. The material of Massenet's *Don Quichotte* is so thin that no performer can transform it into real tragedy, but Nicolai Ghiaurov played its hero with the conviction and assurance in vocal and physical characterization essential to establish and preserve the mood. He was supported by new Pier Luigi Samaritani settings filled with atmosphere and sensitive imagery, and the production had genuine moments of pathos, evoked by a sense of genuine humanity. Jean Fournet conducted, making the most of every opportunity Massenet gave him and his orchestra. Andrew Foldi's Sancho Panza was a splendid mixture of love, honor, and vulgarity, and Viorica Cortez was a gorgeous Dulcinée.

The final production of the season, Wagner's *Götterdämmerung,* marked the completion of Lyric's four-year *Ring* cycle, and it proved to be the finest achievement of the series. With the resplendent Brünnhilde of Birgit Nilsson matched to the heroic looks of Jean Cox as Siegfried, and their singing framed by some outstanding playing under Ferdinand Leitner's leadership, the evening had all the necessary elements of success on a musical level. Visually, like the rest of Lyric's cycle, it proved rather uneven in design and execution. Bengt Rundgren was an ideal Hagen, huge, menacing, and totally depraved, with Peter Van Ginkel's Alberich mild by comparison. Jeannine Altmeyer was a stunning Gutrune with regal Nordic beauty, and Donald McIntyre played Gunther as a greedy man, too soon overthrown by his weaknesses.

In 1975 Alan Stone's Chicago Opera Studio returned with *The Marriage of Figaro,* and again it provided a lot of pleasing opera per dollar spent. Under Illinois Arts Council and other sponsorship, the production also played in the Court Theatre at the University of Chicago and, later in the year, in the university's Mandel Hall.

The first inklings of needed financial caution came as the Lyric Opera announced that its 1975 season would contain not the former eight, but just seven productions. That number of yearly offerings continued through 1979.

The gold curtain on the Civic Opera House stage was bright and new as the Lyric Opera began its 1975 season. Pier-Luigi Pizzi designed a handsome new production of Verdi's *Otello* for the opener, but the visual force of the evening far exceeded its musical and dramatic impact. Giorgio De Lullo's stage direction often was at odds with the libretto and subtleties of the work. A further problem was that the principal roles went to singers whose acting was poor, so definition and development of characters as complex as the work requires were lacking. Carlo Cossutta's Moor was loud and full of gestures, never nuanced. Gilda Cruz-Romo, though she had a lovely voice, portrayed Desdemona as a hard-luck hausfrau, making one feel no real compulsion to become involved with her fate. Piero Cappuccilli's Iago was a malicious hustler, but not one who personified evil. Bruno Bartoletti's conducting was undistinguished and episodic, without a strongly sustained musical line.

More Verdi followed. *La traviata* achieved a certain nobility in the final act, but the essential spark that brings greatness to an opera was missing. Ileana Cotrubas and Alfredo Kraus were the lovers, singing well but conveying too little of either character's passion, and Bartoletti's conducting gave the impression of extreme fatigue.

Lyric's third production of the season, Richard Strauss's *Elektra,* apparently marked the first time Chicago had seen the opera on the stage—sixty-six years after its world première. Despite Nikolaus Lenhoff's meddling misdirection, the audience on opening night responded to the performance enthusiastically, giving the singers the warmest and most unrestrained reception to be heard that autumn. There were three performances in October and four more in December, with three principals of the cast—and the conductor—changing in the process. Brenda Roberts sang the first Elektras in her Lyric debut, doing so with a natural sense of the stage and impressive vocal potential, and Ursula Schröder-Feinen, also making her debut, took the role in December, demonstrating that she had the resources to deal with Strauss's long, soaring phrases, the courage to belt out the high notes with conviction, and the skill to get them right most of the time. The stage direction of the Klytämnestra of Ursula Böse in October made the role more caricature than character, and Frank Little's Aegisth suffered the same fate. By the time Mignon Dunn sang Klytämnestra in December, much of the pretentiousness of the Lenhoff direction had been eliminated or subdued, and the confrontation between mother and daughter was truly powerful. Thomas Stewart made the most of his role of Orest in the first performances but was unable to sing the later ones; he was replaced by Noel Tyl, who was not as effective. There was another debut: Carol Neblett sang Chrysothemis all seven times, her characterization growing with force as the two runs of the opera progressed. Berislav Klobučar conducted the first performances, at times dwarfing dramatic moments with too much orchestra, but the steady impact of the singing, the orchestra, and the action could not help but stir the senses. When Bruno Bartoletti led the later performances, they showed greater care in keeping vocal lines from being submerged in orchestral sound, less rhythmic emphasis, and greater stress on the broad themes and the vocal opportunities they presented.

Jean-Pierre Ponnelle designed and directed a new production of Mozart's *The Marriage of Figaro;* the strength and intensity of his conception yielded a performance of extraordinary effect. John Pritchard conducted a Mozartian-sized orchestra playing elegantly but with somewhat measured tempos. The cast was close to perfection. Geraint Evans was Figaro, and Thomas Stewart's Count Almaviva had the right mixture of all the irreconcilable elements of the character. A notable debut was that of Catherine Malfitano as a pert Susanna; she became one of the most consistently hired singers on the Lyric roster, appearing frequently with the company well into the twenty-first century. Margaret Price brought wonderful qualities of interpretation to her portrayal of the Countess, and Maria Ewing was a marvelous Cherubino. Even the roles that often get neglected were played as forcefully as the others.

Jon Vickers sang the role of Florestan in Beethoven's *Fidelio* quite successfully in the only productions (1961 and 1963) Lyric had given of the opera to date, but his 1975 performances were a revelation. From his sustained outcry of "Gott! Welch Dunkel hier!" through that entire vocal scene, one was riveted to his voice and characterization, bringing tears that surmounted sentimentality. And that seemed to fire his Leonore, Gwyneth Jones, to match him in voice and character. The role of Don Pizzaro was taken by Walter Berry, and he virtually incarnated villainy in the part. Yuri Ahronovitch conducted.

Joan Sutherland and Luciano Pavarotti offered the kind of singing that made them famous in *Lucia di Lammermoor,* but as a totality this was an old-fashioned Italian opera presented in the traditional old-fashioned manner.

For the season finale Pier Luigi Samaritani devised a new production of Gluck's *Orfeo ed Euridice* consisting of a series of tableaux, most of them as evocative and misty as a Watteau painting. Richard Stilwell was a convincing Orfeo, always acting as well as beautifully singing his grief, and he was matched with Ileana Cotrubas's warm, full soprano. Elena Zilio was the Amor, her voice a bit full for the part, and some of conductor Jean Fournet's tempos were quite slow. George Balanchine choreographed the production, and Maria Tallchief's dancers performed the kinds of formal court dance styles he had used in previous ballets, evoking memories of his days with the Imperial Russian court. Sandro Sequi, the production's director, eliminated the opera's closing dance sequences.

It was his company's 1976 repertory that showed plainly where Alan Stone wanted his Chicago Opera

Studio to go, pairing an Italian staple, *The Barber of Seville,* with a major American work, Virgil Thomson's *The Mother of Us All,* the latter an opera Fox would not have presented in a million years. Here was good music, good theater, and the impact was such that the Thomson was seen on television. The University of Chicago's Court Theatre audiences saw the *Barber* production that August.

At this point, Lyric's training wing, LOCAA, was doing more than just behind-the-scenes nurturing of future opera singers. In spring 1975 their charges had performed—and with considerable success—Benjamin Britten's opera *The Turn of the Screw* in the small Civic Theater alongside Lyric's main auditorium in the Civic Opera House building. The year 1976 brought a varied three-show season: Stravinsky's opera *The Rake's Progress,* a performance of Rossini's *Petite messe solennelle,* and Maria Tallchief's presentation of a program of ballets by George Balanchine. Each program was given four times, in a Wednesday-Friday-Saturday-Sunday pattern.

This was a time in which Balanchine, in conjunction with Tallchief, worked with the Lyric to sustain its own ballet company, an arrangement that went on for a number of years until Lyric's financial condition worsened to where it no longer could maintain that wing of its operations. At that point, and for three years, the Boston Ballet came for Lyric productions that needed dancers. Later, the Lyric and Tallchief made an arrangement under which she would prepare a company of Chicago dancers for Lyric's needs in a given season.

At its April 1976 annual meeting, the Lyric Opera of Chicago announced that its books were balanced; in fact, the company had not only achieved a surplus of a little over $3,000 but had as well cut $100,000 from the predicted deficit for the coming year. The Lyric also set a fund-raising goal of $3.1 million to close the gap between box office income and production costs. By the time performances began in September 1976 it was announced that the season was already sold out. The actual number of subscribers, 20,790, was about 120 less than the previous year, but prices had increased, so the income from subscriptions set a new record, $2,132,225. That left 19% of the tickets for the season available for single-ticket sales, and the demand was as intense as ever.

The season opener was a spectacular piece of staging. It was Lyric's first offering of Offenbach's *The Tales of Hoffmann* and was a director's show, a designer's show, and a tenor's show. Virginio Puecher brought one startling effect after another on the Ezio Frigerio set, which looked like a French railway station of the 1870s. You wondered when the blue train was going to arrive, and it *did*—appearing on the stage at the close of the prologue, huffing and puffing great clouds of steam. Plácido Domingo dominated the opera as Hoffmann; no one else onstage was any real competition for audience attention whenever he was singing. The three ladies of the plot were Ruth Welting, perfect as the mechanical doll Olympia; Viorica Cortez, sensuous if lacking vocal warmth as Giulietta; and Christiane Eda-Pierre, dramatically and vocally convincing as Antonia. Norman Mittelmann was a strong presence with a fine voice as Hoffmann's adversaries.

Jean-Pierre Ponnelle was the designer-costumer-director for this season's offering of Rossini's *La Cenerentola*, and it was his show. The comedians dominated: Paolo Montarsolo wonderfully pompous, vain, and muddled as Don Magnifico; Trudy Hines and Nassrin Azarmi lively and pretty little monsters as the wicked sisters; and Timothy Nolen stealing scenes as Dandini. Lucia Valentini-Terrani, the Cinderella, seemed to be saving her voice for the last act's vocal fireworks, which she performed well but without great brilliance. The same could be said of Luigi Alva as her prince, Don Ramiro: he sang well, but without much characterization. The opera has a nice sense of tempo, and that was well served by the conductor, Nicola Rescigno.

Two Verdi operas came next. *Un ballo in maschera* was seen in a respectable production but offered nothing to surpass the finest of several previous Lyric stagings of the work. José Carreras made his only Lyric appearance as Riccardo, Katia Ricciarelli was Amelia, and Renato Bruson debuted as Renato. Jesús López-Cobos conducted. The season's *Rigoletto* was quite another matter, taut in its dramatic line, well paced, well sung, and convincingly achieved in a traditional romantic style. Norman Mittelmann sang the title role in six of the performances, while Matteo Manuguerra made his American debut in the other five (including a student matinée). Elena Mauti-Nunziata's Gilda was her Lyric debut, with Silvana Mazzieri in her American debut as Maddalena. Alfredo Kraus was the Duke, and a Lyric Opera School bass, Gianfranco Casarini, was Sparafucile. Riccardo Chailly's conducting was admirable.

Mussorgsky's *Khovanshchina* was back, with Nicolai Ghiaurov a tower of vocal and dramatic strength as Prince Ivan Khovansky. The other male principals sang well but were no match for him vocally or dramatically. Viorica Cortez as Marfa sang with a presence that commanded the eye and the ear, and Bruno Bartoletti led his excellent chorus and orchestra in a pacing that kept everything moving forcefully.

The Puccini opera of the season was *Tosca*, with Luciano Pavarotti making his first appearance anywhere in the role of Cavaradossi, and Carol Neblett and Cornell MacNeil singing their first Lyric Tosca and Scarpia, respectively. Hearing each of them in this music added a new dimension to one's appreciation of their skills.

This was the year of the American bicentennial, and since the commission Lyric made for the occasion was not going to be ready for this season (two further years had to elapse—more of that later), it was decided to revive the work commissioned by the Chicago Opera in 1921, Prokofiev's *The Love for Three Oranges*. The production was yet another of the many gifted to the Lyric by James C. Hemphill, who died two weeks before it opened. Overall it was one of the happiest things the Lyric had presented in several seasons, a constant delight to the eye, the score a bonanza of bright thematic ideas, with the composer's fantasy and comedy bountifully realized: an uninhibited, free-wheeling Russian opera of the twentieth century, vocally full of good things that, on the whole, were well achieved by a very large and capable cast singing the work in English. Frank Little as the Prince did some of the finest work he achieved in his many years with the company. Jacque Trussel's Truffaldino was a delight to watch and hear, as was Italo Tajo's comic turn as the enormously large Cook. Bruno Bartoletti conducted the production, and Giulio Chazalettes's direction made it the nearest thing to perpetual motion.

Particularly with the Offenbach, Mussorgsky, and Prokofiev scores it had presented (and the excellent stagings it had given them), Lyric proved in its 1976 season that the company was moving away from established patterns such as its previous highly Italianate leanings and traditional stagings and that the audience was not only supporting the change but encouraging it.

In December of 1976 it was announced that WFMT (which was celebrating its twenty-fifth anniversary at the time) would begin national broadcast syndication of Lyric productions, starting with the just completed seven-opera season, to be heard following the Metropolitan's annual on-air offerings. In spring 1977, 206 radio stations across the country carried the sound of Lyric for the first time to an audience in the millions. It was the beginning of a major step in further national recognition of the Lyric and its product. (With a loss of funding sources, the broadcasts ceased after the 2002 spring syndication. At this writing, efforts are still being made to restore both the local and national broadcasts.)

January and April of 1977 found Alan Stone and his Chicago Opera Studio back with a season played in Mandel Hall and Evanston Township High School. This time the repertory included the score that—probably more than any other—was to put the company on the city's operatic map, Lee Hoiby's *Summer and Smoke,* based on the play by Tennessee Williams. Robert Orth, a stalwart of the company from the beginning, made use of his full resources as a singing actor in playing the Doctor, and Carol Gutknecht offered a performance of exceptional depth and range as a young woman unable to come to terms with her sexuality. This was opera drawn from American life and projected as musical theater of remarkable intensity. For contrast there was more Mozart, this time *The Abduction from the Seraglio (Die Entführung aus dem Serail),* and the company policy of singing everything in English brightened the comic moments.

The spring 1977 season of Lyric Opera's training school was less ambitious than before, presenting Cimarosa's opera *Il matrimonio segreto* for two performances and concluding with two ballet nights. The Cimarosa was done well, but its three-hour duration seemed interminable—the opera's fault, not the cast's.

Lyric's press release of its financial picture in May 1977 sent mixed messages. The fund-raising goal of $3.1 million was exceeded by $40,000, and income from operations was $2.75 million against operating expenses of $6.4 million. Fund-raising closed the gap except for $337,398, which was a 12% overrun in expenses. The fund-raising goal had to be increased to $3.4 million. Meanwhile a $140,000 surplus was already used up, so the company secured a $200,000 loan to cover its debts. Another eyebrow-raising fact was that the Lyric was spending $1,028,412 for artists and conductors versus $1,163,168 for administration. That was a very expensive front office.

The 1977 Lyric season got off to a good start with Donizetti's *L'elisir d'amore.* Realism and dramatic credibility made the production more than the usual staging of a score better known today for its vocal than its dramatic potential. Ulisse Santicchi sets, Giulio Cha-

zalettes stage direction, and Duane Schuler lighting presented the work as if it were an example of Italian rural life in the 1830s. The most spectacular singing of the evening came from Luciano Pavarotti as Nemorino (one of his favorite roles). As musical and dramatic entities, the Adina of Margherita Rinaldi and the Dulcamara of Geraint Evans were unified to an exceptional degree: consistent, convincing, and well sung. Lyric's chorus, heard for the first time under its new director, Giulio Favario, was a credit to him.

Mozart's *Idomeneo* had been seen in Chicago in a Northwestern University production in 1966 and a Music of the Baroque offering in 1976, but neither of those was on the level of what the Lyric offered in 1977 in a staging conceived by Jean-Pierre Ponnelle. A giant head of Neptune at the back of the stage dominated the scene, a constant reminder of the tragic vow Idomeneo made to the sea god and how it moved the main story of the opera. Carol Neblett's striking presence and vocal fireworks were the main elements of her Elettra, but she did not project the text with much force. Maria Ewing's Idamante offered superb enunciation of her character and equally commendable singing. Christiane Eda-Pierre sang the first five Ilias (Ellen Shade sang the other two) and was thoroughly notable, as were George Shirley, Frank Little, and Eric Tappy as the powers that ruled Crete. Tappy, as Idomeneo, sustained the burden of the most demanding of the dramatic scenes through excellent singing with the right mixture of formal gesture and expression. The conductor John Pritchard had been associated with the score for some twenty-five years and made it thoroughly his own.

The Lyric successfully revived two of its acclaimed productions of recent years. *Peter Grimes* had basically the same cast as it did in 1974, the major change being Morley Meredith's sharing the role of Captain Balstrode with Geraint Evans. *Orfeo ed Euridice* was given with Ellen Shade as Euridice this time. The whole approach to the opera worked as well as it did two years earlier.

Maria Callas died on September 16, 1977, and on November 1—twenty-three years to the day since Callas made her American debut with the company in 1954—the Lyric Opera staged a tribute to her. The curtain rose to reveal a huge portrait of Callas, which was flanked by two tall trees of roses. After the Lyric orchestra played the overture to Bellini's *Norma* (the opera in which she made her debut), Callas's 1954 recording of "Casta diva" was played. Several people (including the usually stage-shy Carol Fox) spoke, the most touching reminiscences coming from her long-time colleague and friend, Tito Gobbi. The performances were more somber than celebratory. Richard Stilwell's singing of "Che farò senza Euridice" from *Orfeo ed Euridice* and (especially) Jon Vickers's performance of "Total eclipse!" from Handel's *Samson* were outstanding.

The Lyric season continued with a new production of Puccini's *Manon Lescaut.* The Pier Luigi Pizzi sets were handsome and evocative, but they were so cumbersome that the evening's intermissions were tediously long; the opera with about two hours of music was presented in an evening that ran three-and-a-half hours. Maria Chiara, in her American debut, sang Manon with the right vocal quality, but she did not bring the poignancy and depth required for the role. The characters around her were too simply drawn as well. The conductor Nino Sanzogno had a secure grasp of the score.

Rossini's *The Barber of Seville* is an opera constantly degraded by bad productions and a slapstick tradition, but Lyric's 1977 offering of it was directed by Tito Gobbi, and this time he moved to restore it to its proper mood and make it a plausible companion to Mozart's opera on the Beaumarchais characters. Maria Ewing's Rosina was her greatest achievement for the company to date, and Richard Stilwell's Figaro had charm, elegance, and fine, flexible singing. Luigi Alva, Claudio Desderi, and Paolo Montarsolo completed the cast of principals, and Piero Bellugi conducted. With good people such as these—and a skilled director—it was a truly good show.

The Lyric as well as its audience had long wanted the company to produce Wagner's *Die Meistersinger,* which had not been performed in Chicago since 1950. That wish finally was fulfilled as the last production of Lyric's 1977 season, and it was a performance any theater in the world could view with pride. It marked only the third time in opera history in the United States that the score was performed uncut. It was gorgeous to behold (the sets were on loan from the Metropolitan), and the total realization of the score was deeply satisfying for its quality. Of the principals, Karl Ridderbusch's Hans Sachs was close to perfection, and Geraint Evans's Beckmesser was in the same class. Pilar Lorengar was a beautiful Eva, with the many moods of the character reflected in her voice, and William Johns as Walther played her suitor with the right mixture of the nobleman and the artist. The other pair of lovers,

Magdalena and David, were strongly drawn by Sarah Walker and Kenneth Riegel. Under Ferdinand Leitner's baton, the Lyric orchestra made clear that it had become a major civic asset in its own right, and the large chorus matched the qualities of dedication and delivery of all the others onstage.

All in all the 1977 Lyric season seemed to be the great season of the decade. For the first time in memory the company maintained a high artistic level throughout. Notable, too, was the range of the repertory and the sophistication implicit in offering operas of many different periods and styles, addressing all aspects of them on a high artistic level.

In 1978 Alan Stone's company was renamed the Chicago Opera Theater. It had found a venue on the north side, the 925-seat Athenaeum, which had physically inadequate production facilities and smelled of stale popcorn. But it was a home. Stone returned to *The Merry Wives of Windsor,* and this time he did it justice. Nicolai's Falstaff was paired with Donizetti's *Don Pasquale.* Thus began an exciting period in the city's operatic history, since every season Stone was to bring a work the Lyric was unlikely to produce in a performance that demanded attention.

Carol Fox was determined to offer the world première of an opera by a composer of international reputation. A commission for the season of the American Bicentennial was announced, with Krzysztof Penderecki the designated composer. Some asked, "Why this choice? Why not, for this occasion, an American?" The reply was that Penderecki was the most important living opera composer, which not everyone was prepared to accept. The work was not ready in 1976. Instead, after delays, disputes, and difficulties, Fox achieved her première on November 29, 1978, when the Lyric made itself known to audiences in fourteen countries with the presentation of *Paradise Lost,* conducted by Bruno Bartoletti. Nothing comparable had occurred in the city since 1921, when Chicago heard the first performances of Prokofiev's *The Love for Three Oranges.* That event was limited to those present in the Auditorium. *Paradise Lost* was heard internationally in a broadcast produced by WFMT.

The work was a significant step forward from Penderecki's *The Devils of Loudon,* which the Santa Fe Opera had introduced to American listeners. For the composer this was a *rappresentazione* rather than an opera in the traditional sense, a stately, static cosmic drama on a gigantic stage, in which the center of attention was in the music, not the action. In Christopher Fry's libretto, issues and ideas were foremost, not arias and duets. For an audience nursed on *verismo* it presented problems. Some announced it was the worst opera they had ever seen. Others found noble qualities appropriate to the subject but few truly dramatic moments.

The greatest difficulty for the Lyric was Ezio Frigerio's physical production, which had to be modified to fit the stage. (Some of the scenery, reportedly, never was used.) Everything was new to everyone, and an overrun of more than $1 million in the production budget was a portent of the financial problems that were to end the Fox regime three years later. Penderecki, who was on hand to supervise, may have sensed that the piece was too long, but the time for tightening the structure was past. Closer to home were differences with the director, Virginio Puecher, who was replaced by Igal Perry shortly before the première.

For some the greatest moment of the evening was the ballet, choreographed by John Butler, in which Adam and Eve, danced by Dennis Wayne and Nancy Thuesen, came together fresh from creation by the divine hand to affirm the renewing power of the life force. Adam and Eve were human, as was John Milton (Arnold Moss), who narrated and translated God's speeches from Hebrew, but the other characters were symbolic—Sin, Death—or angelic beings. The music called for heroic voices the Lyric failed to supply, although Ellen Shade as Eve and William Stone as Adam were capable and convincing.

The score, the Lyric decor, the Lyric chorus, and the principals of the Lyric cast went to La Scala, Milan, in January and on to the Vatican in February, performing the work as an oratorio. For a Lyric production to rise to these heights of Italian culture must have given Fox an extraordinary sense of achievement. Later in the season the work was heard in Germany and Poland, but apparently it was felt to lack the qualities that would give it a secure place in the repertory.

The season had begun in September with Puccini, *La fanciulla del West,* in a new cost-is-no-object production designed by Eugene and Franne Lee and directed by one of the great names of the New York stage, Harold Prince. Bartoletti conducted. Visually it was always striking, although old-timers might argue that—especially in the final act—the Chicago Opera scenery used by the Lyric in 1956 was more appropriate. Could Carol Neblett, pumping a handcar on a mine railroad in a rush to save her bandit lover sur-

pass the enduring vision of Eleanor Steber riding onstage, a pistol in each hand? Alas, the production dropped to campy comedy in this climactic moment, as it had in the poker game of act 2, when Puccini wanted serious dramatic confrontations.

For Americans, who have well-established ideas about matters Western, *Fanciulla* has always been a problem, and though Neblett played and sang Minnie forcefully enough to carry the show, a heavy Italian tenor (Carlo Cossutta) and a plumper Italian baritone (Gian-Piero Mastromei) were hard to accept as Johnson and Rance, roles that called for tall, lean Americans.

With this Puccini spectacular in the repertory, Fox apparently saw *Madama Butterfly* as a safe box office item that invited economizing. (Ironically three years later that opera was to provide Prince with his most enduring Lyric success.) So it was a sad, poverty-stricken Butterfly who fluttered across the stage in October, with the three principals (Yasuko Hayashi, Giorgio Merighi, and Angelo Romero) falling short of the vocal demands of the large house. Ming Cho Lee's sets (acquired from the Met National Company) were attractive, but the direction was commonplace, and the sluggish conducting by Riccardo Chailly suggested little of his successes in later years.

Chailly returned in November to conduct the venerable coupling of *Cavalleria rusticana* and *Pagliacci,* and here his results were refined and energetic, a testimony to good homework, since he was conducting both operas for the first time. Merighi, having recovered from *Butterfly,* here made a strong impression as Turiddu. *Pagliacci* had the advantage of being a Franco Zeffirelli production on loan from the Met. *Cavalleria rusticana,* from the same source, was ordinary. As Nedda, Teresa Kubiak proved the strongest character in *Pagliacci.* Cossutta, her Canio, had not fully mastered a role he was singing for the first time.

No more than respectable mediocrity was achieved in *Salome,* which was staged much better than it was sung. The sets, by Wieland Wagner, were a strong frame for the action, and the conductor Berislav Klobučar and director Ernst Pöttgen consistently made use of the opportunities offered them. But Grace Bumbry—if she ever could manage Salome with ease—had passed that point, and with the static Jochanaan of Norman Bailey the confrontations the drama required were not present. Ragnar Ulfung and Mignon Dunn as Herod and his queen gave the opera some needed force.

The fear that the Lyric was not going to equal its

best work of the past was dispelled in late October, ironically by a French opera, a restaging of Massenet's *Werther* with the most celebrated protagonist of the title role, Alfredo Kraus, and Yvonne Minton as his lost love. The production, designed and directed by Pier Luigi Samaritani, was gorgeous to see and moved with a sure dramatic pace. The singing was in the great Massenet tradition.

A close rival in the Italian repertory was *Don Pasquale,* which arrived in November with Geraint Evans wonderfully at home in the title role. There was the clever Ezio Frigerio set, with Eduardo De Filippo's staging setting his cast spinning, aided throughout by the bright and lively sounds the conductor John Pritchard brought forth from the pit. Kraus returned as Ernesto, and Judith Blegen, one of the most beguiling sopranos of the day, was a piquant Norina. Richard Stilwell played Malatesta, and the Pasquale-Malatesta duet brought down the house. This production was the vehicle for the only North American tour under Lyric auspices, a visit in April 1979 to the Cervantes Festival in Mexico.

Bill Mason left the Lyric at the end of 1978 to accept the job of artistic administrator at the San Francisco Opera. If his decision was based on personal advancement, it was also spurred by a feeling of deterioration at the Lyric behind the scenes, what with Carol Fox's increasingly difficult behavior and a financial situation that seemed to be leading the company into bankruptcy. But Mason would be back in 1980.

If the Lyric was experiencing problems, small opera companies were thriving. Later in November the other monumental dirty old man of opera, Sir John Falstaff, could be seen on the local educational television channel in Nicolai's rarely heard *The Merry Wives of Windsor.* Eugene Johnson played the title role with appropriate lust and sloth in the Chicago Opera Theater staging.

In 1979 the Opera Theater was producing a spring season that had now grown to three operas (and seventeen performances) a year for a budget of $240,000. The Lyric, to stage its seven productions, required $5 million. Of course there was a difference in the scale of the operations, but the Opera Theater was presenting talented young Americans and hoping there was an economic middle ground in which attractive shows could be produced without spending a fortune.

The repertory consisted of *The Pearl Fishers,* sung in English, of course, as were *Così fan tutte* and *Albert Herring.* The early Bizet score was made dramatically as

plausible as possible and provided an attractive glimpse of the composer on the way to *Carmen.* The staging of *Così* marked five years since the company introduced itself with this work. It was a production the young and struggling Lyric might have been happy to claim. The Britten, however, reaffirmed the special value of the company, its ability to bring the city forceful representations of important works that for one or another reason the Lyric would never stage.

Opera Midwest, an Evanston company, made its debut in July with the dubious premise that Pick-Staiger Hall at Northwestern University might be used as an opera house. It tempted our curiosity with a staging of the original operatic *Barber of Seville,* that of Giovanni Paisiello (1740–1816). (In deference to him Rossini originally called his score *Almaviva.*) In the absence of a pit, the orchestra was placed at the side of the stage, with the result that the singers frequently were not together because they could not see the conductor, Gershon Miklos Braun, and the orchestra was not together because it could. It was a noble try.

In August, downtown, yet another alternative group, the Chamber Opera Theater, introduced itself with Menotti's *The Medium* and Walton's *The Bear.* By December Opera Midwest had moved to Cahn Auditorium at Northwestern University (with a pit and a proscenium stage) to offer an extraordinarily lively staging of *Die Fledermaus.* Winifred Brown of the Lyric was Rosalinda. But the stroke of genius was to have Jerry Hadley (as Alfred) serenade his fellow prisoners with "Nessun dorma." In 1980 the group turned to low-budget and amateurish stagings of works recently heard from the Lyric. This was fatal and prevented it from establishing the firm financial base needed to survive.

The year 1979 brought the twenty-fifth anniversary season to the Lyric, which tended to obscure with celebratory delights the fact that the company faced grave problems. Twenty-five years was a notable achievement—five years more than the most long-lived of the preceding Chicago area opera producers, the Ravinia Opera. Her health failing, Carol Fox was not running the show with her past effectiveness. For a start, she was not planning ahead far enough to secure major talent, which increasingly was engaged three seasons in advance. Still, in 1979 she offered opera fanatics a lineup of all three of what was to become the Three Tenors: Domingo, Pavarotti, and Carreras, along with Vickers and Kraus. Unfortunately, Carreras's health problems forced him to cancel.

The Love for Three Oranges, 1979. Three years earlier Lyric first presented this production, which marked the 55th anniversary of the opera's world première, on this same stage.

I commented at the time: "As we are reminded repeatedly through the season, the Lyric is Carol Fox's opera company. No other opera-producing group in the country, perhaps in the world, is rooted so strongly on a general manager as a cultural heroine-cult figure. The trustees regard her as their leader, not their employee. The Lyric crisis seems to boil down to this. Too much depends on one all-powerful executive. If she cannot function to full efficiency, things slip."

There had to be a party, and it took place on October 14, a concert in the Opera House followed by a champagne reception on the stage, followed by a more intimate gathering for Fox at the Casino Club, where she received Italy's highest civilian decoration.

Princess Margaret of Britain was present. Sir Geraint Evans, a proper Welshman, surveyed the champagne drinkers on the stage and asked, "What, no beer?"

One had to recall the honored dead, among them Jussi Bjoerling, and the conspicuously missing (Boris Christoff for one), but rejoice in those who were present, among them Pavarotti, Vickers, Kraus, Gobbi, and Leontyne Price. "God willing," I wrote, "we will be doing it again [in 2004]." Still, few of those who attended the new production of *Faust*, which opened the season on September 22, would have suspected that this was to be the last group of seven operas under Fox's direction. *Faust*, designed by Pier Luigi Samaritani and directed by Alberto Fassini, departed imaginatively from the usual staging of the opera, never more effectively than at the end when Faust and his nemesis descended straight to Hell. There was even a ballet—seven students from the Lyric School and twenty students from New York—doing Balanchine choreography under the direction of Maria Tallchief.

The conductor Georges Prêtre produced an unusually high standard of vocal and instrumental performance through the evening, but he had prime material to work with: Kraus in the title role, Mirella Freni as Marguerite, and Nicolai Ghiaurov in a performance of Mephistopheles that had grown substantially since his debut in 1963. The Lyric could rejoice that this production, taped for television by Unitel and aired the following January, gave—through ingenious camera angles—an international audience a view of the opera quite unlike any that could be obtained in the theater.

Traditionally, the mayor of Chicago is the honorary chairman of the Lyric board, and, traditionally, the mayor never sets foot in the Opera House. But for this opening night the mayor was Jane Byrne, and she even brought the governor.

Next in line was Prokofiev's *The Love for Three Oranges,* returning three years after the Lyric revived it in 1976. Prêtre was in charge, and the score was presented with all its brilliant complexities shining. Frank Little was once more the Prince. Then there was *Rigoletto* with Pavarotti as the Duke, singing the first performance on his birthday. This was a revival of the 1971 Pizzi staging, conducted with fine measures of lyricism and energy by Chailly. Matteo Manuguerra was a dark eminence in the title role. Judith Blegen's Gilda was a convincing virgin, a vivid contrast to the Maddalena of Kathleen Kuhlmann.

La bohème reaffirmed Fox's belief that popular Puccini could be given indifferent productions. A voice with great promise arrived in *Simon Bocccanegra,* James Morris as Fiesco. Sherrill Milnes had the title role, and Amelia was played, on short notice, by Ellen Shade. Of Margaret Price, who had canceled, Fox ruefully observed, "The artists demand you engage them three years in advance, but they feel free to cancel on you with three days' notice." The problem was that in the Fox years the Lyric rarely had a "cover" (understudy) available for leading roles. Cossutta, momentarily the company's primary Italian tenor, was heard as Gabriele.

Those who had heard Artur Rodzinski's *Tristan und Isolde* at the Lyric might well ask why after twenty-one years the company could not mount a version with equal impact as music and theater. In 1958 one saw the old Civic Opera decor, but it was serviceable. This new production, from Roberto Oswald, was ugly, pretentious, and unsuited to the work. Jon Vickers as Tristan

and, to a lesser degree, Roberta Knie as Isolde, produced some wonderful things, aided by Mignon Dunn as Brangäne and Hans Sotin as King Marke. Siegmund Nimsgern, who was to become an artist of real stature, here proved immature and unconvincing as Kurwenal.

Disappointing as this was, the true disaster of the season came last. *Andrea Chénier* combined proven talents: Bartoletti as conductor, Gobbi as director, and Samaritani as designer. But as in *Paradise Lost* the season before, a vast amount of expensive scenery arrived with no instruction book. The third act looked as though it had been shipped by mistake, appearing to belong to a different opera altogether. Only about half of act 1 could be fitted on the stage. And fussing with all this dubious decor yielded a production that mixed 120 minutes of music with 90 minutes of intermissions.

Musically things were a little better. Plácido Domingo brought the best moments of the evening. The rest of the cast was uneven. Renato Bruson was a weak Gérard, Eva Marton an unconvincing Maddalena. Ironically, while principals were floundering, some of the supporting roles were effectively achieved.

The Chicago Opera Theater, under the banner of "opera for everyone," began an enterprising season, three operas and fourteen performances for a budget of $387,000. Keys to success were a board headed by Joan W. Harris, and what artistic director Alan Stone called "a trim company—modest fees, careful control of production costs, a closely monitored administrative budget, and lots of hard work."

The COT season began in January with Offenbach's *La Périchole,* which the city had not seen in twenty-three years. Company stalwarts Maria Lagios and Robert Orth were the lovers. It was a delicious evening of French comedy. Then the Italians had their turn with Rossini's *The Italian Girl in Algiers (L'Italiana in Algeri).* Like the Offenbach, an English text kept the fun going despite a cast of unequal vocal and acting skills. This led the way to a return of what some regarded as the company's greatest achievement, *Summer and Smoke,* with a number of the original principals.

Only five operas were heard at Lyric in 1980. Opening night, September 20, had *Boris Godunov* in a critical edition based on Mussorgsky's original score. Bartoletti conducted, with Ghiaurov in the title role and a large cast of true merit. The Chicago City Ballet was seen in the Polish act. It was an August Everding production from the Met, with decor by Ming Cho Lee. In terms of time, this was the longest opening night in Lyric history. It lasted until after the midnight witching hour, when overtime began. Artistically it was one of the finest introductions to a new series of performances, and the public responded, demonstrating the sophistication and musical maturity of the audience the Lyric had built in twenty-six years. This was not a group of social butterflies displaying new clothes and eager to get to a party.

The problem with the second production, the company's first staging of *Lohengrin,* was mismatched elements, uniting a splendid conductor perfectly at home in the score—Marek Janowski in his debut performance—with the arrogant scenic mediocrity of Roberto Oswald, whose basic stock in trade was ersatz Wieland Wagner. Janis Martin's Ortrud dominated the opera, with William Johns and Eva Marton as Lohengrin and Elsa constantly overshadowed.

The new Lyric production of the series went to the local première of Verdi's ninth opera, *Attila,* a splendid collaboration between Bartoletti and director Ernst Pöttgen. It offered fresh, effective sets (again by Ming Cho Lee). Ghiaurov, who was to sing the title role, missed the first two performances because of illness, which introduced the Lyric public at last to a major American talent, Jerome Hines. The rest of the strong cast was headed by Gilda Cruz-Romo as Odabella, Veriano Luchetti as Foresto, and Silvano Carrolli as Ezio.

Don Giovanni, charged with the promise of a great evening, came to the Lyric from the Salzburg Festival with a fancy, functional unit set designed by Jean-Pierre Ponnelle and Ponnelle direction that filled the work with flowing life force. John Pritchard conducted and accompanied the recitatives on the harpsichord, recalling Bruno Walter's great days at the Met. Richard Stilwell was the Don, Stafford Dean his servant, and Anna Tomowa-Sintow (Anna), Carol Neblett (Elvira), and Isobel Buchanan (Zerlina) were the three ladies. Hermann Winkler made his American debut as Ottavio.

This was the year of Lyric's first Operathon, an annual fund-raiser, which now consists of a one-day-a-year, continuous sixteen-hour collaboration with WFMT, in which listeners call in with their pledges of support for the Lyric, urged on by the company's performers and staff, from the general director down to the chorus, orchestra, and behind-the-scenes personnel. Representatives of other Chicago cultural institutions and various luminaries appear, and excerpts from past seasons of Lyric broadcasts are heard. Between the listeners' pledges and matching grants

from corporations and individuals, a goodly sum is raised each year, and the event gives the audience a sense of comradeship with the Lyric and the feeling that it is part of the action in supporting the company beyond purchasing tickets.

To wrap up the season, there was Luciano Pavarotti in one of his signature roles, Gustavus III, in *Un ballo in maschera.* After five *Ballo*s set in the improbable locale of Boston, here was the San Franciso production (designed by John Conklin) that put it where Verdi always intended it to be, in Sweden. Pavarotti and Renata Scotto (Amelia) had had quite a row in their recent appearances in *La Gioconda* in San Francisco and were not speaking to one another. Sonja Frissel's direction was hampered in no small way when the two stars kept a distance from each other, even in their big act 2 duet. But musically things came off quite well. Again Pritchard conducted. I had never heard a finer, more carefully realized performance from Pavarotti, and in the duets with Scotto (despite their problems with one another) the heart soared. Leo Nucci was Renato, and Kathleen Battle was pure delight as Oscar.

The season was not completely over. The Lyric was expanding its offerings by presenting four of its major singers (Pavarotti, Kraus, Leontyne Price, and Scotto) in a recital series that ran into January 1981. And Pavarotti organized a special benefit concert for Italian earthquake victims held on December 7, 1980. (Despite their differences, Scotto suggested that—as the two most important stars in the benefit—she and Pavarotti should at least sing one duet. Pavarotti refused.)

Artistic success and a shorter season did not end Lyric's problems. The company had never built a substantial endowment as a backstop. What it had amounted to less than $2 million, and the heavy costs of the Penderecki production and the gala of the 1979 season dipped seriously into what monies were available to the company. Years before, the Kempers had donated the square-block warehouse on 22nd Street and all the opera production content in it to the Lyric. Based on the value of the land and the building itself, the Lyric got a letter of credit for $400,000, one of the things that kept it going. By the end of the 1980 season, the last of those funds had run out. And the Lyric had received a million-dollar Ford Foundation grant with the proviso that it would spend only the interest, not touch the capital itself. But Lyric began taking money from the capital, too. By the middle of the 1981 season even those funds were exhausted. As Danny Newman put it, "We were not only limping, we were flat broke."

"The company is bankrupt," J. W. Van Gorkom of the executive committee told friends. What was needed was the public confidence essential to raising funds and balancing the budget. That required a visible, active, and effective chief executive, a role Carol Fox could no longer play.

At fifty-three she suffered from severe osteoporosis, complicated by her overweight condition. In 1977, while on her annual talent search in Italy, a purse snatcher knocked her down, breaking her elbow. It never fully healed. Early in 1978 she broke her hip, and her recovery was slow and painful. Walking was difficult. She was comfortable only when reclining, and Mimì's couch from *La bohème* was moved to her office. Her ability to work was unpredictable, and her practice of never delegating authority meant that the company ceased to function on her bad days. The staff, headed by Ardis Krainik, kept things stable, often having to do so behind Fox's back.

Early in January 1981 the board told Fox she must retire. "Step down before you destroy what you built," Van Gorkom advised her. "Your place in history is assured." She protested violently. "I *am* Lyric Opera," she told them. But the articles of incorporation said differently. Archie Bow, president of the board, announced on January 9 that "she has relinquished her responsibilities . . . effective immediately."

Aghast, her daughter, Victoria Flanagan, went to the key people of the company, Krainik, Bartoletti, and Newman, urging them to resign in protest. But they had invested too much of their lives in the Lyric and had suffered too much under Fox to destroy the operatic organization that had become central to their lives. Bartoletti had been stung by her contemptuous references to him as "the flute player," and Krainik had been hurt by Fox's referring to her as "the secretary." And certainly Bill Mason was wondering if he had made the right choice in returning to the company that year.

At this point Krainik, who held the official titles of assistant manager and artistic administrator, had had enough of Fox's treatment of her and of the company, and she was about to leave the Lyric to accept the directorship of the Sydney Opera in Australia.

The Lyric board members convinced her that she was the one to take over *their* company, and Krainik was hastily signed on as Lyric's general manager.

On July 22, 1981, Fox had a heart attack in her Lake Shore Drive apartment and was dead on arrival at Northwestern University Hospital.

The thing that sets Fox apart from the ordinary run of upper-class women who must always get their way is that there is no question that at the time of her death she was the most successful opera manager in the history of the city. She did not outlive her myth, but she was soon to be eclipsed by Krainik. During her tenure, the strengths and weaknesses of the Lyric were primarily the strengths and weaknesses of Fox. It was her company. It was as if opera had never existed before her and could not possibly exist without her, and she never saw a Lyric season other than her own work. When it was to her advantage, she could be extraordinarily charming. Her skills as a power broker and politician were impressive. But, as her treatment of Christoff (among others) revealed, where others might have had loyalty and gratitude, she had opportunism.

Her artistic outlook was narrow, but what she knew she knew well. Her social perspective was equally restricted. She did not love her fellow mortals, especially if they were her social inferiors. She was indifferent to the bourgeoisie, but she looked to the middle class to buy tickets and keep her company solvent, and she did nothing in public to offend. Her inner circle—the board members, who supported her for years, and veteran artists like Gobbi—gave her sincere personal loyalty, which she apparently considered her due. But she loved her daughter, and the affection was generously returned.

My considered judgment, after many years, is that Fox was plagued by feelings of inadequacy and tried to hide them under a cloak of megalomania. She fired able people she could not control and hired mediocrities who played to her vanity. She could be self-critical but could not deal objectively with criticism from others. Fox at her worst was paranoid, bullying, and insensitive. You had to respect her best work, but she could not claim affection. The central human element was lacking. She knew success. The question is, did she ever really know happiness?

11

The Krainik Years

1981–1997

Those who attended the annual meeting of the Lyric on the Opera House stage on April 29, 1981, may have sensed that more than change in management had taken place. But few could have realized the company was entering its greatest days artistically, financially, and in terms of impact on the community.

It was the first such meeting that Carol Fox did not attend, although tribute was paid her for services to opera in the city. On the rostrum was her successor as general manager (later general director), Ardis Krainik, and the Krainik approach to administrating the company's affairs was simply stated. "We are going to have firm budgets," she said, "but we are going to have them without trimming quality. We will never trim quality." Krainik's punch line was, "The Lyric will continue to be the best opera company in the world." Certainly new levels of quality were defined.

The financial picture by the end of 1981 was grounds for optimism. The crucial corner had been turned. The season was some $500,000 under budget, and revenues began covering 66% of expenses. (Chapter 14 discusses this in detail.) With Krainik's appointment the Lyric management flourished with the continuity possible only when the top job goes to someone who has been with the organization from the start.

Born in 1929, Krainik was a plump, pretty girl from Manitowac, Wisconsin. Neither of her parents cared for music, but when she began singing in a church choir at seven, her mother found her a voice teacher. There were a few operatic recordings in the house, and *La traviata* became a favorite. But young Ardis was primarily interested in theater, and at eighteen she went to Northwestern University in Evanston, Illinois, with the thought that if she could not have a performing career in the theater, she could

teach the subject. She took part in student shows and her popularity is suggested by the fact she was president of her sorority (Chi Omega). She was also a formidable tennis player and retained an active interest in spectator sports through her Lyric years. (Krainik and Luciano Pavarotti were tennis partners when he appeared in Chicago in Lyric productions.)

Graduation took her back to Wisconsin for two years, where she taught speech and drama in Racine. Only when she began teaching did she become aware that she missed singing and, moreover, had a voice worth training, so in 1953/54 she went back to Northwestern—this time to the music school. As the academic year ended she wondered where to go next and called the newly established Lyric Theater, which hired her as a clerk-typist.

She had only heard three operas. Knowing a lot about opera was originally not part of the job, but learning a lot about opera was. She did office work, sang in the chorus, and played a number of supporting roles before being appointed assistant manager in 1960. Successful work was rewarded in 1975 when the title changed to artistic administrator. Six years later she was the boss. The Lyric grabbed her at the last moment as she was leaving to head the Australian Opera in Sydney.

Krainik's greatest asset was that she was quick to learn and able to view the world with a positive, objective attitude. Where Fox had been paranoid and difficult, Krainik in her mid-thirties turned to Christian Science, which became a source of strength and stability. While retaining the full authority of her job, she was always reasonable and easy to deal with. Her greatest liability was that she had been trained in the limited world of Fox's Italianate company. A year or two at the Met, or in San Francisco under Kurt Herbert

Adler, would have been highly beneficial. For those of us taught by the example of Toscanini, the composer always comes first. For Krainik the Lyric came first. Her most serious weakness, as time proved, was that she would compromise artistic integrity—dedication to the composer—to do things she felt would attract favorable attention to the company.

"It took me a long time to like Mozart," she confessed, "and it's taken me a long time to really like Wagner. I liked Alban Berg before I liked Wagner. But you learn as you grow; there's a place in your life for every kind of music."

Although Fox had studied voice, she never appeared on a Chicago stage, while Krainik will always be remembered for her comprimario parts in a number of operas in Lyric's early years, including Rossweisse in Solti's 1956 *Die Walküre*. She understood singers as only another singer might do—Jessye Norman affectionately called her "Auntie Ardis."

Danny Newman said later of Krainik, "She had a very strong sense of responsibility, and she had one of the most orderly minds I have ever known. She always had a plan. First Things First. She knew the price of every light bulb, what the cost of *everything* was. She had had a tremendous ongoing preparation for her task as general director of Lyric."

"That a singer gets sick is natural," she told an interviewer. "That a singer has some kind of a neurotic something or other, that's also natural. This is a very difficult business . . . the anxieties, frustrations take their toll. That's why performers are a separate kind of creature . . . they need special care, and love is the operative word."

Unlike Fox, Krainik encouraged dialogue within her staff and gladly accepted criticism or disagreement when her plans were discussed. The result was a far more harmonious company than in the past, with a real sense of teamwork.

She set up a kind of quadrumvirate of power, in which she was the general director, Bruno Bartoletti continued as artistic director, Bill Mason was named director of operations (the administrative head of artistic and production matters), and Matthew Epstein became more and more involved as an artistic advisor (and ever more influential in Lyric's taking on new—and sometimes controversial—productions). Like Fox, Krainik had the final word in all matters, but input from all those around her was welcomed.

Krainik had virtually no life apart from her job, and during the season would be in the theater from dawn to dusk on an almost daily basis. And her presence was always felt in what was happening on the stage or what was happening in the Graham Room, where she frequently appeared at intermission. From 1981 to her death in 1997, no one would doubt that it was her opera company.

Jane Byrne was Chicago's mayor in 1980, and in pledging city money to the Lyric to help the company bail out of its financial troubles, she stipulated that some of those funds should be used for Lyric to produce one opera (a "light" opera was agreed on) in the spring of each of the next three years. The first of these, in May 1981, was Franz Lehár's *The Merry Widow,* in a production from the Canadian Opera Company. Lee Schaenen, who had lived and worked in Vienna, conducted, and Lotfi Mansouri directed, with Carole Farley and Evelyn Lear alternating in the title role. It was an interesting contrast. Farley, one of the most beautiful women in opera in this decade, used a well-trained voice effectively. Lear was older but more experienced. She was playing the role of a great beauty, and she made you believe in her. Moreover, she had a bigger, more secure voice, and she projected the spoken dialogue with the effect of a seasoned actress.

Nothing could have been more remote from the world of Carol Fox than Viennese light opera, but the successful move into a tradition and style unknown in the past was a happy prophecy of things to come. The cast was consistently fine, with André Jobin a dashing Danilo, Neil Rosenshein a romantic Camille, and Victoria Vergara, another beauty, Valencienne.

For one May weekend Chicago had two opera companies at work. Chicago Opera Theater offered *The Marriage of Figaro* in a house small enough for the jokes in the English text to have full effect. Earlier in the year the company had offered the Chicago stage première of Puccini's *La rondine,* with an English text that made it good theater. Karen Huffstodt and Richard Leech were the star-crossed lovers. Another important offering from COT in 1981 was the Chicago première of Robert Kurka's *The Good Soldier Schweik.* The opera was completed in 1957, the year of Kurka's death (he was born in 1921), and is based on the satirical antiwar novel by Jaroslav Hašek. It is bitingly Kurt Weillian in its musical dramatics.

The twenty-seventh season of the Lyric Opera, which opened on September 25, 1981, had been planned by Carol Fox and, appropriately, was dedicated to her memory. But there were as many German as Italian works in the seven-opera season, and nearly half the repertory was French, starting with *Samson and Delilah.* Carlo Cossutta and Yvonne Minton were vocally and dramatically convincing as the mighty warrior and the seductive priestess. The final temple crash was eminently satisfactory.

Bruno Bartoletti marked his twenty-fifth season with the Lyric conducting *L'elisir d'amore,* a revival of the 1977 Lyric version. Carlo Bergonzi substituted for an ailing Pavarotti in the first performances. Isobel Buchanan proved a lovely Adina.

Ariadne auf Naxos had been a Lyric success in 1966, and its return with Marek Janowski leading the Lyric orchestra to the top of its form was an occasion for cheering. A miraculous cast, headed by Leonie Rysanek in the title role, swept you along on the high crest of Straussian lyricism. Ruth Welting made her performance as Zerbinetta one of the great experiences of the season, and William Johns was a splendid Bacchus. Yvonne Minton as the Composer projected a vivid character who easily dominated the Prologue.

Verdi's first Shakesperian opera, *Macbeth,* came as a revival from the 1960s, but it was much stronger this time around. Josephine Barstow as Lady Macbeth ruled the stage whenever she was present—no slight achievement, since she was surrounded by strong male characters: Piero Cappuccilli in the title role, Paul Plishka as Banquo, and Frank Little as Macduff. Adam Fischer conducted a strong, idiomatic performance.

A *Fidelio* with Jon Vickers's intense portrayal of Florestan could not fail to make an effect, even though those around him—Johanna Meier as Leonore in the first four performances and Leif Roar as Pizarro—were unable to match him. Eva Marton fared better in her four appearances as Leonore. Gustav Kuhn conducted.

The final two operas of the season were conducted by Jean Fournet. One might argue that Pier Luigi Samaritani's production of Massenet's *Don Quichotte* was his most beautiful, evocative work for the Lyric. First seen in 1974, it was back, with Nicolai Ghiaurov again singing the mad knight, this time with Donald Gramm as his squire and Lucia Valentini-Terrani as his spirit of love. It played well.

The Lyric version of Gounod's *Romeo and Juliet* was hardly a tribute to adolescent love. Both singers in the title roles were grandparents—but listening to Alfredo Kraus and Mirella Freni you would not have guessed it. The passion was there. This opera had opened the seasons in the Auditorium in 1889 and closed them forty years later—Chicago had always

loved it. Yet for this audience it was practically a new work, and, in a production as lyric and poignant as this, a lovely way to close the series.

Inevitably, as the season ended one might prefer some productions over others, but what this first Krainik year heralded was that these preferences were now to be based on the works themselves. Characteristically, every season Fox had one show, usually a staple work, that gave the appearance of being tossed on the stage with minimal fuss and bother. Krainik and her team achieved a striking uniformity in quality through the season. The greatest successes of the past had not been eclipsed, but there was now an artistic product with remarkable consistency.

The following spring the elements that made *The Merry Widow* a success the year before returned in *Die Fledermaus.* Lotfi Mansouri was again in charge of the stage; Lee Schaenen presided in the pit. Winifred Faix Brown was the primary Rosalinda, alternating with Carol Gutknecht. Sunny Joy Langton played Adele. André Jobin, Timothy Nolen, and Tonio di Paolo were Eisenstein, Falke, and Alfred, respectively. For a change, the role of Orlovsky was played by a man, Gerald Issac. You smiled and waltzed all the way home.

The spring season of the Chicago Opera Theater presented one of the most important works it introduced to the city, *Regina,* by Marc Blitzstein (1905–1964), based on Lillian Hellman's play *The Little Foxes.* An acrid study of greed among the magnolias, it was well cast and ably conducted by Steven Larsen. In the title role, Judith Erickson dominated the proceedings. Mozart's *The Abduction from the Seraglio* and Donizetti's *The Daughter of the Regiment* completed the season. In June *Summer and Smoke* came to public television, shot not as an opera seen from a theater seat, but as a highly effective TV film with a moving camera making its own dramatic points. Why was COT on the tube more frequently than the Lyric Opera? It was affordable.

For 1982 opening night at the Lyric there was a festive revival of the 1976 production of *The Tales of Hoffmann.* Bartoletti conducted, with Alfredo Kraus at ease in the title role and three ladies to beguile him: Ruth Welting as Olympia, Marilyn Zschau as Giulietta, and Valerie Masterson as Antonia. Norman Mittlemann played Hoffmann's nemeses. Victoria Vergara was Nicklausse.

In retrospect the 1982 *Tristan und Isolde* (another revival that carried over elements from the 1979 version) was the last Lyric staging of the work to have a musical and visual foundation according with Wagner's view of the opera. This time the intensity of the musical performance permitted one to overlook the failings of Oswald's sets, and Ernst Pöttgen's stage direction was dramatically compelling. Vickers sang Tristan, as he later announced to be his final series of performances in that role, to the youthful and passionate Isolde of Janis Martin. Brangäne was new, too—Nadine Denize. Siegmund Nimsgern's Kurwenal was much more firmly drawn than in 1979, and Hans Sotin made King Marke a far more tragic figure than he is often made to appear. At the final performance the orchestra saluted Ferdinand Leitner with a *tusch* (that disjointed, free-for-all fanfare orchestral musicians give in tribute to a conductor), the first it had given a conductor in many years.

When Tito Gobbi returned to direct *Tosca,* few would suspect that Chicago would never see him again. Recalling that he had sung the role of Scarpia in 879 performances, he laughed as he said, "On 879 nights I got to go home before the end of the opera." Unlike his stagings of *Un ballo in maschera,* his productions of *Tosca* were always set in the correct historical period. "History is history. I insist on accuracy. The dramatic logic of the work requires it." This production involved, in effect, two different casts of principals over its eight performances: Grace Bumbry and Eva Marton as Tosca, Veriano Luchetti and Plácido Domingo as Cavaradossi, and Ingvar Wixell and Siegmund Nimsgern as Scarpia. The stable elements were Julius Rudel in the pit, Gobbi's direction, and the familiar Pizzi decor. They provided consistently exciting evenings.

All later Lyric stagings of *Così fan tutte* have been haunted by the Viennese magic of its first production, in 1959. This version, directed by Graziella Sciutti and conducted by Julius Rudel, offered Gösta Winbergh and Richard Stilwell as the young gentlemen and Rachael Yakar and Anne Howells as their ladies. The decor came from the Met. It wasn't 1959 again, but it was a fine evening.

It was Krainik's idea to pair one of the two most popular of all one-act operas, *Pagliacci,* with a work little known to most operagoers, Poulenc's *La voix humaine.* In a real *coup de théâtre,* Josephine Barstow played the solo role in the Poulenc (and brilliantly, too), then returned as Nedda in the Leoncavallo score, a totally different type of role, which she realized with equal skill. Carlo Felice Cillario conducted both scores with a fine understanding of the distinc-

tive requirements of each. Poulenc and Jean Cocteau had found the essence of the tragedy of a lost love, and the same anguish, in a very different form, poured from *Pagliacci,* with Vickers as Canio and Cornell MacNeil as Tonio.

The year 1982 held the debut of the miraculous Harold Prince production of *Madama Butterfly.* As designed by Clarke Dunham, a little Japanese house on a hilltop overlooking Nagasaki harbor turned on a revolving stage, which often gave an illusion similar to a long moving camera shot in a film. The production based its details on staging elements of traditional Japanese theater, and the action took place in fluid spaces that framed it perfectly. It was the most effective staging of *Butterfly* one was likely to remember, and it had vivid performances by Elena Mauti-Nunziata, Giuliano Ciannella, and Sesto Bruscantini.

Luciano Pavarotti cooked his goose for good when he canceled *Il trovatore* in 1987, but it was at least half done when he canceled *Luisa Miller* in 1982. A primary light in an uneven cast, Ciannella took his place, with Ellen Shade in the title role and Dimitri Kavrakos as the most perfectly named of all operatic villains, Wurm. Miguel Gómez-Martínez, who had conducted the *Butterfly,* conducted again, replacing Bartoletti, who was undergoing heart surgery. The old-fashioned production came from the Met. One was left with the impression of a powerful Verdi score that could have been better served.

In December Light Opera Works, an Evanston company with noble hopes and limited resources, gave the local public its first chance to witness a performance of Leonard Bernstein's *Candide.* Given in Cahn Auditorium with a simple set, it had a big cast that ranged from adequate to excellent in an uneven, but still stageworthy, production. Marcy A. Weckler as the Old Lady stole one scene after another, but when they were alone, David Huff and Elizabeth Gottlieb, as Candide and his beloved, easily held your attention.

A milestone was passed in March 1983 when Claudia Cassidy left station WFMT, where she had served as critic-at-large since her departure from the *Tribune* in 1964. In regard to the Lyric, Cassidy was fighting against those who took Fox's opera company from her and regarded Krainik as part of that plot. This was unfair. Even more unfair was her claim that the company was in a state of decline when, in fact, productions and artists Cassidy found objectionable were there because Krainik was honoring plans and contracts made in the final Fox season.

The early months of 1983 brought a number of attractive performances from smaller opera producers. Those who wanted to judge for themselves the qualities of the Auditorium as an opera house could do so in January, when the New York City Opera National Company brought *Carmen* for two performances. In February the Chicago Symphony presented Schoenberg's *Erwartung* in a concert performance with Hildegard Behrens and with Claudio Abbado conducting. Beautifully achieved, it was wasted on many listeners who would have been much happier with Brahms. Abbado had his revenge the following week when he scheduled Karlheinz Stockhausen's *Gruppen* and played it twice in one concert.

In April, anticipating his debut at the Bayreuth Festival the following summer, Solti conducted *Das Rheingold* with the Symphony with three members of his Bayreuth cast: Siegmund Nimsgern, Siegfried Jerusalem, and Hermann Becht. In Orchestra Hall the three Rheinmaidens appeared in dresses that clashed visually with one another. In Bayreuth Solti had no such problems—there the Rheinmaidens were naked. His Bayreuth performances were heard on American classical music stations when WFMT produced the broadcasts, the first three from a tape delay, but *Götterdämmerung* broadcast live, starting at 8:45 in the morning.

At the end of February a production of *Porgy and Bess* that marked the fiftieth anniversary of the beginning of Gershwin's work on the score passed though Arie Crown Theater on its way to the Radio City Music Hall in New York. It was based on the highly successful 1976 Houston Grand Opera production, and the stature of the work—certainly the best-known American opera—was made perfectly clear in both the singing and the staging. Three days later Robert Gay, the head of the Northwestern University opera department for twenty-four years, offered an effective staging of Janáček's *The Cunning Little Vixen*.

An opera that was once popular and now is all but unknown is *Martha,* which the Chicago Opera Theater produced in February as a frothy, lightweight romantic comedy. In April it brought us Menotti's finest score, unheard in the city for some twenty years, *The Consul,* and found a musical, human, and theatrical scale for the work that was lacking in the later Lyric production of 1996. Finally, in August, the College of DuPage presented a work one never expected to encounter on a stage, Lehár's purported grand opera, *Giuditta.* One of the pleasures of opera in Chicago in the 1980s was that you did see and hear these things. The operatic menu was not limited to what the Lyric chose to produce.

Following vocal studies at Milliken University and then at Chicago Musical College in the 1950s, soprano Norma Williams embarked on a career centered mainly in Europe, especially in Germany. Following that, she returned to the United States to teach in Virginia until she was invited to become a faculty member at the DePaul University School of Music in Chicago in 1978—a position she held until 1982.

Imbued with a sense of entrepreneurship, while at DePaul she began presenting performances of opera, unstaged and with piano accompaniment. The response was encouraging, so in 1983 she established a company she called Lincoln Opera. By 1985 productions of complete operas were staged but had to be given with piano. In 1988, and with expanded staging, they were presented with orchestra.

Season series Chicago performances were given first at Lincoln Park Presbyterian Church, then at Mundelein College, which became the major performing base for the company until 1993. After that, productions were presented at St. Scholastica High School and at the South Shore Cultural Center. The repertoire consisted usually of three productions per season, and, because it utilized local talent, the company claimed that the operation was never in the red. Each production was given four to eight times and included performances in Illinois beyond Chicago (in Rockford, Woodstock, Elgin, and Kankakee).

Lincoln Opera also organized a great deal of education outreach. In its twelve years of existence some 104 schools were involved, with productions adapted to logistical practicality and the attention span of schoolchildren. Some schools witnessed fourteen operas over those years. But the main thrust of the company was professional production for Chicago audiences, and Lincoln Opera grew in audience interest, subscriptions, funding, and internal size. It was the latter aspect that finally led to the demise of the company.

Norma Williams was a strong leader, realistic in her assessment of Lincoln Opera's limitations but demanding in her vision of what both its quality and its aims should be. She found though that, as the company's presence and its obligations increased, behind-the-scenes support did not keep pace. More and more she felt that too much of operational detail and fund-raising fell on her, and in 1995 she closed the company down.

A decisive moment in Ardis Krainik's artistic development took place in May 1983 when for the last of her three spring productions she offered *The Mikado.*

The Triumphal Scene from *Aida*, Lyric Opera of Chicago, 1993, on the set first seen ten years earlier, which is still in use

A traditional presentation seemed inappropriate, so Krainik hired Peter Sellars, a rapidly growing talent with a gift for the unconventional. For him, the piece was set in a fantasy land, a mixture of Victorian England and a Japan that never existed. All the satire was to be carefully preserved, but this became a spoof on modern Japan, with the opening chorus sung by a group in Brooks Brothers suits against a wall of trademarks—Sony, Toyota, Nikon, and so forth. It worked. The show was brisk, lively, unconventional, and funny, without the slightest damage to the music or the words. Donald Adams, a D'Oyly Carte veteran, played the title role, with James Billings and William Wildermann as Koko and Pooh-Bah. Neil Rosenshein sang Nanki-Poo.

That autumn, a year after his heart attack, Bartoletti returned triumphantly with a new production of *Aida* that was so good you feared the rest of the season might prove anticlimactic. The work had not been heard in the city for nearly twenty years, and this was a staging that was at once traditional and in-

novative and avoided the Egyptian kitsch that can plague the work. Luciano Pavarotti sang the opening performances gloriously, but when the role passed to Giuseppe Giacomini the production retained its force. Anna Tomowa-Sintow proved a true princess in manner and force.

Reviving Delibes's *Lakmé*, once quite popular in the city, after forty-five years and putting it right after one of the most powerful Italian scores made it appear terribly slight—almost an operetta. The production came from Trieste, with Michel Plasson conducting and Luciana Serra heading a good cast. A second French revival, *Manon*, returned after ten years, with Renata Scotto and Alfredo Kraus well cast and dramatically effective as the lovers, and with Julius Rudel conducting. The sometimes heavily cut score was heard intact, which greatly enhanced its dramatic force.

San Francisco provided the settings for two operas, both Ponnelle productions. *La Cenerentola* glittered, with Agnes Baltsa in the title role and Rockwell Blake her prince. It was fresh and funny, and it was proof that one of the last great successes of the Fox seasons could return to the stage as attractive as before. Fairly controversial, but unquestionably different, was Ponnelle's staging of *The Flying Dutchman* on a battered old freighter. His viewpoint was that the way to unite supernatural elements with the life of a Norwegian town was to make the action the Steersman's dream. Since dreams do not have intermissions, Ponnelle chose Wagner's original Dresden version, in which the work is in one act. Vocally the performance was uneven, but Siegmund Nimsgern as an effective Dutchman and Hans Sotin (Daland) and Robert Schunk (Steersman and Erik) were excellent foils. Carolyne James was Senta. The Puccini of the season was *La bohème*, with Ileana Cotrubas as Mimì, and it marked

the first time the Lyric offered a matinée performance. For the first few years thereafter the Lyric would proceed cautiously in expanding the number of matinée performances, and at this writing every one of the operas in its eight-per-season offerings has a least one matinée, some get two, and a very few have three.

When the final curtain fell, the fact remained that the great event of the autumn was the original version of Shostakovich's *Lady Macbeth of Mtsensk,* sung in English, with a production from the American Spoleto Festival. Bartoletti masterfully demonstrated his gift for both Russian and twentieth-century music. The performance was powerful in every way: visually, dramatically, and, most of all, musically. Moreover, it demonstrated to Krainik that there was strong operatic

Alfredo Kraus and Renata Scotto in *Manon,* 1983

repertory from the twentieth century and that, given the right staging, these works could claim audience attention as forcefully as older scores. In an excellent cast, Marilyn Zschau was the murderous lady, with Jacque Trussel her lover and Franco Farina her husband.

On December 11 the Lyric joined the Opéra de Paris, Teatro alla Scala, and Royal Opera House, Covent Garden, in "Callas: An International Celebration," a live, international telecast; the Chicago portion included performances by Cotrubas, Kraus, Scotto, and Vickers, with Bartoletti conducting.

In the spring of 1984 the Lyric presented a three-event "Marilyn Horne Festival." May 2 brought a concert performance of Handel's *Rinaldo,* with Horne, Samuel Ramey (in his Lyric debut, stopping the show with his first-act aria), and Carol Vaness among the cast members, Mario Bernardi conducting. Leonard Slatkin led Lyric's orchestra for "Marilyn Horne in Concert" on May 9, and Martin Katz was her pianist for a recital on May 30.

A month before its 1984 season began, the Lyric presented "Luciano Pavarotti in Concert" at the Poplar Creek Music Theatre. Emerson Buckley conducted.

Bartoletti's gifts for Russian music were on view once more in 1984 when the Lyric opened its thirtieth season with the first production by a Chicago company of Tchaikovsky's *Eugene Onegin.* It was a romantic view of the score, very Russian in spirit and sound, beautifully cast. Mirella Freni was radiant as Tatiana, and her husband, Nicolai Ghiaurov, was Prince Gremin. Wolfgang Brendel as Onegin and Peter Dvorský as Lensky were vocally and dramatically outstanding. Taped in performance, the production was broadcast on PBS a year later. This was the first of four operas added to the Lyric repertory, proof that for Krainik innovation was serious business. And Verdi's *Ernani,* not heard in the city for sixty-seven years, might just as well have been a première.

Patrons of German opera must have felt their wildest dreams were being fulfilled when two major works of Richard Strauss, *Arabella* and *Die Frau ohne Schatten,* entered the Lyric repertory in the same year. Under the conductor John Pritchard, *Arabella* poured forth as unending song, and Kiri Te Kanawa and Ingvar Wixell captured the spirit of romance. Unfortunately, the production was just one season too early for supertitles, so much of the humor and irony of the libretto was lost to those unable to follow the words. *Die Frau ohne Schatten* is a very different sort of work, a mythical hymn to life, fertility, and love,

composed during the horrors of World War I. Here again the conductor, this time Marek Janowski, was a central element in the success of the work. William Johns and Eva Marton were the Emperor and Empress, Mignon Dunn the Nurse, and Siegmund Nimsgern and Marilyn Zschau the dyer Barak and his wife.

Mozart's *The Abduction from the Seraglio* was not new to the city but it was to the Lyric, a lively romp through the harem put in motion by the baton of Ferdinand Leitner. The sets and director (John Dexter) came from the Met. Francisco Araiza, Ruth Welting, and Kurt Moll were the principals.

Ernani (in the first production from the new critical edition) was to have been a vehicle for Luciano Pavarotti, but as the work was beginning rehearsals he canceled his appearances. Since *Ernani* is not an opera that is produced all the time (the critical edition was the first occasion it had appeared in print in full score), finding a tenor who is equal to the role, knows it, and is free, is the sort of thing that puts opera managers in early graves, but Lando Bartolini took the stage opening night, faced an audience that had sold out the house in mid-summer expecting Pavarotti, and succeeded. He was part of an ensemble of strong colleagues. Grace Bumbry and Nicolai Ghiaurov joined him to sustain the work.

The Krainik approach was that there had to be some meat-and-potatoes opera, in this case a handsome *Carmen* filled with the physical and emotional heat of Spain in a Ponnelle version with Teresa Berganza and with Plácido Domingo as Don José. *The Barber of Seville* was a frolic through the familiar with J. Patrick Raftery in the title role. Araiza was the Count, and Cesare Siepi—in the noted tradition of major basses taking the role—sang Basilio. Shortly after the season began, the Lyric presented Jon Vickers in a deeply felt and beautifully sung traversal of Schubert's *Winterreise* cycle.

Fine as the Lyric proved to be in 1984, it was a year in which a wide range of opera was heard from a variety of sources. In February the Northwestern University Opera Studio staged Barber's *Vanessa* most effectively from the resources of its School of Music, giving Chicago a welcome look at the work. In April a group calling itself the Opera Theater of Illinois presented *Der Freischütz* in Northbrook and Hinsdale. The last professional performance of the score in the Chicago area had been in 1895. The production was good enough to make one realize the importance of the work.

The Chicago Symphony made the point that if

The Mother of Us All, Chicago Opera Theater, 1984

you wanted to hear opera with conductors of the stature of Solti and Abbado, you had to go to Orchestra Hall. In April Solti conducted and later recorded a concert version of Schoenberg's *Moses und Aron* with spectacular success, and in May Abbado offered a powerful, semistaged production of *Wozzeck* with Benjamin Luxon and Hildegard Behrens. In November he conducted *Boris Godunov* in Russian and in concert form from the critical edition of the 1874 text. Ruggiero Raimondi sang a powerful Boris, and Samuel Ramey was Pimen. In April and May the Volksoper of Vienna waltzed through the Auditorium with *The Merry Widow* and *Die Fledermaus.* Neither production was to be preferred to the Lyric versions, which had the further advantage of being in English.

Finally, Chicago Opera Theater bravely attempted *Don Giovanni* and succeeded in terms of its limited resources. It had moderate success with *The Bartered Bride* but really came into its own with what some regard as the finest American opera, Virgil Thomson's *The Mother of Us All.* Hearing nine operas in addition to the Lyric offerings gave the Chicago area public a rich variety of repertory that, unfortunately, was not to be repeated very often.

In 1984, two years after his final work with the company (directing *Tosca*), the Lyric lost one of its greatest strengths. Tito Gobbi died in March at the age of sixty-eight after an agonizing battle with cancer. Performances of *The Barber of Seville,* the opera in which he made his Chicago debut thirty years before, were dedicated to his memory.

In June 1984 the Chicago Opera Theater founder and artistic director Alan Stone had surgery for a brain tumor. He was working mainly from home as COT's 1985 season began in February. Marc Scorca was named the managing director, coordinating the various aspects of the company's operations. Bizet's *The Pearl Fishers* was given, its English translation showing the glaring weaknesses of the libretto. The production was somewhat campy, but good singing made the performance work. A month later found COT's *L'elisir d'amore* done with taste and style (except for an unnecessary mock bullfight dumped into the early stages of the opera), but once again the singing was excellent. Robert Ward's *The Crucible* was presented in May, in a new version for smaller orchestra. This was the best work the company did all season, and it made a convincing case for American opera as effective music and theater.

COT had now settled into a new basic formula for its seasons: one Italian classic, one romantic opera, and one twentieth-century work.

Spring of 1985 saw two more Lyric presentations of major opera stars in concert, both with the Lyric orchestra. Kiri Te Kanawa sang on March 20, with Marek Janowski conducting. Plácido Domingo (with mezzo-soprano Marta Senn) was heard on April 16; García Navarro conducted.

The next season was not 1985 but 1985/86. After an interim of more than half a century the Chicago opera season ran through the holidays into the new year. Considering the needs of this larger audience, the Lyric tried its first experiment with supertitles. They were so popular that by 1987 they were used in all operas and proved a major factor in establishing a 100% attendance standard the following year.

Plácido Domingo left after the opening night performance of *Otello* and flew to Mexico to assist earthquake victims. William Johns took over forcefully. Margaret Price sang Desdemona, and Sherrill Milnes was Iago.

It was an overwhelmingly Italian season. The one opera sung in another language was *Die Meistersinger,* which came in a handsome production from the Met. Marek Janowski conducted splendidly, with a cast headed by Thomas Stewart as Sachs, William Johns as Walther, and Nancy Johnson and Patricia Wells sharing the role of Eva. Sharon Graham and David Kuebler were the young lovers Magdalene and David.

It must be said of the Italian fare that a third of it was new. Bartoletti conducted Puccini's *La rondine.* The choice seemed a trifle odd, since the Chicago Opera Theater had done the work in 1981, and a major Puccini score, *Il trittico,* had yet to be heard from the Lyric in its entirety.

A more important première was Bellini's *I Capuleti e i Montecchi,* a wonderfully lyric score—bel canto triumphant—made all the more significant by a superlative performance by Tatiana Troyanos as Romeo, with Cecilia Gasdia as Giulietta, and with Donato Renzetti conducting. Donizetti's *Anna Bolena,* another Lyric première, was also a farewell to Joan Sutherland, who brought great dignity to the title role. Two staples, *Madama Butterfly* and *La traviata,* were carried to success by their respective prima donnas, Anna Tomowa-Sintow and Catherine Malfitano. *Madama Butterfly* was taped in performance for television, but it was not seen until some three-and-a-half years later, as a "Great Performances" telecast.

The Handel renaissance advanced with *Samson,* which really wasn't intended to be an opera. The music was glorious, and Vickers was never less than deeply moving as the great warrior, but the work was a rather static piece to witness.

The Chicago Opera Theater longed to perform beyond the confines of the cramped Athenaeum Theater (it is still inadequate in so many ways for the quality of production groups such as COT wanted to offer), and the company's March 1986 season gave it a chance (short-lived, as it proved) to take its work a little farther after its north side presentation. The locale was the Rialto Theater on Chicago's south side. Carlisle Floyd's *Susannah* opened the season in a production that brought out all the beauty and pathos of the score. Gloria Capone's singing of the title role was fully on the level of what Phyllis Curtin had given Chicago in the New York City Opera production some twenty years earlier. Mascagni's *L'amico Fritz* came next, its first production in the area since the Ravinia Festival performance of 1924. It was attractively staged and extremely well sung. Rossini's *The Turk in Italy* came off with fun, froth, and finesse.

Lee A. Freeman Sr. continued as Lyric's chief counsel through the Fox and most of the Krainik regimes, and Freeman and his wife Brena continued to be supportive of the company in other ways. In the early 1980s they funded the inauguration of a composer-in-residence program, in which the designated person would, over a several-year period, have access to the personnel and facilities of the Lyric staff—and especially its training school, the Lyric Opera Center for American Artists (LOCAA)—to envision all aspects of and develop a new opera, in English, to be world-premièred by the Lyric. The opera would (especially in the early years of the program) be performed by LOCAA soloists and would be written for forces and production on less than a mainstage scale, but it would be given a full production at a suitable venue. The first person chosen for the program was William Neil. He wrote an opera titled *The Guilt of Lillian Sloane,* set to a libretto written by himself and Frank Galati (who was also charged with directing the world première). During the course of the composition, some of the music was heard in workshop presentation, with a panel discussion involving the composer, librettist-director, and Lyric staff. The première, consisting of a single performance with Lee Schaenen conducting, was given at Cahn Auditorium at Northwestern University in Evanston on June 6, 1986.

In 1986/87, Krainik, reinforced by twenty-five thousand subscribers, extended the repertory to nine productions, with *The Merry Widow* a holiday show. The joy of the season was *The Magic Flute* in a truly magical production superbly conducted by Leonard Slatkin, whom Chicago previously knew only for symphonic music. It was blessed with a glowing cast headed by Judith Blegen, Francisco Araiza, and Matti Salminen. The other great event was the first Lyric production of *Parsifal* (and the first Chicago hearing of the work in forty years), with Vickers at his best in the title role. These evenings offered what proved to be some of the final—and finest—Lyric performances by Troyanos in her portrayal of Kundry.

The Lyric and the San Francisco Opera joined to build the production of Handel's *Orlando,* memorable music sung by Marilyn Horne in the title role and June Anderson as Angelica, with Charles Mackerras conducting. Bartoletti, the expert on Slavic music, was in charge when Janáček's *Káťa Kabanová* finally was heard in Chicago, a story of far more than the usual operatic complexity forcefully projected, with Ellen Shade and Felicity Palmer featured.

And there was the *Widow*, with Maria Ewing the lady of the title. Four Italian operas balanced this performance: *Bohème, Lucia, Ballo,* and *Gioconda. Ballo* was memorable for, if no other reason, the presence of Luciano Pavarotti in one of his great roles. *Bohème* had two runs, in October and January. *Lucia* came from Dallas, with two prima donnas (Edita Gruberová in November, June Anderson in December) and three conductors. San Francisco loaned Chicago its *Gioconda,* conducted by Bartoletti and sung by Ghena Dimitrova, Giulio Ciannella, Hartmut Welker, Paul Plishka, and Mignon Dunn in principal roles.

The Chicago Opera Theater considered *Così fan tutte* a charmed work for the company ever since it was the first opera COT (as Chicago Opera Studio) ever gave, way back in 1974. But in COT's 1987 revival, you had to wonder whether you were seeing Mozart or the Marx Brothers. It was an over-the-top production that was also the most viciously antifeminine presentation of the score I've ever seen. To top it off, the singing was little better than adequate. Britten's *The Turn of the Screw* was presented (in its Chicago professional premiere) in an acceptable, if understated, performance. Smetana's *The Two Widows* is more like an operetta than an opera, but COT's singing and conducting of it was idiomatic, even though the staging lacked the spark it might have had.

Under James Levine, concert opera had become a regular part of the summer fare at the Ravinia Festi-

val, but in 1987 he decided to remind Chicago that he also did summer opera at Bayreuth and Salzburg and that Ravinia should see this facet of his musicianship in a more three-dimensional manner. *Così fan tutte* and *Ariadne auf Naxos* were presented in semi-staged style that was almost as good as a real opera house production. The casting was sensational. Kiri Te Kanawa and Jerry Hadley in *Così* were two of the singers who were to appear in the work in the autumn Lyric season. Margaret Price was Ariadne, with Kathleen Battle as Zerbinetta and Gary Lakes as Bacchus. Dawn Upshaw was present for her Chicago area operatic debut as Echo.

Luciano Pavarotti opened Lyric's autumn season with a recital that had sold out the Auditorium—with stage seats—months before. He said he had a cold, but he overcame it with a program containing far more songs than arias. "We love you!" someone shouted midway into the evening, but that love turned to irritation when it was learned that Pavarotti would not be returning ten days later for the Lyric's *Il trovatore.* He had not sung the role of Manrico for ten years and had been too busy and ill to relearn it properly. Krainik, who was tired of selling subscriptions with the promise of Pavarotti, only to deal with a cancellation, announced that she would not reengage him for the Lyric Opera. Much was made in the national press of what it seemed to love describing as Krainik's "firing" of Pavarotti.

For many, 1987 will always be the *Lulu* year. Regularly in the history of the company one or another production has been hailed as proof that the Lyric had "finally come of age," but for me this staging of Berg's most mature and demanding work established the Lyric as the peer of any other opera producer in the world. In 1967 the city had heard the score from the short-lived American National Opera Company in the truncated two-act version then in use. Lyric's production of the three-act version was impressive in its full form both as drama and for the large-scale musical development of the score. An unusually large cast had been meticulously prepared. The production came from Turin, the director, Yuri Ljubimov, from Russia, and the conductor, Dennis Russell Davies, from Heaven. Never had the Lyric orchestra played better, and this was a central element in making a conservative audience aware of the significance of the work. The fact that it contained one of the most sexually explicit scenes ever seen on a Chicago stage didn't hurt either.

Catherine Malfitano lived the title role. One can argue today that this was the finest thing, of many fine things, she ever did for the Lyric. Evelyn Lear, in an earlier day a remarkable Lulu herself, now was equally remarkable as Countess Geschwitz. Victor Braun and Jacque Trussel were the Schön family, father and son. Andrew Foldi, internationally acclaimed for his portrayal of Schigolch (the ultimate dirty old man) made this the finest of his many contributions to the company.

Even farther far-out than *Lulu* was Philip Glass's *Satyagraha,* sung in Sanskrit. The story of Gandhi and his developing of passive resistance in India, the opera worked theatrically because of supertitles and the inescapable dramatic interest of the piece. Christopher Keene conducted, and the flowing integration of the orchestra, singing, dance, and stage pictures held the eye and ear. With the retirement of Giulio Favario, Philip Morehead had taken over the position of Lyric's chorus master at the start of the 1986/87 season (and remained in that post through 1990/91). Longtime choristers still speak of learning Sanskrit for the Glass opera as the toughest job they ever had, but they were truly outstanding in bringing it off.

In its specialty, Italian opera, Lyric remained in remarkable form. Bartoletti conducted *Il trovatore* on opening night in a superbly cast production any of the great theaters of the world would have been happy to claim. Giuliano Ciannella was so good as Manrico that you forgot the Pavarotti cancellation. Leo Nucci was a strong Di Luna, Anna Tomowa-Sintow an impressive Leonora. But the most fully developed performance was that of Shirley Verrett as Azucena.

It could have happened again in *Tosca* if conductor Michael Tilson Thomas had shown a more secure grasp of the score, but the singers made up for it. Renata Scotto was the tragic diva, with Sherrill Milnes and Siegmund Nimsgern alternating as her adversary. Ciannella returned as Cavaradossi. On the other hand, Rossini's *L'Italiana in Algeri* was pure joy in a Ponnelle production blessed with Agnes Baltsa, Rockwell Blake, and Simone Alaimo making his American debut as Mustafa.

There was a veteran French conductor, Jean Fournet, in the pit, but otherwise the Lyric's *Faust* was an all-American show. Neil Shicoff was the aging philosopher and Samuel Ramey his diabolical nemesis. Nancy Gustafson could hardly have been better as Marguerite, and Wendy White, a Chicago area singer who made a career at the Metropolitan, was

Siebel. J. Patrick Raftery was a robust Valentin.

The conductor Andrew Davis, in his Lyric debut, contributed mightily to his growing reputation with a realization of *The Marriage of Figaro* that made maximum use of the potential of a remarkable cast. Ramey was back—as a good guy this time—singing Figaro to Maria Ewing's Susanna. They were a great couple, ideally framed by Frederica von Stade as Cherubino, Ruggero Raimondi as the Count, and Felicity Lott as the Countess. It was all set in a new production designed by John Bury and directed by Sir Peter Hall.

The Lyric's *Così fan tutte* had the advantage of supertitles and staging—Ponnelle staging at that—but musically could not always surpass the Levine version heard at Ravinia. John Pritchard conducted, with Kiri Te Kanawa, Jerry Hadley, Anne Howells, Marie McLaughlin, and Alan Titus all in fine form. Timothy Nolen was a properly world-weary Don Alfonso.

Powerful Verdi closed the season: *La forza del destino,* with a remarkably fine cast headed by Susan Dunn, Giuseppe Giacomini, and Leo Nucci, conducted by James Conlon. Few operas are on a larger dramatic scale, and the power and sweep of the score were projected faithfully.

But the season's end signaled Lyric's retreat from presenting nine productions per year. The ever cost-conscious Krainik felt Lyric would be in peril to continue the expansion, and from the next season on well into the new century, Lyric's annual offering was a roster of eight operas.

Productions in which the choreography and dancing are the best part of an opera are in trouble, and that was the case when the Chicago Opera Theater presented *Orpheus and Euridice* as its 1988 season opener. The dark and gloomy production held neither the vocal power (from two of the opera's soloists) nor the conducting that should make the music come alive. On the other hand, *Don Pasquale* was bright and attractive, with the COT regulars Robert Orth and Maria Lagios in fine form. Carlisle Floyd's 1969 *Of Mice and Men* had its Chicago première, presented with the kind of immediacy COT could achieve in its finest hours, with key roles cast perfectly. There were four operas this year from COT, and the last of them was Rossini's *La Cenerentola* in a winning production in which Charles Nelson Reilly's direction was especially effective because it was essentially—if surprisingly—low-key.

There are moments in an opera house when one feels that the most exacting demands of a composer and librettist have been realized. In the 1988/89 season such an experience came at the close of the "Dance of the Seven Veils" in a production of *Salome* originally staged by Sir Peter Hall. I have seen the climactic dance done by Birgit Nilsson (who didn't remove as much as a Band-Aid), but here Maria Ewing did what Strauss must have hoped he might someday see, a sensuous, beautifully choreographed dance sequence, building to a succession of climactic moments as each veil was discarded, and reaching its peak when the seventh was tossed away and Ewing, with a lovely woman's body clothed only in shadows, stood before us for an instant. If Mary Garden had done anything like that (and one suspects she wanted to) there really would have been a riot. Here it was a revelation of beauty. Much of the power of the evening came from Ewing's remarkable musical and dramatic involvement, as well as from Nimsgern as Jochanaan, with the thrust and power of the music fully realized by conductor Leonard Slatkin and the Lyric orchestra.

A notable *Don Giovanni* in the Ponnelle staging had Semyon Bychkov a tower of strength in the pit and Samuel Ramey an equal force as the lecherous Don. In an excellent cast, Claudio Desderi was Leporello, Marie McLaughlin, Zerlina. Carol Vaness and Karita Mattila were Donna Anna and Donna Elvira, respectively, and Gösta Winbergh was Don Ottavio.

After an absence from the repertory of sixty-two years, the city's first opera, *La sonnambula,* returned to open the season. Donato Renzetti conducted with a firm grasp of the style, and Cecilia Gasdia played the sleepwalking heroine. Frank Lopardo, Ruth Welting, and Dimitri Kavrakos joined her in pursuit of the high bel canto style. At the other end of the season, Rossini's *Tancredi* was given its first Chicago performances as a vehicle for Marilyn Horne, who was most certainly in her element. Chris Merritt and Sharon Graham were among those joining her to attempt to bring the opera to life, but one might question why obscure Italian works of this type are offered to the public when major works of the twentieth century remain unheard.

La traviata was given unusual power in a version in which a young man, Neil Rosenshein, is in love with an older woman, Anna Tomowa-Sintow. Conductor Bartoletti insisted that the work be given in three acts, as Verdi intended, rather than the often performed four. The elder Germont, Juan Pons in his Lyric debut, is slightly older than Violetta and might have become involved with her himself in earlier days. Thus he grieves at her death as much as his son does.

Falstaff, the Mozart opera that is by Verdi, came in

a near perfect Ponnelle production in which a true ensemble with vibrant rhythm and energy brought the opera to life. Ingvar Wixell in the title role revealed the richness of Verdi's greatest comedy, but the entire cast was marvelous. Jerry Hadley and Ruth Ann Swenson were the young lovers, Barbara Daniels, Marilyn Horne, and Sandra Walker the merry wives, and Alessando Corbelli sang Ford.

Krainik had been so intrigued by Peter Sellars's *Mikado* in 1983 that she felt she must give him a repertory opera to produce. The choice was *Tannhäuser,* which the Lyric had not staged in twenty-five years. Few things the Lyric had announced produced greater curiosity. Even Georg Solti came to have a look (but left in disgust). Of course, Sellars proclaimed, the original symbolism of the work was now meaningless, so this was a *Tannhäuser* that began in a cheap motel with Venus the queen of sluts and ended at an airport with the protagonist being hauled drunk off a flight from Rome. When he sees a vision of Venus there, she is a stewardess in a tight uniform.

No less than three kinds of supertitles—for translation of the libretto, comments on it, and snippets from various pieces of literature, with a different color for each of the three—kept the audience vigorously dividing its attention: reading, listening, and trying to absorb what was happening on the stage.

Musically this was not a production of the future but a reminder of the Wagner style that dominated Bayreuth in the 1920s, when conductor Ferdinand Leitner was a student there. The orchestra was so impressed that it played a bit of the "Ride of the Valkyries" for him at the close of the evening. Marilyn Zschau's Venus was a magnificent tour de force, and Nadine Secunde's Elisabeth the personification of virtue. Richard Cassiley, here a fundamentalist minister, was truly torn between them. Håkan Hagegård was Wolfram. All sang with mature artistry and beauty.

Finally, there was *Aida,* the sort of thing the Lyric was expected to do well, and it was realized in its full musical and dramatic scale. There were three tenors and three sopranos in a revolving cast. The first pair of lovers, Giuseppe Giacomini and Susan Dunn, was not surpassed. Dolora Zajick (in her Lyric debut) and Siegmund Nimsgern completed the principals. Richard Buckley conducted.

The Chicago Opera Theater opened its fifteenth anniversary season by bringing the city its first staging of Oliver Knussen's *Where the Wild Things Are.* It was given as a Christmas holiday season offering and was presented at the Auditorium Theater for five performances; the last one was added in response to brisk ticket sales. The twelve-foot-tall cartoon monsters of Maurice Sendak's imagination charmed the audience in a production that was successful visually and dramatically. It was well and bravely sung, but the overall weakness was Knussen's music, one of those scores one feels is written against the voice rather than for it, with unnecessary leaps and descents all over the vocal range. As a curtain raiser, COT offered an unstaged performance of *Peter and the Wolf,* with Alan Stone narrating like a friendly uncle.

The COT season included performances in February, March, April, and May. *La finta giardiniera* was Mozart's eighth opera (he was eighteen when he wrote it), and COT gave it its only Chicago professional production to date. If this opera does not have all the hallmarks of what we think of as the best of Mozart, COT's exemplary production brought out the promise and the charm the work holds. It is a long opera, but here the staging, conducting, and a remarkably fine cast showed it in its best light. COT had presented Benjamin Britten's chamber comedy *Albert Herring* ten years earlier, and its 1989 revival was even more fun this time, evidence of the company's continuing professional growth. Gounod's *Romeo and Juliet* ended the season, with youthful passion and poignant quality in a cast largely from members of the Lyric Opera Center for American Artists—most notably Jung Ae Kim and Gregory Kunde as the young lovers—who made their singing alone worth a trip to the theater.

June 17, 1989, brought the première—in, again, a single performance—of the second work completed under the Brena and Lee Freeman Composer-in-Residence Program. Lee Goldstein's opera *The Fan,* with a libretto by Charles Kondek, was given in downtown Chicago at the Blackstone Theatre. As in the 1986 production, the librettist was the stage director, the cast was drawn from LOCAA, and the conductor was Lee Schaenen.

In the 1989/90 season the Lyric again went back to presenting only eight productions a year. A powerful *Tosca* opened the season. It was an opera the Lyric prized and invariably did well. Marton was the lady (Carol Neblett sang two performances later in the season), Kristján Jóhannsson the principal Cavaradossi, and Nimsgern the Gestapo officer Scarpia. Bartoletti conducted. Marton bristled visibly when the audience laughed as the supertitles for Tosca's jealous admonition to Cavaradossi—who was painting the

blonde, blue-eyed Marchese Attavanti—urged him to "blacken her eyes." The supertitle screen was blank at that point for all succeeding performances.

Tosca was followed by a *Rosenkavalier* Vienna could have prized, with Tomowa-Sintow, Anne Sofie von Otter in her Lyric debut, Kathleen Battle, and Kurt Moll. Jirí Kout was the conductor.

There remain Mozart operas that have yet to be heard in Chicago, but his last opera, *La clemenza di*

Longtime friends Ardis Krainik and Alan Stone, 1984

Tito, had its first Lyric performance that season, with Andrew Davis conducting, thus filling a major repertory gap. The production came from Geneva, with an excellent, mostly American cast, including Vaness, Troyanos, Susan Graham, and Susanne Mentzer. The opera is not nearly as powerful as its immediate predecessors; the story seems contrived, the characters shallow. But the music is glorious.

The other two Italian operas were staples, but in new productions: *Don Carlo,* ably conducted by James Conlon, and *The Barber of Seville,* in an extremely imaginative, Magritte-inspired staging. The French repertory was represented by some of its most familiar and least familiar works, *Samson and Delilah,* with Agnes Baltsa and Domingo, and Thomas's *Hamlet,* back after seventy years, as a vehicle for Sherrill Milnes. It was not difficult to understand its neglect, but Milnes did his best to make it look and sound good, as did Ruth Welting as Ophélie. The Christmas cake was *Die Fledermaus* in a run of ten performances conducted by Julius Rudel, with a good cast.

The boldest, most innovative, and, for the city, most influential phase of the Krainik seasons was announced in 1989. In what was called an "artistic initiative," the Lyric accepted a greater commitment both to American opera and opera of the twentieth century than any major opera company had undertaken previously. Called "Toward the 21st Century," the program would for a decade give a quarter of each Lyric season from 1990/91 through 1999/2000 to twentieth-century scores that, in effect, led the way into the century to follow. One American and one European work would be given each season. It was a grand conception of the social and artistic purpose of an opera company, and Krainik's death before it came to a close did not diminish its impact or the importance of her grand design.

The ten American operas produced were all new to the Lyric, although three of them had been heard previously in the city. Whether there were nine or ten twentieth-century European operas is a moot point; the more important fact is that half of them had been part of earlier seasons. One might legitimately ask why scores of the importance of Poulenc's *Dialogues of the Carmelites,* Hindemith's *Mathis der Maler,* or Schoenberg's *Moses und Aron,* to cite a few obvious titles, were permitted to remain unknown territory to Chicago audiences. But, this said, Krainik and her team had to be respected for the scope and strength of the Lyric plans.

The most important of Chicago Opera Theater's 1990 productions was the local première of Peter Maxwell Davies's *The Lighthouse.* It is a powerful piece, and here it was sung, directed, and staged with consistent skill and full dramatic awareness of its force. Nicolai's *The Merry Wives of Windsor* was sympathetically played and sung, and Andrew Foldi directed it with care. *Lakmé* was an opera often shown in the early days of the twentieth century, but it is seldom seen today, many considering its libretto and music (outside of the "Bell Song" and "Flower Duet" perhaps) shallow and passé. COT's 1990 production gave the opera's strengths full value, and its weaknesses were not emphasized. It was well sung, and Fiora Contino's conducting (marking the first time in Chicago history that a woman conducted a production of a resident opera company) was idiomatic and satisfying.

Hoping to bolster its coffers with something to suit the many, Chicago Opera Theater decided to try its hand at bringing a Broadway musical downtown. In June 1990 it offered Rodgers and Hammerstein's

Carousel at the Shubert Theater, with a sixth performance added to the originally scheduled five. It was the first time a professional production of *Carousel* had been seen in Chicago since the 1947 national tour, and though it broke even financially, COT's expectation for considerably more in receipts was a sign of the growing dark monetary clouds that were beginning to close in on the company.

In 1990/91 the American work at Lyric was Dominick Argento's *The Voyage of Edgar Allan Poe,* and between John Conklin's sets and Frank Galati's direction it created a striking impression. *La fanciulla del West,* although dating from 1910, was not officially called a twentieth-century work. Admittedly it is somewhat influenced by Debussy—the wellspring of the twentieth-century style—but the overall manner remains closer to nineteenth-century neoromanticism than anything of the century to come. Zschau and Domingo were the girl and her bandit lover. The rest of the repertory was unlikely to deter the most conservative suburbanite. Gluck's *Alceste,* which opened the season, was unfamiliar but not frightening, seen in a minimalist but evocative production designed and directed by Robert Wilson. In it, Jessye Norman appeared in her only Lyric offering. *Eugene Onegin, Lucia di Lammermoor, Rigoletto, Carmen,* and *The Magic Flute* were the kinds of meat-and-potatoes works Krainik counted on to fill the house for the remainder of the season. *Lucia* was seen in a new production designed by William Dudley, in which a tall set of stairs appeared to collapse as June Anderson, the Lucia, raced down it in the Mad Scene.

In the autumn of 1990 Marc Scorca relinquished the post of managing director of the Chicago Opera Theater to become chief executive officer of Opera America; Mark Tiarks replaced him. There was a thorough audit, and COT found that the company owed $100,000 in unpaid union payroll withholding taxes and had an operating deficit of about $200,000. Some blamed Scorca for overextending the company in such endeavors as the presentation of the Knussen opera at the Auditorium and the *Carousel* production, while others blamed COT's board for both encouraging company growth and not paying the attention it should have to the financial situation.

In December of 1990 COT tried a revival of *Where the Wild Things Are,* this time at the Chicago Theater. There were eight performances, and Alan Stone shared the narration of the curtain raiser *Peter and the Wolf* with various local TV news anchors. Utilization of the services of the mime T. Daniel in the Prokofiev did little to enliven it. The production lost $70,000, and by the time COT was closing its fiscal year in June 1991 the company had a total deficit of $600,000. An emergency board meeting early in the year raised $308,500 in pledges to keep the company alive. A $100,000 matching grant from longtime COT backers Joan and Irving Harris assured the opening of Mozart's *Idomeneo* in February, though the scheduled performances of *Madame Butterfly* (it was to be given in English, after all) and Argento's *Postcard from Morocco* remained uncertain. There was a further fund-raising effort in March, and COT applied for outreach grants (but was not successful in obtaining money for presentations in Chicago schools until 1993). It should be noted that Joan Harris was an especially strong supporter of COT from its earliest days; she was the company's president from 1977 to 1984 and chairwoman of its board from 1984 to 1987; and she was chairwoman emeritus in most of the years 1990–1998.

COT's 1991 *Idomeneo* was done in modern dress, with effective projections and striking direction. The excellent cast sang with beauty, stylistic authority, and powerful dramatic force. *Butterfly* did happen; its first-night audience was told from the stage that if $150,000 could be raised in the next week the company's third planned offering could be staged. Even though the singing did not represent COT at its best, the box office receipts from surefire Puccini emboldened COT to go ahead and present Argento's *Postcard from Morocco*. As so often in COT's history, their production of a twentieth-century work found the company at its best, with Frank Galati directing an excellent cast.

In 1991 discussion began to explore the possibility of providing the city's two major music-producing organizations with new and more adequate housing. Orchestra Hall (1904), home of the Chicago Symphony, had long been recognized as a mediocre hall on an inadequate site, and the Civic Opera House (1929) was unsuited to the type of stagecraft presently utilized at the Metropolitan and in leading European theaters. John H. Bryan, the chief executive of the Sara Lee Corporation, headed a group of leading businessmen with the goal of raising $100 million for this purpose, giving $50 million to each organization (to be matched by the institutions), and by the early months of 1993, $85 million of that sum had been raised.

Planning stalled quickly when it became clear that the trustees of the Chicago Symphony were unprepared to leave Orchestra Hall, which had landmark status. In Europe the façades of older halls had been retained while new theaters were built behind them, and many thought the proper thing to do in Chicago was to retain the Michigan Avenue building with its beloved façade, foyers, and ballroom and tear down everything else so a new, more spacious music room for the orchestra might be built behind it. But this did not take place, even though an appropriate site was secured. It was promised that the old hall would be raised to the level of the finest the orchestra had visited in Europe, a result that could only have been achieved by rewriting some laws of physics. When the results were heard in 1997, some felt the opportunity to build a new hall had been sacrificed to irresponsible nostalgia, and the remodeled hall in many ways fell far short of hopes and expectations. The finished complex did, however, provide considerably more space for activities and amenities, though at this writing attempts are still being made to improve the main hall's acoustics.

The decision of the Symphony trustees left the Lyric with no option but to stay in the Civic Opera House. Modernization was limited by the fact that the building stood on the river, and anything below river level was at the least threatened by invasive water and high humidity. Massive stage elevators of the type found in the Metropolitan Opera House at Lincoln Center would be impossible. But there was room for movement up and back. It was decided to raise $50 million, and this, with the funds from Bryan's colleagues, could make the Civic Opera House as modern as possible.

The first, decisive move was to purchase the theater. In 1993 the Lyric finally acquired its own home for $3.5 million, with the rest of the forty-five-story building the property of Travelers Insurance Company. Renovation was spread over a three-year period with work largely restricted to the months when the house was dark. The first big improvement, a new heating and cooling system, was ready for the 1994 season. When the opening-night audience arrived in September 1996, it found the theater cleaned, polished, redecorated, and restored to its art deco glory, very much as it must have been when it opened in 1929. Stage lighting was modernized, and the elaborate rigging in the stage loft was replaced. But the major work was out of sight—backstage.

The Civic Theater at the north end of the Opera House building at street level was destroyed and the space incorporated into the backstage area of the larger theater. Although 858 seats might have been economically feasible in 1929, the Civic (a charming little house) had long proved to be too small for the final decades of the century. The Civic stage became a large rehearsal space. New backstage working space of 29,000 square feet doubled the room available and provided an area necessary for the storage of large scenery pieces. Some operatic productions the Lyric had wished to borrow previously proved impossible to get into the house, since the door through which assembled scenery was admitted was too small. The back wall of the stage was broken through (Krainik referred to it as the "Big Bang") to allow much easier movement of scenery on and off the stage. The Lyric normally has two operas in production, and scenery for both should be stored in the house. In recent years it had sometimes overflowed, and scenery had been temporarily stored under tarpaulins on Washington Street. In a remodeled backstage building, floors of dressing rooms, rehearsal spaces for singers and orchestra, and new work spaces for wigs, costumes, and props were provided, all linked by new elevators. The company was prepared to enter the new century with the facilities needed to maintain production standards at the level of the other major theaters of the world.

Two works new to the Lyric appeared in the 1991/92 season. Barber's *Antony and Cleopatra* had been the sacrificial victim of mindless overproduction when the new Metropolitan Opera House opened in Lincoln Center in New York in 1966. It was not, as many concluded, so much a bad opera as a fragile one. The Lyric staging of a Barber-Menotti revision on a simple but effective scale appropriate to the work made its many assets clear. Richard Cowan and Catherine Malfitano were the principals, and Richard Buckley conducted. A perfect foil was Prokofiev's *The Gambler,* set to a story by Dostoyevsky. It proved a mixture of romance, irony, and tragedy in a distinctively Russian manner. A large cast, including Felicity Palmer and Jacque Trussel, caught the spirit of the piece, and Bartoletti's conducting was a powerful force in bringing it all to life.

To make the package appealing, if there were two new works, then there must be two Puccini scores in the remaining, largely Italian season. Danielle Gatti made his American debut conducting a revival of the Hal Prince *Madama Butterfly,* with Malfitano and Richard Leech starring, and with Richard Stilwell a wonderfully sympathetic Sharpless. *Turandot* was staged in a brand-new production with extremely colorful designs and costumes by David Hockney and Ian Falconer. Marton was the Ice Princess, with Malfitano as Liù. Lando Bartolini and Kristján Jóhannsson shared the role of Calaf.

The bass Samuel Ramey starred in two productions, the title character in both the season opener, *Mefistofele,* and *The Marriage of Figaro.* The impressive production for the Boito, designed by Michael Levine, was co-owned by the Lyric and the San Francisco Opera. Ramey always reveled—vocally and dramatically—in his roles as the Devil, this one surely one of the finest characterizations of his career. Aprile Millo made her Lyric debut as Margherita. Donald Palumbo was Lyric's new chorus master (a post he still holds at this writing—there is no finer opera chorus in the world than the one Palumbo has built through the years), and the chorus received cheers for the opera's prologue and epilogue. Bartoletti conducted. Andrew Davis led the revival of the Hall production of *Figaro,* and Susanne Mentzer and Frederica von Stade both appeared as Cherubino over the eight-performance run.

June Anderson and Chris Merritt were featured in *I puritani,* Cecilia Gasdia and Jerry Hadley in *L'elisir d'amore.* At the end of the season the Lyric presented Marilyn Horne in a recital billed as a "Rossini Bicentennial Program."

Alan Stone continued to have health problems, so much so that he could not handle the 1992 Chicago Opera Theater season. That year he relinquished the title of artistic director to Steven Larsen, who had become a regular conductor for COT. In February the Chicago Opera Theater gave Chicago its first production ever of Rossini's *Count Ory.* Critiques ranged from negative comments on the silly libretto and COT direction to praise for the cast, which brought the opera off musically. The April offering was *La traviata.* Not only was it good box office, it was a delight to both the ear and the eye for anyone realizing the performers were young, promising American singers. May of that year brought a double bill, starting with more Argento, this time *A Water Bird Talk,* its libretto freely adapted from two unlikely bedfellow sources, Anton Chekov's "On the Harmfulness of Tobacco" and J. J. Audubon's *The Birds of America.* Robert Orth did a virtuoso turn in a virtual one-man show. The other work on the double bill was Menotti's *The Medium,* which brought Mignon Dunn to COT as Madame Flora (Baba).

COT was experiencing seesawing financial fortunes. Subscriptions were down, but single-ticket purchases were up. Corporate giving was down by $60,000, while foundation giving was up by $55,000. Fifty thousand dollars had been raised in the board's spring drive, so the company ended its fiscal year a few thousand dollars in the black, and that money would be used toward whittling down the company's debt, which now was some $247,000. On that news, COT announced a two-opera repertoire for spring 1993.

The young, Chinese-born Bright Sheng served as Lyric's composer-in-residence from 1989 to 1992. The opera he wrote for the Freeman initiative was *The Song of Majnun,* described as "a Persian *Romeo and Juliet,*" its story based on a legend from the Islamic Orient, its libretto written by Andrew Porter. The world première of the seventy-five-minute work this time presented two performances (instead of only one as in the past), given in the Civic Theatre on April 9 and 11, 1992. Richard Buckley conducted.

In a really enterprising move, the Lyric opened its 1992/93 season with the other *Otello,* Rossini's, an opera quite popular in the nineteenth century before it was swept away by Verdi's masterpiece. It contained music that could inspire spectacular singing, and with a cast headed by Chris Merritt in the title role, Rockwell Blake as Iago, and Lella Cuberli as Desdemona, there were the necessary elements for success. The opera had not been heard in Chicago for a century, and one wondered how long it might be before there was a public demand for its return.

In more traditional repertory, the most exciting item in the season's schedule was *Elektra,* with Eva Marton and Marilyn Zschau sharing the title role, Leonie Rysanek (at the close of her career) proving memorable as Klytämnestra, and Nadine Secunde's Chrysothemis beautifully drawn. Hans Schavernoch's sets and Götz Friedrich's direction proved that a strong modern production did not require disregard for the stated intentions of the composer and librettist. Leonard Slatkin was a powerful force in the pit.

Lyric's flair for Italian opera was further demonstrated in *La bohème,* with Giuseppe Sabbatini in his American opera debut, and *Un ballo in maschera* in a Swedish setting and with two casts for December and February dates. Kristján Jóhannsson of the first cast was the most exciting Gustavus III since Luciano Pavarotti; Sharon Sweet made her Lyric debut as his Amelia.

Some feel today that *Pelléas et Mélisande* is so poorly defined in terms of time and place that it is justified to move it to a more concrete setting. The Met in 2000 restaged it successfully in the world of Marcel Proust. The Lyric version, with the incomparable Teresa Stratas in the title role and Jerry Hadley as Pelléas, bloomed under the baton of James Conlon, but Frank Galati's production (designed by Robert Israel) offered modern dress for the men and Victorian costumes for the women against a vague background of gothic opulence. Visually it lacked real focus. Dramatically it was sometimes confusingly scattered, as in the scene where Yniold is supposedly spying on the (offstage) young lovers but in this production is facing the audience alongside Golaud while his part is being sung by someone else standing beside them, and with Pelléas and Mélisande at the other side of the stage, downstage and in full view of the audience.

Lyric's first commission since *The Harvest* of 1961 was William Bolcom's *McTeague,* heard this season in its world première. It faced the inevitable problem of those who wanted not simply an attractive stage work but the Great American Opera, whatever that might be. If you faced it without unreasonable expectations, you heard a fine, solid piece of work with a strong libretto (based on the film *Greed,* which was adapted from Frank Norris's novel *McTeague*) and attractive, singable music that consistently developed the dramatic situation effectively. It was in the hands of first-class people. Dennis Russell Davies conducted, and Robert Altman, one of the librettists, directed. Ben Heppner sang the title role splendidly, well matched by Malfitano and Timothy Nolen. The set designs by Yuri Kuper were wonderfully evocative, especially with Duane Schuler's lighting in the final scene on the desert.

The weakest element of the season was, unfortunately, the first Lyric staging of a work that audiences had requested for years, Smetana's *The Bartered Bride.* It was given in a bad English translation and a so-so production from the English National Opera. But the real fault was that the distinctive Czech spirit of the work was lost. An American cast headed by Barbara Daniels and Neil Rosenshein, directed by Elijah Moshinsky, searched aimlessly for a style.

And there was *Das Rheingold,* the first step toward a new, complete *Ring* cycle to come. Sets were by John Conklin, with stage direction by August Everding. Zubin Mehta conducted in his Lyric debut, and James Morris gave Chicago a chance to see why he was the reigning Wotan of the time. Troyanos was excellent as Fricka, and a young Welshman named Bryn Terfel appeared for the first time on the Lyric stage as Donner. A concert performance of Massenet's *Le Cid* in January found Plácido Domingo at less than his best.

Alan Stone was well enough to return for Chicago Opera Theater's 1993 artistic activities. An anniversary fund-raiser on February 20 netted $20,000 less than hoped for, but the company pressed ahead with the first of its two scheduled productions. One of the things that gave COT its earliest critical successes and widest publicity was its production of the Virgil Thomson-Gertrude Stein opera *The Mother of Us All* in 1976 (revived in 1984). This time COT turned to the first of the two Thomson-Stein operas, *Four Saints in Three Acts,* giving it six very well-received performances. A few days after the last of those, Joseph De Rugeriis—who had been named COT's general manager three months earlier—announced that, in the face of a now $360,000 deficit and dropping subscriber numbers, the company was suspending operations, thus canceling its planned June production of *Don Giovanni.*

The board put the company on hold. Publicly, Alan Stone remained optimistic, as did Charles T. Angell, now board chairman and head of a restructuring task force, who said that a season-long hiatus would give COT time to undertake reviews of a number of aspects of its behind-the-scenes practices as well as time to seek more financial support for what had become the company's $1.2 million annual operating budget.

In May, the COT board terminated all employees (Alan Stone included) except for General Manager De Rugeriis.

COT subscribers were persuaded to donate the amount of nearly $20,000 they had paid for tickets to the aborted *Don Giovanni* production, but it was Charles Angell (the owner of Newly Wed Foods, Inc., and an opera buff) who was the major hero in putting financial matters in order. He suggested that COT pay its creditors twenty cents on the dollar to retire $50,000 in unpaid obligations. He contributed some $2,000 himself, and he got about thirty other members of the COT board to contribute between $1,000 and $2,000 each. Angell also posted $75,000 of his own money to guarantee taxes and union dues, and another board member donated $50,000 to pay singers. Further, Angell housed COT operations at Newly Wed Foods free of charge and even had space cleared at his company for sets and rehearsal space.

In August of 1993 Don S. Dadas, newly named CEO of the Chicago Opera Theater, announced that the company had completely wiped out its debt of nearly $500,000 and was turning its attention to raising money for a 1994 season. Dadas also announced that Alan Stone had been "terminated" because he "had made certain demands the company couldn't meet" and henceforth would remain as artistic director emeritus. Dadas added, "I hope we can find some role for Stone in the company, but I can tell you it won't be in a decision-making capacity."

It was said, but apparently never publicly acknowledged, that the philanthropist Barre Seid was another knight on a white horse in saving the company, or at least helping ensure there would be a 1994 COT season. Seid was a major supporter of the Chamber Opera of Chicago (COC), a much more modest operation than COT. It was speculated that he engineered a transfer of financial assets from the smaller company to the larger one, but some said Seid got involved only after he was assured COT had taken care of its debts. There was speculation that there might be a merger of COT and COC, but that did not occur. What did occur was that COC's conductor Lawrence Rapchak and its director Carl Ratner eventually became the artistic team of COT.

Ardis Krainik opened the 1993/94 Lyric season with the sort of thing the Lyric would be expected to do unusually well, a new production of Verdi's *La traviata,* designed by Desmond Heeley. It had twelve performances—six of them in September and October, the others in January and February. June Anderson sang all the Violettas, and in the first brace of performances Giuseppe Sabbatini was Alfredo and Dmitri Hvorostovsky made an impressive Lyric debut as the elder Germont. Bartoletti conducted. John Nelson took charge of Massenet's *Don Quichotte,* staged as a vehicle for Samuel Ramey, with Susanne Mentzer as Dulcinée and Jean-Philippe Lafont as Sancho Panza. One of the Met's brightest young directors, Lesley Koenig, was in charge. She, Nelson, and Lafont were making their Lyric debuts.

For many the greatest success of the autumn was Carlisle Floyd's *Susannah* in a production shared by the Houston Opera. It was a splendid demonstration that an American can write a glorious lyric opera. The event was the Lyric debut of Renée Fleming, clearly destined to be one of the great sopranos of the day, who made the title role an occasion for remarkable singing and acting. Ramey was back as the lecherous evangelist; Michael Myers was Susannah's brother, Sam. Robert Falls, who had had great

Renée Fleming and Samuel Ramey in the Revival Meeting Scene of *Susannah*, 1993

successes directing theater in Chicago (and else-where), here directed an opera for the first time.

A fussy, overproduced new *Tosca*, directed by Frank Galati and designed by Tony Walton, appeared in both the autumn and winter series. Maria Ewing, singing the title role in the autumn series opposite Kristján Jóhannsson and James Morris, was effective but not at her best. Maria Guleghina, Richard Leech, and Tom Fox made up the second cast. The real melo-dramatic spirit was lacking throughout the produc-tion. Nor was the innate vitality of *Così fan tutte* fully realized in a production conducted by Andrew Davis. Carol Vaness and Delores Ziegler were the sisters, Gi-anna Rolandi their servant, and Keith Lewis and Jef-frey Black the sisters' lovers.

Il trovatore had its foundation in the new critical edi-tion of the score, which meant you heard more of it than on previous occasions. Richard Buckley conducted a cast with Chris Merritt and Paolo Gavanelli as the ill-fated brothers and Ljuba Kazarnovskaya as the object of their lust. Dolora Zajick was a powerful Azucena.

The Lyric originally intended to import Patrice Chéreau's Parisian production of *Wozzeck*, with Daniel Barenboim conducting, a welcome gesture of unity between the Lyric and the Chicago Symphony. (Barenboim had succeeded Sir Georg Solti as the Sym-phony's music director in 1992.) But the Parisian ver-sion was not designed to alternate in repertory with other operas. It demanded rows and rows of lights, and the cost of putting them up and taking them down was prohibitive. So Barenboim and most of the cast canceled, and another *Wozzeck* was hastily as-sembled, with Buckley conducting and Franz Grund-heber debuting at the Lyric in the title role. This, alas, became one of the first memorable disasters of David Alden's direction. Every character became a caricature of what the dramatist and composer intended, and the dramatic force of the work was all but destroyed.

And there was *Die Walküre*, continuing the series of Conklin-designed, Everding-directed, Mehta-conducted productions building toward Lyric's first complete *Ring* since 1974. Highlights were James Morris's Wotan, Eva Marton's Brünnhilde, and Siegfried Jerusalem's Siegmund.

September 1993 brought the Chicago Opera Theater an anonymous challenge grant of $300,000 from one of its board members if COT could mount a 1994 season. The company's annual masked ball gala brought in $80,000 toward that goal, and two operas were announced for the spring of 1994: the local premiere in April of Berlioz's *Beatrice and Benedict,* and a May staging of Douglas Moore's *The Ballad of Baby Doe* (which returned the opera to Chicago after some thirty years). Lawrence Rapchak conducted the Berlioz, and Carl Ratner was the director for the Moore. At the end of the successful season, COT announced the appointment of Ratner as its artistic administrator and Rapchak as musical director. The board threw Alan Stone a bone by announcing "The Alan Stone Debut Artist Series," enabling five young singers to work with Stone in two ten-week series of coachings and recitals and utilizing those singers in cover roles for COT mainstage seasons. It was a short-lived endeavor.

As it entered its 1995 fiscal year COT announced it had balanced its budget and had received another challenge grant, this time $700,000 from board members and other individuals.

October 1994 launched the project, headed by a number of prominent Chicagoans (Joan Harris very much one of them), of building a state-of-the-art performing space for the Chicago Opera Theater and a number of the other, "smaller" performing companies in Chicago. But it would take almost ten years and many starts and stops (as well as proposed location changes) before such a facility would be built and would be open for operation.

The fourth world première in Lyric's Freeman Composer-in-Residence Program occurred on June 10 (and 11), 1994. The composer was Bruce Saylor, who chose J. D. McClatchy to adapt Tennessee Williams's *Orpheus Descending* into an opera libretto. Stewart Robinson conducted the performances in Northwestern University's Cahn Auditorium.

With the 1994/95 season the Lyric celebrated its fortieth anniversary with what appears in retrospect to be the finest series of productions in Krainik's later years. Opening night was given to Mussorgsky's *Boris Godunov* in the rarely heard original version of 1869 (which does not include the Polish Scene or much of the false Dmitri). The glittering production came from the Grand Théâtre de Genève, and though it was faithful to Mussorgsky's original musical ideas, it departed from his dramatic structure by putting the simpleton (David Gordon) all over the place carrying a miniature

Kremlin tower instead of limiting him to the sixth scene. Still, this was a *Boris* in the established tradition of the work. Bartoletti presided, with Stein Winge directing the stage in Göran Wassberg's settings.

George London established the principle that an English-speaking singer could be a powerful Russian Boris, and Samuel Ramey was a monumental presence in the title role. He was surrounded by an admirable cast: Patrick Denniston as the false Dmitri, Dimitri Kavrakos as Pimen, and John Duykers as the oily Shuisky. The lesson here seemed to be that when the Lyric accepts, rather than rejects, tradition, it achieves its best results.

Ramey went from tsar to devil (Nick Shadow) in the Lyric's first production of Stravinsky's *The Rake's Progress.* You would never guess that the opera had been inspired by Hogarth paintings the composer had seen at the Art Institute of Chicago. The production departed completely from that artist in Richard Hudson's designs, which were inspired by the work of René Magritte. It was almost a cartoon fantasy in bright colors and had little relation to the words, music, or original dramatic concept. Still, it was attractive, and the action of the drama moved effectively within its new frame. Jerry Hadley was well cast as Tom Rakewell, with Ruth Ann Swenson his beloved. Felicity Palmer had a few bright moments as the bearded Baba. Dennis Russell Davies conducted and Graham Vick directed.

Giordano's *Fedora* is an opera revived from time to time to please a prima donna who sees it as a vehicle for her special talents. Lyric did it in 1960 for Renata Tebaldi and brought it back in 1994 for Mirella Freni, giving her one super tenor, Plácido Domingo, and a budding star, José Cura, as Loris, in a borrowed production from La Scala. Bartoletti conducted. It was a grand much ado about practically nothing, but a considerable improvement over the 1960 version.

Terrifically strong casts—Thomas Allen and Thomas Hampson as Figaro, Frederica von Stade and Susanne Mentzer as Rosina, and Rockwell Blake as Almaviva—made November and February performances of *The Barber of Seville* a pleasure for the ear. Blake and his audiences seemed to enjoy the inclusion of the often dropped final aria for Almaviva. The autumn series had the further attraction of Nicolai Ghiaurov as Basilio, a role Chaliapin and Christoff loved to sing.

Works of Richard Strauss and Leonard Bernstein represented the season's offerings in the "Toward the 21st Century" initiative.

Andrew Davis established his credentials as Lyric's future chief conductor in his superlative direction of Strauss's most intimate opera, *Capriccio*. Often rejected as unsuited to a large theater, it proved in this production from the 1973 Glyndebourne Festival to work very well in the large house if assisted by supertitles. There were two departures from the original. The work was divided into two acts—a realistic move in terms of audience stamina—and the time frame was moved from before the French Revolution to after World War I. In terms of issues and ideas, nothing was really changed, but the audience could relate to the work more easily in the twentieth-century setting. Felicity Lott was completely convincing and vocally opulent as the Countess, and the young Americans Kurt Streit and Rodney Gilfry, in their Lyric debuts, played her suitors with admirable force. Jan-Hendrik Rootering had the pivotal role of the impresario La Roche. John Cox directed.

Gershwin's *Porgy and Bess*—which the Lyric has yet to do—and Bernstein's *Candide* are two operas that started out as Broadway shows. *Candide* arrived in the opera house after considerable revision, but that is where it belongs, as this bright, zestful, Lyric production made plain. Harold Prince trimmed the score of its weakest pages and set the stage in motion in an innovative production that produced one delightful moment after another. George Manahan's deft handling of some of Bernstein's finest theater music was another major asset. The work is intended for operatic-grade singers, but singers who can make these comic figures real. Barry Banks played the title role, with Elizabeth Futral making her artistic stature clear as his beloved. As the Old Lady, one of the inspired comic creations of the work, Phyllis Pancella excelled. Timothy Nolen played several roles, starting with Voltaire. For sheer delight, the Lyric had not done anything this fine in years.

After these journeys into operatic bypaths, a solid Italian work was in order: *Aida,* with Aprile Millo in the title role, Michael Sylvester her Radames, and Dolora Zajick the jealous Amneris. It was the Lyric's familiar production given to its established standard.

And, of course, there was *Siegfried,* to continue the *Ring* series. Siegfried Jerusalem moved into higher tenor ground portraying the title character, and two of the nine Brünnhilde performances introduced Jane Eaglen to Chicago (the other seven were sung by Eva Marton).

The Chicago Opera Theater found a new, downtown performance space for its 1995 season, the Merle Reskin Theatre (formerly the Blackstone) at the south end of the Loop. Three performances of *The Magic Flute* were given to mixed, but mostly kind, reviews, and the Chicago première of Copland's *The Tender Land* brought praise for the performances but divided opinions on the opera's worth.

The Lyric gave Chicago its first performance ever of *Simon Boccanegra* in 1959 and returned to it for a sixth time to open the 1995/96 season, the last in which Krainik was functioning full time. The production—and some of the cast—came from the Royal Opera in London. Daniele Gatti conducted and Elijah Moshinsky directed. Alexandru Agache drew a powerful figure vocally and dramatically in the title role, with Robert Lloyd a strong match as Fiesco. Michael Silvester and Kiri Te Kanawa, the love interest of the plot, had both taken part in the London production and offered some grand singing in the Verdi style.

Lyric's commitment to Handel revivals continued with *Xerxes* in another British production, this one from the English National Opera. The time leap from classical antiquity to the eighteenth century strengthened the work, which belied its Wagnerian length with the stage briskly in motion, thanks to Nicholas Hytner's direction and strong, idiomatic conducting by John Nelson. Ann Murray sang the title role with Elizabeth Futral as the much-pursued love object.

The American opera was John Corigliano's *The Ghosts of Versailles,* a 1991 Metropolitan commission heard in its 1994 revised version. John Conklin's staging was spectacular, and Colin Graham's direction matched it for imagination and zest. The conductor Leonard Slatkin caught the spirit of the music precisely. With a large and splendid cast headed by Sheri Greenawald, Sylvia McNair, Håkan Hagegård, Dwayne Croft, and Graham Clark, it was a lively evening of effective musical theater.

Don Pasquale, with Paul Plishka in the title role and Ruth Ann Swenson not so much his dream girl as his nightmare bride was a secure audience pleaser. But *Andrea Chénier*—one of those operas that threatens to cease to exist if you don't have the right singers—proved to be good, staple Italian fare without the vocal fireworks required for maximum effect. Kristján Jóhannsson sang the title role, with Aprile Millo and Sergei Leiferkus in the other principal parts.

In contrast, *Don Giovanni,* returning in the Ponnelle production of 1980, had all the vocal power one might desire, with James Morris as the lecherous Don, Bryn Terfel as his servant, Frank Lopardo as Don

Ottavio, and Ljuba Orgonasova, Carol Vaness, and Susanne Mentzer as the three ladies. But Yakov Kreizberg was not an ideal choice as conductor.

Opera producers have been moving *Faust* to the nineteenth century for forty years or more, but here Lyric's version opened in a morgue where, it turned out, Mephistopheles was lying on the autopsy table under a sheet. In time you might wonder if the work really needed to be modernized in this fashion, although the force of the drama was not threatened. Richard Leech sang the title role, with Samuel Ramey his nemesis and Renée Fleming a Marguerite worth damnation. An added delight was Dmitri Hvorostovsky's Valentin. Frank Corsaro directed the stage, and John Nelson presided masterfully in the orchestra pit.

Yet, ironically, the opera to make the greatest stir was a work Chicago had never heard before, Janáček's *The Makropulos Affair.* Both the Lyric and the Metropolitan were staging the work this season. The Met version centered on the vocal powers of Jessye Norman and stayed close to the composer's intentions. The Lyric production was in the expressionistic style and was dominated by Catherine Malfitano. Bruno Bartoletti conducted, and David Alden's revisionism here yielded an expressionistic approach to the work that, thanks to Malfitano, did not divert the dramatic thrust of the libretto too far from its intended objective. Her spectacular performance, vocally and physically striking, commanded the stage, but she had a strong cast with which to interact.

There is no question that Krainik regarded her staging of three complete *Ring* cycles in March 1996 the climax of her career, the realization of a dream she and Bartoletti had shared for many years. This was the first truly cyclical *Ring* ever staged by a Chicago company, although all four operas had been heard in the 1915 and 1916 seasons.

Indeed, for a city with a large German population, the history of the *Ring* in Chicago was strange. It had been heard as early as 1889 from a touring company of the Metropolitan Opera, but the full cycle did not return until 1915 (and 1916). Cycles in which all four operas were heard in the course of a week were—finally—offered by touring companies in 1923, 1929, and 1930, after which the *Ring* operas, *Die Walküre* excepted, were not heard in the city for forty years. The first Lyric *Ring,* spaced over four seasons, was heard from 1971 to 1974.

Krainik prepared for her cycles by offering subscribers *Das Rheingold* in 1992, *Die Walküre* in 1993,

and *Siegfried* in 1994. But subscribers did not get *Götterdämmerung* in 1995/96. Three nonsubscription, non-cycle performances of the opera were offered in February and March 1996, preceding the three full cycles in March. Tickets for the cycles went on sale in May 1995 and were gone in four months. *Ring* cycles that sell out six months in advance have to be regarded as a success on at least one level. Visitors—among them sixty music writers—came from all over the world. If Krainik wanted attention, her wishes were fully gratified.

What you thought of the Lyric's *Ring* as the final curtain descended in March 1996 depended in large part on how many times you had been to Bayreuth in the previous twenty years. This was a *Ring* that glaringly illuminated the strengths and weaknesses of the Krainik administration. The great strength, undoubtedly, was her advocacy of the project and the vigor (while in failing health) with which she saw it through to completion. She wanted a *Ring.* She wanted a *notable Ring.* And here her weaknesses overcame her.

The *Ring* is, first of all, romantic German opera, and a city as unfamiliar with the cycle as Chicago (it was, after all, some twenty years since the previous Lyric staging of these works, and that had been in a freakish, unsuccessful production) should see it in its true terms. But the Metropolitan in 1987 had produced a conservative, romantic *Ring* (a production that was still in use at the turn of the century and highly regarded by the public), so the Lyric *Ring* had to attract attention by being different.

"Different" *Ring*s are commonplace in Europe, where the operas are being staged all the time. Krainik considered the possibility of a Peter Sellars *Ring,* something that would attract worldwide attention. I predicted it would all be under water except, of course, for the opening scene of *Das Rheingold.* Mercifully, Sellars declined the offer to produce it.

Krainik turned to two men who had worked with her before, the designer John Conklin and the veteran Munich producer August Everding. Lest it be thought that I am prejudiced against the latter, I must say that he staged the finest *Tristan* I have ever seen, the 1971 Metropolitan production designed by Gunther Schneider-Siemssen. Duane Schuler did Lyric's lighting which, in many ways, was the best thing about the staging. They all officially went to work to formulate a fresh view of the cycle. Everding's suggestion that he do a gangster *Ring* with Wotan a sort of Al Capone figure may have been a joke, but it does suggest the weary thoughts of some-one searching for a break from tradition. A gangster *Ring* was the last thing Chicago needed.

Although she had visited Bayreuth in her European travels, the *Ring* (indeed, much of German repertory) was an area in which Krainik could not move with confidence. The reason, of course, was that her operatic education had taken place in the Italianate environment created by Fox.

What Chicago got was a production deeply in debt to whatever was presently fashionable in Europe, especially recent Bayreuth stagings of the cycle. It didn't add up to a consistent view of the operas but rather a massive dose of Eurokitsch. The music of the Rhein-maidens was sung by an invisible trio while the visible Rheindaughters were acrobats bouncing up and down on bungee cords. Human-sized giants were followed by huge puppets. The "Ride of the Valkyries" consisted of seven warrior maidens also bounding, but this time on trampolines. Brünnhilde was put to sleep *standing up* in a pyramid. There were aerialists and acrobats in the cast of *Siegfried* and *Götterdäm-merung*. It was a travesty—absurd special effects to amuse ignorant Midwesterners, a joke from a burned-out European (Everding died in 1999). And Krainik, who should have said an emphatic no to this, dutifully penned letters to contributors for special funding ($5,000 worth of trampolines, for example) to pay for these abominations.

Bayreuth has demonstrated that the *Ring* can be staged in contemporary terms and still remain faithful to Wagner's dramatic intent. Harry Kupfer's *Ring*, seen in the late 1980s, was unconventional, challenging, imaginative, and able to reveal new facets of the dramas, things Everding rarely managed. A letter to the *New York Times* following the Met's 2000 *Ring* cycle notes that the Met's conservative production had held, and gratified, its audiences for thirteen years. But Krainik chose Eurotrash.

Musically it was another matter. Krainik engaged Zu-bin Mehta as conductor for the series. He was a major figure, but not one particularly associated with Wagner (whose music he could not play in his primary musical base—Israel). It was clear that these were four years of artistic growth for him. His performances of *Das Rhein-gold* in 1992 were good but not those of a seasoned Wagnerite. By March 1996 he had the style and the spirit fully in hand and directed a powerful cycle.

James Morris, the leading Wotan of the day, was a dominant figure vocally and dramatically. Graham

Clark was Loge in *Rheingold,* Marjana Lipovšek sang Fricka and the *Götterdämmerung* Waltraute, and Ekke-hard Wlaschiha was Alberich. Matti Salminen (who was to return as Hunding, the dragon, and Hagen) and Carsten Stabell were the giants. Stig Andersen, who was to be the Met's Siegfried in 2000, here sang Froh. Jane Eaglen was the Brünnhilde in the final three operas, alternating in that role with Eva Marton. Tina Kiberg and Poul Elming were the tragic Walsungs.

Clark was the Mime of *Siegfried,* with Siegfried Jerusalem in the title role. The former castings carried over for *Götterdämmerung,* in which Alan Held and Elizabeth Byrne were the brother and sister Gibich. Krainik used young American singers in supporting roles (after all, she had been a Valkyrie herself!), and they proved adequate but obviously unequal to more experienced European artists.

For me, this was a *Ring* where you were wise to listen but not look, basically a lost opportunity. Lost because—from the first—the project had been misdirected; rather than serving Wagner, it seemed calculated to bring notoriety and prestige to the Lyric. It was to shock the conservatives. It was to be entertaining. It was not necessarily to touch the heart or mind very profoundly. And, as it turned out, it was not only the twilight of the gods but the twilight of the Krainik regime.

The 1996 season of the Chicago Opera Theater was planned with the triumvirate of Ratner, Rapchak, and Mark Tiarks (who became the general director of the company at the end of that year and held the post until 1998). Each of the three offerings was anything but traditional. Richard Strauss's *Ariadne auf Naxos* became simply *Ariadne,* its action pushed to the late nineteenth century, its comic elements pressed to excess. At least the singing of Judith Raddue as Ariadne and Lorraine Ernest as Zerbinetta saved the musical day. *The Jewel Box* was Mozart (partially) operatic music given in an opera Mozart never wrote. Paul Griffiths created a libretto made out of whole cloth that utilized music—a lot of it concert arias—that Mozart had composed for virtuoso singers of his day, and most of it was late Mozart. The three-hour production was somewhat too much of a good musical thing, but most of the singing pleased, as did the production. Rossini's *The Italian Girl in Algiers,* which COT had presented once before (in 1980), was updated to portray comically such things as Scud missiles and assorted current Middle Eastern events. The production's zaniness was highly praised, as was most of the singing, especially that of Susan Hofflander as Isabella.

Ardis Krainik was gratified to announce that she had not seen a doctor in thirty years, but in 1995 it became clear that she had what a Christian Scientist such as herself would call "physical problems." Like Fox at the close of her life, Krainik was substantially overweight and in 1994 complained of a bad knee. Even after surgery, there was constant pain in one leg, and by 1996 she was obliged to use a wheelchair. The old stamina and the familiar zest for life were failing. You saw she was losing weight and aging rapidly. Many feared cancer in the pelvic region. But she went on boldly and bravely, until it became clear that she had reached her limits. In June 1996 she announced she would retire in April 1997 at the close of her fifteenth season as general director. We must view 1996/97 as a transitional season. Krainik was alive, although hardly functioning, through much of it. Bill Mason faced the responsibility of realizing her plans on the stage. The company honored Krainik with a gala concert on October 13.

The April date proved optimistic. Work became too difficult, and Krainik retired to her apartment, where sedation kept her as comfortable as possible. She died on January 18, 1997, at the age of sixty-seven. There was no funeral. The Lyric was her family, and a week later the company gave a brief memorial program. Her body was returned to Wisconsin, and her ashes were dispersed in Lake Geneva, where she had long had a summer home.

Those who admired Krainik and her achievements will remember her as she was in her prime, striding down the aisle just as the house lights were dimming to take her place in the front row. This was the lady herself in her element. The pathetic, decimated Ardis of the last seasons, slipping into the theater through a side door in a wheelchair after the lights were down, called for our compassion, but it is not the vital person we want to remember. Chicago had had three celebrated women as opera managers. Two—Mary Garden and Carol Fox—led their companies to financial ruin. Ardis Krainik led hers to success on the stage and on the way to the bank.

On opening night 1996 opera competed for audience attention with the blazing bright new look of the refurbished house. *Don Carlo* returned—still without the Fontainebleau Scene—in the 1989 production. This time it seemed to be more about singing than drama; there were few real confrontations between characters. Samuel Ramey was impressive as King Philip, but how impressive depended in part on

whether you had any memories of Boris Christoff or Nicolai Ghiaurov in the role. Indeed, the Lyric *Don Carlo*s of the past were consistently stronger stuff than this one, in which Carol Vaness was Elisabetta, Michael Sylvester (no match for Richard Tucker) sang the title role, and Vladimir Chernov (no Tito Gobbi) played Rodrigo. Dolora Zajick was Eboli.

Considering the Lyric's devotion to Puccini, it is extraordinary that it would wait until its forty-second season to produce *Il trittico* in its entirety. (Bartoletti, who conducted, had long favored the project—and had, in fact, recorded these three operas in a recent set—but apparently there had been some prejudice against *Suor Angelica*.) The evening became a tour de force for Catherine Malfitano, who sang the soprano role in all three scores, heading well-chosen casts that could sing this music with maximum effect. A special delight was to see and hear Rolando Panerai as Gianni Schicchi, and Jean-Philippe Lafont was a powerfully menacing Michele in *Il tabarro*.

The Lyric and the Metropolitan joined in a new production of *Norma,* with June Anderson singing the title role for the first time. She required "Casta Diva" and her duet with Adalgisa to be transposed down a tone. Richard Margison was her Pollione, and Robynne Redman sang Adalgisa. If less than a pure exhibition of bel canto, it still proved effective. The production by Colin Graham and John Conklin moved the action from the Roman conquest of Gaul to Napoleonic France—the last place I would have looked for a Druid priestess.

The two twentieth-century operas fared less well. Menotti's *The Consul* was overpowered by enormous sets; the heroine seemed to be living in a railroad station. Indeed, the whole spirit of the piece seemed to be lost, and Barbara Daniels's aria "To this we've come"—the dramatic high point of the score—was far less than the climax it was intended to be. Emily Golden as the Secretary got the most applause. All in all, the Chicago Opera Theater version of 1983 was considerably better.

Bartoletti had long wanted to do an opera by Luciano Berio, and plans for a production in the mid-eighties had been scrapped because of casting problems. *Un re in ascolto* was effectively staged and was musically everything the composer might have hoped for. Suburban sensibilities were not outraged by "dreadful modern music." Indeed, Berio's music had a sensuality and beauty many did not expect, revealed in large part thanks to the conductor Dennis Russell Davies.

But it is an opera virtually without plot, and the absence of structure produced for many the effect of an evening in which nothing of any particular importance appeared to have happened.

The 1986 production of *The Magic Flute* was successfully revived, with Marek Janowski making a welcome return to the Lyric and Everding reminding us that he can do other things than Wagner. Yelda Kodalli was a viciously effective Queen of the Night. Fantasy and delight were stressed over philosophical elements, making this more of a family show. Elizabeth Norberg-Schulz and Frank Lopardo were the lovers, with Olaf Bär as Papageno and Kurt Moll alternating with Franz-Josef Selig as Sarastro.

A second successful revival was the David Hockney *Turandot* production of 1992, this time with Gabriele Schnaut in the title role and Ben Heppner as Calaf. The you-bet-your-life confrontation scene was quite powerful.

Krainik told her subscribers that "each year we scour the world to find top-notch productions that we think our Chicago public will like." Lyric's 1996 *Salome*, designed by Erich Wonder, came from the Salzburg Festival and, Krainik said, "is one of the most extraordinary shows I have ever seen, filled with fascinating touches, like Herod and Herodias sitting down at the kitchen table to talk about what they're going to do with their very wayward daughter." This was the inspiration of the director Luc Bondy. My mind boggles at what Strauss or, for that matter, Oscar Wilde would have thought of Herod and Herodias at the kitchen table. What would those who were in moral shock anticipating the city's first *Salome* in 1910 have said had they known it contained a kitchen table scene? This was the kind of wild revisionism to which Krainik had become most vulnerable.

Catherine Malfitano had sung the role in a basically traditional production at the Met the previous season. Here she was cast with Bryn Terfel, and they were a powerful combination. Anja Silja, probably the greatest Salome in Lyric's history, was back as Herodias, and Kenneth Riegel joined her at the kitchen table. Antonio Pappano conducted, and musically all went well.

12

A New Beginning

1997–2000

Early in November 1996, William Mason, who had directed operations and productions at the Lyric since 1980, was, at fifty-four, named general director, the second time the leadership of the company had passed to people who had spent most of their professional life in the Lyric organization. Mason's Lyric career had begun as a performer (as noted earlier) when the boy soprano Billy Mason had sung the shepherd in the Lyric's first production of Tosca in 1954, then again in 1956 and 1957. Like Krainik, he knew the view from both sides of the proscenium.

The appointment was a popular one. Joseph Volpe, the general manager of the Met, had begun as a stage carpenter and felt strongly that people working in the house should be permitted to rise to the top. Krainik, whose support of Mason on the search committee was undoubtedly a major factor in its unanimous decision to give him the job, made this—one of her final executive decisions—an affirmation that she wanted the Lyric to be led by someone who knew the company as a veteran insider. Indeed, Mason had been brought back to the Lyric by Krainik after his brief defection to San Francisco, and he served as one of the major architects of her success in the early years of her administration.

Born in Chicago, Mason was a child on Chicago's south side and a teenager on the north side. He was attracted to opera by a performance of *Rigoletto* in one of Harry Zelzer's New York City Opera seasons and became interested in singing. After graduating from Senn High School, he went to the Chicago Musical College at Roosevelt University to study voice. As his instruction progressed he was increasingly convinced that he wanted to make a career in music and increasingly doubtful it would be as a singer. In 1962 Krainik

offered him an opportunity to work backstage with Pino Donati, who found young "Beely" an invaluable aid. For a start, he was willing to learn Italian to spare Donati the problem of mastering English. He stayed with Donati until his mentor died in 1975, perfecting the art of putting an opera on the stage. Without Donati as an interface, life with Carol Fox was not always pleasant. (The way to deal with being fired, Mason discovered, was to keep on coming to work.) Mason briefly sampled life in other opera companies, Cincinnati and the New York City Opera in addition to San Francisco, but he was glad to come home.

As Mason saw it, Krainik's management style was right for the Lyric, and he hoped to continue it. In August 1997 he announced a new staff to lead the company into the coming century. Bruno Bartoletti was to retire in April 1999 after thirty-five years as artistic director, and that title was to go to Matthew A. Epstein, who (as artistic consultant) had served the Lyric since 1982 in matters of casting and repertory. As a vice-president of Columbia Artists Management (CAMI), the largest company of its type in America, he had been regarded by some as the most hated man in American opera. His dual role, managing artists and advising opera companies on whom to engage, would hardly make him popular with singers who were not on the CAMI roster. But he was probably unequalled as a discoverer of new talent, and throughout the world of opera the announcement "Matthew's here" was an inducement for all to put forth their best. His disadvantages, in the eyes of some, were his familiarity with unconventional European approaches to the production of standard works and his zealous interest in making American operatic production less conservative. To come to the Lyric he left his management job.

Left to right—Sir Andrew Davis, Bill Mason, Bruno Bartoletti, and Matthew Epstein, 1997

At the Lyric he would be working closely with Sir Andrew Davis, who was to join the company as music director and principal conductor, an appointment that provided reason for rejoicing. Davis's first appearance in his new roles was directing a concert, "A Date with the Devil," for Samuel Ramey in the 1999/2000 season. Beginning in 2001/02 he would be conducting at least three operas a season.

In the Fox and Krainik regimes titles were not always what they seemed to imply. Although some delegation of responsibility was necessary, the lady in the front office had limitless authority. Bartoletti's title as artistic director was at least 50% decorative. Davis, it can be assumed, will want to play a role in artistic decisions. This means that to talk of Mason seasons—in the same sense that one talked of Fox or Krainik seasons—will be inappropriate. Teamwork will be emphasized.

Since to secure the leading international artists it is now necessary to plan seasons at least three years in advance, it can be taken for granted that the repertory and casting of 1997/98 was firmly in place before Mason took his new job and that 1998/99 was also basi-

cally a Krainik design. The 1981 season presented under Krainik's administration was nearly all Fox's planning. Artistically the first real Krainik season was 1984. But although Fox planned the seasons, Krainik had the job of realizing these plans on stage, and the same applied to Mason in turn. A season both fully planned and staged by him would not be heard until 2000/01.

It was Mason's good fortune to be in charge when the Lyric's composer-in-residence program finally produced a work of unchallengeable merit, Shulamit Ran's *Between Two Worlds,* a retelling of S. Ansky's play *The Dybbuk.* Ran, a Pulitzer Prize-winning composer, revealed known skills (mastery of orchestration) and previously undemonstrated talents, chief of them a gift for vocal writing. Produced by Lyric's Center for American Artists in June 1997, it revealed the remarkable achievements of the young performers as effectively as it drew admiration for the composer. With a few minor revisions, the work might claim a place in the subscription series.

Seemingly emboldened by the success of its updating of Rossini the year before, the Chicago Opera Theater opened its 1997 season turning Offenbach's

La Grande Duchesse de Gérolstein (The Grand Duchess of Gerolstein) into *The Grand Duchess of Helmsley-Stein,* placing it in the corporate New York City setting of the Internal Revenue Service versus the hotel owner Leona Helmsley-Stein, thus spoofing events that were actually transpiring at the time the operetta was being produced in Chicago. The mood was almost over the top, but most of the singing and acting found the audience fully entertained. *Don Giovanni* was the second opera of the season, and the production was not up to the best COT could offer. The Chicago première of Daron Aric Hagen's *Shining Brow* showed once more that an American opera can be both dramatically and musically exciting. Spanning the ten-year period in which the architect Frank Lloyd Wright exposed himself to public scandal by leaving his wife to take a client's wife as his mistress, Paul Muldoon's libretto transcended the details and made one think of the responsibilities famous personages have to the lesser mortals who surround them. The music beautifully mirrored the events and the personalities, and—as he had done so many times before in COT productions—Robert Orth drew raves for his singing and characterization.

In the 1997/98 Lyric season the European opera in the twentieth-century series was Britten's *Peter Grimes,* an international repertory piece that called for revival after twenty years. With the conductor Mark Elder lifting the Lyric orchestra to the heights of its powers, and refined and skillful stage direction from John Copley, *Grimes* rose to its full tragic potential in Ben Heppner's performance of the title role. If he did not duplicate the full power of the mature Jon Vickers and if earlier Lyric versions had stronger castings in supporting roles, this was still a great experience.

The American score was a new Lyric commission, *Amistad,* by Anthony Davis, on a politically fashionable subject that was also being explored in a Steven Spielberg film. *Amistad* proved that a good story is not always good operatic material unless one knows how to write music that develops the big scenes dramatically. The theme of the work, that no human being can be treated as a piece of property, won sympathy, but the balance of words to action weighed heavily in favor of the words, and this, together with a stylistically eclectic score with few truly compelling pages, added up to a disappointing opera. Dennis Russell Davies conducted, with Mark S. Doss, Florence Quivar, and Thomas Young conspicuous for their contributions in the cast.

The season opened with *Nabucco,* Verdi's first great success, in a very up-to-date production directed by Elijah Moshinsky, with sets by Michael Yeargan. Bartoletti conducted and Alexandru Agache sang the title role. Samuel Ramey was predictably effective as the high priest Zaccaria, with Maria Guleghina a dramatic Abagaille who capped the end of act 2 with a high E-flat. To the delight of suburbanites, a quarter of the season went to Puccini, with the Lyric proving that in standard fare it can produce a consistent product as gratifying as an experienced chef's scaloppine. *Madama Butterfly* was back in the familiar, but no less impressive, Harold Prince production, with Catherine Malfatano and Richard Leech a strong combination as the ill-fated lovers. *La bohème* was a trip down memory lane, recalling past Lyric successes with the much-loved score. This version combined Mirella Freni's Mimì with Vincenzo La Scola's Rodolfo under Bartoletti's baton. But not all revivals were so happy. The new production of Bizet's *The Pearl Fishers* added little to lift it beyond the mediocre, though the tenor-baritone duet (sung by Paul Groves and Gino Quilico) brought the expected audience cheers.

If a quarter of the season went to Puccini, another quarter went to Mozart: *Idomeneo* under the strong hand of John Nelson and *The Marriage of Figaro* with Zubin Mehta in the pit and Sir Peter Hall in charge of the stage. *Figaro,* with its incredible music and a strong libretto, need only be given an appropriate cast to reveal its marvels, and with Bryn Terfel in the title role, Elisabeth Futral as his bride, Susan Graham as Cherubino, and Håkan Hagegård and Renée Fleming as Count and Countess Almaviva, success was assured.

Idomeneo is another matter, an *opera seria,* old-fashioned even in Mozart's day. It needed the strength provided by John Conklin's marvelous sets (from San Francisco) and Copley's handling of the stage, but the singing was no less important. Vinson Cole had the title role in the opening performances, followed by Plácido Domingo in less than his most attentive form. Carol Vaness, Vessalina Kasarova (in her American debut as Idamante), and Mariella Devia brought convincing vocal and dramatic characterizations.

As if to remind all and sundry that in Berlin he headed an opera house, Daniel Barenboim chose to close the Chicago Symphony season in May 1998 with a radically deconstructive staging of Beethoven's *Fidelio* in Orchestra Hall, directed by Alexander Schulin. It worked. Beethoven's optimistic faith that liberty would always triumph was tempered by twentieth-century political realities. Waltraud Meier was Leonore, with Thomas Moser her Florestan.

The Chicago Opera Theater's single production in the spring of 1998 was—in effect—a triple bill. Viktor Ullmann's *The Emperor of Atlantis,* a defiant, scathing attack on Adolf Hitler written in the Theresienstadt concentration camp in 1943, was the main offering in what COT termed a "One-Hour Opera Festival." It was given on the main stage of the Athenaeum Theatre. Lee Hoiby's *Bon Appétit!* and Henry Mollicone's *The Face on the Barroom Floor* were performed in smaller spaces in the same building. A ticket for the Ullmann entitled you to see both of the other works as well (and on the same date if seating was available), but since the Hoiby and Mollicone were given in spaces considerably smaller than the auditorium in which the Ullmann was performed—and though they were shown twice on each of the Ullmann dates— extra performances of the shorter works were presented to accommodate all ticket holders. Ullmann depicted an ironic moral universe with music reminiscent of Mahler and Zemlinsky, tinged with Kurt Weillian instrumentation and bite. All the performers involved did COT proud. A sizeable number of discussions (some as post-performance symposia), three films, and brief chamber concerts were offered in various locations in conjunction with the Ullmann for those who wished to put the piece into a historical and musical perspective.

The libretto of Hoiby's frothy one-woman show was an actual recipe from one of Julia Child's television cooking shows, and Karen Brunssen sang and acted (and stirred!) with spirit as Timothy Shandlin's piano kept pace with her. The Mollicone melodrama was given with audience members seated at tables (they were almost part of the action themselves) in a small barroom with the singers, accompanied by a piano sounding for all the world as one would expect it to in an early saloon.

With this, its twenty-fifth anniversary season, the Chicago Opera Theater had—over the years—presented twenty American operas, most of them among the twenty-seven Chicago premières the company had offered to date. COT did not produce again until December 1998, and it was for seven performances of *Hansel and Gretel* (including three "family matinées").

Considering 1998/99 at the Lyric Opera of Chicago one must conclude that no season of recent memory had held greater contrast between success and disaster. Familiar strengths remained. There was Italian

opera on the level that had built and sustained the reputation of the company. Bartoletti conducted an assured opening night success, a remarkable performance by Jane Eaglen in the title role of *La Gioconda.* Johan Botha was the hero and Nikolai Putilin the villain of the piece. Neither was a match for Eaglen.

Verdi's *La traviata* was heard in a rather routine and lightweight production with revolving casts and conductors for performances in the autumn and winter. Ruth Ann Swenson and Frank Lopardo of the second series made the greater impression. Boito's *Mefistofele* returned in a successful restaging of the 1991 production, with Samuel Ramey again dominating the work as the Prince of Darkness. Richard Margison was Faust, and Daniella Dessì was Margherita. Gounod's *Romeo and Juliet* proved a handsome revival of what had years before been one of the city's favorite scores. For half the performances the most famous lovers in history were played to consistent dramatic effect and mostly effective music-making by the currently most publicized lovers in opera, Angela Gheorghiu and her husband, Roberto Alagna, with John Nelson conducting.

The American opera, Marvin David Levy's *Mourning Becomes Electra* (after the dramatic trilogy by Eugene O'Neill) was heard in a very different version from that commissioned for the opening season of the new Metropolitan Opera House in 1967. The composer reorchestrated the work and provided a vocal line he described as "twentieth-century bel canto" rather than the fashionable serialism of thirty years earlier. Those who knew the work in both forms found the revision lighter and more lyric: distinct improvements. For many the opera had real theatrical force, but one might argue that the primary strength of the work remained the libretto. For others the music provided a significant intensification of the drama impossible to achieve in the theater of the spoken word. The strong cast was headed by Cynthia Lawrence and Lauren Flannigan, with Richard Buckley conducting. Liviu Ciulei both designed and directed the production.

Then things started to slide. *Ariadne auf Naxos* was impressively sung by Deborah Voigt, Laura Aikin, Susan Graham, and Jon Villars, and it was opulently staged by John Cox. But the orchestra under Robert Spano seemed at times to be struggling to play the notes.

An important revival and a Lyric "first" were both seriously flawed by ill-conceived revisionist productions that took the works out of their proper frames and placed them in ludicrous new environments. *Die*

Meistersinger, in a production borrowed from Brussels, was moved from 1560—where it made dramatic sense—to the 1840s, where it made no sense at all. It seems possible that the conception offered an opportunity to charge Wagner with antisemitism by suggesting that Beckmesser was a Jew. Someone should have looked the director Kurt Horres in the eye and said, "No!" James Levine has suggested that *Die Meistersinger* is close to being an indestructible opera provided you have singers who can manage their notes. In this case the Lyric had an excellent Eva in Nancy Gustafson, a Sachs of warmth and wisdom, Jan-Hendrik Rootering, and a noble Pogner sung by René Pape, but Eike Wilm Schulte's Beckmesser was unlike any I had seen before. Most of the performances brought Gösta Winbergh as Stolzing. One particularly impressive aspect of the production was the conducting of Christian Thielemann.

For many—Bartoletti among them—who had long urged a Lyric staging of Kurt Weill's *The Rise and Fall of the City of Mahagonny* the English-language version that finally arrived on the Lyric stage was so disastrously bad that one had to regret it had been given at all. This was the worst thing the Lyric had done in at least ten years, the most appalling example of Krainik's approving a revisionist production completely at odds with the traditions and spirit, not to mention the letter, of the work. Director David Alden was the architect of this mess, aided by sets and costumes by Paul Steinberg. Musically the production was crippled by an orchestra and conductor (Sylvain Cambreling) who had no firm grasp of the style. Trapped in this travesty were some fine singers, among them Catherine Malfitano (Jenny), Kim Begley (Jimmy), Felicity Palmer (Begbick), and Timothy Nolen (Trinity Moses). The Cranes duet was too fine musically to fail, but otherwise the *Tribune* headline "Vile Weill" said it all. Truly, it was a lost opportunity.

In spring 1999 Carl Ratner and Lawrence Rapchak presented the last of their seasons as Chicago Opera Theater's artistic team (though the following season's repertory and casting were their work). There were two productions, Offenbach's *The Tales of Hoffmann* and an offering consisting of music by Leonard Bernstein. Ratner's adaptation of the Offenbach turned the protagonist into the young Orson Welles, with the older Welles as his nemesis. The action of the opera was based on aspects of Welles's life as well as ideas from his major films. The concept worked well at times but seemed strained at others. The performances varied in quality, and in this case the decision to use the same singer for the feminine lead in each of the three sections of the opera proved unwise.

There Is a Garden: The Musical Genius of Leonard Bernstein was a concept conceived and directed by Angelina Réaux. In its prologue, six characters each introduced his or her perspective on love in seven Bernstein songs. Next there was a complete performance of Bernstein's chamber opera *Trouble in Tahiti.* The second half of the production, subtitled "Songs, Scenes & Other Amusements," consisted of no less than twenty-four Bernstein songs and scenes from varied sources of his vocal output, in which, the synopsis claimed, "the 'bought-and-paid-for' magic of Tahiti becomes a reality for the performers and the audiences as the real world is left behind and the pure joy of Bernstein's American musical theater, opera and concert works are revealed." If there was more than a little pomposity in that description, and if the revue's three hours made a long evening, an excellent cast and simple but effective staging kept things moving in a lively production.

For the Lyric's 45th season—the 150th season since opera first came to the city—the Lyric announced a new Wednesday matinée series. The immediate response indicated that the company was responding to the interests and needs of many individuals.

It was instructive to consider on this 150th anniversary that—allowing for years when no opera was heard—a third of the opera performed in Chicago from that first year had come from the Lyric organization. The only real rival was not even a Chicago company. Between 1884 and 1962 thirty-six visits by the Metropolitan Opera of New York attested to the close musical bonds that (East Coast-Midwest rivalry notwithstanding) affirmed mutual goals and common values.

The Lyric season that bridged the millenium was a classic Krainik composition, something new, something unfamiliar, and generous servings of standard repertory that would guarantee the return of the conservative listeners. For the second year running, there was no Puccini.

The season opened with an innovative staging of a triumphant masterwork of the Italian repertory, Verdi's *Falstaff.* Frank Philipp Schlössmann, making his American debut as a designer, caught the spirit of Shakespeare's Windsor in terms of contemporary stagecraft, and Bryn Terfel made the protagonist a dirty old man of heroic dimensions. The cast was young. Kallen Esperian (Alice), Patricia Risley (Meg), and Bernadette Manca di Nissa (Quickly) were ladies to melt any heart. Gwyn Hughes Jones and Inva Mula ravished the ear as the young lovers, and Lucio Gallo had the right mixture of wisdom and foolishness required of Ford. Antonio Pappano conducted. The orchestra played this Mozartian Verdi vivaciously.

Those who rejoiced in Krainik's "Toward the 21st Century" project could take satisfaction that it closed with the world première of an American opera possibly destined for international repertory status. Five years in the planning and writing, William Bolcom's *A View from the Bridge* had the unbeatable asset of a strong libretto based on Arthur Miller's play of 1955 about Sicilian passion transplanted to the Red Hook neighborhood of Brooklyn.

The play, especially in the first version that dominated this libretto, was poetic in a manner that could be intensified by music and dramatically strong enough to retain its integrity when compressed into operatic form. Bolcom, the master synthesizer of styles, knew how to dress the words in a variety of appropriate musical idioms and still produce a work with great unity. Fine as his score for *McTeague* might be, *A View from the Bridge* revealed the increasing maturity of a major American talent. In the final scene he could combine ideas from the finales of *Don Giovanni* and *Cavalleria rusticana* in bold dramatic counterpoint and still keep everything unequivocally American.

Further assets were a spectacular unit set by Santo Loquasto that fused projections with solid forms, powerful staging by Frank Galati, and dramatically white-hot conducting from Dennis Russell Davies. The cast could hardly have been better, with Kim Josephson as the tortured Eddie, Juliana Rambaldi as the youthful object of his lust, Catherine Malfitano as his rejected wife, and Gregory Turay (whose singing of the aria "The New York Lights" stopped the show) as the young man who claims the younger woman's love. Timothy Nolen and the chorus viewed the inevitable tragedy with compassionate understanding. Miller, who was an active participant in the project, may have written the shortest and most comprehensive review. "It's a marvelous piece," he said.

The problem of reviving Handel operas was made plain by *Alcina*. The work is as long as a Wagnerian music drama but, alas, it is all music (a succession of some twenty florid arias) and practically no drama at all. The plot, if not the silliest in all opera, is a strong contender for that title. (Alcina, a sorceress, turns her lovers into inanimate objects of various types.) What saved the evening was a consistently remarkable cast that was able to sing the piece as it must be sung. First honors go to Renée Fleming in the title role, but Jennifer Larmore, Natalie Dessay (who almost stole the show with her aria ending the first act), and Rockwell Blake made distinguished contributions. John Nelson's knowledgeable, idiomatic conducting was another impressive aspect of the production.

Those who recalled the Lyric's original production of *Die Fledermaus* in May 1982 might wonder if its vitality could ever be surpassed. It didn't happen this time, although Nolen returned in the role of Franke, and he and Thomas Allen as Eisenstein strove to keep things rolling. The necessary *Wiener Blut* was lacking, partly because Dame Felicity Lott as Rosalinde lost her sparkle in the second act. Leopold Hager conducted.

L'elisir d'amore was another production with a revolving cast and, in this case, a tacky production. The second cast, with Ruth Ann Swenson and Vincenzo La Scola, was somewhat more interesting than the first, which had Elizabeth Futral and Frank Lopardo.

Alden, the destroyer of *Mahagonny* the season before, was permitted to do his worst to Verdi's *Macbeth* with results that were controversial for some and disastrous for others. The production came from Houston, where Franz Grundheber and Catherine Malfitano, Macbeth and his queen in the Lyric staging, had sung it previously. The musical strengths they brought to the work were undeniable if sometimes strained, but this production was maddeningly far from what Verdi intended.

Both the Metropolitan and the Lyric presented *Tristan und Isolde* this season in new productions, with Ben Heppner and Jane Eaglen in the title roles. The Met version, with evocative, abstract scenery, was a notable success. The Lyric had another freakish revisionist production, this one from Seattle, the work of Francesca Zambello and Alison Chitty. It began with the couple on a modern ship and proceeded to greater absurdities. Following a current twist of fashion, the *tod*-less *Liebestod* ended with Isolde alive and on her feet. Compensation was found in lush, romantic orchestral playing under Semyon Bychkov and the presence of the two artists probably best qualified to sing this music today. René Pape found the nobility and beauty (not the boredom) in the role of King Marke.

The Lyric deserved a monumental success to end the season and had it in a sumptuous *Carmen*, conducted by Yoel Levi and directed by John Copley. The physical energy of the production (given to the Lyric in memory of Krainik) was matched by the vocal impact. This time we had a black Carmen, Denise Graves, matched by a black Escamillo, Mark S. Doss. Richard Leech was Don José, Janice Watson sang most of the Micaëlas. Bizet's tragedy retained its original spirit and force.

Mason, asked by the press to discuss his first seasons, politely suggested that he really hadn't produced a season yet. The policies of his management and Messrs. Davis and Epstein would have to be announced at a future date. That came in December 1999 when, in an unprecedented step, the Lyric revealed most of its plans not only for 2000/01 (the period normally discussed at that time of year) but through the fiftieth season, 2004/05.

In the coming decade the repertory would remain balanced between long-established works and new or less familiar operas. Moreover, in what was called the "Renaissance Project," at least eight of the great classics would receive new productions with the expectation that they would be staged from three to five times in a period from ten to twenty years. Mason described these new productions as being "basically representational and in period, but never routine." To say that and then announce that 2000/01 would contain *Rigoletto* in a version in which Christopher Alden in the name of "relevance" moved the action to the nineteenth century and further played havoc with almost every dramatic stage action Verdi called for demolished the credibility of Mason's statement.

Krainik's "Toward the 21st Century" artistic initiative proved in ten years that the public would accept new operas if they were played, sung, and staged to the high standards the company upheld in classic scores. The successor to this project, proposed by Mason, would be "American Horizons," but this effort would be open-ended. Through the first decade of the new century there would be three Lyric commissions. The company's belief, well justified by results, that in William Bolcom it has a composer who can produce significant work in an American idiom was demonstrated by the fact that two of the three commissions would go to him. *A Wedding,* based on a classic Robert Altman film, would be heard in 2004/05, and another Bolcom opera was scheduled for 2009/10.

Significantly, in the five seasons leading up to the fiftieth anniversary, the size of the Lyric repertory each season was not going to increase. The emphasis remained on the economic stability inherent in producing a work and giving it as long a run as appeared to be economically feasible. This left room for seasons to grow in terms of the number of performances, but not in terms of operas staged.

Mark Tiarks left the Chicago Opera Theater in the fall of 1998, and Robert Alpaugh was named administrative consultant to help create a new structure for the company. The board eventually opted for a single manager/general director post to replace the tripartite arrangement that had existed for several years. Lawrence Rapchak and Carl Ratner were each offered the chance to be considered for the new post, but both declined. Enter Brian Dickie in September 1999, and an entirely new—and in many ways quite different—era for COT was launched. Dickie had spent five years as the general director of the Canadian Opera Company and seven years in that position with the Glyndebourne Festival Opera. Long-range plans called for at least a doubling of COT's annual $1.5 million budget and an even longer-range hope to increase the company's offerings from two or three to six productions per year. There was no question that the board wanted to move COT away from being considered a small, local endeavor. As Robert Alpaugh put it, "There's a desire to really make COT a player [on the national opera scene]." Offices had been moved to downtown Chicago, and everyone looked forward to the new performing space it would have (in two years, it was hoped) at the northwest corner of Millenium Park on Randolph Street, just east of Michigan Avenue. (That 1,452-seat theater, the record will show, did not open until early in 2004 and did so under the name of the Joan W. and Irving B. Harris Theater for Music and Dance.)

COT's twenty-sixth season held two productions, given five months apart. Both utilized Rapchak as conductor, with Ratner the stage director for the second one. October 1999 brought four performances of *The Barber of Seville,* and in late March and early April 2000 there were performances of what, on paper, looked like an interesting double bill: Puccini's *Gianni Schicchi* and a one-acter by the composer-librettist Michael Ching, *Buoso's Ghost,* a comic sequel to the Puccini. Outside of Philip Kraus's portrayal of Schicchi, the Puccini lacked vocal allure and power. John von Rhein described Ching's opera as "a pleasing confection . . . charming and unpretentious and mercifully brief," and he found

Chicago's newest venue for opera, the Joan W. and Irving B. Harris Theater for Music and Dance

its eclectic score to be holding "expert" vocal writing. The cast seemed to be more spirited and satisfying in the Ching work than in the Puccini.

Dickie scheduled Philip Glass's *Akhnaten* for production in July 2000, with Kurka's *The Good Soldier Schweik* and Handel's *Acis and Galatea* to be given in the spring of 2001. The new thrust of the Chicago Opera Theater seemed to be set. There would be a major focus on pre-Mozart and twentieth- and twenty-first-century operas. There would be far less reliance on local talent for soloists and conductors. No longer would operas be sung always in English but rather in their original language (with supertitles for all productions), and populist ticket prices would give way to considerably higher costs in light of the more professional productions to be presented. COT was, indeed, moving into new ground on a number of levels, and, with critical comment as favorable as it became from mid-July 2000 on, there was a new cognizance of the presence and the revised stances of what Chicago Opera Theater wanted to be under its new leadership.

The forty-sixth season of the Lyric (2000/01) opened with Tchaikovsky's *The Queen of Spades*, an opera that had never been produced by a Chicago company and, indeed, had not been heard in the city for more than seventy-five years. Davis conducted. Securely fixed in the repertory of many major opera houses (starting with the Metropolitan), it (and *Jenůfa*) represented Danny Newman's category of "dog operas," works that should not be offered without nearly 90 percent subscription because the demand for single tickets would be practically nonexistent.

Inside the Joan W. and Irving B. Harris Theater for Music and Dance

But Newman's opinions are based on his experiences with audiences of sixty years ago. There is reason to think that times have changed. *The Queen of Spades* is unlikely to be a popular opera in the sense that *Tosca* is a popular opera, but it is an opera by Tchaikovsky and for this reason alone should attract interest. *Jenůfa* was last seen at the Lyric in 1959. Since it is an opera by Janáček, whose *The Makropulos Affair* was a major Lyric success in 1995, shouldn't another work by that composer be attractive?

The second opera of the new series was John Harbison's *The Great Gatsby*, commissioned by the Metropolitan and first heard there in 1999. The original sets and costumes were seen and some of the original cast were heard, but Harbison's revisions were included. Four Italian staples were offered: Verdi's *Attila* and *Rigoletto*, Puccini's *Tosca*, and Rossini's *The*

Barber of Seville. Davis made his third conducting appearance in a new production of Wagner's *The Flying Dutchman*.

The 2001/02 series began with Davis's conducting Verdi's *Otello* in a new production with Ben Heppner and Renée Fleming. Davis also conducted Britten's *Billy Budd* (another new production) and Mozart's *The Magic Flute*. Two more Italian operas were on the list, Puccini's *La bohème*—back after an absence of four years—and Bellini's *I Capuleti e i Montecchi*, a noteworthy success of 1985 that called for revival. The two German operas are sharply contrasted. Humperdinck's *Hansel and Gretel* was one of the great showpieces of the Chicago companies of the 1920s; the Lyric was doing it for the first time and with a new, modernized production. There was another new (controversial) production of Wagner's *Parsifal*, the fourth opera for Davis, which meant he conducted half the season. The American opera was Kurt Weill's *Street Scene,* new to the Lyric but not the city, although few would recall the 1960 performance.

The striking item for 2002/03 was Stephen Sondheim's *Sweeney Todd,* a Lyric première in a new production, with Bryn Terfel in the title role. There was an established American opera, Floyd's *Susannah,* in its second Lyric production and fifth Chicago appearance. The season opener consisted of new productions of *Cavalleria rusticana* and *Pagliacci. Un ballo in maschera* returned in a new production. A Mary Garden specialty, *Thaïs,* last heard in 1959, brought Renée Fleming in the title role, with Thomas Hampson, with Davis conducting. Davis was also in charge of *La traviata* and *Die Walküre,* the latter anticipating *Ring* cycles to come. The truly unfamiliar work is Handel's *Partenope.*

Davis opened the 2003/04 season with *The Marriage of Figaro,* and his repertory included *Siegfried* (further anticipation of the *Ring*). Two new productions had been announced but were later dropped for financial reasons: Berlioz's *Benvenuto Cellini,* which has never been staged in Chicago, and Montemezzi's *L'amore dei tre re,* missing from the local repertory for nearly fifty years. They were replaced with *Faust* and Lyric's first Gilbert and Sullivan production ever in their mainstage seasons, *The Pirates of Pensance.* Classic fare includes *Lucia di Lammermoor* and *Madama Butterfly.*

The fiftieth season, 2004/05, announced as a gala, was established as such by opening with a new production of *Don Giovanni* (the company's calling-card opera in 1954), Lyric's first staging of Janáček's *The Cunning Little Vixen,* the world premiere of William Bolcom's *A Wedding,* the Met's new production of *Fidelio,* the revived Zeffirelli Covent Garden sets for *Tosca,* and the addition of *Das Rheingold* as subscription repertory, followed by two performances of *Götterdämmerung* and three complete *Ring* cycles at the end of the season. *Aida* was given, and there was a 50th anniversary gala concert.

The first impression the incoming Mason management troika gave in 1996 was that Davis and Matthew Epstein had artistic control and that Mason saw his role as providing them with an appropriate setting in which to work. As the first five years of that arrangement progressed, however, the balances of power shifted. The Lyric, perhaps spoiled by experiencing greater than 100 percent ticket sales each season, found that percentage decreasing as the financial picture in the United States changed, beginning with the World Trade Center terrorist attack in New York City on September 11, 2001. Money became tighter on all fronts, and Mason began to balk at the more adventurous repertory and staging concepts pursued by Epstein. In December 2004 it was announced that Epstein's contract as Lyric's artistic director would not be renewed when it expired at the end of April 2005.

13

A Changing Repertory
over the First 150 Years

Opera in Chicago began in a time when important new works were being produced regularly. The first year of Chicago opera, 1850, was the year in which what was to be one of the favorite operas in the city, Wagner's *Lohengrin,* was introduced by Liszt at Weimar. The greatest year for opera in the city, 1865, was also the year audiences first heard *Tristan und Isolde.*

The character of the repertory has always been dynamic. As time passed, more and more works became established with the audience, and these became a core group of scores that generation after generation of the local operagoing public wanted to hear. In the first eighteen seasons of local companies in the Auditorium, the opera most frequently presented was *Carmen,* and, not surprisingly, a new, potentially exciting staging of that work was what many members of the Lyric Opera audience most wanted to hear in the season marking the 150th year of opera in the city.

The least interesting seasons of Chicago opera are those in which innovation lagged, but even when the downtown companies seemed deep in stagnation, at Ravinia familiar works were frequently contrasted with new things. Innovation has been characteristic of the last twenty-five years of Lyric Opera seasons, thus it is no surprise that the 150th anniversary was also the year of Bolcom's *A View from the Bridge,* a powerful, distinctively American work that had the potential to make a lasting place for itself.

Making an operatic census requires distinctions between light opera and presumably more serious works, and any two individuals may come up with different totals. For convenience let us adopt a round

number. In 150 years Chicago heard some 350 operas. Again in round numbers, the Lyric Opera of Chicago, in its forty-fifth season the most long-lived resident company in the history of the city, had staged 140 of that group, and 60 (more than 40%) of these productions introduced the work in question to the city. Moreover, nearly all the new works have been accepted by the public, and several have returned in later seasons. Carol Fox brought Chicago *Così fan tutte, Don Carlo, Simon Boccanegra, Elektra, Angel of Fire, Ariadne auf Naxos,* and *Wozzeck*—all great successes—and she produced the first Lyric performances of *Der Rosenkavalier.* Only one or two works might qualify as monumental failures.

Some operas are immediate successes and go on being successful all over the world, year after year. In contrast, some are immediate disasters and quickly depart from the stage, never to return. There are works that are known (at least by reputation) through the operatic world and are produced, somewhere or other, with reasonable regularity. And there are works that are admired, perhaps in one theater or one country, and live on the stage in those locations but are largely unknown to the operatic public at large.

All four groups can be illustrated by the works of Verdi. *Aida* (1871) within a decade of its première had been heard in the major opera houses of the world and was commonly regarded as a repertory piece. In the Auditorium seasons it was the opera heard most frequently after *Carmen. Alzira* (1845) received a few scattered performances after its première and vanished from the stage in 1858. Verdi, who in later life came to regard it as "really ugly," was not surprised. It is the Verdi opera that almost no one knows and, apparently, no one misses. *Luisa Miller,* written five years later, quickly went from its 1849 première in Naples to major European theaters and was heard in New York as early as 1854. Always respected as a major achievement, it is in the repertory of important singers and thus is revived with some frequency, but it is not a standard work. With the advances of modern Verdi scholarship, those seriously involved with his career are familiar with his next opera, *Stiffelio* (1850). In this period Verdi was battling censorship at every turn, and the daring theme of the work, with a Protestant clergyman as its protagonist, was more than convention could accept. With recent revivals it may finally assume some role in the repertory. It has been produced, for example, in New York but not in Chicago.

It is inevitable that tastes change, but in opera the changes can be dramatic. Let us contrast the operas most frequently produced in the 150 seasons of Chicago opera with those staged in the fifty years 1950–2000 (see table 2).

It will be noted that seven of the ten most popular works in the full span of 150 seasons remained among the first ten in 1950–2000. But there are dramatic changes in frequency of production. *Lohengrin,* heard fifty times in 150 seasons, returns only once after 1950. *Martha,* once one of the most popular operas, has all but vanished. *Faust* and *Il trovatore,* the nineteenth-century paradigms of grand opera, have lost that status. Like so much else in the repertory of the nineteenth century, they have been overwhelmed by Puccini, who holds the first three places on the list of recent productions. The most popular Verdi score is now *La traviata.* Mozart, long eclipsed by lesser composers, has come into his own. *Carmen,* often called the indestructible opera, secured a strong position with its first performances and has never lost it. And Wagner, who demands superior voices and a big orchestra, always lags behind the Italians. Not surprisingly, there is no opera by Richard Strauss on either list. He, too, is demanding.

If we turn to the composers most frequently represented in the repertory, we find—no surprise—that Verdi is the most popular, although in the nineteenth century he was known for only ten operas. *I vespri siciliani* has not been heard in Chicago since 1868. *La forza del destino* was produced only once, and *Ernani* lagged behind the seven most popular works. It was in the Lyric seasons that the range and significance of Verdi's work became clear.

The popularity of Massenet corresponds to the peak of the Mary Garden period. His finest opera, *Manon,* has rarely been given in the past fifty years. Donizetti almost became a composer with a single work, *Lucia di Lammermoor,* eclipsing nearly everything else, and Offenbach, known in the nineteenth century for light operas, was not revealed in his full stature until *The Tales of Hoffmann* was produced in 1910.

Chicago heard Wagner's *Rienzi* only in the nineteenth century and had to wait until the twentieth, when the demise of copyrights made *Parsifal* available. Rossini's *Moses in Egypt,* probably his most important serious score, got a single production in 1862—an important omission—but despite that, Chicago operagoers of the past fifty years may have a better idea of the range of his work than their nineteenth-century counterparts. Puccini took off from the moment he was first heard, although *Manon Lescaut* did not arrive until nearly twenty years after its Italian première.

TABLE 2—NUMBER OF PRODUCTIONS OF MOST PERFORMED OPERAS, BY PERIOD

Seasons 1850–2000	Seasons 1950–2000
Faust 90	*Madama Butterfly* 27
Il trovatore 75	*La bohème* 21
Carmen 74	*Tosca* 20
Aida 73	*La traviata* 17
La traviata 73	*Faust* 16
Lucia de Lammermoor 73	*Rigoletto* 15
Cavalleria rusticana 69	*Carmen* 14
Rigoletto 68	*The Marriage of Figaro* 13
Madama Butterfly 62	*Aida* 12
La bohème 60	*The Barber of Seville* 12
Tosca 58	*Cavalleria rusticana* 11
Martha 56	*Don Giovanni* 10
The Barber of Seville 55	*Pagliacci* 8
Pagliacci 51	*Lucia di Lammermoor* 8
Lohengrin 50	*Il trovatore* 6
Don Giovanni 46	*Die Walküre* 5
The Marriage of Figaro 39	*Martha* 2
Die Walküre 39	*Tannhäuser* 2
Tannhäuser 39	*Lohengrin* 1

TABLE 3

Composer with 10 or more operas produced	Produced only in the 19th Century	Produced only in the 20th Century
Verdi 17	1	7
Massenet 14	0	10
Offenbach 13	10	1
Donizetti 11	3	2
Wagner 11	1	1
Rossini 10	1	5
Puccini 10	0	8

For a clear idea of how the repertory changed over the years, four periods must be defined. The longest is the sixty years 1850–1910 in which opera heard in Chicago came off the road, with New York the primary source of supply. Impresarios were interested mainly in making a profit from their run, and repertory was selected on the basis of their often faulty judgment as to what would sell. A similar viewpoint—although reflecting the new century—prevailed in the years 1943–1954, when New York again was a prime source of Chicago opera.

In sharp contrast, the period of the first resident companies in the Auditorium, 1910–1928, reflected the desire of the music producers to respond to the distinctive taste of the Chicago public. Works such as Massenet's *Le Jongleur de Notre-Dame,* never produced at the Metropolitan, might be heard more than twenty times if they featured a singer as charismatic as Mary Garden. Indeed, works as bad as Février's *Monna Vanna* might survive as long as fourteen years so long as Garden was available to sing them.

The first seasons in the Civic Opera House, 1929–1946, paid equal attention to local preferences, but these managements felt that tastes had changed since the earliest years of the century and tried to be responsive to this. Operas that had been popular early in the century vanished from the stage. Composers that had been neglected, Wagner in particular, were heard more frequently.

Once it had found its place in the city of the mid-century, the Lyric Opera was intent on audience building, and repertory was selected with the expectation that it would attract and support a large subscription base. The present Lyric policy is that most of the season will be established works, but there will be room for innovation annually. This balance will change from year to year—an unfamiliar Handel opera is easier to sell and probably cheaper to produce than a work by Shostakovich—but the vitality of dynamic contrast will remain. Still, many feel the Lyric should be more adventurous.

Opera houses are repertory theaters, but as the century advanced they became repertory theaters of a new type. The Chicago opera of 1910 was a house in which more than twenty works, perhaps 70% of what was regarded as established repertory, might be given annually. You did not have to wait very long to hear *Carmen, Il trovatore,* or *Die Walküre.* If it was not scheduled for this autumn, it would probably appear next year. And there were works, often by important composers, that were never heard. Verdi's first great success, *Nabucco,* was unknown, as were important later scores. Wagner's *The Flying Dutchman* was equally neglected. Significantly, there appeared to be little audience pressure to enlarge the repertory by staging works of this type. The choice of repertory was dominated by the wealthy backers of the company, and just as they preferred to hear what Virgil Thomson called "the fifty famous pieces" in symphony concerts, so (except for the Garden vehicles) they were often content with the operas they had known since childhood.

Since 1985 the Lyric Opera has been offering eight works a season. Rarely will it have more than three operas in production at the same time. Several years will pass between the stagings of even such popular works as *Madama Butterfly.* Earlier opera producers, addressing their efforts to a small audience, felt they must change the bill frequently or play to empty houses. The Lyric, with the large (and subscription) audience it has built, can minimize the number of productions (and hence production costs) and give each opera a run. And since production costs can be amortized against a number of performances, production standards can (in theory, anyway) be kept on a high level.

The most important thing is that present-day audiences are well aware of production values and insist on careful preparation. Audiences that went to the opera at the Auditorium early in the century went there primarily to hear singing. The decor was a painted canvas drop that might have been intended originally for another work. The orchestra, if it had been rehearsed at all, was given a superficial run-through on the assumption that it knew the music from past performances. Stage direction was generally rudimentary and often nonexistent. The public accepted this, in large part because it had no alternative approach with which to make comparisons.

Lyric audiences soon came to expect encountering a well-integrated unity of sets, costumes, and lighting, with the movement on stage controlled and shaped by a director. Opera was not just about singing, it was music theater. And opera no longer represents the theater of the past but is part of the theater of the present century; its effect must come from a synthesis of artistic elements that creates maximum musical and visual impact. A production can be undertaken when it is assumed that there are enough potential listeners to justify a number of performances. This was not a requirement in the early Chicago seasons, when a work might be given a single hearing.

In 1850, when opera first came to Chicago, everything was new, and, so far as one can tell, everything was welcome. The early seasons were dominated by bel canto operas because that was the style of the most popular works in the current repertory. Rossini, Bellini, and Donizetti were the most conspicuous figures in Italian opera. Rossini had written his last opera in 1829 and retired to enjoy his wealth in Paris. Bellini's small output (by the standards of the day) ended with his death in 1835. But when opera began in Chicago, Donizetti had been dead only two years, and the last work staged in his lifetime had been heard only seven years before. Facing this body of work were the first fifteen operas of the flaming new talent Verdi. This music began to be heard as early as 1858, and, as the decade closed, the two different approaches to singers and singing became obvious.

Rather than fearing modern music, in the nineteenth century Chicago heard a lot of what has to be described as contemporary opera. For example, *Aida* reached the city three years after its world première. *La bohème* was also only three years old when it first came to Chicago. In the new century, *Tosca* arrived the year after its première in Rome and two years before it was first heard in Paris.

In the mid-twentieth century you could find singers trained (and working) in both the new and the old traditions. The problem in presenting bel canto repertory today is casting, finding singers who can do justice to the roles and the style. This is essential. Bel canto operas were not written for the ages any more than a Gershwin show. They were vehicles for singers, and their only justification was that you had singers to do them justice. You went to the opera house to hear extravagant, florid singing. Adelina Patti was the supreme prima donna. As James Levine has observed, with Wagner, even with a less than ideal cast, you still have an opera. With Bellini, if the necessary cast is not there, neither is much of anything else.

Soon after her debut at the Metropolitan in 1956, Maria Callas was invited to dine with Arturo Toscanini in his Riverdale home. For her it was almost a royal command. Walter Toscanini, the maestro's son, and a most trustworthy source, recalled that all went well until after dinner when the party had retired to one of the three living rooms in the twenty-eight-room house and Callas began to question the Old Man about his repertory.

Why, she wanted to know, had he never in all his years of dedication to Italian opera attempted to revive bel canto works?

"Because, my dear," he replied, "it is impossible to find singers who know the proper style. The tradition was destroyed by the operas of Verdi and his successors, and no one today can sing these operas correctly."

"You mean no one?" she asked.

"Sì," he replied.

At this moment, to prevent a reenactment of the second act of *Tosca*, Walter Toscanini (who had been hovering anxiously nearby) rushed in with a snifter of cognac. "Maria, please, your glass is empty," he said, and she accepted the diversion.

But the Old Man had a point. It is not enough to program bel canto operas, they must be realized musically in the proper style, and this is no easy matter. The impresario of 120 years ago had casting options that have long ceased to exist.

Three operas of Bellini, *La sonnambula, Norma,* and *I puritani,* entered the Chicago repertory between 1850 and 1859, and *La sonnambula* and *Norma* remained current into the early years of the twentieth century. The Lyric has produced both these scores, restored *I puritani* to the stage, and introduced *I Capuleti e i Montecchi* to the city with success. Bellini thus begins opera in Chicago, and a reasonable sample of his work remains before the public today.

Rossini and Donizetti have not fared as well. Nine of Donizetti's more than sixty operas were presented between 1853 and 1865. But for most of this century he was represented by three or four works. *Lucia di Lammermoor* and *L'elisir d'amore* remain basic repertory, *Don Pasquale* is a popular operatic comedy, and *The Daughter of the Regiment* will always be a prized vehicle for the singers who can do it justice. One should note that all four operas can be sung successfully by singers who are not trained as bel canto specialists.

This is not the case in regard to Rossini, who is immortal for a comedy (admittedly a brilliant one), *The Barber of Seville,* and who suffers the indignity of having his most serious works all but forgotten. Five Rossini scores were heard in Chicago between 1858 and 1871, and, small as the group was, it included *Moses in Egypt* and *William Tell,* the two large-scale works in which the substance of his dramatic and musical skills is made plain. In recent years the Lyric has given us a wider view of his achievements, but it is his gift for comic opera that has been stressed.

Composers who continued to be represented in the repertory, even in a misleading fashion, clearly had an advantage over the composers who disappeared. Consider Auber, the great master of *opéra comique,* who had two of his works introduced in 1858. One of them, *Fra Diavolo,* was to remain before the public for seventy-three years. But nothing new of his was heard after 1869. He remains another prolific composer who is remembered, if at all, for a single work. The unfortunate Balfe, who had four operas produced in Chicago between 1858 and 1876, might take pride that *The Bohemian Girl* held the stage for almost sixty years—but performance of his operas ended in 1917. He was the type of composer championed by troupes that sang operas (many of them Italian works) in the English language. So long as English opera companies turned up in Chicago with some frequency, there was a place for Balfe, but he lacked the musical force needed for survival.

Today an opera generally will be given with either the original text or in English translation, but this is a recent practice dating from the middle of the twentieth century. Prior to that, one produced an opera in whatever language was most convenient. *Faust* and *Lohengrin* were frequently sung in Italian. Mary Garden sang *Tosca* and *Salome* in French, the latter in a version prepared by the composer. No American company could deal with any opera in a Slavic language. *The Bartered Bride* was usually heard in German; *Boris Godunov* became an Italian work, though if Chaliapin was the Boris, he, of course, sang in Russian (a practice continued by Alexander Kipnis at the Met into the mid–twentieth century).

The emphasis on securely accepted repertory can be illustrated by the works selected for a three-week visit of Grau's troupe from the Metropolitan Opera in 1889. There were three operas by Wagner, *Tannhäuser, Lohengrin,* and *Die Walküre.* Verdi was represented by *Aida* and *La traviata.* There was Gounod's *Faust* and also his *Romeo and Juliet.* Rossini was presumably epitomized by *The Barber of Seville,* Donizetti by *Lucia di Lammermoor.* Meyerbeer remained in the repertory with *Les Huguenots.* And there was Flotow's *Martha,* in Italian. Mozart's *The Marriage of Figaro* completed the list. There were twenty performances from a group of twelve operas, with *The Barber of Seville* heard three times.

Walter Toscanini once asked his father why this outrageously popular work had never figured in his repertory. "Because, my dear," the son was told, "it is impossible to present it in an appropriate, tasteful manner. It has become so totally corrupted by crude comic business, which the public expects, that if you want to put first emphasis on the beauty of the singing and refined humor, it will never be accepted. I will not be a *pagliaccio.*"

In the first decade of operatic production, 1850–1859, about half of the works heard in Chicago were operas that were to become permanent repertory: *The Barber of Seville, Don Giovanni, Lucia di Lammermoor, Rigoletto, La traviata,* and *Il trovatore* are prime examples. In the following decade they were joined by *Un ballo in maschera, Don Pasquale, L'elisir d'amore, Faust, Fidelio, La forza del destino, The Magic Flute, The Marriage of Figaro,* and *Tannhäuser.* Growth slacked in the 1870s. Here the important new works were *Aida* and *Carmen.* Wagner's *The Flying Dutchman* and *Lohengrin* were introduced to the city, and audiences of the 1880s were to hear his *Ring* cycle and *Die Meistersinger.* Even *Rienzi* appeared briefly. The important new Italian operas were *La Gioconda* and *Mefistofele.*

Then came the new Italian school characterized by realism—verismo. The transition in style from the bel canto composers early in the nineteenth century to the more dramatic style personified by Verdi was nothing in comparison with the changed concept of opera represented by the new Italian composers and their librettists. The nineties heard *Cavalleria rusticana, Pagliacci,* and *La bohème* with devastating effect. There was still a place for the romantics. Massenet became a favorite with *Werther,* his most lasting success. *Lakmé* added a note of French exoticism. Thirty years after its première, Wagner's *Tristan und Isolde* finally reached a Chicago stage. Verdi's late triumphs *Otello* and *Falstaff* were introduced, and there was room for pre-Mozartian opera, Gluck's *Orfeo ed Euridice.*

About half the operas heard in these fifty years, if they hold the stage at all today, do so tenaciously. Weber is generally considered to be the founder of the German romantic school of opera, thus his *Der Freischütz* is historically highly important. But the last, full-scale professional performance of that opera in Chicago was in 1895. (It can be encountered in Europe.) Works such as *Martha,* which once delighted audiences, could not attract a public that had Puccini as an alternative. Its final Chicago performances were widely separated, and the last of them was in 1983.

There are some fine, singable, stageworthy operas that for one or another reason are neglected. Montemezzi's *L'amore dei tre re,* enormously popular in the early part of the century, was scheduled to be revived by the Lyric, but that plan was dropped. It would have been interesting to see if that opera could regain a public. *Louise,* a Mary Garden specialty that was a staple of Chicago opera until 1939, may return after a Met revival with Renée Fleming. But Wolf-Ferrari's *The Jewels of the Madonna,* adored by audiences for more than twenty years early in the century, seems to have disappeared from the international scene. (It figured in the Met repertory for only two seasons.) Lyric's 1950s revivals of *Thaïs* and *Mignon* were unsuccessful.

Generally opera works drop out of the repertory because stronger works replace them. It is the survival of the fittest in the simplest Darwinian terms. *Guy Mannering,* heard in 1859, never returned, the first of many scores that appeared and vanished in the same season. About a quarter century later *Mireille,* by as formidable a talent as Gounod, suffered the same fate. Meyerbeer was a monumentally successful composer in the nineteenth century. Chicago heard six of his works in the 1860s, but by the close of the 1920s he belonged to history.

It is instructive to consider the twenty-seven works most frequently produced in the first forty-five seasons of the Lyric Opera. The number of productions (not performances) is given in parentheses.

La bohème (15)
Tosca (13)
Madama Butterfly (12)
The Barber of Seville/La traviata (11)
Un ballo in maschera (10)
Rigoletto/Carmen (8)

*The Marriage of Figaro/Lucia di Lammermoor/Aida/
    Don Giovanni* (7)
*Così fan tutte/L'elisir d'amore/Il trovatore/Don Carlo/
    Simon Boccanegra/Salome* (6)
*Don Pasquale/Faust/Otello/Falstaff/Die Walküre/
    Cavalleria rusticana/La Gioconda/Andrea Chénier/
    Turandot* (5)

Twelve composers are represented, seven of them Italians. Two are French, two are German, and there is Mozart. Twenty of the operas are Italian, and this group is dominated by Verdi (nine works) and Puccini (four). Donizetti is represented by three works, Rossini, Ponchielli, Mascagni, and Giordano by one. The popularity of Mozart—three works—may surprise some. Bedrock German opera, Wagner's *Die Walküre* and Strauss's *Salome,* received about a third as many hearings as the front-running Puccini scores.

Carol Fox saw Chicago as an Italian opera town, and Italian opera could be produced faster and more inexpensively than German repertory, which called for a different kind of orchestra and a different type of voices. In the Fox seasons, the top seven scores are all basic Italian fare. *Carmen* is the only French opera able to compete in this league. Mozart is then able to make an impression—he was a popular composer in the city if not the suburbs—and finally, toward the end of the list, we encounter Wagner. Fox might have said that she was presenting German opera "for the critics." More to the point was that a city that retained a large German population welcomed an occasional gesture recognizing its existence.

Danny Newman's view of what the public wanted was formed selling New York City Opera productions for Harry Zelzer. There was no subscription, and nearly everything would today be regarded as standard repertory. *La traviata* was clearly easier to sell than *The Love for Three Oranges,* but Zelzer was smart enough to know that there were potential customers who had had their fill of *La traviata* and might welcome something new. The composer featured in the New York seasons who has largely vanished is Menotti. In later years the New York company became a primary source of important American opera and was prepared to tour with this repertory.

Mozart's *The Marriage of Figaro* was the oldest score in the nineteenth-century Chicago repertory until Gluck appeared in 1886. When first heard, it was 124 years old. *Don Giovanni,* 72 years old, arrived in 1859. But much of the music offered to the public had been written within the past 20 years. Bellini's *La sonnambula* was 19 years old when it introduced opera to Chicago in 1850.

What was missing was what Erich Leinsdorf called "the fragmentation of modern composition, something that has never happened before." In the nineteenth century there was an accepted style, admittedly a rapidly evolving one, of operatic composition, and there was a public that followed the new work of living composers with interest and frequently with enthusiasm. The deeply ingrained hostility and suspicion of new work—"dreadful modern music"— frequently encountered in the public today did not exist. Schoenberg's *Moses und Aron* dated from the 1930s, but when James Levine introduced it in 1998/99 to the Metropolitan, there were protests about its modern idiom. No opera of 1832 would have had a comparable effect in 1898. Even Wagner's supposedly unplayable *Tristan und Isolde* of 1865 had been presented in all the major opera houses by the close of the nineteenth century.

A living artistic tradition must constantly be refueled and replenished by new work. In the United States the Broadway musical theater has evolved steadily through the present century. Pivotal works like *Pal Joey* (Rodgers and Hart, 1940) and *Oklahoma!* (Rodgers and Hammerstein, 1943) produced extended controversy and discussion, but they captured and held audiences. The majority of the public soon accepted the innovations. Today the public would reject any return to the typical Broadway musical of the past. Gershwin shows of the 1930s, for example, may be raided for music to go with new story lines, but in their original form they would appear dated. Only truly strong, landmark works (*Show Boat, Kiss Me, Kate,* for example) withstand revival in their original form. *Annie Get Your Gun* must be revised to eliminate racism. New shows that are truly innovative easily achieve public support.

In opera, both composers and listeners are alienated. The living composer objects to the demand that he follow models from the past, although the truly talented have taught us it is not necessary. The listener insists that opera must sing, must offer a vocal line written for, not against, the voice. The Lyric repertory of the 1990s provides strong examples of the strength of recent American operas, and the segment of the public that always fears the unfamiliar has been won over to a remarkable degree. One can find satisfaction that the most popular

American opera in Chicago (with four productions) is Carlisle Floyd's *Susannah* rather than a work of ersatz Puccini by Menotti.

Verdi and Puccini in particular were both great musicians and practical businessmen. They respected the public, and they wanted to write music the public would accept. They also knew that opera was about singing, that they must write music that permitted the listener to appreciate the qualities of an exceptional voice. Far too many composers of the twentieth century never mastered the craft of effective vocal writing. They were afraid of melody, not realizing the many shapes a melodic line can take. *The Rake's Progress* is a major—and characteristic—work by Stravinsky, but it gives a fine singer something to do.

The alienated contemporary composer rejects the demand that he please the public and all too frequently retires to a shelter in the academy to mutter, "If it's popular, it can't be good." But that is not true. Mozart, for one, has been extremely popular for two hundred years and, unquestionably, Mozart is good. The lesson of history is that rejection has never been the distinguishing mark of achievement. Mute, inglorious Miltons generally remain mute and inglorious— and for good reasons.

A critic who reviewed Grau's season of December 1900 in the Kansas City (Missouri) Convention Hall was not impressed with the new work he offered them opening night. It was, for the *Star,* "altogether too scholarly to ever rival *Faust.* It does not stream with melody; there is nothing to whistle unless it is the theme of the duet in the third act. . . . Maybe the masses will learn to love it, however, it is doubtful." The *Journal* felt the music for the leading soprano gave her "very slim pickings" (especially compared with the Mad Scene from *Lucia,* which completed the evening). Her music was not "showey" [sic], nor was her character. The skill with which the work was orchestrated had to be admired, but the music "ranges from light and trifling" to "beautiful [sic] concerted numbers."[1]

What is this tuneless, light-weight exercise in musical scholasticism, apparently destined for rapid oblivion? Puccini's *La bohème.* And what was wrong? The opera was not about vocal fireworks, it was about the things that touch the heart most deeply. And it required singing actors, not singing machines.

From the perspective of the opening of the twenty-first century we can see the broad sweep of the development of Italian operatic writing from Rossini to the present day. To give the Kansas City critic his due, he was suffering from the shock of nonrecognition. Nothing in *La bohème* immediately recalls either the bel canto tradition or the operas of Verdi. Why should it?

Puccini was introduced to Chicago on February 13, 1899, by the Ellis troupe with a performance of *La bohème,* which was then three years old. Melba sang Mimì with great success. In 1901 Grau offered a brand-new Puccini work, *Tosca.* William H. Sherwood, the critic of the *American,* hailed it as "a marvel,"[2] although its style was new and not instantly accessible to some. The Met, convinced it would sell, brought it back in 1904, 1906, 1907, and the spring of 1910, this time giving the title role to its brightest star, Geraldine Farrar. Mary Garden and Farrar symbolized the new prima donna. She drew and held your attention not simply with her voice but with everything: her face, her figure, the way she moved, the way she was costumed, and the stage presence she generated.

The Met season at the Auditorium in April 1907 might be regarded as the cornerstone of Puccini's reputation as a major composer in the city. It contained, in addition to the now familiar *Tosca,* the first local performances of *Madama Butterfly* and the second Chicago staging of *La bohème.* The return of Farrar, the Met's first (and probably greatest) Butterfly, was enough to make that work a major success.

Not until one reviews the repertory lists is it possible to realize the devastating effect of the *verismo* school on lesser composers, who were wiped out, annihilated. Wagner was eclipsed not for artistic but economic reasons. Puccini sold just as well and was far less expensive to produce. His operas were not difficult to cast, although having a Farrar available was advantageous. Distinguished Wagnerian singers were always in short supply and, hence, expensive.

Viewing the success of the Lyric Opera as objectively as possible, the key to everything was audience growth, and much of the credit for that phenomenon must be given to the Puccini repertory, which, for the larger public, had an appeal comparable to the music of Richard Rodgers, Jerome Kern, and even Cole Porter. This was music of high artistic quality that was in no sense elitist. Yet Puccini's texts and the way he treats them are tragedies in the full Aristotelian sense, filling our hearts with pity and fear.

Surveying the eighteen seasons of resident opera in the Auditorium, the figures make plain that for all its dedication to things French it was basically an Ital-

ian company. Nearly sixty Italian operas were heard, along with works like *Boris Godunov* sung in Italian translation. Nine of the ten most frequently performed works were Italian, the exception being *Carmen,* which narrowly beat *Aida* for the top position. But a third of the Italian scores was performed only five times or less. Forty-one operas were sung in French, but this group includes two Russian operas, Rimsky-Korsakov's *The Snow Maiden* and Prokofiev's *The Love for Three Oranges.* In those Auditorium years ten German operas were sung in German, and four German operas—*Hansel and Gretel* (which you might expect), but also *Martha, Die Fledermaus,* and *Lohengrin*—were sung in English. *Die Walküre* with twenty-five performances was the most frequently heard work in either of the German or English groups. The most popular Italian operas were *Aida* (65 performances), *Rigoletto* (55), *Pagliacci* (54), *Tosca* (52), and *Madama Butterfly, La traviata,* and *Cavalleria rusticana* (all tied at 46). In the French repertory the top five were *Carmen* (67) and four scores that all trailed their Italian counterparts, *Faust* (38), *Thaïs* (33), *Samson and Delilah* (28), and *Louise* (27). As the century advanced, the French repertory steadily shrank, due to a degree to a growing international shortage of first-quality French singers.

The nine seasons of resident opera from 1910 to 1919 were years of explosive innovation. Nearly fifty works were introduced, more new music than the city had heard in all the years since Crosby's Opera House burned down. It was the most monumental experiment in repertory growth in the history of the city, and it was a failure. Enduring to be part of the Lyric repertory were *Don Quichotte, The Abduction from the Seraglio, The Tales of Hoffmann, L'Heure espagnole, Samson and Delilah, Salome,* and two works of Puccini, *La fanciulla del West* and *Il trittico. Zazà* might come from Leoncavallo and *Cléopâtre* might be Massenet, but they did not have what it took to last. Massenet might be considered the composer whose popularity has declined most spectacularly. Twelve of his operas have been produced by Chicago companies, but only four have been heard from the Lyric, and just two of those—*Don Quichotte* and *Manon*—have achieved as many as three productions.

The growth of the repertory in the 1920s was due to the united efforts of the downtown companies, Ravinia, and Sol Hurok's touring groups. (How many would guess that, thanks to Hurok, Dargomïzhsky's *Rusalka* would ever be heard in Chicago?) The total of new scores was again close to fifty, with Puccini's *La rondine*, Strauss's *Der Rosenkavalier*, and Tchaikovsky's *The Queen of Spades* (which entered the Lyric repertory in 2000/01) being the most important additions.

In the 1930s repertory growth probably was slowed by the Depression. New productions cost money, and money was tight. The most significant event is that on November 20, 1930, for the first time a resident Chicago opera company staged *Die Meistersinger*. That a work of its stature should wait two decades while *Aphrodite, Gismonda, Grisélidis, Noël*, and their like danced across the stage for one or two performances is a clue to the level of taste. *Aphrodite*, which came and went in one evening, was, naturally, a vehicle for Mary Garden. Garden, I am beginning to think, really didn't care very much for opera in the largest sense. She was interested in those works— whatever their musical or dramatic value—that gave her an opportunity to display her vocal and dramatic resources, and she had an audience that couldn't get enough of them or of her.

Innovation in the 1930s involved *Conchita* (a vehicle for Rosa Raisa) and works like *Lorenzaccio, Mona Lisa, La fiamma, Gale*, and an American opera, *A Man without a Country*. The one novelty that survives internationally, although the Lyric has yet to produce it, is Rimsky-Korsakov's *Le Coq d'or*.

Many factors were involved in the economic failure of the later Chicago opera producers, but the loss of the appeal provided by new works may well have played a part. In this period the San Carlo Opera Company could go on the road successfully with budget-priced ("dollar opera") stagings of basic Italian fare. But the resident company that goes to the public for subsidy and becomes locked into the past cannot survive by routinely duplicating, at higher prices, the works the San Carlo has presented.

In the 1940s the question might still be asked, Why can't one produce works as popular as *Rigoletto* and *La bohème* at a profit? One reason was the dramatic growth in backstage costs. Leading singers demanded more money, but so did orchestra musicians, stagehands, and electricians. And if a new opera required new scenery, you might well wonder if it could be financed without an unacceptable loss.

The five locally produced opera seasons of the 1940s contained three new works, *Halka*, in 1942, and *Amelia Goes to the Ball* and *The Emperor Jones*, a double bill, in 1946. None of them is likely to receive a Lyric production.

During the period 1910–1947 Chicago heard thirty-five seasons of resident opera downtown (one of them consisting of a single performance) and twenty seasons of summer opera at Ravinia. More than half the repertory heard between 1910 and 1947 has never reappeared in the Lyric seasons. The Lyric did not go on duplicating the repertory of earlier Chicago opera producers but shaped a distinctive and attractive repertory of its own. Even if some protested that there was too much Italian music, it brought its listeners seven Verdi operas new to them—doubling the number of his works in the active repertory. Sixty works the Lyric has presented are scores associated in Chicago with this company alone.

In Carol Fox's company there was some French opera, a touch or two of Slavic opera for color, and a modest representation of Austro-German opera, except for Mozart—who prospered. One might plausibly argue that the two most neglected composers at the Lyric were Wagner and Strauss, although in Ardis Krainik's seasons that was corrected. Fox's standard argument was not that these composers did not sell (actually they sold very well) but that they were too expensive to produce. The Lyric was an Italian company—giving it the long-enduring sobriquet "La Scala West."

For Fox there was practically no American opera or twentieth-century opera of any type, not even Italian. Bruno Bartoletti wanted badly to produce *Il prigioniero* by his teacher Dallapiccola, but Fox would not agree. There was even less baroque repertory, although the occasional excursions in this direction were successful. To keep the record clear, earlier Chicago opera producers offered no baroque opera at all. The older companies were, however, more generous with American works and operas composed in the recent past.

In contrast, the Lyric since the beginning of Krainik's regime as director (1981) enjoyed an extraordinary growth in repertory, indeed, the most rapid and significant growth in the history of the company. Since opera involves advance planning three or more years ahead, when Krainik took over, she inherited the advance plans of the Fox administration. These included *Romeo and Juliet* in 1981 and *Luisa Miller* in 1982. She gladly agreed to continue with these productions. But the 1982 double bill of *Pagliacci* (previously planned) with Poulenc's *La Voix humaine* was Krainik's idea.

"I hired Peter Sellars to do *The Mikado* for our spring season in 1983," she recalled in a 1984 interview. "I wanted to make a statement: 'Look, kids, it's not going to be like it was before.'" Some subscribers felt there were going to be many changes they would not like but were delighted, in time, to discover they were wrong.

"About half the 1983 season had been planned in the Fox years," Krainik explained. "Lakmé was primarily her idea, but *Lady Macbeth of Mtsensk* was something Bruno Bartoletti and I wanted to do. But in 1984 the field was mine, and I surprised them with five lovely operas, all standard repertory, *Eugene Onegin, The Abduction from the Seraglio, Ernani,* and two Strauss scores, *Arabella* and *Die Frau ohne Schatten.* These were new but also great successes and the sort of music the subscribers enjoyed." *Onegin* was so popular that it returned in 1990.

Krainik's advance plans dominated the seasons immediately after her death. Bolcom's *A View from the Bridge* was her commission. Of the sixty new works the Lyric has introduced to the city, more than half arrived in the Krainik years. A substantial number of Krainik's new works were from the twentieth century and the baroque, previously neglected areas. Fox introduced twenty-eight operas to Chicago, but with a strong Italian bias. Six of them were works by Verdi. Krainik extended the repertory to include a variety of styles and periods—the days when the Civic Opera House might be regarded as "La Scala West" had ended. The Lyric was a truly international house, a sophisticated and cosmopolitan opera producer, drawing on a wide range of music. Verdi remained the most popular composer in terms of the number of works in the repertory (sixteen operas, nine of them in the top twenty), but Puccini was the composer of the most popular operas.

Krainik selected for revival eighteen operas that had been heard in the city previously but had never been produced by the Lyric. She added to these works thirty scores that received Lyric (if not world) premières. The distribution in this group is eight American, five Austro-German, six Italian, five baroque, three Russian, one French, and two Czech operas. This is the sort of fare one expects from an opera company taking a wide world-view of composers and styles. She also produced the works written in the composer-in-residence program.

Here is the growth of the repertory under Krainik, including posthumous contributions (asterisks indicate operas that had been heard in the city from earlier producers):

Argento—*The Voyage of Edgar Allan Poe*
Barber—*Antony and Cleopatra*
Bellini—*I Capuleti e i Montecchi*
  *La sonnambula**
Berg—*Lulu**
Berio—*Un re in ascolto*
Bernstein—*Candide*
Bizet—*The Pearl Fishers**
Bolcom—*McTeague*
  A View from the Bridge
Corigliano—*The Ghosts of Versailles*
Delibes—*Lakmé**
Donizetti—*Anna Bolena*
Floyd—*Susannah**
Glass—*Satyagraha*
Gluck—*Alceste*
Gounod—*Romeo and Juliet**
Handel—*Alcina*
  Orlando
  Samson
  Xerxes
Janáček—*Kátya Kabanová*
  The Makropulos Affair
Lehár—*The Merry Widow**
Levy—*Mourning becomes Electra*
Menotti—*The Consul**
Mozart—*La clemenza di Tito*
  *The Abduction from the Seraglio**
Poulenc—*La Voix humaine*
Prokofiev—*The Gambler*
Puccini—*La rondine**
  *Suor Angelica** (complete *Il trittico*)
Rossini—*Otello*
  Tancredi
Shostakovich—*Lady Macbeth of Mtsensk*
Smetana—*The Bartered Bride**
J. Strauss—*Die Fledermaus**
R. Strauss—*Arabella*
  Capriccio
  Die Frau ohne Schatten
Stravinsky—*The Rake's Progress*
Sullivan—*The Mikado**
Tchaikovsky—*Eugene Onegin**
Thomas—*Hamlet**
Verdi—*Ernani**
  Luisa Miller
Wagner—*Parsifal**
Weill—*The Rise and Fall of the City of Mahagonny*

The "Toward the 21st Century" project committed the company to offer one American opera and one European opera of the twentieth century each year from 1990 through the decade. The Lyric thus accepted an obligation to the American composer unmatched by any other major American opera producer, and it met it with strong works in forceful stagings that won unusually strong audience support. Fox could not have undertaken such a project, because she was unfamiliar with American music and apparently had no wish to do anything about it. Danny Newman occasionally suggests that in a way the demand that one subscribe forces individuals to buy tickets to operas they really aren't terribly eager to hear and would not support on a single-ticket basis. The counterargument is that if too many unpopular works are offered, the number of subscribers will decline. The success of subscription sales during the "Toward the 21st Century" project suggests that, although some may have objected to one or another new work, the Lyric public as a whole welcomed this expansion of the repertory.

One might have hoped that the European operas would all be relatively new as well, but new work was intermixed with important scores offered in earlier seasons. Hindemith and Schoenberg await inclusion in the Lyric repertory, yet one feels that past sins of omission are being atoned for.

The existence of a composer-in-residence program and the production (by the Lyric's Center for American Artists) of the new works produced by the project is a further demonstration of confidence that the United States can be not merely an opera-consuming nation but can produce operas as well. With Shulamit Ran's *Between Two Worlds (The Dybbuk)* in 1997 the program had produced a score that major opera theaters throughout the world might consider for presentation.

Clearly an essential for more rapid repertory growth would be a lengthened season offering nine or even ten operas instead of the present eight. The question is when the Lyric management will feel free to do this. The issue is more economic than artistic. The Lyric is reluctant to depart from a conservative fiscal policy that has brought it years of security, and change will require two things: confidence that the needed funds can be raised, and strong public demand for more works and more performances.

14

Paying the Bills
and Broadening the Audience

Who is going to support opera twenty years from now? Rising operating costs and, concurrently, rising ticket prices are the main problems opera companies face today with ever increasing intensity. At the same time, society is changing. Audiences are diluted by a myriad of entertainment choices (mostly from the mass media), many of which may be experienced without ever having to leave one's home. Lack of music education in schools leads to less cognizance of operatic and other classical music art forms in young people's early musical experience. These are but a few of the problems facing people and institutions presenting the unique and enriching experiences these art forms offer.

In the nineteenth century it was hoped that classical music might pay its way. Such hopes were frequently disappointed, and in our time they seem completely beyond reach.

In the early 1920s touring allowed resident Chicago opera to break even, because every city visited was required to form a group of guarantors who pledged $15,000 per performance to underwrite any deficits. Thus one views the extensive activities of Chicago companies on the road, 1,225 performances in seventy-nine cities in the period 1910–1929, and realizes that it made sense economically to go to Wichita Falls, Texas, in 1928 with the odd mixture of *Aida* and *Risurrezione*. New York got the most performances, 215, and for a few years the old pattern was reversed and Manhattan was at least partly dependent on Chicago for opera. Along with the Mary Garden vehicles, they heard *The Love for Three Oranges*, which has yet to be staged at the Met.

But in the Auditorium, for all its seats, and later in the new Civic Opera House, Chicago companies were facing financial problems. Early in the twentieth century, when subsidy became essential for survival, opera was taken over by the "swells," as Upton called them. The myth (rampant social Darwinism) was that the very rich were not merely economically superior but culturally superior as well; the vile bourgeoisie had inferior taste. Actually the middle class had been the primary support of all types of theater for 150 years, which is why it is important today that the Lyric not price itself out of the purchasing power of this group.

In the early years of the twentieth century, the difference between box office income and production costs required a higher level of subsidy than the swells could provide. Thus in 1914 and 1921 Chicago opera companies went under; in 1931 two failed (at Ravinia and downtown). A series of short-lived companies followed in 1933–1934, 1935–1939, and 1940–1946.

From its first season, the Lyric Opera has been deeply concerned with survival. Carol Fox had been both president and general manager of Lyric Theater. After 1956 she was general manager under a board of directors. The Lyric was fortunate in this crucial decade to have a board that offered the strongest type of leadership. Thomas I. Underwood was the president in 1956. He was succeeded in 1957/58 by Leonard Spacek, who passed the office to Alfred C. Stepan Jr. from 1959 to 1961. Stepan was a bold leader, as was his successor, J. W. Van Gorkom, who held the post in 1962/63. In 1964 Van Gorkom became chairman, and the presidency went to Daggett Harvey. It was a powerful management combination that more or less insured the survival of the company in the following decade. In 1970 Harvey succeeded Van Gorkom as chairman, and Edward F. Blettner became president. In 1974 Blettner became chairman. T. M. Thompson was the president from 1972 to 1976, and he was succeeded by William F. North, then William O. Beers.

There appeared to be three keys to economic security. First, box office income had to be maximized. There were 3,563 seats in the Civic Opera House, and every one that went unsold symbolized an unacceptable financial loss. Second, production costs had to be kept to a minimum consistent with artistic quality. Third, management costs had to be firmly controlled, and this, it proved, was the Lyric's greatest area of weakness.

Preparing an opera for the stage was a capital investment, a manufacturing operation, and, as in any factory, good management meant you produced the product as inexpensively as possible and then sold all the product the market would buy. From the beginning the Lyric has estimated the potential market for its product in a highly conservative manner. The dollar lost from overproduction proved more frightening than the dollar lost from underproduction. The ticket you might have sold but didn't have to sell was less of a worry than the ticket you had to sell but could not.

This led to the realization in the late 1950s that the market for the product, the Chicago operatic audience, had to expand. The days in which an opera was staged for two or three performances had to end. A well-produced opera ought to fill the house ten times. This permitted productions of unusually high quality within an acceptable ratio of box office income to production costs.

In its early seasons the Lyric walked a tightrope very carefully. It certainly did not want to alienate or offend the city's traditional operagoers, the rich. Their support in the form of ticket sales and philanthropic gifts was essential. On the other hand, the Lyric was socially the most open of all the opera companies the city had seen; anyone who was interested could participate. Unlike some of its predecessors, the Lyric was not anti-Semitic. Jewish subscribers and Jewish patrons were welcomed along with the old-money WASPs. Ironically, for all her devotion to Italy, Fox made little effort to involve Italian Americans—unless they had money. They found the Lyric for themselves, but one might have expected them to play a larger role. A special appeal was made to the black community by the engagement in leading roles of a succession of notable black singers. Leontyne Price was an established star in Chicago before her debut at the Metropolitan. One regrets that a larger black public did not respond to this call. The social penetration of the Lyric Opera into the black, Asian, and Latin components of Chicago's population remains superficial.

Opera subscription lists can be used for sociological research to a degree, but the sample is always changing because of factors that may have nothing to do with an interest in the opera company. Businesspersons are transferred to another city, students complete their studies and take a job elsewhere, a person can no longer afford to buy tickets, or an older subscriber dies. There are many reasons. What was important for the Lyric was that in its earliest seasons it won a core of persons who subscribed year after year, and, over the period of almost five decades, this group has consistently grown.

If in 1954 Chicago had an active operatic audience of about twelve thousand, one can estimate that at the close of the twentieth century that group had increased at least seven times, perhaps even as much as ten times. In relation to the population of the city this group was proportionately smaller than the audience of 1865, but, in terms of the city of the twentieth century, it was the largest, most affluent, and most loyal operatic audience Chicago had known.

How was it created? The Lyric had an advantage none of its predecessors enjoyed. In the day of the 78 rpm record, complete operatic recordings were bulky, heavy, expensive, and scarce. The arrival of the long-playing record in the late 1940s had made available a large number of complete operatic recordings in a compact format at an affordable price, and many persons had become familiar through records with an extensive operatic literature. When *I puritani* opened the 1955 season, it was by no means a totally unfamiliar work, even though it had not been heard in the city since 1883. Callas had recorded it three years before, and the album was well known. In short, a lot of people came to the new company to see staged presentations of operas they knew from recordings.

Moreover, the Lyric had attractive casts. The New York City Opera was a fine, professional organization, but it lacked the glamour of big international stars. Fox sensed that a comparable Chicago company was not called for. Glamour would sell tickets. It had for Mary Garden, and it would do so again.

An additional factor was word-of-mouth advertising. The early Lyric productions were exciting, possibly the most exciting form of theater many of those present had ever seen. Even experienced operagoers sensed a kind of vital energy that had rarely been present in past seasons.

Most of the women who joined the Guild were subscribers and forceful audience builders who encouraged their friends and neighbors to attend, taking a sometimes reluctant husband to the opera house and proving in many cases that the trip was worth the money and time.

The first ten Lyric seasons can be seen as an effort to establish a pattern of production that promised economic stability. The first two Lyric Theater seasons were financially stressful until all the bills could be paid, but in retrospect they had a very positive look. The 84% attendance of the first year was the lowest in the first decade of the company, but it was a cheap season to stage. Operating income covered 75% of operating costs, and the required level of subsidy was almost met by contributions. Some debts could be carried over, but the Lyric Theater debts of $112,000 were fully paid by 1957. In 1955 attendance was up to 89%, but production costs increased 111%; it was what one later came to see (in Dallas) as a typical Lawrence Kelly season. Fortunately, income was up by nearly $200,000, and the required level of subsidy was an acceptable 33%.

In the eight Lyric Opera seasons 1956–1963 under Fox's management there is a steady pattern of audience growth with attendance as high as 96% in 1962. One unsuccessful production could dip the figures significantly. In 1959 it was Janáček's *Jenůfa,* even though three of the critics praised it (one did not). In 1961 it was Giannini's *The Harvest,* commissioned under an ambitious Ford Foundation program to encourage American opera that did produce some notable works—but not in Chicago. Since the foundation was subsidizing the performances, Fox gave *The Harvest* four, when, it proved, two would have been ample. Here Danny Newman experienced his nightmare of the curtain rising on half empty houses. The operating income provided only 46% of the budget, raising the level of subsidy to 54%, the highest of the decade. Attendance in both 1959 and 1961 was 85%.

In 1958 the Metropolitan marked its seventy-fifth season, and the general manager Rudolf Bing announced, "There is no opera worth speaking of outside New York." This was viewed with outrage in both Chicago and San Francisco, where the seasons might not be as long as those at the Met but the artists and productions were often equal, if not finer, than the offerings of the New York house. Bing claimed he had been misquoted. Certainly Fox did not see herself as the head of an inconsequential provincial theater. She was experimenting to find the minimum number of productions consistent with high attendance. The number of productions dropped from thirteen in 1957 to eight in 1963, and as production overhead decreased the seasons slowly grew. In 1956 three operas were given a run of three performances, while the rest remained at two. By 1958 seven of eleven operas were being heard three times, and 72% of the budget came from the box office. So the next year two operas were increased to four performances, and for the last time only two were given two hearings. In 1960 nearly everything was heard three times; two operas had four stagings. By 1962 half the works of the season were being heard four times.

Producing the 1963 season cost $627,397, but there was $423,271 in operating income, and contributions and other income came to $234,879, leaving the company nearly $31,000 in the black. With 67% of the budget earned income, the balance had tipped in the direction of economic security.

In 1963, its tenth season, the Lyric was ready to establish the performance pattern it was to follow with slight modification for the next thirty-five years. The number of productions was down to eight (as in the current seasons), but the number of performances was up to thirty-two, the highest in the history of the company so far. Every opera was heard four times, sustaining four subscription series. The policy thereafter is simply stated: when possible, add performances and increase box office income, but be cautious about adding productions. In 1963 sellouts were the rule rather than the exception, and the season ended with attendance at nearly 97% of capacity.

In 1964 Fox decided to see if nine operas would go for four performances. In the spring of 1964 the annual report told the good news. Attendance was 90%, and box office and related income for the season was $936,027 against $1,218,819 in production costs and $225,755 in management overhead. This meant 64.7% of the budget came from the box office, and contributions of $558,944 left the company with a comfortable $50,399 surplus. The Lyric was functioning on an acceptable level of subsidy.

Fox came back in 1965 with nine more operas, two of them for five performances, another *(Wozzeck)* for three. Subscribers took 73% of the tickets, and overall attendance was almost 99% of capacity. For the first time the operating income of the company exceeded $1 million. A healthy 67% of the budget was earned income. In 1966 *La traviata* was heard seven times without an adverse effect on attendance, which was 97%. Eight other operas were heard at least four times. The box office produced 65% of the budget. This translated into $627,000, the largest amount an organization comparable to the Lyric had ever raised in Chicago to cover an operating deficit.

In 1968, when the Lyric resumed operations after its only dark year (see chapter 10), Carol Fox decided she could probably save money by cutting back her productions to eight, a pattern that was maintained from 1968 to 1974. This let her offer more performances of each opera without lengthening the season beyond a few nights. In 1975 she repeated this maneuver by cutting back to seven productions, the standard for the remainder of her tenure as general manager, with the exception of the reduced season in 1980. In 1985 Ardis Krainik restored the eight-production format, which (except for the 1986/87 and 1987/88 seasons, when nine productions were given) remained until the end of the century. Table 4 tells the story succinctly.

TABLE 4—NUMBER OF LYRIC OPERA PRODUCTIONS AND PERFORMANCES, BY YEAR

Year	Productions	Performances
1954	8	16
1960	10	29
1965	9	39
1970	8	49
1975	7	51
1980	6	43
1985	8	66
1990	8	65
1995	8	76
1999/2000	8	84

Attendance was 91% in 1968, 94% in 1969. Operating income produced nearly 62% of operating costs, but in 1969 it dropped to 58.6%. In 1970 attendance was 93% for forty-nine performances, and operating income produced 52.5% of the budget. This was within the generally accepted limits of fiscal responsibility, as was 52.8% in 1971, when 97% attendance could be maintained even though there were four more performances. But a $175,000 (round number) increase in operating income was wiped out by a $320,000 boost in operating costs. It happened again in 1972 when operating income went up, but so did operating costs, specifically a nearly $200,000 increase in management expenses. This time only 49.6% of the budget was covered by earned income.

In 1973, with the resale of returned tickets, the Lyric for the first time in its history had 102.4% attendance and close to $2 million in operating income, but expenses exceeded $4 million, and the ratio of earned income to expenses dropped to 45.9%. This turned out to be the best figure of this type for the decade. The Lyric had begun a slow, steady slide into bankruptcy.

The problem was the front office. Between 1970 and 1975 management cost increased by $750,000 (round number), from $502,823 to $1,250,193. By 1979 the figure was $2,148,317. In 1974 the Lyric's operating income was slightly under 40% of its budget. The following years the figure leveled out around 42%. But the production of Penderecki's *Paradise Lost* in 1978 brought disaster. Production costs were $6.7 million, and administrative costs exceeded $2 million. Operating income produced 35.5% of the budget. Due in part to the inflation under the Carter administration, this was now a deeply troubled opera company.

In retrospect, 1979 was a twenty-fifth birthday that nearly became a wake. When the balance sheet was revealed at the annual meeting in April 1980, the city learned that the company had ended the performances after a $600,000 overrun in the production budget and a $700,000 shortfall in its fund-raising. Operating income was $3.6 million, up $700,000 from the previous year, but it covered less than 42% of the budget. Administration costs again exceeded $2 million, and production expenses increased by $700,000 to $7.3 million. The company's reserves, the Lyric Opera Foundation, had to be raided for $1,315,000, leaving it with a trifle over $1 million in assets. A mortgage on the warehouse provided some working capital.

The only hope for the company was to reduce the level of its operations, and a shortened season was announced for 1980. It produced an impressive $3.5 million in operating income, about 43% of the budget, but administration was continuing to cost over $2 million a year, and production costs were now nearly 50% more than in 1975—in excess of $6 million. For the trustees, who had given a quarter century to the Lyric, this had to end. Pino Donati was dead, and Fox, on her own, had lost the ability to control expenses, making long-range budget planning impossible.

But before there could be a 1980 season, there had to be a new contract with the orchestra. In 1978, anticipating contract negotiations the following year, members of the Lyric orchestra prepared a report again advocating the extension of the season. The Metropolitan Opera orchestra had recently achieved the goal of year-round employment, and although their Lyric colleagues saw this as an unattainable objective, they saw (correctly) the present pattern of some fifty performances a year as far less than the city could be expected to support.

Analyzing the Lyric annual reports from 1964 to 1976, they found that orchestra costs ranged from 20% to nearly 30% of the company's earned income, depending on the number of performances played. The cost of stage directors and musical staff had more or less paralleled that of the orchestra, while expenses for stagehands, artists, and conductors had increased at a greater rate. But management costs had steadily risen and were now twice that of the first year of the study. The percentage of management costs at the Lyric was double that of the Metropolitan Opera. In fact, the Lyric had a management apparatus capable of handling a much longer season than the one actually produced.

The orchestra members were not the only ones concerned. Supporters of the company, who read annual reports, felt that the reason the company could not mount more new productions was not a lack of public support but a disturbing tendency to let travel and other incidental general expenses get out of hand. A tighter grip on budget controls seemed appropriate.

The core issue was presented by the Chicago Federation of Musicians when it began negotiations for the services of the orchestra in the seasons 1980–82. What was killing the Lyric was cost elephantiasis in Fox's front office. What was needed was a revision of priorities that reflected a budget that placed more emphasis on audience development and income-producing activities. This time talks dragged on past the February deadlines. In 1967, when the Lyric had canceled its season, it had had the resources to keep its staff alive, but a similar move in 1980 would require at least $1 million. Could private philanthropy be asked to raise money that did not go directly to producing opera?

Dramatic rescue came from a mayor who did not just accept an honorary title from the company but actually attended opening night. In March, Mayor Jane Byrne offered the company $200,000 for 1980 and 1981 and $300,000 in 1982, funds from the city hotel tax, on the condition that the Lyric present a short spring season. The Andrew W. Mellon Foundation gave $250,000, and the National Endowment for the Arts contributed nearly the same amount. The Joyce Foundation gave $165,000, and the Illinois Arts Council offered $27,000. It was enough to make a deal.

The 1980 orchestra negotiations demonstrated that one of the greatest advantages the Lyric Opera enjoys in its union contracts is that, unlike the Metropolitan, it can plan a flexible schedule with as little as one performance a week and five the practical maximum. The Met, bound to six evenings and a matinée, has no breathing time from September until May. The Lyric can take two weeks off at Christmas. Operas can be carefully rehearsed without requiring overtime services from the orchestra.

Autumn of 1981 was a new beginning with new management. It was an advantage that artistically the season had been planned by Fox, giving Krainik freedom to concentrate on financial problems. Once more seven operas were produced, and operating revenue exceeded $5 million, nearly 60% of the budget. The company was back on safe ground. The fiscal year ended with the bills carried over from 1980 paid, the Lyric Opera Foundation reestablished with assets of $456,000, and the Lyric in the black with a fund balance of $281,764. With Ardis Krainik in charge, that was the way it was going to be. She brought the Lyric two things essential for its survival and growth: a revitalized repertory and fiscal security.

It was known as the miracle year, and Krainik was called Wonder Woman after the protagonist of a popular comic-book superhero. Two factors cannot be forgotten. Fox had suffered severe physical disabilities in the final three years of her administration, and, what is more important, Krainik was a highly successful fund-raiser because it was easy to like her. She invited you to join with her in the pursuit of mutual goals. Fox gave the impression to many that she was estimating how successfully you could be exploited in the pursuit of her objectives.

Archie R. Boe was the new president, followed in 1983 by Angelo R. Arena. Then, in 1984, William B. Graham became president and proved the ideal partner for Krainik's rehabilitation of the company. It was impossible not to respond positively to Bill Graham and his charming wife, and if he asked you for money it was probably impossible to say no. Quickly he made a place for himself, not only as one of the major benefactors of the company (the Green Room, the private restaurant and bar for major contributors, is now named in his honor) but one of the city's great philanthropists. After he stepped down in 1991, James W. Cozad and (after 1996) Edgar D. Jannotta held the presidency for the balance of the decade.

The following year introduced a pattern of strong, steady growth that was to continue through Krainik's final season, 1996/97. It began with a period in which, predictably, every year established new records for subscription sales, box office income, and fund-raising. This was the result of two things. First, and most important, was the consistent artistic interest and quality of the productions. But, second, Krainik and her associates were far more adept at handling money matters than Fox had been. It must be mentioned, too, that the Lyric, with rare exceptions, was receiving very good press.

In 1982 nearly $6.5 million of operating revenue produced close to 66% of the operating budget, a ratio that was to be maintained—with annual variations of a point or two—through the Krainik regime. Contributions covered the deficit and left a fund balance of more than $1 million at the close of the fiscal year. When the books were closed for the 1983 season, that figure was well over $2 million. And there was $3 million in fund balances after the autumn of 1984.

Krainik was ready to move forward. In 1985 she returned to a season with eight operas and increased the number of performances from fifty-four to sixty-six. This extended the season through the holidays into January, the first time that had happened in fifty-two years. Some twenty-five thousand subscribers took 80% of the tickets, and attendance was 92%. The 60% ratio between operating income and production costs was maintained, despite the increase in production. The 1986/87 season had more operas (nine productions), more performances, sold more

tickets, and won more praise than any other in Lyric's history. The Great Opera Fund, intended to provide the company with long-term financial security, raised more than $20 million.

The year 1987 brought an emphasis on selling more tickets and raising more money in a nine-opera season, sustained by an artistically remarkable series. Attendance was now nearly 96%, there were twenty-five hundred new subscribers, and the Great Opera Fund campaign closed with $26,555,957 raised— more than the initial $25 million goal. The overshoot in the Opera Fund campaign had caused a decline in contributions for the support of the 1986/87 season, resulting in a $997,446 deficit, covered by reserve funds. In 1987/88 the red ink was replaced by a surplus of $1.4 million. "We did it," Krainik reported at the annual meeting, "by selling more tickets than ever before, by raising more contributions than ever before, and by controlling costs more ruthlessly than ever before." Artistic quality remained as high as ever, and attendance was 96%.

The miraculous number—100% attendance— achieved briefly in 1973, returned (and, as it proved, returned to stay) in the 1988/89 season. Attendance was to swing between 100% and somewhat over 103% for the rest of the century. It must be explained how the Lyric arrives at this figure. Attendance can be measured in terms of the number of seats sold, or it can be measured by the box office income achieved in terms of the sum obtained by the sale of every seat. Thus 102% attendance does not mean that (because of ticket returns) 2% more seats than the capacity of the house were sold. Still less does it mean that every performance was played to a capacity audience. The resale of a relatively small number of the most expensive tickets will produce this figure. To translate the figure from dollars to people, one would have to know how the house is scaled in terms of ticket prices. It is statistically possible that in some of these 100%-plus seasons the company has, in fact, played to less than 100% of its possible audience.

In 1988/89 the Lyric went back to eight productions per season (a pattern that survives today), but all past records were broken for subscription sales (28,600), box office income ($9.5 million), and contributions (over $7 million). The thirty-fifth anniversary season closed the decade with further gains: 3,400 more subscribers, more than $10 million in ticket sales, and more than $8 million in contributions.

The annual meeting in June 1991 marked Krainik's tenth year as general director of the company and William B. Graham's election to an eighth term as president of the board. With a decade of historical perspective, we see them as the most influential management combination in the history of the company. The pattern of growth continued. There were now 32,500 subscribers, and box office income exceeded $11 million. Interest and investment income had been part of the Lyric's balance sheet since 1981, but it had now reached an impressive level of $1.5 million. With this advantage, only a third of the budget had to come from contributors.

At the close of the 1991/92 season Krainik announced triumphantly that "every ticket was gone before we even opened the season." Attendance of 253,841 exceeded 100% capacity, and fund-raising exceeded $9 million. On this high note, Graham yielded the presidency to James W. Cozad. Reviewing the 1992/93 season, Krainik announced with deserved satisfaction that the number of subscribers, now 33,800, had increased 35% in five years. And the annual campaign brought in $10 million this time, a level that was to be sustained for three years.

In April 1993 Cozad announced a campaign entitled "Building on Greatness: An Opera House for the 21st Century" to raise $100 million for the purchase and extensive renovation of the Civic Opera House. Half of the money was to come from the Chicago Symphony Orchestra and the Lyric Opera of Chicago Facilities Fund, headed by John H. Bryan. A complex purchase agreement with Travelers Insurance had been signed. "We know of no other major performing arts facility in the world that shares ownership of a major office building," Cozad observed.

Krainik felt that the 1992/93 season, culminating in the purchase of the theater, was the happiest year of her professional life. All the figures were up: 33,800 subscribers, an increase of more than 1,000 from the previous year; attendance over 100% (102.7%) for the fifth consecutive year; and more than $14 million in box office receipts. Investment income exceeded $2 million.

In 1993/94, as Krainik marked her fortieth year with the Lyric Opera, 2,500 more subscribers were added to the list, attendance was 103.2%, and box office receipts exceeded $15 million. Bonds with a value of $62 million were successfully sold to guarantee the availability of funds for the renovation of the theater. A year later, when the report for 1994/95 was in, the ranks of subscribers had risen to 37,400,

marking a 50% increase in subscriptions since 1986. Nearly $17 million was earned by ticket sales.

The crucial balance sheet was to be the one for 1995/96, the year of the *Ring* cycle. Total revenues came to slightly more than $31 million, as opposed to $42.6 million in expenses. In a year of unusually high expenses, the company had secured 66% of its operating budget through the box office and had nearly $3 million of investment income. It was the longest season in the Lyric's history, ninety-one performances, yielding nearly $21 million at the box office. On this note of triumph, after sixteen years as general director (and forty-two years with the company), Krainik stepped down because of her illness. The annual meeting of July 10, 1996, was her last. It was announced that the auditorium of the Civic Opera House would be named in her honor.

Krainik was to die midway into the 1996/97 season, but the fiscal affairs of the company were unshaken by the event. Attendance again exceeded 100%, and ticket sales of more than $19 million and other income paid 65% of the operating expenses. In 1997/98, William Mason's first full year as general director, subscription sales reached a new high, 38,000, attendance was 103.3%, and this time 69% of operating expenses were covered by income. A smooth transition had been made, and later reports produced very much the same figures. No other performing arts company in the world could match the Lyric's record of completely sold-out houses, year after year.

In the 1989 season, when 100% attendance began, the Lyric regretted that thirty-two thousand prospective purchasers of single tickets had to be turned away. The "slothful, fickle, single ticket buyer," in Danny Newman's celebrated phrase, was further rejected by the policy that, when single tickets were available, Lyric contributors and subscribers had first priority in purchasing them.

But thirty-two thousand persons are enough to fill the opera house nine times, and even the most conservative thinkers at the Lyric had to recognize that an opportunity for expansion was at hand. Between 1990 and 1999 the audience grew by more than twenty performances without any increase in the number of productions. Along the way the Lyric offered stopgap measures, for example, the 1993 production of *Tosca,* which sold out before the season opened and was given an extra, nonsubscription performance that—surely to no one's surprise—sold out as well.

As the Lyric management has come to see it, ideally the racks in the box office will be cleaned out for the season before opening night, and thereafter only returned tickets will be available. In theory, this—among other things—liberates the company from spending money for newspaper advertising during the season. Danny Newman deplores the thousands of dollars the Metropolitan spends to advertise the tickets it has to sell, but the Met regards these ads as an essential communications link with the public. Free listings in newspaper guide sections cannot replace them. And, as time has passed, the Lyric has found itself with unsold tickets that required advertising and mail promotion to stimulate sales.

From the twice-sold seats came the annual celebration of attendance in excess of 100%. On a night with superstars there may be few returns; it is not uncommon to see a significant number of persons waiting in vain at the box office for seats—especially seats they can afford. On a night with an unfamiliar opera there may be quite a number of returns. The company insists that it studies this matter carefully, that most of the time persons who come to the box office the evening of the performance armed with enough money (at this writing, an amount of as much as $175 may be required) will get a ticket. But this works because the musical public as a whole has taken the attitude (reinforced by the Lyric's marketing techniques) that admission is so improbable that it is not worth the effort to try to attend. The practical consequences are that some of the returned tickets, especially the most expensive, go unsold.

In my dissenting view the Lyric in its forty-fifth season had become the worst thing it might be, a private club for its subscribers. In 1999 the median individual income in the United States was $33,000, and an opera subscription became a luxury, requiring economies in other areas. The long-term policy of calculated underproduction, added to the unyielding emphasis on subscription, has produced financial security, but at a price that may be harmful to the long-range interests of the company. As of this writing, the Lyric has 757 upper-balcony seats for sale, but about 640 of them will be retained by current subscribers. In short, only a few more than a hundred persons will be able to enter the subscription ranks in the lowest price brackets.

The Lyric, wisely and by choice, makes no effort to challenge the Metropolitan in the scale of its operations. On many occasions it has demonstrated that it can achieve artistic results equal to the older company and, indeed, any major opera producer in the world. But the Metropolitan finds 93% attendance satisfactory, and considers a few unsold tickets (many of them standing room—which the Lyric cannot offer) the price it must pay to have tickets available for visitors to New York and New Yorkers who, for one or another reason, cannot subscribe. Subscription at 100% may offer ultimate financial security, but at the cost of withdrawal from the community. As the Lyric moves toward its fiftieth anniversary, the most hopeful sign in regard to its subscription policies is that it is increasing the annual number and diversity of its shorter subscription series, thus allowing previous subscribers to lock in availability of less than the full season if they wish to do so and, what is perhaps more important, allowing more would-be patrons to find availabilities.

The Lyric has taken the theories of Danny Newman to a *reductio ad absurdum*. A season that is 100% subscribed, offering ultimate financial security and ultimate protection from executioner critics, does so at the cost of withdrawal from the community. Today at the Lyric it is not "subscribe now" but "subscribe or else." The envelope of a May 2000 subscription brochure threatens, "Subscribers get 90% of all Lyric seats. Getting into the Lyric's fabulous 2000/2001 season is going to be a close shave . . . subscribe now." Threats of this type are tasteless and coercive, especially when there are probably many who would like to subscribe but cannot afford the available seats.

The Metropolitan encourages subscriptions by offering some twenty "trios" (packages of three operas) with the thought that in time one may well wish to move up to a longer series. The series are carefully selected to give a full sample of the season repertory.

In the few years preceding the publication of this book, Lyric slowly but greatly expanded its offerings of partial subscriptions, and in fact now offers packages of four, five, six, and seven, or all eight operas of their seasons. Still, I feel that the company, without significant risk, could add one or more performances of each work and rearrange its subscription series to allow for more single ticket sales. The Newman philosophy objects to fragmentizing subscriptions: a trio of *Carmen, Tosca,* and *Aida* might sell, but a trio containing a "dog" opera like *The Queen of Spades* or *Jenůfa* would be difficult to move, leaving empty seats. I disagree. Ideas of what would and would not sell forty years ago do not hold for the interests of the contemporary audience. Unfamiliar operas must be effectively merchandised, but this is one of the basic tasks of any major opera producer today.

Newman estimates that about 30,000 tickets will remain, roughly 350 a performance, after the subscription ranks have closed for the season. Few of these will represent the cheapest seats or the most popular operas. And perhaps half will never get to the box office but will be taken by subscribers and contributors—who have first claim on them—for friends and guests.

In the long-term view, an important loss produced by a lack of tickets is the alienation of local editors and promoters of tourism. An arts editor is not going to give much space to performances that readers will find difficult, if not impossible, to attend. People come to New York with, among other expectations, the wish to hear the Metropolitan Opera, and the company tries to make this possible. Visitors to Chicago are not encouraged to have many hopes about seeing a Lyric performance. The basic question is whether, putting vanity aside, the Lyric today needs to maximize box office income. From all appearances it has sufficient depth of financial security that it is not essential to maintain 100% attendance. The wisdom of the Metropolitan's policy should be recognized. There should be a cap of 80–85% on the level to which the house can be subscribed. This will put tickets in the box office. Instead of announcing two weeks before opening night that the house has been sold out through March, I would like to see a big ad in the Sunday papers saying, "We have great shows, and we have tickets for sale." A period of readjustment and reeducation would be necessary before the public would respond fully, but if the productions are good and the promotion is strong, the seats will sell.

This would deal with the present paradox in the Lyric operations: the company expends considerable efforts to make young people become interested in opera but fails to face the issue of how they are to attend opera in early adulthood. Sociologists tell us that most individuals have established a pattern of attendance at performing arts events by the time they are thirty-five. I am thinking of myself, the typical impoverished undergraduate, in my early years of operagoing. Sustaining my interest demanded that I have reasonable opportunities to hear opera, which meant the ability to buy a ticket I could afford in advance of the performance date. In the 1940s this was possible. With the Lyric today, that would be difficult. Young Bill Mason was attracted to opera attending one of Harry Zelzer's New York City Opera productions. Zelzer had no subscribers and made money even though he rarely was completely sold out. If a Bill Mason of today wanted to hear something at the Lyric, would he get in?

The Lyric's "Operareach 2000" program has the noble goal of providing "opportunities for people of all ages and all backgrounds to experience opera and to provide performance activities which will assure . . . the maximum benefits from [a] visit to the Opera House. These efforts will work in two directions: to take opera to the community, and to bring the community to the Opera House."

The Lyric has had reduced-price performances for high-school and college students for many years, and at this writing is rapidly moving toward expanding this program to include four performances per year to reach an audience of fourteen thousand students annually. This is excellent for those who are able to participate. Free tickets are provided to five thousand senior citizens each season through the Chicago Department on Aging and Disability, and the Lyric Opera Center for American Artists has reached thousands through its appearances in the free summer concerts of the Grant Park Symphony Orchestra (although this is hardly the same as opera in a theater).

Much of the outreach program offers something quite different from what happens on the stage of the Opera House. It is encouraging that in 1998, as part of the "Opera in the Neighborhoods" program, more than twelve thousand city and suburban children saw an English-language version of *The Barber of Seville*. Representing a diversity of performers as well as audience, the cast was listed as "four young African-American and Caucasian singers." Teachers and listeners had been primed in advance with study guides. The singers were in costume, there was a set, and there was piano accompaniment. It is hoped that in time the program will reach twenty thousand students a year. A parallel program casts singers from the Lyric Center in performances of opera in English for a somewhat older age group.

Other elements of the outreach program include the availability of preview materials and lectures (live and on cassettes). The question remains as to how much impact these services have. Only slightly more than 1% of the Lyric audience makes use of the libretto service, perhaps 3% encounter the lectures available on cassettes, and less than 1% attends the preview lectures.

A vital task in Lyric's future is assuring that their outreach attempts result in new audiences, audiences composed of people who are sufficiently touched by this exposure to the art form to take the next step: to buy tickets on their own to see and hear performances in Lyric's main season.

The Lyric can claim no greater achievement than building the largest, best-informed, most appreciative operatic audience the city has known in 130 years. But audiences must be renewed constantly, and one might question whether that renewal is presently taking place on an appropriate scale. I am less sure than I would like to be of Lyric's future, when much of the current audience will be gone. Are an appropriate number of younger people waiting to replace it? The company reports that its subscription audience changes by roughly 10% annually, but can one take for granted that this will continue? The answer might well lie in the present and future demographics of the city.

On the other hand, Chicago has risen, phoenix-like, from a number of calamities on the operatic scene: the destruction of multiple opera theaters by fire, the outmoded idea of opera as entertainment for an elite few, and a string of failed opera companies in the city's past. None of those setbacks quelled either Chicago's interest in, or broad support of, the operatic art form over the past 150 years. Chicago's motto *I Will* seems to work on many levels.

Certainly the Lyric's first 50 years have resulted in more opera being played to more audiences in both number and diversity than Chicago ever experienced previously, and the company has spurred and built on the growing realization of opera as a complete musical and dramatic art form. One can only hope for the enriching experience of a Chicago operatic future of continuity and expansion. Here's to the next 150 years of opera in Chicago!

Overview of Chicago Opera Staging Organizations

CHICAGO GRAND OPERA COMPANY (I) produced four seasons at the Auditorium, 1910–1913.

CHICAGO OPERA ASSOCIATION produced seven seasons at the Auditorium, 1915–1921.

RAVINIA OPERA produced twenty summer seasons at Ravinia Park, 1912–1931.

CHICAGO CIVIC OPERA produced seven seasons at the Auditorium, 1922–1928, and three seasons at the Civic Opera House, 1929–1931.

CHICAGO GRAND OPERA COMPANY (II) produced three seasons at the Civic Opera House, 1933–1935.

CHICAGO CITY OPERA COMPANY produced four seasons at the Civic Opera House, 1936–1939.

CHICAGO OPERA COMPANY produced six seasons at the Civic Opera House, 1940–1946.

CHICAGO SYMPHONY ORCHESTRA produced one performance at the Civic Opera House, 1947.

LYRIC THEATER, begun in 1954—after 1956 **LYRIC OPERA OF CHICAGO**—celebrated its fiftieth-anniversary season in 2004–2005. All performances at the Civic Opera House.

CHICAGO OPERA STUDIO, INC.—after 1978 **CHICAGO OPERA THEATER**—performed at Jones Commercial High School and Mandel Hall of the University of Chicago, 1974–1977; (mainly) at the Athenaeum Theater, 1978–2003 (there were performances for a few years, starting in 1995, at the Merle Reskin Theatre); and at the Joan W. and Irving B. Harris Theater for Music and Dance, beginning in 2004.

There were no opera seasons by a resident company in the autumn of 1914, 1932, 1943, 1948, 1949, 1950, 1951, 1952, 1953, and 1967.

Annals of Opera in Chicago, 1850–2005

Preface

Opera has been produced in Chicago since 1850. Covered here is what is seen as 155 seasons: 1850–1851 to 2004–2005. A season is defined as the period from July 1 through June 30 of the following year. An exception has been made for the summer performances of the Ravinia Opera. In this period (1912–1931) the season begins in June. And there are exceptions when a company (most notably the Chicago Opera Theater) begins its season in June and the season extends into the next month or two. (Notation has been made of which Chicago Opera Theater performances were matinées whenever that information was available to the compilers.) Lyric Opera of Chicago (which began as Lyric Theater in 1954) seasons are numbered in parentheses alongside the listing of the company name in each season of the annals.

In the **Index** readers can go to the listing for the opera that interests them, and they will find all the seasons in which it was heard. They can then turn to the listings in the **Annals** for these seasons to find additional detail. An opera may have been produced by more than one company in a given season.

Editors delight in consistency in style, but English usage is not determined by editors. With respect to operas in languages other than English, there is no consistency in usage. Operas with titles in Slavic languages are invariably translated into English under the assumption that these languages are little known outside the countries in which they are spoken. But with Italian operas usage can be wonderfully inconsistent. No one talks about *The Troubador*—it is *Il trovatore*. But

The Barber of Seville is heard far more frequently than *Il barbiere di Siviglia*. The operas of Mozart are written to texts in Italian and German, and usage mixes these languages with English. *Così fan tutte* generally is regarded as untranslatable, but it is *The Magic Flute* rather than *Die Zauberflöte*. When it appears useful, the original language is provided. Works that are part of the general culture in English-speaking countries—*Cinderella* and *Romeo and Juliet*, for example—when made into operas, need not appear in French or Italian spellings.

In the Index, light operas with the date of the first performance given in parentheses are not listed again unless they enter the repertory of a major opera company. The unbracketed date is the first performance under operatic auspices.

It should be noted that it is impossible to list all the operatic performances in Chicago since 1850. The needed sources do not exist, especially for ethnic and nonprofessional companies. What is found here—I hope nearly complete—are performances by major professional opera-producing groups that were heard in the central city or, for twenty years, at Ravinia. As much as possible this list has been compiled from primary sources, theater programs, and announcements in the press. It should also be mentioned that over the years press coverage of operatic productions has by no means been consistent or comprehensive. Student performances by the Lyric Opera of Chicago are not included.

These Annals do not include cast listings. The Selected Bibliography section of this volume lists several publications in which such information can be found, such as that by authors Cropsey, David, and Moore, as well as the Lyric Opera. The Lyric Opera's website may also be helpful.

Index

Composer—Title—Performances, by Season

Britten	*Albert Herring*	129/139
	Billy Budd	121/152
	Death in Venice	154
	A Midsummer Night's Dream	155
	Peter Grimes	125/128/149
	The Rape of Lucretia	97/98/117/152
	The Turn of the Screw	137/153
Buchalter	*A Lovers' Knot*	66
Cadman	*The Sunset Trail*	78
	A Witch of Salem	77/78
Catalani	*Loreley*	69/78
Charpentier	*Louise*	61/63/64/66/67/68/ 70/73/74/75/76/78/ 80/81/82/89/90
Ching	*Buoso's Ghost*	150
Cilea	*Adriana Lecouvreur*	108
Cimarosa	*Il matrimonio segreto*	91
Copland	*The Tender Land*	145
Corigliano	*The Ghosts of Versailles*	146
Cornelius	*Der Barbier von Baghdad*	40/41
Damrosch	*The Man without a Country*	88
Dargo-mïzhsky	*Rusalka (The Water Nymph)*	72/73
Davies	*The Lighthouse*	140
Davis	*Amistad*	148
Davy	*Rob Roy MacGregor*	10
De Banfield	*Lord Byron's Love Letter*	106
Debussy	*Pelléas et Mélisande*	61/68/70/72/75/76/ 79/80/81/95/96/99/ 103/123/143
De Koven	*Rip Van Winkle*	70
Delibes	*Lakmé*	37/40/60/68/69/70/ 71/73/75/76/79/ 80/81/95/96/134/140

Deller	*Il maestro di cappella*	60
Donizetti	*Anna Bolena*	136
	The Daughter of the Regiment (La Fille du régiment)	9/10/15/18/19/23/ 30/53/77/92/124/ 132
	Don Pasquale	11/15/17/18/28/53/ 56/58/70/71/72/76/ 77/79/80/114/119/ 125/128/129/138/146
	Don Sebastiano	15
	L'elisir d'amore	9/16/17/20/34/60/ 70/71/72/73/74/75/ 76/77/79/87/100/ 106/113/128/132/ 135/142/150
	La favorita	9/13/15/16/17/23/ 28/29/31/34/49/ 115/125
	Linda di Chamounix	15/18/23/30/31/35/ 40/69/71/78
	Lucia di Lammermoor	4/9/10/13/14/15/ 16/17/18/20/24/25/ 26/27/28/29/30/31/ 32/34/35/36/40/44/ 45/46/49/50/51/55/ 57/58/59/60/61/62/ 63/64/66/67/68/69/ 70/71/72/73/74/75/ 76/77/78/79/80/81/ 82/84/86/88/89/90/ 93/95/96/97/98/ 104/105/108/112/ 121/126/137/141/ 154
	Lucrezia Borgia	9/10/13/14/15/16/ 17/18/28
	Maria Stuarda	124
	Poliuto	10/13/15/16
Eichberg	*The Doctor of Alcantara*	18/19/23
d'Erlanger	*Noël*	63
Erlanger	*Aphrodite*	71
Falla	*La vida breve*	77/78/80/81/82
	El amor brujo (ballet with song)	120
Février	*Gismonda*	69
	Monna Vanna	64/66/68/69/70/71/ 72/74/78

Offenbach	*Ba-ta-clan*	(19)	**Puccini**	*La bohème*	49/57/58/59/60/61/
	Barbe-bleue	22/23			63/65/66/67/68/69/
	La belle Hélène	18/19/22/23			70/71/72/73/74/75/
	Les Brigands	22/23			76/77/78/79/80/82/
	Geneviève de Brabant	19/23			84/85/87/88/89/90/
	La Grande Duchesse	18/19/22/23/147			91/92/93/94/95/97/
	de Gérolstein				98/99/100/101/102/
	Le Mariage aux lanternes	(19)			103/104/105/106/
	Orphée aux enfers	(18)			107/108/111/113/
	(Orpheus in the Underworld)				115/116/117/123/
	La Périchole	22/23/107/130			124/130/134/137/
	Robinson Crusoé	(19)			143/145/148/152
	Le "66"	(19)		*La fanciulla del West*	61/64/73/107/
	The Tales of Hoffmann	61/63/64/65/66/67/			29/141
	(Les Contes d'Hoffmann)	68/69/70/71/73/		*Madama Butterfly*	57/59/60/61/64/65/
		74/75/76/77/78/79/			66/67/68/69/70/71/
		80/81/82/84/89/93/			72/73/74/75/76/77/
		94/100/102/127/133/			78/80/81/82/84/85/
		149			86/87/88/89/90/91/
	La Vie parisienne	(19)			92/97/98/99/100/
					101/102/103/104/
Orff	*Carmina Burana*	116			105/106/107/108/
	(vocal and ballet)				109/111/112/113/
					115/116/135/141/
Paderewski	*Manru*	52			142/145/148/154
				Manon Lescaut	63/76/77/80/81/82/
Paër	*Il maestro di cappella*	74			108/119/128
				La rondine	80/81/82/131/136
Paisiello	*The Barber of Seville*	130		*Tosca*	51/54/56/57/61/63/
	(Il barbiere di Siviglia)				64/67/68/69/70/71/
					72/73/74/75/76/77/
Parelli	*A Lovers' Quarrel*	63/64/66			78/79/80/81/82/84/
	(I dispettosi amanti)				85/86/88/89/90/91/
					92/93/94/95/96/97/
Penderecki	*Paradise Lost*	129			98/99/100/101/103/
					104/105/107/108/
Pergolesi	*La serva padrona*	98			111/112/113/115/
					118/119/122/124/
Planquette	*The Chimes of Normandy*	28/29/30/31			127/133/138/140/
	(Les Cloches de Corneville)				144/151/155
				Il trittico (all three operas)	70/147
Ponchielli	*La Gioconda*	34/55/57/58/60/64/		*Gianni Schicchi* (only)	77/78/87/107/109/
		66/69/75/78/80/			121/150
		82/84/88/89/96/97/		*Suor Angelica* (only)	(no separate
		108/110/117/137/			performance)
		149		*Il tabarro* (only)	106
				Turandot	84/85/86/89/101/
Poulenc	*La Voix humaine*	133			109/110/111/121/
					142/144
Prokofiev	*Angel of Fire*	117			
	The Gambler	142	**Rabaud**	*Mârouf*	79/80/81/82
	The Love for Three Oranges	72/100/101/102/			
		103/127/130	**Ran**	*Between Two Worlds*	147
				(The Dybbuk)	

		49/50/51/52/54/56/ 58/60/62/63/65/67/ 71/72/73/74/75/76/ 77/78/79/80/81/82/ 84/85/86/88/89/92/ 95/97/98			Die Walküre	90/91/93/94/97/98/ 109/130/133/150 35/39/40/41/42/45/ 46/48/49/50/52/ 53/54/58/59/60/62/ 63/64/67/71/73/ 74/76/79/80/81/87/ 88/90/91/95/96/ 107/111/123/144/ 146/153/155
	Die Meistersinger	39/40/41/42/45/46/ 48/53/55/59/60/74/ 81/82/89/95/100/ 128/136/149				
	Parsifal	55/59/60/64/66/67/ 73/82/94/96/137/ 152		**Wallace**	Lurline	21
					Maritana	10/16/18/19/20/ 21/23/24/25/27/ 29/31/68
	Rienzi	36				
	Der Ring des Nibelungen (complete cycles)	39/52/66/67/74/79/ 80/146/155				
	"Short" Ring (without Das Rheingold)	41/46/53/54		**Ward**	The Crucible	35
	Das Rheingold	39/66/67/69/74/79/ 80/122/143/146/155		**Weber**	Der Freischütz	9/15/16/19/20/21/ 28/35/42/46
	Siegfried	39/41/42/45/46/47/ 48/49/52/53/54/66/ 67/74/79/80/124/ 145/146/154/155			Oberon	20/21
				Weill	The Rise and Fall of the City of Mahagonny	149
	Tannhäuser	15/21/35/36/39/41/ 42/44/45/46/47/48/ 49/50/51/52/54/56/ 57/66/67/71/72/74/ 75/78/80/81/85/86/ 87/88/90/93/94/96/ 114/139			Street Scene	110/152
				Wolf-Ferrari	The Jewels of the Madonna (I gioielli della Madonna)	62/63/64/65/66/68/ 71/72/75/77/78/ 81/86/91
					The Secret of Suzanne (Il segreto di Susanna)	62/63/65/66/67/68/ 69/70/71/72/73/ 74/75/80/81/82/83
	Tristan und Isolde	41/42/45/46/47/53/ 54/57/58/59/62/63/ 66/67/73/74/75/77/ 80/81/82/85/88/89/		**Zandonai**	Conchita	63/80
					Francesca da Rimini	67/68

Annals

1—1850–1851

BRIENTI, MANVERS, GIUBETTI ITALIAN
OPERA COMPANY
  Bellini: *La sonnambula* July 29/30

2—1851–1852 No opera

3—1852–1853 No opera

4—1853–1854

THE ARTISTS ASSOCIATION
  Donizetti: *Lucia di Lammermoor* Oct 27/Oct 31/Nov 3/Nov 5(?)
  Bellini: *Norma* Oct 28/Nov 1(?)/Nov 4(?)
  Bellini: *La sonnambula* Oct 29/Nov 2(?)/Nov 6(?)
  Rossini: *Stabat Mater* Nov 7

5—1854–1855 No opera

6—1855–1856 No opera

7—1856–1857 No opera

8—1857–1858 No opera

9—1858–1859

DURAND ENGLISH OPERA TROUPE OF NEW ORLEANS
  Bellini: *La sonnambula* Sept 27
  Donizetti: *The Daughter of the Regiment* Sept 28
  Auber: *The Crown Diamonds* Sept 29
  Rossini: *The Barber of Seville* Sept 30
  Balfe: *The Bohemian Girl* Oct 1/Oct 8
  Auber: *Fra Diavolo* Oct 2
  Rossini (probably): *La Cenerentola (Cinderella)* Oct 4/Oct 5
  Weber: *Der Freischütz* Oct 6
  Verdi: *Il trovatore* Oct 7

MAURICE STRAKOSCH OPERA COMPANY (New York)
  Donizetti: *Lucia di Lammermoor* Feb 21/Feb 24
  Donizetti: *Lucrezia Borgia* Feb 22
  Verdi: *La traviata* Feb 23
  Bellini: *I puritani* Feb 25
  Verdi: *Rigoletto* Feb 26
  Verdi: *Il trovatore* Feb 28/Mar 4
  Flotow: *Martha* Mar 1/Mar 3/Mar 7
  Bellini: *Norma* Mar 2
  Bellini: *La sonnambula* Mar 5
  Donizetti: *La favorita* Mar 8
  Mozart: *Don Giovanni* Mar 9/Mar 10

COOPER ENGLISH OPERA TROUPE
  Bellini: *La sonnambula* Apr 11/Apr 18/Apr 19
  Donizetti: *L'elisir d'amore* April 13
  Verdi: *Il trovatore* Apr 14/Apr 22
  Balfe: *The Bohemian Girl* Apr 16/Apr 20
  Haydn: *The Creation* Apr 17
  Donizetti: *Lucia di Lammermoor* Apr 12/Apr 21
  Donizetti: *The Daughter of the Regiment* Apr 15/Apr 23

10—1859–1860

COOPER ENGLISH OPERA TROUPE
  The troupe returned in July to repeat repertory from its previous run. Not reviewed in the *Tribune*.

ESCOTT AND MIRANDA ENGLISH OPERA TROUPE
  Balfe: *The Bohemian Girl* Dec 5
  Wallace: *Maritana* Dec 6
  Verdi: *Il trovatore* Dec 7/Dec 8
  Davy: *Rob Roy MacGregor* Dec 10/Dec 14
  Donizetti: *Lucia di Lammermoor* Dec 11
  Bellini: *La sonnambula* Dec 12
  Donizetti: *The Daughter of the Regiment* Dec 13
  Bishop: *Guy Mannering* Dec 15
  Donizetti: *Lucrezia Borgia* Dec 16
  Gala (operatic excerpts) Dec 9

PARODI ITALIAN OPERA TROUPE
  Verdi: *La traviata* Dec 5
  Verdi: *Ernani* Dec 6
  Bellini: *Norma* Dec 7
  Verdi: *Il trovatore* Dec 8
  Donizetti: *Poliuto* Dec 10

11—1860–1861

COLSON ITALIAN OPERA TROUPE
  Donizetti: *Don Pasquale* Nov 15

ITALIAN OPERA TROUPE (singers and piano accompaniment)
  Donizetti: *Don Pasquale* Apr (date unknown)

12—1861–1862 No opera

13—1862–1863

[JACOB] GRAU-MUZIO ITALIAN OPERA COMPANY
  Donizetti: *Lucrezia Borgia* June 15
  Flotow: *Martha* June 16
  Verdi: *Ernani* June 17
  Meyerbeer: *Dinorah* June 18
  Verdi: *Il trovatore* June 19
  Halévy: *La Juive* June 20

Bellini: *I puritani* June 22
Bellini: *Norma* June 23
Mozart: *Don Giovanni* June 24/June 30
Donizetti: *Lucia di Lammermoor* June 25
Verdi: *La traviata* June 26
Verdi: *I vespri siciliani* June 27
Verdi: *Un ballo in maschera* June 29
Donizetti: *Poliuto* July 1
Rossini: *Moses in Egypt* July 2
Donizetti: *La favorita* July 3
Meyerbeer: *Robert le diable* July 4

14—1863–1864

WOODS MUSEUM
Balfe: *The Bohemian Girl* Nov 26–Dec 3

GRAU ITALIAN OPERA COMPANY
Donizetti: *Lucrezia Borgia* Feb 1
Donizetti: *Lucia di Lammermoor* Feb 2
Verdi: *Il trovatore* Feb 3/Feb 6/May 18
Bellini: *La sonnambula* Feb 4
Bellini: *Norma* Feb 5/May 12
Flotow: *Martha* Feb 7/May 19
Verdi: *Un ballo in maschera* Feb 9
Mozart: *Don Giovanni* Feb 10/May 17
Meyerbeer: *Robert le diable* May 9
Verdi: *Ernani* May 10
Gounod: *Faust* May 11/May 14/May 20
Meyerbeer: *Dinorah* May 13
Meyerbeer: *Les Huguenots* May 16
Auber: *Masaniello (La Muette de Portici)* May 21

15—1864–1865

PHILLIPS OPERA COMPANY
Rossini: *The Barber of Seville* July 7
Donizetti: *Don Pasquale* July 8

GROVER'S GERMAN OPERA COMPANY (McVickers)
Flotow: *Martha* Jan 2/Jan 14
Gounod: *Faust* Jan 3/Jan 12/Jan 21
Boïeldieu: *La Dame blanche* Jan 4
Mozart: *Don Giovanni* Jan 5
Halévy: *La Juive* Jan 6/Jan 20
Flotow: *Alessandro Stradella* Jan 7/Jan 21
Weber: *Der Freischütz* Jan 9/Jan 19
Beethoven: *Fidelio* Jan 10
Meyerbeer: *Robert le diable* Jan 11
Wagner: *Tannhäuser* Jan 13
Kreutzer: *A Night in Grenada (sic) (Das Nachtlager in Granada)* Jan 14(mat)
Rossini: *The Barber of Seville*
   with Wagner: *Tannhäuser* (act 1) Jan 16
Mozart: *The Magic Flute* Jan 17
Meyerbeer: *Les Huguenots* Jan 18

GRAU'S GRAND ITALIAN OPERA COMPANY
(Opening of Crosby's Opera House)
Verdi: *Il trovatore* Apr 20/Apr 22(mat)/June 9
Donizetti: *Lucia di Lammermoor* Apr 21/May 20
Donizetti: *Poliuto* Apr 22/Apr 24/May 12(mat)/June 19
Flotow: *Martha* Apr 25/Apr 29/May 12/June 19
   with Donizetti: *Poliuto* (final act) June 20
Bellini: *Norma* Apr 26/Apr 29(mat)/June 6
Gounod: *Faust* Apr 27/May 10/June 5
Donizetti: *Linda di Chamounix* Apr 28/May 6(mat)
Bellini: *La sonnambula* May 3
Bellini: *I puritani* May 4
Verdi: *Un ballo in maschera* May 5/May 13(mat)
Donizetti: *Don Sebastiano* May 8/May 9/May 18
Donizetti: *Lucrezia Borgia* May 11
Verdi: *Ernani* May 15
Mozart: *Don Giovanni* May 16/June 16
Auber: *Fra Diavolo* May 17/May 19/June 7/June 10(mat)
   with Donizetti: *Poliuto* (final act) June 19(mat)
Verdi: *I vespri siciliani* June 8/June 17(mat)
Donizetti: *The Daughter of the Regiment* June 12
Verdi: *La forza del destino* June 13
Donizetti: *La favorita* June 14
Verdi: *Rigoletto* June 15
Gala (operatic excerpts) May 20

16—1865–1866

CAMPBELL'S AND CASTLE'S ENGLISH OPERA TROUPE
Balfe: *The Bohemian Girl* Sep 25–Oct 16
Wallace: *Maritana* Oct 12(mat)

ROSA COOK ENGLISH OPERA COMPANY
Balfe: *The Rose of Castille* Oct 20
Balfe: *The Bohemian Girl* Oct 21

SMITH AND ZUPORIS ENGLISH OPERA TROUPE
Wallace: *Maritana* Oct 24
Gounod: *Faust* Oct 25
Balfe: *The Bohemian Girl* Oct 25
(Additional repertory of this type may have been offered by the three groups listed above, but it was not covered by the *Tribune*. Apparently Upton regarded them as "scratch troupes.")

GRAU'S GRAND ITALIAN OPERA COMPANY
Verdi: *Il trovatore* Nov 8
Gounod: *Faust* Nov 9/Nov 11(mat)
Verdi: *Ernani* Nov 10/Nov 18(mat)
Donizetti: *Lucia di Lammermoor* Nov 13/Nov 25(mat)
Verdi: *La traviata* Nov 14
Donizetti: *La favorita* Nov 16
Flotow: *Martha* Nov 17/Nov 25(mat)
Donizetti: *Lucrezia Borgia* Nov 20/Dec 2
Donizetti: *L'elisir d'amore* Nov 21/Nov 24
Gounod: *Sapho* Nov 22(mat)
Verdi: *Un ballo in maschera* Nov 22
Donizetti: *Poliuto* Nov 23

Bellini: *Norma* Nov 28
Bellini: *La sonnambula* Dec 1
Meyerbeer: *L'Africana* Jan 17/Jan 18/Jan 19/Jan 20
Gala (operatic excerpts) Nov 24

GROVER'S GRAND GERMAN OPERA COMPANY
Gounod: *Faust* Dec 18/Dec 23(mat)/Dec 26
Weber: *Der Freischütz* Dec 19/Dec 28
Mozart: *Don Giovanni* Dec 20
Flotow: *Martha* Dec 21
Auber: *Fra Diavolo* Dec 22
Kreutzer: *Das Nachtlager in Granada* Dec 23
Boïeldieu: *La Dame blanche* Dec 25
Rossini: *The Barber of Seville* Dec 27
Beethoven: *Fidelio* Dec 29
Mozart: *The Magic Flute* Dec 30
Meyerbeer: *L'Africana* Jan 17–20

GHIONI AND SUSINI GRAND ITALIAN OPERA COMPANY
Donizetti: *Lucrezia Borgia* May 3
Verdi: *Il trovatore* May 4
Gounod: *Faust* May 5
Verdi: *Un ballo in maschera* May 7
Ricci: *Crispino e la comare* May 9/May 10/May 12
Verdi: *Ernani* May 11
Mozart: *Don Giovanni* May 17

17—1866–1867

GHIONI AND SUSINI GRAND ITALIAN OPERA COMPANY
Verdi: *Il trovatore* Dec 24
Ricci: *Crispino e la comare* Dec 25
Meyerbeer: *L'Africana* Dec 26/Dec 29(mat)/Jan 10
Donizetti: *Lucrezia Borgia* Dec 27
Gounod: *Faust* Dec 28
Donizetti: *La favorita* Dec 31
Bellini: *Norma* Jan 1
Auber: *Fra Diavolo* Jan 2/Jan 5(mat)
Verdi: *Ernani* Jan 3/Jan 12(mat)
Verdi: *Un ballo in maschera* Jan 4
Verdi: *La traviata* Jan 7
Donizetti: *Lucia di Lammermoor* Jan 8
Rossini: *The Barber of Seville* Jan 9
Meyerbeer: *Robert le diable* Jan 10
Donizetti: *L'elisir d'amore* Jan 11

STRAKOSCH'S GRAND ITALIAN OPERA COMPANY
Verdi: *Il trovatore* May 20
Bellini: *Norma* May 21
Rossini: *The Barber of Seville* May 22/May 25
Mozart: *Don Giovanni* May 23
Donizetti: *Don Pasquale* May 24

18—1867–1868

LA GRANGE AND BRIGNOLI GRAND ITALIAN
OPERA COMPANY
Verdi: *Il trovatore* Oct 28/Nov 2(mat)

Rossini: *The Barber of Seville* Oct 29
Bellini: *Norma* Oct 30/Nov 9
Donizetti: *Lucia di Lammermoor* Oct 31
Verdi: *Ernani* Nov 1
Flotow: *Martha* Nov 4
Donizetti: *Don Pasquale* Nov 5
Donizetti: *Lucrezia Borgia* Nov 6
Mozart: *Don Giovanni* Nov 7
Bellini: *I puritani* Nov 8

COMBINED OPERA COMPANIES OF LEONARD GROVER
AND MAX MARETZEK
Verdi: *Ernani* Feb 3
Ricci: *Crispino e la comare* Feb 4
Gounod: *Romeo and Juliet* Feb 5
Verdi: *Il trovatore* Feb 6
Auber: *Fra Diavolo* Feb 7
Donizetti: *Lucrezia Borgia* Feb 8(mat)
Gounod: *Faust* Feb 8

THE RICHINGS GRAND ENGLISH OPERA COMPANY
Flotow: *Martha* Mar 9/Mar 18/Mar 21(mat)
Balfe: *The Bohemian Girl* Mar 10
Bellini: *La sonnambula* Mar 11
Wallace: *Maritana* Mar 12
Auber: *The Crown Diamonds* Mar 13
Eichberg: *The Doctor of Alcantara* Mar 14(mat)/Mar 18
Auber: *Fra Diavolo* Mar 14
Gounod: *Faust* Mar 16
Balfe: *The Rose of Castille* Mar 17
Donizetti: *Linda di Chamounix* Mar 19
Donizetti: *The Daughter of the Regiment* Mar 20
Rossini: *La Cenerentola (Cinderella)* Mar 21

GRAND PARISIAN OPERA AND BALLET COMPANY
Three operas by Offenbach (starting dates listed):
    La Grande Duchesse de Gérolstein Apr 13 (12 performances)
    La belle Hélène Apr 20 (6 performances)
    Orphée aux enfers May 4 (6 performances)

19—1868–1869

BATEMAN'S FRENCH OPERA BOUFFE COMPANY
Two operas by Offenbach:
    La belle Hélène Sep 14–17/Sep 19(mat)
    La Grande Duchesse de Gérolstein Sep 18/Sep 21–22

THE MAX MARETZEK COMBINATION GERMAN AND
ITALIAN OPERA TROUPE
Verdi: *Il trovatore* Sep 28/Oct 10(mat)
Gounod: *Faust* Sep 29
Verdi: *Ernani* Sep 30/Oct 3(mat)
Beethoven: *Fidelio* Oct 1/Oct 6/Oct 15
Mozart: *Don Giovanni* Oct 2
Flotow: *Martha* Oct 3
Rossini: *The Barber of Seville* Oct 5
Verdi: *I vespri siciliani* Oct 7
Auber: *Fra Diavolo* Oct 8

Meyerbeer: *Robert le diable* Oct 10/Oct 13
Weber: *Der Freischütz* Oct 12
Verdi: *Un ballo in maschera* Oct 14
Meyerbeer: *The Star of the North* Oct 16
Ricci: *Crispino e la comare* Oct 17

THE RICHINGS GRAND ENGLISH OPERA COMPANY
Flotow: *Martha* Nov 9/Nov 23/Jan15
Lortzing: *Zar und Zimmermann* Nov 10
Ricci: *Crispino e la comare* Nov 11
Auber: *Fra Diavolo* Nov 12/Nov 21
Bellini: *Norma* Nov 13
Balfe: *The Bohemian Girl* Nov 14/Nov 19
Auber: *The Crown Diamonds* Nov 16/Nov 24/Jan 16
Verdi: *La traviata* Nov 17
Wallace: *Maritana* Nov 18
Benedict: *The Lily of Killarney* Nov 20
Bellini: *La sonnambula* Nov 21(mat)
Verdi: *Il trovatore* Nov 25/Nov 28
Donizetti: *The Daughter of the Regiment* Nov 26(mat)
Eichberg: *The Doctor of Alcantara* Nov 26
Balfe: *The Rose of Castille* Nov 27

SALLIE HOLMAN'S OPERA BOUFFE COMPANY
Flotow: *Martha* Jan 15
Auber: *The Crown Diamonds* Jan 16
Offenbach: *La Grande Duchesse de Gérolstein* Jan 25–30

THE SUSAN GALTON ENGLISH COMIC OPERA COMPANY
Four operas by Offenbach:
  Le "66" Mar 15 (4 performances)
  Le Mariage aux lanternes Mar 18 (3 performances)
  Ba-ta-clan Mar 22 (4 performances)
  Robinson Crusoé Mar 27
Levy: *Franchette* Mar 26

GRAND FRENCH OPERA BOUFFE COMPANY
Offenbach: *Geneviève de Brabant* Apr 26–29/May 7
Offenbach: *La Grande Duchesse de Gérolstein* Apr 30/
  May 1(mat)/May 5/May 8(mat)
Hervé: *L'Oeil crevé* May 1/May 6
Offenbach: *La Vie parisienne* May 3/May 4
Lecocq: *Fleur-de-thé* May 8

20—1869-1870

BRIGNOLI'S ITALIAN OPERA COMPANY
Donizetti: *L'elisir d'amore* July 7(mat)
Rossini: *The Barber of Seville* July 7
Donizetti: *Lucia di Lammermoor* July 8

PAREPA-ROSA GRAND ENGLISH OPERA COMPANY
Wallace: *Maritana* Oct 25/Oct 29/Dec 8
Bellini: *La sonnambula* Oct 26/Dec 10/Dec 18
Balfe: *The Puritan's Daughter* Oct 27
Balfe: *The Bohemian Girl* Oct 28/Oct 30(mat)/Nov 5/
  Nov 8/Dec 12
Verdi: *Il trovatore* Oct 30/Nov 4

Auber: *Fra Diavolo* Nov 1/Nov 6(mat)
Flotow: *Martha* Nov 2/Nov 6/Nov 13(mat)/Dec 22
Auber: *The Black Domino* Nov 3/Nov 12
Mozart: *The Marriage of Figaro* Nov 9/Nov 10/Nov 11/
  Nov 13(mat)/Dec 16/Dec 25(mat)
Weber: *Der Freischütz* Dec 23

ENGLISH OPERA AT MCVICKER'S
Balfe: *The Bohemian Girl* Jan 3
Wallace: *Maritana* Jan 4
Auber: *The Crown Diamonds* Jan 5/Jan 13
Auber: *Fra Diavolo* Jan 6/Jan 15
Verdi: *Il trovatore* Jan 7
Bellini: *La sonnambula* Jan 8
Meyerbeer: *Les Huguenots* Jan 10/Jan 12/Jan 16/Jan 20
Flotow: *Martha* Jan 11/Jan 19
Adam: *Le Postillon de Longjumeau* Jan 14/Jan 18/Jan 22
Verdi: *La traviata* Jan 21

INDEPENDENT OPERA COMPANY
Weber: *Der Freischütz* Feb 7/Feb 8/Feb 11/Feb 12/Feb 15

(Another) INDEPENDENT OPERA COMPANY
Mozart: *The Magic Flute* Apr 4/Apr 5/Apr 8/Apr 9

PAREPA-ROSA GRAND ENGLISH OPERA COMPANY
Mozart: *The Marriage of Figaro* Apr 18
Weber: *Oberon* Apr 19/Apr 21
Flotow: *Martha* Apr 20
Balfe: *The Rose of Castille* Apr 22
Balfe: *The Bohemian Girl* Apr 23(mat)
Verdi: *Il trovatore* Apr 23
Flotow: *Alessandro Stradella* May 10

21—1870-1871

COMBINATION TROUPE
Verdi: *Il trovatore* Oct 3
Wallace: *Maritana* Oct 4
Auber: *The Crown Diamonds* Oct 5
Auber: *Fra Diavolo* Oct 6
Meyerbeer: *Les Huguenots* Oct 7/Oct 13
Balfe: *The Bohemian Girl* Oct 8(mat)
Flotow: *Martha* Oct 8
Gounod: *Faust* Oct 10
Verdi: *La traviata* Oct 11
Mozart: *The Marriage of Figaro* Oct 12
Wallace: *Lurline* Oct 14
Adam: *Le Postillon de Longjumeau* Oct 15(mat)
Balfe: *The Rose of Castille* Oct 15

NEW GERMAN OPERA COMBINATION TROUPE
Mozart: *Don Giovanni* Feb 6
Gounod: *Faust* Feb 7/Feb 11(mat)
Beethoven: *Fidelio* Feb 8
Flotow: *Martha* Feb 9
Halévy: *La Juive* Feb 10/Feb 18
Nicolai: *The Merry Wives of Windsor* Feb 11

Meyerbeer: *Les Huguenots* Feb 13
Verdi: *Il trovatore* Feb 14
Rossini: *William Tell* Feb 15/Feb 16
Wagner: *Tannhäuser* Feb 17
Boïeldieu: *La Dame blanche* Feb 18(mat)

GRAND ENGLISH COMBINATION TROUPE
Meyerbeer: *Les Huguenots* Mar 13
Balfe: *The Bohemian Girl* Mar 14/Mar 23
Weber: *Der Freischütz* Mar 15
Flotow: *Martha* Mar 16/Mar 21
Weber: *Oberon* Mar 17
Wallace: *Maritana* Mar 18(mat)
Verdi: *Il trovatore* Mar 18/Mar 22
Mozart: *The Marriage of Figaro* Mar 20
Beethoven: *Fidelio* Mar 24
Auber: *Fra Diavolo* Mar 25(mat)
Bristow: *Rip Van Winkle* Mar 25

22—1871-1872
(Crosby's Opera House destroyed Oct 8)
GRAND GERMAN OPERA COMPANY
Verdi: *Il trovatore* Feb 12/Feb 21
(Scheduled performances of *Les Huguenots*, Feb 16, and
Martha, Feb 17, were canceled.)

GRAND FRENCH OPERA BOUFFE COMPANY
Five operas by Offenbach:
La Grande Duchesse de Gérolstein Apr 8
La Périchole Apr 9
La belle Hélène Apr 10
Les Brigands Apr 11
Barbe-bleue Apr 12

23—1872-1873

MARETZEK ITALIAN OPERA COMPANY
Verdi: *Il trovatore* Oct 11/Oct 12
Bellini: *I puritani* Oct 12(mat)

ENGLISH GRAND OPERA COMPANY
Flotow: *Martha* Jan 6
Wallace: *Maritana* Jan 7
Eichberg: *The Doctor of Alcantara* Jan 8(mat)
Balfe: *The Bohemian Girl* Jan 8
Verdi: *Il trovatore* Jan 9
Auber: *Fra Diavolo* Jan 11

GRAND FRENCH OPERA BOUFFE COMPANY
Offenbach: *La Grande Duchesse de Gérolstein* Jan 20
Hervé: *Le petit Faust* Jan 21
Offenbach: *La belle Hélène* Jan 22
Offenbach: *Geneviève de Brabant* Jan 23
Offenbach: *La Périchole* Jan 24
Lecocq: *Les cent vierges* Jan 25

GRAND ITALIAN OPERA COMPANY
Donizetti: *La favorita* Feb 3
Verdi: *La traviata* (replacing *Il trovatore*) Feb 4
Gounod: *Faust* Feb 5/Feb 8(mat)
Donizetti: *Linda di Chamounix* Feb 6
Mozart: *Don Giovanni* Feb 7
Thomas: *Mignon* Feb 10/Feb 15
Verdi: *Il trovatore* Feb 11
Auber: *Fra Diavolo* Feb 12
Mozart: *The Marriage of Figaro* Feb 14

GRAND PARISIAN OPERA BOUFFE COMPANY
Offenbach: *Barbe-Bleue* Mar 24
Lecocq: *Les cent vierges* Mar 25
Offenbach: *La Grande Duchesse de Gérolstein* Mar 26
Offenbach: *Les Brigands* Mar 27
Offenbach: *La belle Hélène* Mar 28
Offenbach: *La Périchole* Mar 29

OAKES BURLERGO OPERA COMPANY
Gounod: *Faust* May 5
Flotow: *Martha* May 6
Thomas: *Mignon* May 7
Mozart: *Don Giovanni* May 9
Donizetti: *The Daughter of the Regiment* May 10

24—1873-1874

STRAKOSCH GRAND OPERA COMPANY
Flotow: *Martha* Dec 2/Dec 6(mat)
Verdi: *Rigoletto* Dec 3/Dec 12
Gounod: *Faust* Dec 4/Dec 10/Dec 20(mat)
Wallace: *Maritana* Dec 5/Dec 13
Auber: *Fra Diavalo* Dec 6
Donizetti: *Lucia di Lammermoor* Dec 8/Dec 19
Balfe: *The Bohemian Girl* Dec 9/Dec 13(mat)
Verdi: *Il trovatore* Dec 11/Dec 15(mat)
Mozart: *The Marriage of Figaro* Dec 14/Dec 18
Gala (operatic excerpts) Dec 15

HOOLEY OPERA COMPANY
Verdi: *Il trovatore* Dec 21

GRAND ITALIAN OPERA COMPANY
Donizetti: *Lucia di Lammermoor* Jan 12/Jan 21
Flotow: *Martha* Jan 13/Jan 20
Meyerbeer: *Les Huguenots* Jan 14
Thomas: *Mignon* Jan 15/Jan 23(mat)
Verdi: *Aida* Jan 16/Jan 20/Jan 23
Gounod: *Faust* Jan 17(mat)
Verdi: *Il trovatore* Jan 19
Donizetti: *Lucia di Lammermoor* Jan 21
Mozart: *Don Giovanni* Jan 22
Verdi: *La traviata* Jan 24(mat)

INDEPENDENT OPERA COMPANY
Auber: *Masaniello (La Muette de Portici)* Mar 30–Apr 4

25—1874-1875

ENGLISH GRAND OPERA COMPANY
Donizetti: *Lucia di Lammermoor* Oct 5/Oct 10(mat)
Wallace: *Maritana* Oct 6
Flotow: *Martha* Oct 7
Mozart: *The Marriage of Figaro* Oct 8
Gounod: *Faust* Oct 9
Balfe: *The Bohemian Girl* Oct 10/Oct 17
Mozart: *Don Giovanni* Oct 15
Verdi: *Il trovatore* Oct 16
Auber: *Fra Diavolo* Oct 17(mat)
Thomas: *Mignon* Oct 23/Oct 24
Gala (operatic excerpts) Oct 24(mat)

STRAKOSCH GRAND OPERA COMPANY
Verdi: *La traviata* Jan 18
Donizetti: *Lucia di Lammermoor* Jan 19
Gounod: *Faust* Jan 20/Jan 30(mat)
Wagner: *Lohengrin* Jan 21/Jan 25/Jan 29
Verdi: *Ernani* Jan 22
Thomas: *Mignon* Jan 23(mat)
Verdi: *Aida* Jan 23
Rossini: *The Barber of Seville* Jan 26
Bellini: *La sonnambula* Jan 27
Mozart: *The Marriage of Figaro* Jan 28
Marchetti: *Ruy Blas* Jan 30

26—1875-1876

ENGLISH GRAND OPERA COMPANY
Balfe: *The Bohemian Girl* Jan 3
Balfe: *The Rose of Castille* Jan 4
Thomas: *Mignon* Jan 5
Verdi: *Il trovatore* Jan 6
Auber: *Fra Diavolo* Jan 7
Wallace: *Maritana* Jan 8
Balfe: *The Talisman* Jan 10
Meyerbeer: *Les Huguenots* Jan 11
Donizetti: *Lucia di Lammermoor* Jan 12
Gounod: *Faust* Jan 13
Flotow: *Martha* Jan 14
Benedict: *The Lily of Killarney* Jan 17
Mozart: *The Marriage of Figaro* Jan 19
Verdi: *Ernani* Jan 20

27—1876-1877

MAURICE STRAKOSCH GRAND OPERA COMPANY
Bellini: *Norma* Oct 30
Verdi: *Il trovatore* Oct 31
Gounod: *Faust* Nov 1
Donizetti: *Lucia di Lammermoor* Nov 2
Flotow: *Martha* Nov 3
Rossini: *Semiramide* Nov 6
Rossini: *The Barber of Seville* Nov 7
Balfe: *The Bohemian Girl* Nov 10

STRAKOSCH-HESS ENGLISH OPERA COMPANY
Bizet: *Carmen* Dec 6/Dec 11(mat)
Auber: *Fra Diavolo* Dec 7
Verdi: *Aida* Dec 8/Dec 16

RICHINGS BERNARD OPERA COMPANY
Wallace: *Maritana* Apr 30
Balfe: *The Bohemian Girl* May 1/May 2(mat)
Flotow: *Martha* May 2/May 5(mat)
Auber: *Fra Diavolo* May 3
Mozart: *The Marriage of Figaro* May 5

28—1877-1878

PAPPENHEIM-ADAMS GERMAN AND ITALIAN TROUPE
Meyerbeer: *Les Huguenots* Nov 12
Wagner: *The Flying Dutchman* Nov 13/Nov 24
Gounod: *Faust* Nov 14
Wagner: *Lohengrin* Nov 15/Nov 17(mat)/Nov 22
Meyerbeer: *Robert le diable* Nov 16
Auber: *Fra Diavolo* Nov 17
Weber: *Der Freischütz* Nov 18
Verdi: *Il trovatore* Nov 19/Nov 24(mat)
Auber: *Masaniello (La Muette de Portici)* Nov 20
Beethoven: *Fidelio* Nov 21/Nov 25
Meyerbeer: *The Star of the North* Nov 22/Dec 2/Dec 26
Donizetti: *Lucrezia Borgia* Nov 23
Balfe: *The Bohemian Girl* Nov 24/Dec 23(mat)
Flotow: *Martha* Nov 25(mat)/Dec 27
Thomas: *Mignon* Nov 27/Dec 30(mat)
Wagner: *The Flying Dutchman* Nov 29/Dec 22
Donizetti: *Lucia di Lammermoor* Dec 1
Verdi: *Il trovatore* Dec 18
Mozart: *The Marriage of Figaro* Dec 20
Auber: *Fra Diavolo* Dec 29

HESS ENGLISH OPERA COMPANY
Planquette: *The Chimes of Normandy (Les Cloches de Corneville)*
     Dec 10–15/Dec 21/Dec 23
Balfe: *The Bohemian Girl* Dec 17/Dec 22(mat)
Thomas: *A Summer Night's Dream* Dec 18
Maillart: *Villars' Dragoons* Dec 19
Auber: *Fra Diavolo* Dec 20

STRAKOSCH GRAND ITALIAN OPERA COMPANY (Hooley's)
Verdi: *Il trovatore* Feb 4
Donizetti: *La favorita* Feb 5
Gounod: *Faust* Feb 6
Verdi: *Aida* Feb 7/Feb 9(mat)
Balfe: *The Bohemian Girl* Feb 8
Thomas: *Mignon* Feb 11
Bellini: *Norma* Feb 12
Mozart: *Don Giovanni* Feb 13
Gala (operatic excerpts) Feb 15

SUSANI OPERA COMPANY (Haverly's)
Donizetti: *Don Pasquale* July 8
Gala (operatic excerpts) July 9

29—1878-1879

GRAND ITALIAN OPERA COMPANY
Verdi: *Un ballo in maschera* Nov 11/Nov 16(mat)
Gounod: *Faust* Nov 12
Verdi: *Aida* Nov 13
Verdi: *La traviata* Nov 14
Thomas: *Mignon* Nov 15/Nov 23
Donizetti: *Lucia di Lammermoor* Nov 16/Nov 23(mat)
Bizet: *Carmen* Nov 18/Nov 21
Flotow: *Martha* Nov 19
Verdi: *Il trovatore* Nov 20
Donizetti: *La favorita* Nov 22

ITALIAN TROUPE FROM HER MAJESTY'S THEATER
(First Mapleson season)
Bizet: *Carmen* Jan 13/Jan 18
Bellini: *La sonnambula* Jan 14/Jan 18(mat)
Mozart: *The Marriage of Figaro* Jan 15
Donizetti: *Lucia di Lammermoor* Jan 16/Jan 25(mat)
Verdi: *Il trovatore* Jan 17
Verdi: *Rigoletto* Jan 20
Gounod: *Faust* Jan 21
Mozart: *The Magic Flute (Il flauto magico)* Jan 22
Bellini: *I puritani* Jan 23
Meyerbeer: *Les Huguenots* Jan 24
Verdi: *La traviata* Jan 25

STRAKOSCH GRAND OPERA COMPANY
Meyerbeer: *Les Huguenots* Mar 17
Gounod: *Faust* Mar 18
Thomas: *Mignon* Mar 19
Verdi: *Rigoletto* Mar 20
Flotow: *Martha* Mar 22(mat)
Bizet: *Carmen* Mar 22
Farewell Gala for Kellogg Mar 21

HESS OPERA COMPANY
Gounod: *Faust* Apr 7
Planquette: *The Chimes of Normandy (Les Cloches de Corneville)* Apr 8/Apr 12
Massé: *Paul and Virginia* Apr 9/Apr 11/Apr 12(mat)
Verdi: *Il trovatore* Apr 10
Balfe: *The Rose of Castille* Apr 11(mat)

30—1879-1880

STRAKOSCH GRAND OPERA COMPANY
Gounod: *Faust* Oct 20
Verdi: *Il trovatore* Oct 21/Oct 25
Thomas: *Mignon* Oct 22(mat)/Oct 29
Verdi: *Aida* Oct 22/Nov 1
Donizetti: *Lucia di Lammermoor* Oct 24
Flotow: *Martha* Oct 27

Bellini: *Norma* Oct 28
Verdi: *Rigoletto* Oct. 30
Gala (operatic excerpts) Oct 31

EMMA ABBOTT OPERA COMPANY
Massé: *Paul and Virginia* Dec 15/Dec 16
Gounod: *Faust* Dec 17
Planquette: *The Chimes of Normandy (Les Cloches de Corneville)* Dec 18
Gounod: *Romeo and Juliet* Dec 19
Balfe: *The Bohemian Girl* Dec 20

ITALIAN TROUPE FROM HER MAJESTY'S THEATER
(Second Mapleson season)
Flotow: *Martha* Jan 12
Bellini: *La sonnambula* Jan 13
Donizetti: *Linda di Chamounix* Jan 14
Donizetti: *The Daughter of the Regiment* Jan 15
Verdi: *Aida* Jan 16/Jan 21/Jan 24
Gounod: *Faust* Jan 17
Rossini: *Stabat Mater* Jan 18
Donizetti: *Lucia di Lammermoor* Jan 19
Verdi: *Rigoletto* Jan 20
Meyerbeer: *Dinorah* Jan 22
Thomas: *Mignon* Jan 23

31—1880-1881

EMMA ABBOTT OPERA COMPANY
Balfe: *The Bohemian Girl* Sep 20/Sep 25(mat)/Sep 29(mat)
Verdi: *Il trovatore* Sep 21
Donizetti: *Lucia di Lammermoor* Sep 22(mat)/Oct 2(mat)
Massé: *Paul and Virginia* Sep 22/Sep 27
Wallace: *Maritana* Sep 23/Oct 1
Gounod: *Romeo and Juliet* Sep 24/Sep 29
Bizet: *Carmen* Sep 25/Sep 30
Gounod: *Faust* Sep 28
Planquette: *The Chimes of Normandy* Oct 2

ITALIAN TROUPE FROM HER MAJESTY'S THEATER
(Third Mapleson season)
Verdi: *Aida* Jan 31
Donizetti: *Lucia di Lammermoor* Feb 1
Boito: *Mefistofele* Feb 3
Flotow: *Martha* Feb 4(mat)
Donizetti: *La favorita* Feb 4
Bellini: *La sonnambula* Feb 5(mat)
Verdi: *Il trovatore* Feb 5
Rossini: *Stabat Mater* Feb 6
Bellini: *I puritani* Feb 7
Gounod: *Faust* Feb 8
Mozart: *Don Giovanni* Feb 9
Wagner: *Lohengrin* Feb 10
Donizetti: *Linda di Chamounix* Feb 12(mat)
Verdi: *Rigoletto* Feb 12

BEAUPLAN OPERA COMPANY
Meyerbeer: *Les Huguenots* Mar 21
Halévy: *La Juive* Mar 22/Mar 29(mat)
Gounod: *Faust* Mar 23/Mar 30(mat)
Verdi: *Aida* Mar 24
Verdi: *Il trovatore (Le Trouvère)* Mar 25
Verdi: *La traviata* Mar 26(mat)
Meyerbeer: *Robert le diable* Mar 26
Bizet: *Carmen* Mar 28
Meyerbeer: *L'Africaine* Mar 30
Donizetti: *La favorita* Apr 2(mat)
Rossini: *William Tell* (in French) Apr 2

32—1881-1882

ITALIAN TROUPE OF HER MAJESTY'S THEATER
(Fourth Mapleson season)
Thomas: *Mignon* Jan 23
Rossini: *The Barber of Seville* Jan 24
Bizet: *Carmen* Jan 25/Jan 31/Feb 4(mat)
Verdi: *Aida* Jan 26
Gounod: *Faust* Jan 27
Wagner: *Lohengrin* Jan 28(mat)/Feb 2
Verdi: *Il trovatore* Jan 28
Meyerbeer: *Les Huguenots* Jan 30
Verdi: *Rigoletto* Feb 1
Beethoven: *Fidelio* Feb 3
Donizetti: *Lucia di Lammermoor* Feb 4

33—1882-1883

ITALIAN TROUPE OF HER MAJESTY'S THEATER
(Fifth Mapleson season)
Rossini: *William Tell* Jan 15
Rossini: *Semiramide* Jan 16
Meyerbeer: *L'Africana* Jan 17
Verdi: *Il trovatore* Jan 18
Bellini: *I puritani* Jan 19
Verdi: *La traviata* Jan 20(mat)
Gounod: *Faust* Jan 20

34—1883-1884

BOSTON IDEAL OPERA COMPANY
Gounod: *Faust* Nov 9
Boito: *Mefistofele* Nov 10/Nov 13/Nov 17
Balfe: *The Bohemian Girl* Nov 11/Nov 14
Verdi: *Il trovatore* Nov 16/Nov 18

ABBEY GRAND OPERA COMPANY (Metropolitan)
Gounod: *Faust* Jan 21/Jan 26(mat)
Donizetti: *Lucia di Lammermoor* Jan 22
Wagner: *Lohengrin* Jan 23
Mozart: *Don Giovanni* Jan 24
Rossini: *The Barber of Seville* Jan 25
Bizet: *Carmen* Jan 26

Rossini: *Stabat Mater* Jan 27
Ponchielli: *La Gioconda* Jan 28/Feb 2
Bellini: *La sonnambula* Jan 29
Thomas: *Mignon* Jan 30
Verdi: *La traviata* Jan 31
Meyerbeer: *Robert le diable* Feb 1
Flotow: *Martha* Feb 2(mat)

OPERA COMPANY OF HER MAJESTY'S THEATER
(Sixth Mapleson season)
Ricci: *Crispino e la comare* Jan 28
Donizetti: *L'elisir d'amore* Jan 29/Feb 9(mat)
Meyerbeer: *Les Huguenots* Jan 30
Donizetti: *La favorita* Jan 31
Donizetti: *Lucia di Lammermoor* Feb 2(mat)
Bellini: *I puritani* Feb 4
Gounod: *Romeo and Juliet* Feb 5
Verdi: *Rigoletto* Feb 6/Feb 9
Gounod: *Faust* Feb 7
Verdi: *La traviata* Feb 8

35—1884-1885

DAMROSCH GRAND OPERA COMPANY (Metropolitan)
Wagner: *Tannhäuser* Feb 23/Feb 28(mat)/Mar 5
Meyerbeer: *Le Prophète* Feb 24/Mar 4/Mar 8
Halévy: *La Juive* Feb 25/Mar 3
Rossini: *William Tell* Feb 26
Auber: *Masaniello (La Muette de Portici)* Feb 27
Beethoven: *Fidelio* Feb 28/Mar 6
Wagner: *Lohengrin* Mar 2/Mar 7(mat)/Mar 13
Weber: *Der Freischütz* Mar 7
Wagner: *Die Walküre* Mar 10/Mar 11/Mar 14(mat)
Boïeldieu: *La Dame blanche* Mar 12
Mozart: *Don Giovanni* Mar 14

CHICAGO OPERA FESTIVAL (Mapleson)
Rosssini: *Semiramide* Apr 6
Meyerbeer: *L'Africana* Apr 7
Gounod: *Mireille* Apr 8
Donizetti: *Linda di Chamounix* Apr 9/Apr 10(mat)
Donizetti: *Lucia di Lammermoor* Apr 10/Apr 18(mat)
Weber: *Der Freischütz* Apr 11
Bellini: *La sonnambula* Apr 13
Verdi: *Aida* Apr 14
Verdi: *Il trovatore* Apr 15
Bellini: *I puritani* Apr 16
Gounod: *Faust* Apr 17
Wagner: *Lohengrin* Apr 18

36—1885-1886

OPERA COMPANY OF HER MAJESTY'S THEATER
J. M. Hill, manager (Seventh Mapleson season)
Bizet: *Carmen* Feb 5/Feb 8(mat)/Feb 20
Donizetti: *Lucia di Lammermoor* Feb 9

Thomas: *Mignon* Feb. 10/Feb 16/Feb 19
Auber: *Fra Diavolo* Feb 11
Verdi: *La traviata* Feb 12
Gounod: *Faust* Feb 13
Verdi: *Il trovatore* Feb 15
Flotow: *Martha* Feb 17
Verdi: *Rigoletto* Feb 18
Bellini: *I puritani* Feb 20(mat)

METROPOLITAN OPERA HOUSE (New York)
Wagner: *Rienzi* Mar 15/Mar 17/Mar 20(mat)/Mar 27
Wagner: *Lohengrin* Mar 16/Mar 19
Gounod: *Faust* Mar 18
Beethoven: *Fidelio* Mar 20
Goldmark: *Die Königin von Saba* Mar 22/Mar 24/Mar 26/
    Mar 27(mat)
Wagner: *Tannhäuser* Mar 23/Mar 25

THEODORE THOMAS AMERICAN OPERA COMPANY
Wagner: *Lohengrin* May 24/June 2
Delibes: *Lakmé* May 25/June 1
Nicolai: *The Merry Wives of Windsor* May 27
Gluck: *Orfeo ed Euridice* (presumably French version) May 31/
    June 5(mat)
Wagner: *The Flying Dutchman* June 4

37—1886-1887

THEODORE THOMAS AMERICAN OPERA COMPANY
Gounod: *Faust* Dec 6/Dec 10(mat)
Meyerbeer: *Les Huguenots* Dec 7/Dec 15/Dec 18
Delibes: *Lakmé* Dec 8
Gluck: *Orfeo ed Euridice* Dec 9
Wagner: *Lohengrin* Dec 10
Massé: *Galathée* Dec 11
Verdi: *Aida* Dec 13/Dec 18
Nicolai: *The Merry Wives of Windsor* Dec 14
Wagner: *The Flying Dutchman* Dec 17
(Rubinstein: *Nero* was in the company repertory but did not
reach Chicago.)

38—1887-1888 No major opera season

39—1888-1889

STANTON GERMAN GRAND OPERA (Metropolitan)
Seven operas by Wagner:
    Der Ring des Nibelungen
        Das Rheingold Apr 22
        Die Walküre Apr 23
        Siegfried Apr 24/Apr 29
        Götterdämmerung Apr 25/Apr 30
    Die Meistersinger Apr 26/May 1/May 4(mat)
    Tannhäuser Apr 27(mat)/May 2
    Lohengrin May 3/May 4
Beethoven: *Fidelio* Apr 27

40—1889-1890

ABBEY'S ITALIAN GRAND OPERA
(Abbey was not the official impresario at the
Metropolitan that season)
Auditorium Dedication with Patti Dec 9
Gounod: *Romeo and Juliet* Dec 10
Rossini: *William Tell* Dec 11/Dec 19
Gounod: *Faust* Dec 12/Dec 28(mat)
Verdi: *Il trovatore* Dec 13/Dec 20
Donizetti: *Lucia di Lammermoor* Dec 14(mat)/Dec 30
Verdi: *Aida* Dec 16/Dec 26
Rossini: *Semiramide* Dec 17/Jan 1/Mar 15
Flotow: *Martha* Dec 21
Meyerbeer: *Les Huguenots* Dec 23/Dec 31
Verdi: *La traviata* Dec 24
Bellini: *La sonnambula* Dec 27
Verdi: *Otello* Jan 2/Jan 3/Mar 12/Mar 14
Rossini: *The Barber of Seville* Jan 4(mat)
Meyerbeer: *L'Africaine* Mar 10
Donizetti: *Linda di Chamounix* Mar 11
Delibes: *Lakmé* Mar 13

STANTON'S OPERA COMPANY (Metropolitan)
(All operas were sung in German)
Wagner: *Tannhäuser* Apr 21/Apr 26(mat)
Rossini: *William Tell* Apr 22
Wagner: *Die Meistersinger* Apr 23
Halévy: *La Juive* Apr 24
Wagner: *Lohengrin* Apr 25/May 7
Verdi: *Un ballo in maschera* Apr 28
Wagner: *The Flying Dutchman* Apr 29
Beethoven: *Fidelio* Apr 30
Goldmark: *Die Königin von Saba* May 1/May 3(mat)
Bellini: *Norma* May 2
Cornelius: *Der Barbier von Baghdad*
    with Bayer: *Die Puppenfee* (ballet) May 5/May 8/May 10(mat)
Mozart: *Don Giovanni* May 6
Wagner: *Die Walküre* May 9

41—1890-1891

WAGNER OPERA COMPANY
Tristan und Isolde Apr 15
Lohengrin Apr 16
Der Ring des Nibelungen (three of the four operas)
    Die Walküre Apr 17
    Siegfried Apr 18
    Götterdämmerung Apr 19
Tannhäuser Apr 20(mat)
Die Meistersinger Apr 20

THE AUGMENTED J. C. DUFF ENGLISH OPERA COMPANY
Bizet: *Carmen* May 4/May 5/May 7/May 9
Balfe: *The Bohemian Girl* May 8/May 9(mat)
Cornelius: *Der Barbier von Baghdad* May 5(mat)

42—1891-1892

MINNIE HAUK GRAND OPERA COMPANY
Bizet: *Carmen* Sep 28/Oct 3(mat)/Oct 8
Gounod: *Faust* Sep 29/Oct 9
Mascagni: *Cavalleria rusticana* Sep 30/Oct 2/Oct 4/Oct 5/
    Oct 6/Oct 9(mat)
Verdi: *La traviata* Oct 1
Verdi: *Il trovatore* Oct 3
Meyerbeer: *Les Huguenots* Oct 7

ABBEY, SCHOEFFEL AND [MAURICE] GRAU
ITALIAN GRAND OPERA (Metropolitan)
Wagner: *Lohengrin* Nov 9/Nov 14(mat)
Gluck: *Orfeo ed Euridice* Nov 11
Bellini: *La sonnambula* Nov 13/Nov 21(mat)
Gounod: *Romeo and Juliet* Nov 16
Meyerbeer: *Dinorah* Nov 18
Meyerbeer: *Les Huguenots* Nov 20/Dec 5(mat)
Verdi: *Otello* Nov 23
Verdi: *Rigoletto* Nov 25
Gounod: *Faust* Nov 26/Dec 2
Bellini: *Norma* Nov 27
Flotow: *Martha* Nov 28(mat)/Dec 11
Thomas: *Mignon* Nov 30
Mascagni: *Cavalleria rusticana*
    with Verdi: *La traviata* (act 1) Dec 4
Mozart: *Don Giovanni* Dec 5
Concert (Anniversary of Auditorium Dedication) Dec 9
Verdi: *Aida* Dec 10
Wagner: *Lohengrin* Dec 12(mat)

WAGNER OPERA COMPANY
Six operas by Wagner:
    Tristan und Isolde Nov 18
    Lohengrin Nov 19/Nov 29
    Die Walküre Nov 20
    Die Meistersinger Nov 21
    Siegfried Nov 22/Nov 30
    Tannhäuser Nov 28
Beethoven: *Fidelio* Nov 25
Weber: *Der Freischütz* Nov 26

43—1892-1893

No opera. Met destroyed by fire. For the Columbian Exposition, and starting in March 1893, Abbey, Schoeffel and Grau
offered *America*, a "grand historical spectacle." By mid-July of
that year the company had given its 100th performance.

44—1893-1894

ABBEY, SCHOEFFEL AND GRAU ITALIAN GRAND
OPERA (Metropolitan)
Gounod: *Faust* Mar 12/Apr 6
Bizet: *Carmen* Mar 13/Mar 17(mat)/Mar 26/Mar 31/Apr 7
Mozart: *The Marriage of Figaro* Mar 14

Meyerbeer: *L'Africaine* Mar 15
Donizetti: *Lucia di Lammermoor* Mar 16/Mar 31(mat)
Gounod: *Faust* Mar 17/Mar 24(mat)
Wagner: *Lohengrin* Mar 19/Apr 5
Rossini: *Semiramide* Mar 20
Mascagni: *Cavalleria rusticana*
    with Gounod: *Philémon et Baucis* Mar 21
Gounod: *Romeo and Juliet* Mar 22/Apr 7(mat)
Thomas: *Mignon* Mar 23
Verdi: *Rigoletto*
    with Thomas: *Hamlet* (act 4) Mar 27
Leoncavallo: *Pagliacci*
    with Mascagni: *Cavalleria rusticana* Mar 28/Apr 3
Massenet: *Werther* Mar 29
Verdi: *Aida* Mar 30
Meyerbeer: *Les Huguenots* Apr 2
Wagner: *Tannhäuser*
    with Donizetti: *Lucia di Lammermoor* (Mad Scene) Apr 4

45—1894-1895

ABBEY, SCHOEFFEL AND GRAU ITALIAN
GRAND OPERA (Metropolitan)
Meyerbeer: *Les Huguenots* Mar 11/Mar 16/Mar 23(mat)
Verdi: *Otello* Mar 12/Mar 16(mat)
Gounod: *Romeo and Juliet* Mar 13/Mar 29
Verdi: *Falstaff* Mar 14/Mar 23
Verdi: *Aida* Mar 15/Mar 28
Gounod: *Faust* Mar 18/Mar 30(mat)
Verdi: *Rigoletto* Mar 19
Wagner: *Lohengrin* Mar 20/Mar 27(mat)
Mozart: *Don Giovanni* Mar 22
Bizet: *Carmen* Mar 25
Donizetti: *Lucia di Lammermoor*
    with Mascagni: *Cavalleria rusticana* Mar 26
Mozart: *The Marriage of Figaro* Mar 27
Verdi: *Il trovatore* Mar 30

DAMROSCH GERMAN OPERA COMPANY
(All-Wagner season)
Die Walküre Apr 15
Lohengrin Apr 16
Tristan und Isolde Apr 17
Siegfried Apr 18
Tannhäuser Apr 19/Apr 20(mat)
Die Meistersinger Apr 20

46—1895-1896

DAMROSCH GERMAN OPERA COMPANY
Wagner: *Tristan und Isolde* Nov 18
Wagner: *Lohengrin*: Nov 19/Nov 20
Wagner: *Der Ring des Nibelungen* (three of the four operas)
    Die Walküre Nov 20
    Siegfried Nov 22/Nov 30
    Götterdämmerung Nov 27
Wagner: *Die Meistersinger* Nov 21

Wagner: *Tannhäuser* Nov 23/Nov 28

Beethoven: *Fidelio* Nov 25

Weber: *Der Freischütz* Nov 26

ABBEY, SCHOEFFEL AND GRAU ITALIAN
GRAND OPERA (Metropolitan)

Gounod: *Faust* Mar 23

Bizet: *Carmen* Mar 24

Meyerbeer: *Les Huguenots* Mar 25

Verdi: *La traviata*
   with Mascagni: *Cavalleria rusticana* Mar 26

Wagner: *Tristan und Isolde* Mar 27

Bizet: *Carmen* Mar 28(mat)/Apr 4

Verdi: *Rigoletto*
   with Donizetti: *Lucia di Lammermoor* (Mad Scene) Mar 28

Gounod: *Romeo and Juliet* Mar 30

Verdi: *Il trovatore*
   with Massenet: *La Navarraise* Mar 31

Gounod: *Faust* Apr 1

Wagner: *Lohengrin* Apr 2

Donizetti: *Lucia di Lammermoor*
   with Mascagni: *Cavalleria rusticana* Apr 3

47—1896-1897

ABBEY, SCHOEFFEL AND GRAU ITALIAN
GRAND OPERA (Metropolitan)

Bizet: *Carmen* Feb 22/Feb 27(mat)/Mar 4/Mar 9/Mar 19

Meyerbeer: *Les Huguenots* Feb 23/Mar 16

Flotow: *Martha* Feb 24/Mar 13(mat)

Gounod: *Faust* Feb 25/Mar 6/Mar 11/Mar 17

Wagner: *Tristan und Isolde* Feb 26

Meyerbeer: *L'Africaine* Mar 1

Boito: *Mefistofele* Mar 2

Verdi: *Aida* Mar 3

Verdi: *Il trovatore* Mar 5

Massenet: *Le Cid* Mar 8

Wagner: *Lohengrin* Mar 10

Wagner: *Siegfried* Mar 12

Gounod: *Philémon et Baucis*
   with Mascagni: *Cavalleria rusticana* Mar 15

Mozart: *Don Giovanni* Mar 18

48—1897-1898

DAMROSCH AND ELLIS

Verdi: *La traviata* Mar 14

Wagner: *Tannhäuser* Mar 15

Rossini: *The Barber of Seville* Mar 16

Wagner: *Die Walküre* Mar 17

Wagner: *Siegfried* Mar 18

Gounod: *Faust* Mar 19/Mar 23

Meyerbeer: *Les Huguenots* Mar 21

Wagner: *Lohengrin* Mar 22

Wagner: *Die Meistersinger* Mar 24

49—1898-1899

[MAURICE] GRAU GRAND OPERA COMPANY
(Metropolitan)

Wagner: *Lohengrin* Nov 7/Nov 12(mat)

Gounod: *Romeo and Juliet* Nov 8/Nov 17

Wagner: *Tannhäuser* Nov 9/Nov 14

Rossini: *The Barber of Seville* Nov 10/Nov 19(mat)/Nov 24

Gounod: *Faust* Nov 11/Nov 19

Verdi: *La traviata* Nov 12

Donizetti: *Lucia di Lammermoor* Nov 15/Nov 26(mat)

Verdi: *Aida* Nov 16

Wagner: *Die Walküre* Nov 18/Nov 23

Mozart: *The Marriage of Figaro* Nov 21

Flotow: *Martha* Nov 22

Meyerbeer: *Les Huguenots* Nov 25

CHARLES A. ELLIS OPERA COMPANY

Puccini: *La bohème* Feb 13

Wagner: *Tannhäuser* Feb 14

Bizet: *Carmen* Feb 15/Feb 25(mat)

Wagner: *Lohengrin* Feb 16

Mascagni: *Cavalleria rusticana*
   with Leoncavallo: *Pagliacci* Feb 17

Gounod: *Faust* Feb 18(mat)/Feb 22

Gounod: *Romeo and Juliet* Feb 20

Wagner: *Siegfried* Feb 21

Thomas: *Mignon* Feb 23

Rossini: *The Barber of Seville* Feb 24

GRAND FRENCH OPERA OF NEW ORLEANS

Meyerbeer: *Les Huguenots* Mar 20

Halévy: *La Juive* Mar 21

Gounod: *La Reine de Saba* Mar 23/Mar 28

Donizetti: *La favorite* (in French) Mar 24

Verdi: *Il trovatore (Le Trouvère)* Mar 25

Gala (operatic excerpts) Mar 29

50—1899-1900

GRAU GRAND OPERA COMPANY (Metropolitan)

Wagner: *Tannhäuser* Nov 13/Nov 21

Mozart: *The Marriage of Figaro* Nov 14

Meyerbeer: *Les Huguenots* Nov 15

Bizet: *Carmen* Nov 16/Nov 22/Nov 30(mat)

Wagner: *Lohengrin* Nov 17

Gounod: *Faust* Nov 18(mat)

Massenet: *Manon* Nov 18

Mascagni: *Cavalleria rusticana*
   with Rossini: *The Barber of Seville* (acts 2 and 3) Nov 20

Mozart: *Don Giovanni* Nov 23

Wagner: *Die Walküre* Nov 24/Dec 2(mat)

Mozart: *Don Giovanni* Nov 25(mat)

Verdi: *Aida* Nov 25

Gounod: *Faust* Nov 27

Wagner: *Lohengrin* Nov 28

Mozart: *The Marriage of Figaro* Nov 29
Verdi: *Il trovatore* Nov 30
Gounod: *Romeo and Juliet* Dec 1
Verdi: *Rigoletto* Dec 2

GRAND FRENCH OPERA OF NEW ORLEANS
Halévy: *La Juive* Mar 12/Mar 28
Gounod: *Romeo and Juliet* Mar 13
Reyer: *Salammbô* Mar 14/Mar 31(mat)
Verdi: *Il trovatore (Le Trouvère)* Mar 15
Gounod: *Faust* Mar 16
Meyerbeer: *Les Huguenots* Mar 17
Verdi: *Aida* Mar 18/Mar 30
Meyerbeer: *L'Africaine* Mar 19
Mascagni: *Cavalleria rusticana*
    with Massenet: *La Navarraise* Mar 20/Mar 29/Apr 3
Gounod: *La Reine de Saba* Mar 21
Rossini: *William Tell* (in French) Mar 22
Donizetti: *Lucia di Lammermoor* Mar 24(mat)
Thomas: *Mignon* Mar 24
Reyer: *Sigurd* Mar 26
Massenet: *Manon* Mar 27
Leoncavallo: *Pagliacci*
    with Massenet: *La Navarraise* Mar 29
Gala (operatic excerpts) Apr 3

51—1900-1901

GRAU GRAND OPERA COMPANY (Metropolitan)
Gounod: *Faust* Apr 22
Mozart: *Don Giovanni* Apr 23
Donizetti: *Lucia di Lammermoor*
    with Mascagni: *Cavalleria rusticana* Apr 24(mat)
Puccini: *Tosca* Apr 24
Meyerbeer: *Les Huguenots* Apr 25
Wagner: *Tannhäuser* Apr 26
Wagner: *Lohengrin* Apr 27(mat)
Verdi: *Il trovatore*
    with Verdi: *Rigoletto* (act 4) substituting for Leoncavallo:
    Pagliacci Apr 27

SAVAGE'S METROPOLITAN ENGLISH OPERA COMPANY
Verdi: *Aida* Dec 24
Balfe: *The Bohemian Girl* Dec 25
Bizet: *Carmen* Dec 26
Thomas: *Mignon* Dec 27
Wagner: *Lohengrin* Dec 28
Gounod: *Faust* Dec 29
Verdi: *Il trovatore* Dec 30
Arthur Goring Thomas: *Esmeralda* Dec 31

52—1901-1902

GRAU OPERA COMPANY (Metropolitan)
Verdi: *Aida* Mar 31
Wagner: *Tannhäuser* Apr 1
Wagner: *Lohengrin* Apr 2(mat)

Bizet: *Carmen* Apr 2/Apr 9(mat)
Mozart: *The Magic Flute* Apr 3/Apr 11
Massenet: *Le Cid* Apr 4
Gounod: *Faust* Apr 5(mat)
Paderewski: *Manru* Apr 5
Verdi: *Requiem* Apr 6
Wagner: *Der Ring des Nibelungen*
    Das Rheingold Apr 7
    Die Walküre Apr 8
    Siegfried Apr 10
    Götterdämmerung Apr 12
Meyerbeer: *Les Huguenots* Apr 9
Mascagni: *Cavalleria rusticana*
    with Leoncavallo: *Pagliacci* Apr 12(mat)
Rossini: *Stabat Mater* Apr 13

53—1902-1903

MASCAGNI AND HIS GRAND OPERA COMPANY
Cavalleria rusticana
    with part of *Iris* Dec 20/Dec 21

GRAU OPERA COMPANY (Metropolitan)
Donizetti: *The Daughter of the Regiment* Apr 7
Wagner: *Der Ring des Nibelungen* (three of the four operas)
    Die Walküre Apr 8
    Siegfried Apr 15
    Götterdämmerung Apr 18
Wagner: *Die Meistersinger* Apr 9
Gounod: *Faust* Apr 10
Wagner: *Tristan und Isolde* Apr 11(mat)
Verdi: *Aida* Apr 11
Mozart: *Don Giovanni* Apr 13
Verdi: *Un ballo in maschera* Apr 14
Donizetti: *Don Pasquale*
    with Mascagni: *Cavalleria rusticana* Apr 16
Mozart: *The Magic Flute* Apr 18(mat)

54—1903-1904

CONRIED OPERA COMPANY(Metropolitan)
Wagner: *Der Ring des Nibelungen* (three of the four operas)
    Die Walküre Mar 14
    Siegfried Mar 21
    Götterdämmerung Mar 26
Gounod: *Faust* Mar 15
Bizet: *Carmen* Mar 16/Mar 26(mat)
Mozart: *The Magic Flute* Mar 17
Wagner: *Tristan und Isolde* Mar 18
Rossini: *The Barber of Seville*
    with Mascagni: *Cavalleria rusticana* Mar 19(mat)
Wagner: *Tannhäuser* Mar 19
Donizetti: *L'elisir d'amore* Mar 22
Wagner: *Lohengrin* Mar 23
Mozart: *The Marriage of Figaro* Mar 24
Puccini: *Tosca* Mar 25

55—1904–1905

CONRIED OPERA COMPANY (Metropolitan)
Donizetti: *Lucia di Lammermoor* Mar 20
Wagner: *Parsifal* Mar 21/Mar 23(11:30 A.M. mat)
Mascagni: *Cavalleria rusticana*
    with Leoncavallo: *Pagliacci* Mar 22
J. Strauss: *Die Fledermaus* Mar 23
Ponchielli: *La Gioconda* Mar 24
Meyerbeer: *Les Huguenots* Mar 25(mat)
Wagner: *Die Meistersinger* Mar 25

56—1905–1906

CONRIED OPERA COMPANY (Metropolitan)
Goldmark: *Die Königin von Saba* Apr 2
Gounod: *Faust* Apr 3
Donizetti: *Don Pasquale*
    with Humperdinck: *Hansel and Gretel* Apr 4(mat)
Wagner: *Lohengrin* Apr 4
Bizet: *Carmen* Apr 5
Puccini: *Tosca* Apr 6
Flotow: *Martha* Apr 7(mat)
Wagner: *Tannhäuser* Apr 7

57—1906–1907

SAN CARLO OPERA COMPANY
Ponchielli: *La Gioconda* Feb 18
Verdi: *Rigoletto* Feb 19
Verdi: *Il trovatore* Feb 20(mat)
Bizet: *Carmen* Feb 20
Meyerbeer: *Les Huguenots* Feb 21
Rossini: *The Barber of Seville*
    with Leoncavallo: *Pagliacci* Feb 22
Gounod: *Faust* Feb 23(mat)
Donizetti: *Lucia di Lammermoor* Feb 23

CONRIED OPERA COMPANY (Metropolitan)
Meyerbeer: *L'Africana* Apr 8
Wagner: *Tristan und Isolde* Apr 9
Verdi: *Aida* Apr 10(mat)
Puccini: *Madama Butterfly* Apr 10
Wagner: *Tannhäuser* Apr 11
Puccini: *La bohème* Apr 12
Puccini: *Tosca* Apr 13(mat)
Humperdinck: *Hansel and Gretel*
    with Leoncavallo: *Pagliacci* Apr 13

58—1907–1908

SAN CARLO OPERA COMPANY
Ponchielli: *La Gioconda* Jan 20
Verdi: *Rigoletto* Jan 21/Feb 1(mat)
Gounod: *Faust* Jan 22(mat)/Jan 28
Verdi: *Aida* Jan 22/Jan 29/Feb 1
Mascagni: *Cavalleria rusticana*
    with Leoncavallo: *Pagliacci* Jan 23/Jan 29(mat)

Verdi: *La traviata* Jan 24
Verdi: *Il trovatore* Jan 25(mat)/Feb 5(mat)
Donizetti: *Lucia di Lammermoor* Jan 25
Bizet: *Carmen* Jan 27/Feb 5
Rossini: *The Barber of Seville* Jan 30
Meyerbeer: *Les Huguenots* Jan 31
Wagner: *Lohengrin* Feb 3/Feb 8(mat)
Donizetti: *Don Pasquale* Feb 4
Mozart: *Don Giovanni* Feb 6
Concerts Feb 7/Feb 8

CONRIED OPERA COMPANY (Metropolitan)
Puccini: *La bohème* Apr 20
Verdi: *Il trovatore* Apr 21
Gounod: *Faust* Apr 22(mat)
Wagner *Die Walküre* Apr 22
Mascagni: *Cavalleria rusticana*
    with Leoncavallo: *Pagliacci* Apr 23
Massenet: *Manon* Apr 24
Mascagni: *Iris* Apr 25(mat)
Wagner: *Tristan und Isolde* Apr 25

59—1908–1909

THE METROPOLITAN OPERA COMPANY (Gatti-Casazza)
Verdi: *Aida* Apr 12/Apr 23
Wagner: *Die Meistersinger* Apr 13
Donizetti: *Lucia di Lammermoor*
    with Mascagni: *Cavalleria rusticana* Apr 14(mat)
Verdi: *Falstaff* Apr 14
Puccini: *Madama Butterfly* Apr 15/Apr 22(mat)
Wagner: *Die Walküre* Apr 16
Puccini: *La bohème* Apr 17(mat)
Smetana: *The Bartered Bride* (*Die verkaufte Braut*) Apr 17/Apr 25
Wagner: *Parsifal* Apr 18
Mozart: *The Marriage of Figaro* Apr 19
Wagner: *Tannhäuser* Apr 20
Gounod: *Faust* Apr 21(mat)
Wagner: *Tristan und Isolde* Apr 21
Humperdinck: *Hansel and Gretel*
    with Leoncavallo: *Pagliacci* Apr 22
Massenet: *Manon* Apr 24(mat)
Wagner: *Götterdämmerung* Apr 24
Verdi: *Il trovatore* Apr 25(mat)

60—1909–1910

THE BOSTON OPERA COMPANY
Verdi: *Aida* Jan 10
Delibes: *Lakmé* Jan 11
Bizet: *Carmen* Jan 12(mat)/Jan 17
Puccini: *La bohème* Jan 12/Jan 19(mat)
Verdi: *Rigoletto* Jan 13
Puccini: *Madama Butterfly* Jan 14/Jan 22(mat)
Gounod: *Faust* Jan 15(mat)
Meyerbeer: *Les Huguenots* Jan 15
Donizetti: *Lucia di Lammermoor* Jan 18

Verdi: *Il trovatore* Jan 19
Verdi: *La traviata* Jan 20
Wagner: *Lohengrin* Jan 21
Delibes: *Lakmé* (acts 1 and 2)
 with Leoncavallo: *Pagliacci* Jan 22

THE METROPOLITAN OPERA COMPANY
(Final season until 1943)
Ponchielli: *La Gioconda* Apr 4/April 15
Verdi: *Rigoletto* Apr 5
Puccini: *La bohème* Apr 6(mat)/Apr 21/Apr 29
Verdi: *Otello* Apr 6/Apr 14
Donizetti: *L'elisir d'amore*
 with Mascagni: *Cavalleria rusticana* Apr 7
Verdi: *Aida* Apr 8/Apr 13
Franchetti: *Germania* Apr 9(mat)
Flotow: *Martha* Apr 9/Apr 23(mat)
Puccini: *Madama Butterfly* Apr 11/Apr 19/Apr 30(mat)
Verdi: *Il trovatore* Apr 12
Rossini: *The Barber of Seville* Apr 13(mat)/Apr 22
Deller: *Il maestro di cappella*
 (with operatic excerpts) Apr 16(mat)
 with Donizetti: *Don Pasquale* Apr 20
Mascagni: *Cavalleria rusticana*
 with Leoncavallo: *Pagliacci* Apr 16
Wagner: *Die Meistersinger* Apr 18
Gounod: *Faust* Apr 20(mat)
Auber: *Fra Diavolo* Apr 23
Wagner: *Parsifal* Apr 24
Puccini: *Tosca* Apr 25
Wagner: *Lohengrin* Apr 26
Humperdinck: *Hansel and Gretel*
 with Leoncavallo: *Pagliacci* Apr 27(mat)
Wagner: *Tannhäuser* Apr 27
Wagner: *Die Walküre* Apr 28
Smetana: *The Bartered Bride* (*Die verkaufte Braut*) Apr 30

61—1910-1911

CHICAGO GRAND OPERA COMPANY
(First resident Chicago opera company)
Verdi: *Aida* Nov 3/Nov 12(mat)/Nov 21/Nov 30/Dec 24
Debussy: *Pelléas et Mélisande* Nov 5(mat)/Nov 17/Dec 5/Dec 21
Verdi: *Il trovatore* Nov 5/Nov 12/Nov 24(mat)
Mascagni: *Cavalleria rusticana*
 with Leoncavallo: *Pagliacci* Nov 7/Nov 24/Dec 31
Puccini: *La bohème* Nov 8/Nov 16
Charpentier: *Louise* Nov 9/Nov 14/Nov 22/Dec 17(mat)
Puccini: *Tosca* Nov 10/Nov 26(mat)/Dec 3/Dec 19
Bizet: *Carmen* Nov 15/Nov 23
Verdi: *La traviata* Nov 19(mat)/Dec 17
Gounod: *Faust* Nov 19/Dec 1/Dec 13
Strauss: *Salome* Nov 25/Nov 28
Verdi: *Rigoletto* Nov 26/Dec 24(mat)/Jan 7
Puccini: *Madama Butterfly* Nov 29/Dec 7/Dec 12
Donizetti: *Lucia di Lammermoor* Dec 3(mat)

Massenet: *Thaïs* Dec 6/Dec 14/Dec 26/Dec 29/
 Dec 31(mat)/Jan 10
Offenbach: *The Tales of Hoffmann* Dec 15/Dec 20/Dec 28
Meyerbeer: *Les Huguenots* Dec 22
Puccini: *La fanciulla del West* Dec 27/Jan 5/Jan 7(mat)/
 Jan 9/Jan 18
Verdi: *Otello* Jan 11
Gala comprising Offenbach: *The Tales of Hoffmann*
 (acts 1 and 2) and Leoncavallo: *Pagliacci* Jan 16
Verdi: *Un ballo in maschera* Jan 17
Grand Gala (operatic excerpts) Jan 6

ALBORN GRAND OPERA COMPANY (Mid-June for two weeks)
Puccini: *La bohème* (presented as a musical show, with
 matinées Wednesdays and Saturdays)
It should be noted that in this period there were opera
performances from time to time at the White City Amusement Park on the south side of Chicago. The downtown
critics apparently did not consider them important.

62—1911-1912

CHICAGO GRAND OPERA COMPANY
Saint-Saëns: *Samson and Delilah* Nov 22/Dec 1/Dec 12
Bizet: *Carmen* Nov 23/Dec 5/Jan 3/Jan 13/Jan 24
Donizetti: *Lucia di Lammermoor* Nov 24/Dec 9(mat)/Dec 23
Mozart: *The Marriage of Figaro* Nov 25(mat)/Dec 20
Verdi: *Il trovatore* Nov 25
Massenet: *Cendrillon* Nov 27/Dec 2(mat)/Dec 27/Jan 10(mat)
Verdi: *La traviata* Nov 28/Dec 16
Massenet: *Thaïs* Nov 29/Dec 11/Jan 11/Jan 20(mat)
Humperdinck: *Hansel and Gretel* Nov 30(mat)/Dec 9/
 Dec 25(mat)/Jan 1(mat)
Verdi: *Rigoletto* Nov 30/Dec 30
Mascagni: *Cavalleria rusticana*
 with Leoncavallo: *Pagliacci* Dec 2
Rossini: *The Barber of Seville* Dec 4
Delibes: *Lakmé* Dec 6/Dec 14
Wolf-Ferrari: *The Secret of Suzanne*
 with Massenet: *Le Jongleur de Notre-Dame*
 Dec 7/Dec 18/Dec 26/Jan 6(mat)/Jan 27
Herbert: *Natoma* Dec 15/Dec 22/Dec 28/Jan 1/Jan 17
Gounod: *Faust* Dec 16(mat)
Nouguès: *Quo Vadis?* Dec 19/Dec 23(mat)/Dec 27/Jan 4
Wagner: *Die Walküre* Dec 21/Dec 30(mat)/Jan 8/Jan 23
Offenbach: *The Tales of Hoffmann* Dec 25/Jan 9/Jan 20
Wagner: *Lohengrin* Jan 2/Jan 10/Jan 13(mat)/Jan 15
Wolf-Ferrari: *The Jewels of the Madonna* Jan 16/Jan 18/
 Jan 22/Jan 27(mat)/Feb 1(mat)
Wagner: *Tristan und Isolde* Jan 26/Feb 1
Grand Gala Jan 18

63—1912-1913

RAVINIA OPERA
(The Ravinia Opera began offering scenes from operas and—

as time passed—performed more and more of a work until eventually many popular scores were heard in their entirety. In the present listing, only performances in which at least approximately half the work was offered are included. *For complete listings, including cast lists and performance dates, see my* Annals of the Ravinia Opera, *in* Opera Quarterly *13, nos. 3 and 4, through 14, nos. 1 and 2 [1997/98].)*

Donizetti: *Lucia di Lammermoor* Aug 12/Aug 17/Sep 8

Mascagni: *Cavalleria rusticana* (first complete opera at Ravinia) Aug 21/Aug 24/Sep 6

Offenbach: *The Tales of Hoffmann* Aug 26/Aug 29

CHICAGO GRAND OPERA COMPANY

Puccini: *Manon Lescaut* Nov 26/Dec 14(mat)/Dec 20

Bizet: *Carmen* Nov 27/Jan 4(mat)/Jan 13

Mascagni: *Cavalleria rusticana*
    with Leoncavallo: *Pagliacci* Nov 28(mat)/Dec 5/Dec 11/Dec 21
    Cavalleria rusticana (only) Jan 19(mat)
    Pagliacci with ballet Jan 19

Verdi: *Aida* Nov 28/Dec 10/Dec 28(mat)/Jan 4

Verdi: *Rigoletto* Nov 29/Dec 9/Jan 21

Massenet: *Cendrillon* Nov 30(mat)/Dec 18/Dec 26(mat)/Jan 9

Verdi: *La traviata* Nov 30/Jan 18(mat)

Verdi: *Il trovatore* Dec 2

Thomas: *Hamlet* Dec 3

Wolf-Ferrari: *The Jewels of the Madonna* Dec 4/Dec 17/ Dec 30/Jan 11/Jan 25

Goldmark: *The Cricket on the Hearth (Das Heimchen am Herd)* (in English) Dec 7(mat)/Dec 25/Jan 2/Jan 14
    (with *Noël*, see below)

Gounod: *Faust* Dec 7

Offenbach: *The Tales of Hoffman* Dec 12/Dec 28

Wolf-Ferrari: *The Secret of Suzanne*
    with Humperdinck: *Hansel and Gretel* Dec 14.
    Hansel and Gretel (only) Jan 1(mat). *The Secret of Suzanne*
    with Massenet: *Le Jongleur de Notre-Dame* Dec 24

Massenet: *Hérodiade* Dec 16/Dec 21(mat)/Dec 31

Wagner: *Tristan und Isolde* Dec 19

Thomas: *Mignon* Dec 21/Jan 11(mat)/Jan 18/Jan 23/Jan 29

Massenet: *Le Jongleur de Notre-Dame*
    with *The Secret of Suzanne* Dec 24;
    with Parelli: *A Lovers' Quarrel (I dispettosi amanti)* Feb 1

Charpentier: *Louise* Dec 26/Jan 6

Wagner: *Lohengrin* Jan 1/Jan 7

Wagner: *Die Walküre* Jan 3/Jan 16/Feb 1

d'Erlanger: *Noël*
    with *The Secret of Suzanne* Jan 8;
    with *The Cricket on the Hearth* Jan 14

Puccini: *La bohème* Jan 15/Jan 20

Puccini: *Tosca* Jan 17/Jan 22/Jan 30(mat)

Donizetti: *Lucia di Lammermoor* Jan 23(mat)/Jan 27

Parelli: *A Lovers' Quarrel* (with Gala) Jan 24

Massenet: *Thaïs* Jan 25(mat)/Jan 28

Zandonai: *Conchita* Jan 30

64—1913–1914

RAVINIA OPERA

Donizetti: *Lucia di Lammermoor* July 28/Aug 3/Aug 11/Aug 15

Offenbach: *The Tales of Hoffmann* July 30/Aug 1

Leoncavallo: *Pagliacci* Aug 8/Aug 16/Aug 24/Aug 26

Puccini: *Madama Butterfly* Aug 20/Sep 4/Sep 6

Parelli: *A Lovers' Quarrel* Aug 25

Mascagni: *Cavalleria rusticana* Aug 28/Aug 30

CHICAGO GRAND OPERA COMPANY

Puccini: *Tosca* Nov 24

Ponchielli: *La Gioconda* Nov 25

Massenet: *Don Quichotte* Nov 26/Dec 29/Jan 17(mat)/Jan 27

Puccini: *Madama Butterfly* Nov 27(mat)/Dec 11(mat)/ Dec 27/Jan 17

Wagner: *Die Walküre* Nov 27

Verdi: *Aida* Nov 29(mat)/Dec 31

Herbert: *Natoma* Nov 29

Verdi: *Rigoletto* Dec 1/Dec 13(mat)

Saint-Saëns: *Samson and Delilah* Dec 2/Dec 17/Dec 24

Puccini: *La fanciulla del West* Dec 3

Franchetti: *Cristoforo Colombo* Dec 4/Dec 10

Wolf-Ferrari: *The Jewels of the Madonna* Dec 6(mat)/Jan 8/ Jan 21/Jan 26

Bizet: *Carmen* Dec 6/Jan 3(mat)/Jan 12

Puccini: *La bohème* Dec 8/Jan 15/Jan 23

Kienzl: *Ranz des Vaches* Dec 9/Dec 27(mat)

Massenet: *Hérodiade* Dec 11

Gounod: *Faust* Dec 13/Dec 16

Rossini: *The Barber of Seville* Dec 15/Jan 14

Mozart: *Don Giovanni* Dec 18

Leoncavallo: *Zingari* and *Pagliacci* Dec 19/Dec 23

Giordano: *Fedora* Dec 20(mat)/Jan 6/Jan 24(mat)

Goldmark: *The Cricket on the Hearth (Das Heimchen am Herd)* Dec 20

Massenet: *Le Jongleur de Notre-Dame* Dec 22/Jan 13

Humperdinck: *Hansel and Gretel* Dec 25(mat)/Jan 10

Verdi: *Il trovatore* Dec 25

Massenet: *Thaïs* Dec 26/Dec 30(mat)/Jan 1/Jan 10(mat)

Wagner: *Die Walküre* Dec 30/Jan 24

Offenbach: *The Tales of Hoffmann* Jan 3/Jan 29

Verdi: *La traviata* Jan 5/Jan 18

Donizetti: *Lucia di Lammermoor* Jan 7

Wagner: *Parsifal* Jan 11/Jan 18

Massenet: *Manon* Jan 16/Jan 20

Verdi: *Rigoletto* Jan 21

Charpentier: *Louise* Jan 22

Massenet: *Don Quichotte* Jan 27

Février: *Monna Vanna* Jan 28

Parelli: *A Lovers' Quarrel* Jan 29(mat)

Flotow: *Martha* Jan 31

Grand Gala Jan 30

65—1914-1915

RAVINIA OPERA

Offenbach: *The Tales of Hoffmann* July 27
Bizet: *Carmen* July 28/Aug 1/Aug 9
Wolf-Ferrari: *The Secret of Suzanne* July 29/July 30/Aug 7/Aug 13
Leoncavallo: *Pagliacci* July 31/Aug 9
Flotow: *Martha* Aug 3/Aug 6
Mascagni: *Cavalleria rusticana* Aug 4
Puccini: *Madama Butterfly* Aug 5/Aug 8/Aug 12

No season from a resident company downtown

CENTURY OPERA COMPANY (Century Theater, New York)

Verdi: *Aida* Nov 23/Nov 25/Nov 26/Nov 28(mat)
Puccini: *Madama Butterfly* Nov 24/Nov 26(mat)/Nov 27/
   Nov 30/Dec 1/Dec 2/Dec 5(mat)
Bizet: *Carmen* Nov 25(mat)/Nov 28/Dec 17/Dec 19(mat)/Dec 31
Rossini: *William Tell* Dec 1/Dec 3/Dec 4/Dec 30/Jan 1(mat)
Verdi: *Il trovatore* Dec 2(mat)/Dec 5/Jan 1
Wolf-Ferrari: *The Jewels of the Madonna* Dec 7/Dec 9(mat)/
   Dec 10/Dec 12
Offenbach: *The Tales of Hoffmann* Dec 8/Dec 12(mat)
Gounod: *Romeo and Juliet* Dec 9 (celebrating the 25th
   anniversary of the opening of the Auditorium)/Jan 2
Wagner: *Lohengrin* Dec 11/Dec 15/Dec 30(mat)
Puccini: *La bohème* Dec 14/Dec 16/Dec 19
Donizetti: *Lucia di Lammermoor* Dec 16(mat)
   with Van Etten: *Guido Ferrante* Dec 29
Leoncavallo: *Pagliacci* (with Pavlova and a company billed
   as the Imperial Russian Ballet) Dec 18/Dec 21/Dec 24
Gounod: *Faust* Dec 20 (with the Walpurgis Night Scene—
   usually cut—danced by Pavlova and the Imperial Russian
   Ballet)/Dec 23/Dec 25
Mascagni: *Cavalleria rusticana* (and ballet) Dec 23/Dec 27
Humperdinck: *Hansel and Gretel* (and ballet) Dec 25(mat)
Farewell Gala Jan 2

66—1915-1916

RAVINIA OPERA

Verdi: *Aida* July 13/July 24/Aug 26
Gounod: *Faust* July 14
Leoncavallo: *Pagliacci* July 15/July 18/Aug 14/Sep 6
Puccini: *Madama Butterfly* July 17/July 28/Aug 10/Sep 5
Offenbach: *The Tales of Hoffmann* July 20/July 25/Aug 23
Puccini: *Tosca* July 21/July 31/Sep 2
Flotow: *Martha* July 22/Aug 1/Aug 11/Sep 6
Verdi: *Il trovatore* July 27/Aug 8/Aug/12/Aug 18
Wolf-Ferrari: *The Secret of Suzanne* July 29/Aug 7/Sep 3
Mascagni: *Cavalleria rusticana* Aug 3/Aug 15/Aug 25/Aug 30
Verdi: *Rigoletto* Aug 5
Balfe: *The Bohemian Girl* Aug 17/Aug 21/Aug 29
Puccini: *La bohème* Aug 19/Aug 28

BOSTON GRAND OPERA COMPANY AND
PAVLOVA BALLET RUSSE
   (Apparently the ballet company was the same as the one that
   appeared with the Century Opera the previous season)
   Auber: *Masaniello (La Muette de Portici)* Oct 4/Oct 8
   Bizet: *Carmen* Oct 5/Oct 7
   Puccini: *Madama Butterfly* Oct 6(mat)/Oct 9
   Montemezzi: *L'amore dei tre re* Oct 6/Oct 9(mat)

CHICAGO OPERA ASSOCIATION

Ponchielli: *La Gioconda* Nov 15/Nov 27(mat)/Dec 11
Charpentier: *Louise* Nov 16/Nov 22/Dec 2
Wagner: *Tristan und Isolde* Nov 17
Massenet: *Werther* Nov 18/Nov 23
Puccini: *La bohème* Nov 19/Dec 31
Février: *Monna Vanna* Nov 20(mat)/Dec 1/Dec 6/Dec 21
Donizetti: *Lucia di Lammermoor* Nov 20
Verdi: *La traviata* Nov 24
Wagner: *Tannhäuser* Nov 25/Nov 29/Dec 14
Wagner: *Der Ring des Nibelungen*
   Das Rheingold Nov 28
   Die Walküre Dec 5/Jan 16
   Siegfried Dec 12
   Götterdämmerung Dec 19
Puccini: *Tosca* Nov 30/Dec 8/Dec 30/Jan 15
Bizet: *Carmen* Dec 3/Dec 13/Dec 18(mat)/Dec 23/Dec 28/Jan 12
Montemezzi: *L'amore dei tre re* Dec 4(mat)/Dec 7/Dec 22
Verdi: *Il trovatore* Dec 4
Saint-Saëns: *Déjanire* Dec 9/Dec 15
Puccini: *Madama Butterfly* Dec 10/Dec 16/Dec 23(mat)/Dec 27/Jan 8
Thomas: *Mignon* Dec 11(mat)/Dec 18/Jan 6
Wolf-Ferrari: *The Jewels of the Madonna* Dec 20/Jan 1(mat)/
   Jan 4/Jan 22
Parelli: *A Lovers' Quarrel*
   with Leoncavallo: *Pagliacci* Dec 25
Wagner: *Parsifal* Dec 26/Jan 9
Massenet: *La Navarraise*
   with Leoncavallo: *Pagliacci* Dec 29/Jan 3
Verdi: *Rigoletto* Jan 1
Gounod: *Faust* Jan 2(mat)/Jan 8(mat)
Verdi: *Aida* Jan 2
Gounod: *Romeo and Juliet* Jan 5/Jan 13
Massenet: *Cléopâtre* Jan 10/Jan 18/Jan 22(mat)
Massenet: *Thaïs* Jan 15(mat)/Jan 20
Buchalter: *A Lovers' Knot*
   with Puccini: *Tosca* Jan 15
Leoncavallo: *Zazà* Jan 17
Mozart: *Don Giovanni* Jan 19
Mascagni: *Cavalleria rusticana* (part of Grand Gala) Jan 21

67—1916-1917

RAVINIA OPERA

Donizetti: *Lucia di Lammermoor* July 1/July 11/Aug 3
Leoncavallo: *Pagliacci* July 2/July 26/Aug 5
Wolf-Ferrari: *The Secret of Suzanne* July 4/July 20/Aug 8

Verdi: *Il trovatore* July 6/Aug 12
Verdi: *Rigoletto* July 8/July 30
Puccini: *Madama Butterfly* July 9/July 29
Verdi: *Aida* July 13
Flotow: *Martha* July 15/July 19/Aug 6
Balfe: *The Bohemian Girl* Aug 16/Aug 22/Aug 27
Puccini: *Tosca* July 18/Aug 6/Aug 30
Bizet: *Carmen* July 22/Aug 2/Aug 24/Sep 4
Offenbach: *The Tales of Hoffmann* July 23/July 27
Massenet: *Thaïs* July 25/Aug 10/Aug 23
Mascagni: *Cavalleria rusticana* Aug 26
Massenet: *Manon* Aug 29/Sep 3
Puccini: *La bohème* Aug 31

CHICAGO OPERA ASSOCIATION
Verdi: *Aida* Nov 13/Nov 25(mat)/Dec 14/Jan 6
Massenet: *Hérodiade* Nov 14
Giordano: *Andrea Chénier* Nov 15/Nov 27/Dec 5
Meyerbeer: *Le Prophète* Nov 16/Nov 22
Bizet: *Carmen* Nov 17/Nov 28/Dec 25/Jan 6(mat)/Jan 13
Verdi: *Rigoletto* Nov 18(mat)/Nov 29/Dec 13/Jan 9
Humperdinck: *Hansel and Gretel*
  with Herbert: *Madeleine* Nov 18
  Hansel and Gretel (only) Nov 30(mat)
Wagner: *Der Ring des Nibelungen*
  Das Rheingold Nov 19
  Die Walküre Nov 26
  Siegfried Dec 3
  Götterdämmerung Dec 10
Gounod: *Faust* Nov 20/Dec 2/Dec 28
Donizetti: *Lucia di Lammermoor* Nov 21/Dec 4/Jan 7
Mascagni: *Cavalleria rusticana* Nov 23/Dec 9(mat)/Dec 20
Humperdinck: *Königskinder* Nov 24/Nov 30/Dec 6/
  Dec 12/Dec 20(mat)
Verdi: *Il trovatore* Nov 25
Verdi: *La traviata* Dec 1/Dec 21
Massenet: *Manon* Dec 2(mat)/Dec 7/Dec 11
Puccini: *Madama Butterfly* Dec 8/Dec 16
Offenbach: *The Tales of Hoffmann* Dec 9/Dec 19
Gounod: *Romeo and Juliet* Dec 15/Dec 23(mat)/Jan 3/Jan 11
Puccini: *Tosca* Dec 16(mat)/Dec 23
Wagner: *Parsifal* Dec 17
Verdi: *Falstaff* Dec 18
Wagner: *Tannhäuser* Dec 24
Charpentier: *Louise* Dec 30(mat)/Jan 4/Jan 20(mat)
Puccini: *La bohème* Dec 30
Wagner: *Tristan und Isolde* Dec 31(mat)
Massenet: *Thaïs* Dec 31/Jan 10/Jan 16
Rossini: *The Barber of Seville* Jan 1/Jan 14(mat)/Jan 20
Massenet: *Le Jongleur de Notre-Dame* Jan 2/Jan 8
Zandonai: *Francesca da Rimini* Jan 5/Jan 13(mat)/Jan 15
Wagner: *Lohengrin* Jan 7(mat)
Massenet: *Grisélidis* Jan 12/Jan 18
Meyerbeer: *Les Huguenots* Jan 17
Galas Jan 19/Jan 21

68—1917–1918

RAVINIA OPERA
Leoncavallo: *Pagliacci* June 30/July 20/Aug 17
Donizetti: *Lucia di Lammermoor* July 1/July 3/Aug 26
Mascagni: *Cavalleria rusticana* July 4/July 12/Aug 10
Massenet: *Thaïs* July 6/July 17
Offenbach: *The Tales of Hoffmann* July 7/July 24
Puccini: *Tosca* July 8/July 29/July 31/Aug 28
Verdi: *Rigoletto* July 11/Aug 12/Aug 31
Flotow: *Martha* July 12/July 13/Aug 16
Wolf-Ferrari: *The Secret of Suzanne* July 14/July 20/Aug 29
Bizet: *Carmen* July 15/July 27/Aug 23
Puccini: *Madama Butterfly* July 18/Aug 9
Verdi: *Aida* July 22/Aug 3/Aug 25
Verdi: *Il trovatore* July 25/Aug 7/Sep 3
Verdi: *La traviata* July 26/Aug 1/Aug 21/Aug 26
Rossini: *The Barber of Seville* Aug 4/Aug 8/Aug 19
Puccini: *La bohème* Aug 5/Aug 11/Aug 30
Massenet: *Manon* Aug 15/Aug 16
Thomas: *Mignon* Aug 24
Gounod: *Romeo and Juliet* Aug 29

THE BOSTON ENGLISH OPERA COMPANY
  (Each opera was given a one-week run, with matinées
  Wednesdays and Saturdays. Gilbert and Sullivan productions
  were staged weeks of Nov 12, Dec 3, and Dec 17)
Verdi: *Il trovatore* Oct 1
Flotow: *Martha* Oct 8
Gounod: *Faust* Oct 15
Balfe: *The Bohemian Girl* Oct 22
Verdi: *Aida* Oct 29
Bizet: *Carmen* Nov 5
Offenbach: *The Tales of Hoffmann* Nov 19
Wallace: *Maritana* Nov 26
Verdi: *Il Trovatore* Dec 10

CHICAGO OPERA ASSOCIATION
Mascagni: *Isabeau* Nov 12/Nov 17(mat)/Dec 6/Jan 2
Donizetti: *Lucia di Lammermoor* Nov 13
Verdi: *Aida* Nov 14/Nov 20/Dec 1/Dec 30(mat)
Gounod: *Faust* Nov 15/Nov 24(mat)/Dec 8(mat)/Dec 13/Dec 25
Meyerbeer: *Dinorah* Nov 16/Nov 21/Dec 24/Jan 8
Verdi: *Il trovatore* Nov 17
Gounod: *Romeo and Juliet* Nov 18/Nov 27/Dec 3/Dec 12
Puccini: *Tosca* Nov 19/Nov 28/Dec 22(mat)/Dec 29
Puccini: *La bohème* Nov 22/Dec 8/Dec 18/Jan 13
Bizet: *Carmen* Nov 24/Jan 4
Verdi: *Rigoletto* Nov 25(mat)/Nov 29
Meyerbeer: *Les Huguenots* Nov 26/Dec 4
Massenet: *Manon* Dec 1(mat)/Dec 23
Verdi: *La traviata* Dec 2(mat)/Dec 19/Dec 27/Jan 5/Jan 11
Massenet: *Le Jongleur de Notre-Dame* Dec 5/Dec 13
Wolf-Ferrari: *The Jewels of the Madonna* Dec 9/
  Dec 15(mat)/Jan 3

Mascagni: *Cavalleria rusticana*
  with Leoncavallo: *Pagliacci* Dec 10/Dec 22/Jan 6
Charpentier: *Louise* Dec 11/Dec 17/Dec 20
Rossini: *The Barber of Seville* Dec 16(mat)
Delibes: *Lakmé* Dec 21/Dec 31
Hadley: *Azora* Dec 26/Jan 7/Jan 12
Verdi: *Ernani* Dec 29(mat)/Jan 1
Nevin: *A Daughter of the Forest*
  with Massenet: *Le Jongleur de Notre-Dame* Jan 5(mat)
Février: *Monna Vanna* Jan 9
Gounod: *Sapho* Jan 10/Jan 14
Debussy: *Pelléas et Mélisande* Jan 12(mat)/Jan 17
Massenet: *Thaïs* Jan 15
Zandonai: *Francesca da Rimini* Jan 16
Gala Jan 18

69—1918-1919

RAVINIA OPERA

Verdi: *Aida* June 29/July 10/Aug 18
Donizetti: *Lucia di Lammermoor* June 30/July 10
Verdi: *Il trovatore* July 2/July 13/Aug 31
Offenbach: *The Tales of Hoffmann* July 3/July 17
Leoncavallo: *Pagliacci* (complete) July 4/Aug 21/Aug 29
Verdi: *Rigoletto* July 6/July 17/Aug 4/Aug 28
Puccini: *Tosca* July 7/July 16/Aug 13
Gounod: *Faust* July 9/July 30/Sep 1
Mascagni: *Cavalleria rusticana* July 11/July 23/Aug 8
Rossini: *The Barber of Seville* July 14/July 24
Massenet: *Manon* July 18/July 25/Aug 6
Delibes: *Lakmé* July 20/July 28
Puccini: *La bohème* July 27/Aug 1/Aug 27
Verdi: *La traviata* July 31/Aug 14
Montemezzi: *L'amore dei tre re* Aug 3/Aug 20
Gounod: *Romeo and Juliet* Aug 7
Puccini: *Madama Butterfly* Aug 10/Aug 22/Sep 2
Flotow: *Martha* Aug 11/Aug 21
Wolf-Ferrari: *The Secret of Suzanne* Aug 17/Aug 25
Bizet: *Carmen* Aug 18/Aug 24

CHICAGO OPERA ASSOCIATION

Verdi: *La traviata* Nov 18/Dec 11
Puccini: *Madama Butterfly* Nov 19/Nov 30/Jan 10/Jan 18(mat)
Verdi: *Il trovatore* Nov 20/Dec 14
Massenet: *Thaïs* Nov 22/Dec 7
Donizetti: *Lucia di Lammermoor* Nov 23(mat)/Dec 27
Mascagni: *Isabeau* Nov 23/Jan 6
Verdi: *Aida* Nov 25/Dec 28(mat)/Jan 11
Bizet: *Carmen* Nov 26/Dec 6/Jan 9/Jan 18
Rossini: *William Tell* Nov 27/Dec 2/Dec 13
Donizetti: *Linda di Chamounix* Nov 28/Dec 21(mat)
Puccini: *Tosca* Nov 29/Dec 10
Gounod: *Romeo and Juliet* Nov 30(mat)/Dec 9/Dec 21
Puccini: *La bohème* Dec 1(mat)
  with Thomas: *Hamlet* (act 4) Dec 28

Saint-Saëns: *Samson and Delilah* Dec 2/Dec 17/Dec 30/Jan 15
Rossini: *The Barber of Seville* Dec 3/Dec 16/Jan 25
Gounod: *Faust* Dec 4/Jan 4(mat)/Jan 21
Ponchielli: *La Gioconda* Dec 7(mat)/Dec 20/Jan 1
Massenet: *Werther* Dec 14(mat)/Jan 8
Mascagni: *Cavalleria rusticana*
  with Leoncavallo: *Pagliacci* Dec 18/Dec 24/Jan 4
Massenet: *Manon* Dec 23/Jan 7
Ricci: *Crispino e la comare* Dec 25
Meyerbeer: *Dinorah* Dec 31
Février: *Monna Vanna* Jan 3/Jan 11(mat)
Verdi: *Rigoletto* Jan 13/Jan 24
Février: *Gismonda* Jan 14/Jan 20
Catalani: *Loreley* Jan 17/Jan 22
Massenet: *Cléopâtre* Jan 23
Leroux: *Le Chemineau* Jan 25(mat)

70—1919-1920

RAVINIA OPERA

Leoni: *L'Oracolo* (under the auspices of the Scotti Opera Company)
  with Leoncavallo: *Pagliacci* (act 1) June 28/July 4
  Pagliacci (act 2) Sep 1
Donizetti: *Lucia di Lammermoor* June 29
Verdi: *Aida* July 1/July 6/Aug 7
Offenbach: *The Tales of Hoffmann* July 2/July 16
Verdi: *Il trovatore* July 3/July 8/July 15
Rossini: *The Barber of Seville* July 5/July 13
Delibes: *Lakmé* July 9/July 20
Mascagni: *Cavalleria rusticana* July 10/July 22/Aug 6
Puccini: *La bohème* July 12/July 17/Aug 29
Puccini: *Tosca* July 19/July 24/Aug 5
Donizetti: *L'elisir d'amore* July 26
Gounod: *Faust* July 27
Puccini: *Madama Butterfly* July 29/Aug 2
Verdi: *La traviata* July 31/Aug 3
Bizet: *Carmen* Aug 9/Aug 19
Wolf-Ferrari: *The Secret of Suzanne* Aug 10/Aug 20/Aug 30
Massenet: *Thaïs* Aug 12/Aug 27
Montemezzi: *L'amore dei tre re* Aug 13/Aug 16/Aug 24
Leoncavallo: *Pagliacci* (complete) Aug 14
Massenet: *Manon* Aug 17/Aug 21
Gounod: *Romeo and Juliet* Aug 23/Aug 26
Flotow: *Martha* Aug 28/Aug 31

CHICAGO OPERA ASSOCIATION

Montemezzi: *La Nave* Nov 18/Dec 1
Puccini: *Madama Butterfly* Nov 19/Nov 24/Nov 27(mat)/
  Dec 27/Jan 23
Giordano: *Fedora* Nov 20/Jan 3
Verdi: *Un ballo in maschera* Nov 21/Nov 30/Dec 26
Bellini: *Norma* Nov 22(mat)/Dec 16/Jan 12
Donizetti: *Lucia di Lammermoor* Nov 22/Dec 7/Dec 25
Puccini: *La bohème* Nov 25/Dec 3/Dec 13

Leroux: *Le Chemineau* Nov 26/Dec 8
Massenet: *Cléopâtre* Nov 27
Massenet: *Thaïs* Nov 29(mat)
Verdi: *Aida* Nov 29/Dec 18
Massenet: *Le Jongleur de Notre-Dame* Dec 2
Verdi: *Rigoletto* Dec 4/Dec 15/Jan 10(mat)
Puccini: *Il trittico* Dec 6(mat)/Dec 22/Dec 30
Bizet: *Carmen* Dec 6/Jan 11
Verdi: *La traviata* Dec 9
Puccini: *Tosca* Dec 10/Jan 10
Massenet: *Manon* Dec 11
Rossini: *The Barber of Seville* Dec 13(mat)/Jan 24
Bellini: *La sonnambula* Dec 17
  with *The Birthday of the Infanta* (ballet) Dec 23/Dec 29
Gounod: *Faust* Dec 24
Donizetti: *Don Pasquale* Dec 27(mat)
  with Meyerbeer: *Dinorah* (act 2, scene 1) Dec 31
Debussy: *Pelléas et Mélisande* Jan 1
De Koven: *Rip Van Winkle* Jan 2 (première)/Jan 8/Jan 17
Massenet: *Hérodiade* Jan 3(mat)/Jan 7/Jan 22
Ravel: *L'Heure espagnole*
  with Leoncavallo: *Pagliacci* Jan 5
Février: *Monna Vanna* Jan 6
Montemezzi: *L'amore dei tre re* Jan 9/Jan 17(mat)
Gunsbourg: *Le vieil aigle*
  with Leoncavallo: *Pagliacci* Jan 13
Charpentier: *Louise* Jan 14
Thomas: *Hamlet* Jan 15
Messager: *Madame Chrysanthème* Jan 19/Jan 24(mat)
Donizetti: *L'elisir d'amore* Jan 20/Jan 21

71—1920-1921

RAVINIA OPERA
Puccini: *Tosca* June 26/July 9/Sep 3
Massenet: *Manon* June 27/July 8
Verdi: *Aida* June 29/July 4/July 22/Aug 3
Donizetti: *Lucia di Lammermoor* June 30/July 20
Gounod: *Faust* July 1/July 11
Leoncavallo: *Pagliacci* (act 1)
  with Leoni: *L'Oracolo* July 2
Rossini: *The Barber of Seville* July 3/July 25
Verdi: *Il trovatore* July 6/July 15/July 27
Mascagni: *Cavalleria rusticana* July 7/Aug 19/Aug 31
Puccini: *La bohème* July 10/July 18/Aug 13/Aug 24
Leoncavallo: *Pagliacci* (complete) July 13/Aug 10
Verdi: *Rigoletto* July 14/Aug 17
Massenet: *Thaïs* July 16/July 28/Aug 5
Puccini: *Madama Butterfly* July 17/July 24/Aug 18/Aug 29
Bizet: *Carmen* July 21/July 29/Aug 4
Thomas: *Mignon* July 23/Aug 1
Verdi: *La traviata* July 25/Aug 8/Aug 20/Aug 28
Donizetti: *L'elisir d'amore* July 30/Aug 7
Montemezzi: *L'amore dei tre re* Aug 6/Aug 15/Aug 25
Massenet: *Manon* Aug 11
Wolf-Ferrari: *The Secret of Suzanne*

  with Massenet: *La Navarraise* Aug 12/Aug 21
Donizetti: *Don Pasquale* Aug 14/Aug 22
Leoni: *L'Oracolo*
  with Wolf-Ferrari: *The Secret of Suzanne* Aug 27
  with Massenet: *La Navarraise* Sep 6
Leoncavallo: *Zazà* Sep 1/Sep 5
Flotow: *Martha* Sep 4
Massenet: *La Navarraise*
  with Leoni: *L'Oracolo* Sep 6

CHICAGO OPERA ASSOCIATION
Marinuzzi: *Jacquerie* Nov 17/Nov 30/Dec 27
Wolf-Ferrari: *The Jewels of the Madonna* Nov 18/Nov 26/Dec 6/Jan 1
Offenbach: *The Tales of Hoffmann* Nov 19/Nov 27
Puccini: *Tosca* Nov 20(mat)/Nov 29/Dec 14
Mascagni: *Cavalleria rusticana*
  with Leoncavallo: *Pagliacci* Nov 20/Dec 11(mat)/Jan 19
Verdi: *Il trovatore* Nov 22/Dec 4
Leroux: *Le Chemineau* Nov 23/Dec 9
Giordano: *Andrea Chénier* Nov 24/Dec 2
Puccini: *La bohème* Nov 25/Dec 26
Verdi: *La traviata* Nov 27(mat)/Dec 20/Jan 8
Verdi: *Rigoletto* Nov 28(mat)/Dec 18
Donizetti: *Lucia di Lammermoor* Dec 1/Dec 30
Bellini: *La sonnambula* Dec 4(mat)
Verdi: *Aida* Dec 5(mat)/Dec 11
Rossini: *The Barber of Seville* Dec 7/Dec 25
Puccini: *Gianni Schicchi*
  with Leoncavallo: *Pagliacci* Dec 8
Gounod: *Romeo and Juliet* Dec 12(mat)/Dec 22
Leoncavallo: *Edipo re* Dec 13/Dec 21/Dec 25(mat)
Verdi: *Falstaff* Dec 15
Donizetti: *Linda di Chamounix* Dec 16/Jan 5
Delibes: *Lakmé* Dec 18(mat)/Dec 28/Jan 13
Donizetti: *L'elisir d'amore* Dec 23/Jan 3
Wagner: *Lohengrin* Dec 24/Jan 6/Jan 15(mat)
Verdi: *Otello* Dec 29/Jan 16(mat)
Erlanger: *Aphrodite* Dec. 31
Puccini: *Madama Butterfly* Jan 1(mat)/Jan 11/Jan 22
Février: *Monna Vanna* Jan 4/Jan 14
Montemezzi: *L'amore dei tre re* Jan 7/Jan 22(mat)
Massenet: *Manon* Jan 8(mat)
Wagner: *Die Walküre* Jan 10/Jan 18
Bizet: *Carmen* Jan 12/Jan 20
Gounod: *Faust* Jan 17
Thomas: *Mignon* Jan 21

72—1921-1922

RAVINIA OPERA
Rossini: *The Barber of Seville* June 25/Aug 30
Massenet: *La Navarraise*
  with *Thaïs* June 26/July 16/Aug 1/Aug 11
Leoncavallo: *Pagliacci* June 28/Aug 9/Sep 5
  with Mascagni: *Cavalleria rusticana* July 4

Verdi: *Il trovatore* June 29/July 12/Aug 24

Donizetti: *Lucia di Lammermoor* June 30/July 10

Gounod: *Faust* July 1/July 5/July 26/Aug 16

Verdi: *Rigoletto* July 2/July 7/July 28

Verdi: *Aida* July 3/July 19

Bizet: *Carmen* July 6/July 17/July 24

Puccini: *Tosca* July 8/July 14/Aug 19

Gounod: *Romeo and Juliet* July 13/July 25/Aug 5/Aug 25

Donizetti: *L'elisir d'amore* July 15/July 31

Wolf-Ferrari: *The Secret of Suzanne* July 16/July 30/Aug 4/Aug 16

Massenet: *Manon* July 20/July 29/Aug 12

Puccini: *La bohème* July 21

Montemezzi: *L'amore dei tre re* July 22/Aug 18

Thomas: *Mignon* Aug 3/Aug 7

Verdi: *La traviata* Aug 6

Puccini: *Madama Butterfly* Aug 10/Aug 14/Sep 1

Giordano: *Fedora* Aug 13/Aug 21

Flotow: *Martha* Aug 17/Aug 26

Donizetti: *Don Pasquale* Aug 20

Leoncavallo: *Zazà* Aug 27

Wagner: *Lohengrin* Aug 31/Sep 4

Gala Sep 5

CHICAGO OPERA ASSOCIATION

Saint-Saëns: *Samson and Delilah* Nov 14/Nov 23

Puccini: *Tosca* Nov 15/Dec 8/Dec 17(mat)/Dec 24

Puccini: *Madama Butterfly* Nov 16/Nov 26/Dec 5/
   Jan 7(mat)/Jan 17

Février: *Monna Vanna* Nov 17/Nov 29/Dec 7

Verdi: *Aida* Nov 19(mat)/Dec 10/Dec 21

Massenet: *Le Jongleur de Notre-Dame* Nov 19/Nov 28

Verdi: *Rigoletto* Nov 21/Dec 10(mat)/Dec 17/Jan 1(mat)

Puccini: *La bohème* Nov 22/Dec 1/Jan 9

Wagner: *Tannhäuser* Nov 24/Nov 30/Dec 6/Dec 12/Jan 7

Bizet: *Carmen* Nov 26(mat)/Dec 9/Dec 31

Montemezzi: *L'amore dei tre re* Dec 3(mat)/Dec 13/Jan 12

Verdi: *Otello* Dec 3/Dec 14

Gounod: *Faust* Dec 19

Verdi: *La traviata* Dec 20/Jan 20

Gounod: *Romeo and Juliet* Dec 22/Jan 3/Jan 18

Donizetti: *Lucia di Lammermoor* Dec 24(mat)

Massenet: *Manon* Dec 26

Wolf-Ferrari: *The Jewels of the Madonna* Dec 27/Jan 2/Jan 4

Strauss: *Salome* Dec 28

Rossini: *The Barber of Seville* Dec 29/Jan 14

Prokofiev: *The Love for Three Oranges* Dec 30 (world
   première)/Jan 5

Massenet: *Thaïs* Dec 31(mat)/Jan 10

Debussy: *Pelléas et Mélisande* Jan 8

Delibes: *Lakmé* Jan 11

Wagner: *Tristan und Isolde* Jan 13/Jan 21

Leoncavallo: *Pagliacci* (with ballet) Jan 14(mat)

Puccini: *La fanciulla del West* Jan 19

Charpentier: *Louise* Jan 21

HUROK RUSSIAN OPERA COMPANY

Rimsky-Korsakov: *The Tsar's Bride* Mar 20/Mar 29

Tchaikovsky: *The Queen of Spades (Pique Dame)* Mar 21/Apr 1/Apr 6

Dargomïzhsky: *Rusalka (The Mermaid)* Mar 22/Mar 25(mat)/
   Apr 1(mat)/Apr 5/Apr 11

Rubinstein: *The Demon* Mar 22(mat)/Mar 31/Apr 4/Apr 9

Mussorgsky: *Boris Godunov* Mar 23/Mar 30/Apr 7/Apr 12

Tchaikovsky: *Eugene Onegin* Mar 24/Apr 2/Apr 8(mat)/Apr 14

Rimsky-Korsakov: *The Snow Maiden* Mar 25/Mar 28/Apr 3/
   Apr 10/Apr 15(mat)

Nápravník: *Dubrovsky* Mar 27/Apr 1(mat)

Bizet: *Carmen* (possibly sung in Russian) Apr 8/Apr 13

Leoncavallo: *Pagliacci* (possibly sung in Russian) April 15

73—1922-1923

RAVINIA OPERA

Mussorgsky: *Boris Godunov* June 24/July 14/Aug 22

Puccini: *Madama Butterfly* June 25/July 7/Aug 4

Verdi: *La traviata* June 27/July 16/Aug 30

Puccini: *La bohème* June 28/July 11/July 15

Leoncavallo: *Pagliacci* June 29/July 27/Aug 16

Massenet: *Manon* June 30/July 5/Aug 24

Mascagni: *Cavalleria rusticana* July 1
   with Massenet: *La Navarraise* Aug 31

Donizetti: *Lucia Di Lammermoor* July 2/July 13

Verdi: *Il trovatore* July 4/July 26

Offenbach: *The Tales of Hoffmann* July 6/July 12

Flotow: *Martha* July 8/July 18/Aug 17

Verdi: *Rigoletto* July 9/July 25

Giordano: *Fedora* July 15/Sep 4

Gounod: *Faust* July 19/Aug 10

Verdi: *Aida* July 20/Aug 3

Donizetti: *L'elisir d'amore* July 21/Aug 18

Bizet: *Carmen* July 22/July 30

Gounod: *Romeo and Juliet* July 28/Aug 1/Aug 26

Wagner: *Lohengrin* July 29/Aug 8/Aug 13

Puccini: *Tosca* Aug 2/Aug 12

Leroux: *Le Chemineau* Aug 5/Aug 23/Sep 4

Rossini: *The Barber of Seville* Aug 6

Montemezzi: *L'amore dei tre re* Aug 9/Aug 25

Wolf-Ferrari: *The Secret of Suzanne* Aug 11/Aug 31

Leoncavallo: *Zazà* Aug 19/Aug 27

Massenet: *La Navarraise*
   with Wolf-Ferrari: *The Secret of Suzanne* Aug 20

Delibes: *Lakmé* Aug 29/Sep 3

Mascagni: *L'amico Fritz* Sep 2

CHICAGO CIVIC OPERA

Verdi: *Aida* Nov 13/Nov 28/Dec 7/Dec 20

Bizet: *Carmen* Nov 14/Nov 23/Dec 2/Jan 15/Jan 20

Puccini: *La bohème* Nov 15/Nov 25(mat)/Dec 26

Rimsky-Korsakov: *The Snow Maiden* Nov 16/Nov 21/
   Nov 29/Dec 4/Jan 6/Jan 14(mat)

Montemezzi: *L'amore dei tre re* Nov 18(mat)/Nov 25/Jan 10

Wolf-Ferrari: *The Jewels of the Madonna* Nov 18/Dec 2(mat)/Dec 14

Wagner: *Parsifal* Nov 19(mat)/Nov 30/Dec 27

Puccini: *Tosca* Nov 20/Jan 12/Jan 18

Verdi: *Il trovatore* Nov 22/Dec 8/Dec 11/Dec 22(mat)/Jan 2

Puccini: *Madama Butterfly* Nov 27/Dec 9/Dec 21

Wagner: *Die Walküre* Dec 3(mat)/Dec 9(mat)

Puccini: *La fanciulla del West* Dec 5

Verdi: *Rigoletto* Dec 6/Dec 12/Dec 16(mat)/Jan 7(mat)

Mascagni: *Cavalleria rusticana*
  with Leoncavallo: *Pagliacci* Dec 11/Dec 23

Donizetti: *Lucia di Lammermoor* Dec 15/Dec 30

Boito: *Mefistofele* Dec 19/Dec 22/Dec 25/Dec 28/Dec 30(mat)

Verdi: *La traviata* Dec 24(mat)/Jan 1/Jan 13

Massenet: *Manon* Dec 29/Jan 9(mat)

Halévy: *La Juive* Dec 31/Jan 4/Jan 20(mat)

Rossini: *The Barber of Seville* Jan 3

Saint-Saëns: *Samson and Delilah* Jan 5/Jan 8

Verdi: *La forza del destino* Jan 6(mat)/Jan 16

Flotow: *Martha* Jan 11/Jan 17

Stearns: *Snowbird*
  with Leoncavallo: *Pagliacci* Jan 13

Gala Jan 19

HUROK RUSSIAN OPERA COMPANY

Tchaikovsky: *The Queen of Spades (Pique Dame)* Feb 19/Mar 6

Mussorgsky: *Boris Godunov* Feb 20/Feb 22/Feb 24(mat)/Feb 26/Mar 2

Dargomïzhsky: *Rusalka (The Mermaid)* Feb 21

Bizet: *Carmen* (possibly sung in Russian) Feb 23

Rimsky-Korsakov: *The Tsar's Bride* Feb 24/Mar 11

Halévy: *La Juive* (possibly sung in Russian) Feb 25/
  Mar 3(mat)/Mar 9/Mar 17

Tchaikovsky: *Eugene Onegin* Feb 27/Mar 5

Tchaikovsky: *Christmas Eve (Cherevichki)* Feb 28/Mar 12

Rimsky-Korsakov: *The Snow Maiden* Mar 1/Mar 10(mat)/Mar 16

Tchaikovsky: *Mazeppa* Mar 3(mat)

Rubinstein: *The Demon* Mar 3/Mar 8

Valentinov: *A Night of Love* Mar 4/Mar 7/Mar 10/Mar 13/
  Mar 14/Mar 15/Mar 17(mat)/Mar 18

74—1923-1924

RAVINIA OPERA

Verdi: *La traviata* June 23/July 4

Wagner: *Lohengrin* June 24/July 5/July 26/Aug 30

Puccini: *La bohème* June 26/July 14/Aug 16

Donizetti: *Lucia di Lammermoor* June 27/July 1

Bizet: *Carmen* June 28/July 8

Puccini: *Madama Butterfly* June 29/July 19/Aug 7/Aug 29

Massenet: *Manon* June 30/July 10

Mascagni: *Cavalleria rusticana*
  with Massenet: *La Navarraise* July 3/July 12
  with Wolf-Ferrari: *The Secret of Suzanne* Aug 5

Rossini: *The Barber of Seville* July 6/July 15/July 21

Gounod: *Faust* July 7/July 24/Aug 2

Verdi: *Aida* July 11/July 22/Aug 17

Delibes: *Lakmé* July 13/July 17/Aug 21

Puccini: *Tosca* July 18/July 28/Aug 9

Montemezzi: *L'amore dei tre re* July 20/Aug 14

Mascagni: *L'amico Fritz* July 25/July 31

Verdi: *Rigoletto* July 27/Aug 12

Leoncavallo: *Pagliacci* July 29/Aug 24

Offenbach: *The Tales of Hoffmann* Aug 1

Flotow: *Martha* Aug 3/Aug 10/Sep 3

Verdi: *Il trovatore* Aug 4/Aug 19

Donizetti: *L'elisir d'amore* Aug 8/Aug 25

Giordano: *Fedora* Aug 11

Gounod: *Romeo and Juliet* Aug 15/Aug 23/Sep 3

Giordano: *Andrea Chénier* Aug 18/Aug 26/Sep 3

Leroux: *Le Chemineau* Aug 22/Sep 1

Leoncavallo: *Zazà* Aug 28/Sep 2

GERMAN GRAND OPERA COMPANY

Wagner: *Die Meistersinger* Oct 28/Nov 8

Wagner: *Der Ring des Nibelungen*
  Das Rheingold Oct 29/Nov 6(mat)
  Die Walküre Oct 31/Nov 7(mat)
  Siegfried Nov 2/Nov 9(mat)
  Götterdämmerung Nov 4/Nov 10(mat)

Wagner: *Tannhäuser* Oct 30

Mozart: *The Marriage of Figaro* Oct 31(mat)/Nov 4(mat)

d'Albert: *Die toten Augen* Nov 1/Nov 9

Kienzl: *Der Evangelimann* Nov 3(mat)

Wagner: *The Flying Dutchman* Nov 3

Wagner: *Tristan und Isolde* Nov 5

Wagner: *Lohengrin* Nov 6

J. Strauss: *Die Fledermaus* Nov 7

J. Strauss: *The Gypsy Baron* Nov 10

CHICAGO CIVIC OPERA

Mussorgsky: *Boris Godunov* Nov 8/Nov 11/Nov 19/Jan 22

Saint-Saëns: *Samson and Delilah* Nov 10(mat)/Nov 15

Donizetti: *Lucia di Lammermoor* Nov 10/Dec 23/Jan 15/Jan 23(mat)

Gounod: *Faust* Nov 12

Halévy: *La Juive* Nov 13/Nov 21/Dec 10/Dec 29

Boito: *Mefistofele* Nov 14/Nov 17(mat)/Nov 24/Jan 18

Verdi: *Il trovatore* Nov 17/Jan 16(mat)

Wagner: *Siegfried* Nov 18/Nov 24(mat)

Rimsky-Korsakov: *The Snow Maiden* Nov 20/Nov 29/Jan 2(mat)

Gounod: *Romeo and Juliet* Nov 22/Jan 4

Meyerbeer: *L'Africana* Nov 23/Dec 1(mat)/Dec 17

Massenet: *Manon* Nov 26/Dec 5

Giordano: *Andrea Chénier* Nov 27/Dec 6

Verdi: *Aida* Nov 28/Dec 4/Dec 15/Jan 11

Bizet: *Carmen* Nov 30/Dec 8/Dec 30/Jan 24

Verdi: *Rigoletto* Dec 1/Dec 31/Jan 13

Delibes: *Lakmé* Dec 3/Dec 16/Jan 23

Meyerbeer: *Dinorah* Dec 7/Dec 18/Dec 29(mat)

Humperdinck: *Hansel and Gretel* Dec 8(mat)/Dec 20/
  Dec 26(mat)/Jan 9(mat)

Flotow: *Martha* Dec 9/Jan 12(mat)/Jan 17/Jan 26

Février: *Monna Vanna* Dec 11/Dec 26

Verdi: *La traviata* Dec 12/Dec 27/Jan 26(mat)

Verdi: *Otello* Dec 13/Dec 22(mat)/Jan 2

Stearns: *Snowbird* and Paër: *Il maestro di cappella*
   with Mascagni: *Cavalleria rusticana* (triple bill) Dec 15

Verdi: *La forza del destino* Dec 19/Jan 6/Jan 14

Rossini: *The Barber of Seville* Dec 21/Jan 20(mat)

Mascagni: *Cavalleria rusticana*
   with Leoncavallo: *Pagliacci* Dec 22/Jan 10

Charpentier: *Louise* Dec 24/Jan 3/Jan 19(mat)

Humperdinck: *Königskinder* Dec 25/Jan 5

Massenet: *Cléopâtre* Dec 28/Jan 9/Jan 21

Massenet: *Thaïs* Jan 1/Jan 12

Massenet: *Le Jongleur de Notre-Dame* Jan 5(mat)/Jan 16

Bellini: *La sonnambula* Jan 7

75—1924-1925

RAVINIA OPERA

Mascagni: *Cavalleria rusticana*
   with Leoncavallo: *Pagliacci* June 21

Donizetti: *Lucia di Lammermoor* June 22/July 4/Aug 31

Verdi: *Aida* June 24/July 10/Aug 17

Puccini: *La bohème* June 25/July 3/July 24/Aug 24

Verdi: *Rigoletto* June 26/June 29/Aug 19

Puccini: *Madama Butterfly* June 27/July 2/July 27

Massenet: *Manon* June 28/Aug 5

Gounod: *Faust* July 1/July 9/Aug 8

Giordano: *Fedora* July 5/July 15/Aug 22

Bizet: *Carmen* July 6/July 17/Aug 12

Verdi: *La traviata* July 8/July 13/Aug 21

Gounod: *Romeo and Juliet* July 11/July 16

Giordano: *Andrea Chénier* July 12/July 22/Aug 27

Montemezzi: *L'amore dei tre re* July 18/July 31

Wolf-Ferrari: *The Secret of Suzanne*
   with Leoncavallo: *Pagliacci* July 19

Rossini: *The Barber of Seville* July 20/July 30

Massenet: *La Navarraise*
   with Fourdrain: *La Légende du point d'Argentan* July 23

Puccini: *Tosca* July 25/Aug 3

Flotow: *Martha* July 26/Aug 7

Verdi: *Il trovatore* July 29/Aug 10

Donizetti: *L'elisir d'amore* July 30/Aug 9

Offenbach: *The Tales of Hoffmann* Aug 1

Delibes: *Lakmé* Aug 2/Aug 14

Leroux: *Le Chemineau* Aug 6

Mascagni: *L'amico Fritz* Aug 13

Saint-Saëns: *Samson and Delilah* Aug 16/Aug 28

Wagner: *Lohengrin* Aug 20/Aug 26

Auber: *Fra Diavolo* Aug 23/Aug 29

Leoncavallo: *Zazà* Aug 30

CHICAGO CIVIC OPERA

Ponchielli: *La Gioconda* Nov 5/Nov 15(mat)/Nov 30(mat)/Jan 3

Debussy: *Pelléas et Mélisande* Nov 5(mat)/Jan 21

Puccini: *Tosca* Nov 6/Nov 15/Nov 29(mat)/Dec 17/Jan 5

Meyerbeer: *Le Prophète* Nov 7/Nov 17

Bizet: *The Pearl Fishers* Nov 8(mat)/Nov 18/Nov 26/Dec 20

Verdi: *Aida* Nov 8/Nov 23/Dec 15/Dec 30(mat)/Jan 2(mat)/
   Jan 7(mat)/Jan 18

Donizetti: *Lucia di Lammermoor* Nov 10/Nov 20/Jan 7/Jan 22(mat)

Wagner: *Tannhäuser* Nov 11/Nov 27/Dec 8/Dec 21(mat)

Saint-Saëns: *Samson and Delilah* Nov 12/Nov 29/Jan 12

Puccini: *La bohème* Nov 13/Nov 22/Jan 6

Verdi: *Rigoletto* Nov 14/Dec 10

Mascagni: *Cavalleria rusticana*
   with Leoncavallo: *Pagliacci* Nov 16(mat)/Nov 25/Dec 7

Verdi: *Il trovatore* Nov 19/Dec 6

Puccini: *Madama Butterfly* Nov 22(mat)/Jan 4(mat)

Massenet: *Thaïs* Nov 24/Dec 18/Dec 27

Massenet: *Werther* Nov 28/Dec 6(mat)/Jan 15

Verdi: *La traviata* Dec 2/Dec 13/Dec 22/Jan 9

Bizet: *Carmen* Dec 3/Dec 12

Halévy: *La Juive* Dec 4/Dec 20(mat)

Gounod: *Faust* Dec 5/Jan 22

Rossini: *The Barber of Seville* Dec 7(mat)/Dec 25/
   Dec 27(mat)/Jan 20

Boito: *Mefistofele* Dec 9/Dec 31/Jan 10/Jan 19

Delibes: *Lakmé* Dec 11/Dec 23/Jan 3(mat)

Wolf-Ferrari: *The Jewels of the Madonna* Dec 13(mat)/Jan 1

Massenet: *Le Jongleur de Notre-Dame* Dec 14(mat)/Jan 8

Montemezzi: *L'amore dei tre re* Dec 16/Dec 29/Jan 17(mat)

Auber: *Fra Diavolo* Dec 19/Dec 30

Charpentier: *Louise* Dec 24/Jan 11(mat)

Verdi: *Otello* Dec 26/Jan 14(mat)

Humperdinck: *Hansel and Gretel* Dec 28(mat)

Offenbach: *The Tales of Hoffmann* Jan 2/Jan 24

Verdi: *Rigoletto* Jan 10/Jan 13

Flotow: *Martha* Jan 14/Jan 20

Mussorgsky: *Boris Godunov* Jan 16/Jan 24(mat)

Gounod: *Romeo and Juliet* Jan 18(mat)

Gala Jan 23

76—1925-1926

RAVINIA OPERA

Montemezzi: *L'amore dei tre re* June 27/July 28

Flotow: *Martha* June 28/July 8/July 31

Verdi: *Aida* June 30/July 5/Aug 25

Rossini: *The Barber of Seville* July 1/July 11/Aug 9

Gounod: *Faust* July 2/July 15

Puccini: *Madama Butterfly* July 3/July 16/Aug 16

Massenet: *Manon* July 4/July 24/Aug 4/Sep 4

Gounod: *Romeo and Juliet* July 7/July 19

Donizetti: *L'elisir d'amore* July 9/Aug 20

Mascagni: *Cavalleria rusticana*
   with Leoncavallo: *Pagliacci* July 10/July 21

Verdi: *Il trovatore* July 12/July 23

Offenbach: *The Tales of Hoffmann* July 14/Aug 6/Sep 2

Verdi: *La traviata* July 17/July 26/Aug 12/Aug 26

Saint-Saëns: *Samson and Delilah* July 18/July 30

Verdi: *Rigoletto* July 22/Aug 2

Halévy: *La Juive* July 25/Aug 11

Puccini: *La bohème* July 29/Aug 5

Giordano: *Fedora* Aug 1/Aug 19

Delibes: *Lakmé* Aug 7/Aug 18

Leoncavallo: *Pagliacci*
  with Massenet: *La Navarraise* Aug 8

Donizetti: *Lucia di Lammermoor* Aug 13/Aug 23/Aug 28

Puccini: *Tosca* Aug 14/Aug 27/Sep 5

Puccini: *Manon Lescaut* Aug 15/Sep 1

Donizetti: *Don Pasquale* Aug 21/Aug 30

Verdi: *Un ballo in maschera* Aug 22/Sep 3

Bizet: *Carmen* Sep 6

CHICAGO CIVIC OPERA

Strauss: *Der Rosenkavalier* Nov 3/Nov 13/Nov 28(mat)/Dec 6

Bizet: *Carmen* Nov 3/Nov 22/Nov 29/Dec 19(mat)/Jan 16

Puccini: *Manon Lescaut* Nov 4/Nov 16/Jan 2(mat)

Verdi: *Un ballo in maschera* Nov 7(mat)/Nov 18/Dec 14

Verdi: *Rigoletto* Nov 7/Nov 19/Jan 4

Verdi: *La traviata* Nov 8/Nov 14(mat)/Nov 28/Dec 9/Jan 21

Flotow: *Martha* Nov 9/Nov 21(mat)/Dec 5/Dec 13/Jan 10

Verdi: *Aida* Nov 10/Dec 12/Dec 10

Mascagni: *Cavalleria rusticana*
  with Leoncavallo: *Pagliacci* Nov 11/Nov 23/Dec 11

Verdi: *Il trovatore* Nov 12/Nov 15/Nov 21/Dec 21

Puccini: *Tosca* Nov 14/Dec 2/Dec 29/Jan 7

Saint-Saëns: *Samson and Delilah* Nov 15(mat)/Dec 1

Gounod: *Faust* Nov 17/Nov 25/Dec 26/Jan 16(mat)

Giordano: *Andrea Chénier* Nov 24/Dec 5(mat)/Dec 17/Jan 8

Verdi: *Otello* Nov 26/Dec 28/Jan 20

Rossini: *The Barber of Seville* Nov 27/Dec 16/Jan 18/Jan 23

Puccini: *Madama Butterfly* Nov 29(mat)/Dec 10/Jan 2/Jan 17

Massenet: *Hérodiade* Nov 30/Jan 9(mat)

Wagner: *Die Walküre* Dec 3/Dec 13(mat)

Mussorgsky: *Boris Godunov* Dec 7/Dec 22

Donizetti: *Lucia di Lammermoor* Dec 8/Dec 19

Franchetti: *Namiko-San*
  with Leoncavallo: *Pagliacci* Dec 11/Dec 27(mat)
  with Mascagni: *Cavalleria rusticana* Dec 24(mat)

Verdi: *Falstaff* Dec 12(mat)/Jan 13

Massenet: *Werther* Dec 15/Dec 23

Harling: *A Light from St. Agnes*
  with Leoncavallo: *Pagliacci* Dec 26(mat)

Alfano: *Resurrection (Risurrezione)* Dec 31/Jan 6/Jan 11/
  Jan 19(mat)/Jan 23

Humperdinck: *Hansel and Gretel* Jan 3/Jan 9

Debussy: *Pelléas et Mélisande* Jan 5

Wagner: *Lohengrin* Jan 12/Jan 17(mat)

Charpentier: *Louise* Jan 14

Halévy: *La Juive* Jan 15

Grand Gala Jan 22

77—1926–1927

RAVINIA OPERA

Puccini: *Manon Lescaut* June 26/July 6/Aug 31/Sep 6

Puccini: *Madama Butterfly* June 27/July 7/Aug 25

Gounod: *Romeo and Juliet* June 29/July 15/Aug 22

Donizetti: *Lucia di Lammermoor* June 30/July 4

Gounod: *Faust* July 1/July 14

Flotow: *Martha* July 2/July 11

Verdi: *Aida* July 3/Aug 17/Sep 3

Bizet: *Carmen* July 5/July 27/Sep 5

Verdi: *Rigoletto* July 8/Aug 1/Sep 1

Montemezzi: *L'amore dei tre re* July 9/July 17/Aug 19

Saint-Saëns: *Samson and Delilah* July 10/July 18/July 30

Puccini: *La bohème* July 13/July 22/Aug 12

Verdi: *Il trovatore* July 16/July 25

Donizetti: *Don Pasquale* July 20/Aug 6

Rossini: *The Barber of Seville* July 21/Aug 9

Halévy: *La Juive* July 23/Aug 3

Massenet: *Manon* July 24/Aug 4/Aug 18

Verdi: *La traviata* July 28/Aug 8/Aug 28

Puccini: *Tosca* July 29

Falla: *La vida breve* July 31/Aug 11/Aug 16/Sep 2

Wagner: *Lohengrin* Aug 5/Aug 14/Aug 30/Sep 6

Giordano: *Fedora* Aug 7/Aug 15

Giordano: *Andrea Chénier* Aug 10/Aug 27

Auber: *Fra Diavolo* Aug 13/Aug 20

Leoncavallo: *Pagliacci*
  with Mascagni: *Cavalleria rusticana* Aug 21
  with Massenet: *La Navarraise* Sep 4

Giordano: *Madame Sans-Gêne* Aug 24/Aug 29

Offenbach: *The Tales of Hoffmann* Aug 26

CHICAGO CIVIC OPERA

Verdi: *Aida* Nov 8/Nov 16/Dec 5(mat)/Dec 11(mat)/Dec 30

Wolf-Ferrari: *The Jewels of the Madonna* Nov 9/Nov 28(mat)/
  Dec 9/Jan 10

Puccini: *La bohème* Nov 10/Dec 4(mat)/Dec 19/Dec 28/Jan 22

Alfano: *Resurrection (Risurrezione)* Nov 11/Nov 20(mat)/Nov 27

Wagner: *Tristan und Isolde* Nov 12/Nov 29/Dec 29/Jan 11

Verdi: *Rigoletto* Nov 13(mat)/Nov 20/Dec 14

Verdi: *Il trovatore* Nov 13/Nov 23/Dec 19(mat)/Jan 5/Jan 22(mat)

Bizet: *Carmen* Nov 14(mat)/Nov 22/Dec 18/Jan 12/Jan 23/
  Jan 26(mat)

Donizetti: *Lucia di Lammermoor* Nov 15/Nov 21/Dec 11

Montemezzi: *L'amore dei tre re* Nov 17/Nov 30/Jan 20

Donizetti: *The Daughter of the Regiment* Nov 18/Nov 24/Dec 4

Halévy: *La Juive* Nov 19/Dec 1/Dec 13/Dec 25(mat)/Jan 16(mat)

Verdi: *Rigoletto* Nov 20/Dec 14

Saint-Saëns: *Samson and Delilah* Nov 25/Dec 27/Jan 8(mat)

Giordano: *La cena delle beffe* Nov 27(mat)/Dec 16/Jan 18

Rossini: *The Barber of Seville* Dec 2/Dec 25/Jan 23

Mascagni: *Cavalleria rusticana*
  with Leoncavallo: *Pagliacci* Dec 3/Jan 14

Bellini: *La sonnambula* Dec 7/Dec 15

Cadman: *A Witch of Salem* Dec 8/Dec 20
Flotow: *Martha* Dec 12(mat)/Dec 22/Jan 1/Jan 9
Donizetti: *L'elisir d'amore* Dec 18(mat)/Jan 8
Verdi: *Otello* Dec 21/Jan 2(mat)/Jan 17
d'Albert: *Tiefland* Dec 23/Jan 1(mat)/Jan 15
Verdi: *La traviata* Dec 26(mat)/Jan 3/Jan 12(mat)/Jan 16
Mozart: *Don Giovanni* Dec 31/Jan 13/Jan 24
Puccini: *Tosca* Jan 4/Jan 15(mat)
Strauss: *Der Rosenkavalier* Jan 6/Jan 26
Puccini: *Madama Butterfly* Jan 19
Mussorgsky: *Boris Godunov* Jan 19
Gounod: *Faust* Jan 21
Humperdinck: *Hansel and Gretel* Jan 23(mat)
Puccini: *Gianni Schicchi*
   with Honegger: *Judith* Jan 27/Jan 29(mat)
Verdi: *Un ballo in maschera* Jan 29
Grand Gala Jan 28

78—1927-1928

RAVINIA OPERA
Giordano: *Andrea Chénier* June 25/July 5/Aug 23
Gounod: *Romeo and Juliet* June 26/July 8/Aug 3
Puccini: *La bohème* June 28/July 7/Aug 14
Flotow: *Martha* June 29/July 4
Gounod: *Faust* June 30/July 19/Aug 12
Verdi: *Rigoletto* July 1/Aug 7
Verdi: *Aida* July 2/July 10/Aug 28
Bizet: *Carmen* July 3/July 22
Leoncavallo: *Pagliacci*
   with Massenet: *La Navarraise* July 6/Aug 21
Auber: *Fra Diavolo* July 9/July 17/Aug 5
Montemezzi: *L'amore dei tre re* July 12/July 20/Aug 30
Saint-Saëns: *Samson and Delilah* July 13/July 29/Sep 3
Mascagni: *Cavalleria rusticana* July 14
   with Massenet: *La Navarraise* Aug 21
   with Leoncavallo: *Pagliacci* July 30/Sep 5
Puccini: *Madama Butterfly* July 15/Aug 18
Thomas: *Mignon* July 16/July 27
Verdi: *Il trovatore* July 21/Aug 26
Massenet: *Manon* July 22/Aug 29
Giordano: *Fedora* July 23/Aug 21
Rossini: *The Barber of Seville* July 24
Halévy: *La Juive* July 26/Aug 11
Wagner: *Lohengrin* July 28/Aug 6/Sep 2
Donizetti: *Lucia di Lammermoor* July 31
Verdi: *Un ballo in maschera* Aug 4/Aug 13/Aug 31
Massenet: *Thaïs* Aug 8/Aug 17
Puccini: *Manon Lescaut* Aug 9/Aug 20
Offenbach: *The Tales of Hoffmann* Aug 10/Aug 19
Puccini: *Tosca* Aug 15/Sep 1
Falla: *La vida breve* Aug 16/Aug 24
Charpentier: *Louise* Aug 22/Aug 27/Sep 4

CHICAGO CIVIC OPERA COMPANY
Verdi: *La traviata* Nov 3/Nov 20(mat)/Dec 20/Dec 25/Jan 21
Wagner: *Tannhäuser* Nov 4/Nov 13(mat)/Nov 26/Dec 8/
   Jan 2/Jan 14(mat)
Rimsky-Korsakov: *The Snow Maiden* Nov 5(mat)/Nov 21/Nov 29
Rossini: *The Barber of Seville* Nov 5/Dec 5/Dec 18(mat)/Jan 23
Verdi: *Aida* Nov 6(mat)/Nov 12/Dec 7/Jan 26
Puccini: *Madama Butterfly* Nov 7/Nov 23/Dec 3/Dec 24(mat)
Catalani: *Loreley* Nov 8/Nov 16/Nov 28/Dec 10(mat)
Verdi: *Otello* Nov 9/Nov 19(mat)
Gounod: *Faust* Nov 10/Nov 13/Dec 3(mat)/Dec 21/Jan 1/Jan 16
Ponchielli: *La Gioconda* Nov 11/Nov 24/Dec 4/Dec 26/Jan 17
Donizetti: *Lucia di Lammermoor* Nov 12(mat)/Nov 19/Jan 3
Verdi: *Il trovatore* Nov 14/Dec 4(mat)/Jan 5/Jan 14/Jan 25
Flotow: *Martha* Nov 15/Dec 11(mat)/Jan 2(mat)/Jan 28
Puccini: *Gianni Schicchi*
   with Leonvavallo: *Pagliacci* Nov 17
   with Mascagni: *Cavalleria rusticana* Dec 17
Verdi: *Un ballo in maschera* Nov 22/Dec 17(mat)
Puccini: *Tosca* Nov 25/Dec 12/Dec 24/Jan 1(mat)/Jan 13
Verdi: *Falstaff* Nov 26(mat)/Jan 11
Mascagni: *Cavalleria rusticana*
   with Leoncavallo: *Pagliacci* Nov 27(mat)/Jan 11(mat)
Wolf-Ferrari: *The Jewels of the Madonna* Nov 30/Dec 10/Jan15(mat)
Février: *Monna Vanna* Dec 6/Dec 19/Jan 4
Bizet: *Carmen* Dec 9/Jan 8(mat)/Jan 21
Donizetti: *Linda di Chamounix* Dec 13/Dec 28
Charpentier: *Louise* Dec 14/Dec 27/Jan 15/Jan 28(mat)
Verdi: *Rigoletto*: Dec 15/Jan 7/Jan 18(mat)
Massenet: *Le Jongleur de Notre-Dame* Dec 22/Dec 31(mat)
Wagner: *Lohengrin* Dec 29/Jan 10/Jan 25
J. Strauss: *Die Fledermaus* Dec 31/Jan 9/Jan 19
Humperdinck: *Hansel and Gretel* Jan 4(mat)
Gounod: *Romeo and Juliet* Jan 7(mat)
Massenet: *Sapho* Jan 12/Jan 18/Jan 23
Alfano: *Resurrection (Risurrezione)* Jan 20
Saint-Saëns: *Samson and Delilah* Jan 22(mat)
Cadman: *A Witch of Salem*
   with Mascagni: *Cavalleria rusticana* Jan 24
Grand Gala Jan 27

AMERICAN OPERA COMPANY
Gounod: *Faust* Mar 27/Mar 28(twice)/Mar 29/Apr 14/Apr 15
Pucccini: *Madama Butterfly* Mar 30/Mar 31(twice)/Apr 1
Mozart: *The Marriage of Figaro* Apr 2/Apr 3/Apr 4(twice)/Apr 5/Apr 17
Bizet: *Carmen* Apr 6/Apr 7(twice)/Apr 8
Leoncavallo: *Pagliacci*
   with Cadman: *Sunset Trail* Apr 9/Apr 10/Apr 11(twice)
Flotow: *Martha* Apr 12/Apri1 13/Apr 20
Mozart: *The Abduction from the Seraglio* Apr 16/Apr 18(twice)

79—1928-1929

RAVINIA OPERA
Leoncavallo: *Pagliacci* (only) June 23/Sept/2
   with Mascagni: *Cavalleria rusticana* July 14/July 29

Charpentier: *Louise* June 24/July 3
Montemezzi: *L'amore dei tre re* June 26/July 6
Puccini: *La bohème* June 27/July 12/Aug 19
Saint-Saëns: *Samson and Delilah* June 28/July 28
Gounod: *Faust* June 29/July 9
Verdi: *Aida* June 30/July 17/Aug 7/Aug 26
Puccini: *Madama Butterfly* July 1/July 24/Aug 29
Verdi: *Un ballo in maschera* July 2/July 23
Giordano: *Andrea Chénier* July 4/Aug 3/Aug 22
Wagner: *Lohengrin* July 5/July 15/Aug 16
Massenet: *Manon* July 6/July 16/Aug 18
Verdi: *Il trovatore* July 7/July 31
Halévy: *La Juive* July 10/July 21
Flotow: *Martha* July 11/July 22/Aug 8/Aug 30
Gounod: *Romeo and Juliet* July 13/July 18/Aug 28
Auber: *Fra Diavolo* July 19/July 27/Aug 27/Sep 3
Leroux: *Le Chemineau* July 20/Aug 6
Puccini: *Tosca* July 25/Aug 14
Giordano: *Fedora* July 26/Aug 2
Massenet: *Thaïs* July 30
Rabaud: *Mârouf* Aug 1/Aug 9/Aug 13/Aug 31
Donizetti: *L'elisir d'amore* Aug 4/Aug 23
Bizet: *Carmen* Aug 5
Puccini: *Manon Lescaut* Aug 10/Aug 24
Rossini: *The Barber of Seville* Aug 11
Verdi: *Rigoletto* Aug 12
Donizetti: *Lucia di Lammermoor* Aug 15/Sep 1
Ravel: *L'Heure espagnole* Aug 17/Aug 20
Donizetti: *Don Pasquale* Aug 21
Verdi: *La traviata* Aug 25

CHICAGO CIVIC OPERA COMPANY
Bizet: *Carmen* Oct 31/Nov 6/Nov 17(mat)/Nov 24/Dec 23(mat)
Puccini: *La bohème* Nov 1/Nov 10(mat)/Nov 18(mat)/Dec 3/Dec 29
Verdi: *Aida* Nov 3(mat)/Nov 10/Nov 11/Nov 19/Nov 29/Jan 23
Verdi: *Rigoletto* Nov 3/Nov 11(mat)/Nov 28/Dec 2/Dec 13(mat)
Wagner: *Lohengrin* Nov 4/Nov 26/Dec 5/Jan 12(mat)
Gounod: *Romeo and Juliet* Nov 5/Jan 26 (final performance in the Auditorium)
Verdi: *Un ballo in maschera* Nov 7/Nov 17/Jan 13
Puccini: *Madama Butterfly* Nov 8/Nov 25
Verdi: *Otello* Nov 12/Nov 20/Dec 13
Gounod: *Faust* Nov 13/Dec 8
Saint-Saëns: *Samson and Delilah* Nov 14/Nov 22/Dec 1(mat)/Dec 15
Mascagni: *Cavalleria rusticana*
    with Leoncavallo: *Pagliacci* Nov 15/Dec 1/Dec 11/Dec 30
Mussorgsky: *Boris Godunov* Nov 24(mat)/Nov 28/Dec 10/Dec 20
Offenbach: *The Tales of Hoffmann* Dec 2(mat)/Dec 18/Dec 26/Jan 19
Verdi: *Il trovatore* Dec 4/Dec 22
Rossini: *The Barber of Seville* Dec 6/Dec 23/Dec 25/Jan 6
Wagner: *Die Walküre* Dec 8(mat)/Dec 16(mat)/Dec 24/Jan 15/Jan 25(mat)
Delibes: *Lakmé* Dec 9(mat)/Dec 17

Mozart: *Don Giovanni* Dec 12/Jan 1/Jan 14
Halévy: *La Juive* Dec 19/Dec 29(mat)
Donizetti: *L'elisir d'amore* Dec 22(mat)/Dec 30(mat)/Jan 7
Strauss: *Der Rosenkavalier* Dec 27/Jan 6(mat)/Jan 19(mat)
Bellini: *Norma* Dec 31/Jan 17
Massenet: *Sapho* Jan 2/Jan 8
Mozart: *The Marriage of Figaro* Jan 3/Jan 9/Jan 20(mat)
Mascagni: *L'amore dei tre re* Jan 5(mat)/Jan 13(mat)
Debussy: *Pelléas et Mélisande* Jan 10/Jan 21
Puccini: *Tosca* Jan 12
Massenet: *Thaïs* Jan 16/Jan 24
Mascagni: *Cavalleria rusticana*
    with Honegger: *Judith* Jan 18/Jan 26(mat)
Donizetti: *Don Pasquale* Jan 22
Grand Gala Jan 11

HUROK GERMAN GRAND OPERA COMPANY
Wagner: *Der Ring des Nibelungen*
    Das Rheingold Feb 17/Feb 18
    Die Walküre Feb 19/Feb 20
    Siegfried Feb 21/Feb 22
    Götterdämmerung Feb 23 (two performances: 1:00 p.m. and 7:15 p.m.)

80—1929-1930

RAVINIA OPERA
Puccini: *Manon Lescaut* June 22/July 1/Aug 19
Rabaud: *Mârouf* June 23/July 3/July 26/Aug 16/Sep 1
Charpentier: *Louise* June 25/July 8/Aug 27
Auber: *Fra Diavolo* June 26/July 13
Saint-Saëns: *Samson and Delilah* June 27
Montemezzi: *L'amore dei tre re* June 28/July 10/Aug 5
Verdi: *Aida* June 29/July 7
Rossini: *The Barber of Seville* June 30
Wagner: *Lohengrin* July 2/July 21
Gounod: *Romeo and Juliet* July 4/July 14/Aug 1
Giordano: *Andrea Chénier* July 5/July 18
Massenet: *Manon* July 6/July 29
Verdi: *Il trovatore* July 9/July 28
Flotow: *Martha* July 11/Aug 20
Halévy: *La Juive* July 12
Leoncavallo: *Pagliacci*
    with Mascagni: *Cavalleria rusticana* July 15/Aug 2/Aug 30
Puccini: *La rondine* July 16/July 30/Aug 12/Aug 22/Aug 31
Massenet: *Thaïs* July 17
Puccini: *La bohème* July 19/July 27/Aug 28
Puccini: *Tosca* July 20/Aug 7
Verdi: *La traviata* July 24/Aug 15
Puccini: *Madama Butterfly* July 25/Aug 17
Donizetti: *Lucia di Lammermoor* July 31/Aug 18
Gounod: *Faust* Jul 23/Aug 21
Wolf-Ferrari: *The Secret of Suzanne*
    with Falla: *La vida breve* Aug 3/Aug 9/Aug 24

Bizet: *Carmen* Aug 4
Respighi: *La campana sommersa* Aug 6/Aug 13/Aug 26
Verdi: *Un ballo in maschera* Aug 10/Aug 23/Sep 2
Verdi: *Rigoletto* Aug 11
Giordano: *Fedora* Aug 14/Aug 29
Offenbach: *The Tales of Hoffmann* Aug 25

AMERICAN OPERA COMPANY
Gounod: *Faust* Oct 7/Oct 15
Puccini: *Madama Butterfly* Oct 8/Oct 16
Loomis: *Yolanda of Cyprus* Oct 9/Oct 12/Oct 14/Oct 19(mat)
Bizet: *Carmen* Oct 11/Oct 17/Oct 19
Flotow: *Martha* Oct 12(mat)
Mozart: *The Marriage of Figaro* Oct 18

CHICAGO CIVIC OPERA COMPANY
Verdi: *Aida* Nov 4/Nov 12/Dec 7/Dec 22(mat)
Mascagni: *Iris* Nov 5/Nov 10/Dec 21(mat)
Verdi: *La traviata* Nov 6/Nov 14/Nov 18/Nov 28/Dec 8/
    Dec 21/Jan 12(mat)/Jan 28
Gounod: *Romeo and Juliet* Nov 7/Nov 16(mat)/Nov 23/Dec 22
Wagner: *Tristan und Isolde* Nov 9(mat)/Nov 17(mat)/
    Nov 27/Jan 21
Verdi: *Il trovatore* Nov 9/Jan 5/Dec 1(mat)/Dec 18/Jan 5/Jan 23
Bellini: *Norma* Nov 10(mat)/Nov 16/Jan 4(mat)
Strauss: *Der Rosenkavalier* Nov 13/Dec 3/Dec 16
Verdi: *Falstaff* Nov 14/Nov 25/Dec 11/Dec 29
Gounod: *Faust* Nov 17/Dec 14/Dec 29(mat)
Puccini: *Tosca* Nov 19/Nov 30(mat)/Dec 26/Jan 13(mat)
Montemezzi: *L'amore dei tre re* Nov 20/Dec 5
Wagner: *Die Walküre* Nov 21/Nov 30/Jan 29
Charpentier: *Louise* Nov 23(mat)/Dec 2/Jan 14
Verdi: *Otello* Nov 24(mat)/Dec 28(mat)/Jan 15
Massenet: *Le Jongleur de Notre-Dame* Nov 26/Dec 8(mat)/
    Jan 6/Jan 18(mat)
Massenet: *Don Quichotte* Dec 4/Dec 12/Dec 30/Jan 25
Wagner: *Tannhäuser* Dec 7(mat)/Dec 15(mat)/Dec 23/Jan 12
Halévy: *La Juive* Dec 9/Dec 17/Jan 18
Verdi: *Rigoletto* Dec 10/Dec 28
Verdi: *La forza del destino* Dec 14(mat)/Dec 14/Jan 5(mat)
Wagner: *Lohengrin* Dec 19/Jan 4/Jan 19
Mozart: *Don Giovanni* Dec 25/Jan 2/Jan 11(mat)
Zandonai: *Conchita* Dec 31/Jan 8/Jan 8/Jan 16
Rossini: *The Barber of Seville* Jan 1/Jan 11/Jan 25(mat)
Donizetti: *Lucia di Lammmermoor* Jan 7/Jan 20/Jan 26/Feb 1
Massenet: *Thaïs* Jan 9/Jan 26(mat)
Mozart: *Don Giovannni* Jan 11(mat)
Verdi: *La traviata* Jan 12(mat)
Beethoven: *Fidelio* Jan 17
Debussy: *Pelléas et Mélisande* Jan 22/Feb 1(mat)
Ponchielli: *La Gioconda* Jan 24/Jan 27
Donizetti: *Don Pasquale* Jan 30
Bizet: *Carmen* Jan 31
Gala Jan 10

HUROK GERMAN GRAND OPERA COMPANY
Wagner: *Tristan und Isolde* Feb 2
Wagner: *Der Ring des Nibelungen*
    Das Rheingold Feb 3
    Die Walküre Feb 4
    Siegfried Feb 6
    Götterdämmerung Feb 8
Wagner: *The Flying Dutchman* Feb 5/Feb 9(mat)
Mozart: *Don Giovanni (Don Juan)* Feb 7

81—1930-1931

RAVINIA OPERA
Respighi: *La campana sommersa* June 21/July 1
Montemezzi: *L'amore dei tre re* June 22/July 2/Aug 23
Rabaud: *Mârouf* June 23/July 13/Aug 19
Puccini: *Madama Butterfly* June 24/Aug 10
Massenet: *Manon* June 25/July 24/Aug 22
Verdi: *Aida* June 26/July 27
Charpentier: *Louise* June 27/July 28
Verdi: *Il trovatore* June 28
Rossini: *The Barber of Seville* June 29/Aug 9
Puccini: *La rondine* June 30/July 11/Aug 2/Sep 1
Auber: *Fra Diavolo* July 3
Gounod: *Faust* July 4/July 17/Aug 12
Gounod: *Romeo and Juliet* July 5/July 14/Aug 5
Giordano: *Andrea Chénier* July 6/Aug 4
Massenet: *Thaïs* July 7
Flotow: *Martha* July 8
Puccini: *La bohème* July 9/July 18/Aug 15
Halévy: *La Juive* July 10/July 26
Verdi: *Un ballo in maschera* July 12/Aug 24
Donizetti: *Lucia di Lammermoor* July 15/Aug 3
Offenbach: *The Tales of Hoffmann* July 16/Aug 27
Bizet: *Carmen* July 19/Aug 7/Aug 17
Wagner: *Lohengrin* July 20/Aug 28
Vittadini: *Anima allegra* July 21/July 26/Aug 11
Puccini: *Tosca* July 22/Aug 31
Leoncavallo: *Pagliacci*
    with Mascagni: *Cavalleria rusticana* July 23/Aug 13
Giordano: *Fedora* July 25/Aug 25
Verdi: *Rigoletto* July 29
Saint-Saëns: *Samson and Delilah* July 30/Aug 29
Verdi: *La traviata* July 31
Wolf-Ferrari: *The Secret of Suzanne*
    with Falla: *La vida breve* Aug 6/Aug 14/Aug 30
Smetana: *The Bartered Bride* (in German) Aug 8/Aug 16/Aug 20
Puccini: *Manon Lescaut* Aug 18

CHICAGO CIVIC OPERA COMPANY
Moret: *Lorenzaccio* Oct 27/Nov 4/Nov 22
Wagner: *Die Walküre* Oct 28/Nov 10/Jan 10(mat)
Verdi: *La forza del destino* Oct 29
Wolf-Ferrari: *The Jewels of the Madonna* Oct 30/Nov 8/
    Nov 18/Nov 23/Dec 3

Massenet: *Manon* Nov 1(mat)/Nov 9(mat)/Nov 15/Dec 7

Wagner: *Tannhäuser* Nov 1/Nov 23/Dec 2/Dec 17

Montemezzi: *L'amore dei tre re* Nov 2(mat)/Nov 22(mat)

Bellini: *Norma* Nov 3/Nov 12

Beethoven: *Fidelio* Nov 5/Dec 8

Mascagni: *Cavalleria rusticana*
    with Leoncavallo: *Pagliacci* Nov 6/Nov 9/Nov 17/
    Dec 20/Jan 14

Wagner: *Lohengrin* Nov 8(mat)/Nov 24/Dec 21/Dec 23/
    Dec 28/Jan 17

Puccini: *Madama Butterfly* Nov 11/Nov 19/Nov 29/Jan 2

Verdi: *Un ballo in maschera* Nov 15(mat)/Nov 27/Nov 29/Dec 9

Wagner: *Die Meistersinger* Nov 20/Nov 26/Jan 5/Jan 20

Verdi: *Otello* Nov 25/Dec 4/Dec 13/Dec 22

Boito: *Mefistofele* Nov 29(mat)/Jan 10

Verdi: *La traviata* Dec 6/Dec 15/Jan 24(mat)

Forrest: *Camille* Dec 10/Dec 27(mat)/Jan 3/Jan 11/Jan 19

Puccini: *La bohème* Dec 11/Jan 7

Strauss: *Der Rosenkavalier* Dec 13(mat)

Alfano: *Resurrection (Risurrezione)* Dec 18/Dec 29/Jan 6

Verdi: *Il trovatore* Dec 20(mat)/Dec 27

Massenet: *Le Jongleur de Notre-Dame*
    with Massenet: *La Navarraise* Dec 24/Jan 1/
    Jan 17(mat)/Jan 24

Smetana: *The Bartered Bride* (probably in German) Dec 25/
    Jan 3(mat)/Jan 12

Mozart: *Don Giovanni* Dec 30/Jan 8/Jan 17

Verdi: *Aida* Dec 31

Thomas: *Mignon* Jan 13/Jan 21

Wagner: *Tristan und Isolde* Jan 15

Debussy: *Pelléas et Mélisande* Jan 22

Gala Jan 9

HUROK GERMAN GRAND OPERA COMPANY

Wagner: *Tristan und Isolde* Feb 26

Wagner: *The Flying Dutchman* Feb 27

Wagner: *Die Walküre* Feb 28

d'Albert: *Tiefland* Mar 1

82—1931–1932

RAVINIA OPERA

Rossini: *William Tell* June 20/June 29

Verdi: *La traviata* June 21/Aug 6/Aug 16

Puccini: *Madama Butterfly* June 22/July 5

Massenet: *Manon* June 23/July 29

Charpentier: *Louise* June 24

Verdi: *Aida* June 25/July 14/July 19/July 26

Rabaud: *Mârouf* June 26/July 16/Aug 23

Puccini: *Manon Lescaut* June 27/July 9

Rossini: *The Barber of Seville* June 28

Gounod: *Faust* June 30/July 30/Aug 18

Puccini: *La bohème* July 1/July 12

Wagner: *Lohengrin* July 2/July 23/Aug 26

Saint-Saëns: *Samson and Delilah* July 3/July 24

Puccini: *La rondine* July 4/July 20/Aug 17

Offenbach: *The Tales of Hoffmann* July 6

Giordano: *Andrea Chénier* July 7/Aug 7

Flotow: *Martha* July 8/July 27

Puccini: *Tosca* July 10/July 28/Aug 27

Smetana: *The Bartered Bride* (in German) July 11/July 31/Aug 9

Verdi: *Rigoletto* July 13/Aug 12

Montemezzi: *L'amore dei tre re* July 15/July 25

Mascagni: *Cavalleria rusticana*
    with Leoncavallo: *Pagliacci* July 17/Aug 30

Wolf-Ferrari: *The Secret of Suzanne*
    with Falla: *La vida breve* July 18/Aug 24

Donizetti: *Lucia di Lammermoor* July 22/Aug 20

Bizet: *Carmen* Aug 1

Auber: *Fra Diavolo* Aug 2

Taylor: *Peter Ibbetson* Aug 3/Aug 8/Aug 14/Aug 21/
    Aug 29/Aug 31 (marking the end of fully staged
    opera at Ravinia)

Verdi: *Il trovatore* Aug 4/Aug 15

Gounod: *Romeo and Juliet* Aug 5

Halévy: *La Juive* Aug 13/Aug 22

Verdi: *Un ballo in maschera* Aug 19/Aug 28

Massenet: *Thaïs* Aug 25

CHICAGO CIVIC OPERA COMPANY

Puccini: *Tosca* Nov 2/Dec 3

Mozart: *The Magic Flute* Nov 3/Nov 9/Nov 28(mat)/Dec 12

Verdi: *Aida* Nov 4/Nov 12/Nov 21/Dec 5(mat)/Jan 15

Verdi: *Rigoletto* Nov 5/Nov 18/Dec 7

Mussorgsky: *Boris Godunov* Nov 7(mat)/Nov 19/Dec 28

Verdi: *Il trovatore* Nov 7/Nov 16/Nov 25/Dec 17

Donizetti: *Lucia di Lammermoor* Nov 10/Dec 26

Smetana: *The Bartered Bride* Nov 11/Dec 5/Dec 14/Jan 1(mat)

Puccini: *La bohème* Nov 14(mat)/Nov 24/Jan 4/Jan 14

Saint-Saëns: *Samson and Delilah* Nov 14/Nov 23/Dec 16

Wagner: *Tristan und Isolde* Nov 17/Dec 2

Schillings: *Mona Lisa* Nov 21(mat)/Nov 30

Massenet: *Hérodiade* Nov 26/Dec 12(mat)/Dec 19

Verdi: *La traviata* Nov 28/Dec 8/Dec 19(mat)/Jan 6/Jan 28

Leoni: *L'Oracolo*
    with Puccini: *Gianni Schicchi* Dec 1/Dec 9/Dec 21

Wagner: *Die Meistersinger* Dec 10/Dec 23/Jan 2/Jan 26

Flotow: *Martha* Dec 15/Dec 25(mat)/Jan 3/Jan 29

Wagner: *Parsifal* Dec 20(mat)/Jan 12(mat)

Halévy: *La Juive* Dec 22/Dec 30/Jan 9

Rossini: *The Barber of Seville* Dec 24/Jan 5/Jan 16

Puccini: *Madama Butterfly* Dec 29/Jan 9(mat)/Jan 20

Thomas: *Mignon* Dec 31/Jan 19

Mascagni: *Cavalleria rusticana*
    with Leoncavallo: *Pagliacci* Jan 2(mat)/Jan 23

Ponchielli: *La Gioconda* Jan 7/Jan 16(mat)/Jan 25

Wagner: *Lohengrin* Jan 13/Jan 21/Jan 29(mat)

Bizet: *Carmen* Jan 18/Jan 21(mat)/Jan 27

83—1932-1933

CHICAGO OPEN AIR OPERA (Alfredo Salmaggi; Soldier Field)
   Verdi: *Aida* Aug 28

No season from a resident Chicago company

84—1933-1934

SAN CARLO OPERA COMPANY
   Bizet: *Carmen* Sep 18/Sep 26/Oct 4/Oct 13/Oct 18
   Puccini: *Madama Butterfly* Sep 19/Oct 7(mat)/Oct 9/Oct 28
   Gounod: *Faust* Sep 20/Sep 30(mat)/Oct 10/Oct 11/Oct 19
   Mascagni: *Cavalleria rusticana*
      with Leoncavallo: *Pagliacci* Sep 21/Oct 17
   Verdi: *Rigoletto* Sep 22/Oct 7
   Humperdinck: *Hansel and Gretel* Sep 23(mat)/Oct 12(mat)
   Verdi: *Il trovatore* Sep 23/Oct 1/Oct 14/Oct 20
   Verdi: *Aida* Sep 24/Sep 30/Oct 5/Oct 21
   Gounod: *Romeo and Juliet* Sep 25
   Puccini: *La bohème* Sep 27/Oct 12
   Wagner: *Lohengrin* Sep 29/Oct 6
   Verdi: *La traviata* Oct 2
   Puccini: *Tosca* Oct 3
   Offenbach: *The Tales of Hoffmann* Oct 14(mat)
   Donizetti: *Lucia di Lammermoor* Oct 16
   Flotow: *Martha* Oct 21(mat)
   Gala Oct 22

CHICAGO GRAND OPERA COMPANY
   Puccini: *Tosca* Dec 26/Jan 1
   Puccini: *Madama Butterfly* Dec 27/Jan 6
   Puccini: *La bohème* Dec 30(mat)/Jan 8
   Verdi: *Aida* Dec 30/Jan 6(mat)
   Verdi: *Rigoletto* Dec 31/Jan 17
   Bizet: *Carmen* Jan 2
   Mascagni: *Cavalleria rusticana*
      with Leoncavallo: *Pagliacci* Jan 3/Jan 22
   Gounod: *Faust* Jan 9
   Puccini: *Turandot* Jan 10/Jan 16/Jan 27(mat)
   Massenet: *Manon* Jan 13(mat)
   Verdi: *Il trovatore* Jan 13/Jan 25
   Wagner: *Lohengrin* Jan 15
   Saint-Saëns: *Samson and Delilah* Jan 20(mat)
   Ponchielli: *La Gioconda* Jan 20
   Leoncavallo: *Pagliacci* (act 1)
      with Rimsky-Korsakov: *Le Coq d'or* Jan 22
   Flotow: *Martha* Jan 24
   Thomas: *Mignon* Jan 27
   Gala Jan 23

85—1934-1935

PRESENTED BY GRACE DENTON (at the Auditorium)
   Thomson: *Four Saints in Three Acts* (four performances
      beginning Nov 7)

CHICAGO GRAND OPERA COMPANY
   Puccini: *Turandot* Nov 10/Nov 17(mat)
   Giordano: *Andrea Chénier* Nov 12
   Puccini: *Tosca* Nov 13/Nov 21
   Verdi: *Il trovatore* Nov 14
   Leoncavallo: *Pagliacci*
      with Mascagni: *Cavalleria rusticana* Nov 17
   Verdi: *La traviata* Nov 19/Dec 19
   Verdi: *Aida* Nov 20/Dec 1
   Puccini: *La bohème* Nov 24(mat)/Dec 8
   Verdi: *La forza del destino* Nov 24
   Wagner: *Lohengrin* Nov 26/Dec 12
   Bizet: *Carmen* Nov 27/Dec 5
   Strauss: *Salome*
      with Leoncavallo: *Pagliacci* Nov. 28
      with two ballets Dec 3
   Puccini: *Madama Butterfly* Dec 1(mat)/Dec 11
   Flotow: *Martha* Dec 4
   Wagner: *Tannhäuser* Dec 8(mat)
   Massenet: *Manon* Dec 10
   Wagner: *Tristan und Isolde* Dec 15(mat)/Dec 18
   Mozart: *Don Giovanni* Dec 15
   Gounod: *Faust* Dec 17
   Verdi: *Rigoletto* Dec 22(mat)

SAN CARLO OPERA COMPANY
   Puccini: *Madama Butterfly* Apr 30
   Verdi: *Aida* May 1
   Verdi: *Rigoletto* May 2
   Mascagni: *Cavalleria rusticana*
      with Leoncavallo: *Pagliacci* May 3
   Wagner: *Lohengrin* May 4/May 5
   Flotow: *Martha* May 5(mat)

86—1935-1936

SAN CARLO OPERA COMPANY
   Verdi: *Aida* Oct 14/Oct 26
   Puccini: *Madama Butterfly* Oct 15/Oct 24/Nov 2
   Wagner: *Lohengrin* Oct 16
   Bizet: *Carmen* Oct 17/Oct 27/Nov 2
   Verdi: *Rigoletto* Oct 18
   Gounod: *Faust* Oct 19(mat)/Nov 1
   Verdi: *Il trovatore* Oct 19/Nov 3
   Mascagni: *Cavalleria rusticana*
      with Leoncavallo: *Pagliacci* Oct 20
   Saint-Saëns: *Samson and Delilah* Oct 21/Oct 29
   Wagner: *Tannhäuser* Oct 22
   Verdi: *La traviata* Oct 23
   Puccini: *La bohème* Oct 25
   Flotow: *Martha* Oct 26(mat)
   Wolf-Ferrari: *The Jewels of the Madonna* Oct 28
   Puccini: *Tosca* Oct 30

CHICAGO CITY OPERA COMPANY
   Boito: *Mefistofele* Nov 2

Mozart: *Don Giovanni* Nov 4
Bizet: *Carmen* Nov 5/Dec 1
Flotow: *Martha* Nov 6
Mascagni: *Cavalleria rusticana* (with ballet) Nov 9(mat)
Verdi: *Il trovatore* Nov 9/Nov 25
Verdi: *La traviata* Nov 10(mat)/Dec 4
Massenet: *Thaïs* Nov 11/Dec 7(mat)
Wagner: *Lohengrin* Nov 12
Puccini: *La bohème* Nov 13/Nov 26
Strauss: *Der Rosenkavalier* Nov 16(mat)/Nov 18
Verdi: *Rigoletto* Nov 16/Nov 19
Puccini: *Turandot* Nov 20
Verdi: *Aida* Nov 22/Nov 27
Wagner: *Tannhäuser* Nov 23(mat)
Leginska: *Gale (The Haunting)* Nov 23
Donizetti: *Lucia di Lammermoor* Nov 28
Puccini: *Madama Butterfly* Nov 30
Respighi: *La fiamma* Dec 2
Gounod: *Faust* Dec 3/Dec 7

THEATRE GUILD/AMERICAN THEATRE SOCIETY (Erlanger)
Gershwin: *Porgy and Bess* Feb 17–Mar 7 (presented as a
musical show, with matinées Wednesdays and Saturdays)

87—1936-1937

CHICAGO CITY OPERA COMPANY
Respighi: *La fiamma* Oct 31/Nov 6
Massenet: *Thaïs* Nov 2
Flotow: *Martha* Nov 4/Nov 14
Verdi: *La traviata* Nov 7(mat)
Puccini: *Madama Butterfly* Nov 7
Thomas: *Mignon* Nov 9/Nov 21
Charpentier: *Louise* Nov 11/Nov 16
Puccini: *Gianni Schicchi*
with Mascagni: *Cavalleria rusticana* Nov 13
Gruenberg: *Jack and the Beanstalk* Nov 14(mat)
with Leoncavallo: *Pagliacci* Dec 3
Puccini: *La bohème* Nov 15/Nov 24/Dec 6
Donizetti: *L'elisir d'amore* Nov 18
Bizet: *Carmen* Nov 20
Gounod: *Faust* Nov 21(mat)
Rossini: *The Barber of Seville* Nov 23
Verdi: *Aida* Nov 25
Verdi: *Otello* Nov 27
Wagner: *Die Walküre* Nov 28(mat)/Dec 7
Delibes: *Lakmé* Nov 28
Boito: *Mefistofele* Nov 30
Halévy: *La Juive* Dec 2/Dec 13
Smetana: *The Bartered Bride* Dec 4/Dec 12
Wagner: *Lohengrin* Dec 5(mat)
Verdi: *Rigoletto* Dec 5
Verdi: *Il trovatore* Dec 10
Wagner: *Tannhäuser* Dec 11
Saint-Saëns: *Samson and Delilah* Dec 12(mat)

ZELZER OPERA COMPANY
Bizet: *Carmen* Dec 31

88—1937-1938

CHICAGO CITY OPERA COMPANY
Verdi: *Aida* Oct 30/Nov 11
Saint-Saëns: *Samson and Delilah* Nov 1
Verdi: *Il trovatore* Nov 3/Dec 9
Puccini: *Madama Butterfly* Nov 4
Massenet: *Manon* Nov 5/Nov 17
Rossini: *The Barber of Seville* Nov 6(mat)/Nov 18
Damrosch: *The Man without a Country* Nov 6/Nov 19
Verdi: *La traviata* Nov 8/Dec 17
Donizetti: *Lucia di Lammermoor* Nov 10/Dec 4(mat)
Massenet: *Thaïs* Nov 12
Bizet: *Carmen* Nov 13(mat)/Nov 20
Puccini: *Tosca* Nov 13/Dec 1
Montemezzi: *L'amore dei tre re* Nov 15
Wagner: *Lohengrin* Nov 20(mat)/Dec 11
Moniuszko: *Halka* Nov 21
Bellini: *Norma* Nov 22
Wagner: *Tristan und Isolde* Nov 24/Dec 13
Mascagni: *Cavalleria rusticana*
with Leoncavallo: *Pagliacci* Nov 25
Ponchielli: *La Gioconda* Nov 26
Wagner: *Tannhäuser* Nov 27(mat)
Delibes: *Lakmé* Nov 27/Nov 30
Verdi: *Otello* Nov 29
Puccini: *Tosca* Dec 1
Gounod: *Faust* Dec 2
Wagner: *Die Walküre* Dec 3/Dec 7
Halévy: *La Juive* Dec 4
Humperdinck: *Hansel and Gretel* Dec 5(mat)
Strauss: *Der Rosenkavalier* Dec 6
Verdi: *Rigoletto* Dec 8/Dec 19
Flotow: *Martha* Dec 10/Dec 31/Jan 3
Puccini: *La bohème* Dec 11(mat)/Dec 15
Thomas: *Mignon* Dec 16
Gala Dec 18

ZELZER OPERA COMPANY
Moniuszko: *Halka* Dec 31

SAN CARLO OPERA COMPANY
Verdi: *Rigoletto* Jan 3
Mascagni: *Cavalleria rusticana*
with Leocavallo: *Pagliacci* Jan 4
Wagner: *Lohengrin* Jan 5
Verdi: *Aida* Jan 6/Jan 16
Gounod: *Faust* Jan 7
Puccini: *Madama Butterfly* Jan 8(mat)/Jan 14
Bizet: *Carmen* Jan 8/Jan 15(mat)
Verdi: *Il trovatore* Jan 9/Jan 15
Verdi: *La traviata* Jan 10
Puccini: *La bohème* Jan 11

Donizetti: *Lucia di Lammermoor* Jan 12(mat)
Wagner: *Tannhäuser* Jan 12

89—1938-1939

SAN CARLO OPERA COMPANY
  Rossini: *The Barber of Seville* Oct 2
  Verdi: *Aida* Oct 3/Oct 18
  Verdi: *Rigoletto* Oct 4
  Mascagni: *Cavalleria rusticana*
    with Leoncavallo: *Pagliacci* Oct 5
  Puccini: *Madama Butterfly* Oct 6/Oct 19
  Gounod: *Faust* Oct 7
  Flotow: *Martha* Oct 9
  Bizet: *Carmen* Oct 10
  Verdi: *Il trovatore* Oct 11/Oct 20
  Verdi: *La traviata* Oct 12/Oct 21
  Puccini: *La bohème* Oct 13/Oct 22
  Wagner: *Lohengrin* Oct 14
  Puccini: *Tosca* Oct 16/Oct 23
  Donizetti: *Lucia di Lammermoor* Oct 17

CHICAGO CITY OPERA COMPANY
  Verdi: *Otello* Oct 29
  Verdi: *Aida* Oct 31/Nov 26(mat)/Dec 17
  Wagner: *Die Meistersinger* Nov 2/Nov 12(mat)
  Ponchielli: *La Gioconda* Nov 3
  Verdi: *Rigoletto* Nov 4/Nov 10
  Saint-Saëns: *Samson and Delilah* Nov 5(mat)
  Puccini: *Madama Butterfly* Nov 5
  Offenbach: *The Tales of Hoffmann* Nov 7/Nov 17
  Puccini: *Tosca* Nov 9/Nov 14/Dec 1
  Puccini: *La bohème* Nov 11/Dec 5/Dec 15/Jan 9*
  Bizet: *Carmen* Nov 12/Nov 24/Dec 16
  Verdi: *La traviata* Nov 16/Dec 10
  Flotow: *Martha* Nov 18/Dec 8
  Puccini: *Turandot* Nov 19(mat)/Dec 9
  Wagner: *Tristan und Isolde* Nov 19/Nov 25
  Wagner: *Lohengrin* Nov 21
  Donizetti: *Lucia di Lammermoor* Nov 23/Dec 3
  Rossini: *The Barber of Seville* Nov 26/Dec 7
  Wagner: *Die Walküre* Nov 28
  Delibes: *Lakmé* Nov 30
  Gounod: *Faust* Dec 2
  Massenet: *Manon* Dec 3(mat)/Dec 12/Jan 15*
  Verdi: *Il trovatore* Dec 4/Jan 16*
  Humperdinck: *Hansel and Gretel* Dec 9(mat)
  Gounod: *Romeo and Juliet* Dec 10(mat)
  Giordano: *Andrea Chénier* Dec 14
  Montemezzi: *L'amore dei tre re* Dec 17(mat)

  * postseason performance

INDEPENDENT OPERA COMPANY
  Rossini: *The Barber of Seville* Dec 31

90—1939-1940

CHICAGO CITY OPERA COMPANY
  Mussorgsky: *Boris Godunov* Oct. 28/Nov 11(mat)
  Giordano: *Andrea Chénier* Oct 30
  Verdi: *La traviata* Nov 1/Nov 10
  Verdi: *Aida* Nov 2/Nov 11/Dec 2(mat)
  Rossini: *The Barber of Seville* Nov 3/Nov 23
  Charpentier: *Louise* Nov 4(mat)/Nov 11/Dec 16
  Gounod: *Faust* Nov 4
  Thomas: *Mignon* Nov 6/Nov 15
  Puccini: *La bohème* Nov 8
  Mascagni: *Cavalleria rusticana*
    with Leoncavallo: *Pagliacci* Nov 9
  Bizet: *Carmen* Nov 12/Nov 25(mat)/Dec 11
  Donizetti: *Lucia di Lammermoor* Nov 16/Nov 25
  Massenet: *Manon* Nov 17/Dec 6
  Verdi: *Falstaff* Nov 18(mat)
  Flotow: *Martha* Nov 18
  Verdi: *Otello* Nov 20/Dec 13
  Puccini: *Madama Butterfly* Nov 22/Dec 4
  Wagner: *Tristan und Isolde* Nov 24/Dec 1
  Wagner: *Tannhäuser* Nov 27
  Wagner: *Lohengrin* Nov 29
  Smetana: *The Bartered Bride* Nov 30/Dec 15
  Wagner: *Die Walküre* Dec 2
  Puccini: *Tosca* Dec 7/Dec 16(mat)
  Verdi: *Rigoletto* Dec 8/Dec 14
  Verdi: *Il trovatore* Dec 9(mat)
  Gounod: *Romeo and Juliet* Dec 9

ZELZER OPERA COMPANY
  Puccini: *La bohème* Dec 31

91—1940-1941

SAN CARLO OPERA COMPANY
  Bizet: *Carmen* Oct 12(mat)/Oct 18/Oct 26
  Verdi: *Il trovatore* Oct 12/Oct 20
  Verdi: *Rigoletto* Oct 13/Oct 23
  Puccini: *Madama Butterfly* Oct 14/Oct 26(mat)
  Verdi: *Aida* Oct 15/Oct 27
  Gounod: *Faust* Oct 16/Oct 24
  Mascagni: *Cavalleria rusticana*
    with Leoncavallo: *Pagliacci* Oct 17/Oct 25
  Flotow: *Martha* Oct 19(mat)
  Puccini: *Tosca* Oct 19
  Verdi: *La traviata* Oct 21
  Puccini: *La bohème* Oct 22

CHICAGO OPERA COMPANY
  Verdi: *Aida* Nov 2/Nov 13/Dec 9
  Wagner: *Tristan und Isolde* Nov 4
  Verdi: *La traviata* Nov 5/Nov 18/Nov 29
  Verdi: *Il trovatore* Nov 6/Nov 15
  Puccini: *Madama Butterfly* Nov 7

Verdi: *Falstaff* Nov 9(mat)/Nov 22/Dec 4

Massenet: *Manon* Nov 9/Nov 23(mat)

Mascagni: *Cavalleria rusticana*
  with Leoncavallo: *Pagliacci* Nov 11/Nov 20

Bizet: *Carmen* Nov 12/Nov 27

Mozart: *Don Giovanni* Nov 16(mat)/Nov 26

Verdi: *Rigoletto* Nov 16/Nov 25/Dec 6

Puccini: *Madama Butterfly* Nov 19

Montemezzi: *L'amore dei tre re* Nov 23

Strauss: *Der Rosenkavalier* Nov 30(mat)/Dec 11

Wagner: *Die Walküre* Dec 2/Dec 14

Wolf-Ferrari: *The Jewels of the Madonna* Dec 3/Dec 14(mat)

Flotow: *Martha* Dec 7(mat)

Puccini: *Tosca* Dec 7

Strauss: *Salome* Dec 10

Humperdinck: *Hansel and Gretel* Dec 29(mat)

Massenet: *Manon* Dec 31

OPERA THEATER
  Cimarosa: *Il matrimonio segreto* Oct 20

92—1941-1942

CHICAGO OPERA COMPANY
  Verdi: *Un ballo in maschera* Nov 8
  Bizet: *Carmen* Nov 10/Nov 21/Nov 29(mat)
  Gounod: *Faust* Nov 12/Dec 5
  Verdi: *La traviata* Nov 14/Dec 13(mat)
  Donizetti: *The Daughter of the Regiment* Nov 15
  Rossini: *The Barber of Seville* Nov 15(mat)/Dec 8
  Verdi: *Otello* Nov 17
  Verdi: *Aida* Nov 19/Dec 13
  Wagner: *Lohengrin* Nov 22(mat)
  Mascagni: *Cavalleria rusticana*
    with Leoncavallo: *Pagliacci* Nov 22
  Verdi: *Falstaff* Nov 24
  Flotow: *Martha* Nov 26/Dec 6
  Puccini: *La bohème* Nov 28/Dec 6(mat)
  Verdi: *Il trovatore* Nov 29/Dec 12
  Puccini: *Tosca* Dec 1
  Puccini: *Madama Butterfly* Dec 3
  Verdi: *Rigoletto* Dec 10

SAN CARLO OPERA COMPANY
  Verdi: *Aida* Apr 12
  Verdi: *La traviata* Apr 13
  Bizet: *Carmen* Apr 14
  Verdi: *Rigoletto* Apr 15
  Puccini: *La bohème* Apr 16
  Gounod: *Faust* Apr 17
  Flotow: *Martha*
    with Wolf-Ferrari: *The Secret of Suzanne* Apr 18(mat)
  Verdi: *Il trovatore* Apr 18
  Mascagni: *Cavalleria rusticana*
    with Leoncavallo: *Pagliacci* Apr 19

93—1942-1943

CHICAGO OPERA COMPANY
  Verdi: *Aida* Nov 7/Nov 21(mat)/Nov 27/Dec 5
  Verdi: *Rigoletto* Nov 9/Dec 12(mat)
  Donizetti: *Lucia di Lammermoor* Nov 11
  Flotow: *Martha* Nov 13/Dec 7
  Bizet: *Carmen* Nov 14(mat)/Nov 30/Dec 4
  Gounod: *Faust* Nov 14/Nov 23
  Verdi: *La traviata* Nov 16/Dec 12
  Thomas: *Mignon* Nov 18
  Rossini: *The Barber of Seville* Nov 20/Dec 9
  Verdi: *Il trovatore* Nov 21
  Moniuszko: *Halka* Nov 25
  Massenet: *Manon* Nov 28(mat)
  Verdi: *Otello* Nov 28
  Mascagni: *Cavalleria rusticana*
    with Leoncavallo: *Pagliacci* Nov 30
  Puccini: *La bohème* Dec 2
  Puccini: *Tosca* Dec 5(mat)
  Offenbach: *The Tales of Hoffmann* Dec 11

CHERYL CRAWFORD PRODUCTION (Studebaker)
  Gershwin: *Porgy and Bess* Nov 2–Jan 16 (presented as a
    musical show, with matinées Wednesdays and Saturdays)

METROPOLITAN OPERA
  Mozart: *The Marriage of Figaro* Mar 22
  Gounod: *Faust* Mar 23
  Verdi: *La forza del destino* Mar 24
  Verdi: *La traviata* Mar 25/Apr 3
  Mozart: *The Magic Flute* Mar 26
  Bizet: *Carmen* Mar 27(mat)
  Verdi: *Il trovatore* Mar 27
  Wagner: *Tannhäuser* Mar 29
  Rossini: *The Barber of Seville* Mar 30
  Wagner: *Tristan und Isolde* Mar 31
  Verdi: *Aida* Apr 1
  Mussorgsky: *Boris Godunov* Apr 2
  Mozart: *Don Giovanni* Apr 3(mat)

94—1943-1944

GALLO AND ZELZER OPERA COMPANY (Soldier Field)
  Verdi: *Aida* July 24
  Bizet: *Carmen* July 31

No season from a Chicago opera company

OPERA THEATER
  Humperdinck: *Hansel and Gretel* Dec 18

METROPOLITAN OPERA
  Wagner: *Tristan und Isolde* Apr 17
  Verdi: *La traviata* Apr 18
  Mozart: *The Magic Flute* Apr 19
  Thomas: *Mignon* Apr 21

Verdi: *Un ballo in maschera* Apr 22(mat)

Bizet: *Carmen* Apr 22

Puccini: *Tosca* Apr 24

Wagner: *Parsifal* Apr 25

Offenbach: *The Tales of Hoffmann* Apr 26

Verdi: *Aida* Apr 27

Wagner: *Tannhäuser* Apr 28

Puccini: *La bohème* Apr 29(mat)

Verdi: *Rigoletto* Apr 29

SAN CARLO OPERA COMPANY (Soldier Field)

(All-Verdi season)

Aida June 21

La traviata June 22

Il trovatore June 23

95—1944-1945

CHICAGO OPERA COMPANY

Bizet: *Carmen* Oct 16/Oct 25/Nov 3

Verdi: *La traviata* Oct 18/Oct 23/Nov 7/Nov 18

Puccini: *La bohème* Oct 20/Oct 28

Verdi: *Aida* Oct 21(mat)/Nov 1

Wagner: *Die Walküre* Oct 21/Oct 30

Verdi: *Il trovatore* Oct 27/Nov 4

Verdi: *Otello* Oct 28(mat)/Nov 6

Gounod: *Romeo and Juliet* Nov 4(mat)/Nov 11

Debussy: *Pelléas et Mélisande* Nov 8/Nov 13

Gounod: *Faust* Nov 10/Nov 15

Verdi: *Rigoletto* Nov 11(mat)/Nov 17

Puccini: *Tosca* Nov 18(mat)

CHERYL CRAWFORD PRODUCTION (Civic Opera House)

Gershwin: *Porgy and Bess* Dec 4–Dec 10 (presented as a
musical show, with a Saturday matinée)

METROPOLITAN OPERA

Donizetti: *Lucia di Lammermoor* Apr 30

Wagner: *Lohengrin* May 1

Mozart: *Don Giovanni* May 2

Rimsky-Korsakov: *Le Coq d'or* May 3

Wagner: *Die Meistersinger* May 4

Bellini: *Norma* May 5(mat)

Puccini: *La bohème* May 5

96—1945-1946

CHICAGO OPERA COMPANY

Massenet: *Manon* Oct 8/Oct 19

Verdi: *Rigoletto* Oct 10/Oct 15

Verdi: *Il trovatore* Oct 12/Oct 20/Nov 12

Bizet: *Carmen* Oct 13(mat)/Oct 24/Nov 16

Puccini: *Tosca* Oct 13/Oct 22

Rossini: *The Barber of Seville* Oct 17/Nov 2

Wagner: *Parsifal* Oct 20(mat)/Oct 27

Mascagni: *Cavalleria rusticana*
with Leoncavallo: *Pagliacci* Oct 26/Nov 14

Gounod: *Faust* Oct 27(mat)/Nov 3

Verdi: *La forza del destino* Oct 29/Nov 7

Debussy: *Pelléas et Mélisande* Oct 31/Nov 5

Verdi: *La traviata* Nov 3(mat)/Nov 9

Verdi: *Aida* Nov 10(mat)/Nov 17

Mozart: *The Marriage of Figaro* Nov 10/Nov 17(mat)

METROPOLITAN OPERA

Wagner: *Tannhäuser* May 6

Verdi: *La traviata* May 7

Ponchielli: *La Gioconda* May 8

Mozart: *The Magic Flute* May 9

Wagner: *Die Walküre* May 10

Strauss: *Der Rosenkavalier* May 11(mat)

Verdi: *Un ballo in maschera* May 11

97—1946-1947

CHICAGO OPERA COMPANY

Verdi: *Aida* Sep 30/Oct 11

Puccini: *La bohème* Oct 2/Oct 7/Oct 19(mat)

Menotti: *Amelia Goes to the Ball*
with Gruenberg: *The Emperor Jones* Oct 4/Oct 14

Wagner: *Tristan und Isolde* Oct 5(mat)/Oct 16

Verdi: *Rigoletto* Oct 5/Oct 12(mat)

Donizetti: *Lucia di Lammermoor* Oct 9/Oct 25

Puccini: *Madama Butterfly* Oct 12/Oct 21/Nov 2(mat)

Puccini: *Tosca* Oct 18/Oct 26

Bizet: *Carmen* Oct 19/Nov 4

Ponchielli: *La Gioconda* Oct 23/Nov 2

Saint-Saëns: *Samson and Delilah* Oct 26(mat)/Nov 8

Wagner: *Lohengrin* Oct 28/Nov 6

Thomas: *Mignon* Oct 30/Nov 9

Verdi: *La traviata* Nov 1/Nov 9(mat)

METROPOLITAN OPERA

Mussorgsky: *Boris Godunov* Apr 21

Puccini: *Madama Butterfly* Apr 22

Donizetti: *Lucia di Lammermoor* Apr 23

Mozart: *The Marriage of Figaro* Apr 24

Verdi: *Aida* Apr 25

Puccini: *La bohème* Apr 26(mat)

Gounod: *Faust* Apr 26

OPERA THEATER

Mozart: *The Abduction from the Seraglio* (in English) Mar 2(mat)

Britten: *The Rape of Lucretia* June 1

98—1947-1948

SAN CARLO OPERA COMPANY

Bizet: *Carmen* Oct 6/Oct 17/Oct 23

Puccini: *Madama Butterfly* Oct 7/Oct 15/Oct 25(mat)

Puccini: *Tosca* Oct 8/Oct 16/Oct 25

Mascagni: *Cavalleria rusticana*
with Leoncavallo: *Pagliacci* Oct 9/Oct 19

Verdi: *Rigoletto* Oct 10

Gounod: *Faust* Oct 11/Oct 26
Verdi: *Aida* Oct 12/Oct 18/Oct 24
Wagner: *Lohengrin* Oct 13
Puccini: *La bohème* Oct 14
Rossini: *The Barber of Seville* Oct 18
Donizetti: *Lucia di Lammermoor* Oct 22

CHICAGO SYMPHONY ORCHESTRA
Wagner: *Tristan und Isolde* Nov 16

OPERA THEATER
Verdi: *La traviata* (in English) Apr 18(mat)
Britten: *The Rape of Lucretia* May 2(mat)
Pergolesi: *La serva padrona* (in English)
    with Menotti: *The Old Maid and the Thief* May 16(mat)

99—1948–1949

NEW YORK CITY OPERA
Strauss: *Salome* Dec 1
Puccini: *Madama Butterfly* Dec 2/Dec 16
Bizet: *Carmen* Dec 3/Dec 15
Menotti: *Amelia Goes to the Ball*
    with *The Old Maid and the Thief* Dec 4
Mascagni: *Cavalleria rusticana*
    with Leoncavallo: *Pagliacci* Dec 5
Debussy: *Pelléas et Mélisande* Dec 6
Puccini: *La bohème* Dec 7/Dec 19
Mozart: *Don Giovanni* Dec 8
Verdi: *La traviata* Dec 9/Dec 18
Verdi: *Aida* Dec 10/Dec 17
Tchaikovsky: *Eugene Onegin* Dec 11
Puccini: *Tosca* Dec 12
Mozart: *The Marriage of Figaro* Dec 13

CHARLES L. WAGNER OPERA COMPANY
Mascagni: *Cavalleria rusticana*
    with Leoncavallo: *Pagliacci* Mar 5

100—1949–1950

NEW YORK CITY OPERA
Strauss: *Der Rosenkavalier* Nov 23/Dec 12
Bizet: *Carmen* Nov 24
Mozart: *Don Giovanni* Nov 25
Verdi: *La traviata* Nov 26/Dec 11
Offenbach: *The Tales of Hoffmann* Nov 27
Strauss: *Ariadne auf Naxos* Nov 28
Puccini: *Madama Butterfly* Nov 29/Dec 9
Verdi: *Aida* Nov 30/Dec 13
Mozart: *The Marriage of Figaro* Dec 2
Mascagni: *Cavalleria rusticana*
    with Leoncavallo: *Pagliacci* Dec 3
Puccini: *La bohème* Dec 4
Prokofiev: *The Love for Three Oranges* Dec 5
Bizet: *Carmen* Dec 6/Dec 14

Menotti: *The Old Maid and the Thief* Dec 7
Puccini: *Tosca* Dec 10

METROPOLITAN OPERA
Puccini: *Tosca* May 8
Bizet: *Carmen* May 9
Verdi: *La traviata* May 10
Wagner: *Die Meistersinger* May 11
Verdi: *Rigoletto* May 12
Verdi: *Aida* May 13(mat)
Puccini: *La bohème* May 13

101—1950–1951

NEW YORK CITY OPERA
Prokofiev: *The Love for Three Oranges* Nov 15
Bizet: *Carmen* Nov 16/Dec 1
Puccini: *Turandot* Nov 17/Nov 29
Verdi: *La traviata* Nov 18/Dec 3
Puccini: *Madama Butterfly* Nov 19/Dec 2
Mozart: *Don Giovanni* Nov 20
Verdi: *Aida* Nov 22
Gounod: *Faust* Nov 24
Mascagni: *Cavalleria rusticana*
    with Leoncavallo: *Pagliacci* Nov 25
Puccini: *Tosca* Nov 26
Mozart: *The Marriage of Figaro* Nov 27
Puccini: *La bohème* Nov 28

METROPOLITAN OPERA
J. Strauss: *Die Fledermaus* May 10/May 12(mat)
Verdi: *La traviata* May 11
Puccini: *La bohème* May 12

102—1951–1952

NEW YORK CITY OPERA
Massenet: *Manon* Nov 23
Prokofiev: *The Love for Three Oranges* Nov 24(mat)/Dec 5
Puccini: *Madama Butterfly* Nov 24/Dec 4
Puccini: *La bohème* Nov 25
Verdi: *La traviata* Nov 27/Dec 7
Bizet: *Carmen* Nov 28/Dec 8
Offenbach: *The Tales of Hoffmann* Nov 30
Gounod: *Faust* Dec 1
Verdi: *Aida* Dec 2
Mozart: *The Marriage of Figaro* Dec 3
Mascagni: *Cavalleria rusticana*
    with Leoncavallo: *Pagliacci* Dec 8
Verdi: *Rigoletto* Dec 9

BLEVINS DAVIS-ROBERT BREEN PRODUCTION
(Civic Opera House)
Gershwin: *Porgy and Bess* June 25–July 19 (presented as a
    musical show, with Saturday matinées)

103—1952-1953

NEW YORK CITY OPERA
Puccini: *Tosca* Nov 12
Verdi: *La traviata* Nov 13/Nov 22(mat)
Bartók: *Duke Bluebeard's Castle*
  with Menotti: *Amahl and the Night Visitors* Nov 14
Bizet: *Carmen* Nov 15(mat)/Nov 22/Nov 28
Puccini: *La bohème* Nov 15/Nov 30
Mascagni: *Cavalleria rusticana*
  with Leoncavallo: *Pagliacci* Nov 16/Nov 26
Verdi: *Aida* Nov 17/Nov 29
Menotti: *The Consul* Nov 18
Mozart: *Don Giovanni* Nov 19
Gounod: *Faust* Nov 20/Nov 25
Puccini: *Madama Butterfly* Nov 21/Nov 29(mat)
Prokofiev: *The Love for Three Oranges* Nov 23

ZELZER OPERA COMPANY
Verdi: *Rigoletto* Dec 31

104—1953-1954

NEW YORK CITY OPERA
Rossini: *La Cenerentola (Cinderella)* Nov 18
Bizet: *Carmen* Nov 19/Nov 28
Verdi: *La traviata* Nov 20/Nov 29
Humperdinck: *Hansel and Gretel* Nov 21(mat)
Mascagni: *Cavalleria rusticana*
  with Leoncavallo: *Pagliacci* Nov 21
Mozart: *The Marriage of Figaro* Nov 22(mat)
Puccini: *Madama Butterfly* Nov 22
Puccini: *La bohème* Nov 25
Puccini: *Tosca* Nov 27
Verdi: *Rigoletto* Nov 28
J. Strauss: *Die Fledermaus* Nov 29(mat)

LYRIC THEATER ("Calling card" performances)
Mozart: *Don Giovanni* Feb 5/Feb 7

BLEVINS DAVIS-ROBERT BREEN PRODUCTION
(Civic Opera House)
Gershwin: *Porgy and Bess* Mar 2–Mar 22 (presented as a
  musical show, with matinées Saturdays and one Sunday)

METROPOLITAN OPERA
Gounod: *Faust* May 20
Verdi: *Aida* May 21
Donizetti: *Lucia di Lammermoor* May 22(mat)
Puccini: *La bohème* May 22
Verdi: *Rigoletto* May 23(mat)
Verdi: *La traviata* May 23

105—1954-1955

LYRIC THEATER (1)
Bellini: *Norma* Nov 1/Nov 20
Giannini: *The Taming of the Shrew* Nov 3/Nov 13
Rossini: *The Barber of Seville* Nov 6/Nov 10

Puccini: *La bohème* Nov 6(mat)/Nov 13
Verdi: *La traviata* Nov 8/Nov 12
Donizetti: *Lucia di Lammermoor* Nov 15/Nov 17
Bizet: *Carmen* Nov 16/Nov 20(mat)
Puccini: *Tosca* Nov 18/Nov 20

METROPOLITAN OPERA
Giordano: *Andrea Chénier* May 19
Puccini: *La bohème* May 20(mat)
Rossini: *The Barber of Seville* May 20
Bizet: *Carmen* May 21(mat)
Verdi: *La traviata* May 21

106—1955-1956

LYRIC THEATER (2)
Bellini: *I puritani* Oct 31/Dec 3
Verdi: *Aida* Nov 1/Nov 4
Verdi: *Il trovatore* Nov 5/Nov 8
Puccini: *La bohème* Nov 7/Nov 9
Puccini: *Madama Butterfly* Nov 11/Nov 14/Nov 17
Verdi: *Rigoletto* Nov 12/Nov 25
Gounod: *Faust* Nov 15/Nov 18
Puccini: *Il tabarro*
  with Monteverdi: *Il ballo delle ingrate* (masque),
  and Lehar: *The Merry Widow* (ballet) (triple bill)
  Nov 16/Nov 19
Mascagni: *Cavalleria rusticana*
  with De Banfield: *Lord Byron's Love Letter*,
  and *Revanche* (ballet on Verdi: *Il trovatore*) (triple bill)
  Nov 21/Nov 26
Donizetti: *L'elisir d'amore* Nov 22/Nov 30
Montemezzi: *L'amore dei tre re* Nov 28/Dec 2
Verdi: *Un ballo in maschera* Nov 29/Dec 3

ZELZER OPERA COMPANY
Menotti: *The Telephone* and *the Medium* Oct 23

107—1956-1957

LYRIC OPERA OF CHICAGO (3)
Puccini: *La fanciulla del West* Oct 10/Oct 13
Giordano: *Andrea Chénier* Oct 16/Oct 19
Strauss: *Salome* Oct 17/Nov 3
Wagner: *Die Walküre* Oct 20/Oct 22
Verdi: *Il trovatore* Oct 23/Oct 27
Verdi: *La traviata* Oct 26/Oct 31
Mozart: *Don Giovanni* Oct 29/Nov 13
Puccini: *Tosca* Oct 30/Nov 2/Nov 5
Verdi: *La forza del destino* Nov 8/Nov 12
Rossini: *The Barber of Seville* Nov 9/Nov 15/Nov 17
Puccini: *La bohème* Nov 14/Nov 16
Gala Nov 10

PAVANNE OPERA THEATER
Humperdinck: *Hansel and Gretel*
  with Puccini: *Gianni Schicchi* Dec 22

METROPOLITAN OPERA
Puccini: *La bohème* May 23
Verdi: *Il trovatore* May 24
Verdi: *La traviata* May 25(mat)
Puccini: *Madama Butterfly* May 25
Offenbach: *La Périchole* May 26

108—1957-1958

LYRIC OPERA OF CHICAGO (4)
Verdi: *Otello* Oct 11/Nov 14/Nov 18
Puccini: *La bohème* Oct 16/Nov 4
Thomas: *Mignon* Oct 19/Nov 4
Puccini: *Manon Lescaut* Oct 21/Oct 25/Nov 9
Mascagni: *Cavalleria rusticana*
  with Leoncavallo: *Pagliacci* Oct 23/Oct 26
Giordano: *Andrea Chénier* Oct 30/Nov 2
Ponchielli: *La Gioconda* Nov 1/Nov 6
Mozart: *The Marriage of Figaro* Nov 8/Nov 11
Cilea: *Adriana Lecouvreur* Nov 13/Nov 16
Verdi: *Un ballo in maschera* Nov 15/Nov 18
Puccini: *Tosca* Nov 20/Nov 29
Verdi: *Don Carlo* Nov 22/Nov 25/Nov 30
Donizetti: *Lucia di Lammermoor* Nov 23/Nov 27

METROPOLITAN OPERA
Tchaikovsky: *Eugene Onegin* May 22
Strauss: *Der Rosenkavalier* May 23
Puccini: *Madama Butterfly* May 24(mat)
Saint-Saëns: *Samson and Delilah* May 24
Gounod: *Faust* May 25(mat)
Rossini: *The Barber of Seville* May 25

109—1958-1959

LYRIC OPERA OF CHICAGO (5)
Verdi: *Falstaff* Oct 10/Oct 17
Puccini: *Madama Butterfly* Oct 13/Oct 15
Puccini: *Turandot* Oct 18/Oct 22/Oct 27
Verdi: *Il trovatore* Oct 20/Oct 24/Oct 29
Leoncavallo: *Pagliacci*
  with Puccini: *Gianni Schicchi* Oct 25/Oct 31/Nov 3
Wagner: *Tristan und Isolde* Nov 1/Nov 7/Nov 10
Verdi: *La traviata* Nov 5/Nov 8/Nov 14
Rossini: *The Barber of Seville* Nov 12/Nov 21
Verdi: *Rigoletto* Nov 15/Nov 19
Mussorgsky: *Boris Godunov* Nov 17/Nov 22/Nov 28
Verdi: *Aida* Nov 24/Nov 26/Nov 29

POLONIA OPERA COMPANY
Moniuszko: *Straszny dwór* Apr 7
Moniuszko: *Halka* May 16

110—1959-1960

LYRIC OPERA OF CHICAGO (6)
Bizet: *Carmen* Oct 12/Oct 16/Oct 21/Oct 24
Rossini: *La Cenerentola (Cinderella)* Oct 14/Oct 17/Oct 19
Verdi: *Simon Boccanegra* Oct 23/Oct 26/Oct 29
Puccini: *Turandot* Oct 28/Oct 30
Janáček: *Jenůfa* Nov 2/Nov 6
Verdi: *Un ballo in maschera* Nov 4/Nov 7
Mozart: *Così fan tutte* Nov 9/Nov 11/Nov 14
Wagner: *The Flying Dutchman* Nov 13/Nov 16/Nov 21
Ponchielli: *La Gioconda* Nov 18/Nov 20/Nov 28
Massenet: *Thaïs* Nov 23/Nov 25/Nov 27

NEW YORK CITY OPERA
Floyd: *Susannah* Mar 4
Moore: *The Ballad of Baby Doe* Mar 5
Weill: *Street Scene* Mar 6

111—1960-1961

LYRIC OPERA OF CHICAGO (7)
Verdi: *Don Carlo* Oct 14/Oct 21/Oct 24
Verdi: *Aida* Oct 17/Oct 19/Oct 22/Oct 28
Mozart: *The Marriage of Figaro* Oct 26/Oct 29/Oct 31
Puccini: *La bohème* Nov 2/Nov 5/Nov 7
Bizet: *Carmen* Nov 4/Nov 9/Nov 12
Puccini: *Tosca* Nov 11/Nov 14/Nov 19
Wagner: *Die Walküre* Nov 16/Nov 18/Nov 21
Giordano: *Fedora* Nov 23/Nov 25
Puccini: *Madama Butterfly* Nov 26/Nov 28/Dec 2
Verdi: *Simon Boccanegra* Nov 30/Dec 3

METROPOLITAN OPERA
Verdi: *Aida* May 12
Flotow: *Martha* May 13(mat)
Puccini: *Turandot* May 13
Verdi: *La traviata* May 14

112—1961-1962

LYRIC OPERA OF CHICAGO (8)
Donizetti: *Lucia di Lammermoor* Oct 14/Oct 16/Oct 18
Giordano: *Andrea Chénier* Oct 20/Oct 25/Oct 28
Boito: *Mefistofele* Oct 21/Oct 23/Oct 27
Verdi: *La forza del destino* Oct 30/Nov 4/Nov 10
Mozart: *Così fan tutte* Nov 1/Nov 3
Mozart: *Don Giovanni* Nov 6/Nov 8/Nov 11
Beethoven: *Fidelio* Nov 13/Nov 17/Nov 22
Rossini: *The Barber of Seville* Nov 15/Nov 18/Nov 20/Nov 24
Giannini: *The Harvest* Nov 25/Nov 27/Nov 29/Dec 1

METROPOLITAN OPERA
Puccini: *Madama Butterfly* May 27
Verdi: *La forza del destino* May 28
Donizetti: *Lucia di Lammermoor* May 29
Puccini: *Tosca* May 30

113—1962-1963

LYRIC OPERA OF CHICAGO (9)
  Borodin: *Prince Igor* Oct 12/Oct 15/Oct 20/Oct 24
  Puccini: *La bohème* Oct 17/Oct 19/Oct 22/Oct 27
  Puccini: *Tosca* Oct 26/Oct 29/Nov 3
  Donizetti: *L'elisir d'amore* Oct 31/Nov 2/Nov 5
  Mozart: *The Marriage of Figaro* Nov 7/Nov 9/Nov 12
  Saint-Saëns: *Samson and Delilah* Nov 10/Nov 14/Nov 16/Nov 19
  Verdi: *Rigoletto* Nov 17/Nov 21/Nov 23/Nov 26
  Gluck: *Orfeo ed Euridice* Nov 24/Nov 28/Nov 30
  Ballet Gala Oct 21

114—1963-1964

LYRIC OPERA OF CHICAGO (10)
  Verdi: *Nabucco* Oct 4/Oct 7/Oct 11/Oct 19
  Verdi: *Un ballo in maschera* Oct 5/Oct 9/Oct 14/Oct 18
  Gounod: *Faust* Oct 12/Oct 16/Oct 21/Oct 25
  Beethoven: *Fidelio* Oct 23/Oct 26/Oct 28/Nov 1
  Verdi: *Otello* Nov 2/Nov 4/Nov 8/Nov 13
  Rossini: *The Barber of Seville* Nov 6/Nov 9/Nov 11/Nov 15
  Wagner: *Tannhäuser* Nov 16/Nov 18/Nov 24/Nov 27
  Donizetti: *Don Pasquale* Nov 20/Nov 23/Nov 25/Nov 29

115—1964-1965

LYRIC OPERA OF CHICAGO (11)
  Verdi: *Il trovatore* Oct 9/Oct 14/Oct 17/Oct 19
  Donizetti: *La favorita* Oct 12/Oct 16/Oct 21/Oct 24
  Bizet: *Carmen* Oct 23/Oct 26/Oct 29/Oct 31/Nov 4
  Verdi: *Don Carlo* Oct 28/Oct 30/Nov 2/Nov 7
  Strauss: *Ariadne auf Naxos* Nov 6/Nov 9/Nov 14/Nov 18
  Puccini: *La bohème* Nov 8/Nov 12/Nov 17/Nov 24
  Rossini: *La Cenerentola (Cinderella)* Nov 11/Nov 13/
    Nov 21/Nov 23
  Mozart: *Don Giovanni* Nov 16/Nov 20/Nov 22/Nov 25
  Puccini: *Tosca* Nov 27/Nov 30/Dec 2/Dec 5

POLONAISE FOUNDATION
  Moniuszko: *Halka* Dec 13

NEW YORK CITY OPERA
  J. Strauss: *Die Fledermaus* Nov 29(mat)/Dec 31
  Lehár: *The Merry Widow* Nov 29/Jan 2
  Verdi: *La traviata* Dec 26/Jan 1
  Puccini: *Madama Butterfly* Dec 27(mat)/Dec 30
  Gounod: *Faust* Dec 27
  Mozart: *The Marriage of Figaro* Dec 29
  Bizet: *Carmen* Jan 2(mat)
  Verdi: *Rigoletto* Jan 3

116—1965-1966

LYRIC OPERA OF CHICAGO (12)
  Boito: *Mefistofele* Oct 8/Oct 13/Oct 16/Oct 18
  Verdi: *Simon Boccanegra* Oct 11/Oct 15/Oct 20/Oct 23

Puccini: *La bohème* Oct 22/Oct 25/Oct 27/Oct 30
Puccini: *Madama Butterfly* Oct 29/Nov 1/Nov 4/Nov 6/Nov 10
Saint-Saëns: *Samson and Delilah* Nov 3/Nov 5/Nov 8/Nov 13
Ravel: *L'Heure espagnole*
  with Orff: *Carmina Burana* (vocal and ballet) Nov 12/
    Nov 15/Nov 17/Nov 20
Berg: *Wozzeck* Nov 19/Nov 22/Dec 1
Verdi: *Aida* Nov 24/Nov 27/Nov 30/Dec 3/Dec 6
Verdi: *Rigoletto* Nov 26/Nov 29/Dec 4/Dec 8

METROPOLITAN OPERA NATIONAL COMPANY
  Floyd: *Susannah* Apr 18
  Bizet: *Carmen* Apr 19/Apr 22(mat & eve)
  Puccini: *Madama Butterfly* Apr 20(mat)/Apr 21/Apr 23
  Rossini: *La Cenerentola (Cinderella)* Apr 20

117—1966-1967

LYRIC OPERA OF CHICAGO (13)
  Mussorgsky: *Boris Godunov* Oct 7/Oct 12/Oct 15/Oct 17
  Verdi: *Otello* Oct 14/Oct 16/Oct 19/Oct 22
  Ponchielli: *La Gioconda* Oct 21/Oct 24/Oct 26/Oct 29
  Mascagni: *Cavalleria rusticana*
    with Casella: *La giara* (ballet) Oct 28/Oct 31/Nov 2/Nov 5
  Monteverdi: *L'incoronazione di Poppea* Nov 4/Nov 7/
    Nov 9/Nov 12
  Bizet: *The Pearl Fishers* Nov 13/Nov 14/Nov 16/Nov 19
  Mozart: *The Magic Flute* Nov 18/Nov 21/Nov 23/Nov 26
  Verdi: *La traviata* Nov 25/Nov 28/Nov 30/Dec 2/Dec 5/
    Dec 7/Dec 10
  Prokofiev: *Angel of Fire* Dec 3/Dec 6/Dec 12/Dec 14

ZEV BUFMAN–ALLIED ARTS CORPORATION
PRODUCTION (Civic Opera House)
  Gershwin: *Porgy and Bess* June 6/June 7(mat & eve)

METROPOLITAN OPERA NATIONAL COMPANY
  Britten: *The Rape of Lucretia* May 22
  Verdi: *La traviata* May 23/May 25
  Puccini: *La bohème* May 24/May 27
  Mozart: *The Marriage of Figaro* May 26

118—1967-1968

AMERICAN NATIONAL OPERA COMPANY
Puccini: *Tosca* Oct 18/Oct 21(mat)
Berg: *Lulu* Oct 19/Oct 21
Verdi: *Falstaff* Oct 20(in Italian)/Oct 22(mat)(in English)

No season from Lyric Opera of Chicago

119—1968-1969

LYRIC OPERA OF CHICAGO (14)
  Strauss: *Salome* Sep 27/Sep/30/Oct 4/Oct 9/Oct 12
  Bellini: *Norma* Oct 2/Oct 5/Oct 7/Oct 14/Oct 18/Oct 23

Puccini: *Tosca* Oct 11/Oct 16/Oct 19/Oct 25/Oct 28
Verdi: *Falstaff* Oct 21/Oct 26/Oct 30/Nov 1/Nov 4/Nov 8
Verdi: *Un ballo in maschera* Nov 2/Nov 6/Nov 9/Nov 11/Nov 15
Stravinsky: *Le Rossignol* and *Oedipus Rex*
    Nov 13/Nov 16/Nov 20/Nov 22/Nov 25/Nov 30
Donizetti: *Don Pasquale* Nov 23/Nov 27/Dec 2/Dec 4/Dec 7
Puccini: *Manon Lescaut* Dec 6/Dec 8/Dec 9/Dec 11/Dec 14

120—1969-1970

LYRIC OPERA OF CHICAGO (15)
    Mussorgsky: *Khovanshchina* Sep 26/Sep 29/Oct 3/Oct 8/Oct 11
    Verdi: *Macbeth*: Oct 1/Oct 4/Oct 6/Oct 10/Oct 15/Oct 18
    Puccini: *Madama Butterfly* Oct 13/Oct 22/Oct 25/Oct 27/
        Oct 31/Dec 4
    Wagner: *The Flying Dutchman* Oct 21/Oct 24/Oct 29/
        Nov 3/Nov 7/Nov 15
    Bellini: *I puritani* Nov 1/Nov 5/Nov 8/Nov 14/Nov 17
    Mozart: *Don Giovanni* Nov 12/Nov 21/Nov 24/Nov 29/
        Dec 3/Dec 6
    Falla: *El amor brujo*
        with Mascagni: *Cavalleria rusticana* Nov 19/Nov 22/
        Nov 26/Dec 1/Dec 12
    Rossini: *The Barber of Seville* Nov 28/Dec 5/Dec 8/Dec 10/Dec 13

121—1970-1971

LYRIC OPERA OF CHICAGO (16)
    Strauss: *Der Rosenkavalier* Sep 25/Sep 28/Oct 2/Oct 7/
        Oct 10/Oct 15
    Puccini: *Turandot* Oct 5/Oct 8/Oct 11/Oct 14/Oct 17
    Donizetti: *Lucia di Lammermoor* Oct 16/Oct 19/Oct 24/
        Oct 28/Oct 31/Nov 1
    Verdi: *La traviata* Oct 22/Oct 26/Oct 30/Nov 2/Nov 7/
        Nov 11/Nov 14
    Britten: *Billy Budd* Nov 6/Nov 9/Nov 18/Nov 21/Nov 23
    Rossini: *L'Italiana in Algeri* Nov 13/Nov 16/Nov 25/Dec 5
    Puccini: *Madama Butterfly* Nov 20/Nov 28/Nov 30/Dec 3/
        Dec 6/Dec 9/Dec 11
    Bartók: *Duke Bluebeard's Castle*
        with Puccini: *Gianni Schicchi* Nov 27/Dec 2/Dec 4/
        Dec 7/Dec 10/Dec 12

122—1971-1972

LYRIC OPERA OF CHICAGO (17)
    Rossini: *Semiramide* Sep 22/Sep 27/Sep 29/Oct 2/Oct 8/Oct 11
    Verdi: *Rigoletto* Oct 4/Oct 6/Oct 9/Oct 13/Oct 20
    Puccini: *Tosca* Oct 12/Oct 13/Oct 18/Oct 22/Oct 30
    Massenet: *Werther* Oct 23/Oct 27/Oct 29/Nov 2/Nov 5/Nov 8
    Verdi: *Don Carlo* Nov 3/Nov 6/Nov 10/Nov 12/Nov 15/Nov 20
    Wagner: *Das Rheingold* Nov 13/Nov 17/Nov 19/Nov 22/
        Nov 27/Nov 29
    Rossini: *The Barber of Seville* Nov 26/Dec 4/Dec 8/Dec 11/
        Dec 13/Dec 17
    Strauss: *Salome* Dec 3/Dec 6/Dec 10/Dec 15/Dec 18

123—1972-1973

LYRIC OPERA OF CHICAGO (18)
    Verdi: *I due Foscari* Sep 22/Sep 25/Sep 29/Oct 2/Oct 4/Oct 7
    Wagner: *Die Walküre* Sep 27/Sep 30/Oct 3/Oct 6/Oct 9/Oct 13
    Verdi: *La traviata* Oct 11/Oct 14/Oct 20/Oct 23/Oct 27/Nov 4
    Puccini: *La bohème* Oct 21/Oct 25/Oct 28/Nov 1/Nov 3/
        Nov 6/Nov 11
    Verdi: *Un ballo in maschera* Nov 8/Nov 10/Nov 13/Nov 18/
        Dec 1/Dec 4
    Mozart: *Così fan tutte* Nov 15/Nov 17/Nov 20/Nov 22/
        Nov 25/Nov 29
    Debussy: *Pelléas et Mélisande* Nov 27/Dec 2/Dec 6/Dec 9/
        Dec 12/Dec 16
    Berg: *Wozzeck* Dec 5/Dec 8/Dec 11/Dec 13/Dec 16

124—1973-1974

LYRIC OPERA OF CHICAGO (19)
    Donizetti: *Maria Stuarda* Sep 21/Sep 24/Sep 28/Oct 3/Oct 6/Oct 8
    Massenet: *Manon* Sep 29/Oct 1/Oct 4/Oct 8/Oct 15/Oct 17
    Puccini: *Tosca* Oct 10/Oct 13/Oct 15/Oct 19/Oct 22/Oct 27
    Donizetti: *The Daughter of the Regiment* Oct 20/Oct 24/
        Oct 26/Nov 21/Nov 5/Nov 7
    Wagner: *Siegfried* Oct 31/Nov 3/Nov 6/Nov 9/Nov 12/Nov 15
    Bizet: *Carmen* Nov 14/Nov 17/Nov 19/Nov 24/Dec 3/Dec 6/
        Dec 12/Dec 14
    Strauss: *Der Rosenkavalier* Nov 23/Nov 26/Nov 30/Dec 5/
        Dec 7/Dec 10
    Puccini: *La bohème* Nov 28/Dec 1/Dec 3/Dec 7/Dec 11/Dec 15

CHICAGO OPERA STUDIO
    Mozart: *Così fan tutte* Apr 26/Apr 27/Apr 28/May 3/May 4/May 5

125—1974-1975

LYRIC OPERA OF CHICAGO (20)
    Verdi: *Simon Boccanegra* Sep 20/Sep 23/Sep 27/Oct 2/Oct 5/Oct 8
    Britten: *Peter Grimes* Sep 30/Oct 4/Oct 7/Oct 10/Oct 12/Oct 15
    Donizetti: *La favorita* Oct 11/Oct 14/Oct 17/Oct 19/Oct 21/
        Oct 25
    Verdi: *Falstaff* Oct 18/Oct 22/Oct 26/Oct 28/Nov 1/Nov 6
    Donizetti: *Don Pasquale* Nov 2/Nov 4/Nov 8/Nov 11/
        Nov 16/Nov 19
    Puccini: *Madama Butterfly* Nov 9/Nov 13/Nov 15/Nov 23/
        Nov 26/Dec 4
    Massenet: *Don Quichotte* Nov 22/Nov 29/Dec 2/Dec 7/
        Dec 11/Dec 14
    Wagner: *Götterdämmerung* Nov 27/Nov 30/Dec 3/Dec 6/
        Dec 9/Dec 13

CHICAGO OPERA STUDIO
    Mozart: *The Marriage of Figaro* Apr 10/Apr 12/Apr 18/Apr 20/
        Apr 25/Apr 27

126—1975-1976

LYRIC OPERA OF CHICAGO (21)

Verdi: *Otello* Sep 19/Sep 22/Sep 27/Oct 1/Oct 3/Oct 6/
Oct 11/Oct 15

Verdi: *La traviata* Sep 26/Sep 30/Oct 4/Oct 8/Oct 13/Oct 17

Strauss: *Elektra* Oct 10/Oct 14/Oct 18/Dec 3/Dec 6/Dec 9/Dec 12

Mozart: *The Marriage of Figaro* Oct 22/Oct 25/Oct 28/Oct 31/
Nov 5/Nov 8/Nov 17

Beethoven: *Fidelio* Oct 29/Nov 1/Nov 4/Nov 7/Nov 10/Nov 14

Donizetti: *Lucia di Lammermoor* Nov 12/Nov 15/Nov 18/
Nov 21/Nov 24/Nov 28/Dec 1/Dec 4

Gluck: *Orfeo ed Euridice* Nov 22/Dec 2/Dec 5/Dec 8/Dec 10/
Dec 13

CHICAGO OPERA STUDIO

Mozart: *The Marriage of Figaro* Nov 21

Rossini: *The Barber of Seville* Jan 31/Feb 1/Feb 7/Feb 8/
Feb 14/Feb 15

Thomson: *The Mother of Us All* Apr 30/May 1/May 2/
May 7/May 8/May 9

127—1976-1977

LYRIC OPERA OF CHICAGO (22)

Offenbach: *The Tales of Hoffmann* Sep 25/Sep 29/Oct 1/Oct 4/
Oct 9/Oct 12/Oct 15

Rossini: *La Cenerentola (Cinderella)* Oct 2/Oct 6/Oct 8/Oct 18/
Oct 23/Oct 26

Verdi: *Un ballo in maschera* Oct 13/Oct 16/Oct 19/Oct 22/
Oct 29/Nov 1

Verdi: *Rigoletto* Oct 27/Oct 30/Nov 2/Nov 5/Nov 8/Nov 10/
Nov 13/Nov 19/Nov 23

Mussorgsky: *Khovanshchina* Nov 6/Nov 9/Nov 12/Nov 17/
Nov 20/Nov 22/Nov 27

Puccini: *Tosca* Nov 26/Nov 29/Dec 6/Dec 8/Dec 11/Dec 14/
Dec 17

Prokofiev: *The Love for Three Oranges* Dec 4/Dec 7/Dec 10/
Dec 13/Dec 15/Dec 18

CHICAGO OPERA STUDIO

Rossini: *The Barber of Seville* Aug 30/Aug 31

Mozart: *The Abduction from the Seraglio* Jan 22/Jan 23/Jan 25/
Jan 29/Jan 30

Hoiby: *Summer and Smoke* Apr 16/Apr 17/Apr 23

128—1977-1978

LYRIC OPERA OF CHICAGO (23)

Donizetti: *L'elisir d'amore* Sep 23/Sep 26/Sep 28/Oct 1/Oct 4/
Oct 7/Oct 10/Oct 12

Mozart: *Idomeneo* Oct 5/Oct 8/Oct 11/Oct 14/Oct 17/Oct 21/
Oct 24

Britten: *Peter Grimes* Oct 15/Oct 19/Oct 22/Oct 25/Oct 28/
Oct 31/Nov 5

Gluck: *Orfeo ed Euridice* Oct 26/Oct 29/Nov 2/Nov 4/Nov 8/
Nov 11/Nov 14

Puccini: *Manon Lescaut* Nov 9/Nov 12/Nov 15/Nov 19/
Nov 23/Dec 2/Dec 5

Rossini: *The Barber of Seville* Nov 18/Nov 21/Nov 26/Dec 6/
Dec 9/Dec 14/Dec 17

Wagner: *Die Meistersinger* Nov 25/Nov 28/Dec 3/Dec 7/
Dec 10/Dec 13/Dec 16

CHICAGO OPERA THEATER

Donizetti: *Don Pasquale* Jan 18/Jan 20/Jan 21/Jan 22(mat)

Nicolai: *The Merry Wives of Windsor* May 10/May 12/May 13/
May 14(mat)

129—1978-1979

LYRIC OPERA OF CHICAGO (24)

Puccini: *La fanciulla del West* Sep 22/Sep 26/Sep 29/Oct 4/
Oct 7/Oct 12/Oct 16/Oct 20

Strauss: *Salome* Sep 27/Sep 30/Oct 3/Oct 6/Oct 9/Oct 13/Oct 17

Puccini: *Madama Butterfly* Oct 11/Oct 14/Oct 18/Oct 21/
Oct 27/Oct 31/Nov 6

Massenet: *Werther* Oct 25/Oct 28/Oct 30/Nov 3/Nov 7/
Nov 10/Nov 13

Mascagni: *Cavalleria rusticana*
with Leoncavallo: *Pagliacci* Nov 4/Nov 8/Nov 11/
Nov 17/Nov 20/Nov 24/Nov 28

Donizetti: *Don Pasquale* Nov 15/Nov 22/Dec 1/Dec 4/Dec 9/
Dec 12/Dec 15

Penderecki: *Paradise Lost* Nov 29/Dec 2/Dec 5/Dec 8/Dec 11/
Dec 13/Dec 16

CHICAGO OPERA THEATER

Mozart: *Così fan tutte* Feb 23/Feb 24(mat)/Feb 25/Feb 28
(student mat)/Mar 2/Mar 3/Mar 4(mat)

Britten: *Albert Herring* Apr 12/Apr 13/Apr 14/Apr 15(mat)

Bizet: *The Pearl Fishers* May 25/May 26/May 27(mat)/June 1/
June 2/June 3(mat)

130—1979-1980

OPERA MIDWEST

Paisiello: *The Barber of Seville* July 13/July 15

J. Strauss: *Die Fledermaus* Dec 29/Dec 30

LYRIC OPERA OF CHICAGO (25)

Gounod: *Faust* Sep 22/Sep 25/Sep 28/Oct 1/Oct 3/Oct 6/
Oct 9/Oct 15/Oct 19

Prokofiev: *The Love for Three Oranges* Sep 29/Oct 2/Oct 5/
Oct 8/Oct 10/Oct 13/Oct 16

Verdi: *Rigoletto* Oct 12/Oct 17/Oct 20/Oct 23/Oct 26/Oct 29/Nov 2

Puccini: *La bohème* Oct 24/Oct 27/Oct 30/Nov 5/Nov 9/
Nov 14/Nov 17/Dec 7/Dec 13

Verdi: *Simon Boccanegra* Nov 3/Nov 7/Nov 10/Nov 13/
Nov 16/Nov 19/Nov 24

Wagner: *Tristan und Isolde* Nov 15/Nov 20/Nov 26/Dec 1/
Dec 5/Dec 10/Dec 14

Giordano: *Andrea Chénier* Nov 23/Nov 27/Nov 30/Dec 3/
Dec 8/Dec 12/Dec 15

CHICAGO OPERA THEATER

Offenbach: *La Périchole* Jan 11/Jan 12/Jan 18/Jan 19/Jan 20(mat)

Rossini: *The Italian Girl in Algiers (L'Italiana in Algeri)* Mar 14/ Mar 15/Mar 19(student mat)/Mar 21/Mar 22/Mar 23(mat)

Hoiby: *Summer and Smoke* May 23/May 24/May 30/May 31

131—1980-1981

LYRIC OPERA OF CHICAGO (26)

Mussorgsky: *Boris Godunov* Sep 20/Sep 23/Sep 26/Sep 29/ Oct 4/Oct 8/Oct 11/Oct 14

Wagner: *Lohengrin* Oct 10/Oct 13/Oct 18/Oct 21/Oct 24/ Oct 28/Oct 31/Nov 5

Verdi: *Attila* Oct 25/Oct 29/Nov 1/Nov 4/Nov 10/Nov 14

Mozart: *Don Giovanni* Nov 15/Nov 19/Nov 22/Nov 25/ Nov 28/Dec 1/Dec 6/Dec 9/Dec 12

Verdi: *Un ballo in maschera* Nov 26/Nov 29/Dec 2/Dec 5/ Dec 8/Dec 10/Dec 13

Lehár: *The Merry Widow* May 29/May 30/June 3/June 4/ June 5/June 6

CHICAGO OPERA THEATER

Puccini: *La rondine* Feb 7/Feb 8(mat)/Feb 13/Feb 14/Feb 15(mat)

Kurka: *The Good Soldier Schweik* Apr 4/Apr 5(mat)/Apr 10/ Apr 11/Apr 12(mat)

Mozart: *The Marriage of Figaro* May 23/May 24(mat)/May 29/ May 30/May 31(mat)/June 20

132—1981-1982

LYRIC OPERA OF CHICAGO (27)

Saint-Saëns: *Samson and Delilah* Sep 25/Sep 30/Oct 3/Oct 6/ Oct 9/Oct 15/Oct 19/Oct 23

Donizetti: *L'elisir d'amore* Sep 26/Sep 29/Oct 2/Oct 5/Oct 8/ Oct 10/Oct 13/Oct 16

Strauss: *Ariadne auf Naxos* Oct 14/Oct 17/Oct 21/Oct 24/ Oct 27/Oct 30/Nov 2

Verdi: *Macbeth* Oct 28/Oct 31/Nov 3/Nov 6/Nov 9/Nov 13/ Nov 16

Beethoven: *Fidelio* Nov 7/Nov 11/Nov 14/Nov 17/Nov 20/ Nov 23/Nov 28/Dec 1

Massenet: *Don Quichotte* Nov 21/Nov 24/Nov 30/Dec 4/ Dec 9/Dec 12/Dec 18

Gounod: *Romeo and Juliet* Nov 27/Dec 2/Dec 5/Dec 8/Dec 11/ Dec 14/Dec 19

J. Strauss: *Die Fledermaus* May 14/May 15/May 20/May 21/ May 22

CHICAGO OPERA THEATER

Mozart: *The Abduction from the Seraglio* Feb 6/Feb 7(mat)/ Feb 10/Feb 12/Feb 13/Feb 14/Feb 15(mat)

Blitzstein: *Regina* Mar 27/Mar 28(mat)/Mar 31/Apr 2/Apr 3/ Apr 4(mat)

Donizetti: *The Daughter of the Regiment* May 22/May 23(mat)/ May 26/May 28/May 29/May 30(mat)

133—1982-1983

LYRIC OPERA OF CHICAGO (28)

Offenbach: *The Tales of Hoffmann* Sep 18/Sep 21/Sep 24/ Sep 27/Oct 2/Oct 6/Oct 9/Oct 14

Wagner: *Tristan und Isolde* Sep 20/Sep 25/Sep 29/Oct 4/Oct 8/ Oct 12/Oct 15

Puccini: *Tosca* Oct 13/Oct 16/Oct 19/Oct 22/Oct 25/Oct 29/ Nov 4/Nov 8

Mozart: *Così fan tutte* Oct 23/Oct 26/Oct 30/Nov 1/Nov 5/ Nov 10/Nov 12

Poulenc: *La Voix humaine* with Leoncavallo: *Pagliacci* Nov 3/Nov 6/Nov 9/ Nov 13/Nov 16/Nov 19/Nov 22

Puccini: *Madama Butterfly* Nov 17/Nov 20/Nov 23/Nov 26/ Nov 30/Dec 3/Dec 6/Dec 11/Dec 14/Dec 17

Verdi: *Luisa Miller* Dec 1/Dec 4/Dec 7/Dec 10/Dec 13/Dec 15/ Dec 18

(Gilbert and) Sullivan: *The Mikado* May 11/May 13/May 14/ May 18/May 20/May 21

NEW YORK CITY OPERA NATIONAL COMPANY

Bizet: *Carmen* Jan 22/Jan 23

RADIO CITY MUSIC HALL–HOUSTON GRAND OPERA– SHERWIN M. GOLDMAN PRODUCTION (Arie Crown Theatre)

Gershwin: *Porgy and Bess* Feb 15–Mar 13 (presented as a musical show, with matinées Wednesdays and Saturdays)

CHICAGO OPERA THEATER

Flotow: *Martha* Feb 19/Feb 20(mat)/Feb 23/Feb 25/Feb 26/ Feb 27(mat)

Menotti: *The Consul* Apr 9/Apr 10(mat)/Apr 13/Apr 15/ Apr 16/Apr 17(mat)

Rossini: *The Barber of Seville* May 21/May 22(mat)/May 25/ May 27/May 28/May 29(mat)

134—1983-1984

LYRIC OPERA OF CHICAGO (29)

Verdi: *Aida* Sep 23/Sep 28/Oct 1/Oct 4/Oct 7/Oct 10/Oct 14/ Oct 17

Delibes: *Lakmé* Sep 27/Sep 30/Oct 3/Oct 8/Oct 12/Oct 18/ Oct 21

Shostakovich: *Lady Macbeth of Mtsensk* Oct 15/Oct 19/Oct 22/ Oct 25/Oct 28/Oct 31/Nov 2

Rossini: *La Cenerentola (Cinderella)* Oct 26/Oct 29/Nov 1/ Nov 4/Nov 8/Nov 11/Nov 14

Wagner: *The Flying Dutchman* Nov 9/Nov 12/Nov 15/Nov 18/ Nov 21/Nov 26/Nov 29/Dec 2

Puccini: *La bohème* Nov 19/Nov 22/Nov 27(mat)/Nov 30/ Dec 3/Dec 6/Dec 9/Dec 12/Dec 17

Massenet: *Manon* Nov 25/Nov 28/Dec 1/Dec 7/Dec 10/ Dec 13/Dec 16

Handel: *Rinaldo* (concert production) May 2

CHICAGO OPERA THEATER
  Mozart: *Don Giovanni* Jan 28/Jan 29(mat)/Feb 1/Feb 3/Feb 4/
    Feb 5(mat)
  Smetana: *The Bartered Bride* Mar 31/Apr 1(mat)/Apr 4/Apr 6/
    Apr 7/Apr 8(mat)
  Thomson: *The Mother of Us All* May 19/May 20(mat)/May 23/
    May 25/May 26/May 27(mat)

VOLKSOPER (Vienna)
  J. Strauss: *Die Fledermaus* Apr 24/Apr 25/Apr 26/Apr 27
  Lehár: *The Merry Widow* Apr 28/Apr 29

135—1984-1985

LYRIC OPERA OF CHICAGO (30)
  Tchaikovsky: *Eugene Onegin* Sep 21/Sep 24/Sep 29/Oct 3/
    Oct 6/Oct 9/Oct 12/Oct 15
  Strauss: *Arabella* Sep 28/Oct 1/Oct 4/Oct 10/Oct 13/Oct 16/
    Oct 20
  Mozart: *The Abduction from the Seraglio* Oct 19/Oct 23/Oct 26/
    Oct 29/Oct 31/Nov 3/Nov 7
  Verdi: *Ernani* Oct 24/Oct 27/Oct 30/Nov 2/Nov 5/Nov 10/
    Nov 13
  Bizet: *Carmen* Nov 9/Nov 12/Nov 15/Nov 21/Nov 25(mat)/
    Nov 27/Nov 30/Dec 5/Dec 8/Dec 13
  Strauss: *Die Frau ohne Schatten* Nov 19/Nov 24/Nov 28/Dec 3/
    Dec 7/Dec 11/Dec 14
  Rossini: *The Barber of Seville* Nov 23/Nov 26/Dec 1/Dec 4/
    Dec 6/Dec 10/Dec 12/Dec 15

CHICAGO OPERA THEATER
  Bizet: *The Pearl Fishers* Feb 2/Feb 3(mat)/Feb 6/Feb 8/Feb 9/
    Feb 10(mat)
  Donizetti: *The Elixir of Love (L'elisir d'amore)* Mar 16/Mar 17(mat)/
    Mar 20/Mar 22/Mar 23/Mar 24(mat)
  Ward: *The Crucible* May 25/May 26(mat)/May 29/May 31/
    June 1/June 2(mat)

136—1985-1986

LYRIC OPERA OF CHICAGO (31)
  Verdi: *Otello* Sep 21/Sep 25/Sep 28/Oct 1/Oct 4/Oct 7/Oct 11/
    Oct 14
  Puccini: *Madama Butterfly* Sep 27/Sep 30/Oct 5/Oct 9/Oct 15/
    Oct 18/Oct 21/Oct 26/Jan 5(mat)/Jan 10/Jan 15/Jan 18
  Handel: *Samson* Oct 12/Oct 16/Oct 19/Oct 22/Oct 25/Oct 28/
    Nov 1
  Donizetti: *Anna Bolena* Oct 30/Nov 2/Nov 5/Nov 8/Nov 11/
    Nov 14/Nov 19
  Verdi: *La traviata* Nov 6/Nov 9/Nov 12/Nov 16/Nov 20/
    Nov 26/Dec 1(mat)/Dec 5/Dec 9/Dec 13
  Bellini: *I Capuleti e i Montecchi* Nov 15/Nov 18/Nov 23/
    Nov 27/Nov 30/Dec 3/Dec 6
  Wagner: *Die Meistersinger* Nov 25/Nov 29/Dec 4/Dec 7/Dec 11/
    Dec 14/Dec 17
  Puccini: *La rondine* Dec 18/Dec 21/Dec 30/Jan 3/Jan 8/Jan 11/
    Jan 14/Jan 19(mat)

NEW YORK CITY OPERA NATIONAL COMPANY
  Gounod: *Faust* Nov 13

CHICAGO OPERA THEATER
  Floyd: *Susannah* Feb 1/Feb 2(mat)/Feb 5/Feb 7/Feb 8/Feb 9(mat)
  Mascagni: *L'amico Fritz* Mar 15/Mar 16(mat)/Mar 19/Mar 21/
    Mar 22/Mar 23(mat)/Mar 26
  Rossini: *The Turk in Italy (Il Turco in Italia)* May 24/May 25(mat)/
    May 28/May 30/May 31/June 1(mat)/June 4

THE BRENA AND LEE FREEMAN SR. COMPOSER-
IN-RESIDENCE PROGRAM (Lyric Opera of Chicago)
  Neil: *The Guilt of Lillian Sloane* June 6

137—1986-1987

LYRIC OPERA OF CHICAGO (32)
  Mozart: *The Magic Flute* Sep 20/Sep 23/Sep 26/Sep 29/Oct 2/
    Oct 7/Oct 11/Oct 15
  Puccini: *La bohème* Sep 24/Sep 27/Sep 30/Oct 4/Oct 8/Oct 13/
    Oct 17/Jan 18(mat)/Jan 21/Jan 24/Jan 30
  Wagner: *Parsifal* Oct 6/Oct 10/Oct 14/Oct 18/Oct 22/Oct 25/
    Oct 30
  Handel: *Orlando* Oct 24/Oct 28/Oct 31/Nov 3/Nov 8/Nov 12/
    Nov 15
  Donizetti: *Lucia di Lammermoor* Nov 1/Nov 4/Nov 7/Nov 10/
    Nov 16(mat)/Nov 19/Nov 22/Nov 25/Dec 8/Dec 10
  Verdi: *Un ballo in maschera* Nov 14/Nov 18/Nov 21/Nov 24/
    Nov 29/Dec 3/Dec 6
  Janáček: *Káťa Kabanová* Nov 28/Dec 2/Dec 5/Dec 9/Dec 12/
    Dec 17/Dec 20
  Lehár: *The Merry Widow* Dec 13/Dec 15/Dec 19/Dec 30/Jan 3/
    Jan 6/Jan 11(mat)/Jan 14/Jan 16
  Ponchielli: *La Gioconda* Jan 13/Jan 17/Jan 20/Jan 23/Jan 26/
    Jan 29/Jan 31

CHICAGO OPERA THEATER
  Mozart: *Così fan tutte* Feb 14/Feb 15/Feb 18/Feb 20/Feb 21/
    Feb 22/Feb 25
  Britten: *The Turn of the Screw* Apr 4/Apr 5/Apr 8/Apr 10/Apr 11/
    Apr 12/Apr 15
  Smetana: *The Two Widows* May 23/May 24/May 27/May 29/
    May 30/May 31/June 2

138—1987-1988

LYRIC OPERA OF CHICAGO (33)
  Verdi: *Il trovatore* Sep 18/Sep 22/Sep 26/Sep 30/Oct 3/Oct 7/
    Oct 12/Oct 16
  Glass: *Satyagraha* Sep 28/Oct 1/Oct 6/Oct 9/Oct 14/Oct 17/
    Oct 23
  Gounod: *Faust* Oct 13/Oct 18(mat)/Oct 21/Oct 24/Oct 27/
    Oct 30/Nov 2/Nov 7
  Rossini: *L'Italiana in Algeri* Oct 28/Oct 31/Nov 3/Nov 6/Nov 9/
    Nov 13/Nov 16
  Mozart: *The Marriage of Figaro* Nov 14/Nov 18/Nov 21/Nov 23/
    Nov 27/Nov 30/Dec 4/Dec 8
  Berg: *Lulu* Nov 24/Nov 28/Dec 2/Dec 7/Dec 11/Dec 15/Dec 19

Mozart: *Così fan tutte* Dec 12/Dec 16/Dec 20(mat)/Dec 28/
Jan 2/Jan 5/Jan 8/Jan 11

Puccini: *Tosca* Jan 9/Jan 12/Jan 17(mat)/Jan 20/Jan 23/Jan 26/
Jan 29/Feb 1/Feb 5

Verdi: *La forza del destino* Jan 16/Jan 19/Jan 22/Jan 25/Jan30/
Feb 3/Feb 6

NEW YORK CITY OPERA NATIONAL COMPANY
Rossini: *The Barber of Seville* Feb 7

CHICAGO OPERA THEATER
Gluck: *Orpheus and Euridice (Orfeo ed Euridice)* Feb 13/Feb 14/
Feb 17/Feb 19/Feb 20/Feb 21/Feb 24

Donizetti: *Don Pasquale* Mar 5/Mar 6/Mar 9/Mar 11/Mar 12/
Mar 13/Mar 16

Floyd: *Of Mice and Men* Apr 2/Apr 3/Apr 6/Apr 8/Apr 9/Apr 10/
Apr 13

Rossini: *Cinderella (La Cenerentola)* Apr 23/Apr 24/Apr 27/
Apr 29/Apr 30/May 1/May 4

139—1988-1989

LYRIC OPERA OF CHICAGO (34)
Bellini: *La sonnambula* Sep 17/Sep 21/Sep 24/Sep 27/Sep 30/
Oct 3/Oct 7/Oct 11

Verdi: *La traviata* Sep 26/Oct 1/Oct 5/Oct 8/Oct 12/Oct 16(mat)/
Oct 21/Oct 25/Oct 28

Wagner: *Tannhäuser* Oct 10/Oct 14/Oct 18/Oct 22/Oct 26/
Oct 31/Nov 5

Verdi: *Falstaff* Oct 29/Nov 1/Nov 4/Nov 7/Nov 11/Nov 16/
Nov 19(mat)/Nov 26

Mozart: *Don Giovanni* Nov 12/Nov 15/Nov 18/Nov 23/
Nov 27(mat)/Nov 30/Dec 2/Dec 5/Dec 10

Strauss: *Salome* Nov 25/Nov 29/Dec 3/Dec 7/Dec 12/Dec 16/
Dec 19

Verdi: *Aida* Dec 17/Dec 20/Dec 30/Jan 2/Jan 7/Jan 10/
Jan 15(mat)/Jan 20/Jan 25

Rossini: *Tancredi* Jan 14/Jan 18/Jan 21/Jan 24/Jan 27/Jan 30/
Feb 3

CHICAGO OPERA THEATER
Knussen: *Where the Wild Things Are* Dec 17/Dec 18/Dec 21/
Dec 22/Dec 23

Mozart: *La finta giardiniera* Feb 8/Feb 11/Feb 12/Feb 17/
Feb 19/Feb 22/Feb 25

Britten: *Albert Herring* Mar 29/Apr 1/Apr 2/Apr 7/Apr 9/Apr 12/
Apr 15

Gounod: *Romeo and Juliet* May 10/May 13/May 14/May 19/
May 21/May 24/May 27

THE BRENA AND LEE FREEMAN SR. COMPOSER-
IN-RESIDENCE PROGRAM (Lyric Opera of Chicago)
Goldstein: *The Fan* June 17

140—1989-1990

LYRIC OPERA OF CHICAGO (35)
Puccini: *Tosca* Sep 16/Sep 19/Sep 22/Sep 25/Sep 28/Oct 2/
Oct 6/Oct 11

Strauss: *Der Rosenkavalier* Sep 26/Sep 30/Oct 4/Oct 7(mat)/
Oct 10/Oct 13/Oct 16/Oct 20

Mozart: *La clemenza di Tito* Oct 14/Oct 18/Oct 21(mat)/Oct 24/
Oct 27/Oct 30/Nov 4/Nov 8

Saint-Saëns: *Samson and Delilah* Oct 28/Oct 31/Nov 3/Nov 6/
Nov 9/Nov 12(mat)/Nov 15

Verdi: *Don Carlo* Nov 10/Nov 14/Nov 17/Nov 20/Nov 25/
Nov 29/Dec 2

Rossini: *The Barber of Seville* Nov 24/Nov 27/Dec 1/Dec 4/
Dec 7/Dec 10(mat)/Dec 13/Dec 16/Dec 19

J. Strauss: *Die Fledermaus* Dec 9/Dec 12/Dec 15/Dec 30/Jan 3/
Jan 6/Jan 9/Jan 12/Jan 15/Jan 21(mat)

Thomas: *Hamlet* Jan 13/Jan 17/Jan 20/Jan 23/Jan 26/Jan 29/
Jan 31/Feb 3(mat)

CHICAGO OPERA THEATER
Nicolai: *The Merry Wives of Windsor* Feb 7/Feb 10/Feb 11/
Feb 16/Feb 18/Feb 21/Feb 24

Davies: *The Lighthouse* Mar 21/Mar 24/Mar 25/Mar 30/Apr 1/
Apr 4/Apr 7

Delibes: *Lakmé* May 9/May 12/May 13/May 18/May 20/
May 23/May 26

Rodgers: *Carousel* June 9–10/June 13/June 15–17/June 20/
June 22–24

141—1990-1991

LYRIC OPERA OF CHICAGO (36)
Gluck: *Alceste* Sep 14/Sep 18/Sep 22/Sep 26/Oct 1/Oct 5/
Oct 9/Oct 13

Tchaikovsky: *Eugene Onegin* Sep 24/Sep 29/Oct 3/Oct 7(mat)/
Oct 12/Oct 16/Oct 19/Oct 22

Puccini: *La fanciulla del West* Oct 17/Oct 20/Oct 23/Oct 26/
Oct 30/Nov 2/Nov 5

Argento: *The Voyage of Edgar Allan Poe* Oct 27/Oct 31/
Nov 3(mat)/Nov 6/Nov 9/Nov 13/Nov 16/Nov 19

Donizetti: *Lucia di Lammermoor* Nov 10/Nov 14/Nov 17/
Nov 20/Nov 23/Nov 26/Nov 30/Dec 4/Dec 7

Verdi: *Rigoletto* Nov 24/Nov 28/Dec 1/Dec 5/Dec 8/Dec 11/
Dec 14/Dec 17

Bizet: *Carmen* Dec 15/Dec 19/Dec 29/Jan 2/Jan 6(mat)/Jan 9/
Jan 14/Jan 18/Jan 22/Jan 26

Mozart: *The Magic Flute* Jan 12/Jan 15/Jan 19/Jan 21/Jan 25/
Jan 28/Jan 30/Feb 1/Feb 3(mat)

CHICAGO OPERA THEATER
Knussen: *Where the Wild Things Are* Dec 20/Dec 21/Dec 22/
Dec 23/Dec 27/Dec 28/Dec 29/Dec 30

Mozart: *Idomeneo* Feb 13/Feb 16/Feb 17/Feb 20/Feb 22/Feb 24/
Mar 2

Puccini: *Madama Butterfly* Apr 3/Apr 6/Apr 7/Apr 12/Apr 14/
Apr 17/Apr 20

Argento: *Postcard from Morocco* May 8/May 11/May 12/May 17/
May 19/May 22/May 25

142—1991-1992

LYRIC OPERA OF CHICAGO (37)

Boito: *Mefistofele* Sep 14/Sep 18/Sep 21/Sep 24/Sep 27/Sep 30/
Oct 4/Oct 7

Barber: *Antony and Cleopatra* Sep 25/Sep 28/Oct 1/Oct 5(mat)/
Oct 8/Oct 11/Oct 14/Oct 18

Mozart: *The Marriage of Figaro* Oct 12/Oct 16/Oct 19/Oct 22/
Oct 25/Oct 28/Oct 30/Nov 2

Bellini: *I puritani* Oct 23/Oct 26/Oct 29/Nov 1/Nov 4/Nov 7/
Nov 10(mat)/Nov 13/Nov 16

Prokofiev: *The Gambler* Nov 9/Nov 12/Nov 15/Nov 18/Nov 20/
Nov 23/Nov 26/Dec 1(mat)

Donizetti: *L'elisir d'amore* Nov 27/Nov 30/Dec 3/Dec 7/Dec 9/
Dec 13/Dec 16/Dec 18/Dec 21(mat)

Puccini: *Madama Butterfly* Dec 14/Dec 17/Dec 20/Jan 4/Jan 7/
Jan 10/Jan 13/Jan 17/Jan 20/Jan 22/Jan 25

Puccini: *Turandot* Jan 11/Jan 15/Jan 18/Jan 21/Jan 24/Jan 27/
Jan 28/Jan 30/Jan 31/Feb 2(mat)

CHICAGO OPERA THEATER

Rossini: *Count Ory (Le comte Ory)* Feb 15/Feb 16/Feb 19/Feb 21/
Feb 23/Feb 26/Feb 29

Verdi: *La traviata* Apr 4/Apr 5/Apr 8/Apr 10/Apr 12/Apr 15/
Apr 18

Argento: *A Waterbird Talk*
with Menotti: *The Medium* June 12/June 14/June 17/
June 20/June 21/June 24

THE BRENA AND LEE FREEMAN SR. COMPOSER-
IN-RESIDENCE PROGRAM (Lyric Opera of Chicago)

Sheng: *The Song of Majnun* Apr 9/Apr 11

143—1992-1993

LYRIC OPERA OF CHICAGO (38)

Rossini: *Otello* Sep 19/Sep 23/Sep 26/Sep 30/Oct 2/Oct 5/
Oct 10/Oct 13

Strauss: *Elektra* Sep 29/Oct 3/Oct 8/Oct 12/Oct 16/Oct 21/
Oct 26/Oct 30

Smetana: *The Bartered Bride* Oct 9/Oct 14/Oct 17/Oct 19/
Oct 24/Oct 27/Nov 1(mat)/Nov 4/Nov 7

Bolcom: *McTeague* Oct 31/Nov 3/Nov 6/Nov 9/Nov 12/
Nov 15(mat)/Nov 18/Nov 21/Nov 24

Debussy: *Pelléas et Mélisande* Nov 14/Nov 17/Nov 20/Nov 23/
Nov 27/Nov 30/Dec 2/Dec 5(mat)

Verdi: *Un ballo in maschera* Nov 28/Dec 1/Dec 4/Dec 7/Dec 11/
Dec 16/Dec 19/Feb 5/Feb 10/Feb 14(mat)

Puccini: *La bohème* Dec 12/Dec 15/Dec 18/Dec 20(mat)/
Dec 30/Jan 2/Jan 5/Jan 8/Jan 11/Jan 16/Jan 22

Wagner: *Das Rheingold* Jan 23/Jan 26/Jan 29/Feb 1/Feb 3/
Feb 6/Feb 9/Feb 12

Massenet: *Le Cid* (concert production) Jan 25/Jan 28/Jan 31(mat)

CHICAGO OPERA THEATER

Thomson: *Four Saints in Three Acts* Apr 10/Apr 14/Apr 16/
Apr 18/Apr 21/Apr 24/Apr 25

144—1993-1994

LYRIC OPERA OF CHICAGO (39)

Verdi: *La traviata* Sep 18/Sep 22/Sep 25/Sep 28/Oct 1/Oct 4/
Jan 29/Feb 2/Feb 7/Feb 10/Feb 14/Feb 20(mat)

Massenet: *Don Quichotte* Sep 26(mat)/Sep 29/Oct 2/Oct 5/
Oct 8/Oct 11/Oct 15/Oct 18/Oct 22

Floyd: *Susannah* Oct 9/Oct 13/Oct 16/Oct 19/Oct 24(mat)/
Oct 26/Oct 29/Nov 1/Nov 5

Puccini: *Tosca* Oct 23/Oct 27/Oct 30/Nov 2/Nov 8/Nov 12/
Feb 5/Feb 9/Feb 12(mat)/Feb 18

Mozart: *Così fan tutte* Nov 6/Nov 10/Nov 13/Nov 16/Nov 19/
Nov 22/Nov 28(mat)/Nov 30/Dec 4

Wagner: *Die Walküre* Nov 23/Nov 27/Dec 3/Dec 6/Dec 10/
Dec 14/Dec 18/Dec 22

Verdi: *Il trovatore* Dec 11/Dec 15/Dec 19(mat)/Dec 21/Jan 3/
Jan 7/Jan 11/Jan 15/Jan 19/Jan 22

Berg: *Wozzeck* Jan 24/Jan 28/Jan 31/Feb 4/Feb 8/Feb 11/
Feb 16/Feb 19

CHICAGO OPERA THEATER

Berlioz: *Beatrice and Benedict* Apr 15/Apr 17/Apr 21/Apr 23/
Apr 24

Moore: *The Ballad of Baby Doe* May 20/May 22/May 26/
May 28/May 29

145—1994-1995

LYRIC OPERA OF CHICAGO (40)

Mussorgsky: *Boris Godunov* Sep 17/Sep 20/Sep 23/Sep 27/
Oct 1/Oct 5/Oct 8/Oct 10/Oct 14

Stravinsky: *The Rake's Progress* Oct 2(mat)/Oct 4/Oct 6/Oct 12/
Oct 17/Oct 19/Oct 22/Oct 28

Giordano: *Fedora* Oct 15/Oct 18/Oct 21/Oct 24/Oct 26/
Oct 29(mat)/Nov 1/Nov 4/Nov 7/Nov 10

Rossini: *The Barber of Seville* Oct 27/Oct 31/Nov 5/Nov 8/
Nov 11/Nov 16/Feb 4/Feb 8/Feb 11/Feb 13/Feb 17/Feb 19(mat)

Strauss: *Capriccio* Nov 12/Nov 15/Nov 19/Nov 22/Nov 27(mat)/
Nov 30/Dec 2/Dec 5

Bernstein: *Candide* Nov 26/Nov 29/Dec 3/Dec 6/Dec 9/Dec 12/
Dec 14/Dec 16/Dec 18(mat)/Dec 20/Dec 22

Verdi: *Aida* Dec 10/Dec 13/Dec 17/Dec 21/Dec 30/Jan 2/
Jan 7/Jan 10/Jan 14/Jan 19/Jan 22(mat)

Wagner: *Siegfried* Jan 24/Jan 28(mat)/Jan 30/Feb 1/Feb 3/
Feb 6/Feb 10/Feb 14/Feb 18

CHICAGO OPERA THEATER

Mozart: *The Magic Flute* June 2/June 4(mat)/June 8/June 10/
June 11

Copland: *The Tender Land* June 23/June 25(mat)/June 29/July 1

THE BRENA AND LEE FREEMAN SR. COMPOSER-
IN-RESIDENCE PROGRAM (Lyric Opera of Chicago)

Saylor: *Orpheus Descending* June 10/June 11

146—1995-1996

LYRIC OPERA OF CHICAGO (41)

Verdi: *Simon Boccanegra* Sep 15/Sep 19/Sep 23/Sep 27/Sep 30/
Oct 2/Oct 6/Oct 10/Oct 13

Handel: *Xerxes* Sep 22/Sep 26/Sep 29/Oct 5/Oct 7/Oct 9/
Oct 15(mat)/Oct 18/Oct 21

Corigliano: *The Ghosts of Versailles* Oct 14/Oct 17/Oct 20/
Oct 25/Oct 29(mat)/Oct 31/Nov 3/Nov 6

Donizetti: *Don Pasquale* Oct 28/Nov 1/Nov 4/Nov 7/Nov 10/
Nov 13/Nov 17/Nov 20/Nov 25

Giordano: *Andrea Chénier* Nov 11/Nov 15/Nov 18/Nov 21/
Nov 26(mat)/Dec 1/Dec 4/Dec 8/Dec 12

Mozart: *Don Giovanni* Nov 24/Nov 29/Dec 2/Dec 5/Dec 7/
Dec 11/Dec 15/Dec 17(mat)/Jan 4/Jan 6/Jan 10/Jan 13

Janáček: *The Makropulos Affair* Dec 9/Dec 13/Dec 16/Jan 3/
Jan 7(mat)/Jan 9/Jan 12/Jan 15/Jan 19

Gounod: *Faust* Jan 20/Jan 24/Jan 27/Jan 30/Feb 2/Feb 5/
Feb 11(mat)/Feb 14/Feb 16/Feb 19/Feb 23

Wagner: *Götterdämmerung* (nonsubscription) Feb 17/Feb 24/
Mar 9(mat)

Wagner: *Der Ring des Nibelungen*
Das Rheingold Mar 11/Mar 18/Mar 25
Die Walküre Mar 12/Mar 19/Mar 26
Siegfried Mar 14/Mar 21/Mar 28
Götterdämmerung Mar 16/Mar 23/Mar 30

CHICAGO OPERA THEATER

Strauss: *Ariadne auf Naxos* June 7/June 9/June 13/June 15

Mozart: *The Jewel Box* (rarely heard arias of Mozart performed
as an opera, with a libretto by Paul Griffiths) June 14/June 16/
June 20/June 22

Rossini: *The Italian Girl in Algiers* (*L'Italiana in Algeri*) July 5/
July 7/July 11(mat)/July 13

147—1996-1997

LYRIC OPERA OF CHICAGO (42)

Verdi: *Don Carlo* Sep 21/Sep 25/Sep 28/Oct 2/Oct 5(mat)/
Oct 8/Oct 11/Oct 14/Oct 18

Puccini: *Il trittico* (*Il tabarro; Suor Angelica; Gianni Schicchi*)
Sep 30/Oct 4/Oct 9/Oct 12/Oct 15/Oct 20(mat)/Oct 23/
Oct 26/Oct 29/Nov 1

Menotti: *The Consul* Oct 19/Oct 22/Oct 25/Oct 28/Nov2/
Nov 7/Nov 10(mat)/Nov 13/Nov 16

Berio: *Un re in ascolto* Nov 9/Nov 12/Nov 15/Nov 21/
Nov 24(mat)/Nov 27/Nov 30/Dec 2/Dec 6

Strauss: *Salome* Nov 23/Nov 26/Nov 29/Dec 4/Dec 7/Dec 10/
Dec 13/Dec 16/Dec 20

Mozart: *The Magic Flute* Dec 14/Dec 17/Dec 19/Dec 21/Jan 7/
Jan 10/Jan 13/Jan 15/Jan 18/Jan 20/Jan 24/Jan 26(mat)

Puccini: *Turandot* Jan 25/Jan 29/Feb 1/Feb 4/Feb 7/Feb 10/
Feb 14/Feb 18/Feb 21/Feb 24/Feb 27/Mar 2(mat)

Bellini: *Norma* Feb 6/Feb 9(mat)/Feb 12/Feb 15/Feb 19/Feb 22/
Feb 25/Feb 28/Mar 3/Mar 8

THE BRENA AND LEE FREEMAN SR. COMPOSER-
IN-RESIDENCE PROGRAM (Lyric Opera of Chicago)

Ran: *Between Two Worlds (The Dybbuk)* June 20/June 22

CHICAGO OPERA THEATER

Offenbach: *The Grand Duchess of Helmsley-Stein*
(adaptation of *La Grande Duchesse de Gérolstein*) June 5/
June 6/June 7/June 8

Mozart: *Don Giovanni* July 11/July 13/July 17/July 19

Hagen: *Shining Brow* July 25/July 27/July 31/Aug 2/Aug 3

148—1997-1998

LYRIC OPERA OF CHICAGO (43)

Verdi: *Nabucco* Sep 20/Sep 23/Sep 26/Sep 29/Oct 4/Oct 8/
Oct 12(mat)/Oct 16/Oct 21/Oct 24

Britten: *Peter Grimes* Oct 3/Oct 6/Oct 9/Oct 14/Oct 17/Oct 20/
Oct 26(mat)/Oct 29/Nov 1/Nov 7

Mozart: *Idomeneo* Oct 18/Oct 22/Oct 25/Oct 28/Oct 31/
Nov 3/Nov 6/Nov 10/Nov 16(mat)

Puccini: *La bohème* Nov 8/Nov 12/Nov 15/Nov 18/Nov 21/
Nov 24/Nov 28/Dec 3/Dec 6(mat)/Dec 9/Dec 12/Dec 15

Davis: *Amistad* Nov 29/Dec 2/Dec 5/Dec 8/Dec 11/Dec 17/
Dec 20/Jan 9/Jan 11(mat)/Jan 15

Puccini: *Madama Butterfly* Dec 13/Dec 16/Dec 19/Jan 7/Jan 10/
Jan 13/Jan 16/Jan 19/Jan 22/Jan 25(mat)

Bizet: *The Pearl Fishers* Jan 31/Feb 4/Feb 7/Feb 10/Feb 13/
Feb 17/Feb 20/Feb 23/Feb 28(mat)/Mar 5

Mozart: *The Marriage of Figaro* Feb 11/Feb 14/Feb 16/Feb 19/
Feb 21/Feb 24/Feb 27/Mar 2/Mar 4/Mar 6/Mar 8(mat)

CHICAGO OPERA THEATER

Ullman: *The Emperor of Atlantis* June 5/June 7/June 11/June 13

Mollicone: *The Face on the Barroom Floor*
with Hoiby: *Bon Appétit!* June 5/June 7/June 10/June 11/
June 13/June 14

(These three operas were, in effect, presented as a triple bill.
A ticket for the Ullman opera entitled one to see the Mollicone and Hoiby works as well (and on the same date if space
was available), but since the latter two works were given in
spaces considerably smaller than the major auditorium of the
Athenaeum in which the Ullman opera was performed—and
though they were given twice on each of the Ullman dates—
extra performances of the Mollicone and Hoiby operas were
presented to accommodate all ticket holders.)

149—1998-1999

LYRIC OPERA OF CHICAGO (44)

Ponchielli: *La Gioconda* Sep 26/Oct 1/Oct 4(mat)/Oct 7/Oct 10/
Oct 13/Oct 16/Oct 19/Oct 23/Oct 27

Levy: *Mourning Becomes Electra* Oct 6/Oct 9/Oct 12/Oct 18(mat)/
Oct 22/Oct 26/Oct 30/Nov 4/Nov 7

Strauss: *Ariadne auf Naxos* Oct 24/Oct 28/Oct 31/Nov 2/Nov 6/
Nov 12/Nov 15(mat)/Nov 17/Nov 21/Nov 24

Weill: *Rise and Fall of the City of Mahagonny* Nov 14/Nov 18/
Nov 20/Nov 23/Nov 27/Dec 1/Dec 4/Dec 7/Dec 13(mat)

Verdi: *La traviata* Nov 28(mat)/Dec 2/Dec 5/Dec 10/Dec 15/
Dec 18/Feb 22/Feb 26/Mar 2/Mar 5/Mar 8/Mar 12

Boito: *Mefistofele* Dec 14/Dec 17/Dec 19/Jan 6/Jan 10(mat)/
Jan 13/Jan 16/Jan 19/Jan 22/Jan 25/Jan 30

Gounod: *Romeo and Juliet* Jan 23/Jan 26/Jan 29/Feb 1/Feb 5/
Feb 13/Feb 17/Feb 20/Feb 23/Feb 28(mat)

Wagner: *Die Meistersinger* Feb 8/Feb 12/Feb 16/Feb 19/Feb 24/
Feb 27/Mar 3/Mar 6/Mar 10/Mar 13(mat)

CHICAGO OPERA THEATER

Humperdinck: *Hansel and Gretel* Nov 13/Nov 15(mat)/Nov 19/
Nov 21. Family matinées Nov 22/Nov 27/Nov 29

Offenbach: *The Tales of Hoffmann* Apr 30/May 2(mat)/May 6/
May 8

Bernstein: *There Is a Garden: The Musical Genius of Leonard
Bernstein* (including *Trouble in Tahiti*) June 4/June 6(mat)/
June 10/June 12

150—1999-2000

LYRIC OPERA OF CHICAGO (45)

Verdi: *Falstaff* Sep 25/Sep 28/Oct 3(mat)/Oct 6/Oct 8/Oct 11/
Oct 15/Oct 20(mat & eve)/Oct 23/Oct 26/Oct 29

Bolcom: *A View from the Bridge* Oct 9/Oct 13/Oct 17(mat)/
Oct 19/Oct 22/Oct 25/Oct 28/Nov 2/Nov 5

Handel: *Alcina* Oct 30/Nov 3/Nov 6(mat)/Nov 8/Nov 13/
Nov 17(mat)/Nov 19/Nov 23/Nov 26/Nov 29

Verdi: *Macbeth* Nov 18/Nov 21(mat)/Nov 24/Nov 27/Nov 30/
Dec 3/Dec 6/Dec 11/Dec 14/Dec 18

Strauss: *Die Fledermaus* Dec 4/Dec 7/Dec 9/Dec 13/Dec 15/
Dec 17/Dec 19(mat)/Jan 5/Jan 7/Jan 10/Jan 15
with *A Date with the Devil* (concert) Dec 10

Donizetti: *L'elisir d'amore* Jan 14/Jan 19/Jan 22/Jan 24/Jan 28/
Mar 2/Mar 7/Mar 11/Mar 17/Mar 19(mat)

Wagner: *Tristan und Isolde* Jan 31/Feb 4/Feb 8/Feb 13(mat)/
Feb 16/Feb 19/Feb 23/Feb 26/Mar 1(mat)/Mar 4

Bizet: *Carmen* Feb 12/Feb 15/Feb 18/Feb 21/Feb 27(mat)/Feb 29/
Mar 3/Mar 6/Mar 8(mat)/Mar 10/Mar 13/Mar 15/Mar 18

CHICAGO OPERA THEATER

Rossini: *The Barber of Seville* Oct 20/Oct 22/Oct 24(mat)/Oct 28/
Oct 30/Oct 31

Puccini: *Gianni Schicchi*
with Ching: *Buoso's Ghost* Mar 29/Apr 1/Apr 7/Apr 9(mat)

151—2000-2001

CHICAGO OPERA THEATER

Glass: *Akhnaten* July 19/July 21/July 23(mat)/July 27/July 29/
July 30

Monteverdi: *Orfeo* Oct 18/Oct 20/Oct 22(mat)/Oct 26/Oct 28

Kurka: *The Good Soldier Schweik* Mar 21/Mar 23/Mar 25(mat)/
Mar 29/Mar 31

Handel: *Acis and Galatea* June 6/June 8/June 10(mat)/June 14/
June 16

LYRIC OPERA OF CHICAGO (46)

Tchaikovsky: *The Queen of Spades (Pique Dame)* Sep 23/Sep 27/
Oct 1(mat)/Oct 7/Oct 10/Oct 13/Oct 16/Oct 20/Oct 25/Oct 27

Harbison: *The Great Gatsby* Oct 2/Oct 6/Oct 11/Oct 15(mat)/
Oct 19/Oct 23/Oct 28/Oct 31/Nov 3

Verdi: *Rigoletto* Oct 21/Oct 24/Oct 29(mat)/Nov 1(mat)/Nov 4/
Nov 8/Nov 11/Nov 14/Nov 17/Nov 20

Janáček: *Jenůfa* Nov 18/Nov 22/Nov 25/Nov 28/Dec 1/
Dec 4/Dec 8/Dec 13/Dec 17(mat)

Verdi: *Attila* Dec 2/Dec 6(mat)/Dec 9/Dec 12/Dec 15/Dec 18/
Jan 4/Jan 7(mat)/Jan 10/Jan 12/Jan 15

Puccini: *Tosca* Jan 13/Jan 17(mat)/Jan 20/Jan 23/Jan 26/Jan 31/
Mar 3(mat)/Mar 7/Mar 9/Mar 12/Mar 15/Mar 17

Rossini: *The Barber of Seville* Jan 24/Jan 27/Jan 29/Feb 1/Feb 3/
Feb 6/Feb 9/Feb 12/Feb 16/Feb 18(mat)/Feb 21(mat)/Feb 24

Wagner: *The Flying Dutchman* Feb 10/Feb 14/Feb 17/Feb 20/
Feb 23/Feb 26/Mar 2/Mar 6/Mar 10/Mar 14(mat)/Mar 18(mat)

THE BRENA AND LEE FREEMAN SR. COMPOSER-IN-RESIDENCE PROGRAM (Lyric Opera of Chicago)

LaChiusa: *Lovers and Friends (Chautauqua Variations)* June 29/
June 30

152—2001-2002

LYRIC OPERA OF CHICAGO (47)

Verdi: *Otello* Sep 22/Oct 1/Oct 7(mat)/Oct 10/Oct 13/Oct 17(mat)/
Oct 20/Oct 23/Oct 26

Weill: *Street Scene* Oct 2/Oct 6/Oct 9/Oct 12/Oct 15/Oct 21(mat)/
Oct 24/Oct 27/Oct 31(mat)/Nov 3

Bellini: *I Capuleti e i Montecchi* Nov 1/Nov 4(mat)/Nov 7/
Nov 9/Nov 13/Nov 16/Nov 19/Nov 24/Nov 27/Dec 1

Britten: *Billy Budd* Nov 17/Nov 20/Nov 23/Nov 25(mat)/
Nov 28/Nov 30/Dec 3/Dec 7/Dec 10/Dec 15

Humperdinck: *Hansel and Gretel* Dec 8/Dec 11/Dec 13/
Dec 16(mat)/Dec 19/Jan 4/Jan 7/Jan 12/Jan 16(mat)/Jan 19

Puccini: *La bohème* Jan 17/Jan 20(mat)/Jan 23/Jan 26/Jan 29/
Feb 1/Feb 4/Feb 8/Feb 12/Feb 15/Feb 20(mat)/Feb 23

Wagner: *Parsifal* Feb 2/Feb 6/Feb 9(mat)/Feb 13/Feb 18/Feb 21/
Feb 26/Mar 1/Mar 5/Mar 9

Mozart: *The Magic Flute* Feb 16/Feb 19/Feb 22/Feb 25/Feb 27/
Mar 2/Mar 6/Mar 8/Mar 11/Mar 13(mat)/Mar 16(mat)

CHICAGO OPERA THEATER

Mozart: *Così fan tutte* Feb 13/Feb 15/Feb 17(mat)/Feb 21/Feb 23

Britten: *The Rape of Lucretia* Mar 13/Mar 15/Mar 17(mat)/Mar 21/
Mar 23

Handel: *Semele* May 8/May 10/May 12(mat)/May 16/May 18

153—2002-2003

LYRIC OPERA OF CHICAGO (48)

Mascagni: *Cavalleria rusticana*
with Leoncavallo: *Pagliacci* Sep 21/Sep 24/Sep 28/
Oct 2(mat)/Oct 5/Oct 8/Oct 11/Oct 14/Oct 17(mat)/Oct 20
(mat)/Oct 23/Oct 26

Floyd: *Susannah* Sep 30/Oct 4/Oct 6(mat)/Oct 9/Oct 12/Oct 16(mat)/Oct 19/Oct 22/Oct 25/Oct 29

Wagner: *Die Walküre* Nov 6/Nov 10(mat)/Nov 13/Nov 16/Nov 19/ Nov 22/Nov 25/Nov 29/Dec 2/Dec 6

Sondheim: *Sweeney Todd* Nov 18/Nov 21(mat)/Nov 23/ Nov 27(mat)/Nov 30/Dec 4/Dec 7/Dec 10/Dec 13/Dec 17/ Dec 20/Dec 22(mat)

Massenet: *Thaïs* Dec 14/Dec 18/Dec 21/Jan 6/Jan 9(mat)/Jan 11/ Jan 14/Jan 17/Jan 22/Jan 26(mat)

Verdi: *La traviata* Jan 18/Jan 21(mat)/Jan 24/Jan 27/Jan 31/ Feb 4/Mar 5/Mar 8/Mar 12(mat)/Mar 15(mat)/Mar 17/Mar 21

Handel: *Partenope* Feb 1/Feb 5/Feb 8(mat)/Feb 11/Feb 14/Feb 17/ Feb 22/Feb 26(mat)/Mar 1/Mar 6

Verdi: *Un ballo in maschera* Feb 15/Feb 19/Feb 23(mat)/Feb 27/ Mar 3/Mar 7/Mar 11/Mar 14/Mar 18/Mar 22

CHICAGO OPERA THEATER

Britten: *The Turn of the Screw* Mar 26/Mar 28/Mar 30(mat)/Apr 3/ Apr 5

Handel: *Agrippina* Apr 30/May 2/May 4(mat)/May 8/May 10

Martinu: *Comedy on a Bridge* with Krasa: *Brundibar* June 4/June 6/June 8(mat)/June 12/ June 14

154—2003-2004

LYRIC OPERA OF CHICAGO (49)

Mozart: *The Marriage of Figaro* Sep 20/Sep 24/Sep 28(mat)/Oct 1/ Oct 4/Oct 8/Oct 10/Oct 13/Oct 17/Oct 21/Oct 25

Blitzstein: *Regina* Sep 29/Oct 3/Oct 7/Oct 9(mat)/Oct 12(mat)/ Oct 15/Oct 18/Oct 22/Oct 24

Wagner: *Siegfried* Nov 5/Nov 9(mat)/Nov 14/Nov 18/Nov 21/ Nov 24/Nov 29/Dec 3/Dec 6

Gounod: *Faust* Nov 15/Nov 19/Nov 23(mat)/Nov 26(mat)/ Nov 28/Dec 5/Dec 9/Dec 12/Dec 15/Dec 20

Saint-Saëns: *Samson and Delilah* Dec 13/Dec 16(mat)/ Dec 18/Dec 21(mat)/Jan 9/Jan 12/Jan 14/Jan 17/Jan 20/Jan 22

Donizetti: *Lucia di Lammermoor* Jan 24/Jan 28/Jan 31/Feb 4(mat)/ Feb 7(mat)/Feb 10/Feb 13/Feb 16/Feb 20/Feb 24/Feb 28

(Gilbert and) Sullivan: *The Pirates of Penzance* Feb 2/Feb 6/ Feb 12(mat)/Feb 17/Feb 19(mat)/Feb 23/Feb 27/Mar 3/ Mar 6(mat)/Mar 10/Mar 13

Puccini: *Madama Butterfly* Feb 14/Feb 18/Feb 21/Feb 26(mat)/ Mar 1/Mar 5/Mar 9/Mar 12/Mar 15/Mar 17(mat)/Mar 19/ Mar 21(mat)

CHICAGO OPERA THEATER

Monteverdi: *L'incoronazione di Poppea* Feb 18/Feb 20/Feb 22 (mat)/Feb 26/Feb 28

Britten: *Death in Venice* May 5/May 7/May 9(mat)/May 13/May 15

Rossini: *Il viaggio a Reims* May 19/May 21/May 23/May 29

155—2004-2005

LYRIC OPERA OF CHICAGO (50)

Mozart: *Don Giovanni* Sep 18/Sep 22/Sep 26(mat)/Oct 1/Oct 4/ Oct 7/Oct 9/Oct 12(mat)/Oct 15/Oct 19/Oct 22

Wagner: *Das Rheingold* Oct 2/Oct 5/Oct 8/Oct 13/Oct 17(mat)/ Oct 21/Oct 25/Nov 3/Nov 6

Verdi: *Aida* Oct 23/Oct 26/Oct 29/Nov 1/Nov 4(mat)/Nov 7(mat)/ Nov 10/Nov 13/Nov 19/Nov 24(mat)/Nov 27(mat)/Dec 1/Dec 4

Janáček: *The Cunning Little Vixen* Nov 17/Nov 20(mat)/Nov 23/ Nov 26/Nov 29/Dec 3/Dec 10/Dec 13(mat)/Dec 15/Dec 18

Bolcom: *A Wedding* Dec 11/Dec 14/Dec 17/Dec 19(mat)/ Jan 5(mat)/Jan 8/Jan 12/Jan 14/Jan 17/Jan 21

Beethoven: *Fidelio* Jan 18/Jan 22/Jan 26/Jan 30(mat)/ Feb 2(mat)/Feb 5/Feb 8/Feb 11/Feb 15/Feb 18/Feb 21

Puccini: *Tosca* Jan 31/Feb 4/Feb 6(mat)/Feb 9/Feb 12/Feb 14/ Feb 16(mat)/Feb 19/Feb 22/Feb 24(mat)/Feb 26/Mar 1

Wagner: *Götterdämmerung* Mar 19/Mar 26

Wagner: *Der Ring des Nibelungen*
 Das Rheingold Mar 28/Apr 4/Apr 11
 Die Walküre Mar 29/Apr 5/Apr 12
 Siegfried Mar 31/Apr 7/Apr 14
 Götterdämmerung Apr 2/Apr9/Apr 16

Fiftieth Anniversary Gala Concert Oct 30

CHICAGO OPERA THEATER

Handel: *La Risurrezione* Mar 2/Mar 4/Mar 6(mat)/Mar 10/Mar 12

Mozart: *The Marriage of Figaro* May 4/May 6/May 8(mat)/May 12/ May 14

Britten: *A Midsummer Night's Dream* May 18/May 20/May 22 (mat)/May 26/May 28

Notes

INTRODUCTION

1. Helen L. Horowitz, *Culture and the City* (Lexington, 1976), p. 75.

1—THE ROOTS OF A TRADITION

1. George P. Upton, *Musical Memories* (Chicago, 1908), p. 15. The Upton memoirs are the most trustworthy printed chronicle of opera in Chicago in this period, but they do contain mistakes. Many of these can be corrected from Upton's daybooks in the Chicago Historical Society.

2. Napier Wilt, *History of the Two Rice Theaters,* Ph.D. diss., University of Chicago, 1923, p. 2.

3. A piece of local lore is to place the fire in the theater on the opening night rather than the date of the second performance, July 30, hence its inclusion in a much used nineteenth-century history of Chicago, Kirkland and Kirkland's *The Story of Chicago* (Chicago, 1892), giving it unwarranted authority. Kirkland apparently was unaware of the performance on July 29, and authors as scrupulous as Emmett Dedmon (*Fabulous Chicago,* enl. ed., New York, 1981, p. 87) continue the misconception.

4. Karleton Hackett, *The Beginning of Grand Opera in Chicago* (Chicago, 1913), p. 26.

5. Upton, op. cit., p. 228.

6. Theodore Thomas, *A Musical Autobiography* (1905; reprint, New York, 1964), p. 32.

7. Upton was not in the city at this time and apparently was unaware of these performances of *Der Freischütz.* The first he mentions are those of 1865.

8. Although Upton, in his *Musical Memories,* includes *Maritana* in this season, I cannot find a contemporary record of the performance in his notes. The first performance of *Maritana* in Chicago in 1859 may have been that of an English company on December 6.

9. Upton, op. cit., pp. 229–30.

10. Upton, op. cit., p. 230.

11. Upton's memory is playing tricks on him when he says (op. cit., p. 231) the work was performed in its entirety. That is at odds with his own contemporary notes.

12. Upton, op. cit., pp. 231–32.

13. Upton, op. cit., p. 167.

14. Upton, op. cit., pp. 122–25.

2—THE CROSBY YEARS

1. His name is given in various sources as Uranus and Uriah. Uranus is correct.

2. Upton, *Musical Memories,* p. 237.

3. Eugene E. Cropsey, "Mr. Crosby's Temple of Art," *Opera Quarterly* 1 (fall 1995), p. 82; and *Crosby's Opera House* (Cranbury, N.J., 1999). Cropsey, possibly unaware of the Upton daybooks (see note 15), omits some performances.

4. Upton, op. cit., pp. 237–38.

5. Ibid., pp. 238–39.

6. Ibid., p. 241.

7. Ibid., p. 169.

8. Ibid., p. 241.

9. Readers today commonly associate this phrase with trench warfare in World War I. They should be reminded that both trench warfare and the phrase began in the final phases of the American Civil War.

10. Upton, op. cit., p. 244.

11. Prospectus in the Chicago Historical Society.

12. Upton, op. cit., p. 245.

13. Ibid., pp. 250–51.

14. Ibid., p. 250.

15. Upton, *Attractions in Chicago,* manuscript books in the Chicago Historical Society.

16. Upton, *Musical Memories,* p. 251.

17. Ibid., p. 236.

3—A TRADITION REBUILT

1. *Grand Opera* (New York, 1972), p. 114.

4—THE MET WEST

1. Upton, *Musical Memories,* p. 308.

5—A NEW TRADITION

1. Clarence J. Bulliet, *How Grand Opera Came to Chicago* (Chicago: Privately printed, 1942).

2. John F. Cone, *Hammerstein's Manhattan Opera Company* (Norman, Okla., 1966).

3. Edward C. Moore, *Forty Years of Opera in Chicago* (New York, 1930), pp. 60–63.

4. We must be grateful to have a well-researched account of Garden's life, *Mary Garden,* by Michael T. R. B. Turnbull, published in 1997.

5. George P. Upton, *The Standard Operas,* rev. ed. (Chicago, 1910), p. 529ff.

6. Turnbull, op. cit., p. 193.

7. Moore, op. cit., p. 100.

8. Ibid., p. 129.

9. Ibid., p. 167.

10. Ibid., p. 159.

11. Harold McCormick Papers, University of Wisconsin Library, Madison.

12. Ibid.

13. Ibid.

14. Moore, op. cit., p. 208.

15. Ibid., p. 235.

16. Turnbull, op. cit., p. 130.

17. Moore, op. cit., p. 139.

18. Emmett Dedmon, *Fabulous Chicago,* enl. ed. (New York, 1981), p. 313.

19. S. Hurok (with Ruth Goode), *Impresario* (New York, 1946), p. 135. Hurok, dictating to a ghost writer, had memory slips and can be vague about chronology. He appears to compress two tours of the Russian company into one.

20. Ziegler Papers, Archives of the Metropolitan Opera.

21. Moore, op. cit., p. 306.

22. Ziegler Papers.

23. Turnbull, op. cit., p. 159.

24. Ziegler Papers.

25. Moore, op. cit., p. 298.

26. Ibid., p. 300.

27. Ibid., p. 324.

28. Ibid., p. 334.

29. The tour began in Philadelphia and went on to Baltimore, Washington, D.C., Cleveland, Pittsburgh, Milwaukee, Chicago, Indianapolis, St. Louis, and Cincinnati. Hurok, op. cit., p. 137ff.

6—THE RAVINIA OPERA

1. *Ravinia: The Festival at Its Half Century* (Highland Park, Ill.: Ravinia Festival with Rand McNally, 1985), p. 26.

2. Moore, *Forty Years of Opera,* p. 148.

3. Ibid., p. 25.

4. Ibid., p. 33.

5. Ibid., p. 245.

6. Ibid., p. 248.

7—A NEW THEATER

1. Moore, *Forty Years of Opera,* p. 116.

2. Hurok, *Impresario,* p. 146.

3. Ibid.

4. Ibid., p. 147.

5. Ibid.

6. I am aware of the existence of this report because a copy was in the files of my predecessor at the *Chicago Sun-Times,* Dr. Felix Borowski.

8—NEW YORK TAKES OVER

1. Stravinsky, *Selected Correspondence,* vol. 3 (New York: Knopf, 1985), p. 315.

10—THE FOX YEARS

1. Peter Jacobi, "Fox of the Lyric: La Donna Immobile," interview with Carol Fox, *Chicago Scene* (October 1963): 16ff.

13—A CHANGING REPERTORY OVER THE FIRST 150 YEARS

1. Quaintance Eaton, *Opera Caravan: Adventures of the Metropolitan on Tour, 1883–1956* (New York: Farrar, Straus and Cudahy, 1957), pp. 83–84.

2. Ibid., p. 97.

Selected Bibliography

Bulliet, Clarence J. *How Grand Opera Came to Chicago.* Chicago: Privately printed, 1942.

Cropsey, Eugene H. *Crosby's Opera House: Symbol of Chicago's Cultural Awakening.* Cranbury, N.J.: Associated University Presses, 1999. Includes a listing of all opera productions, with performance dates and casts, given at Crosby's Opera House from its opening to its destruction in 1871.

Davis, Ronald L. *Opera in Chicago.* New York: Appleton-Century, 1966. Includes dates and last names of casts and conductors of major presentations by Chicago opera-producing companies from 1910 to 1965.

Dedmon, Emmett. *Fabulous Chicago.* New York: Random House, 1946.

Dizikes, John. *Opera in America: A Cultural History.* New Haven, Conn.: Yale University Press, 1993.

DuciBella, Joseph R., and David R. White. *The Theatres of Chicago: The Complete Illustrated History.* Forthcoming.

Garden, Mary (with Louis Biancolli). *Mary Garden's Story.* New York: Simon and Schuster, 1951.

Hackett, Carleton. *The Beginning of Grand Opera in Chicago: 1850–1859.* Chicago: Laurentian Publishers, 1913.

Hurok, Sol (with Ruth Goode). *Impresario.* New York: Random House, 1946.

Kirkland, Joseph, and Caroline Kirkland. *The Story of Chicago.* 2 vols. Chicago: Dibble Publishing, 1892, 1894.

Lyric Opera of Chicago has published three books on its history and activities:

Lyric Opera of Chicago by Claudia Cassidy. With a foreword by Saul Bellow, recollections by Carol Fox, and graphic design by R. D. Scudellari. Chicago, 1979 (published on the occasion of Lyric's twenty-fifth anniversary). Includes color and black-and-white photographs from productions, 1954–1978, and complete performance dates and cast listings of all Lyric productions to date.

Bravi: Lyric Opera of Chicago by Victor Skrebneski. Chicago, 1994. Includes articles by John von Rhein and Andrew Porter, black-and-white photographs, and complete performance dates and cast listings of all Lyric productions, 1980–1994/95.

Lyric Opera: 50 Years of Grand Opera in Chicago. Chicago, 2004 (published on the occasion of Lyric's fiftieth anniversary). Includes articles on the history of Lyric performances by Fred Plotkin and Gary Wills, reminiscences and anecdotes from various performers, and color and black-and-white photographs of Lyric productions and artists over a fifty-year span.

Their website, www.lyricopera.org, includes complete cast and production personnel lists for all of Lyric's productions from 1954 to the present. To access those, look under "About Lyric," going from there to subheadings "History of Lyric" and "Performance/Cast Listings."

Maretzek, Max. *Revelations of an Opera Manager in Nineteenth-Century America.* With an introduction by Charles Haywood. 1855, 1890. Reprint (2 vols. in 1), New York: Dover Publications, 1968.

Marsh, Robert C. *Annals of the Ravinia Opera.* Parts 1–4. *Opera Quarterly* (Duke University Press, Durham, North Carolina) 13, no. 3, through 14, no. 2 (1997–1998). Includes complete list of works, performance dates, and cast lists over the full span of Ravinia opera performances from 1912 to 1931.

McCormick, Harold. Papers. University of Wisconsin Library, Madison, Wis.

Moore, Edward C. *Forty Years of Opera in Chicago.* New York: Horace Liveright, 1930. Includes "A Statistical Résumé of The Chicago Grand Opera Company, The Chicago Opera Association, and The Chicago Civic Opera Company's performances, November 3, 1910, to March 26, 1929," as an appendix, and year-to-year listings of artists, repertory, and performance dates.

Ratner, Carl. *Chicago Opera Theater: Standard-Bearer for American Opera, 1974–2001.* Ph.D. diss., Northwestern University, 2005.

Ravinia: The Festival at Its Half Century. Highland Park, Ill.: Ravinia Festival with Rand McNally, 1985.

Thomas, Theodore. *A Musical Autobiography.* Ed. George P. Upton. 2 vols. 1905. Reprint (2 vols. in 1), New York: Da Capo Press, 1964, with concert programs from original edition omitted and with new introduction and appendices.

Turnbull, Michael T. R. B. *Mary Garden.* Chicago: Amadeus Press, 1997.

Upton, George P. *Musical Memories: My Recollection of Celebrities of the Half Century, 1850–1900.* Chicago: A. C. McClurg, 1908. (Some of Upton's daybooks are housed in the Chicago Historical Society, as are his manuscript books titled *Attractions in Chicago*.)

Wilt, Napier. *History of the Two Rice Theaters.* Ph.D. diss., University of Chicago, 1923.

Wood, Maude Aurilla. *The Early History of Grand Opera in Chicago.* Ph.D. diss., University of Chicago, 1926.

Index

Permissions

The images found on the jacket and on the indicated pages of this book are offered courtesy / by permission of the following generous people and groups.

ALEX ADDUCCI COLLECTION AND HISTORICAL SCENIC COLLECTION, RARE BOOKS AND SPECIAL COLLECTIONS LIBRARY, NORTHERN ILLINOIS UNIVERSITY

p. 84—Mary Garden, Hector Dufranne, & Jose Mojica in *Salome,* 1921

p. 84—*The Love for Three Oranges,* 1921

p. 107—*Aida,* Civic Opera House, 1929

AP/WIDE WORLD PHOTOS

p. 134—Maria Callas and a process server

THE ART INSTITUTE OF CHICAGO, HISTORIC ARCHITECTURE AND LANDSCAPE IMAGE COLLECTION

p. 8—1st Rice's Theatre (Image Collection #40617)

p. 14—1st McVicker's Theatre (Image Collection #40757)

p. 56—Auditorium Theatre and Hotel Building (Barnum and Barnum, Chicago Photo Image Collection #24816)

p. 56—Auditorium Theatre interior (J. W. Taylor, Image Collection #49665)

CHICAGO HISTORY MUSEUM

pp. ii, 47—Adelina Patti (ICHi-14572)

p. 7—Ad for first opera in Chicago (ICHi-38818)

p. 8—John B. Rice (ICHi-03272)

p. 12—Tremont House (J. Carbutt, ICHi-38544)

p. 12—Young America Hotel and 2nd Rice's Theater (ICHi-38554)

p. 22—*Carte de visite* of Uranus H. Crosby (ICHi-21116)

p. 22—Crosby's Opera House (ICHi-01727)

p. 23 and book jacket—Interior of Crosby's Opera House (ICHi-18413)

p. 37—2nd McVicker's Theatre (A.J. Copelin & Son, ICHi-01757)

p. 38—View of 2nd McVicker's Theatre auditorium (ICHi-31466)

p. 39—Exterior of 2nd Hooley's Theatre (ICHi-18166)

p. 39—Richard M. Hooley (ICHi-38548)

p. 40—Grand Opera House (ICHi-38546)

p. 44—Haverley's Theatre (ICHi-38545)

p. 45—Diagram of Haverley's Theatre interior (ICHi-38543)

p. 50—Interstate Exposition Building (ICHi-38555)

p. 69—Edith Rockefeller McCormick (ICHi-17297)

p. 77—Ernestine Schumann-Heink (DN-0062942)

p. 78—Poster for *Ring* Cycle, 1915 (ICHi-38556)

p. 79—Geraldine Farrar (DN-0067257)

p. 81—Cleofonte Campanini (Moffat, ICHi-14564)

p. 81—Edward C. Moore & opera singers (ICHi-38746)

p. 81—Rehearsing for a 1919 performance of *La Nave* (ICHi-27198)

p. 81—Tito Schipa (DN-0086243)

p. 83—Harold R. McCormick & Mary Garden (DN-0073158)

p. 87—Samuel Insull (ICHi-38551)

p. 89—Giorgio Polacco & Edith Mason (DN-0075146)

p. 91—Claudia Muzio (DN-0082466)

p. 98—Louis Eckstein (ICHi-35454)

p. 105 and book jacket—Civic Opera House building (Chicago Architectural Photographing, ICHi-24213)

p. 152—Régine Crespin & Richard Tucker (ICHi-38831)

p. 153—Reri Grist & Irmgard Seefried (ICHi-38830)

p. 164—Birgit Nilsson (ICHi-17695)

p. 154—Geraint Evans (David H. Fishman, ICHi-36420)

p. 160—David Cornell, Montserrat Caballé, & Edna Garabedian-George (ICHi-38833)

p. 166—Elena Zilio, Julian Patrick, Ileana Cotrubas, & Luciano Pavarotti (ICHi-38832)

CHICAGO OPERA THEATER

p. 188—*The Mother of Us All* (Carol & Weston photo)

p. 193—Ardis Krainik & Alan Stone (Jennifer Girard photo)

CHICAGO PUBLIC LIBRARY, SPECIAL COLLECTIONS AND PRESERVATION DIVISION

p. 14—James H. McVicker

p. 17—George P. Upton

p. 25—Clara Louise Kellogg

p. 84—Program listing for *The Love for Three Oranges,* 1921

CHICAGO SUN-TIMES, INC. © 2005

p. 116—Giovanni Martinelli & Fortune Gallo (Risser)

CROATIAN ACADEMY OF SCIENCE AND ART, ZAGREB, THE THEATER HISTORY DEPARTMENT; BRUCE BURROUGHS

pp. iii, 117—Zinka Milanov

THE JOAN W. AND IRVING B. HARRIS THEATER FOR MUSIC AND DANCE

pp. 212, 213—Exterior & interior of the theater (Jon Miller © Hedrich Blessing)

LYRIC OPERA OF CHICAGO

pp. iii, 142—Boris Christoff & Jussi Bjoerling

p. iii—Marilyn Horne

p. 112 and book jacket—Ardis Krainik Theatre (Dan Rest)

p. 128—Nicola Rescigno, Carol Fox, & Lawrence Kelly

p. 129—Two guests greeting Eleanor Steber

p. 131—Nicola Rossi-Lemeni & Maria Callas

p. 135—Tullio Serafin

p. 141—Danny Newman

p. 143—Bruno Bartoletti, Carol Fox, & Pino Donati (David Fishman)

p. 144—Tebaldi, Gobbi, Canali, Simionato (Nancy Sorenson)

p. 146—*Cosi fan tutte* cast, 1959 (Nancy Sorenson)

p. 149—Jon Vickers (Nancy Sorenson)

p. 149—Leontyne Price

p. 149—Renata Tebaldi & Tito Gobbi

p. 161—Joan Sutherland & Marilyn Horne

p. 162—Sherrill Milnes, Fiorenza Cossotto, Carlo Cossutta, Pilar Lorengar, & Nicolai Ghiaurov (Tony Romano)

p. 176—*The Love for Three Oranges,* 1979

p. 185—*Aida,* Civic Opera House, 1993 (Dan Rest)

p. 186—Alfredo Kraus & Renata Scotto

p. 199—Renée Fleming & Samuel Ramey (Dan Rest)

p. 207—Andrew Davis, Bill Mason, Bruno Bartoletti, & Matthew Epstein (Dan Rest)

METROPOLITAN OPERA ARCHIVES

pp. ii, 60, and book jacket—Édouard De Reszke

pp. ii, 60—Jean De Reszke

p. 11—Italo Campanini

p. 16—Pasquale Brignoli & Marietta Piccolomini

p. 53 and book jacket—Lilli Lehmann

p. 62—Giulio Gatti-Casazza

p. 120—Fausto Cleva

p. 144—Birgit Nilsson & Rosa Raisa

book jacket—Birgit Nilsson

THE NEWBERRY LIBRARY

p. 33—Max Maretzek

PICTURE HISTORY

pp. ii, 31—Minnie Hauk

p. 15—Maurice Strakosch

p. 15—Max Strakosch

p. 43—Col. James H. Mapleson

RAVINIA FESTIVAL

p. 95—The entrance gate to Ravinia

p. 97—Original Ravinia Pavilion

ROSENTHAL ARCHIVES, CHICAGO SYMPHONY ORCHESTRA

p. 52—Theodore Thomas

p. 124—Harry Zelzer

VIRGINIA LOCKE & EUGENE H. CROPSEY

p. 22—Albert Crosby

ANDREW ECCLES/JBGPHOTO.COM

book jacket—Renée Fleming

CHARLES MINTZER

book jacket—Italo Campanini

JON RANDOLPH PHOTO

book jacket—Robert C. Marsh